Warman's DOLLS

A VALUE AND IDENTIFICATION GUIDE

R. LANE HERRON

Published by

**krause
publications**

700 E. State Street • Iola, WI 54990-0001
Telephone: 715/445-2214

Please call or write for our free catalog.
Our toll-free number to place an order or obtain a free catalog is 800-258-0929
or please use our regular business telephone 715-445-2214
for editorial comment and further information.

Library of Congress Catalog Number: 98-84616
ISBN: 0-87069-765-X

Printed in the United States of America

DEDICATED TO

the memory of my beloved parents and grandparents, Charles and Alice Herron, and Robert and Ella Herron...

and to my devoted and most loyal friends...Cliquot, Boo-Boo, and Pinkie.

"What is a doll? It is not a thing, nor is it an object; it is a person; it is the child of the child."

M. Hippolyte Rigualt, French writer

"A thing of beauty is a joy forever; Its lovliness increases; it will never Pass into nothingness."

- John Keats, Endymion

TABLE OF CONTENTS

Foreword 5
Acknowledgement 7
Final Word About Pricing 8
Key to Abbreviations 9
Chapter 1 Boudoir Dolls 10
Chapter 2 Bru (Maison) 17
Chapter 3 Chase, Martha Jenks 20
Chapter 4 China Dolls 21
Chapter 5 Clear, Emma 27
Chapter 6 Dean's Rag Book Co. LTD 28
Chapter 7 Drayton, Grace (Wiederseim) 29
Chapter 8 Effanbee (F&B) 31
Chapter 9 English Dolls 37
Chapter 10 Fabric Dolls 39
Chapter 11 Farmer, Mark 45
Chapter 12 French Miscellany 46
Chapter 13 Gaultier, Francois (Maison) 54
Chapter 14 German Miscellany 57
Chapter 15 Handwerck, Heinrich 65
Chapter 16 Heubach, Ernst 83
Chapter 17 Heubach, Gebruder 85
Chapter 18 Jumeau (Maison) 86
Chapter 19 Kammer & Reinhardt 93
Chapter 20 Kestner, Johannes Daniel 95
Chapter 21 Kewpies 103
Chapter 22 Kruse Kathe 106
Chapter 23 Lenci Dolls 110
Chapter 24 Marseille, Armand 115
Chapter 25 Modern Age Dolls 1930-1945 121
Chapter 26 Moss, Leo B 130
Chapter 27 Novelty Dolls 131
Chapter 28 Odd-Material Dolls 136
Chapter 29 Old Favorites-1896-1930 141
Chapter 30 Oriental Dolls 148
Chapter 31 Papier-Mâché & Composition Dolls (Antique) 152
Chapter 32 Parians or Molded Hair, Bisques and Tinted Bisques 157
Chapter 33 Plastic Age Dolls-1945+ 163
Chapter 34 Popular Baby Dolls 170
Chapter 35 Rohmer (Maison) 179
Chapter 36 Schoenau & Hoffmeister 180
Chapter 37 Schoenhut, Albert 182
Chapter 38 Simon & Halbig 184
Chapter 39 Steiff 190
Chapter 40 Steiner, Jules N (Maison) 191
Chapter 41 Tinies 193
Chapter 42 Wax and Wax-over Dolls 202
Chapter 43 Wooden Dolls 209
Artist Dolls...214
Miscelaneous Dolls...217
Bibliography 219
About the Author 221

FOREWORD

Beginnings:

Collecting dolls for amusement or as decorative objects dates to the nineteenth century and earlier. In the 1890s, doll clubs were being formed in America. In France, Leo Claretie wrote his interesting doll book, *Les Jouets: Histoire - Fabrication* (1894). In 1903, France's most famous doll collector, Henri d'Allemagne wrote, *Histoire Des Jouets*. In 1907, an exclusive male doll club was formed in Paris. Its members: Henri d'Allemagne, Emile Jumeau, Leo Claretie, Fernand Martin, and Arthur Maury (all of whom had written about dolls.) They called their private club, "Amateurs de Jouets et Jeux anciens."

In 1908 doll collector, Laura B. Starr (her collection was later purchased by the late Samuel F. Pryor for his International Doll Library Foundation Museum, Greenwich, Conn.), wrote *The Doll Book*. Also, in 1908, Mrs. Nevill Jackson, of London, England, wrote *Toys of Other Days*. Mrs. Jackson was not only very affluent, but she was likewise a collector on a grand scale, collecting antique lace, fans, china, prints, silhouettes, dolls, and toys. Her articles about antiques appeared regularly in the popular magazine, *Country Life*. Her concept of an "antique" doll was, of course, a Queen Anne or one of the other jointed English woodens—and she saw many of them preserved in the luxurious homes that she visited and wrote about.

The French have always loved and collected dolls, so it was not surprising that when Americans began to search for dolls in earnest they were more plentifully found in France than in any other country. In the 1920s, several more memorable doll books were written: *Dolls and Puppets*, by Max von Boehn, 1929; *Dolls,* by Esther Singleton, 1927; and Gwen White's slim volume, *Ancient And Modern Dolls*, 1927-28.

The first doll collector's exhibit was held at Grand Central Palace, New York City, in March, 1937. This was the inspiration of Mrs. Adele Scott, vice-president of the International Exposition of Arts and Industries. She was aided by Mary E. Lewis, a well-known doll collector and author of the book, *Gallery of Diamonds and Dolls*. Despite wide-spread coverage of this event, Mrs. Scott and Mrs. Lewis gleaned very little response from col-

lectors, and they had a gaping 700-feet of space to fill. At first only three women came forth. Then Mrs. Lewis appeared on the Mary Margaret McBride radio program with her plea, but, again, her invitation was met with a lack of interest—only two more women offered their help (Mrs. Maybelle Cremer and Mrs. Peggy Zerc).

Even when the ladies contacted the Consuls of foreign countries for dolls, few countries responded. In desperation, Mrs. Lewis helped fill the room with her own collection of 500 international dolls. Potato mashers served as "stands". In all, only eight women offered their dolls for the display, but attendance was better than expected, and the exhibit gleaned national coverage in such notable magazines as Life, New York Daily News, etc. Such then was the lethargy of dollers in 1937. Janet P. Johl published her first doll book, *The Fascinating Story of Dolls* in 1941. The success of this book encouraged her to write three others, which were published in 1946, 1950 and 1951. Doll collecting was finally coming out of the closet and gaining respectability.

In the 1950s, however, there was still a limited interest in dolls as an international hobby. In fact, old dolls were difficult to find abroad—except for France - and the French were mainly interested in their clothes! In Spain, the author was told that all antique dolls had been burnt because of the plague. Antique dolls were scarce in England. Shops there, and in other countries had few, if any, dolls for sale. Even museums were barren of dolls and knew very little about them. Again the author was told that since most of the Queens collected dolls, people gave their heirloom and other cherished antique dolls to the Queens (Queen Mary was famous for her collection). In France, Henri d'Allemagne had died, and his son, Jacques, was trying to sell his vast collection of toys and dolls which had been stored in four buildings. Although his collection was famous and rare, and the prices comparatively reasonable, dollers complained about the prices!

Madame de Galea was then the most famous doll collector in Paris. She lived in a luxurious country home at 17 Ville de la Reunion, but most of her collection was displayed in a two-story building in the garden. (It is now on exhibit in a museum in Monaco.) In America, dolls were beginning to bring higher

prices than ever before, but rare hairdo types like parians, chinas, and early papier mache's, were taking precedence over French dolls. The 18th century wooden dolls and the 19th century wax dolls were also favorites. The Jumeau was more popular than the Bru. The value of a dollar bill in 1950 had the value of 18¢ in 1993.

In the late 1950s, Mrs. Joseph Mallon of Philadelphia purchased a rare hairdo blonde china—head doll depicting (supposedly) Queen Mary of England at the Benn auction there for $375 (a large-size, closed-mouth Bru could be had at that time for $250-300), which was more than a month's wages for the average working person. When a woman in California paid $600 for a Bru in the early 1960s, it set the stage for higher prices amongst French dolls. Collectors began to see them with different eyes. The Marque, Huret, A.T., H., and other such dolls were beginning to bring higher prices.

Many collectors feared that the uniting of dolls clubs would commercialize the hobby and destroy it for those who could not afford the better, more expensive dolls. British interest in dolls began to stir as early as 1948 when Lesley Gordon wrote her book *The Pageant of Dolls*. Irene Blair Hickman and Faith Eaton were also well-known British doll collectors.

In the 1960s doll collecting was beginning to gain momentum in both England and America, but it was the 1970s that can truly be marked as the decade that led us all to where we stand today. It was the decade of price guides, reference guides, doll picture books, an abundance of articles about dolls, doll shows, and auctions that catered exclusively to dolls and collectors. A new era had been born. Big business had entered the field and dolls were being considered for their "investment" possibilities—and, of course, this will effect the future of dolls.

The Purpose of Price Guides:

A price guide does not "set" or establish prices, but merely reports them. Prices are culled from auctions, dealer lists, antiques shops, and doll shows. In former years, collectors studied the prices used by Kimport Dolls of Missouri as a guide for selling dolls, as well as auction prices. But prices for most dolls rise in price, then fall.

In 1962 an Izannah Walker doll in good condition sold for $100, today it could sell for upwards of $20,000; whereas one in poor condition might bring $5,000. Prices such as these have remained fairly stable for certain rare old dolls. The modern composition doll is another kettle of fish. A composition Shirley Temple doll made in the 1930s, all original, sold for about $35-$50 (and less) in the late 1960s, sizes 18 to 27 - inches.

In the 1990s these sizes are valued from $1,000-$2,000, all original. However, Shirley Temple dolls aren't selling as quickly as they once did. At least they aren't in the city where I live. In a local antiques shop, three 1930s Shirleys in the 18-inch size, semi-original, have been standing in a display case for almost four years unsold! And this shop gets quite a bit of tourist trade. Their prices vary from $395 to $695.

Price guides do not report falling prices because prices vary from one state to the other. Dolls reach a certain level of "worth" and there is always someone willing to pay the price asked. If a doll can't be sold locally for the going price, one must advertise in the national or international media to find a buyer.

People will always collect dolls, if only for their sentimental value - and a doll will sell quicker than any other saleable item. There is a sort of "competition" amongst collectors. They follow trends and tend to copy one another. The more a doll is pictured in a book and the more it is discussed, the higher the price it will be given in the market place. This trend establishes a doll's popularity, not its ever-lasting worth.

Now that the European and Asian markets have opened their doors, we can expect a continuing rise in doll prices - even for the very commonplace old dolls. Antique and popular modern dolls are more sought than ever before, especially in this new world market. Hence, as these dolls become more and more scarce, their values will become more stable as an "investment."

After the turn of the century, dolls made prior to 1900 will be viewed with the same awe that we now view dolls made in the eighteenth century. Even a doll made in the 1930s will seem as ancient as we currently think of one made in the 1830s. Amazing, but true. It's all only a matter of perspective. Even the marvellous "artist" dolls that are being made nowadays will be placed on a pedestal and will be highly cherished. Dolls will most assuredly have "value" and people will be thankful that they collected. A doll is like having money in the bank, but with better returns!

Who Do Investors Really Want?

When I first started collecting antique dolls I was very particular. A doll had to be as nearly mint and "original" as possible; meaning the wig, eyes, body, clothes, shoes, etc. I didn't care if the wig was sparse and the clothes were threadbare, at least I owned something "old" and "authentic".

If I wanted a new doll I would buy a new doll. I did not want a doll that was semi-old or 50% old. I also wanted a doll that was not cracked or chipped. Even a tiny scratch would send me into a frenzy. But I soon learned that I was bypassing some truly old and valuable dolls with only minor damage. The last straw came when Lena Atkinson, a dealer in Le Grange, CA, offered me a long face Jumeau for $200 in 1969 and I turned it down because she had replaced the original sparse wig with a new human hair wig. A friend of mine in Alameda, CA, bought the doll and was very pleased with it—and think of all the profit she gleaned when she sold it years later!

Today advanced collectors and investors seek dolls that are mint and as near original as possible, and, like myself, they prefer the rare and unusual to the ordinary and mundane. And, like myself, they are learning - the hard way—that if they are too particular, they will bypass dolls that they may never again have the opportunity to buy. Minor flaws like hairline cracks on the shoulders, broken bisque fingers on a French doll, a minute chip on the crown of the head, etc., should not condemn a priceless old relic to the under graduate "class, or, worse yet, the dump heap.

Should Dolls Be Refurbished?

As time marches on, and more and more new sellers of dolls enter the field, there seems to be the desire to "recreate" the old doll. Off with the old wig, off with the old clothes, off with the old shoes and stockings. In short, replace the old and faded and worn with something sparkling new and colorful! I've even heard collectors insist on a new body paint job—because the old body was dingy and scratched—as though they were taking their car to a garage to be updated. Well, a doll is not a car—or a fence.

A true collector of antiques prefers the original patina. Auction house appraisers are especially critical when it comes to refurbishing antiques. A doll's hand—made clothing, original shoes, stockings, and accessories glean the ultimate price at auctions. Stay away

from dealers who prefer the restored doll to the doll that is all original—warts, et al.

A bisque - head doll that has become dirty with age can be easily cleaned with a damp cloth. The body can also be lightly cleaned if it has been varnished. If it has not been varnished, leave it be! Wigs can be carefully removed and washed and then re-set with curlers. Don't wash a wig, however, if it appears to be too rotten; simply curl it. A dress and undergarments can be carefully washed if the material appears to be sturdy. If the dress is in tatters—don't wash it! If you wish to rewig or redress and old doll, keep the original wig and clothing and give it to the new owner when you sell the doll. This also applies to modern dolls.

Today, when the doll's original box has become so valuable, many collectors are fearful of removing their new dolls from their original boxes for display. This is foolish. Merely display the doll and keep the box! All this nonsense destroys the joy of collecting. It will be a hundred years before some of today's mass-produced dolls glean any value at all. Popularity and scarcity makes a doll's value skyrocket, and, like movie stars, only dolls with a very unique personality ever reach the top! Enjoy!

Since a doll's head and face are its most valuable asset, don't wash the face of a fragile doll (composition, papier mâché, wax, etc.), or else you may wash away its features and coloring. And don't ever repaint a doll's face! A light touch-up done by an artist might be necessary, but never repaint the entire face or even have an expert do it. A repainted face is a devaluated doll! Ask any auction house appraiser if you don't believe me. I would never buy a doll that has been completely repainted. It instantly turns me off. To me, it is worthless!

A repainted body does not devaluate a doll, however, but, again, don't paint it! And don't replace bisque lower arms with broken fingers which are attached to kid or cloth bodies. Broken fingers are preferable to a new bisque arm. Kid bodies that are leaking sawdust or those that are rotten, can be re-upholstered with a cloth body. This leaves their value intact. Doll collectors—or any collector of antiques—is a conservationist. We must preserve the past for future generations.

ACKNOWLEDGEMENT

The author wishes to thank the following collectors whose dolls illustrated this book: D. Kay Crow, Trish Kantounatakis (Kay's photographer), Jim and Ruby Ellen Smith, Irene Ortega, Carol Lindberg, Billye Otto (Old Oak Tree Antiques, Albuquerque), Aylene Waite, Linda Martinez Bassi, Connie Baca, Virginia Yates, Victoria Rose, Angela Barker, Janet Johl Weissman, and Rosalie Purvis (Land of Enchantment Doll Museum, Albuquerque). I also want to thank Mike Trompak of Timeless Images, Albuquerque, for his help, and my niece Terri Brickner for running errands for me. Last, but not least, I want to thank my editor Tracy Schubert.

A FINAL WORD ABOUT PRICING

The dolls inspected and catalogued for this book were all in good condition and with their original parts. Some dolls were in excellent or mint condition in their original boxes or trunks. If not in good condition or mint, this is stated, the dolls priced accordingly. It is always up to the owner or seller to place the final price on a doll or product. Old or original clothes enhance the value of antique dolls, but an antique doll is not devaluated if it is sold nude. We are buying the doll, not its clothing.

Well-sewn, handmade clothes are preferable to machine-made clothes. Dolls made in this century, especially after World War One are more desirable with their factory-made clothing, which adds to their appeal. Dolls made after 1930, especially Personality and Character Dolls, glean more money with their all-original clothes, shoes, socks, etc. This is particularly important with dolls made after 1945. Madame Alexander collectors are very fussy when it comes to clothing. Doll-artist dolls are of more value when the doll has been dressed by its maker and, completely conceived by its maker. The one-of-a-kind doll is the most coveted doll of them all, antique or modern. Doll prices vary from state to state, country to country. Some dealers vouch that the value of a doll increases by 10% a year. This is not entirely true with all dolls. I've seen antique and collectible dolls sit for years in shops unsold—with the same prices originally placed on them. French dolls will have to be held at least ten years before they earn further value. The Doll Market, like other markets, fluctuates. If you've paid too much for a doll, or you can't sell it for its current market value, hold on to it until you can glean your asking price. Good dolls are always a good investment. Their appeal never diminishes.

Lastly, it is impossible to list and describe every doll, in every size and variation that was made from the beginning of time. If your favorite doll is not listed here, it is possibly listed in another book. If not all sizes of a doll are priced, use your own judgement.

KEY TO ABBREVIATIONS

BJ. . . . . Ball-jointed or ball-jtd

Ca . . . . Circa

CM. . . . . closed mouth

cir. . . . . circumference

compo . . . . composition

HHW . . . . human hair wig

jtd. . . . . jointed

lt. . . . . light

mache . . . . papier-mache

mld. . . . . molded

O/C mouth. . . . . .open/closed mouth

OCM . . . . .open closed mouth

pc. . . . . .piece

PE . . . . pierced ears

PI. pierced in ears

PN . . . . .pierced nostrils

ptd . . . . painted

PW. . . . . paperweight

sh . . . . shoulders

+-or higher (as in pricing)

+-and onward (as in years)

Chapter 1

~ BOUDOIR DOLLS ~

History:

Boudoir dolls or bed dolls (also Salon Dolls, Parlor Dolls, Pillow Dolls, Decor Dolls, Auto Dolls, Revue Dolls, Sofa Dolls, Lady Dolls, wobblies, etc.) seem to belong to the gaudy, romantic, devil-may-care twenties, as they mirrored the fashions, foibles, and fads of the decade—the cinema, the theatre, musical comedy, sports, etc. They spoofed everything and everybody. Great stars like Mistinguette and the Dolly sisters sang and danced with them in Les Folies du Music Hall, Paris.

Silent screen and early talkie stars were posed with them, and famous beauties collected them. (Joan Crawford decorated her home with many.) As early as 1923, the Ladies Home Journal devoted a full page to these daring ladies. One doll represented Sarah Bernhardt, the "Lady of the Camellias" and she wore a white gown lavished with camellias. A "Butterfly" lady had white silk embroidery floss hair and sported a flowing gown adorned with butterfly bows.

Also, in 1923, Harper's Bazar, ran an advertisement of a lady holding two long-legged dolls garbed in peasant costumes (male and female). The lady had bobbed hair and wore a peasant-style blouse. Harper's went on to say: "...quite the smartest dolls we have seen and much newer than the mournful Pierrot and decadent bad ladies who generally accompany him." The key word for these dolls was "Bad"—these debauchees personified vamps, flappers, fallen women, chorus girls, silent screen stars, Jazz Babies, royalty, etc. They smoked, they bobbed their hair, they wore too much make-up, they wore pajamas in public. They slinked and sashayed. They wound up in the boudoir! Ladies Home Journal described them as "decorative, exotic, elongated, adult."

A 1929 magazine suggested that the dolls be dressed to match their owner's bedroom color scheme. These dolls became more sedate during the 1930s when long skirts replaced pajamas. They were deemed passé during the early forties when they were given away with bedroom sets, became carnival prizes, or were sold in dime stores. They were still around in the 1950s.

Collecting Hints:

There are various grades of quality when judging the boudoir doll: cheap composition, mask faces covered with silk or linen, better quality felt faces. The cheap composition types were usually made in America ca. 1920—early 1950s (these latter had plastic hands and feet). The French also made boudoir dolls with cheap compo. shoulder heads, the only difference being that the French-made dolls were better dressed and with more imagination. America made the pressed mask faces, but so did the French! And the British!

The American pressed faces were usually linen and hand-painted; the French preferred silk or stockinet. Signora Lenci's boudoir dolls were mostly felt and expensive, even in her day. She was copied by the British, Italians, Spanish, and even Americans. These dolls should be judged by their over-all quality and degree of originality. Original clothes, wigs, shoes, etc., are a must, although some were sold nude and were dressed in the home. An old dress is considered "original" even though it might not be fancy. These are fad dolls—and fad dolls come and go.

Companies that made boudoir dolls:

Also designers, etc.

Adler, Alart, American Wholesale Novelty Co., Anita, Arrow Doll Wig Co., Austin Gray Ltd. (England), Baltimore Bargain House/American Wholesale Corp., Beaux Art Shade Co., Wm. P. Beers (Jazette), Blossom Doll Co., Bon Marche (department store, Paris, had dolls made to order for them), Bubenheim or Madame Lenore Art Doll (sprite and winking clown, 1924), Calvare (French art doll), Eisen (imported French boudoir dolls), W.R. Ekart (Pierrot), England Art Toy Mfg. Co., European Novelty Co. (merged with Anita), Kitty Fleischman (Cabret Girls, etc.), Gerzon Co. (Netherlands, 1930), Charles E. Gibson, 1922), Goldberger (Eegee; felt head dolls with cigarettes),

Heho Art Dolls (Germany), Hollywood Imps, Victor Kenny (Keeneye), King Tut Dolls (1926), Konroe Merchants, Lady Godwyn, Levallois, Josef H. Levin (Germany), Louis Sherry candy company (used boudoir dolls in their candy advertisements illustrated by Howard Chandler Christy, 1925), Mizpah Toy & Novelty Co., Morris of California, Los Angeles, (made portrait dolls), Munich Art Dolls (1927-28), Paramount Doll Co. (1926), Paul Poiret (Paris designer, 1910), Pompeian Art Works, Sterling Doll Co., Unique Novelty Dolls, Woman's Home Companion magazine (sold undressed boudoir dolls for $1.75 designed by Madame Lisa des Renaudes of Vienna, 1934).

Reproduction Alert:

Modern artists have tried to imitate some of the French faces of the 1920s boudoir dolls, but they look new, making them no threat to the old product.

BOUDOIR DOLLS

1910-1950s

14" "Utility" Lady. Oval-shaped felt face/head, cupid's bow CM, large brown ptd. eyes/lashes, orange yarn wig with rear chignon, stuffed upper body comprises the felt bodice/long sleeves/ruffled collar, wide puffed skirt in the shape of a pin cushion (actually a hiding place for milady's silk stockings, etc.) She sits on the bed amongst frilly cushions. Ca. 1920s $200

24" Boudoir doll with compo shoulder head, ptd features, inserted eyelashes, blonde mohair wig, cloth body/plastic arms/feet with black ptd/mid high-heeled slippers, pink satin gown/bonnet. Early 1950s $150. (Courtesy of Herron)

26" Boudoir doll with compo shoulder head, ptd features, yellow silk thread hair, cloth body, old clothes, 1920s; 30" boudoir doll with platinum hair, compo shoulder head, cloth body/compo hands/cloth feet/silk stockings/satin high-heeled slippers, pink satin gown. Gorgeous dolls. 1920s $225 each. (Courtesy of Herron)

28" Boudoir doll with platinum wig, ptd features, cigarette has fallen off, cloth body/limbs, lovely clothes, 1920s, $225; 29-1/2" French boudoir doll, O/C mouth/teeth, blues ptd eyes, brown mohair wig, cloth body with wired limbs, lovely clothes, 1920s, $275. (Courtesy of Herron)

24"-25" Boudoir dolls. Larger doll has compo shoulder head, ptd features, brown mohair wig, cloth body/compo hands/feet with mold/ptd black high heeled slippers, original red satin gown, early 1930s; 24" boudoir doll has compo shoulder head, brown mohair wig, cloth body, green satin pajamas, $125, 1920s. Larger doll is $150. (Courtesy of Herron)

31" Boudoir doll with mask face, cloth body/limbs 1920s $250

23" Boudoir doll with compo shoulder head, ptd features, grey mohair wig, cloth body/compo hands/compo feet with black ptd/mld high-heeled slippers, original clothes, early 1930s. $275. (Courtesy of Herron)

24" Boudoir doll with compo shoulder head, ptd features, brown mohair wig, cloth body/compo arms/compo feet with black ptd/mld high-heeled slippers, original clothes. Early 1930s, $225. (Courtesy of Herron)

31" Boudoir doll with ptd mask face, black HHW, swivel neck, cloth body, original clothes, 1920s. $225. (Courtesy of Herron)

35" Boudoir doll with ptd mask face, inserted black eyelashes, blonde mohair wig, cloth body, original black velvet dress, undies, stockings, black high-heeled slippers. 1920s $250. (Courtesy of Herron)

30" Boudoir doll, 1920s. Mask face, ptd features, red mohair wig, cloth body, old clothes. Label on body reads: "Etta Inc. New York." 1927 $225. (Courtesy of Herron)

26-1/2" Boudoir doll with compo shoulder head, ptd features, inserted eyelashes, blonde mohair wig, cloth body/compo arms/compo feet with black ptd/mid high-heeled slippers, original clothes. 1930s $225.

28-1/2" Boudoir doll with ptd mask face, brown mohair wig, cloth body, lovely clothes, 1920s. $225. (Courtesy of Herron)

28" French type boudoir doll, ptd features, brown mohair wig, cloth body, gorgeous original clothes, cloth high-heeled slippers, silk stockings, 1920s $350. (Courtesy of Herron)

15" Spanish Senorita. Compo. head/long swivel neck, blue ptd. eyes, puckered lips hold a cigarette, black yarn wig with center part and styled close to the head with coiled braids over each ear, compo. body jtd.. at neck/sh/hips, original Spanish style dress, black net stockings, black high-heeled slippers with ankle ties. Made by Konroe Merchants, NYC. Ca. 1924.....................$350-$400

18" Bahai Lady. Dark felt molded face mask, large brown ptd. eyes to side, cupid's bow red mouth, black thread wig, felt hands/separate thumbs/stitched fingers, cloth body/long felt limbs, original Bahai costume, red felt high-heeled slippers, basket of fruit atop head. (Resembles a Lenci except for lesser quality doll, better quality costume. Perotti once worked for Lenci.) Made by Joao Perotti Manufactura Orbis, Brazil. Ca. 1930s ....$300-$350

22-1/2" Rudolph Valentino. Papier-mâché head, red CM, brown ptd. eyes, cloth body/long limbs, original black velvet trousers, black velvet vest with gold trim (beads), long-sleeved white shirt, black leather shoes with heels, white stockings. Paper label reads: "GEST-ELZICH." Germany. (Not a true likeness.) 1922 ....$500+

23" Lady. Hard mask face/linen covered, red CM, blue ptd. eyes to side, brown silk wig with coiled braids over each ear, pink rayon body/limbs/skirt (trimmed with lace and 4 strips of blue ribbon on bottom of skirt/ruffled ribbon encircles neck/crocheted garter with crocheted rose. Ca. Early 1920s $225

24" Rudolph Valentino. Simulated felt mask face, molded features, CM outlined with fine red lines, ptd. brown eyes/brown eyeshadow, black hair/long ptd. sideburns, linen-covered hollow card body/long hollow card legs/felt-over-wire arms with second and third fingers indicated by stitches, original costume, hat, boots, etc. Foot label reads: "Made in Italy." Opposite foot label reads: "Aquilla" (Eagle). (Per-

sonifies Valentino in the silent film "The Eagle." Better likeness than the Lenci Valentino and others.) Made by La Rosa Company, Milano—Corso Venezia, Italy. Ca. 1924-25 .... $2,500

25" French Lady. Compo head/hands, O/C mouth/molded teeth, brown ptd. eyes to side, blonde mohair wig, cloth body/limbs, original yellow pajama suit with wide lace collar, wide-brimmed hat, black leather high-heeled slippers, silk stockings; holds original mandolin. (Cloth body wired for positioning.) France. 1920s ....$350-$400

25" The "Banana Man" Musical Doll. Compo head, smiling O/C mouth/ptd. teeth/cigarette, ptd. brown eyes to side,

bald head covered by yellow cap, rosy cheeks, modeled ears, cloth body/long cloth limbs, original Pierrot-type suit with lace collar and cuffs/3 pompons on shirt, silk stockings, black leather shoes; holds original mandolin which plays "Oh, Yes, We Have No Bananas." 1920s ....$500-$600

25-1/2" French Lady. Compo shoulder head, smiling O/C mouth/white ptd. teeth outlined with fine red lines, large ptd. brown eyes to side/long ptd. upper lashes, thin eyebrows, blonde mohair wig, cloth body wired for posing/compo hands with long fingers/cloth feet, original rustic-brown velvet lounging pajamas/wide silk collar trimmed with lace and ribbons, broad-brimmed hat, knitted silk stockings, brown leather shoes, original brown-orange ptd. mandolin that still plays a French tune. France. Ca. 1920s $600

27" "Reco 6 Germany" marked Male. French-type. Compo head, brown ptd. eyes/brown eyeshadow, brown mohair wig, cloth body/limbs, original clothes, hat. (Although dressed as a man, this provocative face could just as well be a woman's.) Ca. 1920s $300

27" Ann Harding. Early screen star. Molded felt swivel head, CM, blue ptd. eyes to side, platinum blonde mohair wig, cloth body/felt limbs, original black taffeta gown trimmed with organdy and pink felt, wide-brimmed picture hat, high-heeled slippers, stockings. Ca. 1930s ....$1,000+

27" Scarlet O'Hara. Compo shoulder head, red CM, large blue ptd. eyes/inserted real lashes, dark brown wavy mohair wig, cloth body/legs/compo ankles and feet (black ptd. high-heeled slippers/comp lower arms, original flowing long dress sprinkled with red flowers/red velvet insert at waist/white net top with red ribbon bow, underclothes, original wide-brimmed straw hat, gold heart sewed to neckline reads: GONE WITH THE WIND. Ca. 1939 Mint. Rare $350

28" Boudoir Bride wearing old cream satin wedding gown. Ptd pottery head, brown mohair wig, cloth body. Early 1920s $250. (Courtesy of Herron)

29" Boudoir doll with long HHW, compo face, cloth body, original clothes, crazed face, $35, 1920s; 26" boudoir doll with compo shoulder head, ptd features, inserted black eyelashes, compo hands/feet/mld/ptd black high-heeled slippers, cloth body, original clothes, early 1930s, $175. (Courtesy of Herron)

30"-Scarlet O'Hara. Compo head, ptd features, black mohair wig, cloth body/compo arms/compo feet/mid-on/black ptd high heeled shoes, original clothes, hat, etc. Heart locket on neck reads: "Gone With the Wind" 1939 Mint $350. (Courtesy of Herron)

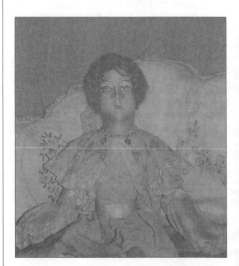

28"Boudoir doll with ptd mask face, inserted eyelashes, brown "marcelled" mohair wig, cloth body/compo hands/cloth feet with silk stockings/cloth high-heeled slippers, original clothes. 1920s $225. (Courtesy of Herron)

23-1/2" French boudoir doll, ptd mask face, pink silk thread wig, cloth body, original clothes, bonnet. 1920s $350. (Courtesy of Herron)

25" Rare ptd pottery head or bisque, black mohair wig, cloth body, original hand-knit outfit, shoes, hat. Probably made in Italy, 1920s. $350

30" Boudoir dolls with compo shoulder heads, ptd features, mohair wigs, cloth bodies, old clothes. 1920s $225 each. (Courtesy of Herron).

27" Boudoir doll. Plastic shoulder head, CM, inset blue plastic eyes, black mohair wig, cloth body/plastic arms/plastic feet/mld on/black ptd high heeled slippers, lovely clothes. Ca. 1940s $150. (Courtesy of Herron)

29" Boudoir doll with ptd mask face, blonde mohair wig, cloth body, original clothes. (She came in her original box.) 1920s $225. (Courtesy of Herron)

23" Compo, shoulder head, ptd feature, broom HHW, cloth body/limbs/compo arms/compo feet/held-on; black ptd high-heeled shoes, bld clothes. Early 1930s $175.

6-1/2" "Made in Japan" all-bisque girl with movable arms set inside original silk cushion, 1920s, $95; 6-1/2" plaster half-doll set inside original cushion, ca. 1925, $125. (Courtesy of Herron)

27" Southern Belle. Compo shoulder head, slightly smiling CM, rare blue glass sleep eyes/real lashes, original brown mohair wig/long sausage curls, cloth body/limbs/compo hands, original long dress, hat, high heels, etc. Probably Anita Novelty Co., NYC. Ca. 1927 .... $500-$600+

27" WW II Patriotic Lady. Compo shoulder head, red CM, large blue ptd. eyes/inserted lashes, white mohair wig with long sausage curls, blue hair bows, cloth body/limbs/molded-on high-heeled slippers, original "patriotic" costume: long satin skirt with vertical red and white stripes/blue border at bottom dotted with white stars/long sleeves/blue blouse dotted with white stars, underclothes, matching hat. (These dolls were given away with bedroom furniture, sold in novelty shops, or were carnival prizes during this period.) Ca. 1941-45 Mint $300

27-1/2" Chinese Man. Yellow sateen pressed mask face, CM, brown ptd. eyes to side, thin high arched eyebrows, black mustache ptd. downward, black mohair wig with long queue, cloth body/limbs, original silk outfit, cap, etc. Ca. 1920s Rare $600

29" "Elka" marked Lady. Compo shoulder head (turned to right side and slightly backwards), red CM, large blue ptd. eyes/black ptd. eye-lashes, dark brown mohair sausage curl wig, cloth body/limbs/compo hands/feet, original gown, etc. (Elka made wax-over-plaster doll heads and half-dolls.) Made in Austria. 1920s $500

Half-doll attached to powder puff and inserted inside pink porcelain powder box, $175, 1920s; (middle) wax-over-bisque half-doll inserted into original cushion/bisque lower arms/legs, grey mohair wig, mark: "BERLIN" (in a triangle), 1920s, $350; 5" half-doll with hands on chest, mark: "Made in France", grey ptd. hair, 1920s, rare, $350. (Courtesy of Herron Photographer: Mike Trompak, Timeless Images, Albuquerque, N.M.)

29" Jeanette MacDonald. Screen star. Molded mask face, red CM, blue ptd. eyes, red mohair wig with 2 long braids, cloth body/limbs, original long black skirt with lace trim, long-sleeved white cotton blouse, shoes, stockings, wrist tag. Costumed as heroine in "The Lottery Bride." (Purchased at the late Francis X. Bushman's REMEMBER WHEN antiques shop in Hollywood.) Ca. 1929 .... $600

29" Pierrette. Companion to Pierrot below. Pressed canvas mask face, large black ptd. eyes, red cupid's bow CM, black beauty spot at corner of right eye, blonde mohair wig, cloth body/limbs, red silk skirt, white silk blouse with black diamond design across front and back and on short sleeves, red cap, red silk slippers. Cloth label reads: "Poupee Gerbs, 29 Rue Gouthey, Paris. Made in France." (Dolls such as this one was used in the musical revues, held by the entertainer.) Ca. 1927 .... $700-$800

29" Pierrot. Pressed canvas mask face, large black ptd. eyes, red cupid's bow CM, beauty spot at corner of right eye, orange silk 2 - pc. outfit trimmed in black with black pompons, black cap, orange silk shoes. Revue doll. Ca. 1927 (Label same as above doll.) .... $700-$800

30" "Saucy" Lady. Molded felt swivel head, CM, brown ptd. eyes/inset lashes, brown mohair bobbed wig, felt body/limbs, original pink satin gown with a ruffled collar and ruffled top, underwear, pink satin high-healed slippers, silk stockings. 1925 .... $1,000

30" French-type Lady. Pressed fabric face, CM, grey ptd. eyes to side/inset lashes, brown silk hair set in tight curls around head at ear level, cloth body/limbs/compo hands/legs, original clothes, hat, fur piece, etc. Possibly French made due to detail. Ca. 1920s $800

30" Male "Groom." Compo shoulder head, CM, blue ptd. eyes, black ptd. hair, cloth body/limbs/compo hands/feet with black ptd./molded-on shoes, original black suit, hat, etc. (He was the groom to a bride doll and bridesmaids in the display window of a florist's shop.) Ca. 1939 (These were cheaply made.).. $250

30" WW II "Victory" Lady. Compo shoulder head, red CM, blue ptd. eye/inserted lashes, blonde mohair wig, cloth body/limbs/compo hands and feet/molded-on high heeled slippers, original white satin gown with a large red "V" printed on the chest, blue satin cape lined with red satin, blue satin cap lined with red satin, apron of gown is

imprinted REMEMBER PEARL HARBOR in red letters. Ca. 1941-45 .. $350

32" Rudolph Valentino. Molded mask face, CM, brown ptd. eyes, black ptd. hair with long sideburns/silk head scarf, cloth body/limbs, original black trousers, white shirt, vest, multicolored scarf tied around waist, long black leatherette boots. Costumed as "The Shiek." (Purchased at Francis X. Bushman's REMEMBER WHEN antiques shop, Hollywood.) Ca. 1921+ (Not a likeness.)........................... $700

34" "Pages Madrid" Lady. Molded felt face, broad smiling mouth/red lips/white ptd.-molded teeth, large blue ptd. eyes to side, blonde mohair wig, cloth body/felt limbs, original felt and cloth outfit, high-heeled slippers, silk stockings, etc. Label reads: "Pages Madrid." (Doll resembles Greta Garbo.) Made in Spain. Ca. 1930s $1,200

36" Valine's Perfume Advertising Lady. Harem Girl type. All cloth, ptd. features/spit curls on forehead and on each cheek/turban conceals rest of hair, long shapely body to waist/long arms/puffed legs represent trouser garment/long slender feet encased in printed ballet-type slippers/printed in vivid Russian ballet colors, printed bracelets on arms (dolls of this type were stuffed and stitched by hand.) Ca. 1920s.. $600+

38" Harlequin. Male. Molded mask face/oval shape, CM, blue ptd. eyes, no wig/wears tight black cap, cloth body/long limbs jtd. at elbows and knees/small waist, original long dress, bonnet, etc. Unmarked. France. ... $900

42" Dean's Lady. Molded cloth mask face, CM, blue ptd. eyes to side, blonde mohair wig, cloth body/limbs, original pajama suit. Dean's Rag Book Co., England. 1920s........................ $1,200

29" Boudoir doll with compo shoulder head, CM, ptd eyes, brown mohair wig, cloth body, lovely clothes. Note 1920s cushions. Cushion on left has mohair wig. $225. (Courtesy of Herron)

Chapter 2

~ BRU ~

History: Bru Jne. & Cie, Paris, and Montreuil-sous-Bois, France, 1866-99.

The Bru story is one of innovation and industry. This was the era when the French doll was finally being made in France—and to French specifications. The French liked to be different. They liked the best and were highly inventive and artistic. They made dolls long before the Germans and resented the German take-over.

The French concept was a luxury doll that must mirror the human being in every way. It must be custom-made and as sturdy as a piece of furniture. It was not enough for the doll to boast paper-weight eyes that were round on the surface and possessed depth and swirling pools of color, but it must walk, talk, eat, drink, sing, cry, and breathe.

Bru tried all mediums for the heads of his dolls: bisque, gutta-percha, wood, composition, and rubber, which was similar to gutta-percha. The Maison Bru was located on the rue Saint Denis in 1868. The rue Saint Denis was famous for its dressmaking establishments, and probably outfitted many a Bru in silks and laces. Like the maisons of Huret, Rohmer, and Jumeau, the Maison Bru was famous for its fashionable Parisiennes and, later, Bebes.

The German tendency to undersell the French—and with a quality product—reduced the French doll maisons almost to poverty in the 1890s. The French were forced into mass-production, and so had to manufacture a cheaper doll, hence the quality of the Bebe Bru declined in the 1890s. Although the "Bru" trademark existed well into the twentieth century, it no longer had much meaning. Late Brus are hardly worth mentioning; one is only buying a "name" and not a tradition.

Collecting Hints:

The Bru lady dolls are instantly recognized by their illusive, almost "secretive" smiles, but not all of these heads have a smiling face. One early "lady" Bru is incised "B. Jne et Cie" and is found with a stationary shoulder head or on a shoulder plate with a swivel head. Sometimes the word "DEPOSE"

is incised on the front of the plate. This doll's face is round and chubby and suggests a teen-age girl or young women rather than a matron. This head is found on a jointed wood body or an all-kid body. A fully articulated wood body is more rare than a kid body, and even in its day, was more pricey. Although the mouth of this young lady is faintly smiling, she is not the lady collectors refer to as the "Mona Lisa" or "Smiling Lady Bru."

That doll is incised with letters from the alphabet. These ladies are always found with a swivel neck. All early Brus usually have pierced ears and all have cork pates. The "Mona Lisa" Bru is found on three body types: all kid; kid body with wood or kid upper arms and bisque lower arms; or the fully jointed wood body.

The Bebe Brevete was Brus offering to the world of baby or child dolls. The first Bebe Brevetes had kid bodies; the wood articulated body was used for a while and is more rare. The Circle Dot or Moon and Crescent Brus are found with kid bodies and bisque lower arms. They are choice and highly sought. The Bebe Teteur (1879+) was Brus most popular model. It was produced for more than twenty years. The early models are the best.

The Bru Jne (1884+) dolls have a slimmer face and neck and a slimmer body shape with a knee rivet joint and wood lower limbs. They depict a somewhat older child than the preceding dolls. Bisque quality declined after 1892. The Brus with the "R" mark and composition bodies do not compare favorably with the dolls that came before. The later ones with sleeping eyes and open mouths are usually the poorest example of a Bru, although popularity of the Bru "name" continues to keep prices high. Brus are not rare.

When buying a Bru for investment purposes choose one with fine bisque quality, original wig and eyes, a firm kid body or good quality composition body, and, if possible original clothes, shoes, etc. The life-size mannequin Brus were for store display of clothes. Some of the ladies have smiling faces. Perhaps they realize that the joke is on us. Are

we paying too much to acquire her and her sisters?

Reproduction Alert:

The Bru is the most reproduced of all dolls. New bisque heads have been attached to old bodies in some instances. Be aware.

BRU (MAISON)

Size 5/0

10-1/2" Smiling Lady Bru. Bisque swivel head on bisque shoulder plate, smiling CM, inset blue PW eyes, PE blonde mohair wig, kid body/limbs, original clothes, bonnet. Unmarked. (This is the 11" size which has shrunk due to settling of sawdust.) 1873+............ $2,900

11" Bru Jne R 3" Bebe. Bisque swivel head on bisque shoulder plate, O/C mouth, inset blue PW eyes, PE, blonde mohair wig, kid body / bisque lower arms, original clothes, etc. Early 1890s (Sold for $3,500 in 1991)........................ $3,700

14"-Bru Jne 3. Pale bisque head/lower arms/kid body, CM, inset blue PW eyes, old clothes, etc. Ca. 1880s $16,500-$17,000. (Courtesy of Linda Martinez Bassi)

11" Bru Jne R//2" Bebe. Walker. Bisque head, CM, inset blue PW eyes, PE, blonde mohair wig, jtd. compo. body / legs attached to hips with metal joints for walking, original 2-pc blue silk outfit, orchid silk blue hat, etc. head mark: "BRU Jne R//2." Paul Eugene Girard, France. Ca. 1890-99 (Sold for $7,000 in 1993)..$8,500

12" "B" incised Smiling Lady. Bisque Swivel head, CM, PE, inset blue PW eyes, brown mohair wig, all-wood articulated body, original clothes, hat. Ca. 1873+...$6,000

12" Bru Jne 1 and "Crescent" mark. Pale bisque swivel head on pale bisque shoulder plate, CM, blue PW eyes, Blonde mohair wig, PE, kid body/bisque lower arms, original clothes, signed "BRU" shoes. Ca. late 1870s $16,000

12-1/2" Smiling Lady. Bisque swivel head on bisque shoulder plate, CM, inset brown PW eyes, PE, blonde mohair wig, gusseted "lady" kid body, original silk walking dress, hat, etc, Ca. 1873+...$3,500

13" "Bru Jne et C" incised Parisienne. Bisque swivel head on kid-lined bisque shoulder plate, CM, inset blue cobalt eyes (cobalt blue), PE, blonde mohair wig, kid "lady" body/tan leather arms, original silk walking dress, bonnet, etc. 1866+............................$3,700-$4,000

13" Bru Jne 2. Bisque head, CM, inset brown PW eyes, PE, blonde mohair wig, BJ compo./wood "walker" body, original silk dress, frilly bonnet, etc. Ca. 1880s $16,000

13" Bru Jne 4 Bebe. Bisque Swivel head on bisque shoulder plate/cork pate (all Brus have cork pates), OM/hole, blue-grey PW eyes, PE, blonde mohair wig, kid body/bisque lower arms, old clothes, etc. (Nursing devise in back of head). Head mark: "Bebe Bru 4." Purple ink stamp on body reads: "Bebe Bru 4." Ca. 1880s $8,000

19" Bru Jne 7. Bisque head, OM/teeth, inset brown PW eyes, blonde HHW, BJ compo body, redressed. Early 1890s $4,000-$4,500. (Courtesy of Connie Baca)

13" Circle Dot Bébé. Bisque swivel head on bisque shoulder plate, O/C mouth/molded ptd. teeth, orange-pink cheek blush, PE, large inset almond-shaped brown PW eyes, early skin wig, kid body/gusseted jts./bisque lower arms, original clothes, bat, signed "BRU" shoes, etc. Ca. late 1870s (Some have kid-lined shoulder plates) $16,000

13-1/2" Parisienne with Trousseaux. Bisque swivel head on bisque shoulder plate, CM, inset blue PW eyes, blonde mohair wig, kid body/wood arms, original clothes plus 3 lavish couturier outfits, parasol, jewelry box, accessories, Bru trunk. Ca. 1866+ (1994 auction price: $16,000).....................$10,000+

14" "Bru Jne" incised Parisienne. Bisque swivel-head on bisque shoulder plate (both incised with BRU-JNE mark), CM, inset blue PW eyes, blonde mohair wig, PE, kid fashion body/gusset jts./kid limbs, original fancy clothes, etc. Ca. 1870s-80s $3,500

14" Smiling Lady Bru. Bisque swivel head on bisque shoulder plate, smiling CM, brown HHW, inset blue PW eyes, PE, fully articulated wooden body/white kid with scalloped edges around shoulders and breastplate, original gown, underclothes. (A doll similar to this one has the "D" mark and Jumeau stamp.) Incised: "D" Ca. 1873+.................$8,000

14-1/2" "B. Jne et Cie" incised Jeune Fille (Young Girl or Teenager). Bisque swivel head on bisque shoulder plate/round full face / long neck / double chin, slightly smiling CM, almond-shaped cobalt blue PW eyes, blonde HHW, kid body/limbs, original clothes, hat, etc. (This doll appears to be a teenager rather than a mature lady type. This face is also found on a stationary shoulder head. The mark "Depose" incised on the front of the chest is likewise found on similar face types. The wood-jointed body is sometimes found with this head.) Ca. 1866+......$4,000+

15" Bebe Teteur or "Nursing Bru." (Bru Jne mould.) Little Girl. Bisque head, OM/hole, inset blue PW eyes, rosy cheeks, blonde mohair wig, kid body/wood lower limbs, original white baby clothes, bonnet, etc. Mark: "Bru Jne 4." Chest label. (This doll appears to be a later model because of the more florid bisque coloring. S.F.B.J. made nursing Brus after 1899.) Ca. late 1890s or later...........................$7,500

15" Smiling Lady Bru. Pale bisque swivel head on pale bisque shoulder plate, smiling CM, inset blue PW eyes, blonde mohair wig, hid body / limbs, original 2-pc cotton dress, etc.; has 2 extra dresses, very elaborate walking dresses, 3 hats, purses, hand mirror, fan, toiletries. Mark: "C." (1992 auction price:. $8,400)...................................$7,000+

15-1/2" "Bru" incised Parisienne. Pale bisque head, slightly smiling CM, large blue PW eyes, brown HHW, PE, kid body/gusseted jts./bisque lower arms, original clothes, hat. Ca. 1866+ $3,600

16" Parisienne. Bisque swivel head on bisque shoulder plate, CM, inset blue PW eyes, blonde mohair wig, PE, kid body/rare articulated wooden arms and legs, original clothes, hat, etc. Ca. 1873+......................................$8,000

17" Parisienne. Bisque swivel head on bisque shoulder plate, CM, inset blue PW eyes, brown HHW, kid body/gusseted jts. original clothes, hat. Head mark: "4." Ca. 1866+.................$4,500

18" Bébé Bru. Rubber head, CM, inset large blue glass eyes, soft blonde mohair wig, unpierced ears, BJ mâché body/legs/feet/arms to wrists made of wood/fine bisque hands, old clothes, etc. Head mark: "BRU." Cal. 1878...................................... $12,000

18" Clarmaid Bébé Bru Reproduction. Negro Girl. Dark brown bisque swivel head on bisque shoulder plate, CM, inset brown glass eyes, brown kid body/gusset jts./dark brown bisque lower arms, old clothes, etc. Head mark: "Clarmaid//1962//Bru Jne//8." Shoulder mark: "Bru Jne 8." Ca. 1962.......................................$1,000+

18-1/2" "Bru Jne & T" incised Bebe Teteur or "Nursing Bru." Bisque head/rubber ball inside head/metal butterfly clip at rear of head for squeezing, OM/hole, inset blue PW eyes, blonde skin wig, kid body/kid-over-wood upper arms/wood lower limbs, original baby clothes, bonnet. Ca. 1878-98 (Early type)...................................$12,000

19" Smiling Lady. Bisque head, smiling CM, inset blue PW eyes, blonde HHW, PE, all-wood articulated body, original clothes, etc. Ca. 1873+...........$12,000

19" Smiling Male. (Female dressed as a male.) Bisque head, CM, inset blue PW eyes, auburn HHW (male cut), PE, kid body/jtd. wood arms/hands, original black 2-pc dress suit/top hat, white shirt, tie, etc. Ca. 1873+............$9,500

20" Bru Jne 7 Bride. Bisque swivel head on bisque shoulder plate, CM, inset blue PW eyes, blonde mohair wig, PE, kid body/gusset jts./bisque lower arms, original Bridal gown, veil, underwear, stockings, signed "BRU" shoes. Late 1870s...................................$10,000+

16" Bru Jne. Bisque head/lower arms (hands)/kid body, O/C mouth, inset blue PW eyes, brown HHW, original clothes, etc. 1880s $18,000. (Courtesy of D. Kay Crow)

20" Parisienne. Little girl type. Bisque swivel head on bisque shoulder plate, CM, inset brown PW eyes, brown HHW, PE, kid fashion-type body/arms, original silk dress, hat, etc. Ca. 1880s $7,000

21" Bru Jne R//9. "Kiss Baby." Bisque head, OM, blue glass sleep eyes, blonde mohair wig, PE, BJ compo. body/straight legs/voice box/throws kisses, original clothes, bonnet, etc. Ca. early 1890s+.......................$5,500

21" Bru Jne R//9. Bisque head, CM, inset brown PW eyes, dark brown HHW, PE, BJ compo. body/straight wrists, old clothes, etc. Incised: "Bru Jne R//O." Ca. early 1890s.........................$8,500

21" Oriental Bru. Olive bisque head on olive bisque shoulder plate, molded bosom, CM, inset brown PW eyes, dark flyaway eyebrows, black HHW, kid body/bisque lower arms/wood lower legs/Bru label, original brownish-silk embroidered kimono, metal fan, signed "BRU" shoes, etc. Head/shoulder plate incised: "Bru Jne N. 7." Ca. 1880s $10,000

21" Parisienne. Bisque swivel head on bisque shoulder plate, CM, inset blue PW eyes, brown HHW, kid body/gusseted jts./leather arms, original clothes, hat, etc. Head mark: "5." Ca. 1866+ ....$6,500-$7,500

22" Bru Jne R//9. Walking/Waving Bebe. Bisque socket head, OM/teeth, blue PW eyes, long curl brown HHW, jtd. compo. walking body/pull-string mechanism, original clothes, hat, etc. Ca. early 1890s $5,500

22" Paul Girard Bébé. Bisque socket head, CM, inset blue PW eyes, brown mohair wig, PE, jtd. compo. French body, original clothes, hat, etc. Mark: "B/P. 13 G." Ca. 1889-99 ....$8,500

22" Portrait Parisienne. Bisque shoulder head, smiling CM, inset blue PW eyes, blonde HHW, PE, kid body/bisque lower arms, old clothes, etc. Mark: "Bebe Bru Bte S.G.D.G." (This is not the usual "Mona Lisa" smiling face.) Ca. early 1880s $15,000

24" Bru Jne R 10.Pale bisque head, OM/molded teeth, brown glass sleep eyes, blonde HHW, PE, BJ compo. body, old clothes, bonnet, marked "BRU" shoes, etc. Ca. 1890s ....$6,500-$7,000

24-1/2" Bru Jne & Cie//9 Circle-Dot Bébé. Bisque swivel head on bisque shoulder plate, slightly open CM, brown PW eyes, blonde mohair wig, PE, kid body/bisque lower arms, original net and lace dress with pink silk liner, fancy hat, etc. Ca. late 1870s $27,000

31" Bru Jne R 14. Pressed bisque head, O/C mouth, blue PW eyes, peach-colored cheek blush, auburn HHW, PE, BJ compo. body, original clothes, etc. Ca. 1890s $15,000

33" Bru Jne Bébé. Bisque shoulder head, CM, large inset blue PW eyes, blonde HHW, PE, kid body/bisque lower arms, old French silk clothes, etc. Mark: "Bru Jne" on head/shoulders. Ca. 1880s......................................$30,000

Reproduction of 28" Bru by Angela Barker, England.

Chapter 3

MARTHA JENKS CHASE

History: 1889+

Martha Jenks Chase, Pawtucket, R.I., began making dolls for her children in the 1870s. A decade later her dolls were being sold through the Jordan Marsh store. Early dolls were primitive and similar to those made by Izannah Walker and Ella Smith. In fact, early Chase dolls were constructed much like the Alabama Babies and it is sometimes difficult to distinguish one from the other. Early Chase dolls had pink sateen bodies. Later bodies were made of a more durable heavy cotton material. Baby dolls are the most commonly found, but black dolls and character types were made in the 1890s and later. The Chase Hospital dolls (1911) seem more difficult to find, and are often confused with the playdolls. (Some of these are adult-size.) The Chase "soft" dolls include Tommy Snooks, Silly Sally, and Bessy Brooks. In 1910, the Chase Company advertised dolls that could be washed in warm water. These were treated with waterproof paint. In modern times, the Chase playdolls were made in plastic and are in no way similar to the old.

Collecting Hints:

Chase dolls were crudely made and painted, but their appeal is universal. Some dolls are badly worn, chipped, and lack their original clothing. These should sell for less than those that have been well-preserved and wear their factory-made clothes (some clothing is marked). All Chase dolls were stamped with the Chase trademark, but some of the body stamps have rubbed off or were washed off. Dolls made in limited quantity (the character types) are the most expensive.

CHASE DOLLS

9"Baby. Hard stockinet head/treated/oil ptd, ptd features, blonde ptd hair, cloth body jtd at sh/hips/elbows/knees/stockinet limbs, old baby dress. Ca. 1890s ....$3,000-$3,500

(Babies similar to above in sizes 13" to 26" vary in price from $700-$1,000, depending on condition and degree of rarity.)

12" Tweedledum and Tweedledee. Alice in Wonderland characters. All-cloth, large round heads, wide CM's, blue ptd eyes, original wigs, original white pants with buttons, blue shirts with white collars (their names embroidered across front), red and white striped socks, black shoes, blue and white baseball-type caps with brims. Ca. 1905-1925 Rare Pair $25,000

16" Little Nell. All-cloth/treated/oil ptd, narrow oval-shaped face, CM, ptd blue eyes, red nostril dots, orange one-stroke eyebrows, orange ptd hair with a center part/brushstrokes/braids molded separately to hang loosely at shoulders and tied with red ribbon bows, jtd cloth body, original cotton dress, etc. Mark on left hip. Ca. 1920 ....$3,000-$4,000

16" Alice in Wonderland. All-cloth/treated/oil ptd, long narrow face, CM, ptd blue eyes with a round shape/ptd eyelashes, orange ptd eyebrows (thicker than Little Nell's), short brown-orange ptd hair/bangs, jtd sateen body/ptd stockinet limbs, original blue cotton dress, white apron, etc. Marked. Ca. 1920 ....$3,000-$5,000

20" Hospital Baby. All-cloth/treated/oil ptd, round face, red CM, ptd blue eyes, yellow ptd one-stroke eyebrows, nostril/ear holes, orange ptd hair/brushstrokes/bangs, ptd waterproof body/limbs, original baby gown, cap. Weighs 16 lbs. Under arm mark: "CHASE HOSPITAL DOLL" (printed on the hat of a round baby doll face), "TRADE MARK" (printed beneath face), "PAWTUCKET, R.I.//MADE IN U.S.A" Ca. 1911+

21" Character Boy. All cloth/treated/oil ptd, molded/ptd face, CM, ptd brown eyes, red nostril dots, dimpled chin, one-stroke yellow eyebrows, brown ptd hair/feathered across forehead in flat brushstrokes, original sailor-type outfit with white tie knotted at throat, etc. Mark: "M.J.C., Stockinet Doll, Patent Applied For." Ca. 1898 .... $4,500

24" Negro Mammy. All cloth/treated/oil ptd, jet black/molded/ptd face, smiling red mouth, ptd black eyes, black wool hair, black ptd/jtd stockinet body/limbs, original red dress, white apron, red bandana, etc. Ca. 1890s $12,500

24" Negro Boy. All cloth/treated/oil ptd, black/molded/ptd face, red CM, ptd large brown eyes, black wool hair, brown ptd/jtd stockinet body/limbs, original clothes, etc. Ca. 1889+ $11,500

32" Negro Boy. All cloth/treated/oil ptd, black/molded/ptd face, red CM, ptd brown eyes, black wool hair, black ptd/jtd stockinet body/limbs, original clothes, etc. Ca. 1890s $15,000

40" Hospital Child. All cloth/treated/oil ptd, CM, ptd blue eyes, applied ears, brown ptd hair with straight bangs, nostril/ear holes, ptd waterproof body/limbs, original white sailor-type suit, etc. (This little boy resembles an older baby, but is meant to be a child about 4-5 years old.) Ca. 1911+ (1911+) $7,000

Chapter 4

~ CHINA DOLLS ~

History:

The manufacture of dolls, like the manufacture of other decorative and functional items, depends upon sales to survive. Hence, it becomes a matter of growth, development, and packaging. The more clever and attractive the package, the better the sales. The stolid faced papier-mâché head dolls with the modish hairstyles made from the 1820s to the 1860s, no doubt influenced the manufacture of dolls with heads of glazed and unglazed bisque (chinas and parians).

The so-called "Milliners' Models," of German origin, were a mere step away from the glorified "Pandoras" or "style" dolls of the 17th and 18th century. The Germans had made dolls with china-heads since circa 1750, but not having proved popular, the doll with the head of wood or papier-mâché soon took precedence.

The popularity of the "Milliners' Models" in the 1820s and 1830s, encouraged the German doll manufacturers to once again revert to old methods and produce artistic dolls of a very superior quality. These 1840s chinas, with their long necks, portraits faces, and timely hairstyles, personified the aristocratic ideal of womanhood; appearing almost "figurine" in their grandeur (some heads were never attached to bodies; serving as "busts" for mantel-piece display). Being carefully and artistically conceived—and time-consuming—their longevity was short-lived.

Although the decorative heads with the elaborate hairstyles and ornamentation continued to be made until the 1880s, they were becoming old fashioned, their very hairdos dating them to the past. In the 1850s, a more simplistic china-head doll was introduced for the masses. These heads depicted matrons with short necks, and young children of both sexes. Hair arrangements were in keeping with the trends favored at the time, and decoration, if any, was kept to the minimum, making them cheaper and easier to produce with two-part molds.

Some of these heads represented peasants in regional attire, but most portrayed the common folk, and not the titled gentry. Occasionally, one of these ordinary shoulder heads would sport a modeled necklace, or one inset with a faux "jewel;" a hairband or ribbon; and, later, would be given names, like Edith, Helen, or Agnes. Heady competition in the 1880s cheapened many of the more common dolls, and by the 1890s a definite "stagnation" had settled in. The china-head dolls with the common low-brown hairdo became a favorite mass-market retail item, and similar heads were made until World War Two, both in Germany and Japan. It was as though all creative genius had absconded the German doll factories.

Collecting Hints

When paying a high price for a doll with a china head study the china quality, painting of features, hairstyle, clothing, body, and limbs. If only the head is old, you are only buying an old head, so the price should not be the same as a doll that is completely original. All dolls made prior to 1900 are old and will soon become scarce and rare (as we move into a new century). This includes china heads with common hairdos.

After World War One china-heads were made in Japan—as well as Germany. And in many instances, the Japanese used old German molds. It was during this period, that dolls were hastily painted; red lid lines, red eye and nose dots, and fine facial detail gave way to sloppy painting. Never pay a high price for a doll that was obviously carelessly conceived. Its value will never amount to much more than what you paid for it.

A china-head doll with a rare hairdo or one with a rare hairdo and unusual decoration, plus an old body, limbs, and clothes, is always the best investment. An all-original antique doll dressed in modern synthetics is not as valuable as one dressed in its original clothing. Such a doll should then be recostumed in antique materials by an expert. But never over-look the nude doll.

Some extremely rare dolls are found in this condition, simply because their clothes either rotted away, or their previous owner simply "borrowed" them for another doll of similar body structure. Some dealers even "strip" dolls bare and sell the antique clothing, stockings, shoes, etc., separately. A nude doll should not sell for the same price as a doll with its old or original clothing.

Reproduction Alert

The china-head has been the most reproduced head of them all—mostly by amateurs. Even molds have been taken off old heads by modern "artists" and reconstructed with a new hairdo and decoration and passed off as an "original." But the new ceramic china heads rarely measure up to antique standards. The old china was not only of a better quality, but oft' times reveals kiln dirt and specks. Early heads were pressed into the molds making them thicker, heavier, and more durable. Many modern "china" heads also crackled with age; old china heads did not. Again, study the painting of features.

Some of the late German-made heads incised "Germany" have been mistaken for "reproductions" made in modern times by amateur artists when

9" Blonde china shoulder head lady, cloth body/china lower limbs, old clothes. Ca. 1860s $225. (Courtesy of D. Kay Crow)

14" China shoulder head with rare blue ptd/mld necklace, cloth body/leather arms, original clothes. Ca. 1860s $450. (Courtesy of Herron)

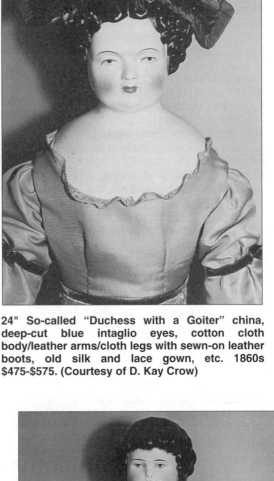

24" So-called "Duchess with a Goiter" china, deep-cut blue intaglio eyes, cotton cloth body/leather arms/cloth legs with sewn-on leather boots, old silk and lace gown, etc. 1860s $475-$575. (Courtesy of D. Kay Crow)

Super-rare china shoulder head doll seated at her original sewing machine. Mechanical doll. Original clothes, etc. Ca. 1860s $5,000+.

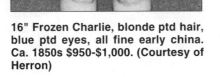

16" Frozen Charlie, blonde ptd hair, blue ptd eyes, all fine early china. Ca. 1850s $950-$1,000. (Courtesy of Herron)

20" Child china, exquisite facial painting, deep breastplate, cloth body/china lower limbs/black ptd boots, old clothes. 1880s Possibly made by Kling (marks unclear) $650. (Courtesy D. Kay Crow)

they are not. One in my collection has a red mouth painted "crookedly," blue painted eyes with black lid lines, and black one-stroke arched eyebrows; the hairstyle is in the familiar "low-brow" mode. Old china heads rarely had painted eyelashes; and when they are found on an old head, the head is considered super-rare. Many old shoulder heads are found on new cloth bodies with new ceramic lower limbs. These additions usually confuse the novice collector, who asks herself: "Is the head also a reproduction?" or: "Are the limbs also 'antique'?" Take the doll into the daylight, if need be, and get out your magnifying glass. There is a difference!

CHINA DOLLS

6" Frozen Charlotte. All china/jtd at sh/hips, CM, ptd. blue eyes, black ptd. hair. (This doll is wire-strung, long arms, chubby legs, well-modeled feet.) Ca. 1850s (super-rare) ....$1,500+

7-1/2" French China Man. Early creamy china shoulder head/pastel coloring, CM, almond shaped ptd. blue eyes/red lid lines, short black ptd. mustache, black ptd. hairstyle (feathered toward face in front of ears), kid body/limbs, original formal attire. (This lovely doll is painted in the delicate, artistic French manner.) Ca. 1840s ($700)

8" "Covered Wagon" China Lady. Pink tint china shoulder head, CM, ptd. blue eyes, rosy cheeks, black ptd. hair/ "Covered Wagon" hairstyle, cloth body, pink tint china lower limbs, original clothes. Ca. 1850s ....$475-$525

8" "Jewel" China Lady. White china shoulder head, red CM, ptd. blue eyes, straight 1-stroke black eyebrows, black ptd./molded low-brow hairdo, cloth

body/white china lower limbs/molded-on gold tinted necklace with an inset imitation "jewel," original cheap factory-made clothes. Distributed by Butler Bros. for Borgfeidt (trademark china). This doll is typical of the hastily painted chinas that flooded the commercial market in the early 20th c. Ca. 1901 ....$150

10" "Kate Greenaway" China. Young girl type. White china shoulder head, red CM, brilliant red cheeks, ptd. blue eyes/no red lid lines, black ptd. common "low brow" hairdo, cloth body and upper limbs printed with Kate Greenaway figures/crude china lower limbs/black ptd. shoes, undressed. Ca. 1890s ....$150-$175

10" "Little Boy" China. Pink tint china shoulder head, wee CM, ptd. brown eyes/red lid lines, black ptd./molded hair, modeled ears, kid/cloth body/leather arms, original 2-pc outfit. (This china head actually looks like a boy; especially the "boy" hairstyle with part and brushmarks surrounding the slender face.) Ca. 1860s $900

11" China Rattle/Whistle. White china shoulder head, CM, ptd. blue eyes, black ptd. common low-brow hairdo, wood handle/whistle/rattle beneath original red skirt/matching red hat/gold trim. Ca. 1890s (Sold for $575 in 1991) Rare item ....$600+

12" "G" incised Lady China. Pink tint china shoulder head (turned almost parallel to the left side)/deeply molded bosom and back muscles, CM, ptd. brown eyes/red lid lines, blonde ptd./molded hairdo with center part/sleek top/side and rear curls, cloth body (with kid)/pink tint lower limbs with realistically sculpted hands and feet, old clothes. Mark: "G." (in black script under the glaze). Ca. 1850s Rare $3,500

12-1/2" "Bald Head" China Lady. China socket head (with rare rotating devise which enables head to turn in any direction) on china shoulder plate, wee CM, ptd. blue eyes/brown ptd. eyebrows, original brown HHW, cloth body/china lower limbs, old clothes. Ca. 1850s (Quality) $900

12-1/2" "Mozart" (so-called) China Man. China shoulder head/long neck, red CM, grey ptd. eyes, modeled ears, dark ptd./curly hair with grey streaks/forelock/sideburns, cloth-covered wire-armature body/china lower limbs/ptd. stockings/purple slippers, old purple velvet suit, hat, etc. Mark: "MEISSEN." Ca. 1840s (Probably made by Teichert) $2,500

13" "Bonnet" China Lady. China shoulder head/oval face/sweet expression/long neck, faintly smiling CM, ptd. blue eyes/red lid lines, black ptd. hair bordering the face in "Scalloped" curls/molded on yellow ptd. bonnet with ruffled edges and blue ptd. band, cloth body/china lower limbs, old clothes. Ca. 1850s $2,500

13" "Bonnet" China Child. White china shoulder head,/squat neck, CM, ptd. blue eyes, blonde ptd./molded "curly" hair sculpted high on head and low on forehead/molded-on wide-brimmed hat atop head (covers rear of head)/wee

red dots painted across brim, cloth body/china lower limbs, old clothes. Ca. 1880-1890s (Sold for $180 in 1992) $350

(More than likely made in the 1890s)

13" "Poupard" China. White china shoulder head, wee red CM, delicate pink cheek blush, exposed ears, large ptd. blue eyes/red dots, red nose dots, 1-stroke upper light brown eyebrows, black ptd./molded short/hairdo with feathered curls framing face and neck, head mounted to a stick with a sound mechanism concealed beneath plain/grey coarse fabric decorated with gold braid and cut to points at waist and hem; lavished with gold braid and wee metal bells. Ca. 1850s ....$900-$1,500

14" "1000" incised China Girl. White china shoulder head, red CM, pale pink cheek blush, red nose dots, ptd. blue eyes/red eye dots/red lid lines/black eyeliner, short blonde ptd./molded hairdo/uneven bangs/curly sides, cloth body/china lower limbs, old clothes. Made by Alt, Beck & Gottschalck, Germany. Ca. 1880 ....$400

14" Frozen Charlie. All-china/no movable joints, ptd. features, ear modeling, blonde ptd./molded hair, Undressed. Ca. 1850s ....$850+

14-1/2" "Molded Teeth" China Girl. White china shoulder head, rare O/C mouth/4 molded upper teeth, rosy cheeks, ptd. blue eyes/black eyeliner, red lid lines, black ptd./molded common "low brow" hairdo, cloth body/china lower limbs, old clothes. Ca. 1890s $400

15" "Civil War" or "Swivel Neck" China. China swivel neck on china shoulder plate, CM, ptd. blue eyes/red lid lines, black ptd./molded flat-top hairdo/center part/short side and rear curls, cloth body/china lower limbs, old clothes. Ca. early 1860s $1,500

15" "Highland Mary" china shoulder head, redressed, 1880s $400. (Courtesy of Ruby Ellen Smith)

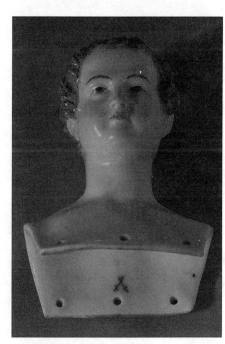

Rare Meissen china head man showing crossed swords mark. Early 19th century. (Courtesy of Janet Johl Weissman)

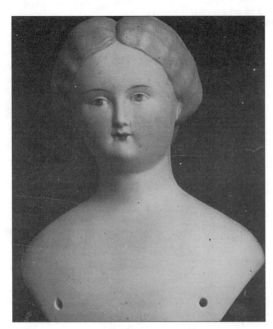

Super-rare 1840s blonde china head with rear bun. (Courtesy of Janet Johl Weissman)

31-1/2" Civil War china lady, original factory-made, heavy-weight body/leather arms/cloth legs with red leather sewn-on boots/blue ribbed sewn-on stockings with floral border, original exquisite clothes. 1860s $1,000-$1,100. (Courtesy of Herron)

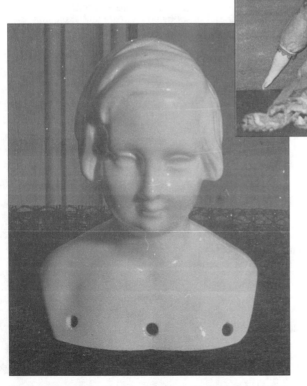

15" "Apple Cheek" china shoulder head, cloth body/china lower limbs lovely, factory-made clothes. Late 1880s $350. (Courtesy of Herron)

Pure white china shoulder head ca. 1840-1850, unpainted. (Courtesy of Herron)

Early untinted white china shoulder head, 1840s (small), 1850s (large). (Courtesy of Herron)

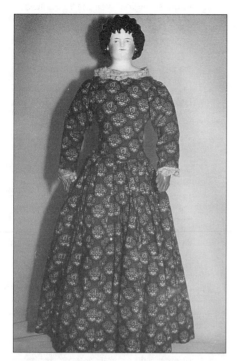

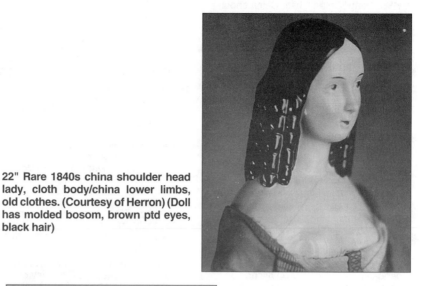

22" Rare 1840s china shoulder head lady, cloth body/china lower limbs, old clothes. (Courtesy of Herron) (Doll has molded bosom, brown ptd eyes, black hair)

21" "Curly Top" china shoulder head, cloth body/leather arms/cloth legs with sewn-on leather boots, old clothes $1,200. (Courtesy of D. Kay Crow)

30" China shoulder head lady, body replaced long ago, old clothes. 1860s $750. (Courtesy of D. Kay Crow)

17" China reproduction of "Grape" lady by La Motte, 1965, cloth body/china lower limbs, original clothes. $350. (Courtesy of D.K. Crow)

20" Lovely china shoulder head lady with Mona Lisa expression, blue intaglio eyes, black ptd hair with gold band, cloth body/leather arms, old clothes. Ca. early 1850s $1,700. (Courtesy of D. Kay Crow)

15" "Whistling" China Child. China shoulder head/hole atop head with metal whistle, blonde ptd./molded common "low-brow" hairdo, cloth body/china lower limbs, old clothes. Ca. 1900-1914 .... $200

15" "Bald Head" China Lady. Pink tint china shoulder head/bald dome head with 4 head holes for wig attachment, red CM, red cheek blush, vivid blue ptd. eyes/fine brown eyeliner/brown lid lines, 1-stroke eyebrows, blonde HHW, cloth body/pink tint lower china limbs/bare feet with toe detail/upturned big toe/flat bottoms, old clothes. Rare type. Ca. 1850s (Quality) ....$1,200-$1,500

15" "Currier & Ives" (so-called) China Child. Creamy china shoulder head/cup-and-saucer neck, tiny rosebud mouth, rosy cheeks, dreamy ptd. blue eyes/black lid lines, exposed ears, black ptd./scalloped bangs/shoulder-length wavy curls behind ears/brushstrokes (not a "spill" curl style), cloth body/china lower limbs, old clothes. Shoulder mark: "3." Ca. 1880s $450

15" Young Queen Victoria China Lady. Pink tint china shoulder head/long neck/sloping shoulders, slightly smiling CM, rosy cheeks, ptd. blue eyes/black lid lines, light brown ptd./molded hairdo/sleek/partially exposed ears (lobes)/looped side braids joining above nape in a V shape, brown eyebrows, pink tint lower arms/open hands/cloth body/legs, original silk walking dress, etc. (Shoulder plate has 8 sew holes. This is an excellent likeness of Victoria except that the nose is too short in profile.) Mark: "JP PAR BREVETE." Made by Jacob Petit, France. Ca. 1843+ .... $7,500+

16" "Dolley Madison" China Lady. China shoulder head/round face/round sloping shoulders, wee CM, ptd. blue eyes/red lid lines, exposed ears, black ptd./molded hair 2 fat curls on forehead/curly sides and back/molded ribbon and bow across front of head, cloth body/china lower limbs, old clothes. Ca. 1870s (Dolley Madison, wife of President James Madison, fourth President of the U.S.A., 1751-1836; wife Dolley, 1772-1849, known for her personality and style. This doll is not a likeness, nor was it ever intended to be her.) Ca. 1870s $575

16" "Long Curl" China Lady. Creamy china shoulder head, red CM, rosy cheeks, ptd. blue eyes/red lid lines, well-defined ears, black ptd./molded hairdo with slightly "puffed" top/long sausage curls sculpted onto shoulder behind left ear, elaborate rear coil of hair, cloth body/white kid arms, original fancy clothes. Ca. 1865-69 .... $900

16" "Lacmann" Lady China. Pink tint china shoulder head, CM, pink cheek blush. ptd. blue eyes/red lid lines, black ptd./molded hair/center part/flat-top/ "winged" curls at sides and rear, cloth body/legs/red leather arms/separated fingers, original well-made, hand-sewn clothes. Jacob Lacmann, Philadelphia, 1860-1883; Philipine Lacmann, successor, 1884-1887. Ca. 1860s ... $450

31" "Glass-eyed" China Lady. Creamy china shoulder head/round, matronly face/thick neck/double chin, rosy cheeks, faintly smiling CM, rare insert brown glass eyes/rare upper and lower eyelashes, black ptd./molded hair/center part/smooth flat-top/scalloped waves framing face/exposed ear lobes, cloth body/china lower arms, old clothes. Ca. 1850s (Eyelashes are a very rare feature on china-head dolls) Inset glass eyes makes it doubly rare. $7,500

32" "Apple Cheek" China. White china shoulder head, red CM, very rosy red cheeks or "apple cheeks," ptd. blue eyes/red lid lines, red nose dots, black ptd./molded flat-top hairdo/center part/vertical side and rear curls, cloth body/limbs/well-sculpted wrists and hands (natural looking), old clothes, leather shoes, stockings. Ca. 1860s (Sold for $1,250 in 1994.) $1,000

36" "Civil War" China Lady. White china shoulder head (deep shoulder plate with semi-long neck), CM, ptd. blue eyes/red lid lines, black ptd./modeled flat-top hairdo/side and black vertical curls, cloth body/china lower limbs, old clothes. Ca. 1860s $1,200

(All listed china-head dolls have their original bodies and limbs.)

Chapter 5

~ EMMA CLEAR ~

History:

Emma Clear was born in St. Louis, MO, April, 1879, the daughter of a prosperous cattleman. Her family moved to Buffalo, New York in 1883. She had always loved dolls, thus when she had a major operation at the age of eight, she spent her convalescence time mending and costuming the little dears. In the 1890s, Emma joined her high school doll club. During the summer months, she repaired and dressed the dolls brought to her. Friends and relatives gave her scraps of material and lace.

After high school she studied commercial law at Vanderbilt University in Nashville. When her college courses were completed she married an Englishman, and they had one child, Henry. In 1908, Emma opened a doll hospital and shop in downtown Buffalo. She imported all the needed parts (wigs, composition and kid bodies, heads, eyes, accessories, etc.,)from Germany and France, hence when World War One curtailed these necessary items, Emma left the business to her sister and moved with her son to Cleveland, Ohio.

With the supply of dolls' parts in short supply, Emma salvaged the better limbs, etc., from severely damaged dolls to mend the better dolls. Emma got a divorce in 1917, and headed for Los Angeles, CA, with Henry. She opened a doll hospital on Hill Street and later moved to a larger shop on Broadway. It had a large display window, which she filled with dolls. She soon discovered that there was very little repair work to be done on children's playthings, but considerable work on collectors' dolls.

She had been again briefly married and divorced when she met Wallace Clear, a local chicken farmer. She had grown weary of dolls and went to work for Clear caring for his ailing wife. The wife died and Emma went back to her doll repair business. She and Clear were subsequently married and she moved to Redondo Beach in 1928.

The Crash of '29 and the subsequent Depression reduced the Clears to extreme poverty. They lost their insurance policies, farm equipment, 2,000 chickens, and had to apply for welfare. Emma also lost her health and

almost died. It was during this period, that she decided to urge Wallace to turn the empty two-story chicken house into a doll workshop. She had a stockpile of fine German clay, doll parts, complete dolls, and trunks filled with old party dresses that she could use to dress dolls.

Wallace painted a sign out of an old dropping board and the Humpty Dumpty Doll Hospital was reborn. Emma operated the kilns and worked the clay, Wallace made molds, and-they hired artists to paint the dolls' hair, feet, and features. Since the clay was the type the Dresden potters had used on their wares, the Clear dolls were decorated with delicate flowers and rushing. All the added decoration had to be done by hand, when the clay was still in the "leather" stage, before drying and firing. Their first successful doll was Jenny Lind.

The Clears produced around 40 different dolls during their reign at HDDH. During World War II, they were awarded military contracts due to the ample supply of clay they had on hand (the Air Force used it for spark plugs). The Clears resumed doll-making after the war. HDDH was sold in 1949.

Clear died November 22, 1952, of cerebral artery thrombosis. Her body was cremated; the ashes interred at Pacific Crest Cemetery. Wallace Clear died in 1965 at age 87. He had remarried. Emma's son, Henry, died in 1981 or 1982.

Collecting Hints:

Most of the Clear dolls were copyrighted and patented. The Clear name was incised on the shoulder plate the year of manufacture. A white cotton HDDH tag stitched on -the bodies. Lillian Smith, who first purchased the business, marked the dolls she made "Clear"-"Smith"— "HDDH." When she sold the hospital 11 years later to Hazel M. Morgan the dolls were marked "Clear" and "1961." When Morgan sold, she and Wallace Clear authorized Clara Wade, once the top designer/ artist at HDDH to use the name. These were marked "Clear" and/or "Clarmaid." The dolls made during the lifetime of Emma Clear are the ones most sought by collectors.

Reproduction Alert:

Some of the Clear dolls are rumored to have been reproduced with her name intact. If suspicious, study the quality of bisque or china.

EMMA CLEAR

1930s-1949

(The following is a list of some of the dolls made by Emma Clear and the Humpty Dumpty Doll Hospital (1930s-1949). Prices vary from $500-$1,700. Some dolls like George and Martha Washington, the Gibson Girls, Danny, Barbary Coast Gent, and the more fancy types will command more money than the plainer types. Since the Clear dolls are not antiques but "replicas" of antiques—discounting the few originals like the Washingtons—their appeal is limited, thus their prices will continue to fluctuate. This also applies to other "artist" dolls.)

- Alice in Wonderland
- American Madonna
- 12"-19"-Barbary Coast Gent
- 14"-16"-27"-Mary Todd
- 15"-Elsa
- 15"-Lady Carolyn
- 15"-Margaret Rose
- 15"-19"-Mary Augusta
- 15"-Parthenia
- 16"-Baby Stuart
- 16"-Danny
- 16"-Gibson Girl (plain shoulders. Sold for $495 in 1994 at auction)
- 17"-Ann Rost
- 17"-Blue Scarf or Louise of Prussia
- 17"-The Kaiserin Augusta Victoria
- 18"-22"-Claudia
- 18"-Coronation Doll
- 18"-Dagmar
- 18"-15"-Diedra
- 18"-22"-Elizabeth
- 18"-Gibson Girl (with corsage. Sold for $695 in 1994 at auction.)
- 18"-Grape Lady 14 1/2-Highborn Lady or Mary Queen of Scots
- 18"-Isobel or Isabel 15"-Ivy Mae
- 18"-23-1/2"-Jenny Lind
- 18"-27"-Mona Lisa
- 18"-21"-Spill Curls
- 18"-Tiara Doll

Chapter 6
DEAN'S RAG BOOK CO. LTD.

History:

Dean's Rag Book Co. Ltd. (subsidiary of Dean & Son Ltd.), 18, Paternoster Square, London, EC. H.S. Dean registered patent no. 25452 on 25th November, 1908, for sheets of-dolls printed on colored fabrics, cut in 6 parts, sewn together and stuffed. (Their "Cut-Out and Sew" doll came out in 1908.) Their trademark, which depicted two dogs scuffling over a rag book, was registered on 8th December, 1909 (no. 319, 017). It was for their new line of dolls, toys, toy animals, toy figures, birds. On the 18th of August, 1913, Dean's registered "Fuz Buz" trademark n. 354, 125, for dolls and toys. Their famous "Tru-to-Life" dolls date to 1913. There were 30 different realistic faces in this collection. Patent no. 100469 (with A. L. Wheeldon) was registered on 17th March, 1916, for stuffed dolls and toy animals with feet patterns that could be cut and sewn in such a manner (with extension pieces) that allowed for free standing. (During World War One, Dean's produced soldier and sailor dolls printed on cloth.) On 14th February, 1917, (with Wheeldon), Dean's obtained patent no. 105888 which stated that the material for making a stuffed doll is shaped so as to form a skirt or other garment in one with the doll. Hilda Cowham, David Brett, Cecil Aldin, Stanley Berkley, and other well-known artists designed for them. Dean's was still making toys at its factory in South Wales in the late 1980s.

Collecting Hints:

Dean's rag dolls are often confused with those made by Chad Valley, Norah Wellings, and other comp.eting companies of the time. When a doll type became saleable, imitations sprang up like dandelions. (This applies to the present day.) When trying to identify an unmarked doll study the marked specimens. When paying a high price seek labels and original clothing. After World War II, they made dolls with hard rubber faces "composition".

1905-1980+

10" Charlie Chaplin. All-cloth, molded mask face, tiny CM, mustache, ptd blue eyes to side, black mohair wig, original black and grey check trousers, black coat, red vest, white shirt, cravat, black derby hat, black shoes. Ca. 1925 .... $800

10-1/2" Puss in Boots. Advertising Doll. All printed/stuffed cloth, limbs apart from body, blue printed belt, black printed boots, blue advertising band printed around neck. Feet marked: "Boots the Chemist, Branches everywhere." Ca. 1912... $225

11" "Knockabout Girl." Ta-Ta series. All printed/stuffed cloth, limbs apart from body, OM/ptd teeth, large blue eyes, brown curly hair bordering face/red scarf tied around head, white and green check skirt with red trim, green bodice laced in front with red ribbon, green socks, black shoes/yellow buckles (nothing is removable). Sole of foot numbered "2215/17." Ca. 1917.... $175

12" Monkey. All soft plush fabric, smiling "line" mouth, inset brown glass eyes, printed-on red jacket/blue trousers. Right foot label reads: "British Manufacture, Hygienic Stuffing. Tru-to-Life. Patent No. 25131/12 U.S.A. Patent April 13, 1915." Left foot: stamped (two dogs, a terrier and an English bulldog, playing tug-of-war with a sturdy Dean's Rag Book; with an oval border composed of: "Hygienic A1 Toys//Dean's Rag Book Co. Ltd.//Trade Mark//Made in England.") 1915+ $225

13" Charlie Chaplin. Pillow Doll. Ail printed/stuffed cloth. Originally made in 1920. Reissued in 1982. .... $85

13" "Tru-to-Life" Girl. Molded/ptd face, short printed hair with tiny ringlets covering head/tiny red bows on each side of head, tiny red CM, brown eyes, printed underwear, printed red shoes/socks, original removable clothes. (These could be purchased in sheet form and made-up at home.) Marked on the sole of each foot. Series of 30 rag dolls. Ca. 1913... $225

14" Lupino Lane. British stage star. All-cloth, molded/ptd face, stuffed body/limbs, needlesculpted hands (one thumb is pointed upwards as though hitchhiking), original black and white striped woolen suit, white shirt, cap, black velvet shoes. Sewn-on waist label reads: "Lupino Lane in 'The Lambeth Walk' Specially made by Dean's Rag Book Co. Ltd. London, Reg. Design 830106." Green Dean's label on shoes. Ca. 1920s........................ $600

15" "Mad Hatter." Molded/ptd face, ptd mouth/4 ptd teeth, large round blue eyes, yellow mohair wig, cloth stuffed body, velvet hands, original checkered trousers, black felt coat, tall felt hat, black velvet shoes. Round tag pinned to coat reads: "Made in England." Ca. 1931 (1931) - Rare ....$1,700-$1,800

15" Chimney Sweep. Molded cloth face, CM, ptd blue eyes to side, brown plush wig, cloth body/limbs/swivel neck, original clothes, hat, chimney brush, sack with sticks. Ca. 1923...........$400-$500

15" Buffalo Bill. Hard rubber head, CM,

brown ptd eyes, brown ptd hair, cloth body/limbs, original blue felt trousers with white plush in front, blue/yellow checkered long-sleeve gingham shirt, yellow waistcoat, red neckerchief with white dots, black felt shoes, socks. Ca. 195l (Also called "Buffalo Billy")... $600

16" Betty Oxo. Cloth mask face, ptd OM/teeth, ptd blue eyes to side, short brown curly mohair wig, sawdust stuffed cloth body/velvet limbs, original pink velvet coat/plush trimmed, matching bonnet, white teddy, velvet leggings/black velvet shoes/3 black buttons on each ankle. (Advertising Doll given free with Oxo labels.) Foot label reads: "Specially made for OXO'LTD. Dean's Rag Book Co. Ltd. London." Ca. 1920s .... $800-$900

17" Becky. Molded felt face, CM, ptd blue eyes, thick brown curly mohair wig, sawdust-stuffed cloth body, velveteen arms, original pink-checked organza semi-long full dress with flounces, pink cotton petticoat with sewn-on underpants, pink wide-brimmed bonnet with pink felt flowers, pink felt shoes, socks. Dean's label on shoe. 1936.................................... $700-$800

18" Dutch Boy and Girl. Hard rubber heads, hand-ptd features, CM, ptd/molded hair, jtd felt bodies, original felt clothes, felt clogs. Dean's foot labels. Ca. 1949. Pr. $600

18" Stella. Molded cloth face, hand-ptd features, CM, rosy cheeks, thick blonde wavy mohair wig, cloth body/felt limbs, original blue print cotton short dress, underpants, blue felt bodice, frilly collar, blue felt shoes, socks. Dean's label sewn on one shoe. Round Dean's wrist tag. Ca. 1949 .... $400

18" Princess Elizabeth. Hard rubber head, hand-ptd features, CM, ptd blue eyes, light brown mohair wig, cloth body/felt limbs, original turquoise-blue felt coat, blue-and-white checked cotton dress, underwear, turquoise-blue felt hat/shoes. Dean's label and handtag. Ca. 1949 Mint (Also called "Lillibet") $1,000

20" Popeye the Sailor Man. Molded/ptd head/pipe/removable cap with name POPEYE on the brown hat band, stuffed cloth body with non-removable brown shirt, light brown or tan trousers, dark brown shoes, red neck scarf. Ca. 1930s... $600

39" Little Girl. Molded mask face, red CM, ptd brown eyes to side, blonde mohair wig, jtd cloth body/legs/arms/stitched fingers with separate thumb, original blue print dress, felt hat, etc. Label. Ca. 1930... $1,700

42" Boudoir Lady or Salon Doll. Molded mask stockinet face, red CM, ptd brown eyes to side, blonde mohair wig, cloth body jtd at neck/sh/hips, original pink satin pajamas, stockings, high-heeled slippers. Ca. 1930.................... $1,500

Chapter 7

GRACE G. DRAYTON ~ (WIEDERSEIM) ~

History: 1909-1990s

Grace Gebbie Drayton (Wiederseim), Philadelphia, PA, 1909-1930s. Born: October 14, 1877. Died: 1936. Although Grace Gebbie loved and understood children and their prankish ways, she had two childless marriages. Her father, George Gebbie was Scottish, her mother, Mary Fitzgerald Gebbie, was Irish. She was educated in private schools within the state of Pennsylvania. She married Theodore E. Wiederseim, April 18, 1900. When Grace was first married, she signed her drawings "Grace G. Wiederseim." The roly-poly children that she drew were actually images of herself as a child, pug nose et al. Grace's early work tends to pass unnoticed because Grace's style had not yet been perfected. In 1903, the *Booklovers Magazine* advertised the "New American Girl Art Calendar" depicting the idealized woman and illustrated by Mrs. Wiederseim. There was also four gorgeous "Out of Door Girls" in color. Grace's "Undiscovered Beauties" series was featured in the New York Herald in 1908.

Grace worked for the *New York Journal* and *Philadelphia Press* from August 30, 1903 until August 21, 1904. Her caption strips were entitled "The Strange Adventures of Pussy Pumpkin and her chum Toodles." The *Sunday Philadelphia Press* editions ran her series "Bobby Blake and Dolly Drake" for two years. "Dolly Dimples and Bobby Bounce and Kittens" and "The Pussycat Princess," were other memorable early Drayton comic strips. Grace illustrated a series of chubby little children and their amusing antics for the Boston Sunday Post magazine circa 1904-1905. In March, 1906, *Ladies Home Journal*, displayed a full page of patterns illustrated by Drayton. It depicted items for the nursery—linen books, pillow shams, bedspreads. Grace's lesser known sister, Margaret Hayes, published a series of verse in the *Associated Sunday* magazine in 1909. It was entitled, "The Terrible

Tales of Kaptain Kiddo" and ran for five years. Of course, Grace was the illustrator. Also, in 1909, the *Ladies Home Journal* published a cover Grace had designed for them. It revealed a very fashionable lady of the day—which looked very much like Grace herself.

Campbell Soup Company representatives later proclaimed that the Drayton Campbell Soup Kids dated to 1900, although 1904 is the date given by earlier company officials. When the Joseph Campbell Company saw the designs of her roly-poly twins they signed Grace to a contract, sensing that her well-fed kiddies would aptly advertise their nourishing soup. (They appeared on cards displayed in street cars.) They first saw the light of day, however, as advertisements in the *Ladies' Home Journal* during 1905. Many of Grace's early drawings and postcards of the Campbell Kids are unsigned. Her association with the Campbell Soup Company may have ceased as early as 1915 or 1916. Other artists copied her style over the years. Her children with the goo-goo or side glancing eyes probably started the googly trend in German doll-making. Grace Drayton was also a prolific book writer/illustrator. Early titles include: *Mother Goose Calender* (1907); *Dolly Drake* (1909); *Bobby Blake* (1909); *Tiny 'Tots* (1909); *Fido* (1910); *Kitty Puss* (1910); *Ducky Daddles* (1911); *Bunykins* (1913); *Teddykins* (1914); *The Baby Bears and their Wishing Rings* (1916); *Let's Go to the Zoo* (1914); *Chicky Cheep* (1915), etc. Grace's books, paper dolls, advertisements, and multitude of other items, including dolls, are all highly prized by collectors.

Collecting Hints:

Grace Drayton designed her first rag dolls in 1909. These were called "Dolly Dollykins" and "Bobby Bobbykins" (Trademark registered by Frank Allison Hayes) and made by the Hayes' "Children's Novelty Co." Other rag dolls include: "Gee Gee Dolly," "Chocolate Drop," "Dolly Dim-

ple," "Bunykins" "Hug-Me-Tight" line, "Mah-Jongg" and "Mah Jongg Kid," "Sis," "Happy Cry," and "Comfy and Friends," Composition head dolls include: "Dolly and Bobby" (1910), "Dolly Drake and Bobby Blake" (reissued by Amberg, 1911), "Baby Beautiful" (1911), "Peek-A-Boo" (1914), "Baby Dingle" (1924), etc.

The valued dolls are the ones made during the lifetime of the artist/originator. If the artist sculpted the doll herself/himself, it is even more valuable. The Campbell Kid dolls issued after Drayton's death are also of value and collectible, but seem to lack the appeal of the old dolls.

Reproduction Alert:

The Campbell Kid/Dolly Dingle type dolls have been reproduced in bisque during modern times, The commercial product is of the most value; especially those of limited edition.

10-1/2" Early Dolly Dingle, "Can't break 'em" type head, incised with a "D", original clothes, cloth body, replaced arm. Ca. 1910 $350 as is. Rare type. (Courtesy R. Lane Herron.)

GRACE DRAYTON

4-1/4" Campbell Kids. Salt & Pepper Shakers. All hard plastic/6 pouring holes in back of each head, brown ptd features, yellow ptd hair/white molded-on caps with red initial "C" on each. Boy wears long white apron and holds a brown spoon with a long handle/ red shirt; girl wears a short white apron and holds a brown bowl and brown spoon/red dress and socks/white shoes. Red stoppers. Possibly 1950s..........................$65 pr.

4-1/2" "September Morn." All-bisque/jtd at sh/hips, tiny red surprised CM, large round black ptd eyes, blonde ptd/molded curly hair, nude. German sticker on body. (Inspired by the "September Morning With Apologies" drawings by Drayton. This doll appeared on postcards, china plates, chalk and metal statuettes, etc.) 4-1/2" $2,000

6"........................$2,500

6" Campbell Kid "Squeak" Doll. All ptd/molded rubber/one arm apart from body and holds a spoon/legs apart/molded and painted clothes and cook's cap with a "C" painted on the front. Ca. 1930s $65

Asst. musical Dolly Dingles, cloth bodies, bisque heads/limbs, 1989 Limited Editions. (Carol Lindberg collection.)

8" "Cheerleader" Campbell Kid. All vinyl/movable arms, ptd features, brown ptd/molded hair/molded shoes and socks, original clothes. Ca. 1950s .$65

11" Puppy Pippin. Compo head, black ptd eyes to side, brown plush cork-stuffed body/jtd legs, sewn-on tail. Head mark: "EIH C (in a circle) 1911." Horsman, NYC, 1911. ....$700-$750

11" Dolly Dingle. All-cloth/movable limbs, ptd features, original clothes. Stamp on torso reads: "DOLLY DINGLE//COPYRIGHT BY//G.G. DRAYTON." Averill Mfg. Co., NYC. 1923..................$500+

11" "Peek-a-Boo" Dolly. Compo head, watermelon mouth, ptd blue eyes to side, ptd/molded hair, cloth upper body/compo lower body and limbs/ bare feet, one-pc. striped summer suit (girls wore polka dot dresses). Also called "Gee-Gee Dolly." (Some of these dolls were dressed only in ribbons.) Cloth label. Horsman, NYC. 1913-15.......$300

12" Campbell Kids. Can't Break 'Em heads, ptd features/hair, CM, pink sateen cork-stuffed bodies/jtd at sh/hips. Boy wears rompers/ girl wears gingham dress/attached shoes. Marks: "C" (in a circle) 1910." Horsman, NYC. 1910-1915 Each $600

12" "Sunbonnet." Dolly Dingle. All-cloth/round body shape covered with pink and white check over white flannelette/sunbonnet/hand-embroidered hair and features. Mark: "Elliott Novelty Mfg. Co., Calif. Ca." 1920s or 1930s..$300

12" Campbell Kid Girl. Spanish Dancer. Compo head, smiling CM, brown ptd eyes to side, orange-yellow ptd/molded bob/molded forelock, chubby compo body jtd at neck/sh/hips, original red cotton 3-tiered skirt with attached black satin bodice and red cotton short sleeves, cotton underpants, red oilcloth tie shoes, white rayon socks with red trim. Body mark: "A//PETITE//DOLL." American Character Doll Co., NYC. Ca. 1928+...$750

12" "Peek-a-Boo" Dolly. Compo head, watermelon mouth, round blue ptd eyes to side, blonde ptd molded hair/original blonde mohair wig, straight-shaped cork-stuffed cloth body/compo limbs original dress. Mark: "E.I.H. 'C' (in a circle) 1915." (This is a later version of the 11" Peek-a-Boo doll described above.) 1915..$300

12" Campbell Kid. Compo head, ptd features, brown ptd/molded bob, compo body jtd at sh/hips/black ptd and molded shoes/white ptd socks, original light blue short pants, striped long sleeve jersey. Unmarked. E.I. Horsman, NYC, Ca. 1948 ....$175

13" Campbell Kid. Compo head/flange neck, small watermelon mouth, ptd blue eyes, blonde ptd/molded bob, cloth body/full compo limbs, original clothes. Neck Mark: "E.I.H. Co. Inc." Horsman, NYC. ca. 1913.............$325

13" Campbell Kid. Compo head/flange neck, small CM, rare blue tin sleep eyes, yellow ptd/molded bob/forelock at side of head, cotton stuffed cloth body jtd at sh/hips, original blue plaid cotton dress with white ruffle trim on pockets and sleeves and neckline, matching teddy, etc. Neck mark: "EIH. INC." Dress label reads: "HORSMAN//DOLL//MFD. USA." Ca. 1920s $400

13" Campbell Kid Girl. Compo head/flange neck, smiling CM, brown ptd eyes to side, light brown ptd/molded bob with curl in center of forehead, cloth body/full bent compo arms/straight compo legs, original dark pink cotton batiste dress/light blue cotton piping trim/red and blue felt squares decorate lower section of dress, matching bonnet, underwear trimmed with blue piping, shoes, socks. Neck mark: "Campbell Kid." American Character Doll Co., NYC. Ca. 1928+............$750

13" Dolly Drake. Compo shoulder head, wee watermelon mouth, ptd blue eyes to front, ptd/molded bob has 3 curved forelocks, cloth body/compo limbs, original clothes. Louis Amberg Co., NYC. Ca. 1928-32 ....$750

13" Campbell Kid Indian. Brown compo head, watermelon mouth, ptd brown eyes, brown ptd/molded bob, cloth body/full compo limbs, original Indian costume: yellow cotton skirt, yellow blouse with long sleeves/ dark yellow trim, cotton teddy trimmed with lace, felt moccasins. Neck mark: "EIH Co INC." Skirt label reads: "HORSMAN//DOLL//MFD IN USA." $500

11" "Chocolate Drop" Averill Mfg. Co., all original, 1923, $600 (Carol Lindberg collection.)

13" "Puppo." Kaptin Kiddo Character. Margaret Hayes, author; Drayton illustrator. Compo head, round brown ptd eyes, molded tongue, extended ears, cloth cork-stuffed body/brown cloth limbs, original shirt, trousers, shoes. Head mark: "EIH c (in a circle) 1915."... $800

13-1/2" Campbell Kid Girl. Compo head, tiny watermelon mouth, rare blue tin sleep eyes, gold ptd/molded bob, cotton stuffed cloth body/compo limbs, original pink pinafore dress, etc. 1925 .... $400

14" "Dolly Dimple" compo shoulder head, tiny watermelon mouth (red line), large ptd blue eyes looking straight ahead/ptd lashes, pug nose, one-stroke blonde /eyebrows, blonde ptd/molded bob /cloth body compo limbs, original dress shoes, socks. Shoulder plate mark: "G G Drayton." Dress label reads: "Horsman." (This doll was issued after the publication of Drayton's book Dolly Dimples and Bobby Bounce.) 1931 .... $600

14" "Bobby Bounce." Compo shoulder head, tiny watermelon mouth (red line), large ptd brown eyes looking straight ahead/ptd lashes, pug nose, one-stroke brown eyebrows, brown ptd/molded hair parted on the side modeled away from forehead, cotton-stuffed cloth body/compo limbs, original outfit: short checkered pants/white top with ruffled collar and semi-long sleeves. Shoulder plate mark: "G G Drayton." Suit label reads: "Horsman." Round card tag pinned to shirt reads: "BOBBY BOUNCE// by Grace G. Drayton." Border of circular tag reads: "PAT APRIL 14 1931 NO.83897//GEO. BORGFELDT & CO. N.Y." 1931 .... $600

Chapter 8

~EFFANBEE~

History: 1912-1997

Fleischaker & Baum (Effanbee or F&B), NYC, 1912-1997; Effanbee trademark registered in 1913. Effanbee is one of the Big Four American doll companies; companies that started before or shortly after World War I and endured long after World War II and into modern times; the other three companies are Alexander, Ideal, and Horsman. All of these durable companies moved with the times; creating doll-types that were popular in each decade. Although many collectors believe that their best dolls were made prior to World War II, many of their plastic dolls are worth collecting.

The Bernard E. Fleischaker and Hugo Baum partnership began in 1910 in a small rented store in New York. It was there they retailed and jobbed toys made by other companies. Their own doll-making business originated in 1913. Their famous trademark Effanbee (F&B for Fleischaker & Baum) also came into being at that time. They wanted a "catchy" name to instantly identify their dolls. Miss Anna Edele dressed the dolls they made and the undressed dolls they purchased from other firms. "Bubbles" was their first major success. (Lenox Inc., Trenton, New Jersey, a pottery company, owned by Walter Scott Lenox, made the F&B bisque-head dolls circa 1914-1920.)

Many of the doll ideas and unique advertising methods were the brainchild of Hugo Baum, who had a theatrical flair and a flamboyance so necessary for success in the competitive toy business. He encouraged his son, Bernard, to work for him, as well as other talented youngsters. Morris Lutz joined the firm in 1923. Bernard Lipfert, often called "The Father of the Doll Industry," designed many famous dolls, not only for F&B, but for Ideal, Horsman, and others. His contributions include "Bubbles," "Patsy," "Dy-Dee Baby," the "Dionne Quints" (Alexander), and the most famous doll of them all, "Shirley Temple" (Ideal).

The "Patsy" doll was actually evolved over a long period of time. We see her "look" emerging as early as 1920 in the guise of "Baby Dainty," a chubby toddler type. Aside from the Shirley Temple doll, the Patsy doll was the most imitated doll in the twentieth century. Every company, large and small, had their version and they all resembled F&B's original—and, more than likely, Lipfert designed them all! Patsy helped pull F&B through the Depression of the 1930s, but World War II almost finished them.

In 1946 the company was sold to NOMA Electric Company, who specialized in Christmas lights. NOMA was mainly interested in "gimmick" dolls, thus doll quality and innovation declined. In 1953, NOMA sold the company back to Effanbee (Bernard Baum, Morris Lutz, and Perry Epstein), and the plastic era had begun—with some very beautiful and memorable dolls. Christmas, 1997, will be celebrated in doll-land with more Patsy reissues: a 13" "Chinese Patsy" with black painted hair, brown painted eyes to the side, and wearing a red silk ensemble; a 13" "Christmas Patsy" sporting an ash blonde bobbed wig, a white fur coat and hat and ice skates; and a 13" "Holiday Patsy with Wee Patsy."

There is also a "Candy Kid Box Set." Candy Kid is also 13" tall and is conceived of the new specially formulated hard vinyl which feels like the original composition. Of course, these dolls are much too expensive to be called children's "playthings," and real children wouldn't relate to them anyhow. They belong to the adult child who lives in all of us.

Collecting Hints:

The most collectible of all Patsys and other famous F&B dolls seem to be those made in the late 1920s to World War Two. To have the most market value, however, these dolls must be in mint or very good condition and wear their original clothes, shoes, socks, etc. Whether their popularity will continue into the next century is questionable. Today's children are not interested in them. They'd much rather relate to a computer.

Reproduction Alert:

F&B issued Limited Editions of Patsy and Skippy in 1976 and 1979. Bisque and composition Patsys may have been made by amateur dollmakers, since it is easy to reproduce an old doll, but such a replica would be obvious and they have no value.

Effanbee

6" Wee Patsy. Compo stationary head, CM, ptd. blue eyes to side, brown ptd./molded bob, compo. body jtd. at sh/hips/straight legs/black ptd./molded-on shoes with straps/white ptd. socks, original red dress/undies. Ca. 1930.....................................$425-$475

7" Baby Tinyette. Toddler. Compo stationary head, CM, ptd. blue eyes, blonde ptd./molded bob, compo. body jtd. at sh/hips, original short playsuit/belt, shoes, socks. Head mark: EFFANBEE. Back mark: EFFANBEE Baby Tinyette. Ca. 1933.............................$350-$400

9" "Patsy Babyette" twins. All compo/jtd. curved limbs, CM, blue sleep eyes/molded lashes, brown ptd./molded hair, original coordinated blue/white outfits (girl wears a dress and a bonnet; boy wears a romper and cap. Girl's clothes are lace-trimmed.) Head mark: "EFFANBEE" and "EFFANBEE//Patsy Babyette" (on the shoulders.) Ca. 1930s.........................$400-$450 each

9" Charlie McCarthy. All ptd. rubber/no movable part/black ptd./molded tuxedo/top hat. Ca. 1938 (Fair condition) $50

9" Patsyette. (George and Martha Washington). All compo/jtd. bodies, CM, ptd. blue eyes to side, brown ptd./molded bob/white mohair wigs, original costumes, hats, etc. Ca. 1932+. $1,200 pr.

Patsyette (Negro) ...... $550-$600

Patsyette (short dress, bonnet, etc.)....................................$450-$500

9-1/2" "Fluffy" (Junior Girl Scout). All-vinyl/jtd. at neck/sh/hips, CM, blue sleep eyes, black rooted hair (short with bangs), original green uniform/green belt/green buttons (opens down front), yellow/green beanie, brown shoes, green socks. Head mark: EFFanBEE//19 C 66. 1966+.....................$85

9-1/2" Black Patsy Baby (Amosandra). Comp head, CM, ptd. brown eyes, black ptd./molded bob/3 black tufts of hair, 5-pc bent-limb compo. body/left arm extended/right arm bent, original clothes. (Made by F&B in the early "Amos and Andy" radio days. Only Sun Rubber had the rights to manufacture the doll legally, thus other companies had their own unmarked versions.) Ca. 1935....................................$550-$600

10" "DY-DEE Baby." Hard plastic head/attached rubber ears, OM, blue sleep eyes/synthetic eyelashes, brown ptd./molded hair, jtd. synthetic rubber body/limbs, original clothes. Back mark: "EFFANBEE//DYDEE BABY//U.S. PAT 1858-485//ENGLAND 880-080//FRANCE 788-980//GERMANY 585-647//OTHER PAT PENDING." Ca. 1950-58 (Good condition)......$125

10" "Tiny Tad//Coquette." Compo head, O/C mouth, ptd. blue eyes to side, blonde ptd./molded hair, cloth body/compo. hands, old clothes, black ptd. shoes. Neck Mark: "D" ("CO" inside the D). Made by Deco for EFFanBee. Ca. 1915 ....$375

10" Boy Puppet. Kit for home assembly. Oval compo. head/hands/feet, red CM, large ptd. grey eyes, light brown yard hair, wood body/upper limbs, original brown short pants, white cotton shirt/ribbon tie, white stockings, large feet with brown ptd./molded shoes. Head mark: "F&B//USA." Ca. late 1930s $125

10" Girl Puppet. Kit for home assembly. Compo head/hands/feet, red CM, large ptd. blue eyes, yellow yarn hair/2 short braids tied with red ribbon, wood body/upper limbs, original white dress with blue polka dots, white ribbed cotton stockings, large feet with black ptd./molded shoes. Head mark: "F&B//USA." (This boxed kit puppet was assembled in the home and dressed in pre-sewn clothing.) Ca. late 1930s $125

10-3/4" "Uncle Sam, Jr." Grumpy Kid Baby. Compo head, disgruntled CM, ptd. blue eyes, blonde ptd./molded hair, cloth body/limbs/short compo. arms, original "Uncle Sam, Jr." outfit: red/white striped lawn rompers, blue jacket with large white stars, matching hat, stockings. Tag reads: EFFANBEE//BABY GRUMPY//TRADE MARK. Ca. 1916 ....$375-$425

11" "Dainty Baby." Compo head, CM, ptd. blue eyes, blonde ptd. hair, blonde ptd. eyebrows, cloth body/legs/compo. arms/metal springs, original red/white checkered cotton dress/white cotton yoke/coarse lace trim. Mark: "Dainty Baby." Label reads: "EFFANBEE DOLL/FINEST & BEST." Ca. 1912-22...............................$125-$175

11" "FLINTEX" Baby. Compo head, O/C mouth, ptd. blue eyes, blonde ptd./molded bob, straw-stuffed cloth body/metal disks/stump hands/straight legs, original dress, etc. Marked: "FLINTEX." Northport Novelty Company trademark, registered in U.S.A., 1913. Wrist tag reads: EFFANBEE//TRADEMARK. A "family doll" and rather ugly. Flintex probably made the

14" Patsy dolls wearing rare original costumes, 1930s. $500-$600. These rare costumes can double the price of these dolls.

doll for F&B. Ca. 1913 ....$375-$425

11" Patsy Baby. Compo swivel head, CM, blue sleep eyes, brown ptd./molded hair swirling onto forehead, compo. bent-limb jtd. body, original clothes. Head mark: "EFFANBEE//PATSY BABY." Back mark: "EFFANBEE//Patsy Baby." Ca. 1932 (Negro version-$550-$600)..................$400-$450

11" Patsy Kins (Patsy Jr.). Compo swivel head, CM, ptd. brown eyes to side, red ptd./molded bob, jtd. compo. body/bend right arm, original checkered dress, apron, etc. Ca. 1930 ....$450/$500

12" Negro "Baby Grumpy" Girl. Black head, CM, ptd. brown eyes, black ptd./molded hair/inset pigtails, black compo. jtd. body, original clothes. Ca. 1925+ ....$375-$425

12" "Candy Kid" twins. All vinyl/fully jtd., CM, blue sleep eyes, blonde ptd./molded hair, original matching red/white gingham outfits, hats, shoes, socks. Marks "FB 33." Ca. 1954 ....$300 pr

12" "DECO" Baby. Compo head/steel strung, O/C mouth/ptd. upper teeth, ptd. blue eyes, thin 1-stroke eyebrows, dark ptd./molded hair, chunky compo. body/spring strung, original lace-trimmed lawn slip. Neck mark: "DECO." Back mark: "DECO." (This is one of F&B's NEXT-TO-NATURE unbreakable dolls advertised by Butler Brothers in 1916.) 1916 ......$375-$425

12" "NEXT-TO-NATURE" Baby. Compo head, O/C mouth/2 upper molded teeth, tiny upturned nose, cheek dimples, ptd. blue eyes, thin 1-stroke eyebrows, light brown ptd./molded hair, ptd. blue eyes, straw-stuffed cloth body/limbs/sewn-on black boots/short compo. arms/metal jointing disks, original dress, cambric slip with blue bow, drawers, etc. Head mark: "52". (These early F&B dolls also had cork-stuffed bodies.) Ca. 1916 ....$375-$425

12" "Snowball" or "Baby Grumpy." Negro baby. Black compo. head, CM, ptd. brown eyes to side, black ptd./molded hair, long cork-stuffed muslin body/cloth arms with compo. hands/stuffed legs of striped material/black sewn-on shoes, original clothes. Neck mark: "172." Ca. 1925+.................................$375-$425

12" Negro "Baby Grumpy" Girl. Black head, CM, ptd. brown eyes, black ptd./molded hair/inset pigtails, black compo. jtd. body, original clothes. Ca. 1925+.................................$375-$425

12-1/2" "Honeybunch" Compo head, OM/teeth, blue tin sleep eyes, blonde ptd./molded hair, cloth body/limbs/compo. hands, original white christening dress, etc. Mark: "EFFANBEE//HONEYBUNCH//MADE IN USA." (Original Bubbles mold) Ca. 1924 ....$375

12-1/2" "Johnny Jones" Character Boy. Compo head, pouty CM, ptd. blue eyes,

13" Patsy, redressed. $300. (Courtesy of Ruby Ellen Smith)

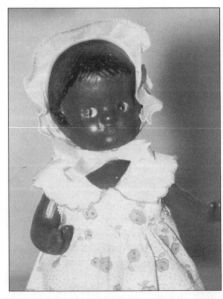

14" V. Austin clown "Clippo". All original $150.

9" Negro Patsyette, all original. 1930s $550-$600. (Courtesy of Rosalie Purvis)

modeled ears, ptd. strawberry blonde/molded hair, straw-stuffed cloth body/limbs/pin-and-disk jts./sewn-on black shoes/stripped stockings, original shirt/overalls. Head mark: "152" Ca. 1915 ....$375-$425

13" "Bubbles." Compo head, O/C mouth/2 ptd. upper teeth/molded tongue, blue tin sleep eyes, blonde ptd./molded curly hair, cloth body/bent cloth legs/full compo. arms, white organdy dress, bonnet. Mark: "EFFANBEE//BUB-BLES." Ca. 1925 ....$375

13" "Bubbles." Compo shoulder plate/very narrow shoulders, OM/2 molded teeth/molded tongue, blue tin sleep eyes, blonde ptd./molded hair, cloth body/full compo. legs/full compo. bent arms, original long white dress with embroidered yoke/shirt lace-trimmed sleeves/ruffled bottom, slip, flannelette diaper, etc. Label reads: "EFFAN-BEE//BUBBLES//COPYR. 1924//MADE IN USA." (Doll has round wrist tag and locket.) Ca. 1928 ....$375

13" "Bubbles." Toddler. Compo shoulder head, OM/teeth, blue tin sleep eyes, blonde ptd./molded hair, cloth body/full compo. bent-arms/straight compo. legs, original clothes. Mark: EFFAN-BEE//BUBBLES//COPYR. 1924//MADE IN U.S.A. Ca. 1926 .$425

13" "Kate." Compo head, CM, brown tin sleep eyes, brown ptd./molded hair, cloth body/compo. hands, original clothes, bonnet, etc. Tag reads: "I am//Katie//with moving eyes//an EF-FanBEE//Durable//Doll." (Mickey's twin sister.) Ca. 1941..................$225-$275

13" Negro Patsy-type. Black compo. head, CM, ptd. brown eyes to side, black ptd./molded bob, black 5-pc jtd. compo. body, original clothes, etc. Unmarked. Ca. 1930s....................................$300

13-1/2" "Candy Kid." Boxer Boy. All-compo./fully jtd. body, CM, brown sleep eyes, brown ptd./molded hair, original

14" "Skippy." All original. Compo sailor. Ca. WW 11 $350-$400. (Courtesy of Rosalie Purvis)

boxing gloves, trunks, shoes, socks. Mark: "FB 22." (This doll came dressed in various costumes as both a boy and a girl. Another "Candy Kid" boy was dressed as a cowboy with a black mask; another in a short-pants playsuit.) Ca. 1946 ....$350-$400

13-1/2" "Emily Ann." Compo head/hands/feet, small CM, ptd. blue eyes, brown ptd./molded hair/molded braids/red satin bow stapled to head, wood body/upper limbs, original blue cotton print dress, blue cotton bloomers, white organdy pinafore, bonnet. Mark: "C//Emily Ann//V. Austin//EFFANBEE." Virginia Austin designed Emily Ann, Clippo, and Lucifer marionettes for EFFanBEE in 1937. A Clippo Circus Tent was also available. 1937 ....$150

13-1/2" "Skippy." Compo swivel head, rosebud CM, ptd. blue eyes to side, brown ptd./molded hair, compo body jtd. at neck/sh/hips/brown ptd./molded shoes and socks, original U.S. Army military uniform, brown leatherette belt, hat, etc. Head mark: "Effanbee Skippy//P.L. Crosby." (Originally issued in 1929. P.L. Crosby was the cartoonist who created Skippy.) Ca. World War II ....$350-$400

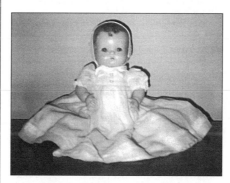

11" Patsy Baby, original clothes. $400-$450. (Courtesy of Ruby Ellen

14" "Baby Dainty." Compo shoulder head, CM, ptd. blue eyes, blonde ptd./molded "Patsy" bob, cloth body/legs/compo. bent arms, original clothes. Shoulder mark: "EFFANBEE." (Early version of this doll. Later versions marked: "EF-FANBEE//BABY DAINTY.") Ca. 1912+...$375

14" "Baby Huggins." Compo head, CM, ptd. blue eyes, orange-blonde ptd./molded hair, cloth body/legs/compo. hands, original clothes. Head mark: "24." (Advertised as "Baby Grumpy in a good humor," although the face looks somber.) Ca. 1915 ....$375-$425

14" "Bubbles." Compo shoulder head/very narrow shoulders, O/C mouth/2 ptd. upper teeth, rare ptd. blue eyes, blonde ptd./molded hair, long cloth body/cloth legs/cry box/full compo. bent arms, original white organdy dress, matching lace-trimmed frilly bonnet, slip, flannelette diaper, leatherette bootees, stockings. Ca. 1927...........................$425

14" "Clippo." Compo head/hands/feet, ptd. features, black ptd./molded hair, wood body/upper limbs, original red cotton/white polka dot clown suit/white or-

gandy neck ruff, white felt cap, control strings. Head mark: "C//EFFANBEE//V. AUSTIN." 1937 ....$150

14" "Dy-Dee-Baby." Hard plastic head/attached rubber ears, OM/tongue, blue sleep eyes/synthetic eyelashes, dark brown/ptd. molded hair, jtd. synthetic rubber body/limbs, original clothes. Ca. 1950-58 Good condition $275

14" "Lucifer." Negro Man. Compo head/hands/feet, CM, large black eyes with whites, black ptd./molded hair, wood body/upper limbs, original blue denim overalls, red checkered cotton skirt, brown ptd./molded shoes. Head mark: "C//Lucifer//V. Austin//Effanbee." 1937...$200

14" "Our Baby." (Smiling Baby Grumpy.) Compo head/full cheeks, O/C mouth/2 upper molded teeth, ptd. blue eyes, brown ptd./molded curly hair with forelock, modeled ears, muslin body/pink cloth/bent legs/compo. hands, old christening dress. (Some versions of this doll came with straight legs.) Ca. 1915...$375

14" "Pat-O-Pat." Cloth mask face, CM, ptd. blue eyes to side, yellow wool hair styled in loops, pink cloth body/limbs/mitten hands/metal body mechanism for "patty-cake" movement, original batiste dress (green, yellow, red dots on white), Valenciennes lace trim, muslin slip, bonnet, green striped bootees. Ca. 1925 ....$425

14" "Suzanne." All-compo./jtd. at neck/sh/hips, CM, blue sleep eyes, brown mohair wig, original pink dress, etc. Effanbee bracelet reads: "EFFan-Bee Durable Dolls." Ca. 1940 ....$350-$375

14" "Suzanne." Compo head, CM, blue sleep eyes, brown mohair wig, slender compo. body jtd. at neck/sh/hips, original long blue dress, wide-brimmed white straw hat, etc. Metal heart reads: "SUZANNE//EFFANBEE MADE IN U.S.A." Ca. 1940 ....$350-$375

14" "Unbreakable Head" Baby or "Buy Me" Baby. Compo head, CM, ptd. blue eyes, modeled ears, brown ptd./molded hair molded forward on forehead, cork-stuffed cloth body/bent cloth legs/cloth arms/compo. gauntlet type hands, original lace-trimmed lawn dress decorated with pink ribbon rosettes, matching bonnet, white socks, pacifier attached to a neck ribbon. Neck Mark: "455." 1916-17 ....$425

14" "Unbreakable Head" Baby. Compo head/sensitive boy face/pointed chin somber CM, ptd. blue eyes, auburn ptd./molded curly hair, straw-stuffed cloth body/limbs/short compo. arms, old clothes. Head mark: "34." Ca. 1916...$275

14" Patsy. Compo swivel head, CM, rare sleep eyes, brown ptd./molded bob, compo. body jtd. at neck/sh/hips, original clothes. Marks: "FB 7." Ca. 1928 ... $500-$600

14-1/2" "Rosemary." Compo shoulder head/very narrow shoulders, red CM, pink cheek blush, ptd. blue eyes/ptd. upper eyelashes, thin eyebrows, brown mohair wig/wig knot inserted through hole atop dome-shaped head, cloth body/compo. lower limbs, original pink organdy dress, matching bonnet, etc.

Mark: "EFFANBEE//ROSE-MARY//WALK-TALK-SLEEP." (in an oval design) "MADE IN USA" (below the oval). Ca. 1924 (Rare) $425

15" "Baby Dainty." Compo shoulder head, CM, ptd. blue eyes, blonde ptd./molded "Patsy" bob, cloth body/straight cloth legs/bend compo. arms, original green dress with lace trim, 1-pc undergarments, original shoes and socks. Mark: "EFFANBEE." Ca. 1912-22 .... $375

15" "Billy Boy." (Solemn Baby Grumpy.) Compo head, CM, ptd. blue eyes, brown ptd./molded curly hair/forelock, cloth body/limbs/compo. disk jts. old clothes. Neck mark: "116." Ca. 1915 .... $375-$425

15" "Bubbles." Toddler. Compo head, OM/2 molded-in teeth/tongue, blonde ptd./molded hair, cloth body/swing leg toddler/full compo. arms/compo. lower legs, original clothes, etc. Ca. 1930s $500

15" "DECO" Baby. Smooth compo. head/long neck, rosebud CM, ptd. blue eyes, thin light auburn eyebrows, sparse auburn ptd. hair, cloth body/limbs/compo. hands, original blue/white striped midday suit. Mark: "DECO." Ca. 1916 .... $400

15" "Dolly Dumpling." Wood-pulp shoulder head, CM, ptd. blue eyes, orange-blonde ptd./molded hair/deep combmarks, cloth body/legs/wood-pulp compo. lower arms, original romper suit. Head mark: "EFFANBEE." Ca. 1918 .... $425

15" "Dy-Dee-Baby." All rubber. Dressed only in a diaper. Mark: "EFFanbee Dy-Dee-Baby, US Pat 1859485." Good condition. (First drink/wet doll; had a hard rubber head/soft rubber body. Compo heads made ca. 1947, but had rubber ears. Head changed to hard plastic in 1950; body remained rubber. Bodies changed to vinyl ca. 1955. Doll was still made in the 1960s. Compo and hard plastic head Dy-Dee-Babies with clothes and layettes sell for about the same price.) Ca. 1933 .... $175

17" "Little Lady" Majorette. All original. 1940 $400-$450. (Courtesy of Rosalie Purvis)

15" "Katie Kroose." Compo head/chubby cheeks/double chin, CM, ptd. blue eyes, molded ears, blonde ptd./molded hair swirled to side, cloth body/metal disk jts. at sh/hips/compo. lower arms/cloth legs with sewn-on shoes, original clothes, hat, etc. (This doll resembles a Kathe Kruse.) Ca. 1918 .... $375-$425

15" "Mary Jane." Compo head, CM, blue sleep eyes, blonde HHW, BJ compo. body, original chemise, old clothes, etc. Round EFFanBee wrist tag. Ca. 1917 Mark: EFFANBEE $300

15" "Merry Sunshine Kid." Compo head/well-modeled "boy" face/full cheeks/pointed chin, O/C mouth/2 molded teeth, cheek dimples, ptd. blue eyes, modeled ears, brown ptd./molded curly hair/forelock, cloth body/limbs/short compo. arms, original pink/blue check gingham romper, matching bonnet, felt shoes, socks. Neck mark: "104." Ca. 1916 .... $425

15" "Pouting Bess." Compo shoulder head, pouting CM, ptd. blue eyes, short blonde ptd./molded bob with bangs swirled to side, cloth body/disk jtd. at sh/hips/compo lower arms/cloth legs/sewn-on shoes, original checkered dress, underwear. (This doll somewhat resembles Orphan Annie.) Ca. 1915 .... $375-$425

15" "Whistling Jim." Compo head, tiny OM, ptd. blue eyes, orange ptd./molded hair, cloth body/compo. lower arms, original blue bib trousers, red/white striped shirt. Ca. 1950 .... $275

15" Anne Shirley. Compo head, CM, blue sleep eyes, strawberry blonde HHW, jtd. compo. body, original clothes based on the 1930s Anne Shirley film wardrobe. (This doll is not a portrait doll of a movie star Anne Shirley; designed to compete with the popular Shirley Temple doll. It had large hands which seem to identify it, even if unmarked.) "FB 31." Ca. 1936 .... $350

15" Charlie McCarthy. Compo shoulder head, red movable mouth, ptd. brown eyes/attached monocle, ptd. brown/molded hair, cloth body/limbs/compo. molded white gloved hands/black molded shoes, original white flannel trousers, blue flannel blazer, red bow tie, white shirt, cap. (There is a 15" size Charlie wearing a white jacket and black trousers, etc.) Mark: "EDGAR BERGEN//CHARLIE MCCARTHY//AN//EFFANBEE PRODUCT." 1937 .... $600

15" Negro "Grumpy" Boy. Compo head, CM, brown ptd. eyes, black ptd./molded hair/forelock, cork-stuffed muslin body/blue and white striped cloth legs/compo. hands/compo. molded shoes, original tan trousers, red jacket with 4 buttons. Neck mark: (reverse) "106." Ca. 1915 .... $425

15" Patricia. Compo swivel head, CM, green sleep eyes, red HHW, jtd. compo. body, original clothes, heart bracelet, etc. Body mark: "EFFANBEE PATRICIA." Ca. 1932 (Advertisements for "Patricia" were titled "Patricia Takes A Bow." She was called the "real American girl.") .... $450-$500

15-1/2" "Coquette." Compo head, O/C mouth/4 tiny teeth, ptd. blue eyes to side, blonde ptd./molded curly hair with indentation around head for placement

of a red hair ribbon bow, cloth body/limbs/compo. hands/molded-on brown compo. boots, original dress with white pinafore, etc. Ca. 1912 $425

16" "Betty Bounce." Compo head, tiny CM, ptd. blue eyes, brown ptd./molded shirt hair/wire loop for ribbon, cloth body/legs/compo. hands, original pink cotton dress, white cotton pinafore, shoes, socks, etc. Neck mark: "DECO." Dress label reads: "EFFanBEE//TRADEMARK." Ca. 1915 ... $425

16" "Bubbles." Luvums mold. Hard rubber compo. head, OM/upper/lower teeth/red metal behind the teeth, brown sleep eyes/real upper lashes, molded ears, ptd./molded hair, rubber body/limbs, original clothes. (These dolls are rarely found in good condition. The rubber deflated.) Ca. 1932 (Good condition) .... $200-$300

13" Patsy, redressed. $350. (Courtesy of Ruby Ellen Smith)

16" "Bubbles" Twin. Compo shoulder plate/very narrow shoulders, OM/2 celluloid teeth, blue sleep eyes, blonde ptd./molded hair, long cloth body/bent cloth jtd. legs/full compo. bent arms, original white christening gown/2 rows of lace above lace trimmed ruffle, wide-brimmed bonnet trimmed with white lace, long muslin slip, flannelette diaper, etc. (Some twins have open-close mouths with 2 upper ptd. teeth and "swing" legs.) Gown label reads: "EFFANBEE//DOLL//FINEST & BEST//TRADEMARK." Ca. 1927. $475

16" "Johnny-Tu-Face" Baby. Rotating 2-faced compo. head, O/C mouth/4 upper and 4 lower teeth, ptd. blue eyes, blonde ptd./deeply molded short hair, cloth body/limbs/half compo. arms (cloth legs are bent), original clothes, bonnet, etc. Ca. 1912 .... $425

16" "Lovums." All-compo. MIB. Box marked: "America Heartbeat." The doll has a toy stethoscope and is wearing her original white dress and bonnet with pink ribbon on bonnet and at waist, original white shoes and socks. Gorgeous doll. Ca. 1935 .... $1,000+

16" "Margie." Compo shoulder head/narrow shoulders, O/C mouth, ptd. blue eyes, molded hair/brown mohair wig, cork-stuffed cloth body/pin and disc jts/cloth upper arms and legs/compo. lower arms/small hands, original gingham dress with white bodice, matching bonnet, etc. Ca. 1921.................. $425

16" "Sweetie Pie." Compo head, CM, blue sleep eyes, caracul wig, cloth body/compo. limbs, original rompers, etc. Mark: "EFFANBEE." Ca. 1942.................................$300-$325

17" "Little Lady" Majorette. Compo head, CM, brown sleep eyes/lashes, pale blonde cotton-yarn braids, jtd. compo. body, original "majorette" costume: short red skirt, white top with long sleeves/gold metal buttons and gold epaulets/tall red felt hat with chin strap, white leather boots. (Hands have mag-

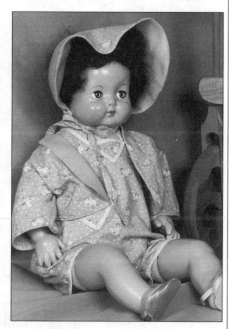

22" "Sweetie Pie", redressed. $475-$525 (if all original). (Courtesy of Carol Lind-

nets which hold her baton. Some Majorettes do not have this feature.) Head back marks: "EFFANBEE//U.S.A." (Although from the Anne Shirley mold, this doll is not considered a true "Anne Shirley.") Ca. 1945 ....$500+

17" "Popeye." Molded cloth-stuffed head/corncob pipe, winking eye/open eye, sewn-on ears, stuffed cloth body/legs/compo. black ptd. shoes/molded cloth-stuffed arms with an "anchor" tattoo on each forearm, original 1-pc sailor suit, white cap. "Spinach" tag reads: "Spinach that makes Popeye strong--POP-EYE AN EFFANBEE DOLL." 1936 ....$400

17" Charlie McCarthy. Compo shoulder head, movable mouth/jaw, ptd. brown eyes, patented monocle over right eye, cloth body/compo. lower limbs, original black suit, vest, white shirt, black top hat. Ca. 1940s.....................$700-$800

17" Negro Patsy Joan. Black compo. swivel head, CM, brown sleep eyes, short black ptd./molded bob, black compo.

body jtd. at neck/sh/hips, original clothes, etc. (Most F&B "Patsy" dolls have a black counterpart.) Ca. 1930s $750

17" White Patsy Joan. Compo swivel head, CM, brown sleep eyes, brown ptd./molded bob (not the same hairstyles as the earlier Patsy Joan, and has a different part), original striped muslin outfit, bonnet, etc. ("Skin" tone has a grey cast unlike earlier versions. Patsy Joans also came with wigs. Some dolls were unmarked.) Mark: "EFFandbee." Ca. 1946-49 (Measures closer to 16").................................$500

18" "Bubbles." Compo shoulder plate/very narrow shoulders, OM/2 upper teeth, blue tin sleep eyes, blonde ptd./molded hair, long kapok-stuffed cloth body/full compo. bent limbs, original clothes, locket, etc. (Bubbles was one of many doll sculpted by Bernard Lipfert. He also sculpted the look-alikes which he sold to competing companies. EFFANBEE filed a $200,000 lawsuit against E.I. Horsman for the look-alike "Bubbles" Lipfert sculpted for them. EFFANBEE won the lawsuit.) 1928........ $450

18" "Honey." All hard plastic/5-pc jtd. body, CM, blue sleep eyes, dark brown mohair wig/pigtails, original clothes, hat, etc. Mark: "EFFANBEE." Ca. 1950...................................$375-$425

18" "Miss Chips." All-vinyl/jtd. body, CM, sleep eyes, dark brown hair, original bridal gown, veil, bouquet, etc. Mark: EFFANBEE 19 C 65" and "1700." (Miss Chips was an innovation when she was first introduced in 1965. She sported the popular "mod look" of mini-skirt, knee-length boots, sunglasses, etc. Later, Miss Chips boasted only a number, no name.) Ca. 1968................$85

18" Anne Shirley. Bride. Compo head, CM, green sleep eyes, light brown HHW/original set, compo. body jtd. at neck/sh/hips, original silk taffeta bridal gown, veil, underclothes, etc. Mark: "EFFANBEE U.S.A." Ca. 1935-1940...................................$450

16" "Bubbles", all original, $400-$450. (Courtesy of Ruby Ellen Smith)

18" Negro "Bubbles." All compo., original clothes, etc. Mint. Super-rare. ....$1,000-$1,200

18" Negro "Rosemary." Black compo. shoulder head/narrow shoulders, OM/4 teeth, brown tin sleep eyes, black HHW, cloth body/full black compo. limbs, original voile dress with design of pink and yellow roses and green leaves/diamonds/white color, muslin slip, etc. Mark: "EFFANBEE//ROSE-MARY//WALK-TALK-SLEEP." (in an oval design) and "MADE IN USA" (below the oval). Ca. 1925+.............. $750

18-1/2" "Lovums." Compo shoulder head, OM/teeth, light green sleep eyes, real eyelashes, blonde ptd./molded hair, cloth body/rear voice mechanism, original clothes, etc. Heart-shaped bracelet reads: "EFFanBEE/Lovums/C/Pat. No.1 285,556." (Voice mechanism is designed to hold records. "Tousle Head" also had this devise.) Ca. 1928-1939 .... $450

18-1/2" "Tintair" Doll. Hard plastic head, CM, blue sleep eyes, blonde synthetic wig, hard plastic jtd. body, original dress, hat, etc., including boxed TINTAIR products and box that came with the doll. Never played with. (This doll is the same as "Honey.") MIB (Rare) (Sold for $450 in 1992) $700

19" "Sweetie Pie." Compo head, CM, brown sleep eyes, CM, brown wig, cloth body, compo. arms/lower legs, original clothes, etc. MIB Ca. 1949 .... $450

19" Anne Shirley. All-hard plastic. Re-issue. Hard plastic head, CM, blue ptd. eyes, light brown HHW (pigtails), jtd. hard-plastic body, original floral print romper, blue coat with large white buttons and white collar, leather shoes, white socks. Ca. 1950 .... $400

19" Negro "Bubbles." Black shoulder head, OM/teeth/tongue, brown tin sleep eyes, black ptd./molded hair, cloth body/black compo. limbs, original tagged gown, bonnet, etc. (Sold for $850 in 1989)...................$900-$1,000

19" Patsy Ann. Compo head, CM, brown tin/sleep eyes, brown ptd./molded bob, compo. body jtd. at neck/sh/hips, original red and white polka dot/floral jumper, matching hat, etc. Metal tag on wrist. (Advertised nationally as "Patsy's Big Sister.") Ca. 1929 .... $600-$650

20" "Bubbles." Compo head, OM/2 teeth/molded tongue, brown glassine sleep eyes, blonde ptd./molded hair, cloth body/compo lower arms, original clothes. Mark: "BUBBLES//EFFAN-BEE." Ca. 1932-33 (Rare) $500

20" "Little Lady." U.S.O. volunteer. Compo head, CM, blue sleep eyes, blonde HHW, compo. jtd. body, original khaki overalls, hat, etc. Ca. WW II $500

20" "Sweetie Pie" Twins. Katie & Mickey. Compo heads, CM, blue sleep eyes (boy)/blue flirty eyes (girl), brown fur wigs, hats, cloth body/compo. limbs/voice boxes, original light brown corduroy coats, hats, leggings; pink skirt/white upper bodice trimmed with pink ruffles (girl) blue pants/white shirt trimmed with blue (boy). Marks: "EF-FANBEE..." Original trunk-box and extra wardrobe attached to lid. Ca. 1946 MIB $1,000

20" Charlie McCarthy. Compo head/hinged mouth/stung at rear of head for operation, ptd. brown eyes, black ptd. hair, black ptd. "Clark Gable" type mustache, original tux, top hat, etc. 1937 ....$700-$800

20" Patsy Joan. Compo head, CM, brown tin sleep eyes, brown ptd./molded bob, jtd. compo. body/bent right arm, original dress with floral print, etc. Ca. 1930. Mark: "FB 16." ....$700-$750

22" "Buttons." The Effanbee Monk. Molded felt face/brown mohair plush head and neck/back of hands, cloth body/limbs/felt tail, original bell-hop uniform: red flannel jacket/cap, black trousers, red oilcloth boots. Button on jacket reads: "BUTTONS EFFANBEE." (Monkey has screech box.) 1923. $400
Sizes: 27" $550; 31" $650

19" Patsy Ann. original clothes, $600-$650. (Courtesy Ruby Ellen Smith)

22" "Rosemary." Compo shoulder head, OM/teeth, grey tin sleep eyes, brown HHW/hair bow, cloth body/compo lower limbs, original pale green dress, bonnet, etc. Ca. 1925.........................$500

22" Patsy Lou. Compo swivel head, CM, green tin sleep eyes/real eyelashes, blonde HHW, jtd. compo. body, original clothes, etc. Marks: "PATSY LOU" and "EFFANBEE PATSY LOU." Ca. 1929-30..............................$625-$650

24" "Baby Catherine." Compo shoulder head/round base, OM, green tin sleep eyes, peach-colored cloth body/upper arms and legs/compo lower arms, brown mohair wig, old white lawn dress, matching bonnet trimmed with val lace, etc. Mark: "EFFanBee." Ca. 1918 (Pacifier missing.) $450

24" "Dolly Dumpling." Compo shoulder head, CM, brown ptd./molded hair, ptd. blue eyes, cloth body/legs/compo. lower arms, original baggy playsuit with wide white collar, shoes, socks, etc. Mark: "EFFANBEE." Ca. 1915.....$650

24" "Mary Jane." Compo head, OM/teeth, blue tin sleep eyes, painted eyelashes, long curl brown HHW, jtd. compo. body/wood arms, original clothes, etc. (This "dolly face" type was EFFANBEE'S imitation of the Jumeau.) Mark: "EFFANBEE" (head and body). Ca. 1917-early 1920s ....$400-$450

25-1/2" Negro "Bubbles." Chocolate brown compo. head, O/C mouth, brown tin sleep eyes, black ptd./molded hair, cloth body/compo limbs, original clothes, bonnet, etc. Ca. 1930s $1,200

26" "Jumbo Infant." Compo shoulder head, CM, ptd. blue eyes, brown ptd./molded hair, white cloth body/pink cloth limbs/mitten hands/cry box, original red and white checkered rompers. (There was also a "Jumbo Infant" with a cloth mask face.) Ca. 1914. Mark: "FB 1." $375

26" Patsy Ruth. Compo swivel head, CM, blue sleep eyes, brown mohair wig, cloth body/compo. limbs, original clothes, etc. Mark: "EFFanBee PATSY RUTH." and "EFFANBEE LOVUMS." Ca. 1935 ....$1,000

27" "Snow White" or "Little Lady" type. Compo head/long neck, CM, brown sleep eyes, black mohair wig, compo. body jtd. at neck/sh/hips, original long dress; black velvet top with short puff sleeves, white full skirt with red flocked dots encircled by a red flocked border and a red bottom ruffle, underclothes, shoes, socks, EFFANBEE metal bracelet. (This doll is said to be EFFanBee's version of Snow White.) 1940s $650

28" NOMA Baby. Electronic Talking Doll. Hard plastic head, OM, blue sleep eyes, dark brown ptd./molded hair, vinyl body/record player, original clothes, bonnet, etc. (Made by F&B for the NOMA Electrical Company who made Christmas tree lights. NOMA purchased F&B in 1946 or 1947 for one million dollars and celebrated Christmas 1950 with the NOMA Talking Doll.) Ca. 1950 (Body has darkened with age)...$85

29" "Mae Starr." Phonograph Doll. Compo shoulder head, OM/4 teeth, brown tin sleep eyes, brown HHW, cloth kapok-stuffed body/compo limbs, talking mechanism inside body/wax cylinder records, original clothes, etc. (This was a premium doll, given free if one sold enough subscriptions to THE PHILADELPHIA LEDGER. Another version of this doll had 2 upper teeth/tongue and had the name MAE STARR embossed on the shoulder plate. F&B had exclusive rights to this doll which was sold only through newspapers until Jan. 1944.) Mark: "FB 9." Ca. 1928-34 ....$1,000+

29" "Melodie." Phonograph Doll. All hard plastic/fully jtd. body, CM, blue sleep eyes, blonde wig, phonograph mechanism inside body/3 records, original dress, bonnet, etc. EFFanBee wrist tag. Ca. 1953 ....$600

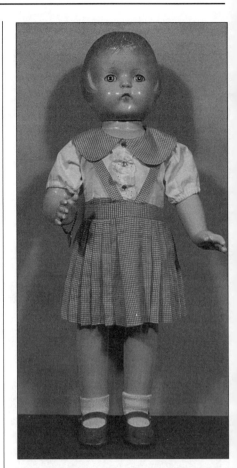

22" Patsy Lou, original clothes, $625-$650. (Courtesy of Ruby Ellen Smith)

22" same doll as above.

Chapter 9

∽ ENGLISH DOLLS ∽

History:

The British have long been known as a maker of fine poured wax and "wax-over" dolls, although the most famous of these wax doll modelers had Italian surnames such as, Montanari, Pierotti, and Bazzoni. British doll-makers also excelled at carved wooden dolls, composition dolls, papier-mâché dolls, and dolls made of fabric.

However, they were never known for their mass-production talents. Hence, with the advent of World War One and the shortage of dolls (the British always purchased the most play-dolls in Europe), they turned their pottery factories into doll-making factories—the result being a rather hastily made, inferior doll. In their attempt to imitate the German product, they even used some old German molds for the socket and shoulder heads and limbs. These were placed on cheap cloth bodies or German ball-jointed bodies (some of their own manufacture).

The dolls had glass or painted eyes, and wigs made either of human hair or the excellent English mohair. But the bisque heads were coarse and "grainy" of texture, the features highly colored. Yet, the bisque-head dolls made in America during this hectic period hardly fare much better.

Since dolls merely mirror the times, and production methods are a result of the times, we must conclude that heady competition, confusion, commercialization, and the desire to manufacture a low-cost "economy" doll—one that everyone could afford—cheapened the product. The era of "luxury" custom-made poupee-beit French or German made—was gone forever (it was conceived expressly for the rich anyhow). Thus, the British-made bisque-head doll is no better or no worse than any other doll made during this frantic war-torn period. World War One was the "war to end all wars;" La Belle Epoque was banished and the harsh "modern" world loomed ahead. The "roaring twenties" would usher in new modes—and problems.

Collecting Hints:

The dolls made by the British during World War One and later, are a step be-low those made in America during this time (Fulper, Bester, Tip Top Toy Co.), and, like their American cousins, prices seem to dangle in the $250-$650 range, depending on size, quality, and rarity. British socket and shoulder heads were duplicated in bisque, pottery, ceramic (glazed), and composition. These heads were placed on cheap cloth bodies or ball-jointed bodies (some of the ball-jointed bodies were old German stock). Wigs were made of human hair and fine British mohair (modeled hair-dos were also common). Since these dolls were made in limited quantity for a brief period of time, they are actually considered "rare" and are worthy of any advanced doll collection—being an example of a particular type doll made during a frantic changing era in history.

Reproduction Alert:

It is doubtful whether any of these old heads have been reproduced in modern times, unless by amateur doll-makers. Examine the painting of the features, especially eyebrows and eyelashes these were professionally painted. Modern bisque would be finer grained and well sanded. Doll "artists"—those who have excelled at making bisque dolls—are too well-trained to waste time on a doll that might be considered "unpopular." Since they charge quite a bit for their reproductions, the "artist" is mainly interested in the most popular and sought-after dolls of the moment.

ENGLISH DOLLS

8" Pearly King. Compo head, CM, large ptd blue eyes, blonde mohair wig, jtd felt body/limbs, original felt black jacket/cap decorated with tiny buttons and sequins, grey felt trousers/buttons on sides of legs, red scarf. Wrist tag reads: "Old Cottage Toys." Made by Mrs. M.E. Fleischmann and her daughter, Susi, Sussex, England. (Sold at Libertys and Harrods in London.) Ca. 1948 ....$150-$175

8"Little Girl. Compo head, CM, large blue ptd eyes, blonde mohair wig/bangs/pigtails, jtd felt body/limbs, original cotton print dress/undies, pink felt shoes, pink felt hat. Wrist tag reads: "Old Cottage Toys"-handmade in Great Britain. "Made by Mrs. M.E. Greta Fleischmann and her daughter, Susi. Old Cottage Toys, Allargate, Rustington, Little-hampton, Sussex, Great Britain." Ca. 1948.....................................$150-$175

8" Norwegian Girl. Compo head, CM, large ptd blue eyes, blonde mohair wig/bangs/pigtails, jtd felt body/limbs, original black wool skirt, white apron, beaded bodice, undies, stockings, black felt shoes, felt bonnet with bead trim. Wrist tag reads: "Old Cottage Toys..." Made by Mrs. M.E. "Greta" Fleischmann and her daughter Susi, Sussex, Great Britain. Ca. 1948 ....$150-$165

8" Indian Girl. Dark compo head, CM, black ptd eyes, black mohair wig, jtd dark felt body/limbs, original Indian or "India" turquoise blue sari, silver lame underwear, shoes. Wrist tag reads: "Old Cottage Toys..." Made by Mrs. M.E. "Greta" Fleischmann and her daughter, Susi, Sussex, Great Britain. Ca. 1948 ....$150-$165

8-3/4 "Young Princess Anne of England. Little Girl. China shoulder head, O/C mouth/teeth, ptd blue eyes, ptd/molded yellow-blonde short hair, full-length china arms/legs/cloth body, original dress, molded-on shoes/socks. Mark: "(Symbols)//MADE FOR DOLL MAKERS//BY CHELSEA ART DOLL MAKERS//1957." (Scarce)........... $750

8-3/4 "Young Prince Charles of England. Little Boy. China shoulder head, CM, ptd blue-grey eyes, ptd reddish-brown/molded hair, china hands/legs/cloth body, original suit. (Companion to above doll.) $750

10" Baby. All-hard plastic/jtd at neck/sh/hips/bent limbs, O/C mouth, blue sleep eyes, orange ptd/molded curly hair, original blue and white romper suit. Mark: "BND London." Made by The British National Doll Co., London, England, Cricklewood, London (before Sept. 1933). Advertised china-head dolls in 1933; mass-produced composition dolls in 1942. Sept. 1933+ located at 4-8 Hutton Grove, Finchley, London N., and 99 Fore Street, London. 1942+ at Acton Lane, Harlesdon, London, NW 10. Ca. 1950 .... $100

13" "Beauty Skin" Baby Doll. Rubber-plastic head, OM/sleep blue eyes/real lashes, orange-brown ptd/molded curly hair, lightweight rubber body/limbs stuffed with kapok, original factory clothes. Made by Pedigree Soft Toys LTD, Merton, London/Canterbury, Kent, 1938-1977+. Ca. 1948 (Good condition) $85

14" Soldier Boy. China shoulder head, CM, ptd blue eyes, blonde ptd/molded hair, cloth body/china lower limbs, original WW1 uniform, hat. Mark: "Willow." Made by Hewitt & Leadbeater, Longton, England. (This company made dolls until 1920.) Ca. 1916.. $350-$400

15" "Goss" Girl. Bisque shoulder head/florid coloring, dark red CM, rosy cheeks, inset brown glass eyes, thick dark brown eyebrows, brown mohair wig, pink cambric body/bisque lower arms, old clothes, etc. Back Mark: "GOSS." Made by W.H. Goss & Co., Falcon Pottery, Stoke-on-Trent, Staffordshire, England, 1858-1944; dolls, 1914-1918 ....$600

15" Little Boy. All-compo/jtd at neck/sh/hips/bent limbs, O/C mouth, ptd blue eyes, black ptd/molded curly hair, original blue checkered shirt, brown short pants, buttoned jacket (matches pants), cap. Unmarked. Possibly Pedigree, 1938 ....$175

16" "Dolly Dimple." Ceramic head/fluid coloring, OM/upper teeth, brown glass sleep eyes, brown mohair wig, BJ compo body, old clothes, etc. Made by Nunn & Smead, Liverpool, England, WW1-1927. Ca. 1921 ....$350

16-1/2" Character Baby. Pottery head, OM/2 lower teeth, vivid blue glass eyes, blonde ptd/molded curly hair, BJ compo toddler body, old clothes, etc. Head mark: "Dollies//4//British." Made by Dollies LTD, Bicester Rd., Aylesbury, Buckinghamshire, England, 1933-1935...................................$400

17" "Little Red Riding Hood." Ceramic or pottery head, OM/4 tiny teeth, inset blue glass eyes, brown mohair wig, cloth body/legs/compo arms, original tucked cotton dress, lace-trimmed drawers/petticoat, red cape with metal button (Willow design)/red hood with red tie ribbons, original shoes and stockings. Made by Willow Pottery Co., tradename for Hewitt & Leadbeater, Longton, Stoke-on-Trent, Staffordshire, England, 1914-1920+. Ca. 1920 ....$400-$425

17" Little Girl. Ceramic shoulder head, O/C mouth, blue glass sleep eyes,

light-brown eyebrows, brown HHW, cloth body/legs/ceramic lower arms, original factory-made dress, etc. Mark: "DU 28 (in a circle) RA." Made by Dura Porcelain Co., Elm St., Hanley, Stoke-on-Trent, Staffordshire, England. Ca. 1915+......................$375

17" "DPC" marked Girl. Bisque head/alert, lively expression, OM/teeth, blue glass sleep eyes, brown HHW, BJ compo body, old clothes, etc. Mark "DPC" and "Hanley, England." Made by Diamond Pottery Co., Shelton, near Hanley, England. (Doll Pottery Company also used these initials. They were located in Fenton.) Ca. 1916+..................$400

17" Little Girl. Flesh-tinted stoneware shoulder head, OM/teeth, blue glass sleep eyes, blonde mohair wig, cloth body/compo lower limbs, old clothes, etc. "Classic" mark. Speights LTD, 16 Bradford Rd., Dewsbury, Yorkshire, England, 1913-1916; 1916-1920s (dolls). 1917+...............................$350

17" Little Girl. Bisque head, OM/teeth, rosy cheeks, blue glass sleep eyes, BJ compo body, long curl brown HHW, old clothes, bonnet, etc. Mark: "Hanley, England." Made by Diamond Pottery Co., Shelton near Hanley, England. (Resembles an Armand Marseille head.) Ca. 1916+.........................$400

17" Little Girl. Compo head, OM/teeth/tongue, blue glass sleep eyes/molded eyelids, blonde mohair wig, BJ compo body, original dress with sash, underwear, socks, buckled shoes. Mark: " "Pedigree no, 620, 731." Made by Pedigree Soft Toys LTD, Merton, London/Canterbury, Kent, England, 1938-1977+. Ca. 1942 ......$225

17" Baby. Compo head, OM/teeth, blue metal sleep eyes, blonde ptd/molded hair, bent-limb compo body, original clothes, bonnet. Mark: "Pedigree." Ca. 1938+...$275

18" Little Girl. Ceramic shoulder head, O/C mouth, ptd blue eyes, blonde ptd/molded hair with curls bordering face/pink ribbon encircling head, cloth body/ceramic hands and feet, original clothes, etc. Mark: "EMPIRE. Stoke on Trent." Made by Empire Porcelain Pottery, Empire Works, Staffordshire, England, 1916-1925. Ca. 1916+................$350

19" Little Girl. Bisque head, CM, ptd blue eyes, brown HHW, cloth body/bisque lower limbs, old clothes, etc. Head mark: "5" (in a circle)/Willow, England. "Made by Hewitt and Leadbeater, Willow Pottery, Longton, England, 1907-1919; 1919-1926 Hewitt Bros." "Willow" mark: 1907-1919...........$350

20" Toddler Boy. All wood flour compo/jtd at neck/sh/hips/bent arms/toddler legs, OM/teeth, blue tin sleep eyes, brown ptd/molded hair, original romper suit, socks. Made by Pedigree Soft Toys LTD, England. ("Pedigree" trademark registered 1942 no. 620, 731 for dolls and toys.) Ca. 1938 (Good condition) $300

20" "Melba" Girl. Ceramic socket head, OM/teeth, inset blue glass eyes, blonde mohair wig, BJ compo/wood body, old clothes, etc. Mark: "Melba 111 5-1/2 England." Made by Mayer & Sherratt, Clifton Works, Longton, Staffordshire, England. Ca. World War One (1915) 1920.. $450

24" Talking Baby. Hard plastic head, OM, blue sleep eyes, brown ptd/molded curly hair with forehead ringlet, hard plastic body jtd at neck/sh/hips/bent limbs/voice box inside body, original clothes. (Some of these dolls had flirty eyes.) Mark: "Pedigree." Made by Pedigree Soft Toys LTD, England. Ca. 1955 (Mint) $200

Chapter 10

~FABRIC~

History:

The fabric or "rag" doll was never mass-produced until the twentieth century. The few people, usually women, who saw the possibilities of a soft doll for the masses, fashioned their dolls in the home. Izannah Walker, a maiden lady who considered herself a housekeeper rather than a "dollmaker," was one of the earliest crafters who tried to reach a broader audience with her unique creations. Her dolls were carefully executed, displaying a definite artistic flair. Martha Chase and Ella Smith, whose dolls were somewhat similar, made their first dolls for children and went on to operate small factories. The doll printed on cloth, which could be cut-out, sewn, and stuffed in the home, became popular in the late 1890s. It was attractive, economical, and, to this day, has survived as an ideal advertising gimmick.

Although dolls with pressed mask faces were made before Signora Lenci of Italy decided to make hers of felt, her dolls paved the way for a more idealized, stylish doll that represented the flamboyance of the Art Deco era. Needless to say, she had many imitators, but none seemed to match her ingenuity and good taste. The mask face with its molded features was an improvement over the rag doll with a flat face and printed or handpainted features, and has continued to be a favorite with doll manufacturers. Children, too, seem to prefer them over the hard-faced dolls.

Collecting Hints:

There is a profusion of cloth dolls out there for collectors—old and new. Some have great value—others have none at all—or very little, at most. Advanced collectors prefer the more costly, vintage types. Those who buy dolls for investment purposes study the market and buy only dolls that have proven their worth, i.e., early American primitives, Lenci's, etc. Dolls who depict well-known personalities like Shirley Temple, Rudolph Valentino, Mary Pickford, etc., are likewise popular favorites. Advertising dolls, old and new, are collectible, as are the early printed and stuffed cloth dolls.

Black dolls have always been made in abundance, yet the few surviving examples made of cloth are always quickly snapped up. A doll in mint or near mint condition will always command top dollar. Mint condition means very little wear, original clothes, and bright colors. But dolls grow old and will sometimes fade, even if kept safely in trunks. The patina of age should never devaluate a truly valuable old doll.

Reproduction Alert:

Some of the early printed cloth dolls have been reproduced in modern times. These have been sold in shops that specialized in vintage reproductions, gift shops, and even in antique shops—where they should not be sold. When in doubt, especially when buying at a flea market or antiques shop, sniff the doll. Old dolls have a musty smell (don't confuse it with a "dusty" smell!). Also, the old dolls were stuffed with cotton and do not have the firm, bouncy feel that modern stuffing allows.

FABRIC DOLLS

5" Little Orphan Annie. Embroidery Set. Cloth Orphan Annie to be cut-out and stuffed, printed-on-cloth wardrobe (dress, apron, pajamas, etc.), metal scissors, embroidery thread, needle. Original box is designed and signed by Harold Gray, creator (depicts Annie as a pirate, and Sandy uncovering a treasure chest.) Made by J. Pressman & Co., New York, New York. 1920s Mint $125

6" "Magis" Girl. Lenci look-alike. Molded felt face, CM, round blue enameled/surprised eyes to side, ptd upper lashes only, blonde mohair wig, cloth body/felt limbs, original felt and organdy German regional costume, hat, etc. Skirt tag reads: "Magis Roma and Dolomiti//Made in Italy." 1930s.................. $65

7" Dolly Dollykins. All cloth, flat lithographed face, tiny watermelon mouth, blue eyes glancing upward, partial wig in front/bow, original clothes, bonnet, lithographed black-strap shoes and striped socks. Grace Drayton design. Children's Novelty Co., Phila., PA. Ca. 1909-11 Rare.............................. $225

7-1/2" Tumbling Doll. Male. Canvas head/face/lithographed hand-drawn features (broad smiling mouth with upper and lower teeth), cardboard cylinder-shape tube constitutes head and body, printed collar and bow tie, blue

felt cap, blue felt clothes with separate machine-stitched felt strip limbs. (Metal ball inside doll enables it to tumble.) Unmarked. Probably J. Gowdey. 1917 Rare... $125

8" 12 Palmer Cox Brownies. John Bull, Uncle Sam, Captain, Dude, Highlander, Policeman, Irishman, Chinaman, German, Indian, Soldier, Sailor. Inspired by the stories written by Palmer Cox for St. Nicholas Magazine. Printed stuffed cloth. Arnold Print Works, North Adams, Mass. 1890s Rare - Set of 12 .... $1,000+

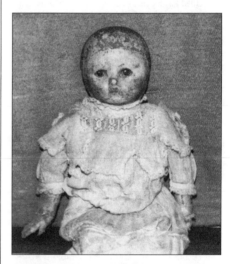

18-1/2" Alabama Baby, all-original, 1899-1905 Made by Ella Smith Doll Co., Roanoke, Ala., 1899-1925.

8-1/2" Dolly Varden. All stuffed cloth, unusual and realistic chromolithograph paper face, open smiling mouth with teeth, large blue eyes, yellow chromolithographed hair, original flannel cape of gaudy design, no arms. Ca. 1898 Rare.................................. $250

8-1/2" Topsy. Negro child. Printed stuffed cotton cloth. Celia M. Smith designer. Arnold Print Works, North Adams, Mass. 1893+ $175

10" "Mawaphil" Girl. All cloth, hand-painted features, blonde mohair wig, original clothes, hat, sewn-on shoes, etc., original tag. (Early dolls were handmade, became more professional looking later on.) Rushton Co., Atlanta, GA, 1924-1930+. Ca. 1920s $150

10" Esther Starring. Child actress. Flat cloth printed doll, holds her doll by its legs, blonde printed hair, smiling face, printed clothes, etc. Mark: "Esther Starring," and "Penny Ross." Penny Ross designer. Live-Long Toys, Chicago, IL, 1923+.. $150

10" Little Girl. Lenci look-alike. Molded felt face, CM, ptd blue eyes to side, blonde mohair wig, felt body jtd at sh/hips, wardrobe and clothes (some are felt). N.D. Cass Co., Athol, Mass., est. 1918-27. Ca. 1920s $700

11" Dottie Dimple. Bucilla Pattern Doll. Flat/cloth printed, embroidered features, printed clothes/shoes/socks. (This doll came in a packaged envelope with a dress.) 1920s Mint $200

11-1/2" Foxy Grandpa. Flat cloth printed doll, original 2-pc black suit, vest, shirt, tie, eyeglasses, hat with striped band. Cartoon character by Carl. E. Schultz. (Foxy Grandpa and his two 9" grandsons came as a set.) Possibly Art Fabric Mills; distributed by Butler Brothers, NYC. Ca. 1903.............................$125

12" "Life-Like" Topsy-Turvey Doll. White girl on one end and black girl face on the other end, hand-painted faces, bonnet/head scarf, cloth arms/no legs, dressed. Babyland Rag Dolls, Horsman, NYC. 1907 ....$900

12" Bing Art Puppen. Boy. Ptd/molded cloth head, CM, ptd blue eyes, ptd brown hair, cloth body/pin jtd sh/hips, original short pants, green suspenders, white shirt, shoes, socks, etc. (Resembles a Kruse.) Bing Werke/Bing Kunstlerpuppen, Nurnberg, Germany. Ca. 1921-32...$650

12" Bing Art Puppen. Girl. Ptd/molded cloth head, CM, ptd brown eyes, ptd short red hair, cloth body/pin jts at sh/hips, original blue and white check dress, etc. (Resembles a Kruse.) Bing Werke/Bing Kunstlerpuppen, Nurnberg, Germany. Ca. 1921-32 ....$650

12" Cuddle Doll. Boxed. Printed-on-cloth doll and wardrobe/cotton stuffing. Stoll & Edwards Co., Inc., NYC. MIB 1920s...................................$200

12" Mickey Mouse. Walt Disney character. Black plush body/yellow "gloves"/short red corduroy pants/dark yellow corduroy "shoes"/black nose, round fabric

22" Spanish Lady, all-original, ca. 1890s One-of-a-kind made by a lady over 70 for a Countess in Spain, molded face, ptd features, red mohair wig, felt-type body, silk stocking, high-heeled slippers, etc. $1,500. (Courtesy of Herron)

eyes. Label reads: "Mickey Mouse copyright Walt Disney Productions" and "Character Novelty Co. License Norwalk, Conn." Ca. 1939-40 ...... $200

12-1/2" "Harwin" Sailor Boy. Steiff look-alike. Felt head/center face seam, ptd CM, round glass eyes, blonde mohair wig, felt body/jtd at sh/hips, round stubby fat fingers, original dark blue felt sailor suit, white felt cap with blue trim, white felt shoes, etc. Harwin & Co., LTD, The Eagle Works, Blackstock Road, Finsbury Park, N., England, 1915-1921. Ca. 1915+ Rare $500

13" "The Drunkards." Character Men. Needle-sculpted stockingnet heads, painted features, bald domes with hair glued to sides of heads, wire-armature bodies/padded, original black suits, white shirts, cravats, spats, wood feet, flowers in lapels. etc. (These two gentlemen, probably the father of the bride and the groom, seem to be celebrating with arms embracing each other. One gentleman holds a bouquet of flowers—probably the bride's father; the other gentleman has a monocle; one smokes a cigar. Foot labels: Made by Kammer & Reinhardt, Germany. 1920s Rare ....$1,000+

13" Airline "Stewardess." Molded mask face, CM, ptd blue eyes to side, auburn mohair wig, cloth body/limbs, original grey skirt, cap, red shirt, shoes, socks. Jacket label reads: "STEWARDESS." Left leg seam label reads: "Mollye's//PRODUCT//(AM)ERICAN MADE." Mollye Goldman, Philadelphia, PA. 1940s $125

13" Brownie Girl Scout. All cloth, mask face, smiling CM, ptd blue eyes to side, yellow yarn hair/pigtails/bangs, original brownie uniform (buttons to waist in front), beanie, underwear, brown shoes, white socks. Unmarked doll. Georgene Novelties, Inc., NYC. 1930s $175

13" Charlie Chaplin. All-cloth/semi-articulated body, embroidered features, black mohair wig, original baggy trousers, jacket, hat, cane, over-sized shoes. Made by Madame Ouvrè, Paris, France. 1916 Rare....................$1,000

13" Daisy Darling. All-cloth cut-out doll/stuffed. Pretty child with printed wavy dark brown hair, fancy printed red dress with blue sash and blue stockings. E.I. Horsman, NYC. 1960+.. $150

13" Little Lulu. All-cloth, long mask face, ptd features, black wool yarn hair, original red dress, drawers, ptd-on shoes/striped socks. Tag reads: "LITTLE LULU//FROM//THE SATURDAY EVENING POST". Opposite side reads: "KNICKERBOCKER TOY CO. INC//NEW YORK." 1939-45 Rare $700

13-1/4" Katzenjammer Kid. Hans. Comic strip character by Rudolph Dirks. All-cloth, ptd features, small round black glass eyes, black ptd hair, original striped trousers (red, blue, green, yellow), red shirt with white color, black bow-tie, black shoes, black felt hat. Yellow paper tag has his name "Hans." Knickerbocker Toy Co., NYC. Ca. 1925...$750

13-1/2" "Marga." Little girl type. Molded felt face/head, CM, large ptd brown eyes to

side, brown mohair wig, cloth body/felt limbs/separate fingers, ornate Hungarian costume. Heart-shaped tag reads: "Marga." Jacket stamped: "Made in Hungary." (Lenci look-alike; some have compo. heads.) Marga Szerelemhegy, Hungry, 1920s-30s. Ca. 1925...... $500

13-1/2" Buster Brown. Advertising Doll. All-cloth, flat face, printed features, printed yellow hair, printed red suit/cap/arms designed onto body. Chest mark: BUSTER BROWN SHOES. 1902+ $500

14" "Alsatian" Girl. Molded cloth/ptd face, CM, blonde mohair wig, cloth body/pin jtd sh/hips, original "Alsatian" costume, shoes, stockings, etc. Bing Werke, Nurnberg, Germany, 1921-32 .... $450-$500

14" "Babyland Rag Doll." All cloth, realistic lithographed baby faces (cry face, smiling face), original white cotton christening gown, bonnet, etc. Original round paper tag reads: "GENUINE BABYLAND..." Original box. E.I. Horsman, NYC, 1901-1918. 1906. $1,200-$2,200

14" "Bye Bye Kids" Doll. Negro Mammy. All-cloth, flat printed face/hair, limbs separate from body, original clothes, bandanna. Mark on back: "BYE BYE KIDS//STRICTLY SANITARY//OLD MAMMY." Bach Bros. & Katzenstein, 1908-1909 Rare........................... $300

14" "Goldilocks." Printed/stuffed cloth. A very pretty little girl. Kellogg Co., Battle Creek, MI. 1925 .... $125

14" "Mama" Bear. Printed/stuffed cloth. Mama holds a labeled Kellogg's cereal bowl and has one paw in the bowl getting ready to eat. She wears a blue print dress sprinkled with flowers and has white stripes. ("Goldilocks and the Three Bears.") Kellogg Co., Battle Creek, MI. 1925 .... $125

14" "Rollinson" Girl. Molded cloth head, CM, large ptd brown eyes, applied ears, thin ptd yellowish eyebrows, yellow ptd hair/brushmarks, cloth body/limbs, old clothes, etc. Stamp mark: (design: doll in center of a diamond shape) and around border: "Rollinson Doll, Holyoke, Mass." Utley Doll Co., Holyoke, Mass. (These dolls have a Martha Chase look; some resemble the Kathe Kruse dolls.) Ca. 1916+ $600

14" "Venus" Bebe. Lenci look-alike. Molded mask face, "bee-stung" red CM, large ptd brown eyes to side/ptd upper lashes, one stroke light brown eyebrows, thick brown mohair wig, cloth body jtd at neck/sh/hips, original pink wool dress, bonnet, etc. Label reads: "Venus." Original box. Made by Adrien Carvaillo, Paris, France, 1920's-1930s. Distributed by Bon Marchè, Paris. Ca. 1928 MIB $550

14" "WRAF" and "WRNS" Girls. Two all-cloth dolls representing members of the WRAF and the WRNS. Similar felt faces, CM, large ptd blue eyes, ptd short hair, long limbs, original velvet uniforms with long-strapped bags attached to shoulders, etc. Norah Wellings, England. (Norah Wellings was the official doll artist to the British Commonwealth of Nations during WW II, thus she created many doll designs repre-

senting members of the different military forces. She marked her dolls with a stitched foot label.) See Norah Wellings section for more of her dolls. Ca. WW II Pair
....$1,200

14" Little Lulu. Cloth swivel head/ptd mask face, cloth body/limbs, original red dress, blue purse with shoulder strap, etc. By Marjorie H. Buell, NY. 1944-51. MIB (This doll gleaned .. $2,000 at auction in 1993.) $800

14" Mary Pickford. Silent Screen Star. Molded mask face, CM, ptd blue eyes, long blonde mohair wig, cloth body/limbs, original costume. Tag reads: "Mary Pickford" and "Dorothy Vernon of Haddon Hall." 1924 Rare
....$1,000

14" Negro Boy. All brown velvet/stuffed/stitched fingers with separate thumb, smiling O/C mouth, ptd brown eyes to side/long eyelashes, black wool wig, original short pants, shirt, belt, hat, etc. Cloth label on sole of foot reads: "FARNELL'S ALPHA TOYS//MADE IN ENGLAND." J.K. Farnell & Co., Alpha Works, Acton, London W3, England, 1871-1968. Ca. 1935+..$350

14" Tubby Tom. Comic character in strip "Little Lulu." Cloth swivel head/ptd mask face, cloth body/limbs, original brown shorts/white shirt/blue jacket. By Marjorie H. Buell, NY. 1944-51 MIB (This doll gleaned. $2,000 at auction in 1993)................................$1,200

14-1/4" Celeste. Jean de Brunhoff elephant character/female companion to Babar (17"). Light brown plush/jtd body, inset glass eyes, OM, original clothes. Made in France. 1937 ....$600

14-1/2" Tubby. Little Lulu's friend. All-cloth, molded mask face, ptd features, dark yarn hair, applied ears, original sailor suit. Made by Georgene Novelties, Inc., NYC. 1944-65 ....$600

14-1/2" Hawaiian Tubby. Little Lulu's friend. All-cloth, molded mask face, ptd features, dark yarn hair, applied ears, original Hawaiian outfit, orange lei, etc. Georgene Novelties, Inc., NYC. 1944-65 ....$800

14-1/2" Cowgirl Little Lulu. All-cloth, molded mask face, ptd features, black wool hair, original black fringed skirt, white long-sleeved shirt, wide-brimmed hat, holster, gun, boots. White paper label reads: "LITTLE LULU//COPR. 1944 MARJORIES H. BUELL." Opposite side: "LITTLE LULU BY MARJO-RIES//GEORGENE NOVELTIES, INC.//NEW YORK CITY//EXCLUSIVE LICENSES MANUFACTURERS." Ca. 1944-1965...................................$800+

14-1/2" Nelke Boy. All-stocking-net/hand-painted, tiny smiling mouth, ptd blue eyes to side, ptd black hair, movable arms/stiff legs/firmly stuffed, original red and green sewed-on suit/cap. 1920s Nelke Corp., Philadelphia, PA. 1917-25+. Ca. 1920s....$800

15" "Brownie" Girl. All-cloth/flat ptd face, wee red mouth, large ptd eyes, brown yarn hair (pigtails), factory made brown uniform, plastic belt with metal buckle, Brownie badge, brown shoes, white socks (sewn to legs). Unmarked. Made in England. 1974..........................$50

15" "Becassine." Book Character Doll. Round molded carton head, ptd features, felt/cloth body, original felt/cotton clothes, cap. Made in France. Character from the book "L'Enfance de Becassine." ("Becassine's Childhood," 1913; Cartoon, 1905.) Ca. 1925 .. $350

15" "Columbian" Baby. Muslin head/oil ptd features, cloth body jtd at sh/hips/knees, original clothes, bonnet. Rear body mark: "Columbian Doll, Emma E. Adams, Oswego Centre, N.Y." Ca. 1890s $5,500

15" "Poulbot" School Girl. All-cloth/needles-culpted face, red heart-shaped mouth, ptd brown eyes, brown yarn wig/bangs, flocked buckram limbs/stitched fingers/separate thumb, original coat, dress, etc. M. Poulbot, Paris, 1908-1930s. Ca. 1908+ ....$2,000+

15" "Raynal" Bebe. Lenci look-alike. Molded felt face/cellulose coating, CM (2 dots on lower lip), ptd brown eyes, brown mohair wig, pink cotton body jtd at neck/sh/hips/rear leg seams/front and back arm seams/mitten hands, original pink taffeta dress trimmed with lace, white cotton teddy, pink felt shoes with buttons similar to the 2 on back of dress. Original box label reads: "LES POUPEES RAYNAL" (the word "RAYNAL" is depicted by a doll figure; "R" being the upper body, etc.). Les Poupees Raynal, Paris, France. Ca. 1938..$500

15" Beloved Belindy. Black mammy doll. All-cloth/printed features, smiling red mouth, original clothes, bandanna. Paper tag reads: BELOVED BELINDY//by//Johnny Gruelle//Copyright 1926//by John B. Bruelle//Made in//U.S.A.//Georgene Novelties, Inc.//Exclusive Licensed Manufacturers." Ca. 1938-1963 Rare
....$1,500-$1,700

15" LIFE SIZE series Girl. Printed/stuffed cloth, printed white underwear with pink ribbon bow, red printed stockings/brown boots, original old clothes. (This big-eyed child has short wavy brown ptd hair with center part.) Art Fabric Mills, NYC; New Haven, Conn.; London. Signed. Ca. 1899-1912.. $175

15" Little Lulu. All cloth/flat face, ptd features, black yarn hair, red dress with white collar/rickrack trim, printed-on black shoes/red socks. Made by GUND. (Marjorie Henderson Buell, cartoonist, introduced Little Lulu, Feb. 1935, in The Saturday Evening Post when Carl Anderson's "Henry" was about to end and the magazine wanted a hasty replacement. The LITTLE LULU comic strip began 1, May 1935, and ran 10 years in the Post. Marge Buell retired in 1972, selling rights to Western Publishing Co. The GUND dolls came in 3 sizes.) Ca. 1972
....$65-$85

15" Scarecrow, The Wizard of Oz. Molded/ptd mask face, cloth body/hands, feet, hat represents "straw" stuffing, felt clothes. Wrist tag reads: "Strawman by Ray Bolger of The Wizard of Oz, Made in U.S.A. Ideal Novelty & Toy Co." MIB 1930s..$600

15-1/2" "Majorette" Little Lulu. All-cloth, molded mask face, ptd features, black wool wig, original majorette costume, hat, etc. (Same red-trimmed white paper label that appears on Cowgirl Lulu, etc.) Georgene Novelties, Inc. NYC. 1944-65 Rare...............................$900

15-1/2" King George VI. Molded felt face, ptd features, felt jtd body, original red plaid kilt, red jacket, tall black head-dress, etc. Wrist tag reads: "H.M. The King. Made in England by J.K. Farnell & Co. Ltd, Acton, London, W.3." 1936+ Rare...........................$2,000+

15-1/2" Hawaiian Little Lulu. All-cloth, mask face, ptd features, black wool hair, original "Hawaiian" costume; lei. Georgene Novelties, Inc., NYC. White tag reads the same as "Cowgirl Little Lulu." Ca. 1944...$800+

16" "Gunther Heine" Character Boy. Pressed cardboard head covered with fabric/ "mumps" cheeks, CM, large ptd brown eyes, large ears, brown ptd/molded hair, jtd cloth body/cloth-covered lower limbs, original clothes, etc. Foot stamp: "Schneider's Kunstpuppen-Atelier Karl Schneider Bad-Kosen Puppenkunst Elizabeth." Heine & Schneider Bad-Kosen, Saale, Germany. 1920-22
....$1,700

16" "Pickaninny" Girl. Printed/stuffed cloth. (This shy little black girl holds a finger to her lips and the other hand holds a fancy wide-brimmed pink bonnet—all printed onto the cloth.) Designed by Celia M. Smith. Arnold Print Works, North Adams, Mass. 1893+.........$275

Little Lulu, 12", all original, ptd mask face, black yarn hair. Made in Poland, ca. 1940s-50s. $100-$150. (Courtesy of Connie Baca)

16" Izannah Walker. Very young child or baby. Round head/very high forehead, ptd blue eyes, light yellowish-brown thin eyebrows, sparse ptd yellowish-brown hair, usual cloth body/stitched fingers/toes, original long-sleeve cotton print pink dress. Izannah Walker, Central Falls, R.I., 1840+. Good condition..........$16,000+

16" Young Boy. Printed/stuffed cloth/6-pc pattern/centre face seam, printed underwear, original blue suit. Ida Gutsell patent, 1893. Lawrence & Company (Cocheco Mfg. Co.), Boston, NY, Philadelphia, 1827. (Miss Gutsell probably designed the "Darkey Doll" as well.) Ca. 1893+ Rare $225

16-1/2" "Poupee Raynal." Lenci look-alike. Molded/felt mask face/pink muslin head, CM, ptd blue eyes to side, blonde mohair wig, faded pink muslin body/rotating limbs/movable head (legs have rear stitching; arms stitched front and back), original felt dress/hat/slippers, white cotton teddy, felt shoes, cotton socks. Dress tag reads: "Les Poupees Raynal//Narque Depose/Made in France." (This doll wears a 1920s style outfit.) Ca. 1925+ $650

16-1/2" "Mrs. Blossom." Cartoon character. Flat stuffed oilcloth, printed long coat with fur and printed hat, black printed hair, holds purse (printed). Mark: "King Mrs. Blossom PAT. APPLIED FOR." Ca. 1930s...............................$225

16-1/2" "Balsam Baby." Molded cloth mask face, red CM, rosy cheeks, ptd brown eyes to side, partial yellow blonde wavy mohair wig, pink cloth body jtd at neck/sh/hips/stitched fingers/separate thumb, original orchid print dress,

30" Pinocchio, all original, ptd mask face, cloth body. Unmarked. Possibly made in Poland. $90-$125. (Courtesy of Connie Baca)

matching bonnet, etc. Square white card tag reads: "PAT. PENDING TRADE MARK REG.//BALSAM BABY//HEALTHFUL CUDDLING DOLL//EASILY CLEANED WITH//art gum//GRE-POIR, INC." Gre-Poir, Inc., France & U.S.A. (These dolls were called this because they were stuffed with balsam needles from the American fir.) Ca. 1930 ....$800-$900

16-1/2" Freddie Bartholomew. Child film star. Pressed felt face, CM, ptd brown eyes to side, brown mohair wig, cloth body/limbs, original "British School Boy" outfit: striped trousers, white patterned shirt with Eaton collar, cutaway jacket, black felt with high top. Trouser tag reads: "To My Dear Friends With Greetings, Freddie Bartholomew (autograph), Geo. Borgfeldt Corp., NY." Ca. 1930s ....$1,000+

16-1/2" Katzenjammer Kid. Fritz. Comic strip character by Rudolph Dirks. All-cloth, ptd features, small round black glass eyes, black ptd hair, original red trousers, white shirt, black coat, black felt hat, black shoes. Yellow paper tag reads: "Katzenjammer//Kids//Fritz//Knickerbocker//Toy Co. Inc.//New York//C Licensed By//King Features Syndicate//Inc." Knickerbocker Toy Co., NYC. 1925 ....$750

16-1/2" Early Lenci Girl. Molded felt head/no neck, CM, ptd brown eyes to side, curly brown mohair wig, jtd felt body, peach and grey felt dress, pink hair-bows, pink felt shoes, etc. Metal button with "Lenci" (script). Ca. 1920..$1,000+

17" "Clelia." Little Girl. Felt head/rear seam/molded/ptd features, ptd blue eyes, CM, blonde wig, 5-pc cloth body/celluloid hands, original sailor suit, hat (inscribed "Normandie"). Marked: "Clelia." (Amilcare Brogli registered a 1926 patent for dolls. He registered "Clelia" for cloth dolls/animals in 1928. He made Snow White and the Seven Dwarfs in 1937). Brogli, Italy. Ca. 1936 ....$600

17" "Peter Pan." Molded felt face, smiling watermelon mouth, round ptd brown eyes, brown mohair wig, jtd felt body/limbs, original green felt clothes, red belt, green hat with red feather, brown shoes. Made by OLIS, France. Ca. 1953 ....$350

17" "Premium" Little Lulu. All-cloth, long pressed mask face, ptd features, black wool yarn wig, rare plaid dress/white organdy collar and cuffs, ptd-on shoes and socks. A premium doll for Saturday Evening Post or Ladies Home Journal. Gold paper tag reads: "LITTLE LU-LU//FROM//THE SATURDAY EVENING POST." Opposite side reads: "KNICKERBOCKER TOY CO., INC.//NEW YORK." Ca. 1939 . $1,000+

17" Babar. Jean de Brunhoff elephant character. Light brown plush/jtd body/inset glass eyes/OM, original 2-pc green felt suit/black buttons, white spats, black felt shoes. Made in France. Ca. 1937 .. $1,000+

17" Little Riding Hood. Printed/stuffed cloth. (Feet are not separated but are part of the forest background. Oval bot-

17" Little Polish Girl, all original, ptd mask face, yellow yarn hair, all-cloth. Made in Poland, ca. 1940s $65. (Courtesy of Connie Baca)

tom is reinforced with an oval piece of card.) Arnold Print Works, North Adams, Mass. 1890s $200

17-1/4" Hungarian Mother and Babe (5-1/4") and little girl (9-1/4"). Mother: round pressed felt face, CM, ptd brown eyes to side, brown mohair wig, jtd felt body/limbs, original ornate Hungarian costume includes white blouse embroidered with flowers, matching embroidered apron, pink pleated skirt, 3 white petticoats, silver necklace, embroidered cap, hand-knit stockings, leather shoes. Baby: compo. head, ptd features, cloth body, original embroidered bunting, pink and white baby dress, white bonnet. Little girl: compo. head/sly expression, CM, ptd blue eyes to side, blonde mohair wig with hair ribbon, white embroidered blouse, white embroidered apron, beige pleated skirt, hand-knit stockings, embroidered shoes. Made by MARGA, Italy. Ca 1939......................................$1,000+

17-3/4" Tom Thumb. Felt head, ptd brown eyes to side, CM, brown mohair wig, pink cloth body/limbs (stitched fingers, separate thumb), original costume: red trousers, white shirt, black vest, black boots, red hat, Raynal, Paris. Ca. 1935....................................$650-$700

18" "Cream of Wheat" Chef. Negro. Cloth/stuffed/printed features, broad smiling mouth/white teeth, brown printed eyes to side, arms printed onto body/hands hold a bowl of Cream of Wheat, loose legs, printed striped trousers/white shirt with 2 buttons, separate white chef's cap and white apron. 1949..$250

18" "Eugene Poir" Girl. Smooth mask face, no ears, CM (mouth has white dots on lower lip), blue eyes to side, brown curly poodle-cut wig, one-stroke eyebrows, cloth body jtd at neck/sh/hips, cloth limbs, mitt hands, original pink organdy dress with two rows of ruffled trim, matching bonnet, etc. Paper label on dress reads: "TRADE MARK//FRENCH DOLL MAKERS//AN ORIGINAL//EUGENIE POIR//MODEL..." 1920s Mint...........................$750

18" "LaMarazzi" Girl. Lenci look-alike. Molded felt mask face, CM, ptd brown eyes to side, short curly brown mohair wig, cloth body jtd at neck/sh/hips/felt limbs, original felt dress, blue felt hair bow, blue felt shoes, socks, etc. Lovely doll. Original box marked: "LaMarazzi Brevettata." 1920s MIB (Italian)

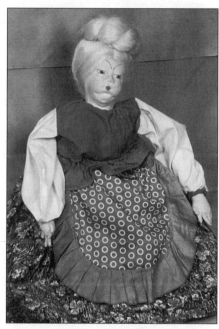

20" Russian Tea Cosy, all original, mash ptd face. Made in Russia. $275 for very old dolls. $75 for newer dolls. (Courtesy of Carol Lindberg)

....$1,000

18" "Poupees Raynal" Girl. Molded felt head, CM, ptd blue eyes to side, blonde HHW, pink cloth body/limbs, yellow taffeta dress, white slip, yellow felt shoes, white socks. Poupees Raynal, Paris, Edouard Raynal, 1922-1930s. Ca. 1922+..$800

18" Alabama Baby. Negro. Molded cloth head ptd black with oils, red CM, large ptd brown eyes with vivid whites, cloth body/tab jtd sh/hips, black ptd hair, applied ears, original clothes, ptd shoes/stockings. Ella Smith Doll Co., Roanoke, Ala. 1899-1925 (Sold at auction in 1996 for $3,000). Good condition ....$6,000-$7,000

18" Dorothy Lamour. Screen star of Paramount Pictures. All-cloth, over-sized head/printed features/broad smiling mouth, brown yarn hair, red floral print sarong. Square tag reads: "Autographed Movie Star Dolls, Dorothy Lamour, Popular Paramount Motion

Picture Star. Made in California by Star Creations of Hollywood." 1940s... $400

18" Izannah Walker. Little Girl. Round head shape, large ptd dark brown eyes, thin red lips, thin eyebrows, black ptd/center part hair/2 sausage curls ptd before crude attached ears/more sausage curls behind ears, muslin body/limbs/stitched fingers/separate thumb, sewed-on shoes, original short sleeve cotton print dress, etc. Ca. 1860s. Good condition

18" Izannah Walker. Very young child or baby. Round shaped head, "sleepy" blue ptd eyes looking downward, sparse feathered black ptd hair, stockinet/oil ptd head/limbs, muslin body/thumb separate, original cotton print dress with long sleeves, bonnet, etc. (Izannah Walker was born, Sept. 25, 1817, in Bristol, RI; died Feb. 15, 1888 in Central Falls, RI.) Ca. 1840s+ ....$18,000+

18" Kamkins Character Boy. All oil ptd cloth, mask face, CM, ptd blue eyes, molded ears, brown mohair wig, jtd cloth body/swivel head, original clothes. Red paper heart on left side of chest. Made by Louise R. Kampes Studios, Atlantic City, NJ. 1920s $1,500

18" Kathe Kruse look-alike. Little Boy. Pressed cardboard head/covered with flesh-colored muslin, CM, ptd blue eyes, ptd blonde hair, pressed cardboard body covered with flesh-colored muslin/limbs, original clothes. Purple foot stamp reads: "Puppen Kunst Elizabeth//Heine & Schneider//Bad-Kosen/Saale" (stars on each side). 1920+.....................................$1,800+

18-1/2" "Raynal" Bebe. Lenci look-alike. Molded felt head/cellulose coating, CM, ptd blue eyes to side, thin eyebrows, blonde mohair wig, pink cotton jtd body/flap attachment arms/rotating leg jts/upper body reinforced by cardboard/molded Rhodoid hands with fingernail detail and dimples/flat bottom cardboard-reinforced feet, original pink organdy dress with attached underskirt, etc. Sole of the white leather shoes reads: "RAYNAL//PARIS." Brass necklace marked: "RAYNAL." Unmarked doll. Made by Poupees Raynal, Paris, 1925-1930s. Ca. 1930s ....$1,000+

19" "Roselina." Eugenie Poir or Gre-Poir, Inc. Molded felt face, CM, ptd brown eyes to side, brown mohair wig, pink cloth body jtd at neck/sh/hips/separate thumbs, original pink and white felt/organdy dress with felt flowers trim, etc. Label reads: "Gre-Poir." Gre-Poir, Inc., NYC, Paris, 1927-1930s. Ca. 1927+..$750

19" Alice in Wonderland. All-cloth/jtd limbs, chubby molded cloth-mask face/dimples, CM, ptd blue eyes, inserted ears, long blonde mohair wig, blue hair ribbon, original pale blue organdy dress, white apron, dark blue strap shoes, white socks. Tag sewn to apron reads: "FARNELL//ALPHA TOYS//MADE IN ENGLAND." Acorn-shaped wrist tag reads: "AN ALPHA JOY-DAY ALICE, MADE IN ENGLAND by J.K. FARNELL & CO. LTD ACTON, LONDON W3." (Alpha Joy Day name registered

on August 2, 1935). Ca. 1935+.............................$900-$1,000

19" Happy Hooligan. Cartoon Character. All-felt, large CM, spherical eyes, black yarn eyebrows, straw-stuffed cloth body/limbs, original coat, shirt, trousers, shoes, red felt hat (resembles a tin can); holds green wooden bottle. Foot mark: "Made in Germany." 1920s...$750

19" Kamkins Girl. Molded mask face, CM, ptd blue eyes, auburn mohair wig/bangs, cloth body/limbs, original clothes, hat, etc. Made by Louise R. Kampes Studios, Atlantic City, N.J., 1919-1930. (The Kampes Studio was on the boardwalk. Miss Kampes designed the doll and clothing. Completely dressed dolls and separate pieces of wardrobe could be purchased in her studio. She was aided by homeworkers; sending them fabric and patterns. Riemann-Seabrey Co. were representatives of the Kampes American Kiddies during the 1920s. Red paper heart sticker read: "KAMKINS A DOLLY MADE TO LOVE PATENTED BY L.R. KAMPES ATLANTIC CITY, NJ.") 1920s.......................................$1,500

19-1/4" "Clelia" Boy. Molded felt head, CM, ptd blue eyes to side, blonde mohair wig, 5-pc cloth body, original "tennis player" outfit: white flannel trousers, white shirt, belt with metal buckle, white cap, white felt shoes, white socks. marked: "Clelia." Made by Amilcare Brogli, Italy, Ca. 1936 ....$800

19-1/4" Little Red Riding Hood. Molded felt head/rear seam, CM, ptd brown eyes to side, brown mohair wig, pink cotton

12" Rag doll by Albert Bruckner, all original. Patd. Jul. 8, 1901 Excellent condition $275-$300. (Courtesy of D. Kay

body/limbs, original outfit, etc. Raynal, Paris. Ca. 1935 .... $800

19-1/4" Little Girl. Lovely molded felt head, CM, ptd grey eyes to side, blonde mohair wig/tight curls, 5 pc./semi-articulated body (cloth), original organdy dress, straw hat, white strap shoes, white socks, etc. Raynal, Paris. 1930s (Raynal Company started by Edouard Raynal, Paris, 1922. Listed under Toy Manufacturers in the Commercial Directory, 1923, with animals made of felt, plush, leather. Advertised dolls made of felt/fabric by 1926. Registered 1930 patent for doll heads coated with a celluloid varnish. His "rhodoid" dolls date to 1935.) 1930s $800

19-1/2" "Rollinson" Boy. Molded/ptd cloth head, red CM, ptd blue eyes, attached ears, brown ptd hair, molded cloth body/ptd limbs, original sunsuit, hat. Mark: "Rollinson Doll Holyoke, Mass" (diamond-shaped stamp with a doll in the center; "Rollinson Doll..." printed around border). 1916+ ..$1,000-$1,300

20" "Dora Petzold" Girl. Molded cloth head/long face/sad expression, CM, ptd brown eyes, blonde HHW/bangs, short straight sides, cloth body/long limbs, original dress, shoes, socks, etc. (Some dolls have compo. heads.) Mark: "DORA PETZOLD REGISTERED TRADE MARK DOLL GERMANY." Ca. 1920+ ....$1,200-$1,500

20" "Rollinson" Girl. Molded/ptd cloth shoulderhead, O/CM/teeth, ptd blue eyes, molded ears, sausage curl brown HHW, sateen body/molded limbs/cupped hands made of ptd stockinet, original clothes, shoes, etc. (Lovely, professionally made doll). Body stamp: "Rollinson Doll Holyoke Mass" (in diamond shape with word Trade Mark and a design of a seated doll with one leg crossed over the other). Ca. 1920 (Gertrude Rollinson designer. Utley Doll Co.) $1,500

20" "Improved Foot Doll." Little Girl. Printed/stuffed cloth, large round printed face, side-parted hair with ribbon, white printed underwear, red printed stockings, black high-top boots, old clothes. Art Fabric Mills, NYC; New Haven, Conn., London. Marked. 1899-1910 .... $185

20" Shirley Temple. Molded lightweight felt mask face, smiling OCM/ptd teeth, ptd eyes to side, curly strawberry blonde mohair wig, cloth body/limbs/mitt fingers/separate thumb, original outfit, hat, etc. Mark: "France-Au Printemps, Paris." By Raynal, Paris. Ca. 1935-36 .... $1,200+

20" Chat botte (Puss in Boots). Character from "Mother Goose Tales" by C. Penault, 1697. Light tan plush body/red high-top boots/red full-length gloves, inset glass eyes, embroidered mouth/nose, long tail. Made in France. Ca. 1900 Rare $1,000

21" "Dinah." Negro girl. All-cloth, hand-ptd features, black mohair wig, original clothes. "Babyland Rag Doll" series. E.I. Horsman, NYC. 1901+ $1,400

21" "Dolores." Felt molded face, CM, rosy cheeks, large ptd blue eyes to side, long sausage curl blonde mohair wig, cloth body/felt limbs/jtd at neck/sh/hips, inside-out seams at rear of head, no ears, mitt hands, hair eyelashes, original silk dress, hat, etc. Tag reads: "Dolores." Eugenie Poir, France. 1920s $850

21" "Ellen Hooker Doll" (Molly H. Cole.) Cloth stuffed head/contoured nose and chin, red ptd cupid's bow mouth, ptd dark brown eyes, cloth body jtd at sh/elbows/dimpled stitched hands/separate fingers/legs cut to reveal knee and calf muscles, original frilly white dress, cream silk brocade bonnet brown ribbed stockings, light brown satin slippers with leather soles decorated with matching ribbon bows and bead buckles. (Roxanna Cole made the Cole rag dolls prior to 1900. Her daughter, Molly Hunt Cole, made the Ellen Hooker rag dolls until her death in 1936.) 1900+ $6,000

21" Jackie Coogan. Silent Screen child star. Molded felt face, CM, ptd brown eyes to side, blonde mohair wig (bangs, straight sides), no ears, well-modeled

21" Russian Tea Cosy, all original. Made in Russia. Ca. 1950s $125. (Courtesy of Victoria Rose, England)

features, jtd felt body/limbs, separate fingers, original clothes from "The Kid:" trousers, turtleneck sweater, cap, shoes, socks, Unmarked. Probably early Lenci. 1920s $2,000

22" "Laubscher's Puppen Fabrik." Little Girl. Molded plaster mask face/covered with cloth/hand-ptd, CM, ptd brown eyes, ptd brown hair, bulky cloth body/sewed-on fat arms and fat bent legs/hip jts, original clothes. Laubsher's Puppen Fabrik, Graaff-Reinet, South Africa. Miss Anna Laubscher founder. Crude doll. Ca. 1915+ .... $1,000+

22" "Venus" marked Girl. Molded felt face, CM, ptd brown eyes to side, brown mohair wig, 5-pc semi-articulated body/celluloid hands, original "First Communion" dress, veil, cross at neck, etc. Adrien Carvaillo, Paris, France. Ca. 1935 .... $800

22" Alabama Baby. Boy type. Cloth molded/oil ptd face/circular head seam, orange ptd CM, ptd blue eyes, brown ptd hair with brushmarks, applied ears, cloth body/limbs/tab jts at sh/hips/bare

feet, original clothes, shoes stockings. Body mark: "Mrs. S.S. Smith Manufacturer and Dealer to The Alabama Indestructible Doll Roanoke, Ala. PATENTED Sept. 26, 1905." 1899-1925 Good Condition $3,500

22" Philadelphia Baby (Boy). Molded cloth shoulder head, CM, large ptd brown eyes, ptd brown hair, applied ears, stocking body/ptd lower limbs, original clothes. Unmarked. (Also called "Sheppard Dolls.") J.B. Sheppard & Co., Philadelphia, PA. Ca. 1900 Good condition .... $4,500+

22" Teddy Bear and Cubs. Uncut fabric with printed brown Teddy Bear and two brown cubs (front and back sides). To be cut-out, stuffed, and sewn at home. Saalfield Publishing Co., Akron, Ohio. 1913... $100

23-1/2" Lenci "British School Boy" Boudoir Doll. #174. Molded felt head, CM, ptd brown eyes to side, light brown mohair wig, felt body/limbs/jtd at sh/hips/arms curved at elbows/very long legs, original beige felt trousers, white cotton shirt/stand-up collar, vest, brown jacket/beige buttons, black tie, beige gloves/black stitching, black patent leather shoes, white spats/five buttons, beige felt hat, black walking stick with white tip, original long ornate box. Ca. 1925 MIB .... $2,500-$3,000

24" "Else Hecht" Lady. Molded felt face/upturned nose/receding chin/open crown, smiling ptd red mouth, blue ptd eyes with black glass bead pupils, blonde mohair wig, wire armature/stuffed felt body/stitched fingers with separate thumbs/large feet, original sewn-on elaborate costume and hat, petticoat, drawers, etc. Original paper tag reads: "HECHI PUPPE ELSE HECHT (script);" illustrated by a doll riding a fish. Made by Else Hecht, Germany, 1920-1940s. (Else Hecht doll workshops became well-known during the "artists revolt" period of the 1920s. She also made puppets, many of which appear crude by today's standards.) Ca. 1920s Rare .... $1,500-$2,000

24" Madame Alexander Boudoir Lady Doll. Cloth mask face/mature look, CM, ptd blue eyes/long applied eyelashes, blonde mohair wig, original cloth body/limbs, original 2-pc outfit, etc. Tag reads: "Madame/Alexander/New York." 1930s...................................... $2,000

24-1/2" Beecher Rag Baby. All pink-stockinet/needlesculped/ptd face, pink CM, large ptd blue eyes/short upper and lower lashes, short looped yarn hair, chubby body, original old nightgown. (Also called Missionary Ragbabies.) Mrs. Thomas K. Beecher, Elmira, NY. Ca. 1893-1910 Rare ..... $3,500-$4,500

25" "Rollinson" Girl. All-cloth, lovely hard-pressed/molded cloth face, OM/teeth, grey glass sleep eyes, brown HHW, cloth body/limbs, original pink organdy dress, bonnet, etc. Stamp mark: Diamond shape with doll design in center, and printed around border: "Rollinson Doll Holyoke, Mass." Ca. 1916-1917 Rare type............. $5,000+

Chapter 11

~ MARK FARMER ~

History:1947-1972

This small ceramic business in El Cerrito, California turned its plant into a doll factory in 1947. The Farmers had been in business a year making high-fire artware, when a friend named "Cyrelle" suggested that they make "49'er" dolls to celebrate the century anniversary in finding gold in California. The Farmers like the idea and began converting their building into one more suitable to doll manufacture. The shoulder head and lower limbs that Cyrelle sculpted was reminiscent of an antique china-head doll. The doll was sold in kits with cloth and body patterns and given the poetic name "Jennie June" which was the name of an Idaho friend's great aunt who had been an editor of Godey's Ladies Book during the Civil War. The doll was a success and the Farmers continued to make other doll types which proved equally appealing to doll collectors. The Farmers loved and "lived" their work; their children growing up midst the clay dust, paint pots, and paper work, the latter of which would alter obscure the former—there would no longer be time to make dolls! The Farmers closed shop in the early 1970s. Their closing was a loss to the doll world.

Collecting Hints:

The china, parian, and molded hair-do bisque dolls made by the Mark Farmer Company are marked on the rear of the shoulder plate. The ceramic glaze on some heads has crazed with the passage of time. Since their dolls are so similar to the antique heads they are often referred to as "reproductions" and are not taken seriously as collector items. However, many of their heads were "original" and are very well-made and collectible. Dolls could be purchased fully dressed from the company or could be dressed at home. Unlike the Ruth Gibbs china-head dolls made in 1946, the Farmer dolls offer the collector more variety both in types and sizes.

MARK FARMER

14" Jennie June. China shoulder head, tiny CM, ptd blue eyes, black ptd hair in the familiar "Covered Wagon" type style (flat top, center part, severe draped sides), cloth body/china limbs, original clothes. (Replica of the rare original Jennie June modeled by Cyrelle in 1947 to celebrate California's Anniversary of the 1849 gold rush.) Late 1960s-early 1970s $150

14" Victoria. Bisque shoulder head/long neck/deep breast plate, CM, ptd blue eyes, blonde ptd/molded hairdo with center part and looped side braids, cloth body/china lower limbs, original clothes. Late 1960s-early 1970s .... $175-$200

14" Kitty. Bisque shoulder head/long neck/head slightly tilted to side, CM, ptd blue eyes, blonde ptd/molded hair with 2 rows of puff curls atop head and in back of head, cloth body/bisque lower limbs, original clothes. Late 1960s-early 1970s $165

15" Thelma. Brown bisque shoulder head, CM, pt brown eyes, black wig, cloth body/brown bisque lower limbs, original clothes. (Thelma, the doll's namesake, was a friend of the Farmer's.) Late 1960s-early 1970s .... $175-$200

16" Ida Ho. Indian maiden. Reddish bisque shoulder head, slightly smiling CM, ptd brown eyes, black wig with 2 long braids, cloth body/reddish bisque lower limbs, original clothes. Late 1960s-early 1970s $175

16" Alice. Pink bisque shoulder head/long neck, CM, ptd blue eyes, blonde ptd hair/molded high atop had/rear shoulder curls, cloth body/bisque lower limbs, original clothes. Late 1960s-early 1970s $175

16" Marie Antoinette. Skin-tone Parian shoulder head/long neck, CM, ptd blue eyes, blonde wig (elaborate), cloth body/bisque lower limbs, original gown, etc. Early 1970s $225

30" Pedlar Lady. China shoulder head, CM, ptd blue eyes, blonde ptd/molded curly short hairdo, cloth body/china lower limbs, original dress, cape, wares, etc. Early 1970s $350

Chapter 12

FRENCH MISCELLANY

History:

Connoisseurs of the "best that money can buy" will always decree that anything made in France comes foremost to mind - be it wine, chocolate, cuisine, bread, perfume, fashion, furniture, design, or dolls. Long before the Germans aggressively took control of the European doll industry, the French were well-known for their "Grand Pandoras," style dolls that expressed the latest modes of the day. However, the French dedication to "fashion" instead of "dolls" per se was almost their undoing. While they sewed and designed clothes for their stick-like poupees, the Germans slaved away perfecting the art of porcelain manufacture, desiring to make dolls that not only resembled real people, but were both durable and beautiful. It was then that the French realized that unless they, too, learnt the new doll-making process, they would forever be at the mercy of the Germans and indebted to them for their very livelihood.

Early French pioneers like Gaultier and Jumeau père worked with the Germans, learning the tricks of the trade, and for the next forty or so years, the French reigned supreme in an industry that was still basically German manipulated. The small French "maisons" made the finest, customized "luxury" dolls, but being too specialized and confined, their success was short-lived. Whether or not they always made their own heads remains a mystery. Did Jumeau, Gaultier, etc., made some of the heads incised "A.T.", "H.", and so on—or were some of them made by Kestner and Simon & Halbig, who worked closely with the French. Now, at this late date, when most French dolls are so expensive only the rich or super-rich can afford them, does it really matter who made what and where? One thing is certain, however, the French doll has come full circle.

Collecting Hints:

Since French dolls bring extraordinary high prices nowadays—at auctions—in order to glean these prices a doll has to be almost mint and original in every aspect. Nobody will pay $10,000 upwards for a "put-together" doll. But, in recent years, we saw a slight change in this demanding criterion: top dollar would be paid for an extremely rare doll with "minor" damage or flaw, but it must be a very unusual doll. Speculators and investors do not want the mundane and ordinary! French dolls with kid bodies cost somewhat less than those will ball-jointed composition bodies, but they are still out of reach of the average wager earner. Late French bisques with open-mouths can still be found under $1,000, but their value and great "worth" will never compare to that of an early closed-mouth French bisque-head doll.

Reproduction Alert:

Doll artisans have learned almost all the old methods of bisque doll reproduction, and in many instances, these new modern reproductions of old French heads, are better conceived than the original models. The modern artisan is a "hobbyist" who has both the time and money to recreate an antique doll, whereas the old-line factory artisan worked under great pressure and discomforting conditions. Hence, the modern reproduction in lieu of the old reproduction, is a near prefect, almost characterless, replica or "copy." Beware of unmarked reproduction dolls. They are usually just that—a "reproduction." Anyone who is proud of their work will gladly sign their name to it.

12" "A.T." marked Bébé. Pale bisque head, CM, inset blue PW eyes, blonde mohair wig, BJ compo body, original clothes, hat, etc. A. Thuillier, Paris, 1875-1893. $30,000+. (Courtesy of Linda Martinez Bassi)

14" Super-rare French pink tint china shoulder head, CM, inset blue sapphire-colored glass eyes, brown mohair wig, pink tint china lower arms, wheels on bottom of base/wind-up key, original cream colored Brussels lace and satin bridal gown trimmed with orange blossom flowers and leaves, etc..
(This mechanical walking doll represents a bride walking down the isle in a wedding ceremony. When wound she glides forward and her hands move up and down. A bellows makes a talking sound as though she is saying "I do" in French. Label reads: "Sivre le 23-8-67" (sold August 8, 1867) "A.M. 180" and "J. Steiner fabricant//Rue de Saintonge No 25 A Paris. Made by Jules N. Steiner, Paris, 1867 $25,000+. (Photo courtesy of Janet Johl Weissman)

15" "Fleur." Parisienne. Very pale bisque swivel head on pale bisque shoulder plate, CM, inset blue PW eyes, blonde mohair wig, kid body, original pale blue silk walking dress, purse, etc. Stamped on stomach in a horizontal oval shape: "AUX GALLERIES DE FER//1989 DES ITALIENS" (borders inside of oval shape) "VERRY FILS" (inside of oval shape). 1865-73 $3,500. (Courtesy of Victoria Rose, England)

20" Rare French doll once owned and dressed (dress is signed) by famous French painter, Marie Laurencin, who collected dolls. Bisque shoulder head, smiling OM/teeth, inset brown glass eyes, blonde HHW, kid body/bisque lower arms, original floral print silk dress, hat. Unmarked head (unless signed under wig). Same head as D. Kay Crow's 20" French doll marked "X7". (Courtesy of Herron)

17" Parisienne marked: "Steiner." Very pale bisque shoulder head, CM, blue PW eyes, brown mohair wig, leather fashion body, original walking dress, etc. All original. Early 1860s Mark: "Steiner X." $3,500. (Courtesy of D. Kay Crow)

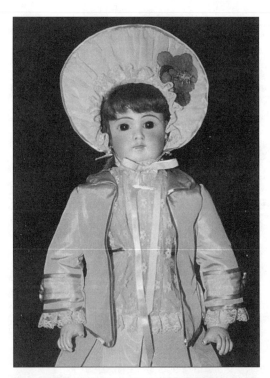

16" Rare antique F.R. incised Bébé. All original. Made by Adolphe Falck, Falck & Roussel, Paris. 1880-1902. Mark: "F7R". $8,000-$9,000. (Courtesy of Linda Martinez Bassi)

25" French Belton marked "117." Bisque head, CM, brown PW eyes, brown HHW, early Jumeau BJ compo body, PE, redressed. Mark: "117" rear of head. Ca. 1880s $4,500. (Courtesy of Ruby Ellen Smith)

12-1/2" "Fanny." Pale bisque swivel head on pale bisque shoulder plate, CM, rosy cheeks, PE, inset large almond-shaped blue PW eyes, blonde mohair wig, original unjtd cloth body/kid arms, original clothes. Mark: "O" on back of head. Possibly early FG or Jumeau. Ca. 1860s $3,000+. (Courtesy of Victoria, Rose, England)

20" Pale bisque shoulder head, OM/teeth, inset brown glass eyes, kid body/bisque lower arms, old clothes. Mark: "X7." $1,500-$2,000. (Courtesy of D. Kay Crow)

15" "Limoges FRANCE" marked Bébé. Bisque head, OM/teeth, inset blue glass eyes, blonde wig, BJ compo body, redressed. Probably A. Lanternier & Cie, Limoges, France, 1891-1925, $775. (Courtesy of D. Kay Crow)

14" "France D.L." incised Man. Bisque head, OM/teeth, inset blue glass stationery eyes, blonde HHW, cloth body, original clothes, hat, etc. Early 20th c. $1,500. (Courtesy of D. Kay Crow)

FRENCH MISCELLANY

8-1/2" Parisienne or Fashionable Lady. All-bisque to waist/turned head/bisque arms attached to shoulders with wooden pegs, CM, ptd. brown eyes, black mohair wig, cloth covered cone-shaped lower body (no legs), original lavish "beaded" costume. Made by E.V. Riera, Paris, 1906-1920s. Ca. 1908 ....$1,000

11" Parisienne "Bride." Bisque swivel head on bisque shoulder plate, CM, blue PW eyes, brown mohair wig, kid body/limbs, original white satin gown, bonnet, leather slippers, etc. Unmarked. Probably early Jumeau. Ca. 1870s (Sold for$1,584 in 1992) ....$3,700+

12" "Bébé Trousseau." Belton-type. Bisque head, inset brown glass eyes, brown mohair wig, BJ compo. body, original clothes, etc. Original box includes extra dress, nightgown, bonnets, etc. Box label reads: "Bébé Trousseau." Ca. 1880s MIB................................$6,000

12" Parisienne. Bisque shoulder head (head turned upwards and to the side)/molded bosom, CM, ptd. blue eyes, auburn HHW decorated with ribbon bow, cloth body/bisque lower arms/black ptd./molded high-heeled pumps, original silk and lace evening gown. Made by Louis-Aime Lejeune, Saint Maur-des-Fosses, France (trademark: a pair of wings). 1915......$1,000

12" Parisienne. Bisque shoulder head/turned/very pretty face, tiny CM, ptd. blue eyes to side, blonde mohair wig, cloth body/bisque lower arms/ptd. high-heeled pumps, original beaded gown. Mark: "Mouley and Schulz."

16" Unmarked Parisienne. Bisque shoulder head, CM, inset blue PW eyes, brown HHW, kid body, original clothes. Probably early FG. Ca. 1860s $2,700. (Courtesy Connie Baca)

Made by Louis-Aime Lejeune, France. Ca. 1915-16 ....$1,000

13" Parisienne. Bisque head, CM, inset blue glass eyes, sparse blonde mohair wig, articulated wooden body, original challis bodice, skirt, flower-strewn bonnet. Unmarked $5,500

14-1/2" "Brevetee" Parisienne. Pale bisque swivel head on bisque shoulder plate, CM, blue PW eyes, blonde HHW, kid body/leather arms, original clothes, etc. Label on body reads: "Brevetee SGDG." Ca. 1870s..................$3,000+

14-1/2" Bébé Jumeau look-alike. Bisque head, CM, large almond-shaped inset brown PW eyes, thin eyebrows, rosy cheeks, mauve eyeshadow, blonde skin wig/cork pate, BJ papier-mâché body/straight wrists, old baby dress, bonnet, etc. Incised: "O." (This Bébé is a twin to the 13-1/2" babe incised "OC" or "CC." Kestner? Ca. 1870s $2,200

15" "A.5T." Babe. Bisque head, CM, blue PW eyes, blond mohair wig, BJ compo./wood body/straight wrists, original clothes, beplumed hat, etc., "A.T." marked shoes, Made by A. Thuillier, Paris, France, Ca. 1875-1893 (Sold for $47,000 in 1989 at auction.) ... $50,000

15" Belton Bébé. Bru look-alike. Very pale bisque head, CM, large blue PW eyes, blonde skin wig, BJ wood/compo. body, old clothes, Ca. 1870s (Sold for$990 in 1986)...$3,500

16" "Favorite no. 2" incised Character Girl. Bisque head/very expressive face, red OM/teeth, rosy cheeks, large inset brown glass eyes, thick light brown eyebrows, thick brown HHW, PE, BJ compo. "lady" body, original clothes, etc. Neck mark: "J.E. Masson" and "A.L. & Co." A Lanternier & Co., Limoges, France, 1891-1925. Head designed by J.E. Masson, a sculptor who made heads in both clay and wax. Ca. 1915...................................$774-$800

16" Jeune Fille (Young Girl). (Francois Gaulthier mark by S.F.B.J.) Bisque shoulder head, CM, huge inset blue glass eyes, thick brown eyebrows, brown HHW, unjointed kid body, original short dress, stockings, shoes, etc. (Doll represents a teen girl or flapper of the 1920s. She has a typical F.G. face. Probably reproduction from an old mold.) 1920s ....$1,000+

16" Parisienne. Pale bisque swivel head on pale bisque shoulder plate, CM, almond-shaped blue PW eyes/black eyeliner, blonde mohair wig, PE, rare carton-moule body covered with drilling (a twill-type fabric)/wooden articulated feet (mortise-and-tenon and boll-joints covered with drilling)/bisque lower arms, original elaborate French-made clothes, shoes, stockings, hat. ca. 1860s Unmarked (Rare) ....$5,000+

16-1/2" Parisienne. Bisque head/round face/full cheeks, CM, blue PW eyes, blonde mohair wig, twill-over-wood jtd. body/bisque lower arms, original French-made clothes, etc. Ca. early 1870s (Rare).................$6,500-$7,000

16-1/2" Parisienne "Clown." White bisque swivel head on bisque shoulder plate, OM/molded teeth, amber-colored inset glass eyes, brown HHW/cork pate, amber-colored clown markings around ear PE, "fashion-type" lady kid body, origi-

nal "clown" long dress, etc. Mark: "E 3 D, Depose." (Body has illegible stamp mark on rear.) Made by Etienne Denamur, Paris, France, 1889+............................$2,000-$3,000

16-1/2" Parisienne. Bisque shoulder head, CM, cobalt blue PW eyes, blonde mohair wig, kid body/limbs (body is designed more for a child than a lady-type), original green silk twill pleated day dress, matching bonnet, etc. Possibly by Duval-Denis who worked for Aine Blampoix, Sr., Paris. Ca. 1868 (sold for $4,450 in 1995)........$5,000+

(Numbers 403 and 406 used by K(star)R; 406 used by Marseille and Heubach)

11" Parisienne. Bisque shoulder head, CM, inset blue PW eyes, blonde mohair wig, kid body, original clothes plus 3 extra outfits. Ca. early 1860s unmarked. Possibly Jumeau. Doll only $2,500-$3,000 $1,000 extra for each dress. (Courtesy of D. Kay Crow)

17" "403 10" incised Belton. Dome bisque socket head #406, CM, large inset brown PW eyes, blonde skin wig, BJ compo. body/straight wrists, original elaborate pink silk dress decorated with tiny rosebuds and old lace, matching bonnet, etc. (This gorgeous doll has an early "Jumeau" look. Possibly a German head made for the French market.) Ca. 1880 (Sold for $3,500 in 1992) ....$5,000+

17" "Bébé Phenix." Bisque head/round face, CM, inset blue PW eyes, blonde mohair wig, BJ compo. body, original ecru dress, bonnet, etc.; has "Bébé Phenix" waist ribbon, Henri Alexandre, Paris, France, 1888-1892; Tourrel, 1892-1895; Jules N. Steiner, 1895-1901. 1889+ ....$4,300-$4,800

17" Negro Character Lady Fashion, Very black bisque shoulder head, OM/2 rows of tiny teeth, inset black glass eyes with whites, black mohair wig, dark brown kid body/limbs, original clothes, hat, shoes, etc. (Probably early unmarked "F.G.") Ca, 1860s... $2,000+

17" Parisienne. Bisque swivel head on bisque shoulder plate, CM, cobalt blue glass eyes, strawberry blond mohair wig, extremely rare Kintzback body/wooden hands, original clothes, etc. Body is marked including trademark and "1874." 1874 ....$6,500+

17-1/2" "Laumont" Lady. Bisque head (sculpted by Jules Edmund Masson, France), O/C mouth/teeth, inset blue glass eyes, jtd. compo. body (lady type;

17" Parisienne. Bisque swivel head on bisque shoulder plate, CM, inset blue PW eyes, brown mohair wig, kid body, original clothes, etc. Kid body marked: "Au Paradis des Enfants 156 Rue de Louvre." Shoes marked: "Au Paradis des Enfants 156 Rue de Louvre." (She has her own wardrobe trunk) Doll only: $3,500+ (originally owned by Janet Johl. (Courtesy of Janet Johl Weissman)

13" Parisienne. Bisque shoulder head, CM, blue PW eyes, PE, dark brown HHW, kid body, elaborate old clothes, etc. Unmarked. Early 1860s $2,700. (Courtesy of D. Kay Crow)

8" "Petite Francaise" marked Bébé. Bisque head, OM/teeth, blue sleep eyes, blonde HHW, BJ compo body, redressed in antique fabrics made by J. Verlingue, Boulogne-sur-Mer and Montreuil-sous-Bois, France, 1915-1921. $450. (Courtesy of D. Kay Crow)

12" "Mon Cherie LP Paris" incised child. Bisque head, OM/teeth, blue glass sleep eyes, PE, blonde mohair wig, cloth body/bisque hands, old clothes. Ca. 1915-1924 $475. (Courtesy of D. Kay Crow)

12" Parisienne. Pale bisque shoulder head, CM, large blue PW eyes, brown mohair wig, kid body/bisque lower arms, original French Provincial costume, black high-heeled slippers with buckles, striped red/beige stockings. Brought from Europe in 1880 Never played with $2,500. (Courtesy of D. Kay Crow)

black painted/molded high-heeled slippers), brown mohair wig, original "regional" costume, hat, etc. Mark: "J.E. Masson S.c. LORRAINE N20 Al & Cie LIMOGE." (Baroness de Laumont/Mme. J. Ferrant, founder of the Ligue du Jouet Francais, 1914. Masson was one of the artists who designed heads for the Baroness; as did De la Boulaye.) Ca. 1913 .... $4,000

16" Parisienne. Bisque swivel head on bisque shoulder plate, CM, inset blue PW eyes, blonde mohair wig, replaced cloth body, redressed. Probably early Jumeau. Ca. 1860s (head). (Courtesy of Ruby Ellen Smith)

18" "Simmone" Parisienne. Pale bisque swivel head on pale bisque shoulder plate, CM, inset blue PW eyes, blonde mohair wig, kid gusseted body/arms, original silk outfit, hat, etc. Mark: "Simonne" blue stamp on chest. 1847-78 (Sold for $10,750 in 1991 at auction.) $5,000

18" Bébé Mascotte. Bisque head, CM, inset blue PW eyes, blonde mohair wig, PE, BJ compo./wood body, original clothes, etc. Head mark: "Mascotte H." Left hip mark: "Paris." Ca. 1901. Made by May Freres Cie, 1890-1897; Jules N. Steiner, 1898+ .... $4,500-$4,800

18" "Simonne" Parisienne. Pale bisque swivel head on pal bisque shoulder plate, CM, large inset brown PW eyes, pale pink cheek blush, brown HHW, PE, gusseted kid body/limbs, original "French" clothes, hat, etc. Head mark: "F.G." Chest stamp: "Simonne 1 a 13 Passage Delorme, Rue de Rivoli, Paris." (The Maison Simone used heads by Jumeau, F.G., and others.) 1847-78 .... $5,000+

18" Character Baby Girl. Bisque head (pretty face), O/C mouth/molded teeth, blue glass sleep eyes, brown mohair wig, bent-limb jtd. compo. body, original "French" embroidered dress, hat, etc. Mark: "Caprice No. 10 Limoges, by Lanternier." Made by A. Lanternier & Cie, Limoges, France, 1891-1925. Ca. 1915-24 .... $1,300

18" Eden Bébé, Bisque head, CM, large inset blue PW eyes, blonde HHW, PE, French BJ compo. body, original clothes, hat, etc. Head incised: "Eden Bébé 1." Made by Fleischmann & Bledel, Furth, Bavaria, Paris, France, 1873; Paris, 1890. Ca. 1890 ..... $2,700

18" Negro Parisienne. Black swivel head on black shoulder plate, CM, inset dark brown glass eyes, black mohair wig, dark brown kid "fashion" body/black bisque lower arms, original clothes, hat, etc. Unmarked. Probably early "F.G." Ca. 1860s $5,000

18" Parisienne. Bisque swivel head on bisque shoulder plate, smiling CM, almond-shaped blue PW eyes, brown HHW, PE/old earrings, kid body/full bisque arms/one arm bent at the elbow and has slightly closed fingers, elaborate original clothes, shoes, stockings. Unmarked. Ca. 1860s (Rare).... $6,500

18" Parisienne. Pale bisque swivel head on pale bisque shoulder plate, CM, inset cobalt blue PW eyes, blonde mohair wig, PE, gusseted kid body/limbs, original elaborate clothes, hat, etc. Foot label reads: "No. 4." Unmarked. Possibly early Jumeau .... $4,000+

18" Parisienne. Unmarked Huret. Bisque shoulder head/full cheeks/double chin, CM, pale pink cheek blush, ptd. blue eyes/liner, blonde HHW gusseted kid body/leather arms, original 2-pc outfit, etc. Ca. 1860 Mark: "F.G." (This is a definite "Huret" head with black eyeliner.) .... $5,000-$6,000

18" Three-Faced Bébé. Fine bisque head/sleep/cry/smile faces, inset glass eyes, composition shoulder plate with a high bosom/ring on wooden peg turns head with swivel joint, kid body/jtd. with wire and steel buttons/fine bisque hands/oblong blue chest label (illegible). Back mark: "CB." Left corner of shoulder mark: "2/0." (This doll is often credited to Bru, the reason it is listed here, but was made by Carl Bergner, Sonneberg, Germany. There are other versions of this doll.) Carl Bergner, Sonneberg, Germany, 1890+. Ca. early 20th c. .... $2,000+

19" "French Provencial" Lady. Bisque shoulder head, CM, large blue PW eyes, brown mohair "curly" wig, PE/original earrings, cloth body/legs/leather arms/separately stitched fingers, original costume: white cotton petticoat, striped silk petticoat, white cotton bloomers, blouse, red shawl, head-dress, stockings, black leather shoes. Mark: "F.G." (in a Scroll). 1887-1900 .... $3,500

19" "Liane" incised Bébé. Bisque head/poor quality, red CM/4 teeth, rosy cheeks, thick brown eyebrows, blonde mohair wig, BJ compo. body, original clothes, etc. Mark: "JV//France/C11/Liane" (anchor design). Made by J. Verlingue, Boulogne-sur-Mer, Montreuil-sous-Bois, France. 1915-21 .... $850

20" "Bébé Francais." Bisque head, CM, inset blue PW eyes, blonde mohair wig, BJ compo. body, old clothes, etc. Head mark: "B.9F." Made by Jumeau (Jumeau used this trademark after 1892.) Ca. 1896 .... $5,500

20" "Eden Bébé." Bisque head/square face, OM/5 teeth, inset blue PW eyes, brown HHW, PE, BJ compo. body, old dress, hat, etc. Mark: "Eden Bébé/Paris/Depose." Ca. 1890 .... $2,100-$2,400

20" "Province of Boulonnouse." Bébé. Bisque head, OM/teeth, brown glass sleep eyes/real eyelashes, brown HHW, BJ compo. body, original regional costume, hat, etc. Mark: "Paris France" (in oval) "71-149" over "301." Tag reads: "Jumeau. 1949." Made by the Société Francaise de Fabrication de Bébés et Jouets, Paris, France, 1899-1958. 1949 .... $1,250

20" Parisienne. Automaton. Bisque head, OM/full row of teeth, inset blue PW eyes, blonde HHW, PE, wood/compo. mechanical jtd. walking body, original bustle-style outfit, hat, matching bonnet, etc. Head mark: "Rabery & Delphieu." Body stamp: "Rabery & Delphieu." Ca. 1870s (Sold for $2,400 in 1995 at auction.) $3,500

21" "Favorite No. 2" incised Character Girl. Bisque head, smiling O/C mouth/molded upper teeth, inset brown glass eyes, brown mohair wig, PE, BJ mâché body, original clothes, etc. Mark: "Depose Fabrication Francaise Favorite No. 2 Ed. Tasson." Ca. 1915 .... $1,100

21" Negro Parisienne. Dark brown bisque swivel head on dark brown bisque shoulder plate, slightly smiling OM/upper and lower molded teeth, inset large brown glass eyes, black mohair wig, PE/old earrings, brown kid/cloth "fash-

18" Paris Bébé. Bisque head, CM, inset blue PW eyes, brown HHW, BJ compo body, original clothes, hat, etc. MIB 1892+ $8,000+. (Courtesy of Linda Martinez Bassi)

ion" body/brown bisque lower limbs/bare feet/toe detail, original clothes, hat, shoes, stockings, etc. Ca. 1860s (Rare) $10,000

21" Parisienne. "F.G." Reproduction. Very fine quality bisque head, CM, inset blue glass eyes (some had brown eyes), dark blonde HHW, well-made white kid body/bisque lower arms, Incised: "F.G." Made in France (Original price: $60 plus post and insurance). 1962 .... $350

22" "Bébé Le Parisienne." Bisque head, OM/6 upper teeth, grey-blue PW eyes, dark brown HHW, BJ compo. body, old clothes, etc. Mark: "MODELE" (red stamp with a star and rectangle similar to the Bébé Phenix.") Hip stamp reads: "Bébé Le Parisienne Medaille D'Or." (This doll has unjointed limbs.) Jules N. Steiner or "Societé Steiner", Paris, 1855+. ("Bébé Le Parisienne" mark or body stamp dates after 1892.) $6,500

22" "Eden Bébé." Bisque head, OM/teeth, inset brown PW eyes, blonde mohair wig, PE, BJ compo. body, original blue velvet pleated dress with a wide lace collar and cuffs, underwear, black shoes, stockings. Mark: "Eden Bébé" and "Paris 9 Depose." Ca. 1890 .... $2,300-$2,500

22" "L. Doléac & Cie" Bébé. Bisque head/round chubby face (has a German look), OM/upper teeth, large inset blue glass eyes, thick dark eyebrows, brown HHW, BJ compo. body, old clothes, etc. Mark: "L.D. DEP. 9." Made by L. Doléac & Cie, Paris, 1881-1908 .... $2,000

22" Character Bébé. Bisque head, CM, inset brown glass eyes, blonde mohair wig, compo. body/straight limbs, old clothes, etc. Mark: "Caprice No. 10 Gilete Limoges." 1915-24 .... $1,400

23" "E.D." Bébé. Bisque head, CM, inset blue PW eyes, blonde mohair wig, PE, BJ wood/compo. body, old clothes, Incised: "E 10 D." Etienne Denamur, Paris, 1889+ $4,500

24" "R.3D." Bébé. Bisque head/square face (jawline)/rosy cheeks, CM, large almond-shaped inset brown PW eyes, brown mohair wig/cork pate, PE, BJ wood/compo. body/straight wrists, original clothes, bonnet, etc. Mark: "R.3D."

Rabery & Delphieu, Paris, France, 1856-1899 .... $4,100-$4,500

25" "Bébé Jullien." Pale satin-smooth bisque head, OM/teeth, large inset brown PW eyes, blonde HHW, PE, BJ wood/compo. body/ma-ma and pa-pa voice box with pull cords (workable), old clothes, etc. Jullien, 1863-1904 .... $2,400

25" "E. 10 D." Bébé. Bisque head, OM/teeth, inset blue PW eyes, blonde mohair wig, PE, BJ compo. body, old clothes, bonnet, etc. Incised: "E. 10. D.//DEPOSE." Made by Etienne Denamur, Paris, France, 1889+ $2,750

25" "Paris Bébé." Pale bisque head/chubby cheeks, CM, inset blue PW eyes, blonde HHW, PE, original clothes, etc. made by Danel & Cie, Paris, Montreuil-sous-Bois, 1889-95; Jumeau, 1892+ $4,700 1860s (Sold for 5,895 in 1989) .... $5,500+

25" "R.3D." Bébé. Bisque head, OM/teeth, inset blue PW eyes, blonde mohair wig, BJ wood/compo. body/jointed wrists/small hands, old clothes, etc. made by Rabery & Delphieu, Paris, 1856-99. .... $2,700

25"(long) "Parasol" Parisienne. Pale bisque head, CM, inset brown glass eyes, blonde mohair wig, PE, original attached hat (maroon silk crown, cream silk brim) matches parasol top with tiny metal bells at the end of each metal folding rod (doll's collar consists of strips of material cut into pointed ends and trimmed with gold braid). Probably unmarked "F.G." head. France. Ca. 1880s (Wood handle) $1,500

20" "PAN" Bébé. Bisque head, O/C mouth, inset blue PW eyes, blonde skin wig, PE, BJ wood/compo. body, original clothes, etc. Mark: "PAN." (in a square with a large X on each side). Ca. 1887 Made by Henri Delcroix, Paris, Montreuil-sous-Bois $15,000

28" "Limoges" Bébé. Bisque head, OM/teeth, inset blue glass eyes/long spider-like eyelashes, auburn mohair wig, BJ papier-mâché body/dainty hands with 2 middle fingers molded together, original clothes, knee-length net stockings, red suede shoes. Head mark: "Limoges, France." Ca. 1915-20s $1,800

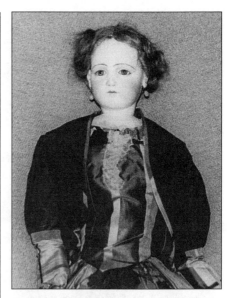

28" "Simonne" marked (stamped on chest) Parisienne. Pale bisque swivel head on bisque shoulder plate, CM, blue PW eyes, PE, brown HHW, kid body, original clothes, leather boots, stockings. This "portrait" head has been seen by the author incised "Jumeau." It is undoubtedly an early Jumeau head. Ca. 1860s $15,000-$20,000. (Courtesy of Herron)

30" "Mascotte" Bébé. Bisque head/round face, CM, large inset blue PW eyes, brown mohair wig, BJ wood/compo. body, original silk and lace dress, etc. Made by May Freres Cie, 1890-1897; J.N. Steiner, 1898+. 1901 (Rare size) $6,500

30" "Olympia" incised (in script) Bébé. Bisque head/full cheeks, OM/row of teeth, brown glass sleep eyes, brown HHW, BJ compo. body, old clothes, bonnet, etc. made by Pierre Muller, France. 1924 .... $2,000+

33" Parisienne. Early pale bisque shoulder head/double chin, CM, inset blue PW eyes, brown HHW, kid body/leather arms (wears original gloves), original clothes, etc. Unmarked. Ca. 1860+ (Rare size) .... $7,000+

Chapter 13

⚬~ FRANCOIS GAULTIER ~⚬

History:

Francois Gaultier (Gautier or Gauthier); changed name to Gaultier in 1875; St. Maurice, Chareton, Seine, Paris, France, 1860-1899; 1899-1930. This pioneer French maison produced doll heads and parts of the finest quality and individuality, selling them to small French factories who made or assembled dolls. Even Bru and Jumeau used Gaultier heads on their early dolls (both companies later made their own heads and bodies). Gaultier made both stationary shoulder heads and swivel heads to be used on bisque or composition shoulder plates. Some dolls had painted eyes. Gaultier heads were pressed into the mold like pie dough until circa 1890 when the pouring method came into use. A pressed head was superior to the thinner poured head, being thicker and more durable (the interior was uneven). Gaultier retired in 1880, and his eldest sons became owners of the factory. They displayed their dolls at international exhibitions and won silver medals: Amsterdam (1883); Nizza (1884); Antwerp (1885); Paris (1889). The brothers merged with other failing French firms in 1899 to form the S.F.B.J. There is a marked difference in quality when one compares the dolls made during the father's reign, and the reign of the sons. Later dolls were more highly tinted and the bisque was more coarse.

Collecting Hints:

E. Gesland, Paris, used Gaultier heads on his unique stockinet bodies from 1860 to 1928. Gesland exported and distributed dolls. He had four doll factories. His doll hospital was very well-known in Paris and was still advertising in the 1890s. The hospital not only replaced broken heads, but repaired damaged heads. Gesland redesigned his stockinet bodies when the little girl or "bébé" types became popular in the 1870s. In the early 1900s, Gesland advertised a wide variety of dolls (he may have used heads made by other firms at this time). Gaultier had a large clientele; many of whom had open charge accounts with him. At least 54 companies owed him money when his estate was evaluated in 1881,

proving how closely related are all French dolls to the Maison Gaultier. The heads Gaultier made for the various small companies (Simmone, Thuillier, Jullien, etc.) were not incised with the initials "F.G."; hence, were probably made expressly for them. This is not to say that these firms did not make their own heads. At least, some of them.

Reproduction Alert:

Reproduction Parisiennes or "French Fashion" lady dolls were reproduced in France after the Maison Gaultier ceased business operations in 1930. These were made in the 1930s, 1950s, 1960s, and were sold as "antiques." Old molds were used, and the new heads were placed on new, but rather inferior, kid bodies. Most were sold undressed. Dealers in the U.S.A. advertised these dolls as "World War One" French Fashions. Some of those heads were glazed bisque or "china" types. Modern doll artists have likewise reproduced "F.G." Parisiennes and Bébé. When in doubt about a doll, don't buy it.

FRANCOIS GAULTIER

1860-99

11" "F.2G." Bébé. Bisque head, CM, inset brown PW eyes, blonde mohair wig, PE, BJ comp body, original silk dress, etc. 1879-87 .... $3,000

12-1/2" Negro Parisienne. Black bisque swivel head on black bisque shoulder plate, CM, large inset black glass eyes, black "wool" wig, black kid body/arms, original outfit, etc. Mark: "F.G." (side of shoulder). 1860s-1870s $3,500

14" Bébé. Bru look-alike. Bisque head/full cheeks, O/C mouth/tongue, large blue PW eyes, blond mohair wig, PE, chunky gusseted kid body/bisque lower arms, original clothes, hat, etc. Mark: "F.G." 1879-87 .... $6,500

14" Parisienne. Very pale bisque swivel head on very pale bisque shoulder plate, CM, blue PW eyes, blonde mohair wig, PE, kid body/limbs, original elaborate 2-pc ivory silk dress with train ornamented with rushing, embroidery, silk flowers and lace (a miniature faux watch in pinned to her bodice), plus additional dresses of wool, parasol, 2 fancy hats, Ca. 1870s. Mark: "F.G." (on side of shoulder). $6,500

15" Parisienne. Bisque swivel head on bisque shoulder plate, CM, large blue PW eyes, blonde mohair wig, PE, gusseted kid body/limbs original blue satin and lace gown, etc. Mark: "2" 1860s $2,650

16" "F.G." Bébé. Bisque head/round full cheeks, CM, large almond-shaped brown PW eyes, thick feathered eyebrows, brown HHW, PE, BJ compo. body, original maroon faille dress, bonnet, etc. 1880s $4,600

21" FG signed lady in original provincial costume. Bisque shoulder head, CM, inset blue PW eyes, PE, brown mohair wig, cloth body/leather arms. Ca. 1860s $3,500. (Courtesy of Herron)

16" Parisienne. Pale bisque swivel head on pale bisque shoulder plate/double chin, CM, large almond-shaped blue PW eyes/black eye liner, upswept blonde mohair wig, PE, gusseted kid body/limbs, original gown, hat, etc. Mark: "F.G." (on side of shoulder). 1860+ $3,000

16" "Promenading Lady with Poodles." Automaton. Parisienne. Fine quality bisque head marked: "F.G."/truncated at the middle of the neck (designed for an automated figure rather than an ordinary playtoy), CM, inset blue-grey PW eyes, brown HHW, enameled hands (hold dog leashes), "walking" legs/articulated by flat metal joints, flock papier-mâché, poodles are designated as to their sex by the colors of the ribbons tied to their tails (pink and blue), and are attached tot he lady by cable-twist wires and a shaft which extends from the lady's body to the axle between the wheels of the dog cart. This elegant Parisienne wears an orange colored silk taffeta walking dress trimmed with lace and decorated with tiny white velvet bows. Dress is the wide crinoline style. Ca. 1866 $12,500

16-1/2"Bébé. Bisque swivel head on bisque shoulder plate/chubby face/double chin, CM, large blue PW yes, brown

56

mohair wig, PE, kid body/bisque lower arms, original taffeta dress, etc. Head mark: "F.O.G." and "F.G." and "O" (on shoulder). Ca. 1879-1887 ....$6,500

17" Parisienne. Pale bisque shoulder head, CM, inset blue PW eyes, blonde skin wig, kid body/leather arms, original elaborate cream silk walking dress, hat, parasol; additional wardrobe includes: 3 gowns, 6 hats, 3 fans, 3 pairs evening gloves. Unmarked. Ca. 1860+ $12,000

17-1/2" Parisienne. Pale bisque swivel head, CM, almond-shaped blue PW eyes, thin light brown eyebrows, pale pink cheek blush, PE, blonde HHW, Gesland stockinet/metal frame body/bisque hands/legs, original clothes, hat, etc. (Early face.) Ca. 1860+ $5,800

18" Parisienne. Bisque shoulder head, CM, blue PW eyes, blonde mohair wig, kid body/bisque lower arms, old clothes, hat, etc. Mark: "F.G." (on side of shoulder). 1860+ $2,800

18" Parisienne. Bisque swivel head on bisque shoulder plate, CM, inset blue

13-1/2" "F.G." incised Parisienne. Swivel bisque head on bisque shoulder plate, CM, inset blue PW eyes, PE, original brown skin wig, cloth body/kid arms, original silk walking dress with bustle, etc. 1860s $2,500. (Courtesy of Herron)

PW eyes, blonde skin wig, Gesland stockinet/metal frame body/molded bosom/bisque hands/bisque lower legs, original clothes, hat, etc. Mark: "F.G." ("Scroll" mark) on shoulder. ("Scroll mark face). Ca. 1860+ $3,500

18-1/2"Bébé. Bisque swivel head/chubby face, CM, brown PW eyes, brown HHW, PE, BJ compo. body, old clothes, hat, etc. Ca. 1879-1887 ....$5,200

21" "F. 9 G." Bébé. Bisque head/square face, CM, large blue PW eyes, blonde skin wig, BJ compo./wood body, original clothes, hat, etc. Ca. 1879-1887 .... $5,500

23" Parisienne. Bisque swivel head on bisque shoulder plate, CM, pale blue PW eyes, blonde mohair wig, PE, kid body/bisque lower arms, original blue sating own, ankle boots, striped stockings, etc. Mark: "F.G." (on side of shoulder). Ca. 1875...........................$3,800

24" Bébé. Bisque swivel head on composition shoulder plate, CM, blue PW eyes, blonde skin wig, Gesland stockinet/metal frame body/wooden hands and feet, old clothes, etc. Mark: "F.G." (head) "Scroll" mark face. Ca. 1860+ $5,500

26" Bébé. Bisque head, CM, inset blue PW eyes, auburn mohair wig, PE, BJ compo. body, original blue silk dress, hat, etc. Mark: "F.G." (in a "Scroll"). Ca. 1887-1900................................$4,400

29" Bébé. Bisque swivel head, CM, large brown PW eyes/mauve eye shadow, brown HHW, chunky BJ compo. body/mamma-papa pull-string, old clothes, etc. Mark: "F.G." (Block letters.) Ca. 1867-1887 ....$8,500

35-1/2" Parisienne. Pale bisque swivel head on pale bisque shoulder plate, CM, almond-shaped blue PW eyes, blonde mohair wig, kid body/limbs, original clothes, hat, etc. Ca. 1860+ $7,500

36" Mannequin Bébé. Pale bisque head/long neck, CM, brown mohair wig, PE, stockinet body/articulated metal joints, jointed wooden fingers with detail and beautifully carved fingernails/brown pt and carved wooden knee-length boots with carved side buttons, original clothes, hat. Head mark: "F.G." (in a "Scroll"). Body stamped: "E.

Gesland" and "Paris..." Ca. 1887+ $15,000

41" Mannequin Garcon (Boy). #4. Pale bisque head/carton plate/flange for removing head, CM, large blue PW eyes, brown HHW, compo. body covered with linen (neck area protected with heavy velvet which prevents wear on the comp from repeating change of clothing, straight legs (no joints)/ptd. stockings/molded-on and ptd. shoes/carved wood ball-and-socket arms covered with linen sleeve for protection/carved hands/jtd. fingers, old clothes. Marked on head/body: "F.G. #4." Ca. 1860+ $20,000

42" Show Doll. Boy. Pale bisque head, CM, blue PW eyes, blonde HHW, stockinet body/carved wood arms/hands/feet, original clothes, hat, etc. Head mark: "F.G." Ca. 1860+ $18,000

11-1/2" Parisienne. "F.G." incised on shoulder, CM, inset blue PW eyes, blonde mohair wig, PE, kid body, original clothes, etc. $2,000. (Courtesy of D. Kay Crow)

Chapter 14

GERMAN MISCELLANY

History:

Since earliest times, the German people have been involved with dolls and toys as a means of livelihood. This was mainly a cottage industry with entire families working around the kitchen table assembling dolls. When dolls became more sophisticated, and materials other than wood and papier-mâché was utilized, the government offered subsidies to encourage more artistic people into the trade.

At one time, Nuremberg was the center of the world's toy business. There had always been a healthy rivalry between the Germans and the French, thus these two countries worked closely together and developed the industry. The Germans, however, wanted a cheaply-made, mass-produced product, while the French desired an expensive, custom-made doll made expressly for only those who could afford it, and when they eventually made a cheaper poupee, it was a sorry example of a doll. The extensive use of papier-mâché in 1810 revolutionized the doll business, even thought it had been in use for toys as early as 1700. By this time, Sonneberg had become the doll-making center or mecca.

Doll manufacture in France was also well-developed, but under the "rapport" of costume. The French poupee was usually made of carton-moule, but intricately dressed in an elaborate, detailed costume. (Fabric was very strong in those days, and some of these original costumes still exist.) Although the German-made papier-mâché/puppe never went out of fashion, and was still being made in the 20th century, it gave sway to the more durable medium of glazed and unglazed porcelain. It was then that the real German-French doll industry began, and it is that phase of history that fascinates doll collectors the most.

Collecting Hints:

When selecting a German-made bisque-head doll for investment purposes the collector/investor seeks a doll with a fine early pale bisque, a closed mouth, inset glass or paperweight eyes, artistic painting of eyelashes and eyebrows, an original wig, an original, well-shaped ball-jointed composition body, and original clothes, shoes, and stockings. Such a doll could be called a "French-type" since it was usually made for the French market. It has also become very pricey and is available to a limited few. Although the doll whose bisque head and shoulders are attached to a cloth or Rid body is older, the price is ssomewhat lower than the above doll. However the swivel head on bisque shoulders has become more desirable to the investment-collector than the stationary shoulder head even though the latter came first.

Since dolls with bisque heads were made until the 1930s, and even after World War II, price the doll accordingly.

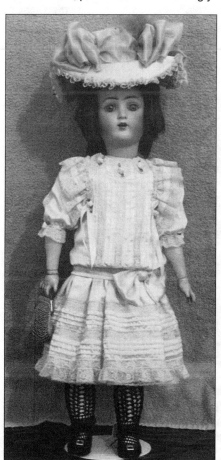

25" "Sweet Nell" (1362). Made by Alt, Beck & Gottschalck, Germany. Dressed by Virginia Yates. $800-$900. (Courtesy of Virginia Yates)

An early doll should never be priced the same as a later doll. Later dolls were more highly colored than earlier versions, and the bisque is usually of a coarser grain. The painting of features, the beauty of a face, an unusual character face, a wig with the original set, elaborate original clothing, degree of over-all originality, all effect the final price of a doll. It is always best to retain the doll's original wig and clothing, regardless of condition. If either must be replaced, keep the original and save it for the next owner. To discard a doll's original parts, clothing, wig, or accessories, is to devalue it.

German dolls with bisque heads and jointed composition bodies that measure over 30-inches in height were sold nude or in chemise, consequently they were dressed in the home in the child's cast-off clothing, shoes, stockings, etc. If such a doll is found in its original factory-made clothing, it was probably used for display or show. Large types served as department store mannequins. Until 1970, these large dolls sold for less than$100. Open-mouth German dolls with bisque heads are quite common and plentiful, and only the larger sizes and character types command high prices. Ordinary examples seem to dangle in the$300-$800 price range.

GERMAN MISCELLANY

9-1/2" Bisque socket head, OM/teeth, inset blue glass eyes, blonde mohair wig or HHW, BJ compo. body/molded-on shoes and socks, old clothes. Mark: (Starburst design with "G." "B." "K." in center.) Ca. 1890+ Made by Gebruder Kuhnlenz, Kronach, Bavaria, 1884~1&. Ca. 1890+ (Well-made body) $375

11-1/2" "247 dep" incised Dolly face Girl. Bisque head/long neck, OM/6 teeth, inset grey glass eyes, PE, brown mohair curly wig, BJ compo./wood body, old clothes, etc. Made by Bahr & Proschild, Germany. (Made for the French market.) Ca. 1888+ .... $650-$700

12" "21 Germany R 13/OA" incised "Zuid-Beveland" Girl. Bisque head. OM/teeth, brown glass sleep eyes, brown mohair wig, cheap comp body/unjointed limbs, original black bodice/skirt, white underbodice, shawl with flower print, striped apron, white lace hat, wooden shoes. Made by Th. Recknagel, Germany, 1886+. 1930s .... `$225

10" "F&W Goebel" incised Girl. Bisque shoulder head/high coloring, inset glass eyes, OM/teeth, blonde HHW, cheap card-type body/arms/legs/mld-on shoes/socks, old clothes. 1900+ $250. (D. Kay Crow)

16" "B-4" marked girl. Bisque shoulder head, OM/teeth, PE, kid body/bisque hands, old clothes. Ca. 1890s $500-$600 (Courtesy of Billye Otto)

18" "Jutta" (1349) by Cuno & Otto Dressel, Germany (Simon & Halbig bisque head). Ca. 1906-1921 $800 (Courtesy of Ruby Ellen Smith)

16" Unmarked turned-head Girl, bisque shoulder head, OM/teeth, inset brown glass eyes, brown HHW, kid body/bisque hands, old velvet/lace clothes, hat, etc. Probably Kestner. 1880s $600-$650. (Courtesy of B. Kay Crow).

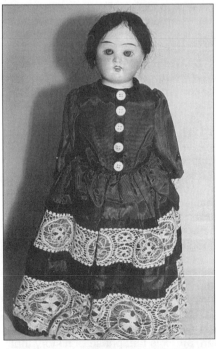

11-1/2" "Goebel" marked Girl. Bisque shoulder head, OM/teeth, blue glass sleep eyes, brown HHW, cloth body/legs/compo arms, original clothes. F&W Goebel, Germany. 1900+ $265 (Courtesy of D. Kay Crow)

24" Early bisque shoulder head, CM, inset brown glass eyes, skin wig, PE, kid body/bisque lower arms, original clothes, etc. Made by Alt, Beck & Gottschalck, ca. 1880 $2,000. (Courtesy of Billye Otto)

26" "Sweet Nell" (1362) by Alt, Beck & Gottshalck, Germany. 1885+ $800-$900. (Courtesy of Ruby Ellen Smith)

20" "Jutta" (1349) by Cuno & Otto Dressel, Germany (Simon & Halbig bisque head). Ca. 1906-1921 $900. (Courtesy of Ruby Ellen Smith)

20" "Cuno & Otto Dressel" marked girl. Bisque shoulder head, OM/teeth, inset blue glass eyes, original grey wig, cloth body/legs/bisque arms, old clothes, etc. 1893+ $550. (Courtesy of D. Kay Crow)

12" "914 DEP R7/O A B" incised Girl. Bisque head, OM/teeth, inset blue grass eyes, blonde mohair wig, BJ compo. body, original 2-pc pink cotton outfit decorated with white trim, matching bonnet, undies, white shoes, white socks. Made by Th. Recknagel, Alexandrienthal, Thur., Germany, 1886+. Ca. 1890s-WWI $300

12" "R7/OA" incised Girl. Bisque shoulder head, OM/teeth, blonde mohair wig, kid body/bisque lower arms, old clothes, etc. Made by Th. Recknagel, Alexandrienthal, Thur., Germany, 1886+. Ca. 1890s+ $250

13" "7234" incised Character Girl. Bisque shoulder/head, CM, inset blue glass eyes, blonde mohair wig, kid body/bisque lower arms, old clothes, etc. (Head is the uncut dome type.) Mark: "7234 Germany SCCP." Possibly Gebruder Heubach, Germany. Ca. 1910 ....$800-$950

13-1/2"Lady Doll. Pale bisque head, O/C mouth/4 molded teeth (lovely shaped lips)/pointed chin, ptd blue intaglio eyes, a light brown HHW, well-molded legs/too short torso/bent arms/no bosom/large buttocks/ original clothes, hat, etc. Mark: "185//26//F.B.//616//2." Made by Fritz Bierschenk, Sonnenberg, Thur., Germany, 1907-1930s. Ca. 1910 ....$1,800

14" "5-1/4" incised Girl. Bisque swivel head on bisque shoulder plate/"mumps" cheeks, OM/teeth, bright pink cheek blush, inset blue glass eyes, blonde mohair wig, kid body/bisque lower arms, original clothes, etc. Ca. 1880's $1,900

14" "DEP/R 5/0" incised Girl. Bisque head, OM/teeth blue glass sleep eyes, original blonde mohair wig, BJ compo. body, original long-waisted red dress

14" Recknagle girl. Bisque head, OM/teeth, blue glass sleep eyes, blonde mohair wig, blonde mohair wig, BJ compo body, redressed. Mark: "R/A DEP 510." 1893+ $325. (Courtesy of Ruby Ellen Smith)

with pink gauze sleeves, gauze drawers, petticoat, shoes, stockings. Mark: "DEP/R 5/0." Made by Max Rader, Germany, 1910-1913 ....$400-$425

14" "R 47 6/0 DEP" incised Girl. Bisque shoulder head, OM/4 teeth, inset brown glass eyes, brown mohair wig, kid body/bisque lower arms, old clothes. Made by Max Rader, Sonnenberg, Germany. Ca. 1910-13 ....$350-$400

14-1/2" "Sears" Girl. Bisque head, OM/4 teeth, blue glass sleep eyes, blonde mohair wig, crude mace or compo. jtd body/limbs/small wooden peg fastenings, original dress, bonnet, etc. Head mark: "Made in Germany/J (flag design) H./2/0." Made by Julius Hering, Koppelsdorf, Germany, 1902+. Ca. 1908-1913 (This was a cheap Sears & Roebuck catalog doll.) $350

16" "1766" incised Girl. Bisque shoulder head, OM/teeth, blue glass sleep eyes, blonde mohair wig, kid body/bisque lower arms, original clothes, etc. Marks: "1776 C.O.D. 0 1/2 D.E.P." Made by Cuno & Otto Dressel, Sonnenberg, Germany, 1873+. Ca. 1890s $395

16" "1916" incised Girl. Bisque head, OM/teeth, brown glass sleep eyes, brown mohair wig, BJ compo. body, original clothes, etc. Head mark: "Waltershausen/Germany/1916/0." Made by C.M. Bergmann, Germany with a S&H head ....$525-$575

17" "275" incised Girl. Bisque shoulder head, OM, inset blue glass eyes, blonde mohair wig, kidbody/bisque lower arms, old clothes, etc. Mark: "275 10/0. Germany." Made by Ernst Heubach, Koppelsdorf, Germany, 1887+ Ca. late 1890s/early 1900s ..$350-375

17" "Bergman" incised Girl. Pale bisque head, OM/teeth, wide set brown glass sleep eyes, brown mohair wig, BJ compo. body, old white-work dress, etc. Mark: "C.M. Bergmann/Waltershausen/Germany/1916/6 1/2." Ca. 1889+ (S&H "1916" head) ....$575-$600

(Heads made by Armand Marseille, Simon & Halbig, Alt, Beck & Gottschalck. Distributed by Louis Wolf & Co., NYC)

17-1/2" "Nanette." Compo. socket head, CM, blue glass "threaded" eyes, brown mohair wig, crude 5-pc unjointed compo. body, original French regional costume, cap, etc. Head mark: "NANETTE//FRANCE//DEPOSE." Probably M. Kohnstamm & Co., Furth, Bavaria, London (Exporter & Manufacturer), 1902-1930s. Ca. 1926 (Rare) $350

18" "2097" incised Character Baby. Bisque head/full cheeks, OM/teeth, brown HHW, bent-limb jtd compo. body, old clothes. Made by Bruno Schmidt, Waltershausen, Germany 1900+ Ca. 1911+ $950

18" "309" incised Girl. Bisque shoulder head, OM/6 molded upper teeth, brown glass sleep eyes, thick light brown eyebrows, brown mohair wig, pink kid body/bisque lower arms, old clothes, etc. (This old doll has a definite "French" look. The 300 series has often been confused with French dolls.)

Made by Bahr & Prochild, Germany, 1871+ Ca. 1888+ $675

18" "915" incised Girl. Bisque shoulder head, inset blue glass eyes, thick brown eyebrows, kid body/bisque hands and wrists, blonde mohair wig, old clothes, etc. Mark: "915 X D.E.P. (head)." Base of shoulder mark: "Inverted J on an L base." Maker unknown. $475

18" "Ruth" incised Girl. Bisque shoulder/head, OM, blue glass sleep eyes, brown mohair wig, kid body/bisque low-

16" Full view of German doll marked "B-4" (see photo 4) $500-$600 1890s. (Courtesy of Billye Otto)

er arms, old clothes, etc. Mark: "Ruth 8/0" ("Ruth" in script). Made by W.A. Cissna & Co., Chicago, IL. Importers/distributors of dolls. "Ruth" advertised in 1898. ....$425

18" "S" incised inside an "H" Girl. Bisque head, OM/teeth, blue glass sleep eyes, HHW, BJ Compo body old cloth headmark: "Germany 7" and an "S" incised inside an "H". Made by Herman Steiner, Neustadt, Germany, 1920+. Ca. 1920s $495

18-1/2" "E.U.St." incised Girl. Bisque head/chubby face, OM/teeth, blue glass sleep eyes, brown HHW, BJ compo. body/wood ball jts, old clothes, hat, etc. Made by Edmund Ulrich Steiner, Sonnenberg, Germany, NYC 1864-1916. ....$550-$600

19" "LA & S" incised Character Girl. Walker. Bisque head, CM, brown glass sleep eyes, blonde mohair wig, BJ compo. body (when legs "walk" the head turns from side to side), original clothes, etc. Mark: "Germany 1924 LA & S-N-Y 50." Made by Louis Amberg & Son, NYC, 1907+. Ca. 1924 ....$750-$850

19-1/2" "890" incised Girl. Bisque head, OM/teeth, blue glass sleep eyes/ptd upper/lower eyelashes/real lashes, blonde mohair wig, BJ compo. body,

26" "Adolph Wislizenus" marked girl. Bisque head, OM/teeth, brown glass sleep eyes, auburn mohair wig, BJ compo body, old clothes, etc. 1894+ $750-$850. (Courtesy of Victoria Rose, England)

16" "KH" marked girl (Kley & Hahn). Bisque shoulder head, OM/teeth, inset brown glass eyes, brown HHW, kid body/bisque lower arms, original clothes, straw hat, etc. 1902+ $450. (Courtesy of Herron)

24" Alt, Beck & Gottschalck marked girl. Close-up described above. $2,000. (Courtesy of Billye Otto)

31" Unmarked German bisque socket head girl, OM/teeth, inset brown glass eyes, blonde mohair wig, BJ compo body, old clothes. Probably Kestner. 1890s+ $1,500. (Courtesy of Ruby Ellen Smith)

18-1/2" "Walkure 250" marked girl (Kley & Hahn). Pale bisque head, OM/teeth, blonde mohair wig, BJ compo body, original silk clothes, hat, shoes, socks. This doll is exquisitely dressed in factory-made clothes. 1902+ $600-$650. (Courtesy

original clothes, bonnet, etc. Mark: "Made in Germany//Metzler//890//E 2 1/2 M." Made by Ernst Metzler, Pressig-Rothenkirchen, Germany, 1909, founded porcelain factory; 1924-1940's, made porcelain and composition dolls. Ca. 1924+ ....$600-$700

19-1/2" "Princess" incised Girl. Bisque head, OM/teeth, blue glass sleep eyes, thick dark brown ptd eyebrows, brown HHW BJ compo. body, old clothes, ext. Mark: "Princess-1-Germany." Probably Borgfeldt. Ca. 1901 (Originally sold for $1.98) ....$600-$700

(This doll was probably made by Hertel, Schwab & Co., although mold number 133 was used by other companies.)

20" "133" incised Girl. Bisque head, OM/teeth, blue glass sleep eyes, brown mohair wig, old clothes, bonnet, etc., BJ compo. body. Made by Hertel, Schwab & Co., Germany, 1910+. Ca. 1910 ....$600

20" "C.O.D." incised Girl. Bisque shoulder head, OM, blue glass sleep eyes, brown mohair wig, kid body/bisque lower arms/compo lower legs, old clothes, etc. Mark: "C.O.D. 93-2 D.E.P." Made by Cuno and Otto Dressel, Germany 1700+. Ca. 1893+ ....$595-$650

20" "DEP//(Horeshoe)" incised Girl. Bisque shoulder head, OM/teeth, blue glass sleep eyes, blonde HHW, kid body/bisque lower arms, old clothes, etc. Made by Ernst Heubach, Koppelsdorf, Germany 1887-1932...$395-$425

20" "K-H" incised Toddler Boy. Bisque head, OM/teeth, brown glass sleep eyes, brown mohair wig, BJ compo. "toddler" body, old boy clothes, cap, etc. Mark: "K-H." Made by Kley & Hahn, Germany. ....$1,850-$2,000

20" "RX 6//R.A." incised Girl. Negro Character type. Black bisque head, O/C mouth/2 molded teeth (lower), brown ptd intaglio eyes, black "wool" mohair wig, black BJ compo. body, old clothes, etc. Mark: "RX 6//R.A." Made by Theodor Recknagel, Alenandrienthal, Germany, 1893-1930. Ca. 1910+ ..$1,500

20-1/2" "A.1. M." Bisque head, OM/teeth, inset brown glass eyes, brown mohair wig, original clothes, shoes, socks, etc. Made by Emil Pfeiffer, Vienna, Austria, 1873+ (used Armand Marseille heads). Ca. 1890s+ $475

20-1/2" "10" incised "Tommy Tucker". Pale bisque head, CM, brown glass eyes, light brown ptd/molded hair with V-shaped forelock, well-modeled eats, thin fly-away light brown feathered eyebrows, BJ compo/wood toddler body, old clothes, etc. Neck mark: "10" (This "Tommy Tucker" type may have been made by Kley & Hahn.) $1,650

22" "275" incised Girl. Bisque head, OM, blue glass sleep eyes, blonde HHW, kid body/bisque lower arms/muslin lower legs, old clothes. Mark: "11 Heubach/275 2/0/Koppelsdorf" Made by Ernst Heubach, Koppelsdorf, Germany, 1887+. Ca. 1888+ ....$395-$495

22" "3090" incised Girl. Bisque shoulder head, OM/teeth, blue glass sleep eyes, thick brown eyebrows, brown HHW, kid body/compo lower limbs, original clothes, green wool braid-trimmed coat/hat, etc. Mark: "3090." Maker unknown. (Doll has a very pretty face; has an Armand Marseille look.) Ca. 1890s+ ....$395-$495

22" "Gans & Seyfarth" incised Girl. Bisque head, OM, rosy cheeks, blue glass sleep eyes, blonde mohair wig, BJ compo. body, old whitework dress, leather shoes, etc. Mark: "Gans & Seyfarth." Made by Gans & Seyfarth, Waltershausen, Germany, 1908-1922. Ca. 1908+ ....$650-$700

23" "1916//6" incised Girl. Bisque head, OM/teeth, brown glass sleep eyes, brown HHW, BJ compo. body, old clothes, etc. Mark: "C.M. Bergmann//Waltershausen//Germany//1916//6." Made by C.M. Bergmann, Germany, 1888+. Ca. 1899+ (Doll has Armand Marseille look). ......$650-$750

23" "29 K H 1" incised Girl. Bisque head, OM/teeth, blue glass sleep eyes, blonde mohair wig, BJ compo. body, old clothes, hat, etc. Mark: "29 K H 1 (the 29 is above a large H with a small K and 1 incised inside the H.) Made by Karl Hartmann, Stockheim, Germany, 1911-1926. (This doll has a "French" look.) Ca. 1911+ $600

23" "2966" incised Girl. compo. head, OM/teeth, blue glass sleep eyes, brown mohair wig, BJ compo. body, original clothes, etc. Maker unknown. Germany. ....$600-$700

23" "8" incised Character Boy. Bisque shoulder head, O/C mouth/teeth, blue ptd intaglio eyes, ptd/molded blonde hair, kid body/compo lower limbs, original 2-pc brown suit, cap. Incised: "8". Maker unknown. Ca. 1890s+ (sold for $800 in 1994) $1,200

23" "Special/Germany" incised Girl. Bisque head, OM/teeth, blue glass sleep eyes, blonde HHW, BJ compo. body, old clothes, bonnet, etc. Mark: "Special/Germany". Made by Adolf Wislizenus, Waltershausen, Germany, 1851 (founded); 1870 (Adolg Wislizenus owner); Spezial Serie, 1919. Ca. 1919+ ....$450-$600

23-1/2" "My Cherub" incised Girl. Bisque head, OM/teeth, blue glass sleep eyes, waist-length brown HHW, BJ compo. body, old clothes, etc. Mark: "My Cherub." Made by Arthur Schoenay, Sonnenberg, Germany, 1884+ Ca. 1912...$600

24" "1909" incised Girl. Bisque head, OM/teeth, brown glass sleep eyes, brown HHW, BJ compo. body, old clothes, etc. Mark: "S(star)H//PB//1909//6//Germany." Made by Schoenau & Hoffmeister, Bavaria, Germany, 1884+, Ca. 1901+ $750

24" "B3" incised Girl. Bisque head, OM/teeth, blue glass sleep eyes, blonde HHW, BJ compo. body, old clothes, etc. Mark: "Made in Germany-B3." Maker unknown. Ca. 1900+ (Probably Borgfeldt) $650

24" "Barclay Baby Belle" incised Girl. Bisque head, OM/teeth, blue glass sleep eyes, long curl blonde mohair wig, BJ compo. body, original clothes, bonnet, etc. Mark: "Barclay Baby Belle/Germany." Made by Bawo & Dotter, Karlsbad, Bohemia, 1838 (porcelain factory); 1860s, NYC import company; 1872, factory in Limoges, France. Ca. 1908........................$850

24" "Dollar Princess" incised Girl. Bisque head, OM/teeth, blue glass sleep eyes, blonde HHW, BJ compo. body, original chemise, no shoes. (Store new) Mark: "The Dollar Princess 62 Special Made in Germany." Made by Kley & Hahn, Ohrdruf, Germany, 1902+. Ca. 1909.......................................$700

24" "My Sweetheart" incised Girl. Bisque head, OM/teeth, large brown glass sleep eyes. brown HHW, thick brown eyebrows, BJ compo. body, old clothes, etc. Mark: "My Sweetheart//BJ & Co//Germany." Made by B. Illfelder & Co., Germany, NYC. ("My Sweetheart" tradename registered in Germany in 1902; in USA in 1905.) Ca. 1910+ ....$650-$750

24" "My Sweetheart" incised Girl. Bisque head, OM/teeth, blue glass sleep eyes, blonde HHW, BJ compo. body, old clothes, etc. Head mark: "101//A.W.//My Sweetheart//BJ & Co//Germany." Made by B. Illgelder & Co., Furth, Germany, NYC, 1862 (export firm established by Leopold Illfelder, owner of a doll factory, distributed dolls made by many German companies until 1930s). Ca. 1910 (Rare mark) ....$650-$750

18" Unmarked girl. Bisque character head, OM/teeth, inset brown glass eyes, PE, brown HHW, BJ compo body. Probably French. $1,000+. (Courtesy of Ruby Ellen Smith)

18" Sonneberger Porzellanfabrik, Sonneberg, Germany marked girl (founded by Carl Muller, 1883, shield SP/S design). Very dark and rough bisque quality, OM/teeth, inset brown glass eyes, dark brown HHW, BJ compo body, old silk dress, etc. Ca. 1893-1913 $700. (Courtesy of D. Kay Crow)

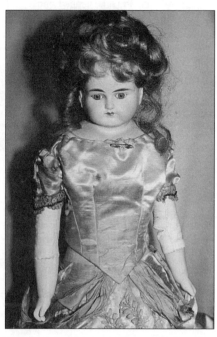

24" Unmarked turned bisque shoulder head girl, CM, inset blue glass eyes, blonde wig, kid body/bisque lower arms, old clothes. Unmarked Kestner. 1880s $1,500. (Courtesy of D. Kay Crow)

12" "R.6" incised "American School Boy" so-called. Pale (almost parian quality) bisque shoulder head, CM, inset blue glass eyes, blonde ptd/mld hair, cloth body/bisque hands/high-heeled leather boots, original clothes, etc. (Max Rader used similar marks, 1910-1913.) $650. (Courtesy of D. Kay Crow)

27" "Max Handwerck/Germany/4" incised girl. Bisque head, OM/teeth, large brown glass eyes, brown HHW, BJ compo body, old clothes, hat, etc. 1899-1920s $800-$900. (Courtesy of D. Kay Crow)

24" "Pansy IV" incised Girl. Bisque head/chubby cheeks, OM/teeth, brown glass sleep eyes, brown HHW, BJ compo. body, old clothes, etc. Tradename registered by George Borgfeldt & Co., NYC, 1910. Ca. 1910+........$650-$700

24" "Walkure" incised Girl. Bisque head, OM/teeth, blue glass sleep eyes, blonde mohair wig, BJ compo. body, old clothes, etc. Head mark: "Walkure/Germany." Made by Kley & Hahn, Germany. Head made by J.D. Kestner. Ca. 1902+ $850

25" "Alma" incised Girl. Bisque shoulder head, OM/6 upper teeth, large blue glass sleep eyes, brown HHW, kid body/bisque lower arms, old clothes, etc. Shoulder mark: "Alma 4." Borgfeldt registered the "Alma" trademark in 1900 with an Armand Marseille head. Ca. 1900+ $600

25" "Queen Louise" incised Girl. Bisque head, OM/teeth, brown glass sleep eyes, applied ears, brown mohair wig, BJ compo. body, old clothes, hat, etc. Mark: "29/Queen Louise/1-1/2/Germany." Made by Armand Marseille (head) for Louis Wolf & Co., Germany. Ca. 1910 ....$650

25" "Taft" incised Girl. Bisque head, OM, large blue glass sleep eyes, BJ turned-wood body/limbs, long curl brown HHW, original clothes, etc. Head mark: "Taft." ....$650-$750

26" "Max Handwerck 2-1/2// Germany" incised Girl. Bisque head, OM/teeth, blue glass sleep eyes, blonde mohair wig, BJ compo. body, old clothes, etc. Made by Max Handwerck, Waltershausen, Germany, 1899-1920s (Used bisque heads made by F&W Goebel.) Ca. 1900+..$700

27" "4703" Character Girl. Pale bisque head/round chubby face, small OM/2 upper teeth, blue glass sleep eyes, brown HHW, BJ compo. body, original clothes, bonnet, etc. Made by Weiss, Kuhnert & Co., Grafenthal, Germany, 1891-1930. (Rare) $1,500

28" "M.O.A." incised Girl. Bisque head, OM/teeth, brown glass sleep eyes, brown HHW (short bob), BJ compo. body, original muslin dress with short puffed sleeves, etc. Head mark: "M.O.A. 200 Germany." Made by Max Oscar Arnold, Germany, 1878+. Ca. 1920s ....$900-$1,100

29" "320" incised Girl. Walker. Bisque head, OM/teeth, blue glass eyes, unusual body construction (compo.)/right hand raises to mouth when she walks, original clothes, etc. Mark: "320 13 DEP."

Head made by Bahr & Proschild or Ernst Heubach; body made by A. Wislizenus. Ca. 1894-1910+ (Probably 1897) (Sold for$3,500.) Rare.. $4,000+

29-1/2" "Kling" incised Girl. Bisque socket head/round face, OM/teeth, blue glass sleep eyes, real eyelashes, blonde mohair wig, BJ compo. body bisque hands/feet, old clothes, etc. Ca. 1890. Made by Kling & Co., Ohrdruf, Thuringia, Germany, 1870+ $1,500

30" "Pansy" incised Girl. Bisque head/highly colored, blue glass sleep eyes, blonde HHW, BJ compo. body, old clothes, etc. Neck Mark: "Pansy//Germany." Made for Borgfeldt. Registered by Borgfeldt in 1910. (May have been made by Schoenau & Hoffmeister.) Ca. 1910+............................$1,100-$1,120

32" "1272" incised Character Boy. Pale bisque head, OM/teeth, blue glass sleep eyes, short brown HHW, chunky BJ compo. body, original clothes, hat, etc. Display or show doll. Mark: "F.S. & Co." Made by Franz Schmidt & Co., Germany, 1890+. Ca. 1910 .....$2,900

32-1/4" "136" incised Girl. Bisque head, OM/teeth, brown glass sleep eyes, brown HHW, BJ compo. body, old clothes, etc. made by Hertel, Schwab & Co., Germany, 1910+. Ca. 1910..$1,100

31" China head dolls, lovely old clothes.
(Courtesy D. Kay Crow)

9-1/2" "Steiner" lady "music"
box. (Courtesy D. Kay Crow)

24" China head child with
molded collar and name:
"Helen", ca. 1905, $400.
(Courtesy of D. Kay Crow)

17" Schoenhut "pouty" child. (Courtesy of D. Kay Crow)

18" Civil War china head lady. (Courtesy of D. Kay Crow)

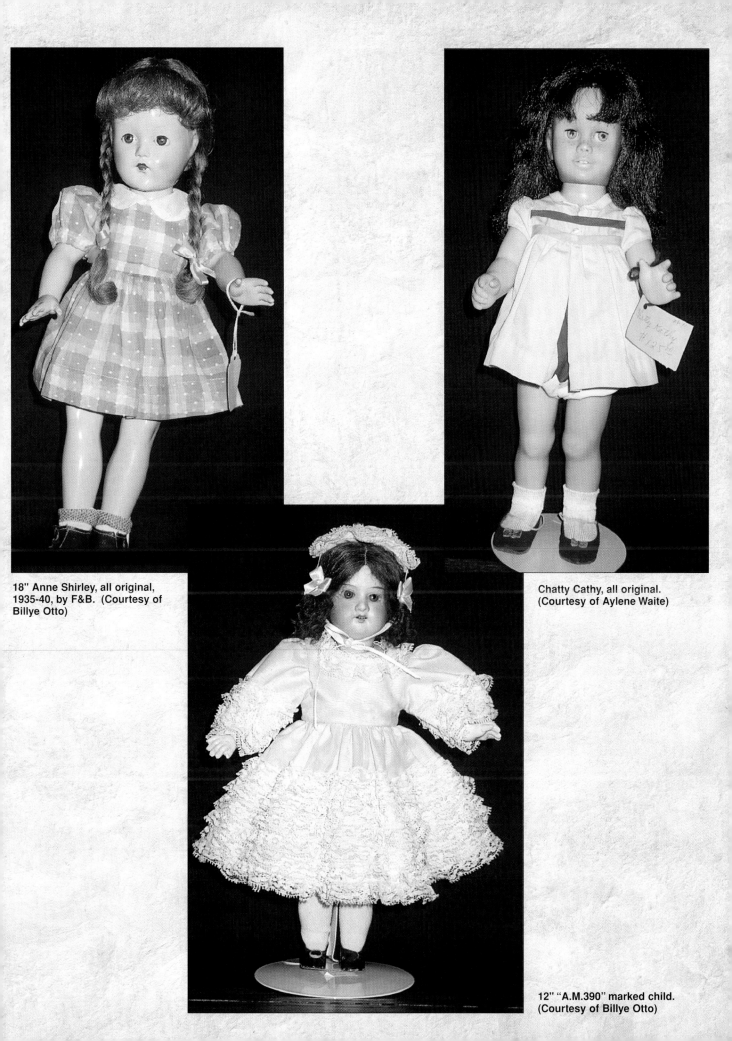

18" Anne Shirley, all original,
1935-40, by F&B. (Courtesy of
Billye Otto)

Chatty Cathy, all original.
(Courtesy of Aylene Waite)

12" "A.M.390" marked child.
(Courtesy of Billye Otto)

24" Rare Alt, Beck & Gottschalck doll with closed mouth, all original ca. 1880, $2,000. (Courtesy of Billye Otto)

Close-up of 24" Alt, Beck & Gottschalck lady doll, 1880, $2,000. (Courtesy of Billye Otto)

Original by John & Angela Barker, England. "Gabrielle" limited edition 39" tall Victorian outfit. $8,000.

20" Kestner child #154. (Courtesy Carol Lindberg)

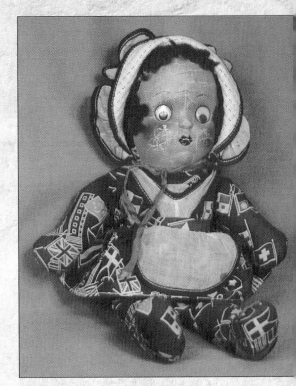

15" Unmarked cloth doll, all original.
(Courtesy of Carol Lindberg)

Original by John & Angela Barker, England-1997. "Rebecca" Limited
edition, Edwardian day dress, 28", $1,800.

Original by John & Angela Barker, England, "Dawn"
Limited edition, 26", $1,800.

Vogue's Ginny dolls. (Courtesy of Carol Lindberg)

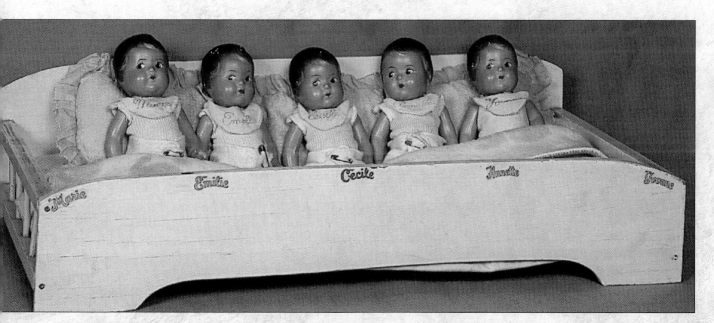

7-1/2" Compo Dionne Quints by Alexander. (Courtesy Carol Lindberg)

14" Dolly Dingles. (Courtesy of Carol Lindberg)

11" Dionne and 17" Dionne, by Alexander. (Courtesy Carol Lindberg)

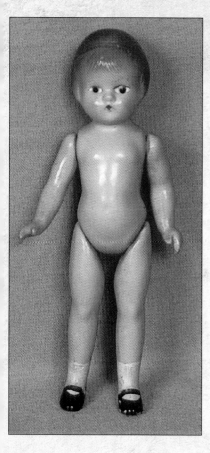

6" "Wee Patsy". (Courtesy of Carol Lindberg)

4-1/2" "189 4/O" marked googly. (Courtesy of Carol Lindberg)

"208" incised Kestner. (Courtesy of Carol Lindberg)

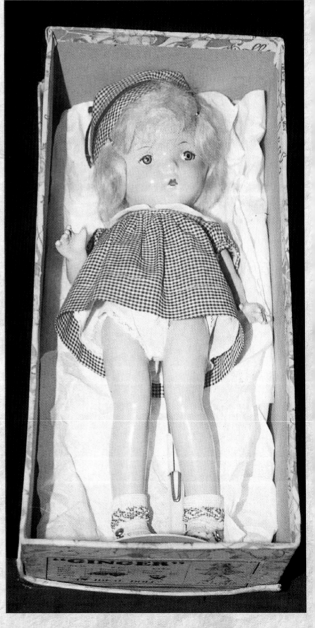

Armand Marseille dolls in regional costumes.
(Courtesy Carol Lindberg)

12" "Ideal" Ginger MIB. (Courtesy Ruby Ellen Smith)

Japanese lady in elaborate headdress made by Aiko Tabata. $2,500.

Japanese boy doll dressed in antique materials
by Aiko Tabata. $2,160.

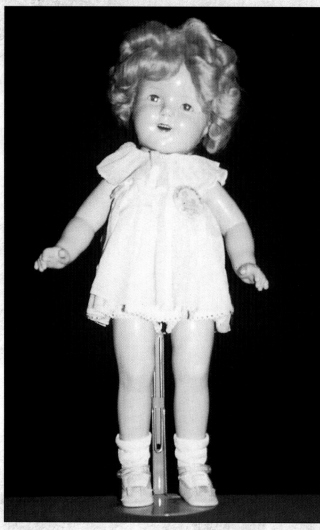

19" Shirley Temple, all original, 1930s. (Courtesy of
Ruby Ellen Smith)

13" F&B's "Patsy". (Courtesy of Ruby Ellen Smith)

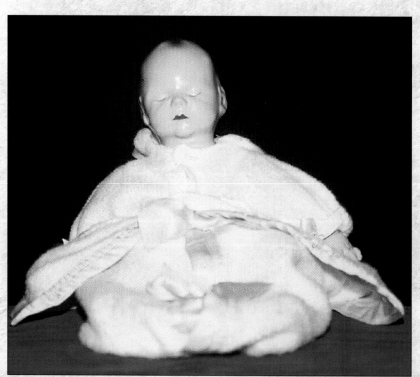

12" F&B's "Babyette".
(Courtesy of Ruby Ellen
Smith)

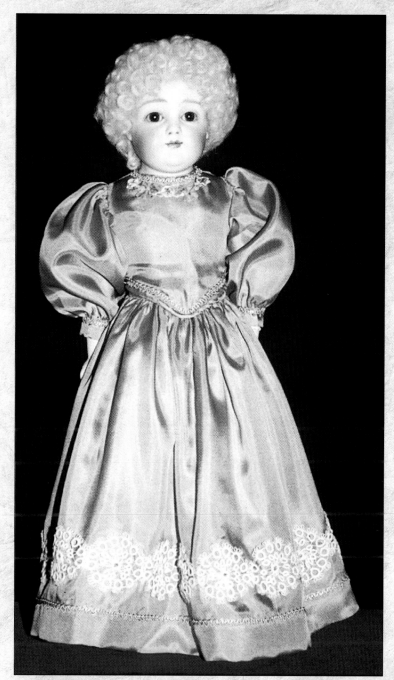

17" Unmarked closed mouth Kestner. (Coutesy of Ruby Ellen Smith)

"Sweet Nell" (1362). (Courtesy of Ruby Ellen Smith)

9" celluloid marked "Made in Japan", 6-1/2" German celluloid, 4-1/2" Nancy Ann.
(Courtesy of Carol Lindberg)

21" All original Jeanne I. Orsini boy doll, ca. 1916-25+.
(Courtesy of Linda Martinez Bassi)

Assorted tinies. (Courtesy of Carol Lindberg)

Japanese lady doll dressed in antique materials by Aiko Tabata, $2,000.

"Buttons the Clown", Irene Ortega, 21", $500.

"Sad Angel", bisque, glass eyes, 24" JR Gale.

Antique Heubach Piano Baby figurines, signed. 6" seated: $350 ea.; 7-1/2" standing: $400. (Courtesy of L.M. Bassi)

Chapter 15

～HEINRICH HANDWERCK～

History: 1885-1932

Heinrich Handwerck, Gotha near Waltershausen, Thur., Germany, 1885; made mohair wigs; made sawdust-stuffed pink cloth bodies and powdered cork-stuffed white calf-skin leather bodies; factories in the Burggasse building and later in the Fullgrabe building; began making ball-jointed composition bodies with wood parts circa 1888; also made the "French-type" bodies; used Simon & Halbig heads; Handwerck registered several patents in 1888 on the process of making bisque heads and composition bodies; the 8-pointed star trademark registered in 1891 in both the German and French language; an 1892 patent was for a ball-jointed doll body with exchangeable head and limbs; the 1892 patent was for a ball-jointed body with thighs and arms of carved wood; Handwerck dolls exhibited at the Columbia Exhibition in Chicago in 1893; Wilhelm Simon of Hildburghausen died in 1894; a new hip joint patent was registered in 1898; Heinrich Handwerck died in 1902, and the factory sold to Kammer & Reinhardt; Heinrich Handwerck, Jr., established a doll factory in Gotha in 1921; the Hanwerck, Jr., established a doll factory in Gotha in 1921; the Handwerck factory was controlled by the Bing conglomerate in the 1920s; the Handwerck, Jr., factory filed for bankruptcy in 1932.

Collecting Hints:

An early photograph of Herr Heinrich Handwerck reveals a handsome man with an imposing handlebar mustache standing before a four-story brick building which one assumes was his doll factory. Another photograph shows two of his workmen with a newly hewn tree which will soon be served by machinery and become wooden parts for doll bodies. It is difficult to associate so cold an image with the body of a beautiful doll. Mold numbers associated with the Handwerck dolls are: 69, 79, 89, 99, 109, 119, 139, 174, 189, 199. Handwerck used the following trademarks to sell his dolls: "Bébé Cosmopolite" (1895); Bébé de Reclame (1898); Bébé Superior (1913); La Belle (1914); La Bonita (1914); Baby Cut (9114); Lotti (1914). French names

helped sell their "French" looking dolls. "La Bonita" was probably for the Spanish market and "Baby Cut" for the English-speaking trade.

Reproduction Alert:

To my knowledge the Handwerck dolls have not been reproduced.

HEINRICH HANDWERCK

13-1/4" "S 5 H 139 DEP"/Negro Girl/brown bisque socket head, OM/teeth, brown glass eyes, black curly mohair wig, dark brown BJ compo body, old clothes, etc. Ca. 1900 .... $850

14" "79" girl. Bisque head, OM/teeth, inset blue glass eyes, blonde mohair wig, PE, BJ compo body, old clothes, etc. 1885+ .... $800-$850

14" "89" Girl. Pale bisque head, OM/teeth, inset brown glass eyes, PE, light brown mohair wig, BJ compo body, old clothes, etc. 1885+ .... $750-$825

16" "6/0" Girl. Bisque shoulder head, OM/teeth, inset blue glass eyes, brown HHW, kid body/bisque hands/cloth lower legs, old clothes. Mark: "Hch 6/0 H.//Germany." 1885+.................... $450

18" "79" Girl. Bisque head/2 rear holes, OM/teeth, blue glass sleep eyes, brown HHW, PE, BJ compo/wood body, old clothes, etc. 1885+ .... $850-$900

18" "89" Girl. Bisque shoulder head, CM, inset brown glass eyes, brown mohair wig, PE, kid body/bisque lower arms, old clothes, etc. 1885+ .... $2,600+

18" "139" Girl. Pale bisque shoulder head, OM, brown mohair wig, PE, kid body/bisque lower arms, old clothes. 1885+ .... $450-$500

18" "189" Girl. Bisque head, OM/teeth, blue glass sleep eyes, brown mohair wig, PE, BJ compo body, original clothes, etc., including original box, booklet, and 12 hand-sewn costumes that correspond with the patterns. Mark: "189-3". 1885+ (Sold for..... $3,900 at auction in 1992) $4,000

20" "79" Girl. Bisque shoulder head, CM, inset brown glass eyes, blonde mohair wig, kid body/bisque lower arms, old clothes. 1885+.......................... $2,700

20" "119" Girl. Pale bisque head, OM/teeth, brown glass sleep eyes, brown mohair wig, BJ compo body, old clothes. 1885+ $1,000

20" "189" Girl. Pale bisque shoulder head, OM/teeth, inset blue glass eyes, blonde mohair wig, PE, kid body/bisque lower arms, old clothes. 1885+ .... $1,100-$1,150

21" "119" Girl. Bisque head, OM/teeth, brown glass sleep eyes, brown HHW, PE. BJ compo body, old clothes, hat, etc. 1885+ .... $1,000-$1,100

22" "109" Girl. Bisque head, OM/teeth, blue glass sleep eyes, blonde mohair wig, BJ compo body, old clothes, etc. 1885+ .... $1,000-$1,100

24" "89" Girl. Bisque shoulder head, CM, inset blue glass eyes, brown HHW, PE, kid body/bisque lower arms, old clothes. 1885+ .... $3,000-$3,500

28" "119-13" Girl. Bisque socket head, OM/teeth, blue glass sleep eyes, brown HHW, PE, BJ compo body, old white cotton dress/sash, original hair bow, etc. Original box marked: "Genuine Handwerck Doll//Handwerck Bebe Cosmopolite." 1895-1902 MIB .$2,500

28" "Hch 7. H.//Germany" girl. Pale bisque shoulder head, OM/4 upper teeth, blue glass sleep eyes, blonde mohair wig, original cloth body/limbs/leather hands, old clothes, bonnet, etc. (Lovely S&H shoulder head). 1885+ ....$1,000+

25" "Heinrich Handwerck/Simon & Halbig" marked girl. Bisque head, OM/teeth, blue glass sleep eyes, brown HHW, BJ compo body, dressed by Virginia Yates. 1885+ $1,000-$1,100. (Courtesy of Virginia Yates)

31" "109" Girl. Bisque head, OM/teeth, blue glass sleep eyes, brown HHW, PE, brown HHW, BJ compo body, old clothes, etc. 1885+ ....$1,700-$1,800

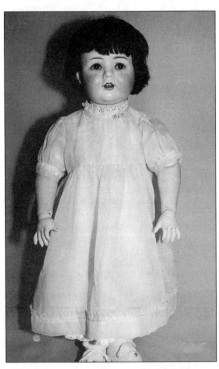

18" F&W Goebel bisque head/Handwerck body, OM/teeth, brown glass sleep eyes, brown HHW, BJ compo body. 1900+ $800-$900. (Courtesy of D. Kay Crow)

28" "119 13" incised girl. Bisque head, OM/teeth, brown glass sleep eyes, blonde mohair wig, BJ compo body, re-dressed. 1885+ Mark: "119 13/Handwerck 5/Germany." $1,300-$1,400. (Courtesy of D. Kay Crow)

31" "6-1/2" Girl. bisque socket head/dimpled chin, OM/4 teeth, brown glass sleep eyes, blonde mohair wig, PE, BJ compo body, original cheap petticoat, socks, kid leather shoes (stamped "HH" in a heart design//6-1/2), old dress (may not be original). Original simulated wood box (metal bound) reads:

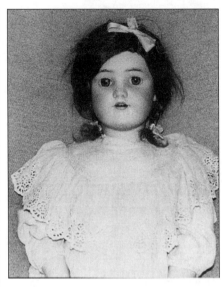

30-1/2" "Heinrich Handwerck/Simon & Halbig. Bisque head, OM/teeth, blue glass sleep eyes, original auburn mohair wig, BJ compo body, old clothes, etc. 1885+ $1,500-$1,600. (Courtesy of Herron)

21" "99" incised Handwerck Girl. Bisque head, OM/teeth, blue glass sleep eyes, brown HHW, BJ compo body, dressed by Virginia Yates Ca. 1885+ $900-$950.

"Bebe Cosmopolite" (trademark design of a baby in an 8-point star). Box also reads: "Eyes are tied through to mouth, cut the string on the corner of the mouth and they will open and close." Neck-mark: "Heinrich Handwerck//Simon & Halbig//6-1/2" 1895-1902 MIB $2,700

32" "99" Girl. bisque head, OM/teeth, blue glass sleep eyes, blonde HHW, PE, BJ compo body, old clothes, etc. Mark: "99 DEP H." 1885+ $1,900

17-1/2" "Hch 6/O H" (horseshoe design) "Made in Germany", incised girl. Bisque head, OM/teeth, inset blue glass eyes, kid body/bisque hands, old clothes, straw hat, etc. 1885+ $450. (Courtesy of Herron)

25" "Handwerck #4" incised girl. Bisque head, OM/teeth, blue glass sleep eyes, brown HHW, BJ compo body, old clothes. 1885+ $1,000-$1,100. (Courtesy of Irene Ortega)

Chapter 16

⌁ ERNST HEUBACH ⌁

History: 1887-1930s

Ernst Heubach, Koppelsdorf, Germany, 1887-1930s. When this small factory first opened, they concentrated on bisque shoulder heads, bisque socket heads, and the then popular bathing dolls. Since their open-mouth dolls (and their closed-mouth infants made in 1925, mold nos. 338, 339, 340, 349, 350) were basically ordinary dolls made for the mass-market, one will find few great rarities made by this company, and, except for very large sizes, and some toddlers and infants, prices remain under $1,000.

In 1895, Heubach employed 250 workers. Their biggest money-makers were their character babies and toddlers. Their black dolls were also very popular (mold Nos. 399, 414, 444, 452, 463). Heubach also manufactured heads for Cuno & Otto Dressel, Gebruder Ohlhaver, Luge & Co., and A. Wislizenus. Their dolls' heads were somewhat similar to those made by Armand Marseille, so it is not surprising that they merged with this firm in 1919 (United Porcelain Factory of Koppelsdorf). Armand's son, Herman, married Beatrix Heubach, which further sealed the business venture. The "Heubach Koppelsdorf" trademark was used after this merger and helps date dolls. This partnership lasted until 1932. Both companies continued to make dolls after that date.

Collecting Hints:

The Ernst Heubach doll was a cheap but lovable doll. Later dolls were coarse grained and highly colored. These dolls are not for the investor per se, but all anitque dolls will in time be of great value and highly sought, regardless of their ordinary qualities. The Heubach doll, like the Armand Marseille doll, has an appeal all its own and is never ignored by the collectors.

Their infant types made in 1925 were in direct competition with the Bye-Lo baby craze. They had sleep eyes, a closed mouth, and painted hair. Their bodies were cloth and their hands were either celluloid or composition. How much closer can a popular doll be emulated? Mold numbers for these dolls are given in HISTORY paragraph. Prices range from $700 upwards. Googly 322 and 419 sell upwards of $1,300 and $3,000.

ERNST HEUBACH

9" "322" incised Googly Girl. Bisque head, watermelon mouth, round inset blue glass eyes to side, blonde mohair wig, compo body jtd at neck/sh/hips/black ptd/molded-on ankle-strap shoes/white socks, original clothes, hat. Mark: "Heubach-Koppelsdorf//322-17/0//Germany." Ca. 1919+ $1,300

9" Negro "Islander" Boy. Dark brown bisque head, OM/teeth, inset brown glass eyes, black ptd hair, dark brown 5-pc compo body, original grass skirt, neck ornament, paper tag, large loop earrings. Mark: "South Seas Baby, Ges. Gesch, Made in Germany." Early 1900s (Sold for $660 in 1989.) ... $850

11-1/4"Toddler Boy. Bisque shoulder head, OM/teeth, blue glass sleep eyes, blonde mohair wig, kidalene body/bisque lower arms, original clothes, hat, etc. Ca. 1935 .... $390

11-1/4"Toddler Girl. Bisque head, OM/teeth, blue glass sleep eyes, blonde mohair wig, BJ compo body, original clothes, bonnet, etc. Mark: "Heubach/Koppelsdorf 417-10/0 Germany." Ca. 1935 .... $500

12" "320" Character Baby. Bisque head/open crown, OM/2 upper teeth, blue glass sleep eyes, PN, brown mohair wig, bent-limb jtd compo body, original clothes, bonnet, etc. Head mark: "Heubach Koppelsdorf//320/5/0//Germany." Ca. 1919+ $425

15" Bisque shoulder head, OM/teeth, brown glass eyes, blonde wig, kid body/bisque lower arms, redressed. 1888+ $275-$325. (Courtesy of Billye Ot-

22" "3022" marked girl. Lovely bisque head, OM/teeth, brown glass sleep eyes, blonde mohair wig, BJ compo body, redressed. Mark: "3022 Kopplesdorf Germany." 1888+ $600-$650. (D. Kay Crow)

15" Same doll as above.

13" "Girl with Pink Bow." Bisque shoulder head, O/C mouth/molded teeth, modelled ears, tiny ptd blue eyes, short 1-stroke eyebrows, blonde ptd/molded bow above right ear, cloth body/legs/compo lower arms, original clothes, etc. Ca. 1910+ (Numbers in this series: 261, 262, 271, etc.) ...$650

13" "Marotte." Bisque head (baby face), OM/teeth, inset blue glass eyes, bald dome head/attached high-peaked gold and red velvet cap with a tiny metal bell on the end, original red and gold velvet costume with 7 pointed ends and 7 metal bells. (Head is attached to a padded stick and has a squeaker.) Ca. 1900 ....$700

18" "Pale bisque shoulder head, OM/teeth, blue glass sleep eyes, blonde HHW, kid body/bisque lower arms, old clothes, etc. Mark: "Germany//275//4/0." Ca. 1888+ $375-$425. (Courtesy of D. Kay Crow)

15" "320" Character Baby. Bisque head/open crown, OM, PN, blue glass sleep eyes, blonde mohair wig, bent-limb jtd compo body, original clothes, bonnet, etc. Ca. 1910+ ..$575

16" "250" incised Child. Bisque head, OM/teeth, blue glass sleep eyes, blonde mohair wig, BJ compo body, old clothes, hat, etc. Ca. 1888+ $450

18" "251" incised Child. Bisque head, OM/teeth, brown glass sleep eyes, brown HHW, BJ compo body, old clothes, etc. Ca. 1888+ $500

18" "300" Negro Character Baby. Dark brown bisque head (dolly face used for white babies), OM/teeth/tongue, dark brown glass flirty eyes, black curly mohair wig, dark brown bent-limb jtd compo body, original clothes, etc. Ca. 1910+ $950

18" "399" Negro Character Boy. Brown bisque dome head (Negroid features) CM, dark brown glass eyes, PE, dark brown bent-limb jtd compo body, original red Moroccan Prince costume, red turban, large loop earrings. (Sold for ... $1,050 in 1994 at auction.) $1,700

19" "275" incised Girl. Bisque shoulder head, OM/teeth, blue glass sleep eyes, blonde mohair wig, kid body/bisque lower arms old clothes. Ca. 1888+ $375

19" "300" Character Baby. Bisque head/open crown, OM/teeth, PN, blue glass sleep eyes, brown mohair wig, BJ compo/toddler body, old clothes. Ca. 1910+ $775

19" "320" Character Baby. Bisque head/open crown, OM/teeth, blue glass sleep eyes, brown mohair wig, BJ compo/toddler body, old clothes, Ca. 1910+ $775

21" "250" incised girl. Bisque head, OM/teeth, blue glass sleep eyes, brown mohair wig, BJ compo body, old clothes, etc. Ca. 1888+ $575

21" "342" Character Baby. Bisque head (painted type)/round face/double toddler chin, OM/teeth, PN, blue glass sleep eyes, brown mohair wig, BJ compo/toddler body, old clothes. Ca. 1919+ $700

21" "Horseshoe" marked Girl. Bisque shoulder head, OM/teeth, brown glass sleep eyes, brown HHW, cloth body/bisque lower arms, old clothes. Mark: "DEP. 1900 (Horseshoe design) 3/0." Ca. 1888+ ....$395-$425

30" "302" Character Baby. Bisque head, OM/4 teeth/felt tongue, blue glass sleep eyes, blonde HHW, BJ compo body, old clothes, etc. Mark: "Heubach//302-9//Koppelsdorf // Germany." (300 series began in 1919) $1,300

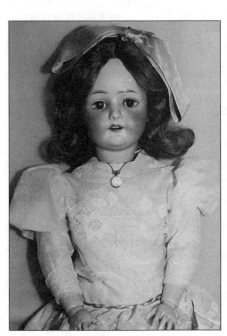

26" "250" incised girl. 1888+ $650-$750. (Courtesy of D. Kay Crow)

Chapter 17

~ GEBRUDER HEUBACH ~

History:

Gebruder Heubach, Lichte, Germany, 1840-1910, porcelain figurines; 1910-1938, bisque doll heads. The Heubach family registered their Sunburst trademark in 1882. The square Heubach trademark was registered in 1910 when they began to manufacture doll heads. Their first heads had painted intaglio eyes which were popular at that time, but it is also possible intaglio eyes were used later on. Heubach made figurines, piano babies, and all-bisque dolls.

Collecting Hints:

Gebruder Heubach company produced socket and shoulder heads in a great quantity and with a wide range of facial expressions. Some of these heads are very scarce, and others have such unusual character faces, that they have become coveted and expensive. Many of their figurines have faces similar to the dolls, but are not always marked. The heads were poured thicker than the figurines, and have a smoother outer surface. The figurines have a "grainy" feel when rubbed, which is similar to the texture inside the dolls' heads. Heubach later colored the slip pink, which gave the dolls a permanent facial coloring and eliminated the extra time spent painting the faces.

This likewise cut costs, enabling the firm to meet the heady competition with cheaper heads. The pink slip was used for heads with both intaglio eyes and glass eyes, and with open or closed mouths. Unfortunately, the dolls' bodies, whether cloth or "composition," were not in keeping with the quality of the heads and were obviously purchased from other companies.

Perhaps, this, too, was another factor in trying to maintain lower costs. Once the doll was dressed, nobody seemed to notice the body. When a Heubach head is found on a superior body, it is more than likely, a replacement, and not the original. Heubach bodies were made from an inferior papier-mâché substance which collectors refer to as "composition." To this pulp mixture was added plaster as a binding agent.

These cheap bodies break easily under pressure of any kind, and are difficult to restring. They cannot be drilled. Even a moist cloth will wash away the painted surface since it was not sealed with a final coat of varnish. Hence, this untreated surface attracts dirt which cannot be removed without damaging the paint and revealing the papier-mâché underneath. These bodies will further soften and deteriorate if stored in a damp basement, etc. Many Heubach dolls are found with sewed-on clothing, which was probably done to conceal the unsightly body which the seamstress felt wasn't the doll's own. The poor quality bodies, however, do not effect the price of the dolls since they are original.

Reproduction Alert:

Many of the Heubach character heads have been reproduced. Again, check the bodies.

GEBRUDER HEUBACH

7" Baby Boy. Solid-dome bisque head, CM, small ptd brown intaglio eyes, blonde ptd hair/brushstrokes, bent-limb jtd, compo body, old clothes. Mark: "Heubach" (in a square). 1910+ .... $375+

7" "Winker" Boy. Bisque head, CM, painted eyes ("winking" eye has more "white" showing), crude 5-pc comp. body, original clothes, bare feet. Ca. 1916+ $1,100

9" "2081" incised Character Baby. Pale bisque head, smiling O/C mouth/molded teeth, ptd blue intaglio eyes to side, blonde ptd/molded hair, bent-limb jtd compo body, old clothes. Mark: "Heubach (in a square) 91." 1910+ $650

10" "9141" incised "Winker" Boy. (Same face as the shoulder head version incised "7"). Bisque socket head, CM, ptd brown eyes, 5-pc compo body, original clothes, shoes, socks, hat. (The bisque is more highly colored than some versions.) 1910+ $1,200

10" Piano Boy. Boy. All-bisque/no movable parts/nude/bent arms modeled towards chest/ wide apart legs/molded-on shoes, ptd features, blonde pts./molded hair. Ca. 1914 .... $650

11" "8774" or "Whistling Jim." Bisque head, OM/hole in center, ptd blue intaglio eyes, blonde ptd/molded hair, cloth body/compo hands, original romper suit, hat, etc. Made for Wagner & Zetsche of Ilmenau. (Wagner & Zetsche purchased heads from Heubach until Ca. 1916) 1910+ .... $1,100-$1,200

11-1/2" "7628" incised Character Boy. Bisque socket head, O/C mouth, ptd blue intaglio eyes, blonde ptd, molded hair, BJ compo body, old clothes, etc. 1910+ $750

12" "8191" incised Character Boy. Solid-dome bisque head, O/C mouth/4 upper teeth/2 lower teeth, ptd blue intaglio eyes to side, blonde ptd/ molded hair, bent-limb jtd compo body, old clothes. 1910+ $1,250

13" "7602" incised Character Baby. Solid-dome bisque head, CM, ptd intaglio blue/eyes, sparse light brown ptd hair, bent-limb jtd compo body, old clothes. 1910+... $900

14" "Coquette" Turned bisque shoulder head, smiling O/C mouth/teeth, ptd blue intaglio eyes, blonde ptd/molded hair/turquoise ribbon, kid body/ bisque arms, original pink silk dress, etc. 1910+.............................. $975-$1,150

14" "4,93,32" incised Negro girl. Black bisque shoulder head, CM, ptd brown intaglio eyes, black mohair wig, black cotton/cloth body/limbs, old clothes. Mark: "HEUBACH (square) 4,93,32 Germany." 1910+ $1,000

14-1/2" "8" incised "Crying" Boy. Solid-dome bisque head, (very realistic face), wide O/C mouth/molded tongue, narrow blue ptd intaglio eyes, forehead wrinkles, well-molded ears, blonde ptd hair, bent-limb jtd compo body, old clothes. 1912 .... $3,000

15-1/2" "7745" or "Laughing" Boy. Bisque head, O/C mouth/molded teeth, squinty ptd blue eyes, well-modeled ears, blonde ptd/molded hair, BJ compo body, old clothes. 1910+........... $1,200

16" "7622 8" incised Pouty. Pale bisque head/angelic face, pouty CM, blue-grey ptd intaglio eyes, modeled ears, blonde ptd/molded wavy hair, BJ compo body, original outfit. 1910+ . $1,400

16-1/4" "6970" incised Character Girl. Bisque head, O/C mouth, blue glass sleep eyes, blonde HHW, BJ compo body, old clothes, etc. 1910+ ... $4,000

17" "7925" incised Lady. Composition shoulder head/head tilted down and turned, CM, large blue glass inset eyes, blonde mohair wig, kid body/leather arms, original clothes. 1910+ (Sold for $1,275 in 1991) $2,000 (This doll may not be incised "7925" but is a duplicate of the bisque version.)

18" "6692" incised Pouty Boy. Pink bisque shoulder head, pouty CM, blue intaglio eyes, flocked hair, kid body/jtd hips and knees/pink bisque hands, old clothes Mark: "5//Germany/6692." (Heubach developed the pink bisque color.) 1910+............................. $1,200-$1,400

Chapter 18

JUMEAU (MAISON)

History: 1842+

Paris city directories (1842-1846) list the names of Jumeau and Belton as partners in a small doll-making business. Like many small doll firms of the time, they assembled dolls with parts purchased from companies who specialized in shoulder heads, kid of cloth bodies, etc. These early Jumeau poupées had heads of wax or papier-mâché, bodies of mouled carton or pink and white kid skin stuffed with sawdust, teeth of straw or enamel, eyes of glass or enamel, hands of wood, papier-mâché, or leather, wigs of hemp or Astrakhan fur (lamb's wool eventually replaced fur). A complete outfit consisted of a dress, underwear, hat, shoes, and stockings and were French-made. Early kid bodies were stiff with no joints.

Although Jumeau père, Pierre, had been working with the Germans, learning the fine art of porcelain manufacture, he was still using German heads in the late 1850s. The German bisque was white or of the type used on the Parian dolls, and not the lovely ground-in color associated with the dolls Jumeau later made.

Jumeau was advertising dolls with kid bodies in 1860. It was during this time, that Francois Gauthier, (St. Maurice, Charenton, Seine, Paris, France), began making porcelain heads and parts, which Pierre purchased for his fine kid bodies. Jumeau began using the swivel head on shoulder plate ca. 1862. The Jumeau "bisque" heads date to 1875.

Pierre Jumeau retired in 1877 and the following year his son, Emile, who had taken over the firm, began advertising dolls with stiff and gusseted bodies, jointed wooden bodies, and the famous fashionable wardrobes. (Jumeau had made some china heads before the 1870 war with Germany.) Emile Jumeau also advertised the Jumeau bisque heads in 1878. Emile was a master showman and a master of French exaggeration. He took the company to the top where it remained for the next twenty years.

America had always been the biggest buyer of German dolls and toys, but when America came upon hard times during the 1890s, people could no longer afford expensive dolls, especially French-made. Hence, the Germans undercut the French price-wise, and flooded the American market with cheaper playthings; the dolls being a poor imitation of the French product. Even the French dolls made by Jumeau were no longer the high-quality of the older types. The starving French manufacturers united and formed the Société Française de Fabrication de Bébés and Jouets. One German house merged with them and after 1900 (until World War One) most "French" dolls were actually made in Germany. When the French began making their own dolls after the war, it was hardly the glorified poupée of yore, but a mere shadow of its former self.

Collecting Hints:

Jumeau's early dolls had heads of wax and papier-mâché, then he used heads made of china and white or "parian" bisque. The wax heads probably came from England and the mâché heads from Germany. Porcelain heads were made in Bavaria, Prussia, Austria, Cobourg, Sonneberg, and Nuremberg. All of these early dolls were unmarked.

Belton's dolls bore a cloth body made similarly to those of kid. The shoes on his dolls were marked "M.B."—or so it has been said. Jumeau bisque had the color ground-in. His dolls, with exceptions, had pierced ears (this uniter had an "EJ" with applied unpierced ears), satin-smooth bisque, and paperweight eyes. There were also eyes with what is called "yeux fibres" (fine lines running from the outer edge of the iris to the pupil), and "feathered" eyes. "Feathered" eyes are deep blue or greenish-grey and the feathering is deep within. Although Jumeaux are not rare and the open-mouth types are fairly common, there are more collectors interested in them and prices have gone over the top. Top price means a top doll—almost perfect and original in every aspect. In fact, condition has to be almost mint and "unplayed with."

Surprisingly, there are many Jumeau that fall into this category. Being expensive, they were "Sunday" dolls—dolls to be handled briefly on Sunday after church. They were also rich people's dolls, and rich children usually had so many dolls they didn't have time to play with them. Late Jumeau had bisque heads of a denser quality and more coarse in texture, and the coloring is more florid and "tartish." Prior to 1970, a 30" closed mouth Tete Jumeau Bébé could be had for $300 or less. Jumeau made prior to 1890 never disappoint the collector.

Reproduction Alert:

The Jumeau poupée has been reproduced all over the world. Some bisque heads are placed on modern composition bodies, others have bodies made of bisque. The modern composition used for bodies is a hard, rubber-like material and quite different than the old product. Old bodies smell old and always reveal wear, especially around the joints. Antique Jumeaux never had bisque bodies. Study the painting of eyelashes and eyebrows and compare with the painting of the old dolls.

Artistic painting requires years of skill and technique, but there are artisans in this era whose work is every bit as fine as that of Jumeau's day. If the bisque inside the doll's head is tinted it is a new head. Old heads were white inside. Precolored bisque was never used in the old days, with the exception of some Heubach heads. New heads have a rim around the top edge, old heads were cut off. Old heads and bodies look clean on the outside because they have been cleaned. But look inside and you will find the dirt of ages.

Modern composition bodies are usually painted with latex and can be wiped with a damp cloth. Old bodies have to be cleaned with wax because the paint used did not have a plastic base. Old dolls had hooks that held the elastic cord, modern bodies have an iron washer in the lower leg and hands. Antique heads are sometimes mounted on new bodies and vice versa. When one buys an expensive reproduction of a French doll one must take into account the high cost of supplies and labor. (The French Society for the Manufacture of Dolls and Toys has the original molds of the Jumeau dolls.)

MAISON JUMEAU

10" Tete Bébé. Size 1. Bisque head, CM, huge inset blue PW eyes, PE light brown feathered eyebrows, blonde mohair wig, BJ compo/wood body/straight wrists, original clothes, etc. Necklace clasp has initial "J." Ca. 1885+ .$5,500

11" "2" incised E.J. Bébé. Pale bisque head, CM, large blue PW eyes, light brown HHW, PE, BJ compo/wood body, original white cotton dress, ruffled bonnet, pink socks, ivory leatherette shoes, etc. Emile Jumeau. Ca. 1881+ ....$6,000-$6,500

11" Bébé. Closed-dome bisque head, CM, inset grey PW eyes, PE, blonde mohair wig, BJ compo/wood body/straight wrists, original clothes, etc. Early doll $7,000

12" "3" incised E.J. Bébé. Bisque head, CM, inset blue PW eyes, blonde mohair wig, PE, BJ compo body/straight wrists, original pink satin dress with pleated front, matching hat, etc. Head mark: "Déposé E3J, H." (in red). Ca. 1885+ $4,500

14" "Jumeau" incised Bébé. Early bisque head, CM, inset brown PW eyes, dark brown HHW, PE, BJ compo/wood body/straight wrists, old clothes, etc. Ca. 1880s $5,500

14" Bébé. Bisque head, CM, blue PW eyes, blonde mohair wig, PE, BJ compo body/straight wrists, old clothes, etc. Mark: "Jumeau Medaille D'Or." Ca.. 1878+ (Jumeau won the gold medal for his dolls in the 1878 Paris Exposition, but this mark was used for many years thereafter.) ....$5,000-$5,500

14" Negro Bébé. Black bisque head, CM, inset brown glass eyes, black wool wig, PE, black BJ compo body/straight wrists and ankles, original clothes, bonnet, etc. Head mark: "Déposé Jumeau 7." Ca. 1886-89.............$6,000-$7,000

14" Tete Bébé. Bisque head/startled expression, OM/teeth, large blue PW eyes, thick dark eyebrows, PE, brown mohair wig, BJ compo body, old white cotton dress, etc. Stamped: "Tete Jumeau, Diplome d'Honneur." (Jumeau was awarded the Diploma of Honor at Antwerp in 1885.) Ca. 1885+ ....$2,400-$2,700

30" Reproduction Long Face Jumeau by John and Angela Barker, England.

15" "1907" incised Bébé. Bisque head, OM/teeth, blue PW eyes, PE, original auburn HHW, BJ compo body, original pink silk crepe dress, bonnet, etc. head mark: "1907 5."; red stamp on body reads: "Tete Bébé." Paper label on dress reads: "Jumeau Diplome d'Honneur." Ca. 1907+ ....$3,000-$3,500

15" Tete Bébé. Bisque head, CM, blue sleep eyes have lever in rear of head, PE, auburn mohair wig, thick/curved auburn ptd eyebrows, BJ compo body, original pink factory chemise, shoes, socks. Mark: "Jumeau, Medaille D'Or, Paris." Ca. 1878+ ....$5,500-$6,000

16" "1" incised Portrait Bébé. Pale bisque head, CM, inset dark brown PW eyes, PE, dark brown mohair wig, BJ compo body, old clothes, etc. (This doll has the choice large almond-shaped eyes and the early unmarked compo body.) Shoes marked: "J" and "1." Ca. 1877-83 (size 1 is usually on 17" size doll.) ....$15,000+

16" "1907" incised Walking Bébé. Bisque head, OM/molded teeth (Upper), inset blue PW eyes, brown HHW, BJ compo body/jtd arms/straight legs, metal wheels beneath feet, original peach satin dress with lace trim, hat, shoes, etc. Head incised: "1907 6." Plate beneath feet incised: "BREVETE 305.249 S.G.D.G." (When key wind is activated arms move, head turns, and doll walks.) Ca. 1907+ ....$5,000-$6,000

16" "Déposé/Jumeau/7" incised Bébé. Pale bisque head, CM, inset blue PW eyes, blonde mohair wig, PE, BJ compo/wood body/straight wrists, old clothes, etc. 1886-89 ....$5,500+

16-1/2" Tete Bébé. Bisque head, O/C mouth, large blue PW eyes, thick dark eyebrows, PE, dark brown mohair wig, BJ compo body, old clothes, etc. Mark: "Tete Jumeau Bte S.G.D.G. 7." Ca. 1885+ $4,500

17" "1" incised Portrait Bébé. Early pale bisque head, unusually large almond-shaped eyes (brown PW), thin light brown eyebrows, CM, blonde mohair wig, PE, BJ wood body, old clothes, etc. Body mark: "Jumeau." Ca. 1877-86 ....$15,000-$16,000

17" Ethnic Bébé. Light brown bisque head, OM/teeth, inset brown glass eyes, black mohair wig, brown tinted BJ body, original Asian costume (possibly Algiers): embroidered silk baggy trousers, gilt embroidered top with long sleeves, cap decorated with spangles and faux coins, etc. Incised: "6." Ca. 1885+ ....$4,000+

17-1/2" Bébé Samaritaine. Bisque head, OM/teeth, blue glass sleep eyes, PE, brown HHW, BJ compo body, original chemise, shoes, socks. (Made by Jumeau company for Samaritaine department store.) 1897+ $3,500

18" Early Bathing Beauty Bébé. Bisque head/flange neck/bisque shoulder plate, wee CM, blue ptd eyes, brown mohair wig, kid body/bisque lower arms, original bathing suit, oilskin cap, shoes. Shoes marked: "Jumeau." Early 1860s $10,000

18" Tete Bébé. Modern Reproduction. Hard vinyl head, orange-red CM, auburn ptd eyebrows, blue blown glass eyes, brown synthetic wig, hard plastic fully-jtd body/spring and metal washers/straight wrists/swivel

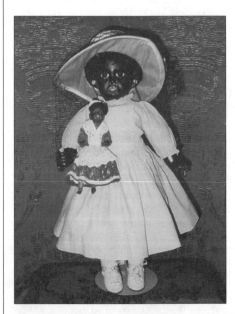

18" Negro Emile Jumeau. Black bisque head, pink CM, PE, large inset brown PW eyes, wig, black mohair wig, BJ compo body, original clothes, etc. 1880+ $35,000. (Courtesy of LInda Martinez Bas-

23" "Jumeau" marked Jumeau Bébé. Bisque head, CM, inset brown PW eyes, brown mohair wig, PE, BJ compo body, original clothes, etc. $8,000-$10,000. (Courtesy of Linda Martinez Bassi)

20" "Depose Tete Jumeau Bte S.G.D.G." marked Bébé. Bisque head, CM, inset blue PW eyes, brown HHW, PE, BJ compo body, redressed. 1885+ $4,700-$5,000. (Courtesy of Connie Baca)

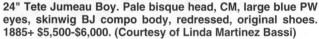

24" Tete Jumeau Boy. Pale bisque head, CM, large blue PW eyes, skinwig BJ compo body, redressed, original shoes. 1885+ $5,500-$6,000. (Courtesy of Linda Martinez Bassi)

Close-up of Long Face or "Cody" Jumeau reproduction. Dressed in antique fabrics, laces, trim, by John and Angela Barker, England.

waist/high-modeled "flapper" knees, original maroon cotton dress, white cotton pantalets, white stockings, brown velvet shoes, straw hat. head mark: "Collector's Dolls CD-#2." Original box has a photo of the doll in an oval and the words: "Collector's Doll." (The head is low-cut with a vinyl crown. Body looks German.) Ca. 1977 MIB $700

19" "137" incised Belton-type Bébé. Very pale bisque head, CM, pastel pink cheek blush, grey PW eyes, long brown HHW, PE, BJ compo body/straight wrists, old clothes, etc. (Resembles a Long-Face Jumeau.) Ca. 1875 ....$4,200-$4,500

21" "Depose Tete Jumeau Bte S.G.D.G." stamped (on head) Parisienne. Bisque swivel head on bisque shoulder plate, CM, inset blue PW eyes, PE, brown HHW, kid body (Parisienne type), old clothes, etc. 1885+ $5,000+. (Courtesy of Herron)

19" Parisienne. Bisque head on bisque shoulder plate, CM, blue PW eyes, PE, blonde mohair wig, kid fashion body/limbs, original black silk 2-pc walking suit, hat, black leather shoes, etc. Stamped: "Jumeau Medaille D'Or Paris." Ca. 1880 ....$4,000-$4,500

19-1/2" "Dep/8" incised Bébé. Bisque head, OM/4 teeth, brown glass sleep eyes, real eyelashes, PE, brown HHW, BJ compo body/pull string for working voice box, old clothes, etc. Body mark: "Bébé Jumeau//Diplome d'Honneur//Dep//8//." Ca. 1885+ ....$3,000-$3,500

19-1/2"Early Parisienne. Pale bisque shoulder head, CM, blue PW eyes, brown mohair wig, PE, kid body/limbs, elaborate old gown, hat, original long black net gloves, etc. Mark: "Déposé." (Jumeau's early Parisiennes had shoulder heads, although these were also made later. The swivel-neck dates 1862+.) (Lovely face) $4,500

20" "9" incised Tete Bébé. Bisque head, CM, inset blue PW eyes, PE, brown mohair wig, BJ compo body, old clothes, etc. Mark: "Déposé Tete

Jumeau S.G.D.G. 9." (plus Jumeau check marks). Ca. 1885+ ....$4,700-$5,000

20" "9" incised Tete Bébé. Bisque head, CM, light brown arched eyebrows, brown PW eyes, PE, brown HHW, BJ compo body, original white and blue cotton chemise, original shoes, socks. Original box has two labels which extol the Jumeau Bébé; illustrates available clothing and footwear. Ca. 1890 MIB $6,000

20" "E.J." incised Parisienne. Bisque swivel head on bisque shoulder plate, CM, inset blue PW eyes, PE, brown mohair wig, kid gusseted body, original clothes, etc. Original box stamped: "Medaille D'Or 1878 8 Poupee Jumeau." 1878 MIB ..$15,000-$20,000

20" Bébé Louvre. Bisque head, CM, large brown PW eyes, blonde HHW, PE, BJ compo body, original velvet and silk outfit, etc. Mark: "B.9L." (Made for the Louvre department store, Paris.) Ca. 1880s ....$5,000-$5,500

21" "1907 8" incised "Kiss" Bébé. Bisque head, OM/teeth, blue flirty glass eyes, auburn HHW, BJ compo body/key wind on hip, original factory dress: pink silk trimmed with lace, hat, etc. Ribbon tied across front of dress reads "J'Evoie Des Baisers" (I send kisses). Ca. 1900 ....$5,000

22" "10" incised Tete Bébé. Bisque head, O/C mouth, inset brown PW eyes, blonde mohair wig, PE, BJ compo body, old clothes, etc. Mark: "Déposé Tete Jumeau Bte S.G.D.G. 10." Ca. 1885+.............................$5,000-$5,500

22" Tete Bébé Jumeau. Bisque head, CM, inset blue PW eyes, brown mohair wig, PE, BJ compo body/straight wrists, old blue silk dress, bonnet, etc. Stamped: "Bébé Jumeau Hors 1889." (Jumeau was a member of the Jury and Hors Concours at the Paris Expo of 1889.) 1889..............................$5,000-$5,200

22" Tete Bébé. Bisque head, CM, inset blue PW eyes, dark brown mohair wig, PE, BJ compo body, original maroon silk dress with lace trim, hat, etc. Mark: "Déposé Tete Jumeau 10." Ca. 1885+ ....$5,000-$5,500

22" Tete Bébé. Bisque head, OM/teeth, inset blue PW eyes, PE, brown HHW, BJ compo body, original clothes, etc. Red stamp head mark: "TETE JUMEAU." Yellow body label: "BÉBÉ JUMEAU//DIPLOME D'HONNEUR." Dress label reads: "au Louvre//Paris//15 Fr 50." (The Louvre dolls made by "Jumeau" were actually of German manufacture; especially after 1900.) Ca. 1916 ....$3,000

23" 208 incised Character Bébé. Bisque head/rosy cheeks, O/C mouth/tongue/upper teeth, squinty glass eyes, blonde mohair wig, BJ compo body, original clothes, bonnet, etc. (This crying child has a wide-open mouth.) Ca. 1900 ....$50,000+

23" Portrait Bébé. Bisque head, CM, inset round-shaped blue PW eyes, PE, blonde mohair wig, BJ compo body/straight wrists, old clothes, hat, etc. Mark: "3, Jumeau Medaille D'Or Paris." Ca. 1878-83 ..$11,500-$12,000

23" Portrait Parisienne. Pale bisque swivel head on pale bisque shoulder plate, CM, inset blue PW eyes, blonde skin wig, gusseted kid body/leather arms, original clothes, etc. Ca. 1860s $9,000

23" Tete Bébé. Bisque head, CM, brown glass sleep eyes motivated by a lever at the rear of the neck (open-close), PE, auburn HHW/cork pate, BJ compo body, original clothes, etc. Stamped: "Déposé Tete Jumeau Bte S.G.D.G. 10" (red check marks). Size 10 is usually 21"-22". Ca. 1885+ $6,000

24" "Bébé Jumeau" marked Bébé. Bisque head, CM, blue glass sleep eyes, blonde HHW, PE, BJ compo body, original clothes, etc. Head and body marks: "Bébé Jumeau" and "Tete Jumeau." Ca. 1890s ....$5,000-$5,500

25" Tete Jumeau. Bisque head, CM, inset blue PW eyes, brown HHW, PE, BJ compo body with a small waist and a large bosom/wooden limbs with ball joints, original white satin gown, long blue kid gloves, white satin slippers with blue pompons and French heels, etc. Head mark: "Déposé Tete Jumeau Bte S.G.D.G." Shoes marked: "France." Blue oval body stamp: "Bébé Jumeau Diplome d'Honneur." Ca. 1885+ ....$7,000-$10,000

26" "Déposé E.12J." incised Bébé. Bisque head/chubby cheeks, CM, inset blue PW eyes, PE, blonde HHW, BJ compo body/straight wrists, original silk dress, etc. Ca. 1881-86 ....$8,000-$8,500

26" "Déposé Jumeau 12" incised Bébé. Bisque head, O/C mouth, PE, blue PW eyes, applied PE, blonde mohair wig, BJ compo body/straight wrists, original clothes, etc. Ca. 1886-1889 ....$8,000-$8,200

26" Smiling Boy. Bisque head, OM/teeth, large brown PW eyes, PE, brown HHW,

15" Emile Jumeau Bébé. Pale bisque head, CM, blue PW eyes, PE, blonde mohair wig, BJ compo body, original clothes, etc. 1881-1886 signed inside head, back of neck and on body. Choice $9,500-$10,500. (Courtesy of Linda Martinez Bassi)

23" Tete Jumeau Bébé. Bisque head, OM/teeth, inset blue PW eyes, blonde HHW, BJ compo body, re-dressed. $3,500 1885+. (Courtesy of Irene Ortega)

17" "Jumeau" incised Bébé. Bisque/shoulder/head, OM/square teeth, inset blue PW eyes, PE, brown HHW, kid body/bisque hands, original clothes, etc. $2,500. (Courtesy of D. Kay Crow 1885+)

11" Negro Tete Bébé Jumeau. Brown bisque head, OM/teeth, large brown PW eyes, black mohair wig, brown BJ compo body, dressed. 1880+ $2,000-$3,000. (Courtesy of Linda Martinez Bassi)

30" Tete Bébé Jumeau. Pale bisque head, OM/teeth, inset brown PW eyes, blonde HHW, BJ compo body, old clothes, etc. Ca. 1885+ $3,800-$3,900. (Courtesy of Victoria Rose, England)

BJ compo body/wooden limbs, original white satin trousers, jacket, vest, shirt, bow tie, white satin hat, blue kid gloves, silk stockings, white satin shoes/blue pompons, red satin arm band imprinted "Bébé Jumeau." Head mark: "Déposé Tete Jumeau Bte S.G.D.G." Body mark: "Bébé Jumeau, Diplome d'Honneur." Ca. 1887 ....$4,000+

26" Tete Bébé #12. Bisque head, OM/teeth, dark blue PW eyes, heavy feathered eyebrows, brown HHW, BJ compo body, original white and blue cotton chemise, marked "Jumeau" shoes. Head mark: "12." Body stamp: "Bébé Jumeau Bte S.G.D.G. Déposé." 1890s ....$3,600-$3,800

26" Tete Bébé. Bisque head, CM, inset blue PW eyes, PE, blonde mohair wig/bangs, BJ compo body, old clothes, etc. Mark: "Déposé Tete Jumeau Bte S.G.D.G. 12." Ca. 1885+ ....$5,700-$6,200

27" "Paris Bébé." Bisque head, CM, inset blue PW eyes, PE, auburn HHW, BJ compo/wood body, original outfit: gold skirt with brown velvet stripes at bot-

tom, gold and brown velvet top, tricorn hat, etc. (Doll has a jaunty Vive la France air.) Incised "11." Body mark: "Jumeau." 1892+ (Trademark also used by Danel & Cie, Paris.) ....$8,000-$8,500

27" Early Parisienne. Bisque head on bisque shoulder plate, CM, inset blue PW eyes, thin light brown eyebrows, blonde mohair wig, cork pate, applied PE, BJ wood fashion body/tendon jts at sh/hips/elbows/swivel jtd upper arms/thighs, original clothes, hat, etc. Ca. Late 1860s+ ....$18,000-$20,000

30" "DEP" incised Bébé. Bisque head (Has an S&H look), OM/teeth, blue glass sleep eyes, brown HHW, BJ compo body, original clothes, etc. Ca. 1900..............................$3,000-$3,200

30" "DEP" incised Bébé. Bisque head, OM/row of teeth, blue glass sleep eyes, blonde HHW, BJ French compo body, old embroidered white net dress, hat, etc. (This head has a Simon & Halbig look.) Ca. 1900 ....$3,000-$3,200

30" Tete Bébé. Bisque head, OM/teeth, blue PW eyes, PE, brown HHW, BJ compo body, original silk dress, matching hat, etc. Ca. 1885+ . $3,800-$4,000

32" "Tete Bébé 32" marked Bébé. Bisque head, CM, blue PW eyes, PE, applied ears, brown mohair wig, BJ compo body, old clothes, etc. Mark: "Déposé Tete Jumeau S.G.D.G. 14." (Jumeau check marks). Ca. 1885+ ....$6,500-$6,800

42" Walking/Talking Bébé. Bisque head, OM/teeth, brown glass eyes, black HHW, PE, cheap card or mâché body stapled together at shoulder area/round hole in center of back contains a voice box imprinted "Barcelona"/long cardboard legs wired to body/unjointed compo arms, original Spanish costume, mantilla, etc. Assembled and sold in Spain for the Spanish trade. (Head turns from side to side as she walks.) Early 1900s ....$6,000-$7,000

18-1/2" "Marigold." Early "Portrait" Jumeau. Parisienne. Pale bisque swivel head on pale bisque shoulder plate, CM, PE, large inset brown PW eyes, blonde mohair wig, kid body, original Breton peasant outfit. Body stamped: "Jumeau, Paris." 1860s $7,000-$8,000. (Courtesy of Victoria Rose, England)

21" Bébé. Bisque head, CM, blue PW eyes, brown HHW, BJ compo body, redressed in antique fabrics. Red stamp: "Jumeau." 1885+ $6,200-$6,500. (Courtesy of D. Kay Crow)

16" "Portrait" Bébé Jumeau. Pale bisque head, CM, large blue PW eyes, blonde skin wig, BJ compo body, old clothes, etc. 1877-83 $15,000+. (Courtesy of Linda Martinez Bassi)

Chapter 19

⌁KAMMER & REINHARDT⌁

History: 1886-1930s

Kammer & Reinhardt, Waltershausen, Germany, 1886-1930s. Founded by sculptor Ernst Kammer and businessman Franz Reinhardt. The firm had ruled the market with a single doll model until 1909, when they began manufacturing their controversial character dolls which were registered in 1909 as "Charakterpuppe."

Their story begins in 1908 when an important exhibit of dolls was held at the Hermann Teitz department store in Munich. The so-called "artistic" dolls on display were creating quite a stir amongst the observers, but when Kammer and Reinhardt inspected them, they found the dolls' faces harsh and ugly. They felt that the success of the dolls was mainly due, apart from their newness, to the artistic "arrangement" and development of colors in the costumes.

Kammer and Reinhardt agreed with the doll-makers that a staleness had settled upon the doll industry, and perhaps something good existed in the new movement or "rebellion." It was nigh time for a new doll image and realistic faces and body shapes might be the answer to the current unrest and stagnation. They sought an employed Berlin sculptor who had been recommended to them, and the sculptor showed them a bronze bust of a six-week-old baby (his own son) which he felt would make a perfect character head for their new series. This became the famous "Baby" or number 100 mold.

Although Herr Kammer and Herr Reinhardt liked the head, they held the opinion that it was too "realistic" to be successful, and were surprised with the favorable results. The Berlin artist completed other heads for them, and Kammer and Reinhardt held a small exhibit of their new character dolls and products at the Hermann Tietz store for a select group of invited guests. The composition bodies of the dolls had been restyled to simulate the bodies of real children and babies. Also, in keeping with the somber character faces, the dolls had been given painted eyes which were considered more expressive than glass eyes. Re-

action to the dolls was mixed. Some critics decreed that the dolls would be a great success, others felt that the dolls would fail; recalling that the Germans had failed in the 1880s when they first introduced character faces. Demand for the dolls was low in 1909, but a year later, 1910, the Sonneberg Chamber of Trade and Commerce reported that the dolls were out-selling Teddy Bears and traditional dolls.

Success was short-lived, however, because by 1911, sales has plummeted, and Kammer and Reinhardt blamed it on the painted eyes. Children, they reasoned, wanted sleeping eyes. Painted eyes were no eyes at all. J.D. Kester and Franz Schmidt of Germany had anticipated this public reaction, producing character heads with sleeping eyes and rushing them into the waiting market. This was in 1911.

Mr. Halbig, Kammer and Reinhardt's business advisor, agreed with these changes, and in 1912, Kammer and Reinhardt unveiled a doll head that was a combination of the traditional head and the character head (mold 117). This head had everything (molds 117A, 117n): closed or open mouth, sleep eyes or flirty eyes. Since market turnover had been calculated at 10 percent in 1910, and only 3 percent in 1912, it was gratifying when sales for this new compromise head was up by 40 percent in 1913. The baby doll was the only doll that survived this critical period without financial failure. It undoubtedly financed the experimental "art" or "character" dolls that had been foisted upon the doll buying public.

During this trying period, Kammer and Reinhardt even sought out Kathe Kruse, offering her a contract. But her mass-produced "Baby Bauz" (1911) was not successful. When made in quantity, the Kruse dolls lost their hand-made appeal. Frau Kruse was not happy with the results, and agreed with the cancellation of her contract. It was not in her stars to be in partnership with anyone. After her departure, however, Kammer and Reinhardt produced a doll that closely resembled her Doll 1. Even Marion Kaulitz accused the firm of having imitated her dolls (and perhaps they did), but the accusations

were counterclaimed with the fact that K (star) R had made character heads in the 1880s.

Other companies who made character heads: J.D. Kestner, Franz Schmidt & Co., Gebruder Heubach (who produced over 10,000 different heads), Ernst Heubach, Bahr & Proschild, Max Handwerck, William Goebel, Kley & Hahn, Simon & Halbig, Armand Marseille, Hertel, Schwab & Co., Schoenau & Hoffmeister, Swaine & Co., and Bruno Schmidt.

Although these companies manufactured a vast and wide-variety of doll heads, the success of the character face was brief; thousands of heads were destroyed; accounting for the extreme rarity of some heads at the present time.

Collecting Hints:

Collectors should not confuse Simon & Halbig doll heads with the character heads they made for Kammer & Reinhardt. The latter heads were made from Kammer & Reinhardt molds and models. Although Kammer & Reinhardt purchased Simon & Halbig in 1920, each firm remained independent of the other, producing their own doll types.

Kammer & Reinhardt claimed to have been the first company to put teeth in open mouths, and gramophones in talking dolls. They likewise claimed to have invented the bent-limb baby body. Their babies had natural-looking bodies with roils of fat and dimples. In the 1920s, when skirts climbed above the knee, their dolls were given longer legs with joints above the knee. Kammer & Reinhardt registered Edmund Steiner's MAJESTIC trademark in 1902; DIE KOKETTE trademark was registered in 1907, and DER SCHELM trademark was registered in 1908.

Reproduction Alert:

The Kammer & Reinhardt Character Dolls have been reproduced; be wary of closed mouth "pouty" types.

KAMMER & REINHARDT

8" "114" or "Hans." Bisque head, CM, ptd blue eyes, blonde mohair wig, BJ compo body, original clothes, hat, etc. Ga. 1909+..$2,500

8" "192" Girl. Bisque head, OM, blue glass sleep eyes, PE, blonde mohair wig, compo body/limbs, original clothes. Ca. 1886-95.......................................$750

8-1/2" "101" or "Peter." Solid-dome bisque head, CM, blue ptd intaglio eyes, close-cropped brown flocked hair, BJ compo body, original bridegroom outfit, top hat, etc. Signed: "Karl Kellner." Foot sticker reads: "Cunique Des Poupees, Lausanne, Place Pallio (Switzerland)." ("101 X" means "experimental.") Ca. 1909+..$2,500

8-1/2" "101" or "Marie." Bisque head, pouty CM, ptd blue eyes, blonde mohair wig, BJ compo body, old clothes, bonnet, original leather shoes. Ca. 1909+ $2,400

8-1/2" "192" Girl. Bisque head, rosy cheeks, CM, inset blue glass eyes, PE, blonde mohair wig, BJ compo body, original clothes, bonnet, etc. Ca. 1886-1895 ....$875

10" Negro "100" Baby. Black bisque head, OM, ptd brown eyes, well modeled ears, black ptd hair, black bent-limb compo body, old clothes. Ca. 1909+ ....$800-$900

10-1/4" White "100" Baby. Bisque head, OM/molded tongue, large ears, ptd grey eyes, blonde ptd hair, bent-limb compo body/dimpled knees, old clothes. Ca. 1909+ $650

11" "101" or "Marie." Pale bisque head, CM, blue glass eyes, pale blonde mohair wig, BJ compo body, old clothes, etc. Ca. 1909+ Mark: "101 26."........$3,000

11" "114 X" Character Boy. Bisque head, CM, brown flocked hair, blue ptd intaglio eyes, BJ compo body, original clothes, etc. Mark: "K (star) R 114 X 26." Ca. 1909+ $3,500

13-3/4" "126 28" Character Girl. Bisque head, OM/upper teeth, flirty blue glass eyes, blonde HHW, BJ compo/wood body, old clothes, etc. Ca. 1909+ $750

14" "118A" Character Baby. Pale bisque head/chubby cheeks, OM/2 upper teeth, large blue glass eyes, blonde mohair wig, bent-limb compo body, old clothes. Mark: "118/A 32." (118 A). Co. 1909+ $2,000

14" "701" Character Boy. "Peter." Celluloid head, CM, ptd blue eyes, blonde HHW, BJ compo body, original striped 2-pc sailor suit with wide collar and belt, hat, etc. Mark: "K (star') R 701 Germany." (In the 1920s Kammer & Reinhardt advertised celluloid versions of their character mold numbers which had been previously reproduced in bisque. Celluloid heads were given 700 numbers to distinguish them.) 1920s $1,400

14-1/4" "131" Googly Girl. Bisque head, watermelon mouth, rosy cheeks, inset round brown glass eyes, blonde mohair wig, BJ compo body, old clothes, etc. Mark: "K (star) R Simon & Halbig 131." Ca. 1914 ....$8,000

(The boy version wears his original sailor suit, cap.)

15" "115" Character Boy Toddler. Solid-dome bisque head, OM, inset blue glass eyes, ptd brown hair, BJ compo

toddler body, original clothes, etc. (This head was inspired by the sculpture created by Flemish artist Francois Duquesnois (1594-1643). He is better known by the name "Fiammingo.") Ca. 1909+ ....$6,500-$7,000

16" "115 A" Toddler Girl. Bisque head/open crown, CM, inset blue glass eyes, brown mohair wig, BJ compo body, original clothes, etc. (This is the female version of the doll head inspired by the early sculpture by Fiammingo. S&H made this head for Kammer & Reinhardt who owned the mold and made the body.) Ca. 1909+ ....$5,500-$6,000

16" "116 A" Toddler Boy. Bisque head, O/C mouth/2 molded teeth, blue glass sleep eyes, blonde HHW, BJ compo toddler body, original white sailor suit, cap, etc. Ca. 1909+ ....$3,500-$4,000

16-1/2" "114" or "Gretchen." Bisque head/sad expression, pouty CM, ptd blue eyes, blonde mohair wig/bangs, BJ compo body, old clothes, etc. Mark: "K (star) 2, 114, 43." Ca. 1912 ....$4,700-$5,000

17" "321" or "Pumpelchen." Celluloid head, O/C mouth/1 upper tooth/tongue, blue glass flirty-sleep eyes, pink cloth body, original cotton fleece 2-pc outfit, bonnet, etc. (Doll has "ma-ma" voice box.) Mark: "K (star) R 32-1/4". Tag reads: "Pumpelchen." Ca. 1910+............$700

17-1/4" "122" Character Baby. Bisque head, OM/spring tongue, brown glass sleep eyes, brown mohair wig, bent-limb compo body, old clothes. Mark: "K (star) R Simon & Halbig 122." Ca. 1909+ ....$1,350+

18" "107" Character Girl. Very pale bisque head/sad face, CM, pale pink cheek blush, ptd blue eyes, blonde HHW, BJ compo body, old clothes, etc. Ca. 1909+...................................$40,000+

18" "114 46" or "Hans." Pale bisque head, pouty CM, shaded blue ptd eyes, light brown mohair wig, BJ compo body, original Scot outfit: black coat, red plaid kilts, cap, plaid border atop stockings, shoes, etc. Mark: "K (star) R 114 46." Ca. 1911 ....$5,500+

18" "115 A" Character Boy Toddler. Bisque head, CM, weighted blue glass eyes, light brown mohair wig, BJ compo/wood body (toddler type), original black wool jacket with tails, trousers, etc. Ca. 1909-11 ....$5,500-$6,000

18" "122" Character Toddler Girl. Bisque head/round chubby face, OM/teeth, brown glass flirty eyes, blonde mohair wig, BJ compo toddler body, old clothes, bonnet, etc. Ca. 1909+ ....$1,500+

18" "246" Girl. Bisque shoulder head (mark "246" in front of plate and "Simon & Halbig K (star) R" in back), OM/teeth, large brown glass sleep eyes, thick dark eyebrows, kid body ("scallops" around chestplate and kid around upper arms)/bisque lower arms, lovely old clothes, etc. Ca. 1888+.......$650-$700

18" "728" Toddler. Celluloid head, OM/2 upper teeth/celluloid tongue, blue glass flirty eyes, ptd/real eyelashes, blonde HHW, compo body/un limbs, original clothes, etc. Head mark: "K (star) R

728, Germany 43-46." Body mark: "K (star) R 7." Ca. 1910+.................$500

19" "117A" or "Hein Liebling." Bisque head, CA, blue glass sleep eyes, brown HHW, BJ compo body, old clothes. Ca. 1912...$5,700

20" "126" Character Baby. Bisque head, OM, blue glass sleep eyes, blonde mohair wig, bent-limb compo baby body, aid clothes, etc. (This doll/mold number was so popular in its day that it was mass-produced to such an extent that it is quite common. Its popularity however, almost obscured the dolls that came later.) 1914-1930 ....$950-$1,000

20" "402" Girl. Bisque head, OM, brown glass flirty eyes, PE, blonde mohair wig, BJ compo body, old clothes, etc. Mark: "K (star) R//402." Ca. 1895-1930s...............................$1,000

22" "104" Character Boy. Bisque head, smiling O/C mouth, ptd blue eyes, brown mohair wig, BJ compo body, old clothes, etc. Ca. 1909+ (Rare) ....$75,000+

22" "106K" or "Heinz." Character Girl. Bisque head, O/C pouty mouth, chubby/rosy cheeks double chin/dimple, blue-grey ptd eyes, brown mohair wig, large ears, BJ compo/wood body, old clothes, etc. Mark: "106K. R53." (Mold number 106 was called "Heinz.")" Ca. 1909-1910 (Rare) ....$75,000+

22" "115A" Character Girl. Bisque head, pouty CM, blue glass sleep eyes, blonde HHW, BJ compo toddler body, original clothes, hat, etc. Mark: "K (star') R, S&H 115A."....$7,000-$7,500

22" "117" Girl. Bisque head, pouty CM, blue glass sleep eyes, blonde HHW, BJ compo body, old clothes, etc. Mark: "K (star) R //S&H//117." Ca. 1909 ....$6,800-$7,200

22" "127" Character Boy. Bisque head, OM/2 upper teeth, blue glass sleep eyes, blonde ptd/molded hair, molded ears, chubby 5-pc compo toddler body, old clothes, etc. Ca. 1909+ ....$1,900-$2,100

22" "151" Character Boy. Bisque head, OM/6 teeth, ptd blue eyes, round dimpled chin, molded ears, brown HHW, BJ compo body, original clothes. (Modeled from life: Reinhardt's nephew.) Ca. 1909+...$900

22" "192" Girl. Bisque head, OM/teeth, blue glass sleep eyes, pale blonde mohair wig, PE, BJ compo body, old clothes, etc. Ca. 1886-95 ....$1.600-$1,800

(Another original version of Carl wears original wool jacket, knickers, etc.)

23" " 121" Character Girl. Pale bisque head/full cheeks/slight double chin, OM/4 upper teeth/spring tongue, brown glass sleep eyes, brown HHW, bent-limb compo body, old clothes. Ca. 1910+...........................$1,500-$1,700

23" "107" or "Carl." Bisque head, CM, ptd blue intaglio eyes, blonde wig (sits atop head in a "country bumpkin" style), well-modeled ears, BJ compo body, original clothes: too short jacket, too short trousers, long socks, laced shoes, Mark: "K (star) R//107//54." (Sold for...$40,700 at auction in 1989.) $55,000+

Chapter 20

JOHANNES DANIEL
~ KESTNER ~

History: 1816-1930s

Johannes Daniel Kestner, Jr., Waltershausen, Thuringia, Germany, official of Saxony, and founder of the Waltershausen doll and toy industry. Kestner, Jr., opened a small business in 1805, where he turned wooden buttons and toys on a lathe and made papier-mâché slates. Wooden dolls were advertised in 1816, and papier-mâché dolls were advertised with ladies' apparel in 1823. The Kestners not only made dolls' heads and parts, but leather bodies, and dressed dolls.

In 1824, Kestner, Jr. built a larger building and employed locals, which was a boon to the area. When wax dolls became popular he dipped his papier-mâché heads and added them to his growing line of toys. By the 1850s Kestner, Jr. was buying china-heads and parts and attaching them to his fine muslin bodies. Kestner, Jr. died in 1858 or 1859, and the following year his widow purchased a porcelain plant in nearby Ohrdruf, which she and the deputy directors managed and operated.

In 1872, the grandson, Adolf Kestner, took control of the factory. By that time, the Kestner bisque formula and techniques had been developed and they were manufacturing their own dolls' heads, parts, and bodies. These unmarked dolls can be identified by the parian whiteness and smoothness of the bisque and painting or technical skills. Kestner, like Simon & Halbig, produced parians with fancy, molded hairdos. The bisque quality of the latter firm was more "oily" and the heads more highly tinted.

The decades from 1870 to 1890s proved to be the most profitable for Kestner & Co. They manufactured more dolls than any other company and boasted the greatest variety. Kestner was the "Jumeau" of Germany, his only rivals in his own country being Simon & Halbig and Armand Marseille, who only made dolls' heads and parts - no complete dolls. The popularity of the Bébé Jumeau in the 1870s, inspired the Kestner children of the 1880s. Kestner had not been above emulating the French poupées, but neither had the French been above emulating him. Some Jumeaux not only possess the Kestner bisque quality, but the Kestner techniques. C'est la vie.

Collecting Hints:

Although J.D. Kestner Company made dolls of wood and papier-mâché before venturing into the glazed and unglazed bisque medium, it is his chalk-white and satin-smooth bisque of the "parian" dolls that influenced the color and texture of the later Kestner child dolls. Before the 1890 Tariff Act, Section 6, which stipulated that on or after March 1, 1891, all articles of foreign manufacture "had to be marked by the country of origin, etc." Imported dolls were unmarked by maker and country, and only a few bore an incised mold number, hence, when one comes across such a doll, one must scrutinize it carefully and search for tell-tale signs of its manufacture (every top doll company had its own individual style, although a lot of pirating was going on). Consciously or unconsciously, the old German and French manufacturers left an indelible mark on their dolls, and this can be seen not only in the sculpture, but in the painting technique and bisque or china quality. This is what a collector must seek. Jumeau, for instance, pierced his doll's ears, Kestner did not, but there are Kestners made for other companies or the French market, that had pierced ears. Other Kestner traits to look for are these: bisque color and texture; chubby faces with dimples and double chins and rolls of baby fat on the nape of neck; the delicate shading of lips, cheeks and eyes; the long sweeping light brown eye-

19" "171" incised Kestner child, bisque head, OM/teeth, brown glass eyes, blonde HHW, BJ compo body, dressed by Virginia Yates. 1892 $900-$1,000. (Courtesy of Virginia Yates)

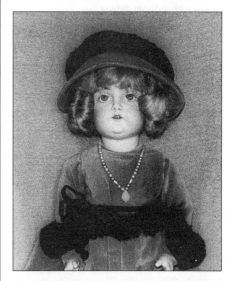

21-1/2" "1 Made in Germany 13" marked girl, OM/teeth, blue glass sleep eyes, blonde HHW, BJ compo body, old velvet outfit, hat, etc. 1892 $1,000-$1,200. (Courtesy of Herron)

brows with feathered edges and the straight bottoms; mohair wigs, also wigs of human hair and sheepskin (on babies); grey or blue-grey glass eyes, also threaded eyes, and French paper-weight eyes on "French" dolls; turned heads, plaster domes; small ears and small eyes (an enlarged eye socket changed the entire face of a doll, giving it a "French" persona); chunky, custom-made, high-quality bodies.

Eyebrows were given a glossy glaze to accentuate them. Nostril openings have a tiny red dot, as do eye corners; usually the same color as the lips. Early kid bodies were gusseted (some with cloth lower legs), next came the kid body with the "hinged" joint which was more pricey. (Ne Plus Ultra, 1883+.) The Universal joint was used after 1895 on the knees and elbows; Ne Plus Ultra joint used for the hips. The EXCELSIOR jointed composition body was patented by Kestner in1892. (The Ne Plus Ultra joint is also called the rivet hip joint or swivel joint. Sara Robinson patented the Ne Plus Ultra joint in the U.S.A. in 1883.)

Early Kestners are found with the straight wrists, which is also found on early French dolls. We find a particular head made for a socket remodeled to form a shoulder head, or a bald head sculpted for a wig remodeled with a molded hairdo. Kestner not only used Jumeau molds and incised his name on them, but made heads for Jumeau with the Jumeau stamp. He borrowed from Schmidt, Bru, and Thuillier, but always with good taste and flair. Today Kestner dolls are priceless collector items.

Reproduction Alert:

The dolls made by the J.D. Kestner firm in Germany have been reproduced in the United States and abroad. These modern Kestner dolls, for the most part, have been expertly duplicated and signed by the maker. Frauds have also been expertly reproduced with the original Kestner markings left intact on the back of the doll's head or shoulder plate. The latter types are the ones a collector must be wary about.

Study the painting of the eyebrows, eyelashes and lips. Careless painting is easy to detect, artistic painting is not. Look inside the doll's head. If the bisque has been colored, it is a reproduction. Old bisque was white. Modern bisque is more perfect than the old. Old bisque is dirt pitted, the inside of the head looks dirty. The old dolls (in the larger sizes) never had bisque bodies. This would make them too heavy for shipment. Old composition bodies re-veal wear around the joints, fingers, and toes, and are usually chipping and cracking. New bodies are painted with latex and don't feel as solid as the old. Remember: popular dolls are always the most copied. Beware of baby dolls and character types, especially.

J.D. KESTNER

7"-8" "155" incised Girl. Bisque head/slim cheek line, OM/teeth, blue glass sleep eyes, blonde mohair wig, compo body/pegged arms/knee jts, original white linen dress, bonnet, etc. Ca. 1892.....................................$900-$950

7" "143" incised Girl. Bisque head, OM/teeth, inset brown glass eyes, blonde mohair wig, compo body/peg jts. at sh/ball - jts. at hips/knees, original clothes, etc. Early 1890s.....$800-$825

9" "134" incised Negro Girl. Black bisque head, OM/teeth, large dark brown glass sleep eyes, black curly wig, black BJ compo body, old clothes, etc. Ca. 1920's $1,000

10" "143" incised Girl. Bisque head, OM/teeth, blue glass sleep eyes, blonde mohair wig, compo body/peg jts. at sh/ball, jts. at hips/knees, original clothes, etc. Mark: "B Germany 3 143." Early 1890s...................$1,000-$1,100

11" (8-1/2" cir. head) "K" incised "Century" Baby. Bisque head, CM, brown glass sleep eyes, brown ptd/mld hair, rosy cheeks, cloth body/compo hands, old baby dress, bonnet. Mark: "K (in a dia-

27" "164" incised Kestner child, bisque head, OM/teeth, brown glass eyes, brown wig, BJ compo body, dressed by Virginia Yates. 1892 $1,200-$1,300. (Courtesy of Virginia Yates)

mond-shaped design) Century Doll Co.", NYC (used Kestner heads). Ca. 1925....................................$600-$650

11" "5" incised Girl. Bisque head/long face, CM, large blue PW eyes, blonde mohair wig, BJ compo body/straight wrists, original clothes, etc. Ca. 1880...$2,500

26" "140" incised Kestner child, bisque head, OM/teeth, blue glass eyes, blonde HHW, BJ compo body, dressed by Virginia Yates. $1,200-$1,300. (Courtesy of Virginia Yates)

11" 7" incised J.D.K Baby. Solid-dome bisque head (face similar to baby incised "14"), O/C mouth/molded tongue, small blue ptd eyes/black eye liner/ red eye liner, well-modeled ears, ptd blonde hair, bent-limb compo body, original factory-made dress, etc. 1910+.................................$750-$800

12" "186" incised Character Girl. Bisque head (slimmer cheeks than most character types), O/C mouth/6 mld teeth (uppers)/slightly smiling expression, brown ptd eyes, brown mohair wig, BJ compo body, old clothes, etc. 1909+ ....$2,000-$2,500

12" "184" incised Character Girl. Bisque head, CM, blue ptd eyes, brown mohair wig (center part, coiled braids above ears), BJ compo body, original checkered woolen dress, etc. Ca. 1920 ....$2,000-$2,500

12" "190" incised Character Girl. Bisque head (round pretty face), O/C mouth/mld tongue/mld teeth, blue ptd eyes, brown mohair wig, BJ compo body, old clothes, bonnet, etc. 1909+...........................$2,000-$2,500

12" "B6" incised Negro Girl. Black bisque head/chubby cheeks, OM/teeth, brown glass sleep eyes, black mohair wig (curly), BJ black compo body, old white cotton dress, etc. Ca. 1890s ....$1,400-$1,500

12-1/2" "143" incised Girl. Bisque head, OM/teeth, brown glass sleep eyes, brown HHW, BJ compo body, old clothes. Early 1890s..................$1,200

12-1/2" "260" incised Character Baby. Bisque head, OM/4 upper teeth, blue glass sleep eyes, lt brown eyebrows, well-modeled ears, rosy cheeks, brown HHW, bent-limb compo body, old clothes. Mark: "Made in Germany

22" "195" incised Kestner child. Bisque shoulder head, OM/teeth, brown glass eyes, brown HHW, inserted fur eyebrows, kid body/bisque lower arms/crown label on chest, old clothes, hat, etc. 1910+ $750-$850. (Courtesy of Herron)

J.D.K. 260." 1910+ ....$850-$900

13-1/2" "171" incised Girl. Bisque head, OM/4 teeth, blue glass sleep eyes, brown mohair wig, BJ compo body/toes outlined in red, old clothes. Mark: "A Germany 5 171." Ca. 1892 .$750-$850

14" "260" incised "Flapper." Bisque head/ruddy complexion, OM/teeth, brown glass flirty eyes, short brown curly wig, unusual compo body (long and slim with jts. above rouged knees/no ankle jts), original factory dress, etc. Late 1920s/early 1930s ....$1,200-$1,500

15" "234" incised Character Baby. Solid-dome head/double chin, large uneven ears, OM/2 teeth, small brown sleep eyes, blonde ptd hair/mld forelock/blonde ptd eyebrows/eyelashes, kid body, rivet jts, compo lower limbs/bent left arm/crown and streamers chest label, original factory-made clothes. (This doll has a rare shoulder head and unusually constructed kid body. Not a popular doll at the time, it is infrequently found nowadays.) Rare. 1910+ Mark: "J.D.K. 234".........$1,250

15" "4" incised Girl. Pale bisque head/"mumps" cheeks, O/C mouth/white line, blue glass sleep eyes, blonde mohair wig, kid body/bisque lower arms, old clothes, Mark: "a Germany 4." 1880s ....$800-$850

15" "5" incised Girl. Pale bisque shoulder head/long face, CM, grey glss sleep eyes, brown HHW, long kid body, long limbs/bisque lower arms, old clothes. 1880s ....$1,000-$1,200

15-1/2" "Bru" type Girl. Bisque/fat cheeks, O/C mouth/mid teeth, blonde mohair wig, plaster dome, BJ compo body/jtd ankles, old clothes, etc. 1880 ....$3,500-$4,000

16" "J.D.K." incised Baby. Solid-dome bisque head, O/C mouth, brown glass sleep eyes, rosy cheeks, blonde ptd hair/molded forelock, well-shaped kid body/rivet jts/compo lower limbs, original factory-made clothes, etc. (This baby appears to be a later, cheaper-priced doll.) Back stamp reads: "D.R.G.M. 442910." 1910+ .$700-$750

16" "169" incised Character Girl. Very pale bisque head, CM, large almond-shaped grey glass/sleep eyes, pastel pink cheek blush, brown mohair wig, plaster dome, BJ compo body (EXCELSIOR stamp), old clothes, etc. Mark: "B1/2 Made in Germany 61/2 169." Ca. 1892+ ....$2,500-$2,700

16" "247" incised Character Baby. Bisque head/chubby cheeks/double chin/dimples, OM/2 upper teeth/tongue, large brown glass sleep eyes, brown mohair wig, bent-limb compo body, original baby clothes, 1910+ $2,300

16" "G" incised Girl. Bisque turned shoulder head, CM, blue glass sleep eyes, blonde mohair wig, kid body/bisque lower arms, old clothes, hat, etc. Mark: "Made in Germany G." Early 1890s ....$1,000-$1,200

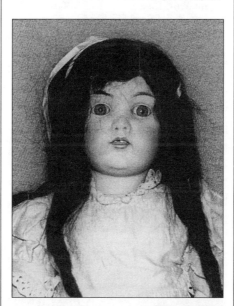

28" "214" incised Character Girl by Kestner. Bisque head, OM/teeth (1 tooth missing in front to give doll realism), blue glass sleep eyes, original brown HHW, BJ compo body, old clothes, etc. 1892 $1,000-$1,200. (Courtesy of Herron)

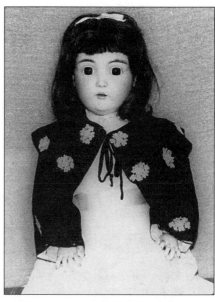

24-1/2" "171" incised Kestner. Pale bisque head, OM/teeth, large brown glass eyes, brown HHW, BJ compo body, original clothes, cape, shoes, socks. 1892 $1,100-$1,300. (Courtesy of Herron)

16" "J.D.K." incised Character Boy. Toddler. Bisque head, OM/teeth, blue glass sleep eyes, brown skin wig, BJ compo body, original shirt, knee-length striped trousers, stockings, shoes, blue neckerchief, white cap. Mark: "J.D.K." Ca. 1912..............................$1,000-$1,100

16" "X1" incised Girl. Early pale bisque head, small CM, blue glass sleep eyes, heavy dark eyebrows, blonde mohair wig, plaster dome, BJ compo body/straight wrists, old clothes, etc. 1880... $3,600

17" "128" incised Character Girl. Pale bisque head, CM, blue glass sleep eyes, brown mohair wig, plaster dome, thick brown eyebrows, BJ compo body, EXCELSIOR mark, old clothes, etc. (The EXCELSIOR mark is common to Kestner dolls. Kestner patented his EXCELSIOR jointed composition bodies in 1892.) Ca. 1892+......$2,500-$2,700

17" "237/245" incised Hilda Baby. Solid-dome bisque head, OM/teeth, blue glass sleep eyes, blonde mohair wig, bent-limb compo body, old clothes, etc. Ca. 1914+.....................$4,500-$4,900

17" "257" incised "Dolly face" Baby. Bisque head/round face/slim cheeks, lovely OM/2 upper teeth, brown glass sleep eyes, brown mohair wig, bent-limb compo body, old clothes, etc. (This appears to be a later doll, both in modernized modelling technique and facial coloring.) Ca. 1920-1932 ....$1,000-$1,100

18" "129" incised Girl. Very pale bisque head (size G 11), OM/teeth, pastel pink cheek blush, blue glass sleep eyes, brown mohair wig, BJ compo body, original clothes, etc. 1892 ....$1,200-$1,350

18" "143" incised Character Girl. Bisque head/bulbous cheeks, OM/teeth, large blue glass sleep eyes, blonde mohair wig, BJ compo body with EXCELSIOR mark, old clothes, etc. (Resembles a Drayton character.) Early 1890s ....$1,350-$1,400

18" "144" incised Girl. Bisque head, OM/4 upper teeth, brown glass sleep eyes, brown mohair wig, BJ compo body, old clothes, etc. 1892......................$1,100

18" "148" incised Girl. Pale bisque shoulder head, OM/4 teeth, blue glass sleep eyes, auburn mohair wig, kid body/bisque hands/cloth legs, old clothes. Mark: "148" and low on shoulder plate: "Made in Germany" 1892+ ....$600-$650

23" (23) "154" incised Kestner girl. Bisque shoulder head, OM/teeth, blue glass sleep eyes, blonde mohair wig, kid body/bisque lower arms, redressed, $700-$750. (Courtesy of Irene Ortega)

18" "162" incised Lady. Bisque head (resembles a child), OM/4 upper teeth, blue glass sleep eyes, blonde mohair wig, BJ compo body/long limbs mld bosom/wasp waist round stomach, original clothes, hat, etc. Mark: "Made in Germany 8.162." 1910+ $2,500-$2,700

18" "171" incised "Daisy." Bisque head, OM/4 teeth, blue glass sleep eyes, blonde mohair wig, BJ compo body, original, clothes, etc. (This mold "171" was used for the famous "Daisy" doll in the LADIES HOME JOURNAL "Lettie Lane" paper doll series, 1911. It is common, but desirable, with a slimmer, expressive face.) Ca. 1911 ....$1,200

18" "172" incised Gibson Girl. Bisque shoulder head, CM, blue glass sleep eyes, original mohair wig, kid body/bisque lower arms, original clothes, hat, etc. Ca. 1910 ....$3,600

18" "214" incised Character Girl. Bisque head/round full face double chin, OM/4 teeth/tongue, brown glass sleep eyes, brown HHW, BJ compo body, old clothes, etc. 1892................$750-$850

18" "226" incised Character Baby. Bisque head/bulbous lower cheeks, OM/2 upper teeth, small blue glass sleep eyes, brown mohair wig, bent-limb compo body, original clothes, etc. (This is still

another version of mold 211.) 1910+ ....$1,000-$1,100

18" "J.D.K." incised Baby. Solid-dome bisque head (similar to 211 mold), O/C mouth, blue glass sleep eyes, ptd blonde hair/mld forelock, bent-limb compo body, original baby clothes, etc. 1910+..................................$850-$950

18-1/2" "169" incised Girl. Bisque head, CM, brown glass sleepeyes, black mohair wig, BJ compo body, old clothes, etc. 1880 ....$2,700-$2,800

19" "10" incised Girl. Bisque head/square cheeks, CM, blue glass sleep eyes, blonde mohair wig, BJ compo body, original clothes, etc. 1880 ....$3,200-$3,500

19" "143" incised Boy. Bisque head, OM/teeth, brown glass sleep eyes, brown HHW, BJ compo body, old 2-pc suit, long black stockings, leather shoes, etc. Incised: "G Germany 143". Early 1890s...................$1,500-$1,600

19" "149" incised Girl. Bisque head (resembles mold 143), OM/teeth, large blue glass sleep eyes, blonde mohair wig, BJ compo body, old clothes, etc. 1892+............................$1,250-$1,400

19" "160" incised Girl. Pale bisque head, OM/4 teeth, blue-grey glass sleep eyes, brown mohair wig, lt brown curved eyebrows, BJ compo body, old clothes. (Except for the fine bisque quality, this doll does not have the familiar "Kestner" persona or "look"; just another "dolly" face.) 1890s+.... $1,350

19" "167" incised Girl. Bisque head/pert expression, OM/4 teeth, large blue-grey glass/sleep eyes, blonde mohair wig, BJ compo body, old clothes, etc. 1892..................................$950-$1,050

19" "174" incised Girl. Bisque head, tiny OM/4 teeth, large brown glass sleep eyes, brown mohair wig, BJ compo body, old clothes, etc. Scarce mold number. 1892................$1,300-$1,500

19-1/4" "13" incised Girl. Bisque head, CM, rosy cheeks, blue PW eyes, long brown

29" "146" incised Character Kestner. Bisque head, OM/teeth, blue glass sleep eyes, brown HHW, BJ compo body, old clothes, etc. 1892 $1,500-$1,700. (Courtesy of Herron)

eyebrows with straight bottoms, short upper/lower eyelashes, blonde mohair wig, BJ compo body/straight wrists, old whitework dress, etc. (Same as mold "X1" 15-1/4") 1880 ....$3,800-$4,000

20" "1/13" incised Girl. Bisque head, OM/teeth, blue glass sleep eyes, blonde HHW, BJ compo body, old blue velvet dress trimmed with fur, matching hat, original underwear, leather shoes, stockings. 1892 Mark: "1 made in Ger-

17" Early unmarked Kestner, pale bisque shoulder head, CM, brown glass sleep eyes, blonde mohair wig (new), kid body/bisque lower arms, redressed. 1880s $1,100-$1,200. (Courtesy of Ruby Ellen Smith)

many 13".......................$1,000-$1,200

20" "154" incised Girl. Pale bisque shoulder head, OM/teeth, brown glass sleep eyes, blonde mohair wig, kid body/rivet jts, bisque lower arms, old white brocade wedding gown, etc. Mark: "Dep 7 154" and low on shoulder plate: "Made in Germany." 1892............$650-$750+

20" "195" incised Girl. Bisque head/double chin, OM/4 upper teeth, inset blue glass eyes, inserted brown fur eyebrows, brown mohair wig, kid body/rivet jts, bisque lower arms, Kestner crown and streamers label on stomach, old yellow dress with brown velvet ribbon trim, matching bonnet, etc. 1910+ ....$700-$750

20" "211" incised Character Baby. Pale bisque head/chubby, expressive face/double chin, O/C mouth, blue glass sleep eyes, blonde mohair wig, plaster dome, bent-limb compo body (highest quality), original clothes. (This face is prettier than some of the other 211 babies.) 1910+.......$1,100-$1,350

20" "263" incised "Catterfelder Puppenfabrik" Baby. Bisque head, OM/teeth, wobbly tongue, brown HHW, bent-limb compo body, old clothes, etc. Mark: "CP//263//50//Made in Germany." Catterfelder Puppenfabrik, Catterfelder,

26" "166" incised Kestner, bisque shoulder head/Kestner crown on breastplate, OM/teeth, blue glass sleep eyes, blonde wig, kid body/bisque lower arms/"Florodora" label on body (body is original. Borgfeldt registered this trademark; using heads made by various companies), original clothes, etc. 1901-1909+ $1,000-$1,100. (Courtesy of D. Kay Crow)

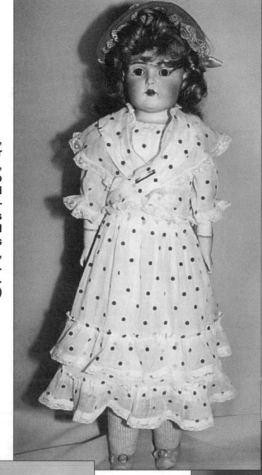

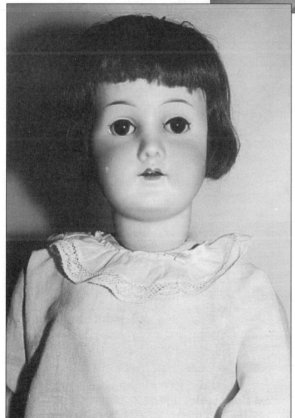

22" "B5" marked Kestner. Bisque head, small OM/teeth, brown glass sleep eyes, brown HHW, BJ compo body, old clothes. $900-$1,000. (Courtesy of D. Kay Crow)

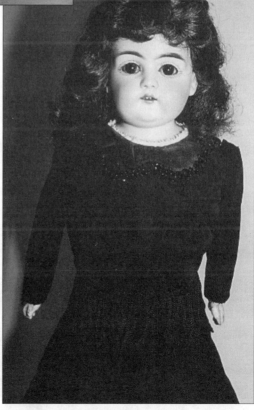

16" "Kestner 147" marked girl. Bisque shoulder head, OM/teeth, brown glass sleep eyes, brown wig, kid body/bisque lower arms, redressed. $600-$650. (Courtesy of D. Kay Crow)

20" "DEP 7-1/2 195" marked Kestner. Bisque shoulder/head, OM/teeth, blue glass sleep eyes, inserted fur eyebrows, brown HHW, kid body/bisque lower arms, old clothes. 1910+ $700-$750. (Courtesy D. Kay Crow)

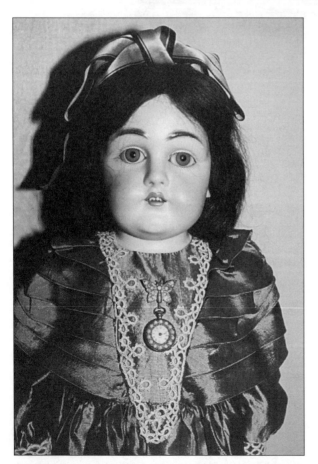

14" "Germany C 2/O" incised Kestner boy, original clothes, etc. 1892 $800. (Courtesy of D. Kay Crow)

30" "Kestner 154" marked girl. Bisque shoulder head, OM/teeth, blue glass sleep eyes, brown HHW, kid body/bisque lower arms, old clothes. $1,300-$1,500. (Courtesy of D. Kay Crow)

Thur., Germany. (Kestner made some of the heads used on their dolls.) 1910+ ....$1,000-$1,150

20" "263" incised Character Baby. Bisque head/round face/chubby cheeks/fat creases, OM/2 upper teeth/tongue, blue glass sleep eyes, blonde mohair wig, bent-limb compo body, old clothes, etc. Ca 1920s $1,100

21" "281" incised "Ma-Ma" doll. Bisque shoulder head, tiny OM/4 tiny teeth, blue sleep eyes, rosy cheeks, blonde HHW, cloth body/voice box, original factory-made clothes, bonnet, etc. Mark: "CENTURY DOLL CO."; CDC NYC, 1909+. (Used Kestner heads). 1920s ....$800-$850

22" "154" incised Girl. Bisque head, OM/teeth, large brown glass sleep eyes, brown mohair wig, kid body/UNI-VERSAL knee-jts, old clothes, etc. Ca. 1895+ (This is a rather common, but very popular mold number and a very lovely face.) ....$800-$850

32" "O Made in Germany" marked Kestner. Bisque head, OM/teeth, blue glass sleep eyes, brown mohair wig, pink kid body, old clothes, etc. 1892 $1,500. (Courtesy of Irene Ortega)

22" "166" incised Girl. Bisque shoulder head, OM/teeth, brown glass sleep eyes, blonde mohair wig, gusseted kid body/bisque hands and wrists old clothes, hat, etc. Scarce mold number. 1892 ....$700-$750

22" "195" incised Girl. Bisque shoulder head, OM/4 teeth, blue glass sleepeyes/real hair lashes, inserted brown fur eyebrows, brown mohair wig, kid body/rivet jts, old clothes, etc. Kestner crown and streamers label on stomach. 1910+ ....$750-$850

22" "214" incised Girl. Bisque head, OM/teeth, brown glass sleep eyes,

brown HHW, BJ compo body, old clothes. Ca. 1892................$800-$850

22" "215" incised Girl. Bisque head/round full face similar to mold 214, OM/teeth, large blue glass sleep eyes/real eyelashes/fur eyebrows, brown HHW, BJ compo body, old clothes, etc. 1910+ ....$900-$1,000

22" "262" incised Character Baby Girl. Bisque head/round face/cheek dimples/fat creases, OM/2 upper teeth, large brown glass sleep eyes, brown mohair wig, bent-limb jtd compo body, original factory dress, bonnet, etc. Ca. 1920s ....$1,000-$1,200

22" "H" incised Girl. Pale bisque turned head on a deep shoulder plate, OM/4 upper teeth, blue glass sleep eyes, brown HHW, original cloth body/leather arms/sewn-on leather boots, old clothes, etc. Ca. 1890s .$1,350-$1,400

22" "R.3-5B" incised Girl. Bisque head/very pretty face, OM/4 upper teeth, blue glass sleep eyes, kid body/bisque lower arms, old clothes. Made by Kestner for R. Backhausen, Berlin, Germany. Ca. 1890s ....$900-$1,000

22-1/2" "15" incised Pouty Girl. Very pale bisque head, CM, brown glass sleep eyes, dark brown mohair wig, BJ compo body/straight wrists, old French-style clothes, frilly bonnet, etc. (Called the "Schmitt/Schmidt" Kestner by collectors, it actually resembles a "Jumeau".) Ca. 1880.................$4,000

23" "B.5" incised Girl. Bisque head, OM/teeth, blue glass sleep eyes, blonde mohair wig, BJ compo body, old clothes, etc. Mark: "B.5/Germany Ca. 1896-1916.....................$1,200-$1,500

23" "15" incised Girl. Fine quality bisque head, tiny CM, (mouth ptd a lt pink with a darker shade of pink liner), almond-shaped blue glass sleep eyes, brown HHW, unpierced ears, pale pink cheek blush, roll of nape fat, BJ compo body/straight wrists, original silk dress, etc. (Made for the French trade.) Ca. 1885...$4,000

23-1/4" "128" incised Girl. Pale bisque socket head/deeply mld shoulder-plate/long face, CM, pale pink cheek blush, inset blue PW eyes, original cloth body/bisque lower arms, original white linen dress, etc. (Exquisite doll with a soulful, sad expression.) 1880..............................$3,500-$3,800

24" "164" incised Girl. Bisque head, OM/teeth, blue glass sleep eyes, long curl brown mohair wig, BJ compo body, old clothes, etc. Ca. 1892 ....$1,100-$1,300

24" "168" incised Girl. Bisque head, OM/4 teeth, large blue glass eyes (sleep), thick eyebrows, brown mohair wig, BJ compo body, old clothes, etc. (Scarce mold number). 1892+..........$850-$950

24" "196" incised Girl. Bisque head, OM/teeth, blue-grey glass sleep eyes, real eyelashes, blonde mohair wig, inserted fur eyebrows, BJ compo body, old clothes. (Dolls with fur eyebrows intact are scarce and choice collectibles.) 1910+..................................$900-$950

24" "260" incised Character Girl. Toddler. Bisque head/chubby cheeks/double chin, OM/4 upper teeth, large brown

glass sleep eyes, blonde "bobbed" mohair wig, BJ compo body, original factory-made clothes, hat, etc. (This late Kestner has the persona and clothing style popular in the 1920s.) Head mark: "JDK 260"; Neck mark; "Made in Germany 62." Ca. 1925-1932 ....$1,200-$1,300

24" "J.D.K." incised Character Baby. Pale bisque head, OM/2 teeth/movable tongue, well-modelled ears, brown glass sleep eyes, blonde ptd hair, bent-limb jtd compo body, old clothes. Mark: "J.D.K." 1910+ ....$1,600-$1,800

32" "Germany" marked early Kestner, pale bisque turned shoulder head, blue glass sleep eyes, blonde mohair wig, kid body/bisque lower arms, redressed $1,500. (Courtesy of D. Kay Crow)

Close-up of above doll.

24-1/2" "171" incised Girl. Bisque head, OM/4 upper teeth, brown glass sleep eyes, dimpled chin, brown HHW, BJ compo body, original whitework dress with lace inserts, black silk cape, pink beribboned underwear, old leather shoes, knit socks. 1892.$1,100-$1,300

25" "226" incised Baby. Bisque head, OM/2 upper teeth/wobble blonde skin wig, brown glass sleep eyes, bent-limb jtd compo body, old clothes, etc. Mark: "J.D.K. 226." 1910+.......$1,600-$1,900

25" "J.D.K. 20" incised Baby. Bisque head, OM/2 lower teeth, blue glass sleep eyes, blonde ptd/molded hairdo/brush-strokes, bent-limb jtd compo body, original baby gown. (This is the 1910-1912 largest size of this Kestner mold.) 1910-12..........................$1,700$1,900

25" "K" incised Girl. Pale bisque turned shoulder head, OM/square-cut teeth, blue glass sleep eyes, brown mohair wig, plaster dome, pink kid body/bisque lower arms, old clothes, etc. (Turned head Kestners were made with both open and closed mouths and are found on bodies of kid or cloth. They are usually incised with letters of the alphabet or unmarked.) Ca. 1890s
....$1,700-$1,800

25" "O" incised Character Bebe. Pale bisque turned shoulder head, CM, pastel pink cheek blush, large almond-shaped brown glass eyes, thick brown eyebrows, dark brown HHW, plaster dome, gusseted kid

body/bisque lower arms, old silk dress, hat, etc. (This doll has a "Jumeau" face.) Ca. 1880s ....$1,700-$1,750

26-1/2" "245" incised Hilda Baby. Solid-dome bisque head, OM/2 teeth, brown glass sleep eyes, brown HHW, bent-limb jtd compo body, old clothes, etc. 1910+ ....$7,000-$8,000

27" "143" incised Character Girl. Bisque head, OM/teeth, blue glass sleep eyes, brown HHW, BJ compo body, old clothes, etc. (Rare size for this model.) Early 1890s...................$1,900-$2,000

27" "164" incised Girl. Bisque head, OM/teeth, brown glass sleep eyes, blonde HHW, BJ compo body, old clothes, etc. 1892..........$1,200-$1,400

28" "211" incised Character Baby. Solid-dome bisque head, O/C mouth/teeth, blue glass sleep eyes, blonde mohair wig, bent-limb jtd compo body, old clothes, etc. Mark: "Made in Germany 20//211 JDK." 1910+
......................................$2,000-$2,200

28" "214" incised Character Girl. Bisque head, OM/3 upper teeth (this model would ordinarily have 4 upper teeth, but one tooth is deliberately missing, giving the doll a realistic look and more character), large blue glass sleep eyes, original long curl brown HHW, BJ compo body, old ivory cream brocade dress, old underclothes, shoes, socks. 1892..............................$1,000-$1,200

28" "260" incised Character Girl. Toddler. Bisque head/round chubby face/double chin, OM/4 teeth/molded tongue, brown glass sleep eyes, blonde HHW, Bj compo toddler body, old clothes, etc. 1909+...........................$1,700-$1,800

28" "Dainty Dorothy." Bisque head, OM/4 teeth, blue glass sleep eyes, blonde sausage curl mohair wig, kid body/bisque lower arms, old ivory silk dress trimmed with lace, etc. 1910+
......................................$1,100-$1,200

29" "Dolly face" Girl. Bisque shoulder head, OM/teeth, blue glass sleep eyes, brown mohair wig, inserted fur eyebrows, kid body/rivet jts, bisque lower arms, old clothes, etc. (Kestner crown and streamers label on chest.) 1910+
......................................$1,200-$1,300

32" "164" incised Girl. Bisque head, OM/4 teeth, blue glass sleepy eyes, blonde HHW, BJ compo body, old clothes, etc. Red stamp on upper hip reads: "Excelsior Germany 7." Head mark: "Made in//17 1/2 Germany 16/2//164." Ca. 1904.............................$1,600-$1,800

32" "196" incised Girl. Bisque head, OM/teeth, blue glass sleep eyes, blonde HHW, BJ compo body, old clothes, etc. 1892+ ....$1,200-$1,300

33" "171" incised Girl. Bisque head, OM/teeth, blue glass sleep eyes, brown HHW, BJ compo body, old clothes, etc. 1892 Mark: "Made in 76-1/2 Germany 16-1/2 171 N."...............$1,600-$2,000

Chapter 21

KEWPIES

History: 1913+

Rose O'Neill, born: June 25, 1874; died 1944; father, William Patrick O'Neill; mother, Alice Asenath Cecilia Smith. Rose O'Neill was born in Emerald Cottage, Meade Street, Wilkes Barre, PA, in 1874. Although Rose only lived briefly in Emerald Cottage, the octagonal living room had a motif of cupids and wreaths of roses. Whether this left an impression on her young mind is not known, but she often dreamt of cupids in later years. (In the Victorian era cupids adorned everything.) Needless to say, her drawing ability sprang forth at age seven, and, despite her father's eager attempts to make an actress of her, Rose was determined to be an artist on paper only. (She appeared briefly on stage at seventeen, but when the tour ended she was offered an illustrative assignment by the *Chicago Juvenile Magazine*.) In 1905, Rose illustrated an advertisement for the Folding Brownie Camera by Eastman Kodak Company, which appeared in 30 November issue of *Youth's Companion*. The baby in the illustration was inspired by her baby brother and looks very much like her "Kewpies" which would make their debut four years later.

Bonniebrook in Branson, MO was also a source of inspiration for Rose's art. It burnt in 1947, three years after Rose's death, as though fate had stepped in to obliterate her memory, but collectors deemed otherwise. At the turn of the century, tourists were drawn to Lake Taneycomo in Branson for its water sports and fishing. Today the Shepherd of the Hills Pageant, Silver Dollar theme park, and the country-western live theatre district attracts even more tourists to the small town of Branson. In 1966, Pearl Hodges founded an organization to preserve the works of Rose O'Neill. This celebration was called "Rose O'Neill Days (April 1 to April 8, 1967). This local group expanded to become the International Rose O'Neill Club. Rose is buried at Bonniebrook in a private cemetery where five other family members repose.

Collecting Hints:

In the 1960s, when the price of dolls was beginning to escalate to a noticeable degree, dealers vied with each other in setting doll prices. Kewpie dolls (the bisque variety) were becoming very popular and sought after, thus it was decided that they should be priced at $10 per inch! The majority of collectors complained at so heady a price for something so common and easily found. Today tiny Action Kewpies cost hundreds of dollars and a 12" size is worth over $1,500! Are we all mad or do we simply have too much money? A Kewpie Mountain, all-bisque, sold at auction for $17,000 in 1991. It was adorned by 23 Action Kewpies, a Doodledog, and a parrot. Only four were made, they said. The question in the minds of many is a simple one: "Will this Kewpie mania continue to endure the years? Or will tomorrow's youth turn a cold shoulder?" After all, they played with Miss Piggy! Rare Kewpie items, like perfume bottles, candy containers, banks, etc., are eagerly desired, as are all Kewpies in mint or near mint condition—and signed.

15" Compo "Scootles", redressed, by Cameo, NYC. 1922+ $750 (Courtesy of Ruby Ellen Smith).

Reproduction Alert:

Bisque Kewpies and Scootles were reproduced in their day and in our day. The Japanese bisque is usually coarser than that made in Germany. But there have been reproductions of Kewpie made in Germany in the 1950s and these are of superior quality--and sold as "old" types. Some reproductions were sold unmarked, others incised with the Rose O'Neill signature. Always look for wear when examining an old doll; ingrained dust and dirt are other signs of old bisque; oil from the hands can permanently soil a doll. When in doubt about a high-priced doll--don't buy it!

KEWPIES

3-1/2" Kewpie Perfume Bottle. All ptd. bisque/arms at sides/together legs, watermelon mouth, brown ptd. eyes to side, orange ptd. hair/topknot/cork at rear of head. (Resembles a doll.) (Sold for $1,800 in 1997) .... $700+

3-1/2" Kewpie Huggars. All bisque/ptd features.................................... $250-$300

4-1/4" Kewpie Farmer. Action Figure. All-bisque/no movable jts/together legs/1 arm behind back/1 arm stretched forward with a hole in the first (to hold a pitchfork)/yellow molded-on wide-brimmed hat, wings, red chest label: "KEWPIE Germany." .... $500-$600

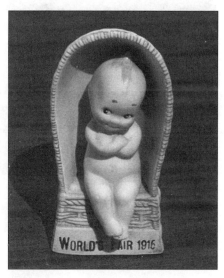

4-1/2" Kewpie. Souvenir of World's Fair 1916 (Courtesy of Connie Baca).

4-1/4" Kewpie Pincushion. Pale bisque/no jts/apart limbs/bowed legs with big toes touching, watermelon mouth, large brown ptd. eyes to side, blonde ptd. hair, original diaper fastened with a large safety pin, pink satin cushion, red "Kewpie" chest sticker. (Sold for $625 in 1997.) $400

4-1/2" Kewpie Doll. All-bisque/movable arms/together legs/brown ptd. 1-strap shoes with bows/white socks with pink stripes, tiny pink wings, smiling watermelon mouth, roguish blue eyes ptd. to side. Nude. ....$175-$200

4-1/4" Kewpie Sweeper. All-bisque/no jts/holds broom....................$500-$600

4-1/2".. "Scootles" or "Kewpie's Big Sister." All-bisque/poor quality/movable arms only/apart legs/lowered head, ptd. features, blonde ptd/molded hair. Nude. Foot mark: "O'Neill." Back stamp: "JAPAN." 1925+ $350

5" "Kewpie Hero" as a bellhop. All bisque/red-orange molded cap. $3,000

5" Kewpie Doll. All-bisque, watermelon mouth, blue ptd. eyes to side, blonde ptd/molded hair, jtd arms and rare jtd legs, original clothes, original pink wicker crib. (Sold for $650 in 1992) . $1,000

5" Kewpie with umbrella. Signed O'Neill on base. $850-$900 (Courtesy of Connie Baca).

5" Kewpie Doll. All-celluloid/movable arms only/together legs, watermelon mouth, large black ptd. eyes to side/brown eyeshadow, orange ptd./molded topknot/side and rear tufts, no wings. (Doll's body painted black to simulate a tuxedo/glued-on white crepe paper front piece.) Party favor. Made by Karl Standfuss, Deuben, near Dresden, Saxony, Germany, 1898-1930. Ca. 1926 ....$100

5" Negro Kewpie. All black bisque/jtd arms only/head molded to side, watermelon mouth, black ptd. eyes to side, black topknot, starfish hands/together legs. Nude. Rare. Ca. 1914 (9" size $1,400) $650

5-1/2" Kewpie Doll. MIB. All-bisque/movable arms only/together legs, watermelon mouth, large blue ptd. eyes to the side,

blonde ptd. hair, original wool outfit with pink bows/3 safety pins in different sizes. Original box............................$725

5-1/2" Kewpie Bride and Groom. All pale bisque/movable arms only/together legs, watermelon mouths, blue ptd. eyes to side, blonde ptd/molded hair, black painted coat and white painted vest on groom/attached top hat, white bridal veil on bride who holds a bouquet..............................$800-$1,000pr.

6" Kewpie Doll. MIB. All-bisque/jtd arms only/together legs, brown ptd. eyes to side, watermelon mouth, red heart chest sticker. Box label reads: "Kewpie Doll Trade Mark Germany." Accompanying verse reads in part: "You ask why we are hurrying so, We're going to be dolls, you Know, Rose O'Neill has shown us how; Look inside and see one now--For Children Dear, we've always Known, Need Kewpies of their very own; So, really, the best way with them Is just to come and play with them, Turn into Dolls and stay with them..." Heart label reads: "From Kewpie you'll not wish to part, But when you've learned his smile by heart, just give that little smile away to everybody, everyday (and with each smile, I hope you'll feel The Kewpish love of Rose O'Neill)." Chest label reads: "Kewpie Germany." Round shoulder label reads: "Design Patented." MIB $800

7" Kewpie Doll. All-bisque/movable arms/together legs, watermelon mouth, blue ptd. eyes to side/head slightly turned and lower than most, dark blonde ptd/molded hair/topknot, blue wings. Nude. Made in East Germany, near Bonn. (These Kewpies were originally stamped "Germany" in washable ink, so most are found without the tell-tale stamp, and are dated earlier. The bisque is fine quality.) 1951 .. $350

7-1/2" Kewpie Bride and Groom. All-bisque/jtd arms, watermelon mouths, blue ptd. eyes to side, blonde ptd/molded hair, original clothes: bride wears a white silk crepe gown, white satin slip, lace veil with silk flowers, glass beads; groom wears a black satin suit, white silk shirt, black bow tie, black silk top hat. Ca. 1920s $1,200

3-1/2" Huggers. Rose O'Neill paper label on back. 1913+ $250-$300 (Courtesy of Connie Baca).

7-1/2" Kewpie Doll. All-bisque/movable arms only/together legs, molded blue ptd. wings, blonde ptd/molded hair/topknot, watermelon mouth, blue ptd. eyes to side. Nude. Incised: "Rose O'Neill." $500

8-1/2" Kewpie Doll. All compo/rigid body/together legs/movable arms, downcast head, smiling watermelon mouth, blue ptd. eyes to side, blonde ptd/molded hair, original bride costume consisting of pink satin ribbon, bridal wreath, maline veil, marabou trim (some dolls wore ballet outfits of satin ribbon and marabou trim, checkered aprons and bonnets, or could be purchased nude.). 1921.. $275

5" Kewpies marked O'Neill on feet, $200 each (Courtesy of Connie Baca).

8-1/2" Kewpie Doll. Molded cloth head, watermelon mouth, blue ptd. eyes to side, kapok-stuffed soft jersey body and back of head. (This type also came in size 12".).....................................$200

9" Kewpie Doll. MIB. All vinyl/apart limbs, watermelon mouth, brown ptd. eyes to side, blonde ptd/molded hair, original clothes. Made by Remco. 1950s . $225

9" Kewpie Doll. All-bisque/movable arms only/together legs/molded blue ptd. wings, blonde ptd/molded hair/topknot, watermelon mouth, blue ptd. eyes to side. Nude. Incised: "Rose O'Neill." ....$700-$750

10-1/2" Kewpie Doll. compo head, watermelon mouth, blue ptd. eyes to side, blonde ptd. hair, cloth body jtd at sh/hips/compo hands, original checkered dress with lace trim, underwear, white cotton socks. (Sold boxed) 1921 MIB $500 ....$325

10-1/2" Kewpie Lamp Base. Cream painted cast metal with 6-1/2" Kewpie. Watermelon mouth, brown ptd. eyes to side, blonde ptd. hair, outstretched arms/together legs/feet molded onto a decorative base. $1,500

11" Kewpie Doll. Bisque head, watermelon mouth, inset large round blue glass googly eyes, blonde ptd/molded hair, BJ compo body (toddler). Undressed. Made by J.D. Kestner, Germany. Mark: "Ges gesch//O'Neill J.D.K.".......$6,500

11" Kewpie Doll. All-compo/jtd arms only/apart legs, watermelon mouth, black ptd. eyes to side (right)/long ptd. eyelashes, orange ptd. toplock/side tufts/back tuft. Nude. Red heart sticker on chest. Blue ptd. wings.... $225-$275

12" Cuddly Kewpie Doll. Painted mask face, stuffed cloth body/limbs/small wings/peaked cap. Made by Richard G. Krueger, NYC. Ca. 1929 ....$275

12" Kewpie Doll. All-bisque/movable arms only/together legs/molded blue ptd. wings, watermelon mouth, blue ptd. eyes to side. Nude. Signed: "Rose O'Neill." 1913+ ....$1,400-$1,600

12" Kewpie. All-compo, original outfit, box. Design & Copyright by Rose O'Neill. Cat. No. 9703. Cameo. 1948 MIB $400

13" Kewpie Doll. compo head, watermelon mouth, blue ptd. eyes to side, blonde ptd/molded hair, jtd compo body, original dress, etc. Made by Cameo Doll Co., NYC. 1940s (1946)...............$350

13" Kewpie Statuette Lamp. Carnival-type. Hand-painted pink chalkware/movable arms/together legs with rouged knees/round yellow base/downcast head, watermelon mouth, brown ptd. eyes, yellow ptd. hair, original red crepe paper dress/light bulb socket at top of head/electric cord attached to base. 1920s...$450

13" Kewpie Statuette. All cast iron/out-stretched arms. Made by Middleton Iron Works, Middleton, Ohio. 1930s $700

13" Kewpie Statuette. Carnival-type. All-chalk/movable arms only (attached with elastic)/together legs molded onto dark green ptd. round base, original light blue satin dress trimmed with tiny silk roses. Ca. 1922. (This figurine has a straight mouth, dark ptd. eyes to right side, orange ptd. topknot/tufts, black dots for eyebrows, and written on the bottom in original script are the words: "Fun Day.")...................................$300

13" Negro Kewpie Doll. All black ptd. compo/movable arms only/apart legs, brown ptd. eyes to side (right), brown ptd/molded topknot/side tufts, red heart-shaped chest label. Nude. Ca. 1920s $450

13" Negro Scootles. Chocolate brown swiv-el head, smiling CM, brown ptd. eyes to side, black ptd/molded hair, compo body jtd at neck/sh/hips, original romp-er, shoes, socks. Made by Cameo Doll Co., NYC, 1922+ ....$900-$950

14" Scootles. compo head/cheek and chin dimples, red CM, blue ptd. eyes to side, orange ptd/molded hair, compo body jtd at neck/sh/hips, sunsuit. Made by Cameo Doll Co., NYC, 1925+...... $700

15" Cuddle Kewpie. Molded/ptd cloth face, watermelon mouth, ptd. blue eyes to side, crushed plush body/limbs/back of head. (Cheapest version of this doll was covered with velvet.) Ca. 1928 .... $350

20" Kewpie Doll. Heavy compo head, wa-termelon mouth, large blue ptd. eyes to side, bald head, cloth body/legs/toes pointed outward (heel to heel)/cloth up-per arms/compo lower arms, original pink checkered cotton dress, under-clothes. (This Kewpie was part of the TINY TOTS line advertised as having the new "Bisc Finish Hard-to-Break" washable head. There is also a 13" size.) 1913 .... $600

Chapter 22

~KATHE KRUSE~

History: 1910-1990+

In a 1912 issue of *Ladies Home Journal* magazine (USA), Frau Kathe wrote of her beginnings as a dollmaker. There was an exhibit of homemade toys in Berlin, and she was asked to bring the dolls she had made for her children. She thought of the dolls as being pretty, washable, unbreakable, and was surprised at the enthusiastic response they gleaned. By 1912 when the article was published, her dolls were being sold all over the world.

From her first doll made with a towel there had been five years of thought and work. She claimed to have had no assistance with the dolls, except for that of her husband, Max, a professional sculptor who had advised her and given suggestions about the features. Each doll went through her hands at least twenty times, and each carried her name and number on the side of its left foot. (The International Studio Magazine, April 1911, had an article and photographs about Max Kruse and his work. Frau Kruse's dolls were also mentioned.)

Kathe (Kaethe) Kruse's autobiography was published in 1951. It gives more details about her life and career. She tells of her struggles during World War One, and the devaluation of the German Mark in 1923. Making the dolls by hand, protected the workmanship of each when a copyright was infringed. Those who tried to imitate her dolls made replicas that revealed imperfections. Still, Frau Kruse was forced into legal action to cease the making of lookalikes. Herr Kruse, who wasn't much older then Kathe, died in 1941 at the age of 90 in Berlin. Frau Kruse lived in her home at Bad Koesen with her children, where she had her doll workshop.

In 1950, she was coerced to leave her home and possessions. It was during these later years, that she made her mannequins for department store displays. There were both adult types and children's mannequins. Her son Friedebald, the playdoll, became a life-size model. At the close of her autobiography, Frau Kruse stated: "Again I am at the beginning of new work. Somewhere I have read that one dies when one ceases to begin. One must continue to begin to follow new interests. He who gives up is finished." Frau Kruse died on July 19, 1968.

Collecting Hints:

The prices that the older Kathe Kruse dolls bring in the secondary market nowadays never fails to amaze me they were so simply and cheaply made. When found undressed and tossed in a bin in a Goodwill or Salvation Army store in the 1960s and 1970s, they were often overlooked by collectors; their prices usually under $5. It was the growing number of dealers and picture book compilers who promoted them to glory and higher prices. The more often a doll is pictured in a doll book, the more expensive and sought after it becomes.

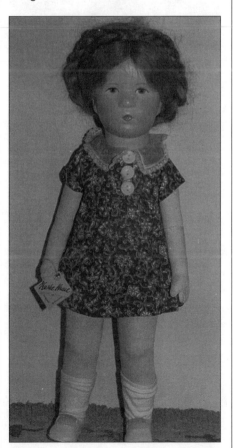

Old Kathe Kruse, auburn HHW, wrist tag. See Kruse section for prices. (Courtesy of Herron).

But the Kruse dolls did have character and they do look like real children, which we can't say about most commercially-made dolls. Although Kathe Kruse's dolls, both old and new, bear a definite family resemblance, there are certain peculiarities one can find when inspecting the entire range:

Doll 1 (1911) had the usual hand-painted (in oils) molded cloth face and head and washable body, but the body has 7 pieces, the legs have 5 pieces, and the arms have 2 pieces; fingers stitched individually with a sewn-on thumb. Early dolls wore woven straw shoes. "Schlenkerchen" or Doll 11 was also called "Little Happy Doll." The cloth head had a rear seam, painted hair, painted eyelashes, and a rare smiling open-closed mouth. The legs were loosely sewn to the body for added realism. It was first made in 1922 and production continued until 1936. Doll V and Doll V1 have the same heads. "Traumerchin (V)" had open eyes, and "Du Mein" (V1) had closed eyes. Heads were sewn loosely. "Traumerchin" was called "Sand Baby" because the body was filled with sand. Hair was painted until 1930, then hand-knotted wigs were utilized. Some dolls boasted the heavy Magnesit heads in 1935. These were soon replaced with cloth heads which were used until 1940. (Collectors sometimes call these "Magnesit" heads composition.)

Doll V11 had a smaller Doll 1 body, but less seams, wide hips, sewn-on thumbs. The first version dates to 1927; the second version, early 1930s, was a slimmer doll. This doll is often mistaken for Doll 1. Doll X is a smaller version of Doll 1 and has swivel neck. It dates to 1935-1952. Doll 1X is a smaller "German Child"; wigged, swivel neck, slender body, modeled after Friedebald, 1929-1930s. Doll V111 or "German Child" has the above features, 1929+; had the smooth mask face, one crooked arm, mitt hands with stitched fingers, wig, disc-jointed legs. Doll X11 or "Hampelchin" and "Little Jumping Doll" had a cloth head with three vertical seams at rear of head, human hair wig, loose legs, button and band on the back (other sizes 16", 14", and 18"). Early 1930s-1940s.

Reproduction Alert:

Kathe Kruse dolls were imitated in their day and modern doll artists have tried to imitate them in our day. The latter, however, were signed by the makers, as were the imitators in Kruse's day, i.e., Bing Art Dolls, Nurnberg, Germany, Heine & Schneider Art Dolls, Bad-Kosen, Germany, and various unmarked types. Many authentic Kruse dolls are also found unmarked.

KATHE KRUSE

13" .... "Schlenkerchen." Model 11. Molded muslin head, smiling O/C mouth, ptd brown eyes/rare ptd eyelashes, brown ptd hair, jtd cloth body, old pink cotton dress with embroidery trim, etc. Marked on foot. (Silk stockinet covered head.) 1922-1936 Good condition .... $8,000-$10,000+

14" Anneliese or Leopold. Called "Du Mein" type (has Du Mein head). Model V11. Molded muslin head, CM, ptd blue eyes, brown ptd hair, jtd cloth body, original print dress, white pinafore, pointed cap with side wings, etc. Ca. 1928-30 Good condition $2,700-$3,200

14" "U.S. Zone Germany" Girl. Model 1X or X. Molded muslin head (some have Magnesit heads), CM, ptd blue eyes, brown HHW, jtd cloth body, original white dress with multi-colored flowers, red apron, red hat, red socks, white ankle-strap shoes. Tag reads: "Made in US Zone Germany." MIB: $2,500 Doll alone: $1,400-$1,800 (1945-1951) ..... $1,400-$1,800

Magnesit head, excellent condition: $1,000 Hard plastic head $850

14" Doll X. Smaller Doll 1. Swivel head. Ca. 1935 Excellent condition $3,200

15-1/4" "Gretchen." All celluloid-plastic or Tortulon, CM, blue sleep celluloid eyes, blonde HHW, celluloid body jtd at neck/sh./hips, original floral and stripe print skirt, white cotton blouse with red and blue lace, green cotton apron, red leather shoes, white knitted socks. Head mark: "T 40" (with a turtle in a diamond frame). Yellow round wrist tag reads: "Eine Schildkrot-Puppe// turtle in

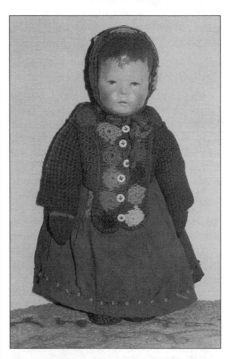

Old Kathe Kruse boy. See Kathe Kruse section for prices. (Courtesy of Herron).

a diamond//Modell Kathe Kruse." (Gretchen had a twin brother named "Karl" who was made and marked similarly.) 1955-61 .... $650-$750

16" "Duquesnois" type Boy. Model 1. Molded muslin head/full lower cheeks, small CM, ptd blue eyes, modeled ears, orange-blonde ptd hair, jtd cloth body/ very wide hips, original clothes. (This familiar face was inspired by the famous head sculpted by Francois Duquesnois, 1594-1643, Vatican artist of Flemish descent, known as "Fiammingo." This doll was dressed as a boy or girl and was later wigged.) Ca. 1910-29. Excellent condition: $5,500-$6,000+; Doll 1 (slimmer hips) Excellent condition: $4,200-$4,500 (1929+); Doll 1H (with wig) Excellent condition: .... $3,500-$3,700

18" .. Little Girl. Hard plastic head, CM, ptd blue eyes, brown HHW (2 long braids), jtd cloth body, original pink open-worked white dress, tartan lined grey coat with tartan collar/cuffs, matching hat, red leather shoes, (sandals), white socks, etc. Left foot stamp reads: "550586 US Zone." 1945-51 .... $3,500

18" ..Little Boy. Hard plastic head, CM, ptd blue eyes, strawberry blonde HHW 'short with straight bangs), jtd cloth body, original grey shorts, jacket, white shirt, white leather sandals, socks. Left foot stamp reads: "550815 US Zone." 1945-51 .... $3,500

18-1/2" "Slim Grandchild" Girl. Hard plastic swivel head, CM, ptd blue-grey eyes, auburn HHW, pink muslin body jtd at neck/sh./hips, original pale blue polka-dot dress, white leather shoes, pearl necklace, etc. Tag. Ca. 1952-75 .... $700-$750

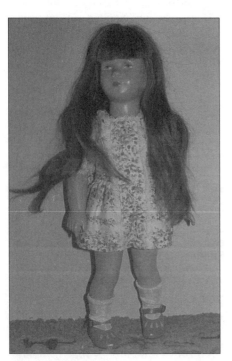

Celluloid Kathe Kruse girl, all original, brown HHW. See Kruse section for prices. (Courtesy of Herron).

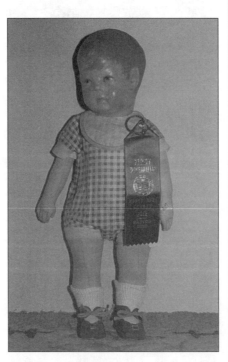

Old Kathe Kruse boy, all original. See Kruse section for prices. (Courtesy of Herron).

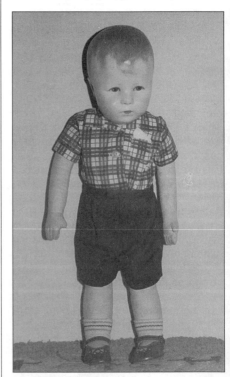

Old Kathe Kruse boy, all original. See Kruse section for prices. (Courtesy of Herron).

18-1/2" "Traumerchin." Sleeping New-Born Babe. Model V. Molded muslin head, CM, closed eyes, yellow ptd hair, jtd cloth body weighted with sand, 5-1/2 lbs., old nightgown, etc. (Second version of this doll was unweighted and had open eyes. It was named "Du Mein"; there were other variations.) Ca. 1925 .... $4,500

23" "Du Mein." Translated: "You are mine." Model V1. Molded muslin head, CM, Ptd blue eyes, brown ptd hair, cloth body, original rompers, hat, etc. foot has Kruse stamp. (Counterpart of "The Little Dreamer" or "Traumerchin.") Ca. 1925 .... $4,500

23" ... "Du Mein" Sand Baby. #549. Molded muslin head, CM, ptd grey eyes, brown ptd hair/brushstrokes, stockinet-covered body filled with sand/floppy neck, original clothes. Sole of foot mark: "549." Ca. 1925+ $4,500

Modern Kathe Kruse dolls, all original, ca early 1970s. (Courtesy of Herron) See Kruse section for prices.

32" Kathe Kruse mannequin girl, brown HHW, all original Ca./1914 $5,000+. (Courtesy of Herron).

16" Celluloid girl by Kathe Kruse, all original. See Kruse section for prices. (Courtesy of Herron).

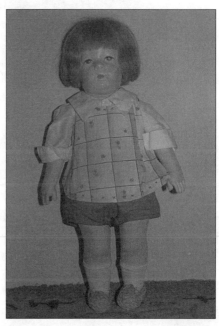

Old Kathe Kruse boy, all original. See Kruse section for prices. (Courtesy of Herron).

Chapter 23

~⚬LENCI DOLLS⚬~

History: 1919-1990's

Signora Lenci (christened Helenchen Elena von Koernig, the latter surname shortened to Konig), was of German and Austrian ancestry. Although born in Turin, Italy, she grew up in Germany and studied art in Dusseldorf. Her father, Francesco, was a chemistry professor. Before her marriage to Enrico Scavini, Elena resided in Germany and worked part-time as a photographer for ten years. The Lenci company was founded in the Scavini apartment in 1919.

Elena and her brother had been experimenting with felt as a medium for the dolls she planned to make. Elena's early dolls were crude and ordinary compared to the decorative and sophisticated dolls that were shortly to come. By 1922, the "Lenci" name was world famous. The twenties decade was an era of innovation and daring, and the Lenci creations captured the spirit of the times. Even dolls her company made during the bleak years of the Depression never failed to capture the zest and flair of earlier years. Lenci, a fan of the stage and screen, merely focused her attention on the glamour that still existed in shadowland and in her vivid imagination. The Signora survived World War Two, although the dolls made by her former company were no longer as well-made or as striking as the product of old. She died in February 1974, at the age of 88.

Collecting Hints:

The value of a Lenci creation depends upon degree of originality and brightness of color, but as more collectors join the collecting ranks, expect the faded and moth nibbled examples to escalate in price. This happened to American primitives, which are not only faded for the most part, but downright rotten. These dolls were very well made and have a charm many dolls lack.

Reproduction Alert:

Lenci dolls have been reproduced by the Lenci firm in Italy and are very collectible. But do not confuse the old with the new.

LENCI DOLLS

7-1/2" Character Sailor. All felt/short fat body/short limbs, broad smiling mouth/pipe, small blue eyes, original blue felt sailor suit: trousers, jacket with striped collar, striped shirt, felt shoes, etc. 1930s ....$400-$450

7-1/2" Sir Cupid. 276. All felt, CM, blue ptd eyes to side, knotted red felt strips hair, yellow/orange/red decorated wings, dark blue felt jacket decorated with embroidered hearts, brown felt trunks/brown felt sandals/red felt gloves/wood sheath holding 4 wooden arrows; holds bow in one hand and arrow in the other. All original. Ca. 1930s $4,000

8" "Pan." All felt, head turned to side, O/C mouth/ptd mouth, ptd brown eyes to side, felt hair, maroon felt horns, long donkey ears/tail/wooden hooves, original felt peplum jacket/white mittens. (Pan, according to legend and Greek mythology, was the god of forests, flocks, and shepherds.) There is another version of Pan with gold woolly hair and woolly legs. Ca. Early 1950s $1,500

9" "Miniature 78" Girl. Molded felt head/jtd at sh/hips/swivel neck, O/C mouth, ptd blue eyes to side, blonde mohair wig attached in strips, cloth body/legs/felt arms, original white organdy dress with crisscross stripes, red felt poke bonnet/red feather, white organdy underwear, etc. Round silver-colored paper tag sewn to skirt reads: "Ars Lenci//Made in Italy Torino//New York. Paris. London." Ca. 1935-early 1940s ....$400-$500

9" Little Girl with Cart. All felt/jtd at sh/hips/swivel neck, O/C mouth, ptd blue eyes to side, blonde mohair wig, original felt and rayon outfit, felt sandals, wooden cart with 2 wheels and felt flowers. Foot mark: "Lenci." (Surprised facial expression.) 1930s $1,200

10-1/2" "Winking" Boy. All felt/jtd at sh/hips swivel neck, O/C smiling mouth/ptd teeth, ptd brown eyes to side/one eye half-closed/lashes, auburn "curly" mohair wig, original felt trousers, shirt, vest, etc. Ca. 1920 ....$1,200

11" Fascist Boy. All felt/jtd at sh/hips/swivel neck, CM, brown ptd eyes to side, brown mohair wig, original 2-pc suit with button-down pockets/gold insignia on left arm, cap with gold metal insignia pin, leather lace-up shoes, etc. 1930s $1,400

11-1/2" "Amore." Smooth felt face, CM, ptd blue eyes to side/white threads on iris, blonde floss curls, muslin body/felt limbs, original felt/fabric clothes, bonnet (decorated with multi-colored felt flowers), etc. Her cardboard hatbox is

imprinted with word "Amore" and has felt ribbon handle. Signed foot and hatbox. 1930s $1,500

12" Little Girl. All felt/jtd at sh/hips/swivel neck/stitched fingers and separate thumb, CM, blue ptd eyes to side, blonde curly mohair wig, green felt dress with white felt trim (cut in points), matching felt hat with 2 tiny red felt roses, white cotton apron with lace trim/pink felt straps, green felt shoes, etc. 1920s ....$950+

13" Boy with Scarf #163. All felt/jtd at sh/hips/swivel neck, CM, blue ptd eyes to side, blonde mohair wig, original short felt pants, short felt jacket, plaid felt scarf with fringe, felt hate, felt shoes, etc. Label reads: "Lenci, E. Scavini, Torino N. 163." Ca. 1925 $950

13" Peasant Girl. All felt/jtd at sh/hips/swivel neck, CM, large brown ptd eyes to side, black mohair wig/bangs/realistic cloth hands, original felt regional costume, etc. Mark: "Lenci." Tag reads: "SARDA." 1930s $1,000

14" Lady type. All felt/jtd at sh/hips/swivel neck, CM, brown ptd eyes/molded eyelids, brown mohair wig, original clothes, bonnet, etc. Rare size for lady dolls $1,000

14" Scarlet O'Hara or "Southern Plantation Girl." All felt/jtd at sh/hips/swivel neck, CM, dark mohair wig, blue ptd eyes to side, original long dress, large wide-brim hat. Ca. 1938 ....$2,000

15" Irish Girl #300. All felt/jtd at sh/hips/swivel neck, CM, blue ptd eyes to side, blonde mohair wig, original Irish regional costume: dark green felt with bright green shamrock design, short light green jacket, white blouse, green hat, green shoes, etc. Holds a felt ball. 1920s.......................................$2,600

16" "Matador" Boy. 300 series. Molded felt face, pouty CM, brown ptd eyes to side, black mohair wig, muslin body/limbs, original red and black felt outfit including cape, hat, shoes, etc. Ca. late 1920s-1930s............................$3,200

16" Baby. Compo head, CM, ptd blue eyes, blonde ptd hair, pressed cloth ptd body/limbs, original clothes. (Resembles the di Fiammingo bust.) Ca. 1930 Rare $1,500

16" Smiling Girl. All felt/jtd at sh/hips/swivel head, OM/molded/ptd teeth, ptd blue eyes, blonde mohair wig, original pink felt short dress with applied flowers, pink felt bonnet, pink felt shoes, etc. 1930s Rare type $3,000

17" Dutch Twins. Boy and Girl. Series 300. All felt/jtd at sh/hips/swivel necks, CM, ptd blue eyes to side, chubby cheeks; boy has brown mohair wig, girl has a blonde mohair wig with short sausage curls, all original clothes, caps, etc. Ca. 1930 ....$5,000

17" Gaucho Boy. 300 series. All felt/jtd at sh/hips/swivel neck, CM, brown eyes to side, black mohair wig, original South American "Gaucho" outfit: trousers, shirt, vest, wide-brimmed black felt hat, boots, spurs, etc. (This head faintly resembles Francois Duquesnois bust owned by Lenci company, which was obviously an inspiration for many of their dolls.) 1920s......................$3,000

17" Goose Girl. All felt/jtd at sh/hips/swivel neck, pouty CM, blue ptd eyes to side, blonde mohair wig/braids, original blue felt skirt, beige felt apron, white cotton blouse with small organdy neck ruffle, black felt vest, black felt shoes, white stockings, original "goose." Ca. 1925 ....$2,500

17" Jump Rope Girl. 1500 series. Molded felt face, CM, ptd brown eyes to side, brown mohair wig, pigtails, hollow felt body jtd at sh/hips/neck/slightly bent arms/straight legs, original pink and tan check felt dress, white organdy apron, pink felt shoes, white socks, original pink jump rope. Ca. 1930..........$2,500

17" Jump Rope Girl. Molded felt face, CM, brown ptd eyes to side, brown mohair wig, muslin body/felt limbs/jtd at sh/hips/neck, original red felt dress with applied orange, blue and yellow flowers and green stems/white organdy sleeves and neck trim, white chemise, white cotton slip sewn onto skirt waist, yellow felt broad-brimmed sun hat, red felt shoes, white socks, jump rope with blue/green wooden handles. 1920s Mint $2,500

17" Little Boy. 300 series. All felt/jtd at sh/hips/swivel neck, CM, ptd brown eyes to side, light brown mohair wig, original tan felt short pants, black wool sweater with brown trim, etc. Late 1920s $2,200

17" Little Girl. All felt/jtd at hips/sh/swivel neck, CM, ptd blue eyes to side, blonde mohair wig, original bright pink felt bodice/appliquéd felt flowers, organdy sleeves, organdy ruffled skirt trimmed with matching felt piping, bright pink felt bonnet, pink shoes with straps, etc. Ca. 1925-30 ....$1,000

17" Military Boy. All felt/jtd at sh/hips/swivel neck, CM, ptd brown eyes to side, black mohair wig, original Italian military uniform with red/white/green insignia on sleeve, hat boasts a pin, etc. 1930-32 ....$2,000

17" Spanish Girl with Rooster. All felt/jtd at sh/hips/swivel neck, CM, brown eyes to side, black mohair wig, original felt costume, felt rooster. 1920s $3,000

17" Turkish Boy. 300 series. Molded felt face, CM, ptd brown eyes to side, brown mohair wig, hollow felt body jtd at sh/hips, neck, original blue felt outfit with gold trim, yellow sash, pink felt hat with blue tassel, etc. Ca. 1925..$3,200

17-1/2" "Golf" Boy. 300/F number in Lenci's 1927/28 catalog. All felt/jtd at sh/hips/swivel neck, CM, ptd brown eyes to side, blonde mohair wig, original checkered knickers, jacket, shoes, stockings, golf club/bag, wrist tag, etc. Ca. 1927 ....$3,000

17-1/2" Russian Girl. 300 series. Molded felt face, CM, ptd brown eyes to side, quality blonde mohair wig with 2 long braids, hollow felt body/jtd at sh/hips/neck, original ornate felt skirt, vest, organdy long-sleeved blouse, teddy/pantalets, slip, red leather boots, felt head-dress. Soles of feet marked: "Lenci." Ca. 1925 ....$2,800

17-1/2" Scowling Tot. 1500 series girl. Molded felt face/"mumps" cheeks, CM, prominent nostrils, ptd brown eyes to side, brown mohair wig/small mohair clumps sewn into head, PE/hoop earrings, hollow felt body/jtd at sh/hips/neck/unusual separately stitched big toes, original pink and tan felt dress, half slip, waist, drawers, pink shoes, white socks. Ca. 1930 ....$2,000-$2,500

25" Reissue Lenci. Reissued from original 1930 model (using original mold). 1985 Sold for $1,200. Came in original box with certificate. (Courtesy of D. Kay Crow)

18" Fascist Boy. All felt/jtd at sh/hips/swivel neck, CM, ptd blue eyes to side, blonde mohair wig, original black long-sleeved shirt/blue neckerchief or tie, knee-length grey felt pants, hat with tassel, black leather shoes, grey socks with black check design at tops. 1930s $2,500

18" French Revolutionary Boy. 300 series. All felt/jtd at sh/hips/swivel neck, CM, ptd brown eyes to side, blonde short hair with bangs, original felt military uniform with metal buttons, felt hat with yellow tassels, etc. Ca. 1925-30 (Very sad face) $3,200

18" Tennis Player Boy. All felt/jtd at sh/hips/swivel neck, CM, blonde mohair wig, original red felt short pants, red sweater with white stripes and diamond design white shirt, red cap, shoes, socks, tennis racket. Number 5 on the sole of 1 shoes. Ca. 1925...$2,500

18-1/2" Josephine Baker. Negro star of Les Folies du Music-Hall, Paris, 1920s. All

brown felt/swivel limbs/chubby legs, bent arms, smiling O/C mouth/molded teeth, black eyes to side, curly black mohair wig, original yellow grass skirt, red gloves, etc. Ca. 1925........ $2,500+

19" Bavarian Girl. All felt/jtd at sh/hips/swivel neck, CM, ptd blue eyes to side, blonde mohair wig with coronet braids/4 gilt hairpins, green felt dirndle skirt, white cotton blouse, embroidered fichu, organdy apron, bead necklace. Ca. 1930s $1,000

19" Italian Peasant Girl. All felt/jtd at sh/hips/swivel neck, CM, ptd brown eyes looking straight ahead, black mohair wig, original costume of southern Italy: black felt long skirt, white blouse with long sleeves embellished with black felt and rickrack trim, red felt apron decorated with braid embroidery, red felt head scarf, gilt hoop earrings. Ca. 1930s $1,000

19" Little Girl. All felt/jtd at sh/hips/swivel neck, CM, ptd blue eyes looking straight ahead, blonde mohair wig with coronet braids, original red jumper (2 attached tags), white short-sleeved blouse, shoes, socks, etc. Ca. 1930...$1,200

19-1/2" Josephine Baker. 554 Negro star of Les Folies du Music-Hall, Paris, 1920s. Dark brown felt/jtd at sh/hips/swivel neck/"knock" knees, red CM, ptd black eyes to side, ears/hoop earrings, short black bobbed mohair with forehead spitcurl, original felt banana costume, yellow top, bracelets. 1927-28 (Child-like version)................... $2,500

20" "Flirty-eyed" Girl. Molded felt face, O/C pink mouth, rare inset brown glass eyes/round shape/eyes move, black mohair wig sewn in strips to the head, ptd/molded "surprised" eyebrows, muslin body/felt limbs/separate fingers, original red and black skirt, embroidered cotton overskirt, white cotton blouse, half-slip, pantalets, etc. Round silver card label read: "Lenci//Torino//Made in Italy." Rectangular label reads: "Fobello." Cloth label reads: "Lenci//Torino//Made in Italy." Ca. 1930s.......................................$3,200

20" Bon Vivant. Male. All felt/jtd at sh/hips/swivel neck, CM, large round blue "surprised" eyes, brown mohair wig, original blue felt trousers, white shirt, brown jacket, button-hole (boutonniere) on lapel for red flower, felt top hat, original suitcase. 1930s $3,500

20" Italian "Cowboy." All felt/jtd at sh/hips/swivel neck, CM, ptd blue eyes to side, rosy cheeks, brown mohair wig, original felt clothes, hat, sheepskin chaps, leather-laced boots, rope lariat. Stud on vest reads: "Lenci." Ca. 1920...$4,000

20" Native Girl. All brown felt/jtd at sh/hips/swivel neck, CM, brown ptd eyes to side, black mohair wig, original native costume: green and yellow felt leaves and red felt roses decorate "skirt," necklace, hair-band, etc. Ca. 1920.......................................$2,000

20" Old Lady. Felt head, O/C mouth, round blue glass googly eyes (startled expression), blonde mohair wig, cloth body/felt limbs, original long dress, fancy hat, etc. Signed. MIB Ca. 1930s $5,000

20" Opium Smoker. Molded felt face/slim shape, ptd brown "sleepy" eyes to side, CM, opium pipe, thin jtd felt body/limbs, original felt robe, turban, etc. Sits in old wooden chair. Ca. 1920 ....$4,000

20" Pierrot. All felt, CM (disdainful, down-turned lips), ptd blue eyes to side /half-closed eyelids, attached ears, bald head/black cap, felt Pierrot costume with ruffled collar, felt shoes, original mandolin (wood). Ca. 1920 Rare $2,000

21" "Flirty-eyed" Girl. All felt/jtd at sh/hips/swivel head, CM, blue glass movable eyes, original regional costume, etc. Ca. 1935+ $3,000

21" Jackie Coogan. All felt/jtd at sh/hips/swivel head, CM, ptd brown eyes to side, blonde "Dutch cut" wig, original felt clothes, cap, etc. dressed as he looked the THE KID. Ca. 1921 ....$5,000

22" Boudoir Lady. Showgirl type. Molded felt face, CM, large ptd blue eyes to side, blonde mohair wig (red felt rose near right ear), cloth body/felt limbs/bent right arm (wears long elbow-length lace gloves)/long limbs, original pink tired-organdy hoop skirt appliquéd with felt flowers, matching broad-brimmed felt picture hat lined with organdy and trimmed with scalloped felt edging, pink high-heel slippers, pearl necklace. 1930s ....$1,600+

22" Girl with Candlestick. All felt/jtd at sh/hips/swivel neck, CM, ptd blue eyes to side, brown mohair wig with coiled braids over each ear, original felt pajama trousers, top, felt shoes, etc. Clothes have floral design. Original candlestick. Tag reads: "Lenci Made in Italy 109-73." 1920s Mint $1,800

8" early Lenci, all original $400-$450. (Courtesy of D. Kay Crow)

22" Japanese Lady. All felt/jtd at sh/hips, swivel head, CM, brown ptd eyes to side, black felt hair, original black kimono, black felt head-dress. Ca. 1920s $4,000

22-1/2" Little Girl. All felt/jtd at sh/hips/swivel neck/chubby cheeks, CM, ptd blue eyes to side, auburn mohair wig, original/hot pink organdy dress with white stripes and white short puff sleeves, flower adorned white organdy bonnet, pink felt shoes, white socks. Original ornate box marked "La Grande Maison De Blanc" (Paris department store on the Place de L'Opera). Ca. 1930 ....$3,500

22-1/2" "Tom" Italian Paper Boy. 500 series boy. Molded felt face, CM, ptd brown eyes, blonde curly mohair wig, muslin body/felt limbs, original light blue felt outfit with dark blue trim and white collar, teddy, brown felt apron embroidered in red with the name "Tom," light blue felt shoes, white socks, folded "newspaper" hat. (The large apron pocket contains a brown piece of paper which reads: "Italian Paper Boy. Notice the hat of Italian newspaper. The hat is not a real newspaper but an old Lenci advertisement.) Ca. 1927-28 ....$3,000

23" "Skier" Boy. 109 series. All felt/jtd at sh/hips/swivel neck, CM, ptd blue eyes to side, yellow mohair wig with bangs, original long felt trousers, green felt long-sleeved shirt with checkered front and white collar, yellow gloves, checkered hat with yellow band, wooden skies, etc. Ca. 1927-28 Mint $3,000

23" Cowgirl. Molded felt face/long neck, CM, ptd brown eyes to side, brown mohair wig, long cloth body/long felt limbs, original felt trousers, blouse, chaps, hat, lariat, etc. (Resembles the cowgirls of the silent screen.) 1920s.......$2,000

23" Lillian and Dorothy Gish. Stars if stage and screen. Boudoir type ladies. Molded felt faces, CM, blue ptd eyes to side (Dorothy's eyes are half-closed), blonde mohair wigs, muslin bodies/felt limbs, original clothes, bonnets, etc. (Lillian came in two versions: long braids or long curls. Lillian's dress has long sleeves with puff tops, long skirt, bonnet, felt shoes, etc. Dorothy wears a long dress with narrow sleeves, bonnet, etc. Original cloth tags. These lovely dolls are not likenesses.) 1920s or early 1930s Each...$2,500

23" Little Girl. 109/46 series. All felt/jtd at sh/hips, CM, ptd blue eyes to side, blonde long curl mohair wig, original pink felt dress, grey coat with a pink tie/pink buttons/appliquéd flower design on pocket, matching grey felt hat with turned up broad brim, grey felt shoes, white socks, etc. 1920s . $1,800

23" Little Girl. 109/54 series. All felt/jtd at sh/hips/swivel neck, CM, ptd blue eyes to side, blonde long curl mohair wig, original white dress with black/grey/red trim, red felt coat with black/grey fur trim, grey felt hat with black trim/appliquéd rooster, black felt shoes, socks. Early 1930s...............................$1,800

23" Teenage Girl. Boudoir type. Long oval-shaped molded felt face, CM, ptd brown eyes to side, blonde mohair wig,

long felt body/felt limbs, original black felt coat with pink rickrack trim, black felt tam, leggings, black felt shoes, stockings. Ca. 1923+ $2,000

24-1/2" Manulita. 165/8 series. Spanish boudoir doll. Molded felt face, smiling CM, ptd brown eyes to side, black mohair wig, large hoop earrings, muslin body/long felt limbs, original long red dress with flounces on skirt, matching petticoat with lace trim, wide-brimmed black felt hat decorated with tassels, embroidered fringed shawl, black felt high-heeled slippers, stockings. Ca. 1927-28 ....$2,000+

25" Harlequin. Female. Molded felt face, CM, ptd blue eyes to side, blonde mohair wig, linen body/long felt limbs, original cream-colored skirt with 3 flounces trimmed in black satin, long-sleeved blouse with wide collar, knee-length bloomers, cream-colored felt slippers, head-dress with black pom pons. 1920s..$5,000

25" Harlequin. Male. Molded felt face, CM, ptd blue eyes to side, brown mohair wig, linen body/long felt limbs, original cream-colored costume with black trim and designs, cream-colored head-dress, black felt shoes, wooden mandolin. 1920s $5,000

25" Spanish Lady Dancer or Pola Negri. Molded felt face, O/C mouth/molded teeth, "hooded" lids/ptd brown eyes to side, black mohair wig/ptd spit curls on cheeks, long muslin body/long felt limbs, original red felt outfit, shawl, hat, fan, high-heeled slippers, etc. (Resembles silent screen beauty Pola Negri in her film "The Spanish Dancer," 1923). Ca. 1923+ $2,500

26" Boudoir Lady. Molded felt face, smiling O/C mouth/ptd teeth, half-closed ptd blue eyes to side, blonde mohair wig with curls, cloth body/felt limbs, original pink organdy gown with appliquéd felt flowers on skirt, ruffled hat, etc. Lenci label. 1930s $2,200

26" Little Girl. 109/75 series. All felt/jtd at sh/hips/swivel neck, CM, ptd brown eyes to side, strawberry blonde mohair wig, original green and beige check jacket, green and beige check pleated short skirt, felt bodice with belt, brown felt shoes, scalloped white socks, etc. Ca. 1927-28............................$2,000

26-1/2" Sonia. Russian Peasant Lady. All felt/jtd at sh/hips/swivel neck, O/C mouth/teeth, ptd blue eyes to side, carrot red mohair wig, original multi-colored/layered felt and fabric skirt/jacket, elaborate hat; every item embroidered and appliquéd in the Lenci style. Ca. 1927-28 ....$2,000

27" Lillian Gish. Stage and Screen Star. Molded felt face/oval shape/demure expression, CM, slightly half-closed ptd blue eyes to side, yellow blonde sausage curl mohair wig (sewn to head in small clumps), hollow felt body with small waist and molded bosom/long shapely limbs, original yellow organdy gown with turquoise dots and stripes and ruffles with scalloped edges, matching bonnet, matching petticoat/pantalets, turquoise slippers with high heels, silk stockings, faux pearl necklace. Square card tag reads:

"Bambola-Itala//Lenci//Torino//Made in Italy//L Gish 16." (This doll is very lovely but does not resemble Miss Gish.) Ca. 1920s ....$4,000-$6,000

27-1/2" Madame de Pompadour. 165/16 series. Molded felt face, O/C mouth, half-closed ptd blue eyes to side, blonde mohair wig, cloth body/long felt limbs, original voluminous shirt trimmed with roses and lace, etc. Ca. 1927-28......................................$2,000

28" Louise Brooks. 579 series. Silent cinema and early talking picture star. Molded felt face, O/C mouth/ptd teeth, blue eyes to side, black mohair bobbed wig with straight bangs, original red evening gown with voluminous skirt/large red rose attached to waist, red slippers, etc. (Doll holds a red rose in her red gloved hand and a cigarette in the other red gloved hand. This same mold was used for the Marlene Dietrich dolls. The Art Deco cowgirl (1931) is also supposedly Louise Brooks, as is the Girl with Watering Can, flower pot, and wearing a huge yellow felt picture hat and bib trousers.) 1930/31 ..$5,000

28" Marlene Dietrich. German silent cinema and American talking picture star. Molded felt face, O/C mouth/ptd teeth, ptd blue eyes to side, short parted blonde mohair wig, felt body/limbs, original flaring net dress/waistband has wooden cut-outs of men, high-heeled slippers, etc. Ca. 1930 ..$4,000-$6,000

28" Marlene Dietrich. Molded felt face, smiling CM/cigarette, short blonde bobbed mohair wig with side part, long felt jtd body/long felt limbs, wears original turquoise flapper dress with flounced, ruffled skirt/low-cut rounded neckline, felt neck band, two-strands of pearls, ruffled turquoise petticoat, turquoise ruffled garters, high-heeled slippers, stockings. (This doll is reputed to be the

real Lenci "Dietrich," although Dietrich didn't smoke on screen until 1928. More than likely the doll was inspired by Clara Bow who smoked earlier on screen. Advertised in the Lenci catalogs of 1926-27.)...........$4,000-$6,000

28" Raquel Meller. Spanish dancer. Molded felt face, CM, brown eyes to side, black hair with a redish glint, muslin body/rotating joints/felt limbs, original full shirt gown with green felt bodice, wide-brimmed picture hat with 2 red felt roses, pantalets, parasol, etc. Ca. 1925-26 (This is a good likeness of Miss Meller.) $4,000

28" Spanish Dancer. Molded felt face, CM, ptd brown eyes to side, black mohair wig/long black spit curls on cheeks, original organdy and felt costume decorated with roses (large red felt rose in hair and another at waist), holds castanets. Ca. 1930 ....$2,000

29" Spanish Senorita. Molded felt head turned to side, CM, half-closed brown ptd eyes, black mohair wig, jtd felt lady body/long felt limbs, original long black felt gown with lavish flower design, black mantilla, high-heeled slippers, etc. 1927-28.............................$2,500

30" Rudolph Valentino as "The Shiek." Molded felt face/long neck, CM, ptd brown eyes to side, dark brown hair, jtd felt body/limbs, original cream-colored costume adorned with embroidery, stripes, gold braid, felt appliqués, high-topped maroon boots with tassels, etc. (An impressive "art" doll but not a good likeness.) Ca. 1927-28
....$6,500-$7,500

32" Shirley Temple. Molded felt face, CM, brown ptd eyes to side, tightly curled mohair wig, stuffed felt body/limbs/separate fingers/rotating joints at sh/hips/neck, original orange organza short dress trimmed with felt flowers,

lace trimmed teddy and slip, black oil-cloth strap shoes, white socks. (Another impressive doll but not a likeness. Only the tight curls distinguish her as the little star.) 1930s $5,000

34" Little Bo-Peep. Molded felt face, CM, ptd blue eyes to side, blonde mohair wig with coiled side braids, jtd pink muslin body/felt limbs, original floor-length white organdy dress, black felt vest, appliquéd floral design on skirt, white organdy bonnet tied with blue ribbon. 1930s ....$2,500-$2,800

35" Little Miss Muffett. Molded felt face, CM, ptd blue eyes to side, blonde mohair wig with coiled side braids, pink muslin body/long felt limbs, green felt dress with white skirt squares out-lined with black (a spider web effect), green drawers, white stockings, black felt shoes with ankle straps, large black yarn spider. Ca. 1927-28
....$2,600-$2,900

36" Teenage Girl. All felt/jtd at sh/hips/swivel neck, CM, ptd blue eyes to side, long neck/long body/long limbs, strawberry blonde mohair wig, original orange organdy knee-length party dress with ruffles on sleeves and around bottom of skirt/red felt roses pinned to waist, petticoat, long white stockings, black felt shoes with ankle straps, black felt picture hat, etc. 1930s................... $3,000

40" Boudoir Lady or Salon Doll (Poupee Salon). Molded felt face, CM wide apart ptd blue eyes looking ahead, long blonde mohair curls, muslin body/long limbs, graceful hands, original black felt dress trimmed with light blue felt/flower decoration on skirt, matching light blue picture hat, double strand of pearls adorn neck, wooden "Dutch" type shoes, wooden pail with flat back. 1930s (This doll has a "surprised" facial expression.) .... $3,500-$5,000

Chapter 24

~ ARMAND MARSEILLE ~

History: 1890-1950s

Armand Marseille, Koppelsdorf, Thur., Germany; toy factory, 1884; porcelain factory (pipe heads and jugs), 1885; bisque doll shoulder heads, 1890. Armand was also known by the surname "Herman" in Germany, thus one can assume he changed his name to Marseille to bolster the sales of his French-looking dolls. Early factory workers claim he also made ball-jointed composition doll bodies, but as this has not yet been proven, we can refer to him as a maker of dolls' "heads" only.

Certainly his dolls' heads surface attached to all types of bodies from French bodies to cheap all-cloth bodies with mitten hands and even crude papier-mâché bodies. Bisque quality varies from smooth finely-grained bisque to rough textured and highly colored bisque. In other words, Armand manufactured dolls' heads priced for the level of every pocketbook: the rich, the poor, and the middle-class. He made heads for other doll companies and distributors. In this quest to reach every market, he became a very wealthy and famous man. His twenties dolls mirrored the times and became "flappers" or "ma-ma" dolls. He made both bisque and composition dolls in the thirties. The firm closed in 1937, but doll heads made in the 1950s were still comprised of bisque and incised "A.M." or "SP" (recycled from old molds). To keep abreast of the times, Armand, like his competitors, was not above imitating the most "popular" doll of the moment, e.g., Jumeaux, characters, Heubachs, Kewpie, Campbell Kids, googlies, Bye-lo Baby, Patsy, Shirley Temple, etc. These dolls, when found today, are considered rare and pricey collector items. Armand Marseille was indeed an astute business man.

Collecting Hints:

The ARMAND MARSEILLE doll has always been the poor man's "French" poupée, but since early molds were used for decades, it is oft' times difficult to precisely date a doll. The "390" head was particularly popular and had a long life span. Early models have worn, somewhat soiled kid bodies or aging composition bodies. Imitation kid was used on later dolls and later "kid" was made differently than the early kid bodies. A doll that has never been played with usually wears its original factory-made clothing, shoes, and stockings. If so, dolls made in the 1890s, teen years, 1920s, and 1930s, are dressed in materials that were used in their heyday. Look through old catalogs, like Wards and Sears, and see if you can find your all original doll illustrated. This helps place the doll in a particular time period. The letters DRGM were used on dolls from 1909+; DRMR mark dates dolls from 1910+.

Reproduction Alert:

Armand Marseille bisque heads were reproduced during World War One by the British, Japanese, and some American companies, but since these heads are marked by the companies who used them with the name of the company, they are not considered a threat to the buyer, but rather just another "old" doll to be cherished and collected. Some of the more rare Armand Marseille character heads have been reproduced in modern times, but these are usually marked by the maker. "Frauds" made to deceive are usually made of precolored bisque (if the inside of the head is colored it is a reproduction, old dolls were made of white bisque). Old heads are also dirty on the inside and dirt collects in ridges and around eyes. Even the bisque itself on the antique dolls is dirt-pitted. It is a custom nowadays for dealers to remove old bisque arms with hands that have broken fingers and replace them with new bisque arms. Be wary of an old doll that has a very worn kid body (or composition) and bisque arms that appear too perfect. A "worn" doll usually looks "worn" all over.

ARMAND MARSEILLE

5" "351" Negro Baby. Chocolate brown bisque head, OM/2 lower teeth, inset black pupil-less glass eyes, black ptd hair/solid dome, bent limb brown jtd rubber body/wire hooks, old clothes. Head mark: "AM//GermanY//351//10/0." Ca. 1913+ (Good condition.) $200

5-1/2" "200" Baby Girl. All-bisque/5-pc body, CM, inset blue glass eyes, blonde mohair wig, old clothes. Mark: "200/A6/OM/Germany/DRGM/243." (This mold number 200 was used on all-bisque bodies and 5-pc papier-mâché bodies. DRGM is the registered mark number 243.) Ca. 1911+ $350

6-1/2" "252" Googly. Bisque head, smiling CM, blue ptd intaglio eyes, brown ptd hair/molded topknot, bent-limb compo body/bare feet, old clothes. Ca. 1912+ .... $1,000+

6-1/2" "255" Baby Boy. Pale bisque head, smiling CM, blue ptd intaglio eyes, modeled ears, sparsely ptd hair/round head, cardboard body jtd at neck/sh./hips/brown ptd shoes, old baby gown. Mark: "255 DRGM 2// A 11/OM//Germany." Ca. 1925 ... $1,000

7" "320" Googly Boy. Bisque head, smiling CM, ptd blue intaglio eyes to side, modeled ears, blonde ptd/molded "mohawk" hairstyle, compo body jtd at neck/sh./hips/bare feet, old clothes. Mark: "320//A 11/ OM//Germany." Ca. 1913+ $1,100

8" "390" Boy Scout. Bisque head, OM, /teeth, brown mohair wig, BJ compo body/molded-on and brown ptd boots and knee-length stockings, original brown short pants, shirt, jacket, red neckerchief, black felt hat. Ca. 1900+ $350

12" "A.M. 390" marked girl, bisque head, OM/teeth, blue glass sleep eyes, brown wig, BJ compo body, redressed. 1890+ $325-$350. (Courtesy of Billye Otto)

8" "390" or "Marken" Dutch Girl. Painted bisque head, 0M/teeth, brown glass sleep eyes, dark brown mohair wig, cheap compo body/unjtd limbs, original "Markent" (an island in the old Zuider Zee) costume: blue skirt, red and brown floral print bodice with a plastron, apron 'kith checkered top, elaborate hat consisting of linen, gauze, lace, chintz, etc., wooden shoes, stockings. Ca. 1930s $250

8-1/2" "390" or "Gaucho." Bisque head, OM/teeth, inset brown glass eyes, brown mohair wig, BJ compo body/straight wrists, original "Gaucho" or South American cowboy outfit: brown loose trousers, belt, shirt, red neckerchief, wide-brimmed felt hat, molded/ptd shoes and stockings. MIB. Ca. 1900+ $400

18" "Florodora" marked girl. Bisque head, OM/teeth, brown HHW, stick body, redressed. 1890+ $275-$300. (Courtesy of Billye Otto)

8-1/2" Emil Pfeiffer-Armand Marseille Girl. Bisque head, OM/teeth, inset blue glass eyes, brown HHW, BJ toddler body, original chemise, (Originally sold in France with French labels.) Emil Pfeiffer, Vienna. Ca. 1920s (This 560A head made by Marseille company.) $400

9" "985" Baby. Bisque head/dimples, OM/mouth/2 teeth, blue glass sleep eyes, brown HHW, bent-limb jtd compo body, old clothes. Neck mark: "Germany//985//7/O.M." Ca. 1913+ $400

9" "1894" Soldier Boy. Bisque head, OM/teeth, inset blue glass eyes, reddish mohair wig, BJ compo body/brown ptd/molded-on boots, original "Boer War" uniform felt hat. Mark: "AM O DEP 1894." 1894 ....$375

9-1/2" "430" Baby. Bisque shoulder head/dimples, O/C mouth/2 teeth, deep blue ptd intaglio eyes, blonde ptd hair, kid body/cloth feet/ tiny bisque hands, old clothes. Mark: "430 Germany

A.O.M." (Resembles a Heubach baby). Ca 1926+ $375

10" "985" Character Baby. Bisque head, 0M/teeth, blue glass threaded eyes, brown HHW, bent-limb jtd compo body, old clothes. Mark: "Germany//A 985 M." Ca. 1913+ $425

10-1/2" "351" Baby. Solid-dome bisque head, OM/2 lower teeth, blue glass sleep eyes, blonde ptd hair, bent-limb jtd compo body, old clothes, bonnet. Head mark: "AM//Germany//351/2/OX K." Ca. 1913+ $400

10-1/2" "390" Scottish Laddie. Bisque head/high coloring, OM/teeth, blue glass sleep eyes, brown mohair wig, BJ compo body, original kilts, jacket, headdress, footwear, etc. Ca. 1890+ .. $350

11" "390" Girl. Painted bisque head/high coloring, red CM, ptd blue eyes, brown mohair wig, tightly-stuffed pink cloth body/straight cloth limbs, original cotton dress, bonnet, white shoes, white socks. 1930s $200

11" "390" Girl. Painted bisque head/rosy cheeks, blue glass eyes, CM, blonde mohair wig, cheap pink cloth body/jtd limbs/mitten hands, original cotton dress, bonnet, white shoes, white socks. Ca. 1930s $225

11" American Indian Child. Reddish tan bisque, red OM/teeth, forehead frown lines, inset dark brown glass eyes, black mohair wig/large holes above the ears, reddish tan compo body peg-jtd at sh./hips/yellow ptd shoes with heels, original tan felt outfit trimmed with multicolored fringe, stapled-on oilcloth belt, headband attached to a paper crown. (Clothes tacked to body). Mark: "AM.//x Germany/'/4/0." Ca. 1900+ $250

11-1/2" "343" Baby Girl. Bisque head/full cheeks/) pointed chin, OM/2 teeth, blue glass sleep eyes, blonde mohair wig, cloth body/limbs/ compo hands,

30" "390" incised A.M. 1890s+ $1,000-$1,100. (Courtesy of Irene Oretga)

original long christening gown. Head mark: "A.M. Germany 343/3." Ca. 1924+... $400

12" "323" Googly Girl. Bisque head, smiling CM, large blue glass eyes to side, blonde braided mohair wig, BJ compo toddler body, original clothes. Ca. 1913+....................................... $2,000+

12" "390" "Turkish" Girl. Stock bisque head, OM/teeth, brown glass sleep eyes, brown mohair wig, BJ compo body, original "Turkish" costume: ecru-lace dress decorated with bead necklaces, beaded head-dress, etc. (This is an ordinary little German girl dressed in a faux "Turkish" costume. The bisque is pinkish, not brown tinted.) Ca. 1900+ $300

26" "390" incised A.M. 1890s+ $650-$700. (Courtesy of D. Kay Crow)

12" "390" "Voldendam" Boy. Painted bisque head, OM/teeth, rosy cheeks, blue glass sleep eyes, brown mohair wig, cheap compo body/straight wrist, legs, original "Voldendam" regional costume: black felt trousers/2 silver buttons on the waistband, black felt jacket (blempie) with silver buttons, red and white striped cotton shirt, black fur cap (ruigie), cotton stockings, wooden shoes. 1930s $325

12" "390" Girl. Papier-mâché head, inset blue glass eyes, OM/teeth, blonde mohair wig, papier-mâché jtd body/limbs (short arms with small hands), original "Scottish" type costume, hat, glued-on fabric boots that match skirt. Mark: "Germany//390//A 710 M." (An all-original but cheaply made doll.) Ca. 1930s $275

12-1/2" "390" "Mexican" Girl. Painted bisque head, OM/teeth, brown glass sleep eyes, black mohair wig with 2 long braids, BJ compo body, original Mexican regional costume: red skirt, white blouse, etc. Mark: "Armand Marseille//Germany//390//A 5/0 M." Ca. 1930s.. $375

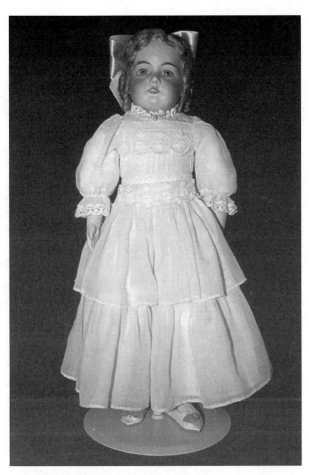

20" "370" incised A.M. bisque shoulder head, OM/teeth, blue glass eyes, blonde mohair wig, replaced cloth body, dressed by Ruby Ellen Smith. (Courtesy of Ruby Ellen Smith)

16" "390" incised A.M. MIB label on box reads: "DRESSED DOLLS" Blue satin dress with ecru lace, etc. All original $650-$700. (Courtesy of D. Kay Crow)

24" "370" incised girl (7 has the French crossbar). Bisque shoulder head, OM/teeth, inset brown glass eyes, long brown HHW, kid body/bisque lower arms, original clothes, wool cape, leather shoes, red-ribbed stockings. (This doll was dressed for the French market. Her clothes are exquisite, maroon dress with pleated skirt, maroon wool cape, etc.) Mark: "370//A6M//Made in Germany." 1890+ $595-$695. (Courtesy of Herron)

31-1/2" "A13M" incised girl. Bisque head, OM/teeth, brown glass sleep eyes, blonde mohair wig, BJ compo body, old clothes, etc. $950-$1,000. (Courtesy of Victoria Rose, England)

23" "Queen Louise" marked girl. Bisque head, OM/teeth, brown glass sleep eyes, red mohair ramshorn wig, BJ compo body, redressed. Mark: "QUEEN LOUISE-GERMANY." 1910. (Courtesy of Ruby Ellen Smith) $625.

22" "390" incised A.M. bisque head, OM/teeth, blue glass sleep eyes, blonde wig, BJ compo body, dressed by Virginia Yates. $550. (Courtesy of Virginia Yates)

12-1/2" "390" Girl. Bisque head, OM/teeth, brown glass sleep eyes, brown mohair wig, BJ compo body, original cheap clothes, etc. Mark: "Armand Marseille, made in Germany, DRGM 246/1, 390." (Dolls were first incised DRGM in 1909.) Ca. 1909+ $375

13" (head cir.) "Baby Phyllis." Solid-dome bisque head, CM, blue glass sleep eyes, blonde ptd hair, cloth body/compo hands, original clothes, etc. Mark: "BABY PHYLLIS//Made in Germany 24014." 1925 .... $525-$550

13" "341" or "Kiddiejoy." Solid-dome bisque head, CM, blue glass sleep eyes, blonde ptd hair, bent-limb jtd compo body, original clothes, etc. Mark: "341/3K." (Hitz, Jacobs & Kassler, NYC, Furth, Bavaria, 1918-1920s, distributed this line of dolls, which were made in 182 European factories and 200 U.S. factories, and in 3 sizes. Armand Marseille company made some of these heads.) C a. 1920 .... $475

13" Musical Marotte. Bisque head, OM/teeth, inset blue glass eyes, blonde mohair wig, pink silk and lace dress/bonnet. Ca. 1890s $700

18" "370" incised girl. Bisque shoulder head, OM/teeth, blue glass sleep eyes, blonde mohair wig, kid body/bisque lower arms, beautiful old clothes, bonnet, etc. 1890s $375-$425. (Courtesy of Herron)

13-1/2" Marotte Boy & Girl. Bisque heads, OM/teeth, inset blue glass eyes, blonde/brown mohair wigs, stick bottoms. (Girl wears a pink and white costume consisting of long pointed streamers trimmed with silver braid and wee metal bells sewn to the tip of each end. Boy wears a similar blue and ivory silk streamer/bell costume. Ca. 1890s Girl $900; Boy: $800

14" "1894" Character Boy. Pale bisque head, OM/4 molded teeth, dimpled chin, blue glass sleep eyes, brown HHW, BJ compo body, original clothes, etc. Mark: "A.M. 1894 D.E.P." $650

14" "258" Googly. Bisque head, smiling CM, inset blue glass eyes, brown HHW, bent-limb jtd compo body, old clothes. (Dolls with sideglancing or "flirty" eyes were referred to as "goo-goo" eyed as early as 1904 in the trade magazines.) Ca. 1911+ $3,500

14" "3200" Girl. Bisque shoulder head, 0M/teeth, inset blue glass eyes, brown mohair wig, kid body/limbs/bisque hands, old clothes, etc. Mark: "A.M. 3200 DEP 2/O/Made in Germany." 1895-1910 .... $325

14" "985" Character Baby. Bisque head, OM/teeth, blue glass sleep eyes, brown HHW, bent-limb jtd compo body, original clothes, bonnet. Mark: "Germany 985, A 2 M." (This doll is closer to Ca. 1913+ $525

15" "431-14" Baby. Bisque shoulder head, CM, inset blue glass eyes, cloth body/legs/compo hands, original clothes. Mark: "A.M. Germany 431-14." Ca. 1926+ $750

15" "600" Character Boy. Bisque shoulder head/4 sew holes, slightly smiling CM, ptd blue eyes, modeled ears, blonde ptd/molded hair/ brushstrokes at hairline, cloth body/compo lower arms, old clothes. Ca. 1910+ $750

15" "Girl's Brigade" Child. Bisque head, OM/teeth, blue glass sleep eyes, brown mohair wig, BJ compo body, original "Girl's Brigade" uniform: white long-sleeve blouse, navy blue pleated skirt, black stockings, black shoes, blue felt hat. (390 number). 1890s....... $400

16" "351" Negro Baby. Black bisque head, smiling OM/2 porcelain teeth, brown glass sleep eyes, black ptd/molded hair, cloth body/ limbs/compo hands, old baby clothes, bonnet. Mark: "A.M. Germany 351/4." Ca. 1913+ (This doll probably dates ca. 1924+) $550

16" "390" Girl. Bisque socket head, OM/teeth, blue glass sleep eyes, brown mohair wig, BJ compo body, old clothes. Mark: "390-A 4-1/2 M." Ca. 1900 .... $425

16" "Baby Gloria." Solid-dome bisque head, OM/2 upper teeth blue glass sleep eyes, blonde ptd/molded hair dimples, cloth body/compo limbs, original clothes, etc. Mark: "Baby Gloria Germany." Ca. 1910 (Round metal dress pin reads: "Baby Gloria.") $950

16" Baby. Compo head, OM/teeth, blue tin sleep eyes, blonde ptd/ molded hair, bent-limb compo body jtd at neck/sh./hips, original christening dress/bonnet, etc. (Marked. Armand Marseille's contribution to the compo baby doll popularity of the 1930s). 1930s $600

17" "990" Character Toddler. Bisque head, OM/teeth, brown glass sleep blonde mohair wig chubby BJ compo toddler body, original sailor suit, cap, etc. Ca.. 1913+ $625

17" "1894" Girl. Bisque shoulder head, OM/teeth, blue glass sleep eyes, blonde mohair wig, kid body/bisque lower arms, old clothes. Mark: "1894//AM 0 DEP." Ca. 1894+ $425

17" "3500" Girl. Bisque shoulder head, OM/teeth, blue glass sleep eyes, brown mohair wig, kid body/bisque lower arms, old clothes, etc. Ca. 1895-99 .... $375

17" "3700" Girl. Bisque shoulder head, OM/teeth, inset blue glass eyes, brown HHW, kid body/bisque lower arms/compo lower legs, old clothes.

Mark: "3700 A.M. 310 + DEP Made in Germany." 1895-99 .... $375

17-1/2" "1894" or "Hindu." Boy-type. Brown mat finish head, red OM/ teeth, brown glass sleep eyes/brown waxed eyelids, black knitting yarn wig, brown BJ compo body, original blue satin trousers, aqua satin jacket lined with buckram, white head scarf, white cape, black cotton stockings, tan kid boots with paper soles. Mark: "1894 AM//AM/2/0 DEP." Ca. 1894+ .... $650-$700

18" "1894" Girl. Bisque shoulder head, OM/teeth, inset blue glass eyes, brown HHW, kid body/bisque lower arms, original clothes, hat, etc. Mark: "A.M.//1894 Germany." Ca. 1894+ $425

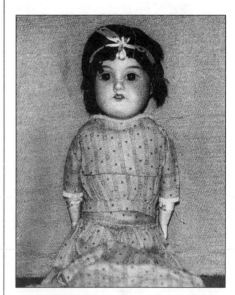

17" "DRGM-2010-A.2/OM." incised girl. Bisque head (top of head cut for insertion of voice mechanism), OM/teeth, brown glass eyes, original brown mohair wig, kid body/bisque lower arms, original factory-made clothes, etc. 1890s $800. (Courtesy of Herron)

18" "3200" Girl. Bisque shoulder head, OM/teeth, inset brown glass eyes, kid body/cloth feet/bisque lower arms, blonde mohair wig, old clothes. Ca. 1895-99 .... $375

18" "A.M.1" Girl. Bisque shoulder head, OM/teeth, grey glass sleep eyes, black HHW, kid body/bisque lower arms, old clothes. Head mark: "A.M.1 D.E.P./Armand Marseille/Made in Germany." Ca. 1890+ $450

18" "Crying" Girl. Bisque head/square cut-out space atop forehead/handle inserted into hole at rear of head to work inner crying mechanism, inset blue glass eyes, blonde mohair wig, pink muslin body stuffed with mohair/cloth limbs/compo hands and upper wrist area, old clothes, cotton stockings, oilcloth shoes. Mark: "A.4.M.//D.R.G.M. 201013." Ca. 1909+.................... $650

18" "Florodora" Girl. Bisque head, OM/teeth, brown glass sleep eyes, brown mohair wig, BJ compo body (stick legs), old clothes, etc. Mark:

"Made in Germany//Florodora//A 4 M." Ca. 1890+ $400

19" "390" Girl. Bisque head, OM/teeth, blue glass sleep eyes, blonde mohair wig, BJ compo body, old clothes, etc. Mark.* "390-A 4-1/2 M." Ca. 1900 .$475-$550

19" "980" Character Baby. Pale bisque head/chubby face, OM/teeth, blue glass sleep eyes, blonde mohair wig, bent-limb compo body, old clothes, etc. Ca. 1913+ ....$650-$700

19" "Baby Betty." Bisque shoulder head, OM/teeth, large blue glass sleep eyes, blonde HHW, kid body/bisque lower arms, old clothes, etc. Mark: "Made in Germany 'atop' Baby 0 Betty (enclosed in an oblong circle) "A" and "M" on each side of oblong and D.R.G.M. at bottom of oblong." Ca 1912+ (Sold for..$1,500 in 1993 at auction) (Gold sticker on body reads: "BABY BETTY" WITH CROWN DESIGN) $675

19-1/2" "2010" Girl. Bisque head/square-cut section atop forehead holds a voice box, OM/teeth, blue glass sleep eyes/open and close when a cord is pulled, brown mohair wig, kid body/bisque lower arms, old clothes, etc. Mark: "DRGM 2010/3." Ca. 1895-99 ....$1,000+

20" "350" Baby. Solid-dome bisque head, OM/2 upper teeth, blue glass sleep eyes, blonde ptd/molded hair, cloth body/compo lower limbs, original clothes. Head mark: "AM Germany 350." Ca. 1913+ (This doll is a 1924+ reissue head.) $850

20" "390" Girl. Bisque shoulder head, OM/4 teeth, inset blue glass eyes, brown mohair wig, kid body/bisque lower arms and lower legs, original clothes, etc. Mark:, "Made in Germany//390 A.G.M." Ca. 1890s+ $500

20-1/2" "Nun" Girl. Bisque head, OM/teeth, blue glass sleep eyes, BJ compo body, original "nun" attire. Ca. 1890+ ...$900

21" "3200" Girl. Turned bisque shoulder head, OM/teeth, brown glass sleep eyes, long brown HHW, kid body/bisque lower arms/cloth feet, old clothes, etc. Mark: "AM 2 DEP." Ca. 1895-99 ....$425

21-1/2" "370" Girl. Bisque shoulder head, OM/teeth, inset brown glass eyes, blonde HHW, kid body/bisque lower-arms/cloth feet, old clothes, etc. Mark: "370 A.M. 2 DEP/Made in Germany." Ca. 1913+ $450

22" "390" Girl. Bisque head, OM/teeth, blue glass sleep eyes, red mohair wig, BJ compo body, old clothes, etc. Mark: "Armand Marseille, Germany 390 A 9 M." Ca. 1890+ $550

22" "1901" Girl. Bisque shoulder head, OM/teeth, inset blue glass eyes, brown mohair wig, kid body/bisque lower arms, old clothes, etc. Mark: "1901//7/0//Made in Germany (horseshoe mark)." Ca. 1901 ....$450

22-1/2" "390" Girl. Bisque head, OM/teeth, blue glass sleep eyes, brown mohair wig, BJ compo body, old clothes, etc. Mark: "Armand Marseille, Germany 390 A 7 M." Ca. 1890+ $550

23" "266" Character Baby. Compo head, OM/teeth/tongue, blue glass sleep eyes, ptd/molded brown hair with molded side braids, 5-pc bent-limb compo body, original organdy dress, bonnet, etc. Mark: "266." Ca. 1925+ (Rare) $400

23" "370" Girl. Bisque shoulder head, OM/teeth, inset brown glass eyes. brown HHW, kid body/bisque lower arms/ cloth lower legs, old clothes, etc. Mark: "370 AM 3 DEP/Armand Marseille, /Made in Germany." Ca. 1913+ $450

23" "990" Character Baby. Bisque head, OM/teeth, brown glass sleep eyes, brown mohair wig, chunky bent-limb compo body, old clothes. Ca. 1913+ ..$850

23-1/2" "A.6M." Girl. or "Florodora." Bisque shoulder head, OM/teeth, inset brown glass eyes, thick dark brown eyebrows, brown HHW, imitation "kid" body/bisque lower arms, old clothes, etc. Mark: "Florodora A.6M./Made in Germany." Ca. 1890+ $525

24" "A.M. 201013" Girl. Bisque shoulder head, OM/teeth, inset blue glass eyes, blonde mohair wig, kid body/bisque lower arms/cloth feet, voice box, original clothes, bonnet, etc. Mark: "A.G. M. D.R.G.M. 201013." (Head has wired wooden talking devise inside head and handle protruding from hole in rear of head.) Ca. 1909+ $950

24" "3700" Girl. Bisque shoulder head, OM/4 teeth, brown -lass sleep eyes, brown mohair wig, rare jtd kid body designed to sit, /bisque lower arms/compo legs, original clothes, etc. Mark: "3700/AM) 01/2 DEP." Ca. 1895-99 ....$575

28" "390" Girl. Bisque head, OM/teeth, brown glass sleep eyes/real eyelashes, brown HHW, BJ compo body, original organdy dress, straw hat, etc. Ca. 1890+ (This doll is a later type, possibly 1920s). $700

28" "390" Girl. Bisque head, OM/teeth, brown glass sleep eyes, brown HHW, BJ compo body, old whitework dress with lace insertions, etc. Other marks: "D.R.G.M. 946" and "A9M." Ca. 1909+ $850

28" "Queen Louise." Bisque head, OM/teeth, dimpled chin, brown glass sleep eyes, long curl brown HHW, BJ compo body, original clothes, etc. 1910+..$850

31" "390" Girl. Bisque head, OM/teeth, blue glass sleep eyes, blonde mohair wig, BJ compo body, old whitework cotton dress, matching hat, etc. Ca. 1890s ....$1,000-$1,100

32" "390" Girl. Bisque head/florid coloring, OM/teeth, blue-grey glass sleep eyes, long brown sausage curl HHW, BJ compo body, old clothes, etc. Ca. 1900+ ....$950-$1,000

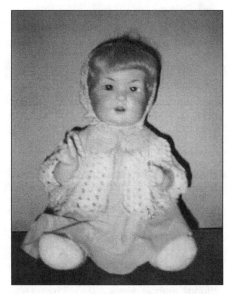

15" "Germany 971//A5M DRGM 264" marked baby. Bisque head, OM/teeth, blue glass sleep eyes, blonde HHW, 5-pc bent-limb compo body, redressed. (Cryer in body). 1910+ $475-$525. (Courtesy of Ruby Ellen Smith)

Chapter 25

∽ MODERN AGE DOLLS ∽

History: 1930-1945

The dolls manufactured after the 1929 stock market crash mirror the times. Despite their cheap retail/catalog look they possess the intrinsic beauty and glamour that was part and parcel of the day. It was an era of rich, glamorous movie stars and poor, struggling people who stood for long hours in soup or bread lines. And, although a Sears or Montgomery Ward doll might cost 69¢ or a hefty $2.95, a hamburger sandwich cost a nickel and a haircut cost a dime. Hence, many children went without dolls or settled for a 5-cent "Made in Japan" all-bisque or a welfare castoff.

Nowadays these dolls bring extremely high prices at auction and are the most requested dolls on collector want lists. Despite the fragility of the composition used during the thirties and early forties, Depression dolls fetch prices in excess of those made prior to 1930; and to find one in its mint or all-original condition is not unlike opening a time capsule. It instantly takes the adult back to childhood and recaptures memories too precious to forget.

Collecting Hints:

Mention the word "composition" and some collectors visibly cringe; associating it with a substance akin to wax. But, like wax, there are prime examples that have survived over 200 years in pristine condition. The very meaning of the word connotes its own use: a mixture of substances; and there were as many formulas made as there were people experimenting with them. Some formulas were perishable; others were durable and rock hard like the "Can't Break 'Em" formula. But, regardless of the quality of the composition used, an old doll must be cared for in the proper manner. Composition dolls require a temperature controlled atmosphere—meaning not too cold and not too damp. Even extremely dry air will effect the surface paint and cause peeling. Plastic bags should never be used as dust covers and plastic cases should not be used for display. Dolls concealed behind glass seem to fare better.

Never repaint a doll's face—or any part of the doll. The original patina and painting of features, even if blurred, re-

tains a doll's value. A repainted and restored doll, regardless of its superb "art" work-is just that-a "restored" doll, and should never sell for the same price of a doll in its original condition. Likewise a doll in its original clothing, shoes, socks, wigs, etc., is far more valuable than one that has been beautifully redressed in modern material and wearing a modern wig.

A light touching-up of lips, if not detracting, does not drastically devaluate a doll, but, as I said, leave her "as is." Also, never clean a composition or papier-mâché doll with a damp cloth, simply "dust" her with a dry one. Cleaning also may wash away the painted features and cheek blush. Dolls are expensive—protect your investment.

MODERN AGE DOLLS

7" "Eugenia Doll." Baby type. Compo head, pouty CM, ptd blue eyes, blonde ptd/molded hair, compo body jtd at neck/sh./stationary straight legs/blue painted-on shoes, original long dress, bonnet, etc. Head mark: "Eugenia Doll." Heart-shaped arm tag reads: "Love lee Doll by W.T. Grant Co." (Grant Co. was a dime-store chain.) Made by Eugenia Doll Co., NYC. Late 1930s or early 1940s (Mint) $125

7-1/2" Dionne Quintuplets. Toddlers. Compo heads, CM, painted eyes, dark brown mohair wigs, compo bodies jtd at neck/sh./hips, original sunsuits, bracelets, etc. Head marks: "Dionne//Alexander." Body marks: "Alexander." Tag read: "Dionne Quintuplets//Madame Alexander//New York." 1935 . $350-$400

8" "Sunshine Baby." All-compo/curved baby legs/right arm bent at elbow, CM, ptd blue eyes to side, medium brown ptd/molded hair with slight nape wave and forehead ringlets, original pink organdy outfit, matching embroidered bonnet, slip, chemise, rayon socks with ribbon ties. (Sunshine Babies made their debut with the compo Toddles and are similar except that Toddles had straight legs. They resemble "Baby Tinyette" (F&B) and the "Dionne Quints" (Alexander), etc. Head mark: "VOGUE." Lower back mark: "DOLL CO." 1937-1948 .... $400-$425

8-1/2" Negro "Puz." Black compo head, OM/no teeth, cloth body/black compo bent limbs, original shirt, romper drawers, bib, box. Unmarked. Box label reads: "803 13/1." Made by Kammer & Reinhardt, Germany. Ca. 1930s (Sold for $350-$375 MIB in 1992) Doll $400-$425 MIB .... $700-$725

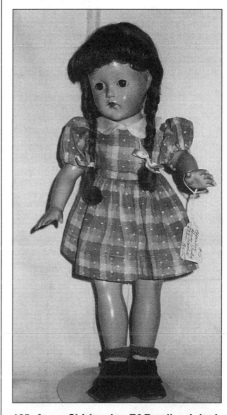

18" Anne Shirley by F&B, all original, $375-$400. (Courtesy of Billye Otto).

18" Anne Shirley by F&B (close-up of above doll).

9" "Carmen Miranda." Compo head, CM, brown sleep eyes, black mohair wig, compo body jtd at neck/sh../hips, original clothes, turban, hoop earrings, etc. Head mark: "MME ALEXANDER, N.Y. U.S.A. ALL RIGHTS RESERVED." 1942 (Size: 14"-15" $400-$450)
....$300-$350

9" Patsyette. "Ann of Green Gables." Compo head, CM, blue ptd eyes to side, molded bob/glued-on red mohair wig with 2 long braids, compo body jtd at neck/sh./hips, original checkered dress, round felt bowler hat, etc. (This doll was the first version of Anne Shirley in ANNE OF GREEN GABLES.) Ca. 1934....................................$400-$450

9" "Little Betty." Compo head, CM, ptd blue eyes, blonde mohair wig, compo body jtd at neck/sh./hips, original clothes: McGuffet Ana's dress, pinafore, pants, etc. Body mark: "Me Alexander, New York." Ca. 1938...................$300-$350

9" Snow White's "Seven Dwarfs." All-compo/jtd arms only, ptd features, mohair wigs/beards, brown ptd/molded shoes, original cotton velvet trousers, jackets, caps (each cap is imprinted with the dwarf's name). Made by Knickerbocker Doll & Toy Co., NYC. 1937 .$350-$375

16" Ideal Shirley Temple, all original, 1930s. See "Modern Age Dolls for prices." (Courtesy of Irene Ortega)

9" "Topsy." Black Baby Doll. All compo/jtd limbs only, CM, ptd brown eyes, black ptd/molded hair/3 inserted pigtails (top and sides of head), original red check dress, etc. Tag reads: "Topsy//Made by R.A.F." Made by Franklin Studios, Covington, GA.; distributed by American Wholesale Co. (These dolls were made for "Century of Progress-Chicago." 1933 (Mint)...................................$150

9-3/4" Little Red Riding Hood/Grandma/Big Bag Wolf. Patsy-look alike Red Riding Hood. All compo/jtd at neck/sh./hips/bent arms/Patsy-type bodies. LRRH has CM, ptd blue eyes, brown ptd/molded bob; BBW has a

dark brown ptd body and a "Wolf" head; Grandma has a smiling CM, ptd blue eyes to side; original dress, cape, shoes, socks, etc.; original "Wolf" overalls; original "Mother Hubbard" type outfit, bonnet, etc. Unmarked. Possibly Freundlich Novelty Corp., NYC, 1923+. Ca. 1930s (Mint) ....$675-$875

10" "Margie." Compo head, smiling CM, ptd blue eyes to side, blonde ptd/molded hairdo/ groove for hair bow, segmented wood body strung by elastic, original short lawn skirt with ribbon band trim. Heart-shaped red chest label reads: "MARGIE//DES. & COPYRIGHT//BY JOS. KALLUS." Designed by Joseph Kallus. Body made by E.B. Estes & Sons. Cameo Doll Co., NYC, 1922+. Ca. 1929-1930s ....$300-$350

10-1/2" "Pop Eye."/All-wood segmented, ptd features/pipe, tattoos on arms, ptd-on clothes/hat. Feet Marks: "KING FEATURES" and "C.J. CHEIN & CO. HARRISON, N.J. JO HEINZ, COLORADO." 1930s $350

10-1/2" "Pete." Cartoon Character. Round compo head/protruding ears, smiling watermelon mouth, round ptd eyes to side, compo body jtd at neck/sh./elbows/ wrists/waist/hips /knees/ankles, original clothes. Mark: "DES copyright by J.L. Kallus." (Since this comic-strip character was never published, the doll was not popular and discontinued.) Scarce (Sold for .. $475 in 1994 at auction)....................................$425-$575

11" "Dream Baby." All-compo/jtd at neck/sh./hips/toddler body, OM, ptd brown eyes, dark brown ptd/molded hair, original clothes. Head/body marks: "Dream Baby." Made by Arranbee Doll Co., NYC. 1940s (Scarce) ....$275-$300

11" "Dream Baby." Toddler. Compo head, OM/tongue, ptd blue eyes to side, black ptd hair, 5-pc compo body/straight legs, old clothes. Head mark: "Dream Baby." Arranbee Doll Co., NYC, 1922-1960 (R&B). There is a version of this doll with celluloid-over-tin/sleep eyes and a version with bent legs, and the same head on a different body, ca. 1935) 1934-41 ....$275

11" "Scarlet O'Hara." Compo head/jtd compo body, blue-green sleep eyes, black HHW, original tagged long gown, wide-brimmed hat, etc. 1937 Made by Madame Alexander, NYC. 1937
....$600-$650

11-1/4" Dionne Quintuplets./All-compo, OM/4 teeth, brown sleep eyes/eyelashes, black ptd curly hair, original flower-print dresses, etc.; pins. Back marks: "Madame/Alexander." Dress tag reads: "Genuine/Dionne Quintuplets Dolls//All Rights Reserved/Madame Alexander--N.Y." 1935
....$475-$525

(Costume colors for Dionne Quints: Yvonne (pink); Cecile (green); Emelie (lavendar); Marie (blue); Annette (yellow).

11-1/2" "Bobbie-Mae." Compo head, ptd features, blonde ptd/molded hair, ptd/molded compo dress "sways" when gentle touched. Inside dress marks: "Pat. Pending #2." Paper label on bottom of feet reads: "Bobbie Mae//Swing 'n Sway doll/inspired by//Sammy

Kaye//Patent Pending//Manufactured by//WONDERCRAFT CO.//NEW YORK." (Sammy Kaye was a band leader in the 1930s-40s. His theme song was "Swing and Sway with Sammy Kaye." Song or not, the phrase introduced his band.) Ca. 1935 ...... $250

12" "GEM" embossed Baby. All-compo/jtd at neck/sh./hips, CM, ptd blue eyes, blonde ptd/molded hair, original clothes. Made by Gem Toy Co., NYC. Ca. 1930s ....$250-$300

12" "Baby Snooks" or Fanny Brice. Compo head, smiling mouth, ptd blue eyes, brown ptd/molded short hairdo, wire-mesh body/flexible metal cable limbs/compo hands and feet, original clothes. Head Mark: "IDEAL." Round

14" Scarlet O'Hara by Madame Alexander, all original, $800-$850. (Courtesy of Connie Baca)

14" Scarlet O'Hara by Alexander, all original. (Same doll as above)

paper tag reads: "FLEXY--an Ideal Doll Fanny Brice's Baby Snooks." 1938+ ....$300-$325

12" World War II Soldier Boy. Compo head, watermelon mouth, ptd blue eyes, brown ptd/molded hair, wire-mesh body/flexible metal cable limbs/compo hand and feet, original uniform, cap. Head mark: "IDEAL DOLL." 1942 ....$300-$325

12" "Nancy Lee." Patsy look-alike. Compo swivel head, CM, ptd blue eyes, brown ptd/molded bob, jtd compo body, original clothes, etc. Arranbee Doll Co., NYC. Ca. 1930s. Mark: "ARRANBEE" or "NANCY." ....$225-$250

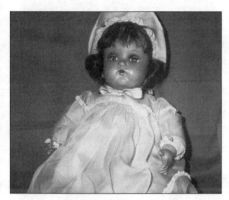

14" "Little Genius" by Madame Alexander, all original, 1940s, $300-$350 ($300-$350). (Courtesy of Connie Baca)

12" "Sweetums". Drink/Wet Baby. Compo head, OM, blue sleep eyes, brown ptd/molded hair, cloth body/full compo bent limbs/hole between legs for water drainage, original clothes, etc. Tag reads: "Sweetums//DRINKS HER BOTTLE//WETS HER DIAPER//GOES TO SLEEP." (Original box top has some working and "patent 2,040,20//May 12, 1936"). 1936 MIB ....$500+

12" "Dopey." Snow White's Dwarf. Compo head, O/C mouth/molded tongue, round ptd blue eyes looking upward, large ears, cloth body/limbs, original long green jacket, etc. Made by Mme Alexander. Ca. 1938 ....$450-$475

12" "Slumber mate." Baby. Compo flange head, CM, closed (sleep) eyes, dark ptd/molded hair, cloth body/compo limbs, original long organdy trimmed baby gown, slip. Neck mark: "Alexander." Ca. 1942 ....$300-$350

13" "Nurse." All compo/jtd body, CM, ptd blue eyes, blonde wig, original nurse uniform, cap, etc. 1935. Made by Mme Alexander, NYC. $800

13" "Betty." Patsy look-alike. All-compo/jtd at neck/sh./hips, CM, ptd blue eyes to side, blonde ptd/molded bob, original clothes, hat, etc. (This doll also came with sleep eyes and a wig.) Ca. 1935 ....$375-$400

Made by Mme Alexander, NYC. (19" size: ....$775-$825)

13" "Amberg" Girl. Patsy look-alike. Compo head, ptd blue eyes to side, brown ptd/molded bob, compo body jtd at neck/sh./hips, original dark blue sail-

or-type outfit with white braid trim, etc. (Doll is chubbier than the regular Patsy and has a "fuller" face, chubbier limbs, and more character.) Mark: "AMBERG DOLLS THE WORLD STANDARD MADE IN U.S.A." Ca. 1929-30 ....$300-$400

13" "A/2" embossed Patsy look-alike. Compo head, tiny heart-shaped CM, ptd blue eyes to side, brown ptd/molded bob (hair swirled across forehead in a "bangs" style), compo body jtd at neck/sh./hips, original striped dress, matching bonnet, et. Made in Germany. 1930s ....$300-$400

13" Bye-Lo Baby. Compo head, blue sleep eyes, CM, ptd blonde hair, cloth body/compo hands, original white hospital gown, pink receiving blanket with blue trim. Made by Cameo Doll Co., NYC, 1924. Ca. 1942-43 (Sold for $800 in 1993) ....$500+

13" "Little Colonel." Shirley Temple look-alike. Compo head, OM/6 teeth, blue tin sleep eyes, blonde mohair wig set in Shirley curls, compo body jtd at neck/sh./hips/straight legs, original "Little Colonel" outfit: dress, pantalets, ruffled bonnet, etc., wrist tag. Unmarked doll. made by Regal-Horsman (Regal Doll Co. and Horsman), NYC. 1936 ....$350-$400

15" Unmarked baby (similar to "Bubbles" and "Happytot"), original clothes. $250. (Courtesy of Ruby Ellen Smith)

13" "13" marked Shirley Temple. (This look-alike Shirley Temple is not from the original Shirley mold, but probably one of the early/rejects made by Bernard Lipfert.) Compo head, OM/teeth, blue metal sleep eyes, brown curly mohair wig, original dress, bonnet, shoes, socks, etc. Mark "13." Ideal. (Shirley temple body with her name obscured.) Ca. 1940 ....$350-$400

13" Judy Garland as "Dorothy." Wizard of OZ. Compo head, OM/6 upper teeth/felt tongue, brown glassine sleep eyes/hair lashes, brown HHW/pigtails, red blush on cheeks/knees, original

11"-13" Shirley Temple dolls, compo, 1930s, all-original. 11"-$1,000-$1,100 13"-$1,000-$1,100 (Courtesy of Connie Baca)

blue and white checked rayon jumper sewn onto organdy blouse with frilly collar and sleeves, leather shoes, white socks. Head mark: "IDEAL DOLL." Back mark: "18//IDEAL DOLL//MADE IN USA." Made by Ideal Novelty & Toy Co., N.Y. 1939 ....$475-$525

13" "Snow White." Compo head, CM, brown sleep eyes/real upper lashes, rosy cheeks, black mohair wig/pink hair ribbon, 5-pc compo body, original tagged costume, etc. Made by Madame Alexander, NYC. 1937 ....$475-$520

13-1/2" "Whistler" (Soldier Boy). compo head, OM/puckered, blue ptd eyes to side, black ptd hair, cloth body/legs/coiled springs with bellows/squeeze leg and the soldier whistles for girls/full compo bent arms, original cotton U.S. Army military uniform, cap, etc. Mark: "U.S.A." (Ideal used this mark on some of its dolls, especially those dressed by a well-known firm; in this instance, Madame Hendren.) WW 11 (Mint) ....$300-$350

14" "Wendy-Ann." Compo head/slim oval face/pointed chin, ptd eyes, ptd/molded bobbed hair, jtd compo body/swivel waist, original clothes, etc. Back mark: "Wendy Ann//MME Alexander//New York." 1936 ....$500-$550

14" WAAC. "Wendy-Ann" face. Compo head, CM, blue sleep eyes/lashes, brown mohair wig, compo body jtd at neck/sh./hips, original tagged "WAAC" uniform, hat, purse with shoulder strap, etc. (There was also a WAAF, WAVE SOLDIER.) 1942 Made by Mme Alexander, NYC. $800

14" Deanna Durbin. Compo head, OM/teeth, blue sleep eyes/real eyelashes, brown HHW, dimples, compo body jtd at neck/sh./hips, original dress with belt, matching jacket with patch pockets, underwear, black suede shoes, white socks, round Deanna Durbin button pinned to jacket. (This doll is dressed in a replica of one worn by Deanna in one of her films. It was given as a free gift for 4 five-year subscriptions to Country Gentleman at $1 each, or 2 one-year Saturday Evening Post subscriptions, sold at $2 each.) 1939 ....$650-$700

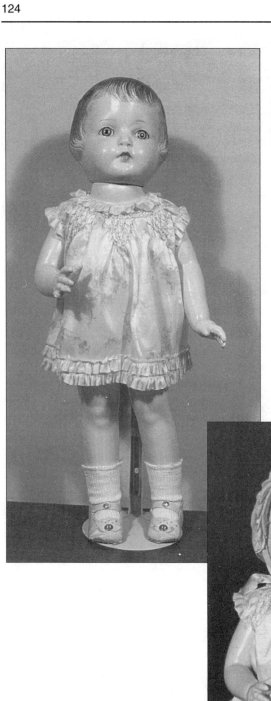

19" Patsy look-alike, all original. Unmarked $375-$400. (Courtesy of Ruby Ellen Smith)

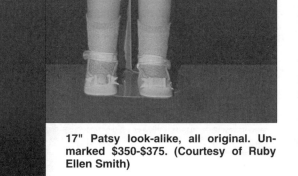

17" Patsy look-alike, all original. Unmarked $350-$375. (Courtesy of Ruby Ellen Smith)

19" Patsy look-alike, original clothes, bonnet, etc. Unmarked. $375-$400. (Courtesy of Ruby Ellen Smith)

18" 18"-22"Shirley Temple dolls, all original, 1930s. $1,100-$1,300 (Courtesy of Connie Baca)

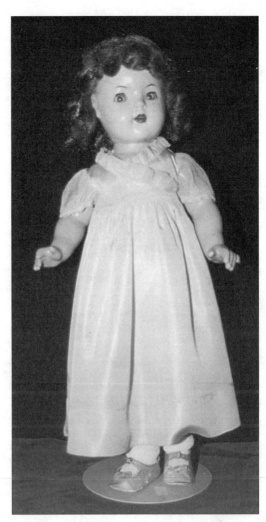

18" "Princess Elizabeth" by Madame Alexander, original tagged clothes. $550-$600. (Courtesy of Ruby Ellen Smith)

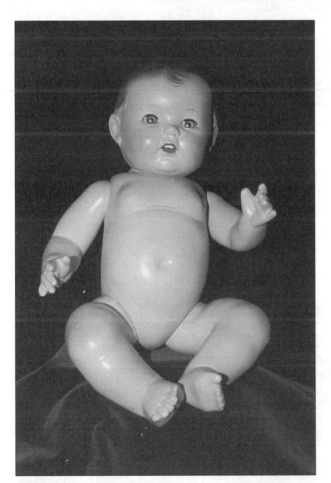

17" "Toodles", all compo, blue sleep eyes, brown ptd hair. Advertised in 1938. American Character Doll Co., NYC $300. (Courtesy of Ruby Ellen Smith)

11-1/2"-13-1/2"-14" Child dolls made in Old Mexico, compo shoulder heads/cloth bodies/compo limbs, original regional costumes, etc. $45 each. 1940's. (Courtesy of Herron)

14" "Bright Star." Compo head, OM, blue sleep eyes, blonde HHW, compo body jtd at neck/sh./hips, original wedding gown, veil, etc. Made by E.I. Horsman, NYC. 1940 ....$300-$350

14" Betty Boop. All-compo/molded hands on hips/stationary together legs/molded base, ptd features, black ptd hair, short red ptd/molded dress. (A carnival type doll.) 1930s (Scarce) ....$400+

12" Dionne toddler, all-original, by Mme Alexander, 1935. $475-$525. (Courtesy of Herron)

14" "Peaches." Patsy look-alike. All-compo/jtd body, CM, blue tin sleep eyes/real lashes, strawberry blonde fur wig, original pink and blue flounced print dress with an organdy collar with a felt rosebud/matching teddy, etc. Head mark: "A. Co. Inc." Made by Averill Company, Inc., NYC, 1915+. (This is a Horsman mold. "Tousle head" is the name given dolls wearing these fur wigs.) 1930s ....$350-$400

14" "WAAC" Girl. compo head, OM/teeth, blue sleep eyes, blonde mohair wig, jtd compo body, original WAAC uniform, shoulder-strap purse, hat, etc. Vogue sticker on dress. Made by Vogue Dolls, Inc., Medford, Mass., U.S.A. Ca. WWII ....$375-$425

14" "Fairy Princess." Compo head, CM, large blue sleep eyes,/lashes, blonde mohair wig, compo body jtd at neck/sh./hips/long straight legs, original pink satin dress with embroidered pink and blue garlands/front panel, etc. Madame Alexander, NYC. 1942 ....$300-$400

14-1/2" "Dimmie." Patsy look-alike. Compo head, CM, large blue ptd eyes to side, brown ptd/molded bob, compo body jtd at neck/sh./hips/twist waist, original clothes, hat, etc. Madame Hendren, NYC. 1927 (Listed here as it resembles Patsy during her 30s hey-day) ....$500-$550

15" "Betty." Compo head, CM, blue sleep eyes, thick blonde wig, cloth body/compo limbs, original blue dress, bonnet, etc. Tag reads: "Madame Alexander." (One of the innumerable "blank" dolls

Mme. Alexander dressed during this period.) Ca. 1935 ....$425

15" Shirley Temple Wardrobe Doll. All-compo/jtd body, OM/teeth, sleep eyes, blonde mohair wig, original red polka dot dress with red ribbon trim; trunk includes extra dress, pajamas, playsuit, hat, pin, etc. Mint-in-trunk. 1930s $2,000

15" "Kewty." Patsy look-alike. Compo head, smiling mouth, rare blue sleep eyes (most have painted eyes), blonde ptd/molded short hair, jtd compo body, original clothes, etc. Made by Domec Toy Co., NYC. (Arranbee also made a "Kewty" type with wardrobe trunk.) 1930s $300

15" Sabu. Compo head, CM, ptd brown eyes, jtd compo body, original harem pants, jacket, turban, shoes, paper wrist tag. (This black boy doll supposedly represents film actor, Sabu, in the 1940 movie, "The Thief of Bagdad." Dressed by Mollye Goldman, clothes designer for her "International Doll Co., Philadelphia, PA" Ca. 1940. $650-$700

15-1/4" "SIC." Patsy look-alike. Celluloid head, tiny CM, round ptd blue eyes to side/ptd upper eyelashes, blonde ptd/molded bob, red nostril and eye dots, celluloid body jtd at neck/sh./hips/long limbs, original white and blue sailor suite, cap, etc. Mark: "SIC (in a diamond shape) 40." Made by Société Industrielle de Celluloid or Sicoine, France. 1930s $300

15-1/2" WW II Sailor Boy. All-compo/jtd/jtd body, smiling red O/C mouth/ptd teeth, ptd blue eyes, blonde ptd/molded hair/white cap, original sailor suit with chest label: "Praise the Lord and pass the ammunition." Made by Freundlich Novelty Corp., NYC, 1923+. Ca. 1942 (Mint)...........................$300

16" "Mammy." Compo head, red smiling O/C mouth/teeth, black ptd eyes, black mohair wig, cloth body/black compo arms/black ptd/molded shoes, original dress, apron, bandanna, etc., and tag. Designed by Tony Sarg for Borgfeldt, NYC. Ca. 1939.............................$400

16" "Sally Jane." Shirley Temple look-alike. All heavyweight "Paratex"/jtd at neck/sh./hips, OM/6 teeth, blue sleep eyes, blonde mohair wig with bangs and 2 ponytails, original dress, white

16" All-compo toddlers, all-original. Boy tagged "Petz." Ca. 1930s Possibly Italian make. $225 each. (Courtesy of Carol Lindberg)

shoes, socks, etc. American Character Doll Co., NYC. Ca. Late 1930s.... $450

16" "Nancy." Compo head, OM, blue sleep eyes, blonde HHW, compo body jtd at neck/sh./hips, original dress, hooded coat, etc. Head mark: "Nancy." Made by Arranbee, NYC. 1930 .... $350-$375

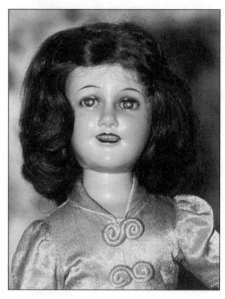

21" Deanna Durbin, all original, 1939. See "Modern Age Dolls" section for prices. (Courtesy of Rosalie Purvis)

16" "Baby Buttercup." Compo head, OM, blue tin sleep eyes, blonde ptd/molded hair/deep combmarks/nape curls, cloth body/legs/compo arms, original clothes, bonnet, etc. Neck mark: "H." Made by Horsman, NYC. 1932.... $350

16" "Betty Jane." Compo head, OM/teeth, blue sleep eyes, blonde mohair wig with 2 long pigtails tied with blue ribbons, compo body jtd at neck/sh./hips, original cotton dress printed with multi-colored flowers, white organdy pinafore, tan straw hat with green ribbon, etc. Body mark: "USA//16." Round wrist tag reads: "AN UNTRAFINE PRODUCT..." Made by Ideal Novelty & Toy Co., NYC. 1930s.................$400-$425

16" "Little Angel." Compo head, CM, brown sleep eyes, dark brown hair, cloth body/compo arms and legs above knees/cloth thighs, original lace net dress with pink rayon ribbon trim, shoes, socks. Made by Arranbee Doll Co., NYC, 1922-60. (This standard baby type was called "Dream Baby" in 1940 and earlier. Hard plastic "Little Angels" came later as toddlers.) Ca. 19402.................$300-$350

16" "Little Orphan Annie." Compo shoulder head, CM, large ptd blue eyes, orange ptd/molded bob, cloth body/legs/arms/compo hands, original red dress, etc. Back mark: "Famous/Artists Synd." Ca. 1931 ...... $350

16" "Carrie Joy." Compo head, wee CM, blue sleep eyes, brown HHW, compo body jtd at neck/sh./hips, original pink and white muslin dress hat, black Mary Jane shoes, socks. Mint. (The original price for this doll was ..$3.00, but if you purchased$10 worth of other Ideal dolls and had the card punched by the store to record each purchase, you got "Carrie Joy" for only 99¢.) 1930s $300-$350

16" "Buttercup" Baby. Compo head, OM/tongue, green glassine sleep eyes, blonde ptd/molded hair, cloth body/compo bent limbs, original white organdy dress, matching bonnet trimmed with lace, batiste petticoat, flannel under shirt/diaper, white shoes, socks. Neck mark: "E.I.H. Co." Cloth dress tag reads: "HORSMAN QUALITY DOLL." Box reads: "I'm called Little Buttercup,//Deer Little Buttercup,//Sweet Little Buttercup I." Made by E.I. Horsman, NYC. 1932 (MIB) $600

16" "Miss Charming." Shirley Temple look-alike. Compo head, OM/teeth, sleep eyes, brown mohair wig with Shirley curls, jtd compo body, original clothes, shoes, socks, etc. Mark: "E.G." (Originally called "Little Miss Movie." A lawsuit changed this name to "Little Miss Charming.") 1930s ...... $400-$500

16" Nurse and (8") Baby. Compo shoulder head, CM, ptd blue eyes, blonde mohair wig, cloth body/compo limbs/large hands (for holding the all compo/jtd baby, original uniform, apron, cap, etc. Unmarked. (Probably represents a Dionne Quint and her nurse.) 1935 .... $400+

16" "Meg." Character in "Little Women." Pressed felt mask face, tiny CM, brown ptd eyes to side, braided auburn mohair wig, pink muslin body/limbs, original white organdy dress with tiny red flocked flowers and white organdy collar decorated with red rickrack, white cotton petticoat/attached drawers, black leather shoes, white socks. Label reads: "Meg//Little Women//Copyright//Madame Alexander N.Y." 1933 (Mint) .... $750-$800

16" "Jo." Character in "Little Women." Pressed felt mask face, tiny CM, brown ptd eyes to side, brown mohair wig, pink muslin body/limbs, original blue cotton dress with rickrack trim and

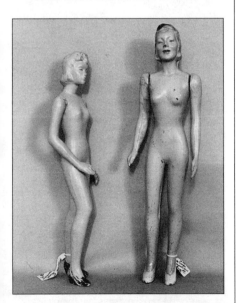

11-1/2"-13" Composition lady mannikin dolls for children's sewing kits, early or mid-1940s. $85-$125. (Courtesy of Herron)

white organdy collar, white organdy apron printed with red and blue flowers, white cotton petticoat/attached drawers, black patent leather shoes, white socks. Label reads: "Jo//Little Women//Copyright//Madame Alexander. N.Y." 1933 .... $750-$800

16" "Beth." Pressed felt mask face, tiny CM, brown ptd eyes to side, brown mohair wig, pink muslin body/limbs, original white organdy dress with red and pink crisscross pattern and wide organdy collar, white cotton petticoat/attached drawers, black patent leather shoes, white socks. Label reads: "Beth//Little Women//Trademark Pending//Madame Alexander N.Y." 1934 .... $750-$800

17" "Rosi." Compo head, OM/teeth, blue glass sleep eyes, thick brown HHW, compo body jtd at neck/sh/hips/wrists/1-pc legs, original clothes, etc. Neck mark: "Rosi." (Resembles an ordinary dolly-face open-mouth German bisque head doll.) Made in Germany. 1930s $400

17" Canadian Mountie. Compo head, CM, blue ptd eyes, brown ptd/molded hair, cloth body/legs/compo arms, dressed as a "mountie." (Same doll was also sold dressed as a Texas Ranger, The Lone Ranger, Scotsman, etc. Mark: "Reliable of Canada." (Eisenmann & Co., England, was the agent for the Reliable firm.) Ca. 1938 .... $400

17" "Fashion Jane" Mannequin Lady. Compo head, CM, blue ptd eyes, blonde "embroidery floss" hair, cloth body/compo arms/feet, original clothes, hat. Label reads: "Fashion Jane//Made in U.S.A." Made by Merrimac, NYC. 1940s $225

18" "Ice Skater." (Often called "Sonja Henie"). Compo head, CM, blue sleep eyes, blonde mohair wig, compo body jtd at neck/sh./hips, original "ice skater's" costume, boots with ice skates attached, etc. Mark: "R&B." Made by Arranbee Doll Co., NYC, 1922-1960. Ca. late 1930s $400

18" "Princess Elizabeth." Compo head, OM/teeth, large blue sleep eyes, blonde mohair wig, compo body jtd at neck/sh./hips, original floor-length white lace gown trimmed with pink ribbons, silver slippers, etc. Label reads: "Princess Elizabeth, Madam Alexander, New York." (Represents Princess Elizabeth at the Coronation of her father to the throne of England.) 1937 (Mint) .... $550-$600

18" "Debu' Teen." Compo swivel head/shoulder plate, CM, blue sleep eyes, brown HHW, cloth body/compo limbs, original yellow taffeta and net formal, etc. Unmarked. Made by Arranbee Doll Co., NYC. 1938+ .... $300-$325

18" "Betty Jane." Shirley Temple look-alike. Compo head, OM/teeth, blue sleep eyes, real eyelashes, brownish mohair wig, compo body jtd at neck/sh./hips, original clothes, etc. Mark: "IDEAL 18." (This doll is often found with flirty eyes.) 1930s $500-$525 Size 14".. $400-$425

18" "Nancy Lee." Compo head, CM, blue sleep eyes, blonde mohair wig, compo body jtd at neck/sh./hips/long legs, original ice-skating costume of velveteen, ice-skating boots, socks, cap, etc.

Head mark: "R&B." Round paper tag reads: "NANCY LEE//AN//R&B//QUALITY DOLL." (This beautiful doll is often called a "Sonja Henie." Only Madame Alexander made authentic Sonja Henie dolls. This doll is much prettier than the Alexander doll.) Arranbee Doll Co., NYC, 1922-1960. Early 1940s (Mint) .... $400-$450

18" "Bye-Lo" type. Compo head, CM, brown sleep eyes, ptd/molded hair, cloth body/limbs, original long white christening gown, bonnet, jacket with lace trim. Head mark: "American Character Doll." American Character Doll Co., NYC, 1919+. (This doll came in 3 sizes. It was exhibited at the Toy Fair in March 1942.) Ca. 1942 .... $250-$300

11-1/4" All original Carmen Miranda, 1939. $125. (Courtesy of Herron)

18" "Little Angel Baby." Compo head, CM, blue sleep eyes, rosy cheeks, blonde ptd/molded hair, cloth body/compo lower limbs, original dress, bonnet, etc. (This same doll was sold through SEARS catalog in 1940 and called the "Million Dollar Baby." There were also sizes 16", 21", and 22".) Arranbee Doll Co., NYC, 1922-1960. Ca. 1940 .... $350-$400

18" "Baby Charming." Dionne Quintuplet look-alike. Compo head, OM/teeth, brown sleep eyes, black ptd/molded hair, compo body jtd at neck/sh./hips/straight legs, original pink organdy dress, pink organdy bonnet/blue trim, white socks, white shoes, etc. Round dress button reads: "Everybody loves me//Baby Charming." Made by Eegee. NYC. 1936 .... $400-$450

18" "Nun" Doll. Little Girl type. Compo head, CM, blue tin sleep eyes,/read eyelashes, bald head/no wig, compo body jtd at neck/sh./hips, original "nun's" habit, cross, etc. Tag reads: "A Dillon Doll Creation//Our//Little//Sister." 1938 .... $250-$275

18" "Betty Jane." Shirley Temple look-alike. Compo head, OM/teeth, blue flirty eyes/real lashes, brown mohair wig, compo body jtd at neck/sh./hips, original clothes, etc. Mark: "IDEAL 18." Made by Ideal Nov. & Toy Co., NYC. 1930s ....$475-$525

19" Negro Girl. Shirley Temple look-alike. Brown compo swivel head/dimples, OM/teeth, brown tin sleep eyes, black mohair wig, brown compo body jtd at sh./hips/bent arms/long straight legs, original red dress with tiny white polka dots and broad white collar, white shoes, white socks, etc. Yellow Pin on dress reads: "COLORED DOLLS BY LUJON, N.Y." Luzon Doll Co., NYC. Late 1930s (Scarce).....................$700

19" Baby Sandy. All-compo/jtd at neck/sh./hips, OM/teeth, sleep blue eyes, brown ptd/molded hair, original clothes, etc. Mark: "Baby Sandy." Made by Freundlich Novelty Corp., NYC, 1923+. 1939-1942.........................$500

(Baby Sandy was a screen star in the late 1930s.)

19" "A.C. INC." marked Girl. Patsy look-alike. Compo head, CM, ptd blue eyes, brown ptd/molded bob with bangs brushed to the left side of forehead, original clothes, etc. Mark: "A.C. INC." Probably American Character Doll Co., NYC, 1919+. 1930s.......$375

19" "Lolly." Baby. Compo head, smiling mouth, blue sleep eyes, brown ptd/molded hair, compo body jtd at neck/sh./hips,/bent arms/straight legs original lace-trimmed full skirt dress with a high yoke and puff sleeves matching bonnet, etc. Neck mark: "Madame Alexander." (The original bodies of these dolls was made of "Lov-le-tex", a rubber product which did not prove durable despite its lovely texture.) 1941+.................................$500-$600

20" "Alice in Wonderland." All cloth/jointed, CM, ptd blue eyes, yellow yarn hair,

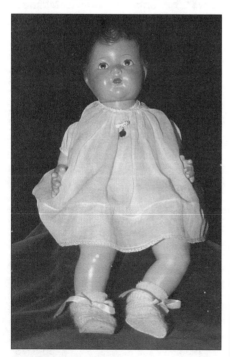

18" "Dionne" Quint by Mme Alexander, original tagged clothing, gold pin reads: "Yvonne." Marked on head $500-$550. (Courtesy of Ruby Ellen Smith)

original blue and white polka dot dress (tagged), white organdy apron, black shoes with ankle straps, white socks, etc. Made by Madame Alexander, NYC. 1933+ (Good condition)...... $500

20" "The Lone Ranger." Compo head/hands/feet/cloth body, CM, ptd blue eyes/black mask, original plaid shirt, bandanna, chaps, belt/gun/holster, trousers, white hat, etc. Unmarked. 1938 (Mint)............$800-$900

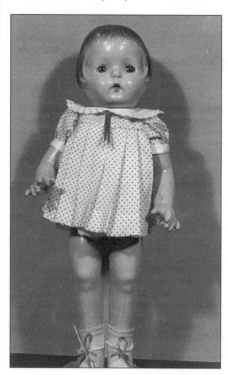

18" Patsy look-alike, redressed. $275. (Courtesy of Ruby Ellen Smith)

20" Little Girl. Compo head, OM/2 teeth, blue sleep eyes, blonde mohair wig, jtd compo body, original outfit includes velvet coat and hat, etc. Made by Horsman; dressed by "Molly-e" or Mollye Goldman, International Doll Co., Philadelphia, PA., 1920s+. High quality doll. 1938.. $300

20-1/2" "Petite" Girl. Compo shoulder head, OM/teeth, brown glassine sleep eyes, long sausage curl brown HHW, cloth body/compo limbs, original short dress, bonnet, etc. head mark: "PETITE." Wrist tag reads: "How do you do//My name is 'Petite'//Don't you think//I'm very sweet?" American Character Doll Co., NYC, 1919+. Ca. 1930s ....$350-$400

20-1/2" "Molly-e" Girl. Compo head/long neck, CM, large brown eyes, blonde HHW, compo body jtd at neck/sh./hips/well-sculpted hands, original clothes, etc. Unmarked. Label reads: "I have human hair." Probably made by the Joy Doll Company, NYC for Mollye Goldman and dressed by Molly-e's Doll Outfitters. Ca. 1940s $350

20-1/2" Snow White. Compo head, OM, brown sleep eyes/real lashes, black mohair wig, compo body jtd at neck/sh./hips, original clothes, etc.

Mark: "WALT DISNEY KNICKER-BOCKER TOY CO." 1937 .... $600

21" "Sally Joy." Patsy look-alike. Compo head, OM/teeth, blue glassine eyes (sleep type), brown sausage curl wig, compo body jtd at neck/sh./hips, original dress, bonnet, etc. Head mark: "PETITE SALLY." Wrist tag reads: "LOVABLE PETITE DOLL//SALLY JOY." Made by American Character Doll Co., NYC, 1919+. 1930 $375-$400

21" Judy Garland. Compo head, OM/teeth, sleep eyes, brown HHW, compo body jtd at neck/sh./hips, original clothes, etc. Head mark: "Ideal Doll Made USA." Back mark: "Ideal Doll." (This size is referred to by collectors as the "teen" doll due to its slender body. The 1939 version of the doll had the body used on their Shirley Temple dolls which was a chubbier child-type.) Early 1940s .... $1,000+

21" Deanna Durbin. Compo head, smiling OM/teeth, blue sleep eyes, brown HHW, compo body jtd at neck/sh./hips, original outfit: plaid jacket/cap, skirt, etc. original round metal button reads: "DEANNA DURBIN, IDEAL DOLL, U.S.A." 1938 .... $900-$1,000

22" "Baby Genius." Compo head, CM blue sleep eyes, brown ptd/molded hair, cloth body/compo limbs, original clothes, etc. Head mark: "Madame Alexander." Ca. 1937............. $500-$600

22" "Special girl." Patsy look-alike. Compo swivel head on compo shoulder plate, CM, brown sleep eyes, blonde mohair wig/pigtails/ bangs, cloth body/compo arms/cloth and compo legs, original clothes, bonnet, etc. 1942 Made by madame Alexander, NYC ....$600-$650

19" Ideal Shirley Temple, all original, marked, 1930s. $1,300. (Courtesy of Ruby Ellen Smith)

23" "Unica" Girl. Papier-mâché socket head, OM/teeth, blue glass sleep eyes, brown mohair wig, BJ compo body, original clothes, hat, etc. Neck mark: "Verhoye Courtray Made in Belgium" (in a circle) and "Unica/60//BR.//415.013" (in the middle). Made by Unica, Belgium, 1921-1940; 1947-1965. Ca. 1930 ....$350

24" "PAT APPLIED FOR" embossed Girl. Patsy look-alike "sitter." Compo head, CM, blue sleep eyes, strawberry blonde ptd/molded bob, compo jtd body with swivel hips that enable doll to sit/bent compo arms/straight toddler compo legs, original clothes, etc. Maker unknown. Ca. 1929-30.............$500

24" "Dimples." Toddler. Compo head/long neck, OM/2 teeth, blue sleep eyes, brown ptd/molded hair, firm cloth body/bent compo arms/long straight compo legs to above knees/cloth upper legs, original clothes, frilly bonnet, etc. Neck mark: "E.I.H. Co. Inc." Cloth label reads: "Dimples." E.I. Horsman, NYC, 1927-30 ....$600

24" "Baby Dimples." Compo head, OM/2 teeth, large blue flirty eyes/real lashes, brown ptd/molded hair, cloth body/compo limbs, original clothes, bonnet, etc. Mark: "A Horsman Doll." (This is the second version of "Dimples" by Horsman.) E.I. Horsman, NYC. 1937 ....$450-$500

24" "Sweetheart." Compo swivel head/long oval face/long neck, OM/6 teeth, green flirty glass eyes/real lashes, blonde mohair wig, long jtd compo body/long compo legs/long rubber arms, original dress, rayon slip, shoes, socks. Unmarked doll. (This doll's hard rubber arms were called "Kantbreak.") Made by E.I. Horsman, NYC. 1939 ......$350

25" Shirley Temple. Compo head, small OM/teeth, green flirty/sleep eyes, blonde mohair wig, compo body jtd at neck/sh./hips, original "Wee Willie Winkie" costume: pleated plaid skirt, tan cotton twill jacket with belt/brass buttons, blue velvet plaid cap, original black ankle-strap shoes, reddish stockings. Round Shirley Temple button pinned to jacket. 1930s Mint (Sold for $3,885 in 1996 at auction) ......$3,000+

25" Shirley Temple. Compo head, OM/teeth, green flirty/sleep eyes, blonde mohair wig, compo body jtd at neck/sh./hips, original pale blue organdy dress, combination teddy/petticoat, shoes, socks. Mark: "Shirley Temple" (head and body). 1930s (Mint) . $1,600

25" "Baby Gloria." Compo head, OM/teeth, blue sleep eyes, blonde ptd/molded hair, cloth body/compo limbs, original clothes, etc. Mark: "200." Paper tag reads: "Baby Gloria, Dolls of Distinction, Maxine Doll Co., N.Y." 1930s ....$475-$525

25-1/2" Shirley Temple look-alike. Compo head, OM/teeth, blonde mohair wig, blue flirty eyes, compo body jtd at neck/sh./hips, original clothes, shoes, socks, etc. Made by "BONNIE", Italy. 1930s.................................$650-$700

36" "Skookum" Indian Chief. Brown ptd compo head, CM, ptd brown eyes to side, black mohair wig/braids, cloth body covered by a floor-length brightly designed woolen Indian blanket. (Mary McAboy registered "Skookum" trademark in 1913, and designed the early dolls. H.H. Tammen Co., manufacturer; Arrow Novelty Co., distributor.) 1930s $700

Chapter 26

~ LEO B. MOSS ~

History: Late 1890s+

Leo B. Moss, Macon, Georgia, late 1890s-1930s. Leo B. Moss, a black man, was born in America's colorful southland, growing up in Macon, Georgia. Although known as a "handyman", he began making dolls while still a young man. His early dolls were made from paper boiled into paste (papier-mâché) and modeled like clay. Poor people in those days lined the walls of their drafty frame shanties with newspapers to keep warm. There were usually many layers of newspaper on the walls, thus Leo would scrape off the top layers and make his clay.Like most doll-makers, his first dolls were crude and not well-sculpted, and are almost indistinguishable from his later, more professional work. When his skill improved, Leo began sculpting the faces of children and adults he saw around him. The dolls were either given to the people they depicted, or traded for vegetables and poultry. Leo married and had six children, and, although he continued to create dolls, he took part-time handyman jobs to supplement his meager doll income. His baby and child dolls became so popular that he accepted commissions from parents to model dolls of their offspring, inscribing the doll with the child's name and date.

A New York toy salesman visited Macon when he heard of the extraordinary dolls being made there by a local citizen. He was so impressed with the dolls he purchased some, subsequently selling them to European toy dealers, who then commissioned some white dolls. It was during this time that

Leo began using ball-jointed bodies on his dolls (sold to him by the salesman). Leo painted the bodies black to match the heads. Leo's life was turned upside down when the salesman ran off with his wife. Thereafter, the Moss dolls became known as the "Crying Dolls" (they had molded tears on their cheeks) In later years, Leo stopped making dolls and began to drift around the country. The dates on his later dolls prove that he was still making dolls during the Depression. He died in poverty in 1937.

Collecting Hints:

Most of Leo B. Moss' dolls are marked with the initials "L.M." But there are also unmarked Moss dolls, yet these are unmistakably his work. The Moss dolls have been commanding high prices at auctions for many years and are considered choice collector items. Early dolls had cloth bodies as did later dolls. Dolls made in the "in-between" period had the ball-jointed composition bodies. I doubt Leo could afford these bodies in the later years, especially during the Depression where every nickel counted.

Reproduction Alert:

These dolls have not been reproduced in modern times, but they were obviously imitated during their hey-day.

LEO B. MOSS

16" "Crying" Girl. Black compo head/"mumps" cheeks/two white tears, down-turned CM, inset dark brown glass eyes, slanted eyebrows, black ptd/molded curly hair, cloth body/com-

po lower limbs, old clothes, etc. Mark: "1901, LM." $7,500
16" "Crying" Toddler Girl./Black compo head/tears, down-turned CM, inset brown glass eyes, PN, black ptd/molded curly hair, brown cloth body/black compo limbs, original clothes. Head incised: "L.M." Cloth label on body reads: "Vesa, 1930." $4,500
16" "Happy" Boy. Black compo head, O/C smiling mouth/6 molded upper teeth, inset brown glass eyes, black ptd/molded curly hair, brown cloth body/black compo lower limbs, old boy clothes, etc. Unmarked. $8,000
20" Little Girl. Black papier-mâché head, OM/white ptd teeth, inset brown glass eyes, black wool wig, black BJ compo body, original red print dress, underwear, bonnet, etc. Head mark: "L.M." $5,000
21" "Crying" Baby. Smooth papier-mâché head, CM (down-turned lips), inset brown glass eyes/3 tears on cheeks, black ptd/molded curly hair, brown cloth body/black bent lower compo limbs, original clothes. (Only the date 1932 can be read on the faded cloth patch stitched to chest.) Head mark: "LM" $5,000
24" "Pouty" Boy. Black compo head, pouty CM, inset brown glass eyes/3 molded cheek tears, black ptd/molded hair, black BJ compo body, original clothes, etc. Head mark: "L.M." $8,500
25" "Crying" Toddler. Girl. Black compo head, CM (down-turned lips), inset brown glass eyes/3 molded cheek tears, black ptd/molded hair, brown cloth body/black compo lower limbs, original checkered dress, underclothes, bonnet, etc. Cloth label on stomach reads: "Vesa, 1930." Head incised: "L.M." $9,000
26" Baby. Black ptd papier-mâché head, CM, inset brown glass eyes, black ptd/molded hair, cloth body/compo lower limbs, old white cotton baby gown, etc. Head mark: "L.M." $9,000

Chapter 27

～NOVELTY DOLLS～

History:

The "novelty" doll was just that a "novelty"—conceived mainly for adult amusement (some were downright "naughty" and were called "naughty dolls"), enjoyed for a moment, then cast away with yesterday's newspapers. Oftentimes they spoofed the headliner of the day, be it an actress, actor, politician, football star, aviator, comic strip or cartoon character, etc. Silent screen comedians like Charlie Chaplin were good targets, as was Theda Bara, Mae West, Mistinguette, Shirley Temple, and so on. Even such popular figures as Kewpie wound up in chalk.

Boudoir dolls in all shapes and sizes were manufactured; flaunting their mute sex appeal with carefree abandon. The more expensive boudoir dolls were cast in china and called half-dolls since they were only sculpted to the waist and hollow. This made them ideal decorations for all sorts of functional items. These were sold in posh department stores, hair dressing salons, perfumer's shops, and even at cosmetic counters. Max Factor's Make-up Studio in Hollywood sold the pin cushion types in their showrooms inside the glass display cases alongside their Art Nouveau and Art Deco perfume bottles and cold cream jars (1919-1930s). A 1919 photograph of their celebrity-themed display windows reveals a haughty half-doll in a long, billowy skirt presiding over a cosmetic and hair color exhibit. She appears to be the chalk or poured wax type with mohair wig attached to a wire form.

Theatre lobbies (the Ziegfeld Theatre), boardwalks dime stores, novelty shops, carnivals, and "cheapie" catalogs were all prime sources to find one of these fashionable damsels. Oddly, they rarely appealed to little girls, being much too sophisticated and risqué for their delicate tastes. Novelty dolls, however, trite as they may seem, are much more than mere "frivolities", they express the temper of the times and are as timely as a tabloid. They also remind us of America's more colorful past, when "wit" and "charm" and "romance" were more than merely words in the dictionary:

Collecting Hints:

Until the advent of price guides and auction houses, novelty dolls, regardless of quality or rarity, were not taken seriously by advanced doll collectors (prior to 1975), and were labeled "secondary" dolls. They abounded in antiques shops, thrift shops, and secondhand stores and were usually priced from $5-$10. Then, quite suddenly, some astute person began to point out their heretofore unseen "virtues" and the race was on! It was deemed unanimously by this unknown jury, that glazed porcelain half-dolls were of the most value if their dainty arms were extended away from their body (this required more intricate molding by those long dead German workman who would no longer gain any profit from their labor). If the hands touched the body and the elbows were away from the body, the doll was worth somewhat less. And if the doll and her arms were modeled onto the body with no extended parts, the doll was of the least value of the three types. This is not to say, that some of the latter are quite lovely and interesting and should be priced accordingly.

Elaborate hairdos, a bald head with an original wig, jointed arms, a swivel neck, inset glass eyes, an open mouth with teeth, unusual facial expressions,

Left to right: 5-1/2" all-bisque/movable arms, gold ptd hair, original crepe paper costume/hat; 8-1/2" (middle) all-bisque/moveable arms, original dress; 5-1/2" all bisque, original pink crepe paper dress over cone shaped bottom. 1920s party favor dolls. $65-$75 each. (Courtesy of Herron)

9-1/4" pin cushion doll, china head/satin body, pre-1920s era, $65; Spanish lady and man, Chinese lady and man, all 6" high, ca. 1932, $35 each. (Courtesy of Herron)

great beauty, etc., all add-up to more and more dollars. A pink tone china is more valued than a common white china. Ethnic chinas (Negroes, etc.) are very rare, as are men, boys, babies, animals, and what have you. France made half-dolls in bisque, china, and wax, but try finding one marked! A "MADE IN FRANCE" half-doll is super-rare.

The most valuable bed-dolls are the ones with heads made of bisque, painted pottery, or poured wax. (Some have china heads.) The nude bathing beauties (some wear swim suits) are choice and pricey. Chalk and plaster of paris half-dolls attached to pin-cushions, cushions, lamps, etc., are more desirable than a chalk carnival figurine. The "value" of the latter is more "nostalgic" than monetary. In the long haul, the value of any doll always depends on just how much it is worth to the person who desires it the most and finally buys it.

Reproduction Alert:

Since we live in the "reproduction" age, be wary of any doll that appears too "new". Some half-dolls have been reproduced, especially in the 1970s and 1980s. I have seen the larger sizes with painted grey hair and some smaller "Spanish" lady types with a pink tone china finish. Look inside the hollow doll for signs of age and dirt along the ridg-

French half-doll utility cover, wax over plaster, ptd features, blonde mohair wig, velvet covering over wire frame, 11", 1920s, $125; 6-1/2" felt French provincial lady power box cover stamped "Made in France", 1920s, $45. (Courtesy of Herron)

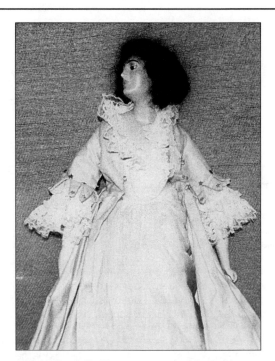

17" Lady doll. Plaster to waist/bisque lower arms, mohair wig, kid body, exquisite clothes, very well cut and sewn. 1920s $150-$225. (Courtesy of Herron)

Two 1920s doll lamps, 13" size, plaster of paris half doll, white mohair wig, metal frame, original covering, lamp cord, $135; 15" lamp doll, wax-over-plaster, brown mohair wig, compo half arms attached with wires, wire base, original covering, 1920s $165. (Courtesy of Herron)

12" "Buddy Lee." All compo/movable arms, original clothes, hat. $350. (Courtesy of Ruby Ellen Smith)

es. Buddy Lee has been reproduced. Some modern doll artists, like Niesje Wolters-van Bemmel of the Netherlands, have made boudoir dolls with china heads and lower limbs, but these are usually signed by the makers and are not reproductions of old dolls but modern dolls conceived in the old manner.

The Shirley Temple figurine or statuette cast in a pure white substance (she holds the ends of her outstretched dress) was reproduced in the 1960s and later (the casting material resembles marble).

NOVELTY DOLLS

2-1/4" "Powder Puff Bag." Half-doll. Bucilla set #5989. Lady-type china half-doll/black ptd hair/orange sleeveless blouse with a yellow collar/arms molded onto doll. Original box contains two embroidery hoops, material for yellow rayon-taffeta skirt. The powder puff pockets are to be embroidered. Instruction book. 1920s MIB $125

13" "Sheba Doll" 1920s, $125; 13" "Sheba Doll" with original feathers, 1920s $150. These "vamp" kewpie types were carnival prizes. (Courtesy of Herron)

6" All-bisque/jtd arms only, made in Germany (marked), original skirt, hat. This boudoir doll was placed on the bed amongst cushions. 1920s $150. (Courtesy of Herron)

3-3/4" Shirley Temple. Figurine. All-bisque with a glaze/blue skirt. Shirley holds the ends of her outstretched skirt/together legs molded onto base. 1930s $35

3-3/4" "Goebel" Marie Antoinette. Half-doll. Delicate glazed china/four sew holes/arm away from body (one hand holds a letter or note which she appears to be placing inside her bodice)/turned head/hair ornamentation. Goebel mark incised on rear near the base. Made by F.&W. Goebel, near Coburg, Thur., Germany. 1915 ... $300

4" Lady. Half-doll. White china/raised head/long neck/stationary arms attached to body at hands (one hand on hip; other hand raised to shoulder), CM, blue ptd eyes, bald head/soft brown mohair wig/straw hat/ptd jacket. Mark: "Germany." 1920s $150

4-1/4" Powder Box Lady. Half-doll (2-3/4") attached to original pink and white powder puff/pink blouse top/ arms molded onto body. The half-doll "puff" concealed inside a pink porcelain-china skirt or "box"; the "lid" has a hole in the center which fits down over the lady and serves as the top of her "skirt." Very dainty. 1920s $175

4-3/4" French Lady. Half-doll. White china/nude to waist/hands conceal bare bosom/elbows away from body, wee red mouth, blue ptd eyes/red lid lines, straight black eyebrows, grey ptd/molded hair in the late 18th century mode. Mark: "Made In France" (inside base). 1920s or earlier. Super-rare $350

4-3/4" "D.R.G.M. 6295" incised Flapper Powder Jar. Hand-ptd china "reclining" lady with removable legs and attached "puff." Black ptd bob with bands (a la Colleen Moore), blue ptd skirt/red blouse top with shoulder straps/long bare limbs/black ptd high-heeled slippers. Made in Germany. 1920s .. $150

4-3/4" French girl. Bust. Wax-over-plaster/sculpted below bosom, smiling O/C mouth/white space, blue ptd eyes, light brown curly mohair wig, wires protruding from base for attachment to a torso. Stamped "France" on the bottom (This is the face of a young girl). 1920s $150

5" "Elka" marked Lady. Wax-over-plaster/sculpted below bosom/round, sloping shoulders, rosebud mouth, large blue ptd eyes to side/brown eyeshadow, pink, cheeks, wavy auburn mohair wig, shoulder wires for attachment to a torso, wire lamp base, pin cushion, etc. Back mark: "52" and triangular sticker which reads: "Made in Austria" and "Elka." Gorgeous doll. 1920s $125

5" Lady. Half-doll. All-bisque to waist/nude/jtd bent arms (jtd at shoulders), CM, over-sized blue enameled eyes, original elaborate mohair wig with long sausage shoulder curl and coronet braid across top of head. Unmarked. Mint. rare type. 1920s $400

5" "Melanie//Southern Miss" marked Girl. Nancy Ann Storybook Doll look-alike. All painted bisque/jtd arms only, CM, ptd blue eyes, long blonde mohair wig, original long plaid taffeta gown, original glass jar that holds the doll. Jar Mark: "#161 MELANIE//Southern Miss-Civil War." Doll mark: "K&H." Kerr & Hinz

Company, Santa Clara, CA. Ca. 1939 Mint $500

6" Pierrette Wax-over-plaster/modeled below bosom/shoulder and bottom wires for attachment to lamp, O/C mouth/white space, ptd blue eyes to side, black ptd skull cap with black spit curls on forehead and at sides of face. 1920s $75

6-3/4" Shirley Temple. figurine. Plaster of paris/ptd/molded in one piece/together legs/separate molded arms holds the end of her ruffled skirt/molded red roses on the sides of the pedestal on which she stands. 1930s $45

Left to right: 3-1/4" pin cushion doll made in Germany, $45, 1920s; 6" high (middle) pin cushion lady trimmed with white marabou, all original, made in Japan, 1920s, quality $85 6" pin cushion lady, all original/elaborate cushion, made in Germany, 1920s, $125. (Courtesy of Herron)

7" Lady. Half-doll. All-bisque to below waist/turned head, CM, ptd blue eyes, white silk wig, raised stationary arms/4-sew holes. (Arms away from body.) Mark: "Germany" and "Goebel" crown mark. Floral design on base. F.&W. Goebel, near Cogurg, Thuringia, Germany. Ca. 1915 .... $450

7" "Columbine." Half-doll. All-bisque/bent arms modeled away from body/delicate separated fingers/bald head, O/C mouth/white line, ptd blue eyes/ptd black mask, large black beauty spot on face, white mohair wig, pin cushion lower body covered with original lace skirt. 1920s.. $175

8" "Madame Pompadour" Powder Box Lady. All glazed porcelain. Top half removable for puff. Mark: "Madame Pompadour//Dresser Dolls//E&R//Germany." 1920s $65

7-1/2" and 6-1/2" "Sit Me" dolls, 1920s. $65 each. (Courtesy of Herron)

Plaster half dolls, 1920s. Pin cushion doll, original skirt and decoration, 11-1/2", $125; half dolls without pin cushion, 7" high. Brunette half doll incised "KC" on back $75 each. (Courtesy of Herron)

1930s Dresser Dolls. 15" $65; 8" $45. (Courtesy of Herron)

18-3/4" high metal half doll/metal lower arms/metal cage, ptd features brown mohair wig, old outfit. Lamp type, 1920s, $175; plaster of paris half doll, ptd features, white mohair wig, compo lower arms, red silk "dress", 1920s, lamp with cord, $165. (Courtesy of Herron)

Left to right: plaster "Sit Me" doll with brown mohair wig, 1920, $175; (middle) 11-1/2" "Tinker Bell", 1920 or earlier, $225; 6-1/2" "Tease Me" with hand on cheek, 1920s, $85. (Courtesy of Herron)

Plaster of paris half dolls 4"-6" high, mohair wigs, ca. 1925, $45 each; half doll with black mohair wig made of papier-mâché, $35, 1920s; half doll with shoulder curl made of papier-mâché, $35, 1920s. (Courtesy of Herron)

9" x 8-5/8" "Sandy." Little Orphan Annie's Dog. Stuffed oilcloth/stenciled in bright colors/made to stand alone. 1927 $300

9-1/2" "Johnny the Page Boy." Philip Morris Advertising Hand-Puppet. Compo head, red CM, ptd blue eyes, brown ptd/molded hair/molded-on black cap, red flannel "glove-type" body with two brass buttons/attached white felt gloves. Unmarked. (There is also an open-mouth version of "Johnny" with a cloth body. Late 1930s $350

9-3/4" "Skeezix and Dog" (8-1/4" X 6-1/2"). Cartoon Characters. Oilcloth/stenciled in bright colors/Skeezix has apart legs. 1927-28 Pr. $500

10" Charlie McCarthy. Plaster of paris/no movable parts/white ptd/molded tuxedo and top hat, ptd features. (Carnival prize.) 1940s $65

Left to right: half doll scent bottle, 4-1/2" $65+; hat pin holder, 6", $65; little girl scent bottle, 5-1/2", $85+. (Courtesy of Herron)

11" "O-U-Kid" Chubby Girl Statuette. All plaster/composition/movable arms/together legs molded onto round green base, CM, rosy cheeks, large ptd blue eyes to side, auburn mohair wig/hair ribbon, nude. (Carnival type doll.) Gem Toy Co., NYC. 1919 ....$150

11" Pin-cushion Lady. All-bisque to waist, shin slightly raised and head turned, stationary arms (lovely modeling), ptd blue eyes/half-closed eyelids, white mohair wig, original "skirt" conceals cushion. (Arms apart from body.) Possibly German. 1920s $125

11" "Mon Cheri" Party Favor. Bisque head attached to wire-armature body/wire limbs wound with red silk fabric/red silk short dress/red cap, no wig, CM, inset black glass eyes, PE/earrings. Head mark: "MON CHERI LP PARIS 0 3 (L. Prieur)." 1920s $350

11-1/2"Pin-cushion Lady. Wax shoulder head/bald head, red CM, ptd blue eyes, black beauty mark on chin, white mohair wig with fine hair net, lovely bisque lower arms and hands, original necklace with blue enameling on chain, original blue silk bodice and skirt which

5" high wax-over-plaster lady bust with original black mohair wig, ptd features, incised "KW", made in Germany, 1920s, $65; 6-1/2" pin cushion doll (head only), all original, 1920s $65. (Courtesy of Herron)

conceals cushion. German or French. Unmarked. 1920s $125

11-1/2"Charlie McCarthy. Hand-puppet or glove-type doll. Compo head/molded-on black top hat, ptd features/black monocle, black cloth "glove" body/white gloves. Head mark: "CHARLIE MC-CARTHY." Made by Ideal Toy Co., New York. 1938 ....$125

13" Drum Majorette. All ptd chalk figurine/arms molded close to body/together legs modeled onto base/red ptd outfit. 1930s $65

13-1/2"Shirley Temple Carnival Figurine. All ptd chalk/red ptd dress/green ptd pedestal and base/outstretched arms hold ends of ruffled skirt/bow at waist. 1930s or early 1940s $175

13-5/8" "Little Orphan Annie." Cartoon/comic strip character. Stuffed oilcloth/stenciled in bright colors (wears a fur-trimmed coat and cap with pompons). 1927 ....$350

14" Pinocchio. All painted chalk/arms modeled close to body/hand holds an apple/together legs. 1930s $85

14-1/2"Donald Duck. All ptd chalk/together legs modeled to base/arms modeled close to body, large black ptd eyes to side, wears short black jacket and bow tie. 1930s $75

14-1/2"Popeye. All ptd chalk/one arm modeled to side, the other arm's hand holds a pipe/together legs. 1930s ...$65-$75

14-1/2"The Lone Ranger. All ptd chalk/arms modeled close to body/hands on holsters/black ptd boots modeled to base, red O/C mouth, black mask, yellow cowboy hat, red shirt, blue vest, blue bandanna, white chaps. 1945 ....$125

15" "Hula Girl" Carnival Figurine. All ptd chalk/arms bent toward upper chest and touching hair/no movable parts/together legs, red CM, large ptd blue eyes to side, yellow-orange ptd/molded

curly hair, real silk string skirt glued to upper and lower torso. 1920s or 1930s (This doll figurine may have been inspired by Clara Bow in the film "Hula," 1927. Does not resemble her.) $85

15-1/2"Charlie McCarthy. All composition/jtd head only/hands in pockets, black ptd tuxedo and top hat, ptd features. Head mark: "CARNIVAL NOV CO." Early 1940s $85

15-1/2" "Nize Baby." Milt Gross cartoon character doll. All cloth/cry box, ptd features/hair, original baggy bloomer-pants, felt shoes. ("NIZE BA-BY" printed on bib top.) Madame Hendrem, NYC. 1927 ....$350-$400

16" "MUNZERLITE" Lamp Lady. Half-doll. Ptd plaster of paris/modeled to waist/turned head/molded bosom, CM, ptd blue eyes/brown eyeshadow, auburn mohair wig with rear sausage curls, wired/ptd metal lower arms/wire frame/socket for bulb situated at base of doll's torso, original "skirt" or lampshade. Back mark: "MUNZER-LITE//PATENT//PENDING." Germany. 1920s $175

24" "Baby Vamp." Little Girl type. All-compo/jtd at shoulders only/stationary legs molded apart/ptd black shoes/socks/fat protruding lower stomach, tiny CM, ptd blue eyes to side, short molded hair beneath blonde mohair wig, fancy feathered dress/feathered head-dress. Made by Imperial Novelty Doll & Toy Co., NYC. (Probably a spoof of Mae West in "The Mimic World of 1921"). 1921 ....$300

17" Turned head (plaster) on a kid body, expertly sewn and styled clothes. 1920s. $150-$225.

Chapter 28

~ ODD-MATERIAL DOLLS ~

History:

The designers and manufacturers of children's playthings have always sought the "perfect" toy—the "indestructible" toy—the "unbreakable" toy—a low-cost toy that would reach the masses and help finance the more costly, artistic toys that appealed to a more high-class, sophisticated segment of the public who had the means to purchase anything they desired, thus constantly sought the unusual and thought provoking.

Yet, despite this insatiable quest for the lasting, durable toy, or doll, in this instance, the manufacturers realized that such a doll was impracticable, especially if they wished to continue to earn money in the business—and doll manufacture is a big business—a billion dollar industry. Consequently the companies experimented with alternative substances over the years and touted them all as "indestructible": pewter, tin, wax, rawhide, rubber, celluloid, vinyl, plastic, etc.

But, to their dismay, these "indestructibles" proved even more fragile than the more common mediums: bisque, china, mâché, and compo Bisque and china will break when dropped, but it will not melt, chip, or

116" Little girl with "turtle mark", all-celluloid/jtd body, CM, blue ptd eyes, white ptd/mld hair, original clothes, etc. $225 (Courtesy of Irene Ortega)

peel; nor does this medium attract rodents. In 1925, Kathe Kruse said: "Celluloid is an unsuitable and wrong material. The only advantage is, it is more durable than bisque. A celluloid doll does not give the soft warm feeling; it is like a breeze." She forgot to mention that celluloid was highly flammable and sometimes split at the mold seams. (In 1955 at the Nurenberg Toy Fair the Kruse celluloid dolls made by Rheinische Gummi und Celluloid Fabrik Company were exhibited and were highly acclaimed. They were made from Tortulon, a celluloid substitute.)

In early times dolls were made from ivory, bone, wood, clay, and bread crumbs—and children loved them all. It was not the components that mattered to the child, nor even the doll's beauty, it was far more complex than that. Perhaps it was the doll's soul—something the manufacturers knew nothing about.

Collecting Hints:

Here are a few hints: a rawhide or rubber doll with a marred face is preferable to one that has been repainted—and has more value. Ditto the tin head doll. (Or any doll, for that mater.) Celluloid dolls have always been considered "secondary" in the eyes of the collector, but now that the hard plastic doll has become a popular favorite, perhaps collectors will realize the value and beauty of her older sisters. The hard plastic doll has fallen victim to nostalgia--reason for the over-pricing in that area of collecting. A marked doll is always a prized possession, but some of the most beautiful and valuable dolls are unmarked. As time goes on and old dolls become more scarce, all dolls, common or not will be considered "rare."

ODD-MATERIAL DOLLS

3" "Max." Book character created by Wilhelm Busch, 1865, All-celluloid/jtd at shoulders only, ptd features, brown ptd/molded hair, original felt outfit. Germany. 1920s $200

3-1/2" Boy Clown. Molded in one piece/movable arms/apart legs, molded-on costume/long sleeves/blue, red, green dots/molded-on hat with pointed top/3 red dots. Body mark: "(turtle design)//Germany." Rheinische Gummi

and Celluloid Fabrik Co., Germany. 1900+ $165

4" "Minerva" marked girl. Metal shoulder head, CM, ptd blue eyes, blonde/molded common hairdo, old home-made cloth body, original clothes. (Dolls' House doll.) Buschow & Beck, Germany, 1888+. Rare size $65

4"(approx.) Shirley Temple Soap Figurine. All white untinted soap/molded in one piece. Shirley's head is slightly tilted to the side/bent arms. 1936+ Mint $35

4" Charlie McCarthy. All-soap figurine/no movable parts, black ptd tux/top hat. (Color worn.) 1939+. Mint $35

5-1/4" Shirley Temple Soap Figurine. All painted soap/no movable parts/tied with original red ribbon. Shirley has raised arms and holds the ends of her pleated skirt in a familiar pose. Ca. 1936... $50

6" Swimming Baby. Celluloid head/body/legs/metal arms/green ptd and molded bathing suit/wind-up key/mechanism on underside, CM, ptd brown eyes, orange ptd/molded hair. Workable. Japan. 1920s $125

6" Metal creeping baby, original clothes with Steiff pigeon. Baby only $75.

6" Crawling Baby. All-celluloid/swivel neck/movable limbs/key wind/mechanism, O/C mouth, ptd blue eyes, protruding ears, blonde ptd/molded hair/curly forehead locks, original romper suit with wide white collar. Foot stamped: "Made in Japan." Ca. 1940 (Workable). $110

6-1/2" Chauffeur. Plaster head/cap, ptd features/hair, ball-jtd metal body/limbs, original grey felt uniform (double-breasted coat with black bead buttons, black imitation long leather leggings, black ptd shoes, grey ptd hat with black ptd visor. Original box marked: "SABA (illustrated with figure), Made in Switzerland, Schwerz Nr 93'. 600 Pat D.R. P. Nr 353'855 U.S.A. demandet Brevets-England Nr. 177'739-France NR. 536'593 27th June 1921 SABA." 1920s MIB $700

7" Betty Boop. All-celluloid, ptd features, black ptd hair, red ptd/molded dress, head nods from side to side/stationary arms/together legs. Original box has Betty Boop on front. 1930s MIB .$600+

7-1/2" Action Man. Compo head/comical face, watermelon mouth, round blue eyes with black pupils, modeled ears, orange ptd/molded toplock/side and back hair, 1-pc metal body/round and square metal parts compose posable limbs/compo hands and feet, no clothes. Mark: "Serba." Serba of Switzerland. Ca. 1921+ Rare..............$300

8" French Girl. All-celluloid, CM, inset brown glass eyes, blonde mohair wig, jtd at neck/sh/hips/ptd/molded shoes and stockings, original French regional outfit, hat. Mark: "SICOINE." Société Industrielle de Celluloid, France, Ca. 1916-20 ....$100

8" "Minerva" Baby. Boy. All-celluloid, CM, blue intaglio eyes, blonde ptd/molded hairdo, jtd at sh/hips/bent limbs, old clothes, etc. Mark: "Minerva (Helmet symbol), 23 Germany." Buschow & Beck, Germany. 1910+ $95

8" "Maiden America." Googly-type. All-compo/jtd arms/together legs, ptd features, ptd topknot, original red, white, blue ribbon tied around body and reads: "Maiden America." Sticker reads: "Des. Pat. 8-24-15. Kate Silverman." Maiden Toy Co., NYC, 1915-17; Maiden America Toy Mfg. Co., 1918-19. ("The National Doll.") 1915 ....$225

8-1/4" "Gretel." Character from the book "Mon Village ceux qui n'oublient pas," by Hansi, 1920. All ceramic/jtd at neck/sh/hips, smiling ptd mouth, ptd blue eyes to side, ptd brown hair, original outfit made of silk, cotton and velvet, black Alsatian head-dress, red umbrella/school slate ptd/molded shoes and striped socks. (Yeri and Gretel date to 1913 as book characters.) Made by P. Gallais, France. Ca. 1916 Rare ....$1,000+

8-1/2" "Whistler" Boy. Celluloid head, O/C mouth (pursed lips), ptd brown intaglio eyes to side, no ears, dome-shaped head/blonde mohair wig, wire-frame body with crêpe paper/cardboard feet, original Little Lord Fauntleroy-style costume. Mark: "BAITZ" (on top of head in black letters.) Ca. 1900+.......$85-$125

9" "Art" Doll. Lady type. All-silk paper, small molded silk paper head, ptd features, black wool bobbed hair, orange silk paper hat, wire-armature body/limbs (covered with orange silk paper), elaborate orange silk paper dress with black rim. Doll attached to a stand. Ca. 1919-1920. Made by Erna Muth. Dresden, Saxony. Rare ....$500+

9" 4-headed doll. Two little girls with blonde ptd/molded hair, one little girl with brown mohair wig, one little boy with black ptd/molded hair, all-celluloid/jtd bodies, ptd features, no clothes. Back shoulder marks: (turtle design) "Schutz Marke" (German for Trademark). Rheinische Gummi and Celluloid Fabrik Co., Germany. Ca. 1900+............$200

9-1/2" "Diddums." All-celluloid/movable arms only, CM, ptd blue eyes, blonde ptd/molded hair, yellow ptd romper suit, yellow ptd socks, black ptd shoes. (Pale green celluloid painted a flesh color.) Mabel Lucie Attwell design, England. 1927+ Rare $300

10" Character Baby Boy. Celluloid head, CM, ptd blue eyes, dark blonde ptd/molded hair, cloth body/limbs, old clothes. (Resembles Kathe Kruse Doll I based on the Flammingo bust.) Mark: (turtle design). Rheinische Gummi and Celluloid Fabrik Co., Germany. Ca. 1920s $125

10-1/4" "Parsons-Jackson" Baby. Biskoline head/double chin, O/C mouth/molded upper teeth/molded tongue, ptd blue eyes, blonde ptd hair, bent-limb Biskoline body jtd at neck/sh/hips/steel spring jts, old clothes/molded blue shoes/socks. Mark: (stork design) and "Trade Mark//Parsons-Jackson Co./Cleveland, Ohio." 1910-1919 $225

10-1/4" "Sleep" Baby. All-rubber/stationary body, O/C mouth, closed eyes, blonde ptd/molded hair, molded-on blue pajamas. Mark: "Pat. Pending." Ca. 1920s-30s $65

10-1/2" "Snow Baby." Celluloid mask face/cloth head, CM, ptd blue eyes, blonde ptd/molded bangs/sewed-on red plush hood, cloth body/limbs/sewed-on red plush snow suit with large white mitten plush hands/white feet. Unmarked. Ca. 1905...$150

11" "203" marked Kestner Baby. Celluloid head/animated facial expression/cheek dimples, O/C mouth/molded teeth/tongue, inset blue glass eyes, blonde mohair wig, plump celluloid body jtd at neck/sh/hips, old clothes. Back mark: "J.D.K.//203//3//Germany." (This doll is expertly sculpted with dimples and creases; realistic face, hands, feet, etc.) Ca. 1910+ $300

12" Mickey Mouse Club Girl. All rubber/jtd at neck/sh/hips, smiling mouth, round ptd blue eyes to side, brown ptd/molded hair/white ptd shoes and socks. Mickey Mouse head molded on chest in raised relief form. Sun Rubber Co., Barberton, Ohio. Ca. 1950 ....$85

12" "Decker" Girl Doll. All-leather, molded head/seam down middle of face, tiny CM, ptd black eyes, ptd black hair, no attached ears, flat-type leather body/stuffed/laced up front/separate limbs/no jts/12 holes on front of body for lacing, old clothes, etc. Gussie D. Decker, Chicago, Ill./M.S. Davis Co./patent by Gussie D. Decker. Ca. 1902-1909 Super-rare ....$3,000+

12" "717" embossed Character Girl. Celluloid head, OM/teeth, blue glass sleep eyes, blonde mohair wig/2 long pigtails, celluloid body jtd at neck/sh/hips, original clothes, etc. Mark: (turtle design) "K(star)R, Germany." Rheinische Gummi und Celluloid Fabrik Co., Germany, for Kammer & Reinhardt. Ca. 1910+ $400

12-1/2" "Bubbles." All-celluloid, OCM/teeth, ptd blue eyes to side, reddish molded hair in upswept hairdo (braids)/red satin bow glued to head, jtd body/stationary head, original clothes. Mark: "3/8." Ca. 1951 ....$65-$125

13" "Baby." (Same head as K(star)R #100 mold.) Celluloid head, O/C mouth, ptd blue eyes, large ears, blonde ptd hair, bent-limb compo body, old clothes. Mark: "K(star)R 700-22" (turtle design). Ca. 1909+.....................................$600

13" "Helmet" marked Boy. Metal head, CM, ptd blue eyes, blonde ptd/molded "boy" hairdo, American-made cloth body/metal lower limbs, original black velvet 2-pc suit trimmed with lace, etc. (the white shirt has the lace trim). Mark: "Helmet symbol." Buschow & Beck, Germany. Ca. 1920 (No chips or scratches) $175

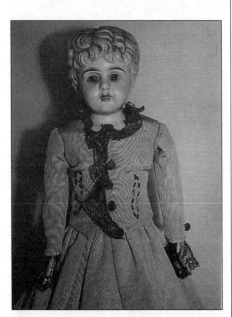

17" Metal shoulder head, O/C mouth, inset blue glass eyes, blonde ptd/mld hair, cloth body/bisque lower arms, old clothes. 1888+ $200-$225. (Courtesy of D. Kay Crow)

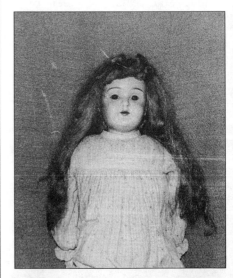

23-1/2" Tin shoulder head girl, OM/teeth, inset blue glass eyes, long wig, kid body/bisque lower arms, original clothes. (This doll's face and shoulders are mint, no scratches.) Unmarked. 1888+ $400-$450 (Courtesy of Herron)

13" "Inge" Girl. Havalit celluloid-compo head, O/C mouth, blue intaglio eyes, exposed molded ears, blonde ptd/molded hairdo with coiled braid encircling crown (top), kidaline body with jts at hips/knees/Havalit hands, original clothes, etc. Mark: "2 Inge W.Z." Wagner & Zetzche, Germany. Ca. 1924 ....$225

13-1/2" Lambeth Delft Doll. Peg-wooden look-alike. All tin-glazed earthenware/no movable parts/static seated position, sharp red line mouth, ptd black eyes, black ptd hair, yellow-orange cheek blush, black ptd shoes, nude. Ca. 1700 Super-rare (Speculative) $3,000

13-1/2" Toddler Girl. Walker. Celluloid head, red CM, ptd blue eyes, brown ptd/molded hair, exposed ears, metal body/clockwork mechanism/celluloid limbs, original red and white check skirt, white blouse, red and white check hat, red metal shoes, socks, etc. Mark: "JAPAN." Good working condition. Ca. 1950 ....$150

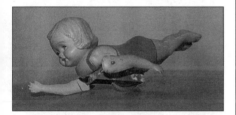

8" Celluloid swimming doll. Ca. 1920s-30s $125.

13-3/4" "Nouveau Nes" (newborn). Light pink celluloid head, OM/pacifier, inset blue glass eyes, light brown ptd hair, light pink celluloid jtd bent-limb body, original pink jacket, etc. Mark: "(head of an eagle design)35." (Babies with sleep eyes were named "Bébé, Dodo.") Petitcolin, France. 1913+ $275

14" Little Boy. Celluloid head, CM, inset brown glass eyes, brown ptd hair/2 stray forehead locks, hollow cloth body/cotton-stuffed legs, original clothes. Unmarked. (A rubber "bladder" fits into the hollow body. When blow-up it fills out the body.) Possibly German. 1920s $300

14" Little Girl. Rubber shoulder head, red ptd mouth, ptd blue eyes, blonde ptd/molded short hairdo, cloth body/limbs/leather lower arms with tiny wooden sticks to support fingers/sewn-on leather boots, old print dress, etc. Mark: "NEW YORK RUBBER CO. GOODYEAR'S PAT. 444." New York Rubber Co., NYC, 1851-1917. (Body made by Philip Goodsmith, Cincinnati, Ohio, 1870-1894.) Ca. 1870s Fair condition ....$1,000+

15" "Dominique." Patsy look-alike (the French version). All celluloid/matte finish, tiny red CM, inset round blue celluloid eyes/real eyelashes, brown ptd bob with bangs (upside down V-shaped part), fully jtd body/long straight legs, black ptd/molded shoes/white socks, original clothes, bonnet. Mark: "SNF (in a diamond design) 40." Made by the

Societe Nobel Francaise (SNF), Paris, France, 1927................................$500

15-1/4" "406/1" marked Girl. Celluloid head, OM/teeth, blue glass sleep eyes, blonde HHW, original BJ compo body, old clothes. Mark: "K(star)R 406/1 and turtle." Rheinische Gummi and Celluloid-Fabrik, Bavaria, for Kammer & Reinhardt, Germany. Ca. 1910+ $600

15-1/4" "36/40" marked character Girl. Celluloid head, red CM, inset blue glass eyes/real upper lashes, brown ptd/molded bob with swirls on forehead and sides of face, celluloid body jtd at neck/sh/hips/bent arms/straight toddler legs/ptd-on ankle-strap shoes, original clothes. Mark: "SCHUTZ-MARKE// (heart design)//36/40//Germany 4." 1930s $350

15-1/4" Snow White and the Seven Dwarfs. Painted carton or papier-mâché head, CM, ptd blue eyes/ptd upper lashes, dark brown mohair wig, cloth body/limbs/tiny celluloid hands, original white rayon long dress with cape and red sleeve inserts, black shoes, hair ribbon, etc. (The Seven Dwarfs have heads made of felt or carton and felt costumes, hats, shoes.) Cotton labels on Snow White and the Dwarfs reads: "Made in France." 1937 Mint.....$2,000

15-1/2" Negro Baby Boy. all black celluloid/fully jtd body, CM, flirty glass eyes, black ptd/molded hair/eyelashes, original baby dress, bonnet, etc. Head mark: "France (diamond design with S/C in the center and one at the side)." Societe Industrielle de Celluloid, France; used trade-name "Sicoid" and "Sicoine" for their celluloid dolls; a "winged dragon" symbol also used. (This firm gleaned a gold medal for their baby dolls at the Leipzig Expo in 1913.) ca. 1928 ....$450

16" "721" marked character Girl. Celluloid head, OM/teeth, blue glass sleep eyes, brown long curl HHW, kid body/wood lower arms, old clothes, etc. head mark: "Tortoise." Kammer and Reinhardt, Germany. 1910+.......$350-$400

16" Little Boy. All-celluloid/swivel neck/unjtd limbs, CM, inset blue glass eyes, luminous white ptd hair, original clothes. Head mark: "(turtle) 36/41." body mark: "(turtle) T44." (Body has voice box, squeak holes.) ....$225-$325

16" "WZ" marked Toddler boy. Heavy celluloid head, red CM, rosy cheeks, ptd blue intaglio eyes, blonde ptd/molded hair/stippling, oilcloth body jtd at hips/knees/ball-jtd arms/hands, original clothes. Mark: "5//Harald//WZ." Wagner & Zetzche, Germany. Ca. 1915 . $250

16" "Minerva" marked Girl. Metal shoulder head, OM/teeth, inset blue glass eyes, blonde mohair wig, cloth body/legs/compo lower arms, old clothes. Buschow & Beck, Germany. Ca. 1900+ (No chips)...................$300

17" Little Girl. Metal swivel head, CM, inset blue glass eye, blonde mohair wig, metal body jtd at neck/sh/elbows/wrists/hips/knees/ankles, old clothes, etc. (Slight nose rub.) Metal Doll Co., Pleasantville, New Jersey, 1902-1903. (This is one of their All Steel Dolls invented by Vincent Lake.) 1902-03 rare type $550

17" "Baby Bo Kaye." Celluloid shoulder head, O/C mouth/2 molded lower teeth, inset brown glass eyes, modeled ears, brown ptd/molded hair, cloth body/compo limbs, original clothes. Designed by J.L. Kallus; had made in Germany. 1925 ....$850

17" "Jacky." Negro boy. All-dark brown celluloid/shiny finish, red CM, large inset brown celluloid eyes, black ptd/molded hair/deep comb marks, fully jtd body/bent legs, original clothes. Mark: "SNF (in a diamond design) 45." Société Nobel Francaise, 67 Bld Haussmann, Paris (same address as Societé, Génerale de Dynamite); also Societé, Industrielle de Celluloid office at 326 rue Saint Martin (Impasse de la Planchette). 1927+ $850

17" "Monique." All-celluloid/matte finish, red OM/upper teeth, brown glass sleep/flirt eyes, brown HHW, fully jtd body/long straight legs, original clothes. Mark: "SNF (in a diamond design) 45." Ca. 1950s $275

10-1/2" Boy and Girl made of stuffed oilcloth-type material, ptd features, ptd hair, original clothes. Probably German. Ca. 1930s $65 each. (Courtesy of Carol Lindberg)

17-1/4" Little Girl. Rhodoid (a celluloid material) head/arms, OM/2 upper teeth, brown side-glancing eyes, cloth body/legs, original clothes, bonnet, et. (Raynal, Paris, introduced his new line of rhodoid dolls in 1935. There were both children and babies. Raynal produced dolls until 1975.) Ca. 1935 $400

17-1/2" Chat botté, (Puss in Boots). Molded/ptd carton/jtd head and limbs/long stuffed cloth tail/walking devise. Made in France by G. Cesan (mask-maker). Ca. 1947 Rare ....$700+

17-3/4" "Colette." Celluloid swivel head, CM (thin lips with upturned corners), large green glass sleep eyes, brown ptd/molded short bob, jtd celluloid body/straight legs, original clothes. Mark: "(head of an eagle design) 45." Petitcolin, France. Ca. 1920s ....$500-$550

18" "Raynal" Baby Girl. Celluloid head (very pretty face), OM/teeth, blue glass flirty eyes, blonde wig, celluloid body jtd at neck/sh/hips/bent limbs, original organdy dress, matching bonnet with frilly border and ribbon ties, underclothes, etc. Metal Raynal pin on dress; paper tag reads: "POUPÉES RAYNAL." (Gorgeous doll.) Les Poupées Raynal, France. 1930s $600

18" French Girl. Flesh-tone rhodoid head/pointed chin/urchin-type face, smiling OM/ptd teeth, blue glass sleep/flirty eyes, blonde HHW, short body jtd at neck/sh/hips/unjointed wrists/short limbs, small nose/red dots, red ptd fingernails, original clothes, etc. Mark: (fox symbol with a sunrise in a circle and marque déposée). Made by Renard, Paris, France. 1930s $550

18" Negro Girl. Black celluloid head, OM, large brown flirty eyes/waxed metal eyelids, 1 PE, black HHW, black celluloid body jtd at sh/hips/long hands/center fingers joined, original clothes. Mark: "(turtle design) and Tortulon 46." Rheinische Gummi........................ $600

18" Negro Girl. Celluloid black head, coral-tinted OM, flirty blue glass eyes/metal wax-covered eyelids, long straight black HHW, slender black celluloid body/1-pc limbs/long hands with 2 center fingers joined together, original clothes. Head mark: "(turtle design) and Tortulon 46."......................... $600

8-1/2" Unmarked girls with oilcloth-type limbs, mask/ptd faces, cardboard bodies, mohair wigs, undressed. Made in Spain or Italy. Ca. 1930s $65 each. (Courtesy of Carol Lindberg)

18-1/2" "Averill" Boy. Celluloid shoulder plate/shiny finish, O/C mouth/molded teeth, large inset blue glass eyes, modeled ears, blonde ptd/molded short tousled hair, cloth body/full compo arms, old clothes. Mark: "GERMANY//(turtle design)//16-1/2." Designed by Georgene Averill, NYC, 1920s .... $600-$650

19" "Cellba" Girl. Celluloid head, CM, inset blue glass eyes, blonde ptd/molded hairdo with center part and 2 long molded braids across top of head, celluloid body jtd at neck/sh/hips, original high-necked dress, etc. Head Mark: "46"; Body mark: "46/45 (mermaid symbol). Cellba Works, Babenhausen, Germany. Ca. 1900+ $300

20-1/2"Little Boy. Celluloid shoulder head, CM, ptd blue eyes, blonde ptd/molded hair in a Dutch boy cut with bangs, swirled to the side, kid body/celluloid lower arms, original clothes, shoes, stockings. Shoulder mark: "GERMANY//7." 1900+ .... $300-$325

21" Little Girl. Celluloid head/chubby face, CM, blue ptd intaglio eyes, blonde ptd/molded bob/bangs, celluloid body jtd at neck/sh/hips/bent arms/chubby toddler legs, original clothes, etc. Mark: "Schutz Marke (heart outline), H/50 Germany." Same mark on body. Ca. 1910+... $300

21-1/4" "Chemiso" Baby. Heavy celluloid head, smiling O/C mouth/teeth/tongue, ptd black eyes, brown ptd/molded hair, heavy celluloid body jtd at neck/sh/hips (bent limbs)/molded-on chemise with molded ribbon at neckline. Mark: "Depose 54." Made by Anel & Fraisse, Oyonnax (factory), 37 Bld de Strasbourg, Paris (head office), 1877-1928. Founded by Charles Bernadac; partnership with L. Croise, 1878; Charles Tissier succeeded Bernadac, 1893. Tissier sold talking dolls and automata, patented S.G.D.G. Tissier advertised celluloid toys and balls in 1900. Tissier succeeded his son, 1905. Ca. 1913+......$350+

22" "Minerva" marked Girl. Metal shoulder head, OM/teeth, inset blue glass eyes, thick brown feathered eyebrows, exposed ears, blonde ptd/molded short hair/bangs/front hair deeply sculpted with petal curls, kid body/bisque lower arms, old cotton print dress, etc. Buschow & Beck, Germany. 1900+ .... $325-$350

23" "Saucy Walker" look-alike. Celluloid head. OM/teeth, flirty glass eyes, mohair wig/2 long pigtails, celluloid jtd body/limbs, original white polka dot dress, bonnet, etc. Mark: "777 K&W Germany." Konig & Wernicke, Germany. Ca. 1920s..................... $550-$600

23" Little Girl. Aluminum head/hands/feet/jtd wood body, OM/teeth, blue glass sleep eyes, blonde mohair wig, old clothes, etc.

Head Mark: "(6 pointed star with G in the middle) 22 U.S. PAT." incised beneath star. Giebeler-Falk Doll Co., NYC, 1918-21 .... $500

24" Little Girl. Compo socket head on compo shoulder plate, CM, inset blue glass eyes, brown HHW, tightly packed kid body/limbs, old clothes, etc. Made by Alkid Doll Co., Portland, Ore., 1920-1921 .... $500

24" Little Girl. Celluloid shoulder head, OM/teeth/tongue, brown ptd eyes, black mohair wig, cloth body/legs/leather arms, old clothes. Mark: (turtle design). Made by Rheinische Gummi und Celluloid Fabrik Co., Bavaria. 1900+ $400

24" Commemorative Character Boy. Celluloid head, CM, ptd blue eyes, well-modeled/black ptd hair/forehead tendrils, 5-pc compo body/bent limbs, original South African Springbok rugby uniform, shoes, socks. (This excellent character doll has a very expressive face, and is well-dressed. It commemorates the 1937 visit of the South African Springbok rugby game in New Zealand.) Mark: "Made in Japan." 1937....... $700

21" "K (star) R 255" marked girl. Celluloid shoulder head, OM/teeth, blue glass sleep eyes, blonde mohair wig, cloth body/legs/bisque hands, old clothes. $425-$475. (Courtesy of D. Kay Crow)

Chapter 29

∽ OLD FAVORITES ∽

History: 1896-1930

Since a doll has to be 100 years old to be considered "antique", the dolls made in the 100 year period before 1930 are simply "old" Old and beloved. Those halcyon days (except for World War One) saw the end of the domination of the toy and doll market by the Germans and the French, and the development of the great American doll industry. American dolls were not made of bisque, nor were they as durable and well-made as the German and French product, but despite these factors they literally wiped-out the foreign doll market. The doll with the head of bisque and china was still being made in the 1930s, but was more popular abroad than in America. This new doll, made in Germany and France, had a "modern" look in imitation of the American ma-ma doll, and when found today, mint and in full-regalia, we realize that it was just that, an "imitation"—and a poor one at that. Children much preferred the composition doll. There was something "warm" and "familiar" with a doll made in America.

Collecting Hints:

Composition dolls made prior to 1930 are not as popular with the majority of collectors, as those made after 1930, especially the personality dolls discussed elsewhere in this book. Composition dolls made prior to 1920 fare even worse, and their prices seem to dangle in the lower composition doll brackets. And this is a shame, since the composition of the early dolls is harder and more durable than that made later. Many of these early dolls are still found uncracked or crazed and in an almost "mint" condition. Their appeal should be considered historic, if nothing else.

OLD FAVORITES

3" "Mibs." All-bisque, ptd features, mld/ptd blonde hair, jointed at shoulders only/slightly bowed legs/pink mold socks/green ptd shoes with ankle straps. (Bisque is pink tinted/rubber jtd at shoulders.) Mark: "C (in a circle)//L.A. & S. 1921//Germany." Hazel Drukker designer. A "Phyllis May" doll. Ca. 1921-23 .... $300

8" "Blink." Gene Carr's Cartoon Character. Compo head, watermelon mouth, closed ptd eyes, brown ptd hair, cloth body/compo hands, cloth "clothes", cap, etc. Bernard Lipfert designer. (Other characters in this series: Skinny (closed eyes), Mike and Jane (open eyes), and Snowball, a Negro boy, etc.) Ca. 1916 8" .... $250; 13"-14" $375

8" "Tiny Tot." Body-twist type. All-compo/jtd at neck/sh/waist/hips, CM, ptd blue eyes to side, blonde ptd/molded bob/bangs, original sunsuit, etc. (She had a twin brother who came in the same box with additional clothing.) Louis Amberg & Son, NYC. 1920s $225

8" Little Girl. Bisque head, OM, inset blue glass eyes, brown mohair wig, BJ compo body, old clothes, etc. Made by Carl Hartmann, Stockheim, Bavaria. ca. 1914-1920s $375

9" "PAT. APPLIED FOR" marked Girl. patsy look-alike. All-compo, CM, ptd blue eyes to side, auburn ptd/molded "Patsy" bob, 1-pc head/body/legs/body twists from side to side, pink bow nailed to head, pink sunsuit, booties. Ca. 1928 .... $300

10" "Kweenie." seated flapper girl holding a red ball. Blonde mohair wig. bottom label reads: "Kweenie-Pat. applied for-Republic Dolls-152-156 Wooster St." Republic Doll & Toy Co., NYC, 1919-21. "Kweenie" trademark registered in 1919. Kweenie was made in sizes 14" and size 10". ...... $150-$200

10" "Tynie Baby." Bisque head, CM, sleep blue glass eyes, blonde mohair wig, bisque body jtd at neck/sh/hips, original clothes. Bernard Lipfert designer. Germany. 1924 .... $2,500

10" German Toddler. Compo head, CM, ptd blue eyes, blonde ptd/molded hair, cardboard body/compo limbs, original clothes, etc. Head mark: "Germany//E 2." ca. 1910+ $250

10" German Toddler. Compo head, inset blue glass eyes, blonde ptd hair, cardboard body/compo limbs, original clothes. Head mark: "60 5 (in a circle) 2//Germany." ca. 1910................ $250

10" Negro Child. Stationary black compo head/body, red CM, ptd brown eyes, black ptd/molded hair, compo limbs/metal springs, old cotton print blue dress. Back mark: "A.G.D. (enclosed in a large C)." Arthur Gerling Doll Company, NYC, 1919. Rare. $350

11" "Ideal" marked Girl. Compo head/flange neck, smiling CM, dimples, blue tin sleep eyes, ptd blonde/molded bobbed hair, cloth body/compo hands/cloth legs/compo boots glued to legs, pin and disc hold limbs to body, original cheap factory clothes. Head mark: "Ideal (in a triangle)." Ca. 1916...................... $200

11" "Teenie Weenie" baby. Bye-lo look-alike. Compo head, CM, squinty blue sleep eyes, brown ptd/molded hair, cloth body/legs/upper arms/compo lower arms, original clothes. neck Mark: "Teenie Weenie." Probably American character Doll Co., NYC, 1919+. Ca. $225

11" Perry Winkle. Comic strip character, in "Winnie Winkle" by Wm. and Eileen Benoliel.; 1922-1930s. flat oil-cloth/printed/stuffed/printed red and blue suit, Eton jacket. Marked: Live-Long toys, Chicago, Ill. ca. 1929-30. .... $225

12" "Baby Bumps." Resembles Kammer & Reinhardt's Baby #100. compo head, O/C mouth, ptd blue eyes, blonde ptd/molded hair/pink sateen body/limbs/no fingers/pin and disc joints, original checkered gingham romper suit. made by E.I. Horsman Co., NYC. 1910+ .... $275-$300

12" "Baby Bundie." Kewpie type. All-wood-pulp comp/movable arms only, CM, ptd blue eyes to side, blonde mohair wig, undressed. Foot label reads: "Baby bundie..." Made by Rex Doll Co., 1919-21; Mutual Doll Co., 1922-25+; Cameo Doll Co. Designed and copyrighted by Joseph Kallus. Distributed by Borgfeldt. (The 16" size had movable arms and legs with coiled

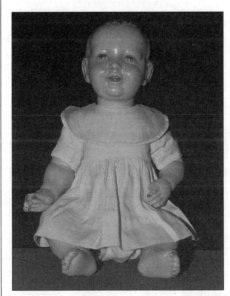

19" Unmarked early, heavy compo spring-strung baby, blue ptd eyes, blonde ptd/mld hair, redressed. Quality doll. Ca. early 1920s $350-$400. (Courtesy of Ruby Ellen Smith)

spring joints. She has painted hair.) 1918+ $700

12" "Chubby" Girl. Comp head/round chubby face/dimples, CM, ptd blue eyes, blonde ptd/molded bobbed hair with molded bow loop, jtd compo body/short bent arms/small hands/straight comp legs, original clothes, etc. Toy Products Mfg. Co., NYC. 1920s $225

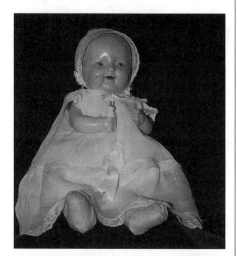

16" "Happy-tot" by American Character doll Company. Compo shoulder head/arms, cloth body/legs, blue tin sleep eyes, original tagged dress, bottle, etc. Mark: "PETITE. AMER. CHAR. DOLL CO." 1923+ $350. (Courtesy of Ruby Ellen Smith)

12" "Janie." Toddler Baby. All-omp/jtd at neck/sh/hips, CM, brown sleep eyes, blonde ptd/molded hair, original yellow and blue playsuit, matching bonnet, shoes, socks. Eugenia Doll Co. Late 1920s $165

12" "Steppin' Baby." Mechanical. Compo head/arms, ptd tin body/attached tin shoes, CM, ptd blue eyes, brown ptd hair, original baby dress, bonnet. (Doll wobbles when wound.) E. Goldberger, 307 Richardson St., Brooklyn, NY. 1926 ....$250

12" American Doughboy. Compo swivel head, CM, ptd blue eyes, blonde ptd hair, 5-pc compo body/molded-on/ptd uniform/felt hat/right arm bent for the "salute" position when raised. (Also called "Liberty Boy.") Mark: "IDEAL" (In diamond design) and "US of A" on the 4 outside corners. Ca. 1917 (Used to sell War Bonds.) $550

12" Negro Girl. Dark brown compo head/flange neck, CM, ptd brown eyes to side, black ptd/molded bob, cloth body/cloth legs/black printed shoes/compo hands/pin and disc jts. cheap factory clothes. Mark: "HCQ//1916." Hi Quality Doll Co. (Resembles a Campbell Kid.) 1916 ...$300

12" Puggy. Compo head, CM, rosy cheeks, ptd blue eyes to side, brown ptd hair, jtd compo body, original clothes, shoes, socks. Tag reads: "A Petite Doll, Campbell Kid, Permission of Campbell Soup Company, U.S.A." Mark: "A Petite Doll." A Charles Twelvetrees inspiration. (Puggy was the "man" of the

Campbell Kid family.) American Character Doll Co., NYC, 1919+. Ca. 1928 ....$550-$600

12-1/2" "Mitzi." Patsy look-alike. Toddler. compo head, CM, ptd blue eyes, brown ptd/molded hair (bob), compo body jtd at neck/sh/hips/one bent arm/one straight arm, original clothes, etc. Back mark: "Mitzi, by Maxine." Ca. 1928 ....$300

13" "Bonnie Girl Scout." Compo shoulder head, smiling CM, ptd blue eyes, blonde ptd/molded hair, cloth body/cry box/compo limbs (straight toddler legs), original brown uniform, belt, brown felt hat, yellow neck tie, dark brown strap shoes, brown socks, etc. Shoulder plate mark: "by grace Corry." Body mark: (stamped) "Genuine Madame Hendren Doll//Made in U.S.A." Ca. 1928+ (Mint)..................................$450

13" "Grumpy Baby." Can't Break 'Em head, OCM, ptd brown eyes, original cork-stuffed, bent-limb plush "teddy bear" type body, original neck bow. E.I. Horsman, NYC, 1878+. Ca. 1910 $700

13" "Little Fairy Soap" Girl. Can't Break 'Em head, CM, ptd blue eyes, blonde ptd/molded bob/forelock, cloth body/limbs/comp "Campbell Kid" type hands, original white cape with hood, etc. Helen Trowbridge designer (modeled from life). This head also used on Polly Prue, Nancy Lee, and Annette. copyrighted and registered by E.I. Horsman, NYC. Doll represented the child in the N.K. Fairbanks Co. "Little Fairy Soap" advertisements.) 1911-1915............................$600-$700

13" "Little Sister." Compo head, red smiling CM, rosy cheeks, ptd blue eyes/blue-grey eyeshadow, orange ptd/molded hair combed forward/pink satin hair bow stapled to head, cloth body/full compo arms/compo "sing" legs, original pink party dress and combinations, original pink shoes with ribbon ties and socks. Mark: "C//BY//Grace Corry." Made by Averill Mfg. Co., NYC, 1915+. Ca. 1927 . $450

13" "Whistler" Boy. Comp shoulder head/narrow shoulders, ptd blue eyes, puckered OM/center hole, orange ptd/molded hair combed toward forehead/deep comb marks, cloth body/full compo bent arms, original white 2-pc cotton sailor suit with blue flannel trimming on cuffs, black neckerchief, matching hat, shoes, socks. Body stamped: "Genuine//Madame Hendren//Doll//patented Feb. 2, 1926//Made in U.S.A." (The legs are constructed with springs and bellows. When pressure is placed on the legs he dances, and whistles.) 1925-29 ....$300-$325

13" Negro "Baby Bumps." black comp head, O/C mouth, ptd brown eyes, black ptd/molded hair, white cloth body/brown cloth bent limbs, original romper suit. Label reads: "Genuine Baby Bumps TRADEMARK." (Resembles Kammer & Reinhardt's Baby #100.) Ca. 1912 ....$350-$375

13" White "Baby Bumps." comp head, O/C mouth, ptd blue eyes, blonde ptd/molded hair, cloth body/bent limbs, original romper suit. Label reads: "Genuine

Baby Bumps TRADEMARK." (Resembles Kammer & Reinhardt's Baby #100.). Ca. 1912 ....$300

13-1/2" "Whistling Rufus." Negro Boy. Black compo head, OM/center hole, ptd brown eyes to side, black ptd/molded hair, cloth body/legs/compo arms, original clothes, cap. Unmarked. Tag reads: "I whistle when you dance me on one foot and then the other.//Patented Feb. 2, 1926//Genuine Madame Hendren Doll." Madame Hendren, NYC. 1925-29 ....$500

14" "Fan Kid." Compo head/flange neck, O/C mouth, ptd blue intaglio eyes, brown ptd/molded hair, dimples, cloth body/legs/compo lower arms (cloth legs have striped stockings and shoes sewed-on), original grey flannel suit with red collar and cuffs, coarse cotton catcher's apron imprinted: "FAN KID, MASCOT." Mark: (red ink) "TRADE FAN KID MARK//MASCOT//PAT. Applied for//STRAUSS MFG. CO. N.Y." Adolph Strauss & Co., NYC, 1857-1925+. Ca. 1915.................$400

14" "Zaiden" Baby Boy. Compo socket head, CM, ptd black eyes, blonde ptd/molded hair, bent-limb compo body, original outfit, cap, etc. Body mark: "Zaiden//Doll//Colonial Toy Mfg. Co." Colonial Toy Mfg. Co., NYC, 1915-20. Ca. 1916......................$600

14" Charlie Chaplin. Compo head, O/C mouth/black mustache, ptd brown eyes to side, black ptd hair, cloth body/compo hands, original clothes, hat. Cloth label reads: "CHARLIE CHAPLIN DOLL/World's greatest Comedian/Made Exclusively by Louis Amberg/& Son, N.Y./by Special Arrangement with Essamay Film Co." 1915..................................$650-$700

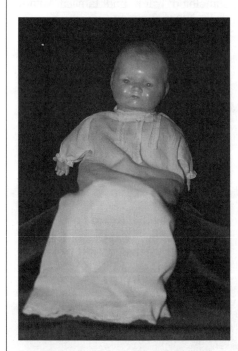

14" "Baby Petite" by American Character Doll Company, NYC, 1923+ Compo flange head/hands, cloth body/legs, blue tin sleep eyes, blonde ptd hair, redressed. Mark: "Petite Amer. Char." $275. (Courtesy of Ruby Ellen Smith)

14" John Bunny. Silent Screen Comedian. Compo head/expressive face, red O/C mouth/molded upper/lower teeth, ptd grey eyes, brown ptd hair, muslin/cork-stuffed body/cloth legs/compo hands/metal buttons and wire attachments, original clothes. Head mark: "C (in a circle) 34.//L.A.S. 1914." Louis Amberg & Son, NYC. 1914 (Rare) ....$750+

14" Little Girl. Compo shoulder head, CM, inset blue glass eyes, brown HHW, cloth body/legs/compo arms, original clothes, etc. Marked. Made by First American Doll Factory, Brooklyn, NY, 1892-1908. Rare Ca. 1890s.........$600

14" Munich "Art" Character Girl. Compo head, CM, ptd blue eyes, rosy cheeks, blonde mohair braided wig, BJ compo body, original clothes, black leather shoes with bows, stockings. Signed on neck. Paul Vogelsanger designer. Marion Kaulitz, Germany. 1908-12 . $2,700

14-1/2" Little Orphan Annie. Comic-strip character. Compo head/arms, CM, ptd blue eyes, orange wig, cloth body/legs/jtd at sh/hips, original clothes, etc. Ca. 1919 ....$600

14-1/2" "Naughty Marietta." Resembles the famous "Coquette" by G. Heubach. Compo head, smiling mouth, ptd blue eyes to side, blonde ptd/short molded bob with headband, cloth body/legs/arms/tiny compo hands/compo boots, original clothes. Ca. 1910+ (Ideal Toy Co.) $450

18" "Rosebud" by E.I. Horsman. Compo head on shoulder plate, OM/teeth, blue tin sleep eyes, blonde HHW, cloth body/compo limbs, original dress. Mark: "Rosebud" (head). $350. (Courtesy of Ruby Eller Smith)

15" "Billiken." Can't Break 'Em compo head, broad smiling CM, squinty eyes, large protruding ears, plush "teddy bear" body jtd at sh/hips/neck. Heads made by Aetna Doll & Toy Co. Copyright c (in a circle) G. 30334 by the Billiken Sales Company, Chicago, ILL, July 22, 1909. Horsman obtained sole rights to manufacture and sell Billiken in the U.S.A. and Canada, later world rights. 1909-10 ....$600

15" Character Baby Boy. Compo head/double chin, CM, blue tin sleep eyes brown ptd/molded hair, exposed ears, cloth body/legs/compo arms, original blue checkered rompers, leather shoes, stockings. Head mark: "IDEAL" (in a diamond design) and "U.S. of A." embossed on the outside corners. Early 1920s $300

15-1/2" "Raggedy Man." James Whitcomb Riley poem character. Compo head, CM, ptd blue eyes with black lid lines, one-stroke eyebrows, yellow ptd/molded hair, cloth body/limbs/well-shaped compo hands, original black trousers with striped knee patch, jacket, etc. (Dwarf-life in appearance.) Ca. 1916 ....$600

16" "Bubbles" look-alike. Compo head, OM/teeth, blue tin sleep eyes, blonde ptd/molded hair, original oilcloth body/compo limbs, original clothes, bonnet, pillow, etc. Unmarked. (Lovely doll.) 1925+..................................$250

16" "Chubby." Compo head, long neck, O/C mouth, ptd blue eyes, blonde ptd/molded hair, BJ compo body, old baby clothes, etc. (The too long neck detracts from the beauty of this doll, but distinguishes it.) Mark: "ELECTRA/T.N.C.//COPRY." Electra Toy & Novelty Co., NYC, 1912-20. (Electra was one of the first companies to make all-compo American dolls.) Ca. 1916 ....$275

16" "Chubby." Compo head/long neck/chubby cheeks, O/C mouth/teeth, ptd blue eyes, brown HHW/bangs, compo body jtd at neck/sh/hips, old clothes. Mark: "E.T. & N. Co. N.Y." Made by Elektra Toy & novelty Co., NYC. Ca. 1916.............................$275

16" "Cuddles." Compo head, OM/2 upper teeth, sleep blue tin eyes, blonde ptd/molded hair, cloth body/compo legs/rubber arms (some also had rubber legs), original pink and white organdy dress, bonnet, etc. Round tag pinned to dress. Body mark: "U.S.Patent/1621434// 17993395." Pat. dates: 1927-31. Ideal Toy & Novelty Co., N.Y. $250

16" "Dimples." Compo head, OM/teeth, blue tin sleep eyes, blonde ptd/molded hair, cloth body/compo limbs, original clothes, bonnet, etc. Head mark: "E.I.H. Co. INC." E.I. Horsman, NYC, 1878+. Ca. 1928 ....$300

16" "E.I.H." marked Girl. Compo head, CM, blue tin sleep eyes, auburn HHW, BJ compo body (toddler type), original factory clothes, bonnet, etc. Head mark: "E.I.H.//Co." Made in Germany for E.I. Horsman, NYC. (This doll is well-sculpted, superior quality compo) 1920s ....$350-$400

16" "Little Mary Mix-Up." Brinkerhoff Character Doll. Compo head, wee CM, ptd blue eyes, ptd/molded hair, cloth body/legs/compo arms/jtd at sh/hips, original clothes, etc. Label. (A more expensive version had glass sleep eyes and wore a wig.) 1919-24. Made by E.I. Horsman, NYC, and Aetna Doll & Toy Co., Brooklyn, N.Y. $350

21" "Baby Dimples" by E.I. Horsman. Compo head, OM/teeth, blue celluloid sleep eyes, blonde ptd hair, cloth body/compo limbs, redressed. 1928 $275 (Courtesy of Ruby Ellen Smith)

16" "Metropolitan" marked Girl. Compo shoulder head, CM, ptd blue eyes, orange-blonde ptd/molded bob/molded compo loop for ribbon, cloth body/legs/applied brown boots/full compo arms, original flower print dress with red trim, etc. Made by Metropolitan Doll Co., N.Y. 1920s $275

16" "Petite" Baby Girl. Compo head, CM, ptd blue eyes, blonde mohair wig, cloth body/compo limbs/crier, original clothes, etc. Mark: "Petite-Amer. Character Doll Co." American Character Doll Co., NYC, 1919+. (A "Wonder Doll." Same face used on their "Sally" doll with molded "Patsy" bob.) Ca. 1928-29 ....$275

16" "Soozie Smiles." Two-faced baby. Compo head/flange neck/smile face/cry face, ptd blue eyes tightly closed eyes, ptd brown/molded hair, cloth body/cry box/compo lower arms, original red checkered romper suit, leather shoes. stockings. Unmarked doll. Wrist tag. Ideal Novelty & Toy Co., Brooklyn, N.Y., 1907+. Early 1920s $350

16" "The American Beauty." Little girl type. Bisque head, OM/teeth, blue glass sleep eyes, kid body/bisque lower arms, original clothes, etc. Label on front of dress reads: "The American Beauty//Copyright 1910 by Sears, Roebuck and Co.//Germany F 70-45." Back shoulder

144

mark: "Heubach" and "42 Germany." (These Sears dolls were advertised in 1910 and have been found with the names of different German manufacturers. American Beauty Babies were advertised in 1920.) 1910 ....$500

16" "Tickletoes." Compo head, OM/teeth, flirty blue tin sleep eyes, brown ptd/molded hair, cloth body, rubber bent arms/compo legs, original clothes, bonnet, etc. Head mark: "IDEAL." Ideal Novelty & Toy Co., Brooklyn, N.Y., 1907+. Ca. 1929 ....$300

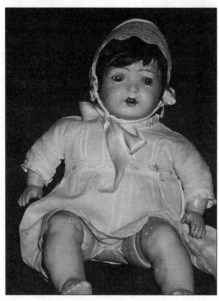

16" Madame Hendres "Ma-Ma" baby doll. Compo shoulder head/limbs, cloth body, OM/teeth, blue tin sleep eyes, brown HHW, original clothes. Mark: "Madame Hendren Doll." 1920s $300. (Courtesy of Aylene Waits)

16" "Trion" marked Baby Boy. Compo head, CM, ptd blue eyes, blonde ptd/slightly molded hair, modeled ears, long pink cotton body/straight limbs (limbs are over-sized and hands are mitten-type), original romper suit. Head mark: "Trion Toy Co." Trion Toy Co., Brooklyn, N.Y., 1915-21. 1915.....$275

16" Dutch Boy & Girl. Googlies. Hard compo swivel heads/chubby cheeks, ptd blue eyes to side, brown ptd/molded hair, cloth bodies/limbs/disc jts, original "Dutch" costumes, wooden shoes. (Boy wears red trousers, black jacket, black cap; girl wears red dress printed with tiny blue and white flowers, white apron, white bonnet.) Unmarked Pr. $1,000

16-1/2" "Berthe Noufflard" Girl. Smooth compo/plaster head/pointed chin (Urchin or "pixie" type face), rosy cheeks, red CM, pointed nose, tiny brown ptd eyes with an Oriental slant, auburn mohair wig, heavy compo/plaster ptd body jtd at sh/hips, original clothes, etc. Signed. (Berthe Noufflard, born 1886, was one of the artists in the Puppen Reform movement. She was a portrait painter. Her first dolls date to 1915 and were exhibited in the Musée des Arts Decoratifs in Paris and one model was accepted by Sévres. She tried unsuc-

cessfully to interest SFBJ in her dolls. Only 3 different head types have been found.) Ca. 1916 ....$3,000

17" "Hendren" Baby. Round head/chubby cheeks, OM/teeth, blue sleep eyes, blonde ptd/molded hair, cloth body/compo lower limbs/crier, original white cotton dress, bonnet, etc. Label reads: "Everybody Loves the Madame Hendren Dolls." Averill Mfg. Co., NYC, 1915+..$375

17" "Peter Pan." Compo head, smiling CM, blue tin sleep eyes, blonde ptd/molded hair, cloth body/limbs/compo hands, original "Pan" outfit, hat. Marked. Ideal Toy & Novelty Co., Brooklyn, N.Y. 1920s Mark: "Peter Pan//Reg. U.S. PAT. OFF.//PATENT PENDING/IDEAL" (in a diamond) and a large heart shape encompasses all. 1929 .....$300

17" "Fulper" Character Doll. Bisque head, O/C mouth/molded upper teeth, ptd blue eyes to side, brown ptd/molded curly hair, BJ compo body, old clothes, etc. Marked. Fulper Pottery Co., Flemington, N.J., 1918-21.1918+ $750

17" "Georgy Porgy." Compo head, puckered OM (for kissing), ptd blue eyes, dark blonde ptd/molded hair, long excelsior-stuffed cloth body/short cloth upper arms/short compo lower arms/long cloth legs/pin-and-disc jts, original clothes, hat, etc. Mark: "TRION TOY CO." Trion Toy Co., Brooklyn, N.Y. Ernesto Peruggi designer. (Slogan: "Dolls That Delight.") Ca. 1915 ....$300

17" "Kiddie Pal Dolly." Compo shoulder head, CM, ptd blue eyes, blonde ptd/molded hair (short wavy bob with side part and no bangs), cloth body/full compo limbs, original clothes, etc. made by Regal Doll Mfg. Co., NYC. (Successors: German American Doll Co.) 1925 ....$300

17-1/2" "Brunson" stamped Girl. Light-weight compo head, O/C mouth/ptd upper teeth, ptd blue eyes, coarse brown HHW, sateen-covered cloth body/compo lower limbs, old clothes, etc. Body stamp: "Brunson Doll, Holyoke, Mass." (This doll is constructed similarly to the Martha Chase dolls; may have been an early experiment.) Ca. 1910+ $600

18" "Dolly face" Baby. Compo head/lovely smooth finish, CM, ptd blue eyes, blonde mohair wig, firmly-packed excelsior/cork-stuffed body/upper arms/compo hands/firmly-packed peach-colored muslin legs, original white linen dress, bonnet, etc. Acme Toy Mfg. Co., NYC, 1908-25+. Ca. 1914-15.......................................$300

18" "Dolly Walker." Compo shoulder head, CM, ptd blue eyes, molded hair/brown HHW, all-wood body except for center area with window screen wire mesh/arms bend at elbows/knees/springs at hips/head attached to body by 2 screws in front and 2 screws in back, old clothes. Block between legs reads: "September 1919" and "Patents Applied for in other countries." Harry H. Coleman, Wood Toy Co., NYC, 1917-23 ....$700

18" "Happy Tot." "Petite" line. Baby-type. Compo head, OM, sleep blue eyes, ptd

brown/molded hair, cloth body/compo limbs, original pink organdy dress, bonnet, shoes, socks, etc. Also original baby bottle with "milk" and rubber nipple. American Character Doll Co., NYC, 1919+. Ca. 1923+ $300

18" "Judy." Patsy look-alike. Compo head, CM, sleep blue eyes, brown ptd/molded bob, cloth body/compo limbs, original polka-dot organdy Swiss dress with wide lace-trimmed collar, etc. Effanbee, NYC. (Advertised as "The Girl Friend.") 1928 ....$600

18" "MB" JAPAN Girl. Bisque shoulder head, orange ptd OM/4 upper teeth, inset blue threaded glass eyes, blonde mohair wig, kidaline jtd body, old clothes, etc. Neck mark: "5 MB (in a circle with design) Japan 4." Morimura Bros. (Japanese Import Company.) 1915-22 ....$400

18" "NAJO" marked Girl. Compo head, OM/teeth, blue tin sleep eyes, blonde mohair wig, BJ compo body, original clothes, etc. Head mark: "19C." Back mark: "NAJO." Buttocks mark: "4618." Made by the National Joint-Limb Doll Co., NYC. Ca. 1917-18................$325

18" "Pretty Peggy." Pale bisque head/flange neck, CM, rosy cheeks, brown glass sleep eyes, blonde mohair wig, cloth body/full compo bent arms/straight compo legs, old clothes, etc. Neck mark: "Copr by//Grace C. Rockwell//Germany." (Originally named "Betty Jean.") Distributed by George Borgfeldt & Co., NYC. 1926 ....$5,000

18" "Rockwell" marked Girl. Bisque head, CM, sleep blue glass eyes, blonde ptd/molded bobbed hair/comb marks, cloth body/compo limbs, old clothes, etc. Incised: "Copr. by Grace C. Rockwell, Germany. (These dolls were made in limited quantity.) Grace Corry Rockwell, NYC. 1920-30 ....$5,000+

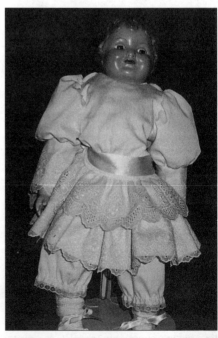

16" Marked "Ideal" ma-ma doll. Compo head/lower limbs, cloth body, redressed. 1920s $275. (Courtesy of Aylene Waits)

18" "TTT" marked Girl. Heavy compo shoulder head, OM/teeth/tongue, grey tin sleep eyes, brown HHW, kid body/compo arms jtd at sh/elbows/wrists/compo lower legs, old clothes, hat, etc. Head mark: "TTT (inside a toy "top" shape). Tip Top Toy Co., NYC, 1912-21." Ca. 1918 ....$350

18-1/2" "Raleigh" Girl. Compo head (resembles Shirley Temple minus the dimples), smiling O/C mouth, ptd blue eyes, brown HHW (curls in front and braids in back), cloth body/spiral spring jts/compo limbs, original white low-waisted frock, etc. Heavy doll, high quality. (These dolls are usually unmarked; are recognizable by their realistic portrait faces. Most have molded/painted hair.) Jessie McCutcheon Raleigh, Chicago, ILL. 1916-20 ....$1,000

14" Gene Carr Character "Jane", compo, all original. Made by E.I. Horsman, 1916. $400-$450. (Courtesy of Rosalie Purvis)

19" "Kiddie Pal Dolly." Patsy-type. Compo shoulder head, O/C mouth, ptd brown blue eyes, thin one-stroke eyebrows, dimples, blonde ptd/molded bob/well-defined bangs, cloth body/compo limbs, original pink cotton dress, matching bonnet, black oilcloth shoes, white cotton socks. Unmarked. Original box label reads: "KIDDIE PAL DOLLY" (in a heart design). Regal Doll Mfg. Co., NYC. Ca. 1929-early 1930s $500

19-1/2" "76616" marked Girl. Bisque head, OM/2 teeth, brown glass sleep eyes, brown HHW, BJ compo body, old whitework dress, etc. Mark: "Nippon 30/5 no. 76616 (Y symbol)." Made by Yamato Importing Co., NYC. 1919 ....$475

20" "Baby Peggy." Silent Screen Child Star. Compo head, smiling CM, ptd brown eyes, brown ptd/molded bob, cloth body/compo limbs, original clothes, etc. 1923 ....$850

20-1/4" Queen Mary of England. Compo shoulder head, CM, ptd blue eyes, reddish mohair wig/molded crown, wire-armature cloth body/compo hands,

original elaborate coronation robe of silk and velvet plush, etc. Probably made by Werksatten for L.&R. Baitz, Berlin, Germany. Early 1920s. $1,000+

20-1/2" "Phyllis." Bisque shoulder head, tiny OM, tiny almond-shaped blue glass eyes, light eyebrows, blonde ptd/molded bob/bangs, kid body/compo lower limbs, original clothes, etc. Mark: "Phyllis//Made in Germany." Baby Phyllis Doll Co., Brooklyn, N.Y., 1919-1929. Ca. 1920s $500

21" "Flossie Flirt." Walker. Compo shoulder head, CM, blue sleep eyes/flirty eyes, brown mohair wig, cloth body/compo hands, original clothes, bonnet, etc. (This is the closed mouth version of Flossie.) Ideal Novelty & Toy Co., Brooklyn, N.Y. 1924-25................$425

21" "Trego" Dolly-face Girl. Thin compo socket head/long neck, OM/teeth, blue sleep eyes, blonde HHW, BJ compo body/wood jtd arms, old clothes, etc. Mark: "TREGO//MADE IN USA." Trego Doll Mfg. Co., NYC, 1918-21. 1918+ $350

21" "Woodtex" Girl. Compo shoulder head/narrow shoulders, red OM/teeth, blue tin sleep eyes/real lashes, brown HHW, cloth body/full compo bent arms/straight legs jtd above knees (for short flapper skirts), original pink dress, matching bonnet, etc. Shoulder mark: "WOODTEX, N.Y." Woodtex Co., NYC, 1922-23........................$400

21" Fulper-Amberg Baby. Bisque head, OM, sleep blue eyes, brown mohair

wig, bent-limb compo body, old clothes. Mark: "Amberg//Dolls//The World//Standard" and "Fulper" (incised within a design) and "Made in U.S.A." Good quality. (Fulper made heads for Amberg.) Fulper Pottery Co., Flemington, N.J., 1918-21 ....$850

22" "Baby" look-alike. Resembles Kammer & Reinhardt's Baby #100. Compo head, red CM, ptd blue eyes, brown ptd/molded hair, excelsior-stuffed cloth pink body/mitten hands, old romper suit. Mark: "ELEKTRA, T.N.C.,//N.Y.//Copyright." Elektra Toy & Novelty Co., NYC, 1912-20 ....$450

22" "NIBUR" marked Girl. Ma-Ma type. Compo shoulder head/sliced-off crown for eye insertion, CM, shiny blue tin sleep eyes, auburn mohair wig, cloth body/compo limbs, original pink dress, matching frilly bonnet, etc. Head Mark: "NIBUR." Nibur Novelty Co., NYC, 1923-25 ....$450

22" "Posable" Baby. Compo head, OM/molded tongue, blue tin sleep eyes, brown mohair wig/pate, sawdust stuffed cloth body/steel frame inside for posing, compo lower limbs/movable wrists, original clothes, bonnet, etc. Possibly a Zaiden Doll by Colonial Toy Mfg. Co., 352-66 W. 13th Street, NYC. Ca. 1916+ $450

22" "Woodtex" Phonograph Girl. Compo shoulder head, OM/teeth, blue-grey sleep eyes/lashes, blonde mohair wig, cloth body/compo limbs, back opening for phonograph cylinder devise/cylinder records/horn in doll's head/clockwind, original clothes, bonnet, etc. Neck Mark: "Woodtex, N.Y." Woodtex Co., NYC, 1922-23 (made dolls' heads and limbs.) Ca. 1922-23 ....$500-$600

23" "Bester" Girl. Plaster-compo head, orange ptd OM/4 flat inserted celluloid teeth, blue tin sleep eyes, real eyelashes, brown HHW/long sausage curls, BJ compo body, old clothes, hat, etc. (Face similar to 26" ARTCRAFT doll.) Mark: "BESTER DOLL CO. BLOOMFIELD." Bester Doll Co., Newark, Bloomfield, N.J., 1919-21 ... $400-$425

23" "Chuckles." Baby type. Compo shoulder head/narrow shoulders OM/teeth, blue sleep eyes/no lashes, blonde ptd/molded hair, modeled ears, chubby cloth body/full compo limbs/voice box, original dress with ruffles and lace, fancy bonnet, etc. Mark: "Chuckles//A Century Doll." Century Doll Co., NYC, 1909+. Ca. 1927 ....$475-$500

23" "Little Boy Blue." Pretty compo head, inset blue glass eyes, blonde ptd/molded hair with forehead spitcurl, firmly-stuffed oilcloth body/legs/compo hands, original "Little Boy Blue" costume, straw hat, metal horn, etc. Satin streamer on shoulder reads: "Storybook doll//Bergfeld & Son//Brooklyn, N.Y." 1923-25 ....$400

23" "The Eugenic Baby." All hard compo/metal springs (smooth, uncrazed), O/C mouth/molded teeth, ptd blue eyes, light brown ptd hair, well-modeled ears, jtd at neck/sh/hips, original clothes, cap, etc. Mark: "The Eugenic Baby." (This natural and well-sculpted doll was the first all-compo baby doll made in America with detailed figures,

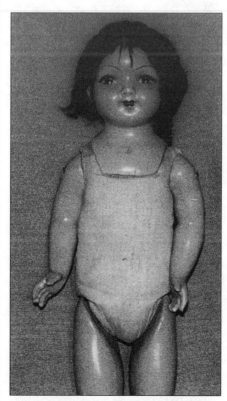

23" Mexican "ma-ma" doll. Compo shoulder head/limbs, straw-stuffed cloth body, black silk-type hair, ptd features, undressed. Very rare. Made in Old Mexico, 1920s. $225 as is or $350 dressed. (Courtesy of Herron)

toes, and realistic baby contours. These are usually found unsigned.) Fair Amusement Company, 142 Fifth Avenue, NYC, 1914. 1914 (Rare) ....$600+

24" "American Doll Co." Boy. Compo shoulder head, small CM, round brown decal eyes, brown ptd/molded wavy hair, ears close to head, (body construction same as below doll except shoes are painted blue), original blue cotton suit. Shoulder mark: "Am. Doll Co." American Doll Mfg. Co., NYC, 1912-1930s $600

24" "American Doll Co." Girl. Compo shoulder head/round face, smiling CM, large blue decal eyes/thin eyebrows, blonde ptd/molded hair in the "Marcel wave" style, papier- mâché body jtd at neck/sh/hips/mâché legs/compo arms/small hands/pin-and-washer joint attachments/elastic, original pink rayon dress trimmed with lace/attached blue cotton underpants, pink ptd/molded shoes/socks. Shoulder mark: "Am. Doll Co." American Doll Mfg. Co./American Doll Co., NYC, 1912-30+. Ca. 1920s $600

24" "Arranbee" Baby Boy. Pale compo swivel head, OM/teeth, blue sleep eyes, modeled ears, yellow ptd/molded hair, cloth body/bent compo limbs, original white baby gown decorated with open work and lace, etc. Head mark: "Arranbee Doll Company." Arranbee Doll Co., NYC, 1922-1960 (R&B). Ca. 1920s $375

24" "Baby Dimples." Compo head/dimples, OM, blue tin sleep eyes, modeled ears, blonde ptd/sparse molded hair, cloth body/compo limbs, original clothes, bonnet, etc. Mark: "E.I.H. CO. INC." 1928 ....$450-$500

24" "Baby Horsman." Compo head/round chubby face, CM, blonde ptd/molded hair, blue sleep eyes (some had painted eyes), highly rouged cheeks, cloth body/limbs/compo hands, original clothes, bonnet, etc. Tag reads: "Baby Horsman//Trademar,//Head copyrighted//1923." Head mark: "E.I.H." Edith Hitchcock designer, 1923. E.I. Horsman, NYC. Ca. 1923....................$375

24" "Halbig-Arranbee" Girl. S&H bisque head, OM/teeth, flirty blue glass eyes, blonde mohair wig, cloth body/compo lower limbs, original clothes, etc. Mark: "SIMON & HALBIG ARRANBEE PATENT GERMANY." 1920s (This bisque head was Simon & Halbig's contribution to the ma-ma doll market.) $450

24" "Rosebud." Compo head/flange neck, shoulder plate, smiling OM/3 teeth, felt tongue, blue tin sleep eyes, brown HHW/bangs, cloth body/compo lower limbs/voice box, original clothes, etc. Upper leg stamp reads: "C (in a circle)//E.I.H. CO. INC." Body mark: "PATENT APPLIED FOR." (Lovely doll.) E.I. Horsman, NYC. Ca. 1929 ....$425

24" "Royal" marked Girl. Compo shoulder head, OM/teeth, blue tin sleep eyes, brown long curl HHW, cloth body/thighs/compo lower legs/full compo arms, original white cotton dress printed with flying bluebirds, bonnet,

etc. Neck Mark: "Royal." Crier mark: "1915." Royal Toy Mfg. Co., NYC, 1913+. Ca. 1923 ....$450

25" "Acme" marked Girl. Compo head, OM/teeth, brown HHW, cloth body/compo limbs, original ruffled organdy dress, organdy bonnet, etc. Mark: "Acme Toy Co. Acme Toy Mfg. Co., NYC," 1908+. (Acme used voice boxes made by "Voices, Inc."). Ca. 1927 ....$400

25" "Artcraft" Baby Girl. Compo head/pretty character face, blue tin sleep eyes, brown HHW, BJ compo body, old clothes, etc. Head mark: "Artcraft Co. Made in USA 10." Artcraft Toy Products Co., NYC, 1918-20; Artcraft Playthings Corp., Brooklyn, N.Y. 1920-21. (This doll-face baby has character and is truly "artistically" painted.) 1918-20.. $400

23" "BesterDoll Co." doll. Compo socket head, OM/tin teeth, blue sleep eyes, brown HHW, BJ compo body. Mark: "Bester Doll Co." (neck). Made by Bester Doll Co., Bloomfield, New Jersey, 1919-1921 $400-$425. (Courtesy of Herron)

25" "Baby Horsman." Compo shoulder head, red CM, rosy cheeks, blue metal/celluloid eyes (sleep type)/real lashes, cloth body/compo hands, blonde ptd/molded curly hair, original faded factory clothes, etc. Mark: "E.I. c (in a circle) H. Co." Made by E.I. Horsman, NYC. An Edith Hitchcock design. (Resembles a Gerber Baby. This doll has a slightly different mark than the 24" size.) 1923 ....$375

25" "Taft" marked Girl. Bisque head, OM/6 teeth, brown glass sleep eyes, real eyelashes, brown HHW, BJ compo body, old clothes, etc. Mark: "Taft//1910//6." $500

25" Negro Girl. Dark brown shoulder head, OM/teeth, brown sleep eyes, long black mohair wig, brown cloth body/voice box/brown compo lower limbs, original clothes, bonnet, etc. Label reads: "Suntan Dolls by Luzon." 1920s $700

25" Smoking Flapper Lady. Compo head/long neck, CM/puckered lips/attached cigarette, brown ptd eyes to side, brown bobbed mohair wig/bangs, jtd compo body/long limbs, original orange 2-pc pajama suit with black buttons and black trim, high-heeled slippers, orange necklace Mint. Probably Mutual Novelty Corp., NYC. 1926 ....$600

26" "Artcraft" Girl. Smooth compo head/glossy finish (resembles an Armand Marseille bisque-head girl), orange ptd OM/4 upper teeth, blue tin sleep eyes, brown HHW/open crown/card plate, BJ compo body, old clothes, bonnet, etc. Back mark: "Artcraft U.S.A." Artcraft Toy Products Co., NYC, 1918-20. (This doll is still another attempt of American doll companies to produce dolls in imitation of the popular German bisque. The head is probably from a Marseille mould.) Ca. 1918 ....$600

26" "Dolly face" Girl. Compo socket head, OM/4 upper teeth, blue tin sleep eyes, rosy cheeks, blonde HHW, BJ compo body, original clothes, hat, etc. Mark: "FAM DOLL CO., 26." FAM DOLL CO., NYC. (These heads were made from old German moulds.) Ca. 1915 ... $500

26" "Dolly Record." Phonograph doll. Brightly ptd compo head (shoulder head), O/C mouth/2 upper teeth/molded tongue, blue tin sleep eyes, blonde HHW, cloth body with 4 metal sound horns in front/phonograph mechanism in back/metal crank on right side of body/6 round records/compo limbs, original pink and white dress, etc. Back stamped: "GENUINE//MADAME HENDREN//DOLL//226//Made in U.S.A." Ca. 1922 (1922)..................$700-$800

26" Harold "Red" Grange. All-American half-back at the University of Illinois, 1920s. Bisque head/round chubby face, broad smiling O/C mouth/molded teeth, ptd blue eyes to side, jtd compo body/straight limbs, original football outfit (jersey has number 77 printed on the chest), helmet, etc. (Clothes are all intact and in excellent condition.) Made by Sterling Dolls, NYC. Ca. 1930 or late 1920s ....$1,000+

27" "Googly" Girl. Plaster-compo shoulder head/3 sew holes, smiling CM, rosy cheeks, oversized round blue glass threaded stationary eyes, one-stroke eyebrows, black ptd/molded hair/center part/smooth draped sides with a puff over each ear/topknot on crown, hard-stuffed cloth body/toes indicated by stitching/compo lower arms, old clothes, shoes, stockings. Unmarked doll. Ca. 1911 ....$1,000+

28" "Carnival" Doll. Hard compo shoulder head (smooth, uncrazed), red smiling O/C mouth/ptd teeth, large narrow ptd blue eyes, orange-blonde ptd "Buster Brown" hairdo/comb marks in bangs and on short sides, double chin, coarse excelsior-stuffed cotton body (shoulder head nailed to body), compo lower arms/small hands, original clothes. Unmarked. Probably made by Fair Amusement Co., NYC. Ca. 1914. $400

28" "Century" marked Girl. Compo shoulder head, OM/teeth, blue tin sleep eyes, blonde HHW/original wide pink bandeaux, cloth body/cry box/compo lower limbs, original pink organdy dress, etc. Mint. Doll and original box marked: "Century Doll, Lancaster, PA." 1920s ....$750+

28" "Dorothy Darling Doll." Compo head, OM/teeth, blue sleep eyes, auburn mohair wig, cloth body/compo limbs, original pink silk dress, etc. Gold medal pinned to dress reads: "Dorothy Darling Doll." 1920s ....$500-$550

28" "FIBEROID" Girl. Compo shoulder head, OM/teeth, sleep blue tin eyes, brown HHW (long sausage curls), cloth body/cry box/compo limbs, original pink dress, bandeaux, etc. Mark: "FIBEROID." K& K Toy Co., NYC, 1915-25+. Ca. 1923 ....$500-$550

28" Amberg's Walking Doll. Little Girl. Compo shoulder head, OM/2 upper teeth, blue sleep eyes, brown HHW, cloth body (cork filled) to waist/unusually long jtd compo legs/compo jtd arms, original dress, etc. Unmarked. Dress tag only. Louis Amberg & Son, 101 East 16th St., NYC. (patented June 11, 1918). Ca. 1920 Good condition .$600

30" "Jockey" Boy. Compo head/flange neck/round chubby face, O/C red mouth, ptd blue eyes, one-stroke eyebrows, reddish blonde ptd/molded hair, excelsior-stuffed cloth body/limbs/disc jts/compo hands, original "jockey" outfit, cap. Head mark: "ELEKTRA T. NC. NY." Elektra Toy & Novelty Co., NYC, 1912-20. (This head was used as a Scotch Bonnie Laddie, Boy Scout, Yama Yama, Base Ball Boy. Sculpture of face also similar to 32" Dutch Girl.) Ferdinand Pany designer. Ca. 1914 ....$400

30" "Yama Yama" Boy. Compo head, CM, ptd blue eyes, well-modeled ears, brown ptd/molded hair, excelsior-stuffed cloth body/legs/arms/compo hands, original black/white striped lawn costume, white lawn neck ruff, and two white pompons on shoes. Royal Toy Mfg. Co., NYC, 1916. Distributed by Butler Bros., NYC. 1916...............$400

30" Babe Ruth. Baseball Star, 1920s. Large compo head, O/C smiling mouth/ptd teeth, large ptd blue eyes to side/ptd upper lashes, dark brown ptd hair, cloth body/limbs, original baseball outfit, cap, (There was also a Jack Dempsey doll; made during this period.) Late 1920s ....$700-$800

30" Carnival Doll. Compo shoulder head, CM, ptd blue eyes, blonde ptd/molded hair, straw-stuffed cloth body/compo lower arms, cheap factory-made clothes, etc. Head Mark: "FAIR AMUSEMENT CO." Made by Fair Amusement Company, 142 Fifth Avenue, NYC, 1914. (They made dolls for carnivals.) 1914 ....$400

30" Charlie Chaplin. Portrait face. Compo shoulder head, O/C mouth/molded teeth, dark brown ptd eyes to side/black eyeliner, thin one-stroke eyebrows, black ptd/molded hair/black ptd mustache, excelsior-stuffed body/limbs/compo wrists and hands/pin-and-disc jts, original trousers, jacket, white shirt/necktie, black felt derby hat, black shoes Butler Bros., Sonneberg, Thur., NYC., 1877-1925+ ....$800-$1,000

30" Red Grange. Football Star, 1920s. Large compo head, O/C smiling mouth/ptd teeth, large ptd blue eyes to side/ptd upper lashes, dark brown ptd hair, cloth body, original football outfit, helmet (letter "7" on shirt front.) Late 1920s ....$650-$700

30" Soldier Boy. Compo head, red CM, ptd blue eyes, modeled ears, brown ptd hair with side part, excelsior-stuffed cotton body/compo limbs/compo hands, original khaki uniform with red "V" for victory sewn on sleeve, hat. Head mark: "ELEKTRA//T. ("N" backwards). C. N.Y.//Copyright." Elektra Toy & Novelty Co., NYC. Ferdinand Pany designer. Copyright 1914 ....$400-$500

30" Train Engineer Boy. Compo head, red O/C mouth/4 ptd teeth, ptd blue eyes, red ptd/molded short hair, modeled ears, long cloth body/cloth legs/upper arms/compo lower arms/metal disc at sh/hips, original train engineer uniform, cap. Unmarked. (Carnival prize.) Ca. WW 1 ....$400

32" Dutch Girl. Compo head/flange neck, round chubby face, red O/C mouth, ptd blue eyes, one-stroke eyebrows, reddish blonde ptd/molded bob/2 forehead curls/blue ribbon and bow molded across hair, excelsior-stuffed cloth body/upper arms/black legs/compo hands, original dress, Dutch-type shoes. Mark: "ELEKTRA T.N.C. NY COPYRIGHT." Ferdinand Pany designer. 1914 ....$425

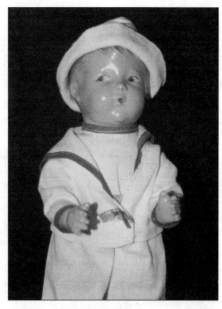

12" Unmarked "Whistling Jim". Compo head/arms, cloth body/legs, blue ptd eyes to side, whistling open mouth, red ptd/mld hair, original clothes. Made by Georgene Averill, NYC. 1925-29. $300-$325 (Courtesy of Ruby Ellen Smith)

32" Exposition Boy. Compo head, CM, ptd blue eyes, blonde ptd/molded hair, excelsior-stuffed body/limbs/compo hands, original 2-pc chinchilla cloth suit/belt, cap, white stockings, leather shoes. Royal Toy Mfg. Co., NYC, 1913-1930 .... $450

32" Uncle Sam. Compo head, CM, ptd blue eyes, blonde ptd/molded hair, excelsior-stuffed cloth body/limbs/compo hands, original red trousers, blue coat with white stars, white shirt/gold buttons, white high-topped hat/blue band with stars, etc. Made by Royal Toy Mfg. Co., NYC, 1913-1930. Ca. 1914.. $500

33" "Amberg" marked girl. Pale bisque head, pastel pink cheek coloring, OM/teeth, brown glass sleep eyes, blonde mohair wig, BJ compo body, original clothes, etc. Mark: "Louis Amberg & Son." Ca. 1920s $1,700

Chapter 30

～ ORIENTAL DOLLS ～

History:

Ancient Chinese dolls were not for play at all, but fashioned as a tutelary deity. These protective guardians or divinities were made from steotite and agalmatolite, and were worshipped and honored with presents. The Chinese believed that these deities brought them good luck and good health. The most valued of these deities date to the sixteenth, seventeenth, and eighteenth centuries.

The Chinese "voodoo" doll dates as early as 100 BC. These were carved from wood or modeled from clay in the image of the accursed, and taken to a witch to be endowed with evil, or the heart pierced with a sharp knife and the effigy buried. Straw dolls, dressed in material from the clothing of the person sinned against, were pierced with needles. Wives made paper dolls in the image of their husband. The paper doll was hung upside down until the husband's heart was changed from bad to good. Paper images were also burnt to remove disease from an ailing person's body. For these reasons dolls were considered effigies, and looked upon with awe by little girls, thus were not considered "playthings."

Not until the commercialization of dolls in the nineteenth century did the Chinese craftsmen contemplate making dolls for decorative purposes. These were usually carved from wood, stained, costumed, and shipped to the west. Other types were modeled from clay. In the twentieth century, dolls were still being made from wood and clay, but composition was becoming popular in the 1920s. The Chinese cloth doll was also a popular item in Oriental gift shops which thrived in large cities like New York, San Francisco, etc.

The Japanese doll also dates from ancient times. Their dolls developed along two distinct lines: the ritual doll and the decorative doll; the ritual doll taking first priority. The ritual figure was an effigy. The Japanese believed that a man's sins could be transferred to a doll simply by rubbing it. When this effigy was thrown into the river, it carried away the man's sins and other problems. The Japanese always admired beautiful objects and were very artistic. Their "decorative" dolls were sold alongside lacquered boxes and bolts of silk brocade. These dolls were popular amongst the elite who purchased them for gift giving.

One such "court" or "palace" doll was gosho ningyo. It dates to the Edo Period (1615-1867) and became a favorite with the nobility. The gosho ningyo represented a chubby baby boy; baby boys being a symbol of good luck in Japan. They were carved from a block of wood, sanded, and given many layers of gofun, and then decorated. Other ornamental dolls made during this creative era were the saga ningyo and ukiyo-e ningyo.

The saga dolls, like other dolls made in the 18th century, are considered very rare and expensive when found nowadays. They were also intricately carved from wood and lavishly decorated. These figurines stood under twelve inches high and were carefully painted and then highlighted with gold leaf. Sumino Ryoi, a famous Japanese artist and craftsman who lived during the Kanei Period (1625-43) originated these display dolls. They depicted tradespeople, warriors, actors, puppeteers, mythological characters, etc.

Another doll-type that dates from the Edo Period is the kimekomi ningyo, which were inspired by the saga ningyo. Their wooden bodies were grooved with a sharp knife and strips of silk fabric was inserted into the slits and glued; the material draped and folded around the figure in a naturalistic manner. The ukiyo ningyo is similar in construction to the kimekomi ningyo except that there is less body structure and more layers of clothing. Doll-making became such a highly respected skill in Japan that it was handed down from father to son, generation after generation. "Dairi hina" dolls likewise date early in Japanese history. They were made expressly for the "Girl's Festival." The Japanese Doll Festival is called "Hina Matsuri" and is celebrated on 3 March each year. This is a family celebration and everyone participates. The overwhelming demand for play-dolls in America and England in the twentieth century gave rise to the mass-produced commonplace doll which lacked all the qualities that made the dolls of past centuries so compelling to the eye. (The exception being the character dolls made in Germany and France.)Gone was the fine craftsmanship and detail, and in its place came a vapid doll that possessed very little artistic merit at all. After World War One, a lovely, but cheaply-made "souvenir" doll was sold in Japanese gift shops and in gift shops in this country (usually located in the Oriental sectors of large cities like New York and San Francisco). The product cheapened even further after World War Two, making the pre-war dolls look almost "custom-made" by comparison. But collectors and layman alike see what they wish to see in doll faces, and, with the fleeting passage of time, every doll, regardless of rank or quality, finds its niche in history.

Collection Hints:

Oriental dolls, those made in the Orient, are valued according to age and quality. Dolls made prior to the twentieth century are the best. Carved wood types are very scarce, as are those with faces made from pulverized oyster and egg shell. The more common Japanese dolls are those with faces made of hand-painted silk (some date to the 1920s), and those with the composition or plaster heads. These later dolls were dressed in brocade or silk. A better quality silk was used in the 1920s, and when these dolls are found today, the silk has become very faded. The workmanship is also superior to that of later dolls. The hand-carved wooden Chinese doll is of more value than those duplicated in composition. Many Chinese dolls were made from fabric, their faces hand-painted or embroidered.

Reproduction Alert:

Commercially-made Oriental dolls have not been reproduced in this country. Modern day doll artists in Japan are making traditional dolls in the old style, but these are not considered reproductions. Oriental dolls made by Kestner, Simon & Halbig, etc., might have been reproduced. Be wary of those.

ORIENTAL DOLLS

3-1/2" Japanese Twins. Boy & Girl. All-stone bisque/jtd at sh./hips with fine wire, ptd features; boy has black mohair wig with queue/black cap; girl has black ptd hair/headband; both wear matching sateen costumes of coarse fabric/ptd black shoes. Tags read: "Made in Japan." 1920s ....$175 pr

4"Japanese Boy. Papier-mâché head, CM, inset brown glass eyes, long black horsehair queue, cardboard body/paper jts/mâché hands/feet, original cotton kimono with Japanese design. Ca. 1900 ....$200

5-1/2"Japanese Babies. Boy & Girl. Bisque socket head, CM, brown glass sleep eyes, black HHW, bent-limb jtd compo bodies, cotton sateen costumes (boy wears black cap, girl wears headband). 1920s ....$300 per pair

16" (standing) Chinese girl, all original, $85; 16" (sitting) Chinese Girl, original dress. Both dolls have black yarn hair. Standing doll has ptd features; seated doll has embroidered features and was probably made by Lutheran World Service, 1920s, $225 (Courtesy of Herron)

9"Chinese Couple. Man & Woman. Compo heads, ptd features (delicate and artistic painting/modeling)/lady has chubby face and double chin/gentleman has black glued-on mustache/amused expression, black ptd/molded hair, compo/wire/paper bodies/ptd and molded black shoes/black wooden base, original faded silk outfits. Early 20th$600 pr

10" "Amah and Baby" or "Nursemaid and Child." Compo heads/round, chubby faces, red CMs, slanted black ptd eyes, short curved eyebrows, black ptd hair (both), cloth bodies/compo hands/bare feet (some have black ptd shoes), removable clothes. Paper tag reads: "Chinese Character Doll//Amah with Child.//No. 158//Made in Hong Kong." 1920s-30s $350

10-1/2" Chinese "Actress" Lady. Molded/ptd pin-jtd clay head/bright colors, smiling CM, slanted brown ptd eyes/molded lids, elaborate molded/black ptd hairstyle called "Ta-Fa" (molded clay bun attached with glue)/bun decorated with simulated gold filigree, floss pompons, paper, fabric, tiny green glass beads, etc., wood-

en block upper body/unstuffed upper arms,/glued-on compo lower arms/flat metal strips serve for "thighs" with wooden dowels at knees/carved wooden shoes/cloth-covered, original elaborate silk costume. (Opera doll from the Haiking Mission School, Province of Hanan, China.) 1920s $300

10-1/2" "The Last Empress." Opera Doll of China. Represents "T'su Hsi." Body constructed similarly to above doll. Empress has a white painted face. Each doll's face is painted in a different shade to denote age of character portrayed. Clay head, ptd features, black ptd hair/elaborate molded hairstyle, original robes of state; embroidered with designs on sleeve and in center of robe. Haiking Mission School, Province of Hanan, China. 1920s $400

11" Chinese Man. Compo head, CM, ptd brown eyes, black ptd hair, cloth body/limbs/compo hands and feet, original clothes. Round label reads: "A Michael Lee//Chinese Character Doll//Micale//Handmade in China." ....$65-$85

12" Japanese "Traditional" Girl. Bisque socket head, CM, PN, black glass sleep eyes, black HHW, sawdust-compo body/compo lower limbs/textile joints/squeaker, original faded silk kimono. Ca. 1908 (late Meiji period). Good condition.............................$600

13" Chinese Girl. All-compo/movable arms only, CM, ptd brown eyes, black ptd/molded hair, original cotton costume with embroidered dragon on front/long sleeves/ptd shoes. Tag reads: "Hoo Choy" and on border: "The Little Goddess of Good Luck", backside reads: "Hoo//Choy//(means)//Good Luck//Health//Happiness/Prosperity//Long Life." (Chinese character design). American-made. 1920s......$125

11" "Hi Flo" Chinese Girl, all original, sold by the Lutheran World Service to raise funds for their mission, Ca. 1920s-1930s $225. (Courtesy of Victoria Rose, England)

13"Japanese "Traditional" Girl. Gofun head (powdered oyster shell mixed with glue), CM, inset brown glass eyes, coarse HHW with straight bangs, cloth body/upper limbs/compo lower limbs/well-sculpted hands and feet, original silk kimono. Ca. 1920s.... $600

14" Ichimatsu Boy. Sawdust-compo socket head, O/C mouth/teeth, PN, black HHW, sawdust-compo body/lower limbs/textile joints/wired-cloth upper arms, inset black pupil-less glass eyes, faded cotton kimono. Ca. 1868 or late Edo period (1615-1867).............$750+

14" Yamato Ning-yo. Compo head, CM, inset brown glass eyes, black HHW, cloth body//limbs//compo hands and feet/squeaker, original silk kimono. Ca. 1920s-30s...................................$125

16" Ichimatsu Girl. Sawdust-compo socket head, CM, inset black pupil-less glass eyes, black HHW, sawdust-compo body/lower limbs/textile joints, original silk kimono with long sleeves. Ca. 1900 (late Meiji Era). Good condition ... $650

16" Japanese Girl. Bisque head, OM/4 teeth, brown glass sleep eyes, black HHW, BJ compo body, original silk kimono. Head mark: "6MB (in a circle with upper and lower curved lines and a straight line through the center separating the M and B) Japan." Morimura Brothers, NYC, importers/suppliers of Japanese-made dolls, 1915-22 ... $450

17-1/2" Chinese Mandarin (Man). Molded clay head/pink flesh-tone color/smooth finish, faintly smiling CM, ptd black eyes/black eyeliner, black fly-away eyebrows, top of head painted black and covered by a gold painted ornamental head-dress, wood-block body/wood lower arms/long fork-like fingers/wooden feet (carved boots), original green silk robe with elaborate embroidery design, blue trousers. (This Mandarin doll is one of many Chinese Opera dolls from the Haiking Mission School, Province of Hanan, China.) 1920s... $400

110" Chinese Baby, all original, black yarn hair, probably made by Quan-Quan Co., Los Angeles, San Francisco, CA. Ca. 1930. All compo/jtd body $225. (Courtesy of Herron)

22" Friendship Doll. Japanese. Smooth papier-mâché head, CM, inset brown glass eyes, black HHW, jtd mâché/wood body, original silk kimono. Ca. 1920s (Sold for $725 in 1987) ....$800+

22" (standing) old Japanese lady doll, all original, embroidered features, black yarn hair, old silk kimono, unmarked. $125 21" (seated) lady has felt head, closed eyes, original costume. Lower part of body is a zippered hideaway for pajamas or such. Unmarked. $150.

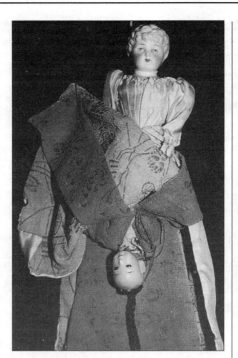

Super-rare antique Topsy-Turvey dolls. Molded bisque head on one end and Oriental man on the opposite end. Brought from Europe in 1880, all original, never played with. German $2,500+. (Courtesy of D. Kay Crow)

23" Japanese lady, ptd features, all original. CA. WW 11, $150. (Courtesy of Ruby Ellen Smith)

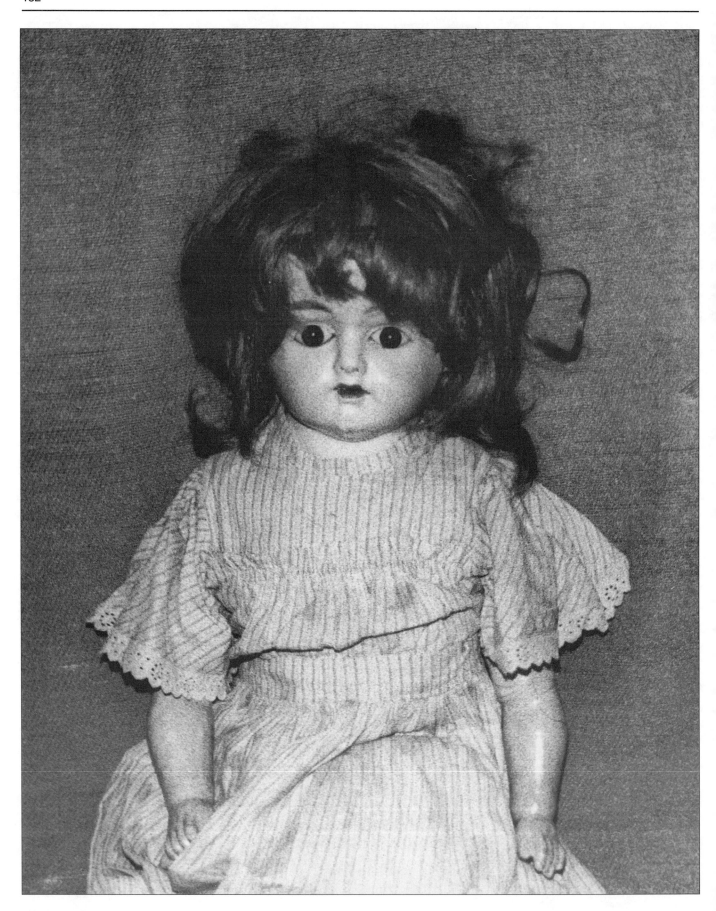

Chapter 31

(ANTIQUE) PAPIER-MÂCHÉ & COMPOSITION DOLLS

History:

The extensive use of papier-mâché, in 1810 revolutionized the European doll industry. As early as 1700, a Mr. Watson, in England, was engaged in a paperware business. A rare 34" fashion or "style" doll in the collection of the late Henri d'Allemagne had a head and lower limbs made from papier-mâché. The wood body was jointed and covered with burlap. It was signed "Nuon Angelye 1734"; the lovely head was signed "A. Latticilli" and wore its original human hair wig. A third party made the doll's elaborate costume, in Italy.

Papier-mâché for common usage, was nothing more than waste paper ground to a pulp and mixed with paste or glue. Sometimes ground chalk, clay, and fine sand was added to the mixture. Dried in a mold, under pressure, the object was tough and hard, resembling wood. When sanded and coated with gesso, then oil painted, decorated, and varnished, it became an ideal medium for dolls and toys.

Although the French had made dolls of carton-moulé, in the 18th century, it

25" Compo shoulder head, OM/teeth, inset brown glass eyes, original brown mohair wig, kid body/compo lower arms, old clothes, hat, etc. Ca. 1880s $900-$1,000. (Courtesy of Herron)

was the Germans who mastered mass-production techniques, and made Sonneberg the toy capitol of the world. The French were natural-born dressmakers and designers, doll-making per se was not their forte. In fact, they considered it a waste of time; the doll merely a form on which to display their carefully executed clothes. The Germans, on the other hand, had little interest in the time consuming process of outfitting a doll. Their aim was great wealth, and production on a grand scale. They developed skills other countries could not match; desirous of reaching the masses with a quality product, all the while keeping costs at a minimum. Their best dolls are every bit as fine as those made by the French, and doll-making in the two countries became so closely intertwined it is sometimes difficult to distinguish one unmarked doll from the other.

Collecting Hints:

Many contemporary collectors are wary of dolls made from papier-mâché, or composition, fearing they will eventually completely deteriorate. This fear is groundless and foolish. The very fact that so many have survived this long (pristine examples date several hundred years), is testimony of their durability. The composition and papier-mâché formulas used for the early dolls is not the formulas used in the 20th century (some of these later dolls were made of composition conceived mainly of glue and sawdust). If a doll conceived in one of these mediums endures 25-50 years, then it will more than likely endure a hundred or more years.

Varnish also sealed in the gesso and surface paint, providing the shoulder head with a hard, smooth, protective veneer that discouraged insect infestation and protected the surface from moisture, which would soften the head and peel away the paint. A thick varnish overcoat could also be cleaned with a damp cloth, whereas an unvarnished head is easily soiled and cannot be

cleaned lest the paint wash away (this applies to some of the 20th century dolls). In the past, before people began to collect and display dolls, dolls were carefully wrapped and stored in trunks when the child was no longer interested. As the years passed, the doll became a family heirloom, to be handed down from generation to generation.

In modern times, with so many people collecting and exhibiting their dolls, the doll has fallen prey to sunlight and air-pollution. This damaging pollution has infiltrated our household dust and is destructive to the already rapidly aging doll. Dolls should then be kept dust free and kept away from direct sunlight. Do not cover their heads with plastic bags. Plastic draws moisture from the air and will crack the doll's composition parts. (Plastic is even more damaging to plastic or vinyl dolls!)

The most desirable of the early papier-mâché and composition dolls are those with rare hairdos. However, do not over-look the more common types made from the 1860s to 1900. These are truly historic old dolls and add quality to any collection.

(ANTIQUE) PAPIER-MÂCHÉ & COMPOSITION DOLLS

7-1/2" Milliner's Model Lady. Papier-mâché shoulder head/long neck/oval face, CM, large ptd blue eyes, brown ptd hairdo/molded rear hair with molded coronet braid on crown/matching human hair inserted on each side of front part and curled, kid body/wood lower limbs, original dress with large puff sleeves, etc. German. Ca. 1830s .... $900+

8-1/4" Milliner's Model Lady. Papier-mâché head, CM, ptd blue eyes, ptd dark brown hair/center part/braided chignon, kid body/wood lower limbs/tan ptd shoes, original long tan calico dress, etc. German. Ca. 1840s............. $850+

8-1/2" Milliner's Model Lady. Papier-mâché shoulder head, CM, ptd blue eyes, black ptd/molded hairdo with center part/smooth top/draped sides, partly exposed ear lobes/double looped braids over each ear/bun of small rear curls/3 nape curls/comb marks on crown, kid body/wood lower limbs/rose ptd shoes/rose colored paper bands above knees and elbows, original floral print cotton dress, petticoats, percale pantalets. German. Ca. 1833+..$1,200

9" Milliner's Model Lady, Gent. Bride and Groom. Papier-mâché shoulder heads, ptd features, black ptd hair is almost concealed by glued-on corn silk wigs, kid bodies/wood limbs/legs attached to wood stands, clothes consist of corn husks (elaborate and artistic). German. All original. Ca. 1810 Rare types Pr. $2,000

9" Negro Milliner's Model Lady. Black ptd shoulder head (papier-mâché)/short neck, CM, ptd black eyes with whites, black ptd/molded hairdo, dark brown kid body/black ptd wooden lower limbs, original clothes. German. Ca. 1850s Rare type ....$2,000+

9-1/2" Lady. Papier-mâché shoulder head, CM, ptd blue eyes, brown HHW, pink kid body/ papier-mâché lower limbs, original clothes. Ca. 1840s. German $1,000

9-1/2" Milliner's Model Lady. Papier-mâché shoulder head/long neck/oval face, CM, ptd blue eyes, black ptd/molded evening head-dress/sausage curls on each side of face in diagonals/bunch of curls atop head/rear hair upswept, kid body/wood lower limbs/green ptd shoes, original plain flower print blue voile dress, pantaloons. (Head-dress does not compliment clothes, but clothes are original.) Ca. 1828. German ....$800-$950

10" Skipping Girl. Compo head, ptd features, black ptd hair/"scallops" bordering face, wooden body/jtd at sh/hips/black ptd shoes marked "Patent" on one sole, original cardboard bonnet with flower decoration, original red pinafore. (Wires attached to arms. Doll "skips" when wires are extended and the wooden handle is turned.) Ca. 1885. German $1,000

10-1/4" Fashionable Lady. Papier-mâché shoulder head/pastel coloring, CM, ptd blue eyes, molded ears, black ptd hairdo/molded high atop crown with molded braid at rear of head and molded comb, original cloth body/limbs, old orange silk dress, etc. Ca. 1820s. German $1,000

11" Milliner's Model Lady. Papier-mâché shoulder head, CM, ptd blue eyes, black ptd/molded hairdo/center part/flat smooth top/draped and puffed sides (wings) pulled into a rear bustle of tiny curls (hair outlined in grey), kid body/wood lower limbs, original gingham dress, etc. German. Ca. 1838 ....$1,500

11" Milliner's Model Lady. Papier-mâché shoulder head/long neck/wide shoulders, tiny smiling mouth, ptd blue eyes, black ptd/molded hairdo/center part/bunches of tiny curls concealing ears on each side of face/coiled and braided rare bun, kid body/wood lower limbs, original green cotton dress, pantaloons, green ptd shoes. German. Ca. 1837 ....$1,000

11" Negro Boy. Black ptd papier-mâché shoulder head, CM, large inset dark brown glass eyes, black ptd/molded hair, Motschmann-type cloth body/cloth jts/black compo hips/black compo lower limbs, original clothes. German. Ca. 1850s Excellent condition $1,500

11" Peddler Woman. Papier-mâché head, CM, ptd blue eyes, black ptd/center part/molded short hair, Grodnertal jtd wooden body, original Welsh outfit, cape (red silk lined), original tray of wares (cards, brushes, purses, scent bottles, books, etc.) Original glass dome. Ca. 1840 ....$2,000+

11-1/2" Negro Girl. Black ptd papier-mâché shoulder head, O/C mouth/2 rows of teeth, inset black pupil-less glass eyes, thick black ptd eyebrows, red eye/red nose dots, black wool wig, original black ptd muslin-gauze body stuffed with straw/ papier-mâché lower limbs/molded boots, original clothes, bandanna, etc. Unmarked. German. Ca. 1870s ....$600+

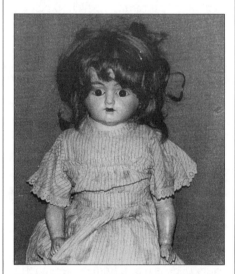

30" Compo shoulder head, OM/teeth, large inset brown glass eyes, brown HHW, cloth body/legs/compo lower arms, original clothes. Ca. 1880s $1,200. (Courtesy of Herron)

11-1/2" Fashionable Lady. Varnished compo shoulder head/broad forehead/v-shaped face with narrow chin, CM, ptd blue eyes, black ptd/molded hairdo in "Apollo's Knot" (bunches of curls on each side of face for width, coiled braids atop head), kid body/wood lower limbs/carved hands, original elaborate gown, apron, pantalets, etc. Ca. 1828 ....$1,200

12" French "Fashion" Lady. Papier-mâché shoulder head, red CM, ptd brown eyes, dark brown mohair wig, cloth body/mâché lower limbs/molded and ptd high-heeled slippers, original clothes. Made by Baroness de Laumont, Paris. Ca. 1916 ....$1,000+

12" Poupard Boy. All molded papier-mâché/straight arms jtd at sh/unjointed "apart" legs, well-sculpted face, red CM, ptd brown eyes, blue ptd/molded cap/straggly blonde ptd hair tendrils on forehead and sides, ptd/molded clothes (blue shirt and yellow short

pants), blue ptd shoes with ankle straps, white stockings. France. 19th c. ....$3,000+

12" Squeeze Toy. Little Boy. Compo head, CM, ptd blue eyes, brown ptd/molded curly hair, cloth body/smooth wood lower limbs/tiny bells attached to hands/black ptd boots, original "jester-type" outfit/molded-on jester cap with tiny metal bells attached to the 3 pointed ends. (When bellows in chest is pressed the jester or clown turns his head, walks, shakes his arms and squeaks.) 1850s $1,200

13" "Apollo's Knot" Style Lady. Papier-mâché shoulder head/long neck, CM, large ptd blue eyes, black ptd/molded hairdo/center part/clusters of small curls on each side of face/rear hair brushed high off neck and braided, the braids twisted around a form to simulate a high tuck comb, wasp-waisted kid body/smooth lathe-turned lower limbs/blue paper bands conceal elbow and knee attachment of wood to kid/blue ptd shoes, original cotton floral print long dress, petticoats, pantalets. (This lady is in the Milliner's Model category.) Ca. 1830s $1,400

13" French Lady. Papier-mâché socket head, CM, ptd blue eyes/molded, think one-stroke eyebrows, brown HHW, shapely cardboard body/stuffed cloth upper limbs/compo lower limbs/molded high-heeled pumps/black ptd stockings to knees, elaborate original clothes. (This doll has all the traits of having been made in France.) Ca. 1850s $1,500

13" Nurse Pushing Baby Cart. Papier-mâché shoulder head, CM, exposed ears, ptd blue eyes, black ptd/molded short curly hairdo, cloth and metal body, original skirt, high-buttoned blouse with necktie, petticoat, drawers, black ptd/molded boots, metal cart with 2 large wheels at rear and one small wheel in front. (Clockwork mechanism. When activated, the cart moves forward and the doll's metal feet lifts in a walking movement. Metal hands are attached to cart.) German. Ca. 1860s Rare ....$2,000-$2,500

13-1/2" Poupard Boy. All molded papier-mâché (head and body modeled in 1 piece, no movable parts.), red CM, ptd blue eyes/black eyeliner, straight black eyebrows, black ptd hair with scalloped bangs, carved "stub" nose, no clothes. France. 19th c. $2,500

13-1/2" Oriental Boy. Papier-mâché shoulder head (yellowish tint), CM, large inset brown glass bulging eyes, black mohair wig, "scowling" 1-stroke black eyebrows, cloth body/compo lower limbs, original Chinese outfit; cap, shoes. Ca. 1880s........................$750

14" "4/0" incised Lady. Portrait-type. Turned compo shoulder head (smooth, high quality)/long neck, CM, small inset light blue glass eyes, blonde HHW, cloth body/compo lower limbs/yellow ptd high-topped molded boots with silver buckles/vertically striped stockings/blue tops, original clothes. (Supposedly "Princess May of Teck" or Queen Mary.) German............$2,000+

14" "Flirty-eyes" Milliner's Model Papier-mâché shoulder head/sloping shoulders, smiling CM, inset brown pupil-less glass flirty eyes, black ptd/molded hairdo (Apollo's Knot with short side curls, upswept nape hair and twisted braids atop head), kid body/wood lower limbs/red ptd shoes, original clothes. Ca. 1826-32. Super-rare $2,500

14" Louis & Philippe Period Lady. Papier-mâché shoulder head, tiny prim mouth, ptd blue eyes/molded eyelids, black ptd/molded hairdo/center part/draped sides/rear bun, mortise-and-tenon jtd wood body, original 18th style open robe with quilted petticoat, etc. Ca. 1840s $2,000

14-1/2"Louis & Philippe Period Lady. Papier-mâché shoulder head, long neck, CM, ptd blue eyes, black ptd/molded hairdo with side curls/coronet braid, kid body/wood lower limbs, original "rotten" dress, pantalets, etc. Ca. 1840 . $3,200

14-1/2" "Bonnet" Lady. Papier-mâché shoulder head (smooth, hard, early type), tiny prim CM, inset dark brown pupil-less glass eyes, rosy cheeks, exposed ears, unusual brown ptd bonnet with widow's peak in center of forehead (bonnet not molded, but painted directly onto egg-shaped head), no hair, cloth body/legs/papier-mâché lower arms/well-shaped hands/separate thumb, original clothes, etc. Ca. 1835 .... $3,000+

15" "Apollo's Knot" Lady. Varnished compo shoulder head/oval face, ptd blue eyes, short one-stroke eyebrows, tiny pink cupid's bow mouth, original HHW in the "Apollo's Knot" evening head-dress (center part, tight curls on each side of face, topknot is a mass of twisted braids and loops), cloth body/compo lower limbs, original commercially-made clothes. Ca. 1820s $1,800

15" "Glass-eyed" Greiner. Smooth papier-mâché shoulder head, CM, large inset brown pupil-less bulgy glass eyes, exposed ears, black ptd/molded hairdo/center part/flat curly top and sides, cloth body/original china lower arms, old clothes. Ca. early 1850s $2,000

15" French Lady. Papier-mâché shoulder head, CM, ptd blue-grey eyes, brown ptd hair, kid body/leather arms, original regional clothes, bonnet. Ca. 1850s (This could be a French-type.) .. $1,300

15" German Lady. Papier-mâché shoulder head, CM, black enamel eyes, black ptd/molded hair do/flat-top/center part/draped sides/rear bun, cloth body/mâché lower limbs/black ptd heeled shoes, original German "regional" costume, head-dress, etc. Ca. 1850s $1,000

15" Lady. Papier-mâché shoulder head, smiling CM, inset black pupil-less glass eyes, glued-on brown HHW braided in coils around each ear, kid body/wooden lower limbs/tiny feet, original clothes, etc. German. Ca. 1840s $2,000

16" "Covered Wagon-type" Lady. Papier-mâché shoulder head/cup-and-saucer neck/deep sloping shoulders, CM, ptd black eyes, light brown eyebrows, black ptd/molded hairdo/center part/molded smooth to head with vertical curls arranged around lower part of head, cloth body/wasp waist/broad hips/wood lower limbs/spoon hands/red ptd flat-soled shoes, original red print dress. German. Ca. 1850s $950

16" French Lady. Papier-mâché shoulder head, CM, ptd blue eyes, black ptd/molded hair/center part/draped sides and plaited rear bun, kid body/limbs, original "regional" outfit: black net skirt, black velvet bodice decorated with flowers/metal thread/blue silk bows, underclothes, cap, leather shoes, stockings. Ca. 1840s (German) 1840s $2,000

17" "Kitchen Helper" Lady. Papier-mâché shoulder head, tiny CM, inset blue glass eyes, black ptd/molded hairdo/flat-top, cloth body to waist/wooden cage-type lower body lined with fabric and concealed by original skirt (skirt opens to reveal original mini wooden table and utensils, a tea set, etc., mâché lower arms. 1850s ..... $12,000+

17" Andreas Voit-type Lady. Smooth papier-mâché shoulder head/long neck, smiling CM, ptd blue eyes, thin one-stroke eyebrows, slight ear modeling, "hair" ptd black on round smooth head with an inverted "V" shape emanating from center part/hairline brush-strokes, cloth body/wood lower limbs/flat-soled ptd shoes, old clothes. Probably Andrea Voit, Germany, 1835-55. Ca. 1840s $2,000

17" Gibson Girl Lady. Compo shoulder head/long oval "pretty" face, CM, molded ears, blonde upswept mohair wig in Gibson style (high bun on crown and curls bordering forehead), cloth body/limbs/compo hands, elaborate original gown, etc. German. Ca. 1905 .... $900

17" Grandma. Papier-mâché shoulder head/pale coloring/forehead lines, OM/straw teeth, original white rabbit fur wig, kid body/leather arms, original cotton nightgown, cap, underwear. French-type. Possibly German. Ca. 1840's Rare $2,500

17" Little Girl. All cardboard, CM, ptd blue eyes, thick dark eyebrows, orange ptd/molded bangs/molded/ptd white bonnet, jtd at shoulders only, bent arms, wears molded-on/ptd "sailor" dress with broad collar, large chest bow, low ptd belt, dress molded below knees, ptd/molded shoes. Ca. 1880s Rare .... $600+

17" Milliner's Model Lady. Papier-mâché shoulder head, CM, ptd blue eyes, black ptd/molded "Apollo's Knot" (very high atop head with large puffs on each side of head above ears), kid body, stiff wood lower limbs/ptd shoes, original clothes. Ca. 1830 .... $2,000-$2,200

17" Milliner's Model Lady. Papier-mâché shoulder head, CM, ptd blue eyes, black ptd/molded hairdo/center part/flat-top/3 sausage curls in front of each ear/rear chignon, kid body/wood lower limbs/ptd shoes, original clothes. Ca. 1840s $1,900

18" "Patent Washable" Baby. Papier-mâché shoulder head, OM/teeth, inset blue glass bulging eyes, curly skin wig, cloth body/legs/mâché lower arms, original white cotton gown, etc. Ca. 1880s .... $600+

18" "Patriotic" Boy. Papier-mâché shoulder head, CM, ptd blue eyes, black ptd hair/brush strokes, stiff kid body/wood lower limbs/slender feet/ptd blue shoes original 2-pc red/white/blue outfit: trousers and jacket (blue jacket printed with white stars, red-and-white stripe trousers) Jacket trimmed with metallic silver paper. German. Ca. 1850s $2,000+

18" Adult Male. Compo shoulder head, CM, inset brown glass eyes, brown ptd hair/brush marks, pink leather body/limbs, original suit, elaborate silk brocade vest, shirt, large neck bow. Ca. 1840 .... $2,000

26" Greiner No. 9 (Pat. Mar 30. Ext. 72") marked lady. Papier-mâché shoulder head, CM, blue ptd eyes, rare blonde hairdo (unusual style), cloth body/leather arms, old clothes. $800-$900+ (Courtesy of D. Kay Crow)

18" Lady. French-type. Shiny, hard compo shoulder head, CM, huge almond-shaped threaded blue glass bulging eyes, upper/lower ptd eyelashes, black ptd/molded hairdo, exposed ears, cloth body/limbs/sloping shoulders, original clothes. Ca. 1880s $2,000

18" Milliner's Model Lady. Papier-mâché shoulder head, CM, large ptd blue eyes, black ptd/molded hairdo/center part/exposed ears/hair draped on sides of face and over ears/long rear curls, kid body/wood lower limbs, original 2-pc cotton skirt/bodice, net over-blouse, net pantaloons, red ptd shoes. Ca. 1844 .... $1,200

18-1/2" "Black Cap" Lady. Papier-mâché shoulder head/long neck, CM, sharp features, large inset black glass eyes, round dome-shaped head painted with a black skull or bathing cap with a pointed widow's peak and fancy bow tied beneath chin, kid body/limbs, old clothes. Ca. 1830s Rare type ....$3,000+

18-1/2" Lady. Smooth papier-mâché shoulder head/long neck, ptd blue eyes, black ptd/molded hairdo/center part/smooth top/exposed ears/2 fat curls behind each ear/rear hair upswept with braided and coiled "Victoria" bun/many brushstrokes/deep comb marks, kid body/wood lower limbs, old clothes. 1840s...........................$2,500

18-1/2" Haughty Lady. Compo shoulder head, tiny red heart-shaped CM, ptd blue eyes, one-stroke brown eyebrows, brown HHW decorated with old feathers, bead rings/bead earrings/bead headdress, kid body/limbs, separate fingers, original silk brocade court outfit, 2 short linen petticoats (to calves), silk stockings, black silk shoes with buckles. All original including watch on chain attached to waist ribbon. Ca. 1780 ....$4,000

19" "French-type" Lady. Smooth papier-mâché shoulder head, tiny red CM, small inset brown pupil-less glass eyes, slightly modeled ears, sparse black ptd hair/center part/high forehead/no curls/brush marks, fine kid body/limbs/long separated stitched and wired fingers, original mousseline (muslin) gown with puffed sleeves, underwear, etc. (This fine quality doll and attention to detail places it in the authentic "French" or "French-type" class; the Germans made such dolls for the French trade.) Ca. 1837 ....$2,500

20" "Enigma" Girl (resembles a Greiner). Papier-mâché shoulder head, CM, inset black pupil-less glass eyes, black ptd/molded hairdo/flattop/side and rear curls, cloth body/upper limbs/mâché lower torso/wood lower limbs/crier, old clothes. Ca. 1860s Rare type..$2,000+

20" "Holz-Masse" signed Girl. Compo shoulder head/expressive face, smirking CM, large blue ptd eyes/heavy molded eyelids (similar to a Huret), blonde mohair wig, cloth body/compo lower limbs/molded/ptd boots, old clothes. Ca. 1875+ (Cuno & Otto Dressel)..................................$1,000+

21" "Bristol" marked Girl. Hard compo shoulder head/ptd white, CM, ptd/molded blue eyes, soft blonde mohair wig, leather body/limbs, old clothes. Paper sticker on shoulder plate reads: "BRISTOL'S UNBREAKABLE DOLL//273 HIGH ST. PROVIDENCE, R.I." Made by Emma L. Bristol, Providence, R.I., 1886-1900. Ca. 1886+ Rare ...$3,000+

21" "Flirty-eyed" Pre-Greiner. Papier-mâché shoulder head, CM, almond-shaped blue "flirty" glass eyes, black ptd severely molded hairdo styled closed to head, exposed ears, cloth body/leather arms, old clothes. Ca. early 1850s (pre 1858 label) ....$3,000+

21" "Glass-eyed" Milliner's Model. Papier-mâché shoulder head, CM, rare inset brown glass eyes, black ptd/molded hairdo with center part/smooth flat-top/drooping waves in front of ears/long sausage curls on nape of neck, kid body/wood lower limbs/ptd shoes, original clothes. Ca. 1840s $3,500

21" "Glass-eyed" Pre-Greiner. Papier-mâché shoulder head, CM, inset brown pupil-less glass eyes, exposed ears, black ptd/molded hairdo/smooth top/center part/short rear ringlets, cloth body/leather arms, old clothes. Ca. early 1850s (pre 1858 label) $2,600

21" Milliner's Model Gentleman. Papier-mâché shoulder head/cup-and-saucer neck, small CM, ptd brown eyes, modeled ears, black ptd/molded male hairdo/center part/hair swirled onto forehead with 3 curls on each side of part, kid body/wood lower limbs, original trousers, wool jacket, shirt, vest, black silk cravat, black ptd shoes. Ca. 1829 ....$3,000+

23" "Eyelash" Greiner. Papier-mâché shoulder head, CM, ptd blue eyes/rare ptd upper eyelashes, exposed ears, black ptd hairdo/center part/smooth flat-top/draped sides/behind-the-ear curls, cloth body/leather arms, old clothes. 1858 label..................$2,000+

23" "Glass-eyed" Pre-Greiner. Papier-mâché shoulder head/very pale/delicate pastel coloring, CM, large inset pupil-less brown glass eyes, black ptd/severely molded hairdo/center part, exposed ears, cloth body/leather arms/sloping shoulders, old clothes. Ca. early 1850s (pre 1858 label). Greiners made by Ludwig Greiner, Philadelphia, Pa.; 1840-74; 1874-1883; knell Bros. or Francis B. Knell, successor, 1890-1900 (Greiner's brother-in-law). $3,500

23" "Queen Adelaide-type" Lady. Papier-mâché shoulder head/long neck/oval face, CM, large ptd blue eyes, black ptd/molded hair/side part/draped front/wide side puffs/s coronet braids atop head with a high tuck comb (all ptd black), cloth body/leather arms, original clothes. (This is still another version of the coveted "Apollo's Knot" hairstyle, although here the tuck comb adds to the height.) 1830s $4,500

23" "The Smoker." Automaton. Negro man. Black compo head, OM, inset brown glass eyes, black mohair wig, compo body/bisque hands/legs mounted to velvet-covered wooden base, original form-fitting black breeches, black pumps, red satin cutaway coat, ivory satin vest, white tie, white shirt with French cuffs and cuff-links. Activate key and arms move up and down; one hand holds a lorgnette, the other hand is for a cigarette. French. Ca. 1880s $12,000

23" Black Mammy. Black ptd compo shoulder head, red CM, inset brown glass eyes, burly black mohair wig, dark cloth body/black compo hands/dark cloth limbs, original checkered cotton dress, white lace-trimmed apron, red neckerchief. Ca. 1860s......................$1,000+

23" Greiner Lady. Papier-mâché shoulder head., CM, ptd brown eyes, exposed ears, black ptd hairdo/center part/flat-top/8 vertical curls, cloth body/leather arms/sewn-on stockings and leather boots, original print dress, etc. Back of shoulder head stamped: "PATENT HEAD." (This is one of Greiner's early pre-1858 heads.) Ca. early 1858........................$2,000

24" "French-type" Lady. Papier-mâché shoulder head/smooth texture, OM/bamboo teeth, PN, inset black pupil-less glass eyes, nailed-on brown HHW, pink kid body/limbs, original clothes. Ca. 1840s...................$2,500

24" "M&S//Superior//2015" labeled Lady. Papier-mâché shoulder head, wee CM, ptd brown eyes/grey eyeliner, black ptd/molded hairdo/center part/scalloped curls framing face, cloth body/leather arms/sewed-on stockings and leather boots, old clothes. Made by Muller & Strasburger, Sonneberg, Germany, 1850-1870. Ca. 1860s ... $1,600

24" Character Girl. Molded/ptd plaster head/oval face/sharp-pointed chin, ptd blue/molded eyes, brown ptd hair/center part/looped braids with red bow in front of molded ears/braided curl on nape, BJ compo body, original print dress, etc. (Face similar to one in Carl Larsson's "Lie-abed's Sad Breakfast.") Probably Marion Kaulitz, Germany. Ca. 1908-12 ....$5,000

25" "French-type" Child. Smooth papier-mâché shoulder head/high forehead, OM/upper and lower bamboo teeth, small inset black pupil-less glass eyes, black ptd hair/painted high off forehead with many fine brushstrokes, gusseted kid body/leather arms, old clothes, etc. (This round face and sparse hair detail indicates that of a small child. Possibly German with a French body.) Ca. 1830s-40s ... $2,600

25" "Greiner" Lady. Papier-mâché shoulder head, CM, rare ptd brown eyes, black ptd/molded hair do/flat-top/"scalloped" curls bordering forehead to ear tops, partially exposed ears, cloth body/leather arms/deep shoulder plate, sewn-on stockings and leather boots, original plain print dress, etc. Paper sticker reads: "Manufactured for Wm. A. Harwood." (Doll made by Greiner for Wm. A. Harwood, NYC, importer of toys from Germany, France, England, and agent for several American toy firms.) Ca. 1862-1877 Rare type $2,000

26" Blonde Greiner. Papier-mâché shoulder head, ptd blue eyes, tiny CM, blonde ptd/molded hairdo/styled high and wide on sides, cloth body/kid lower arms, original clothes. Label reads: "GREINER'S PATENT DOLL HEADS//Pat. March 30 '58, Ext. '72." Ca. 1872+ $950

26-1/2" Greiner look-alike. Composition shoulder-head, CM, ptd blue eyes, black ptd/molded hairdo, shapely cloth body/legs/leather lower arms, old clothes. Paper sticker on back reads: "AMERICAN//MUSLIN-LINED HEAD//No. 9// Warranted Fast Oil Colors." J. Adler & Co. Ca. 1850s+ Rare type..$2,000

27" Motschmann or "Taufling" Baby. Hard smooth compo head (swivel type) on compo shoulder plate, wee CM, red nose dots, inset almond-shaped brown glass eyes, bald-dome with brushstrokes above flat molded ears, cloth upper body/compo hips/wood jtd limbs/compo hands and feet, old clothes. Ca. 1850s Good condition $3,000

Chapter 32

PARIANS or MOLDED HAIR
BISQUES & TINTED BISQUES

History: 1850s-1870s+

The white bisque shoulder head dolls with the elaborate and highly decorated hair styles (and sometimes shirtwaist) that collectors refer to as "parians" were originally inspired by the parian ware and busts made in the Spode factory in England. William Taylor Copeland, a potter in the firm, invented the formula and made the first pieces. The Copeland formula called for two parts of feldspar and one part fine white clay. This mixture was ground, and when high fired in a kiln, produced an object that resembled the Carrara marble used by Praxitiles on the Greek Island of Paros. The Copeland clay was fine and smooth and proved ideal for modeling delicate ornamental figurines. The dolls collectors fondly call "parians" were not made from the Copeland recipe, hence are not really parian ware but untinted bisque doll heads.

True parian products are then more associated with England than with Germany or France. In 1856 John Ridgeway of England (Cauldon Potteries) advertised parian ware, and in 1858 Goss & Company (Falcon Pottery) founded their factory in Stoke-on-Trent, Staffordshire, for the manufacture of "parian" and "ivory" porcelain busts. It was about this time that the untinted bisque shoulder heads were being made in Germany, thus it is without a doubt that parian ware was the inspiration for these dolls. The intricate hairdos with the added decoration was very time-consuming, which placed the dolls out of reach of the average wage earner. The heads and the complete dolls (lavishly costumed) were sold in the salons that catered to the elite. The more common hairdo types, devoid of ornamentation were made for the mass-market.

When a pink tint was added to the bisque the dolls were still being called "parians", even as late as 1870 when *Harper's Bazar* mentioned them in their advertising as "parian dolls with a pink,

flesh-like hue." Today we collectors prefer to call the shoulder heads with molded hairdos as "tinted" bisques or "molded hairdo" dolls. Even when a bonnet or hat has been modeled onto the head, it still seems to fall into the same category and who shall say them nay?

Collecting Hints:

Parians or untinted and molded hairdo dolls are difficult to precisely date because sculptors oftentimes modeled hairdos from a previous decade or bygone period, and a popular head might be sold for years with only a change of hair color or decoration to update it. They are likewise difficult to price due to their ever-constant rise and fall in popularity with collectors. Prior to 1965, they were more in favor than French dolls (French Fashions, Jumeaux, Brus), and their prices were excessive when compared to other old dolls.

In our times, they are more desired by the "advanced" collector who has collected all types of dolls and has come to appreciate these dolls for their artistry (not all dolls are "artistic") and beauty. Hence, the price of parians like china-head dolls varies from state to state, and from one sector of the country to the other. Auctions glean the highest prices for dolls because auctions attract the serious, moneyed collector; collectors who come from all parts of the world to bid on dolls. Auctions also dote on frenzied competition, and in these heated moments a doll might command a price that is out of keeping with its true worth. But when a doll sells for a particular price, that price seems to establish the doll's value in the minds of collectors and investors.

On the other hand, if you are trying to sell a rare hairdo parian in your home town, and it isn't particularly popular there, it might bring a lesser price than the one suggested in a price guide. This brings us back to the old chestnut: "An item is worth only what you can sell it for." Parians and other molded hairdo dolls have a "figurine"

essence about them and they seem to appeal to people who collect figurines.

Reproduction Alert:

Parians have been the most reproduced of all dolls. Some are so beautifully reproduced they could fool an expert. Beware of those with eyelashes that are painted in a sloppy manner. Always study the body and limbs. A new body might be a dead giveaway. There again, old heads and limbs were placed on new bodies when old bodies fell apart.

PARIANS or MOLDED HAIR BISQUES & TINTED BISQUES

8" "Babushka" Parian Lady. Bisque shoulder head/round shoulders, CM, pale pink cheeks, ptd blue eyes/light brown eyeliner/red lid liners, brown eyebrows, rare dark brown ptd/molded/glazed hairdo/fine brushstrokes bordering face/molded scarf or babushka molded close to head/blue back side with yellow trim/molded rose tassel in rear/yellow ribbon ties with pink bow, cloth body/bisque lower limbs, old clothes. Ca. 1850s $800

8" "Scarf" or "Fanchon Bonnet" Parian Lady. White bisque shoulder head/round shoulders, CM, ptd blue eyes, rare black ptd/molded forehead locks/rear hair confined within a molded yellow net scarf with a pink fluted ribbon bordering face/pink ribbon ties with bow/rear tassels, cloth body/bisque lower arms, old clothes. Ca. 1857 $800

10" "Bald" Parian Lady. White bisque shoulder head/bald dome, wee CM, ptd blue eyes, black eyebrows, brown HHW/center part/elaborate coiled rear braid chignon, cloth body/bisque lower limbs, original silk and cotton gown, etc. Ca. 1865 .... $650

10" Male Parian. Pink tinted bisque shoulder head, CM, black ptd/molded hair/black ptd/molded handlebar mustache/goatee, ptd blue eyes, cloth body/pink tinted bisque lower limbs, original 2-pc red velvet military uniform. (The term "parian" is generic and applies to both the dead white bisque color which resembles marble and the "tinted" bisques; both types usually sport molded hairstyles.) Ca. 1865 .... $1,000

158

10" Male Parian. Scottish Boy. Pink tinted bisque shoulder head, CM, ptd blue eyes, blonde ptd/molded hair/curls with fullness around head, rosy cheeks, cloth body/pink tinted bisque lower arms/legs/black ptd shoes/white ptd stockings, original "Scots" costume. Ca. 1880s $1,000

10" Parian Lady. Pink tint shoulder head, CM, ptd blue eyes, blonde ptd/molded hairdo with braids, curls, puffs/blue ribbon decoration, rare molded bead necklace, PE, cloth body/pink tint lower limbs, old clothes. Ca. 1860s (Sold for $1,100 in 1990) $1,500

10-1/2" "Autoperipatetikos" Parian Lady. White bisque shoulder head/long neck, CM, ptd blue eyes, blonde ptd/molded hairdo w/center part/concealed ears/large bun in back, clockwork mechanism inside body/round base/protruding metal feet/brown leather arms, original clothes. Base mark: "Patented July 15, 1862, also in Europe, 20, Dec. 1862." 1862+ (sold for .. $570 in 1987) $2,500

10-1/2" "Straw Bonnet" Parian Lady. White bisque shoulder head/oval face, CM, pale pink cheek blush, ptd blue eyes, blonde ptd/molded wavy hair framing face/tan ptd/molded bonnet with molded roses above forehead beneath the brim/ribbon ties/luster plume, cloth body/bisque lower limbs, original clothes, Ca. 1863 ....$2,500

11-1/2" "Autoperipatetikos" or "Bald" Parian Lady. White bisque shoulder head, CM, large inset almond-shaped inset cobalt blue glass eyes, blonde skin wig, clockwork inside body/round base/protruding metal feet/leather arms, original clothes. Base mark: "Pat. July 15, 1862." (Working mechanism.) Made by Daniel & Cohen/Joseph Lyon & Co., NYC; Martin & Runyan, London, etc. Enoch Morrison patented the doll design in both America and England, 1862+ $3,000

12" "Plaited Bun" Parian Lady. Very white bisque shoulder head, tiny prim CM, ptd blue eyes, chestnut brown ptd/molded hairdo/fine temple and forehead brushstrokes/plaited bun, cloth body/chubby bisque lower limbs/black-ptd flat-soled slippers, original gown, etc. (This doll has a long, thick neck with deep round shoulders.) Ca. 1850s $1,200

12" "Princess Augusta" Parian. White bisque shoulder head, tiny CM, rosy cheeks, ptd blue eyes, blonde ptd/molded hairdo, PE/earrings, cloth body/leather lower arms, old clothes. (This hairdo is sculpted in a high pompadour with deep comb marks, waves, and curls. A bead tiara encircles front of hair. There is a molded, ruffled collar and molded cross.) Ca. 1870 ......$900

12-1/2" "K" incised Parian Lady. White bisque shoulder head/long face, ptd blue eyes, blonde ptd/molded hair, old clothes. Mark: "K" (incised on the underside of shoulder plate with a scroll or bell design). Possibly early Kling & Co. doll. Ca. 1880s $750

13" "Band Comb" Parian Lady. Bisque shoulder head/round shoulders, tiny CM, rosy cheeks, ptd blue eyes/red lid lines, rare dark brown ptd/molded glazed hair/molded band comb across crown, cloth body/bisque lower limbs/black ptd heel-less shoes. Ca. 1850s $1,300

14" "Bald" Parian Lady. White bisque swivel head on white bisque shoulder plate, CM, inset blue glass eyes, original pale blonde silk floss wig with a braided nape bun and nape curls, PE, cloth body white bisque lower limbs, old fancy clothes. Mark: "12" (incised at the top of rear crown which has a small opening.) This "French" or "French-type" parian is a good example of why these elaborate dolls were called "fancies" and sold in perfume shops or at the confectioner. Ca. 1850s ....$5,000+

14" "Eugenie" Parian Lady. White bisque swivel head on white bisque shoulder plate (back ribbon concealing joint), CM, pink cheek blush, blonde painted/molded hairdo in "Eugenie" style, PE/earrings, cloth body/bisque lower arms, old clothes. Ca. 1870s $1,500

14" "Fortune-Telling" Parian Lady. White bisque shoulder head/long neck, CM, ptd blue eyes, yellow ptd/molded hairdo has center part/full sides, cloth body/bisque lower limbs/green ptd boots, original elaborate "French" gown, etc. (The petticoat consists of many leaves of white paper covered with green paper. Each white paper leaf reveals a fortune written in artistic script.) Ca. 1860s ....$2,000+

14" "Franklin Pierce" Male Parian. White bisque shoulder head, CM, pastel pink cheek blush, modeled ears, blonde ptd/molded hair with small curls cascading from each side of part/glazed molded collar, cloth body/white bisque lower limbs, elaborate antique "Regen-

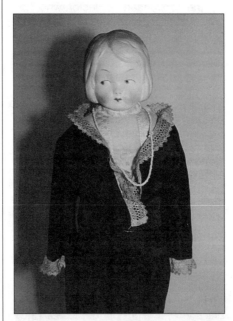

16" Parian boy, side glancing blue ptd eyes, blonde ptd hair, cloth body/bisque lower limbs/ptd black shoes with pink bows, old clothes. Ca. 1870s $1,500. (Courtesy of D. Kay Crow)

cy" style costume: trousers, brocade vest, silk-lined waistcoat, etc. (Franklin Pierce, 1804-1869, 14th president of the United States, 1853-1857. This doll is not a likeness.) Ca. 1860s (Quality) $1,600

14" "Gilded Earrings" Parian Lady. White bisque shoulder head/oval face, tiny CM, large ptd blue eyes, short blonde ptd/molded hairdo has center part/waves/blue and red molded flowers atop head/molded ears with molded/gilded earrings/molded black ptd necklace with molded cross, cloth body/bisque lower limbs/well-modeled hands, original silk gown, etc. Ca. 1870 ....$3,000+

14" "Gold Necklace" Parian Lady. Bisque shoulder head/long neck, CM, ptd blue eyes, pink cheek blush, light brown eyebrows, rare brown ptd/molded hairdo/center part/loose side waves/long rear sausage curls ornamented with unpainted beads (6)/pink Dresden flowers encircle top of head/glazed gold molded necklace/exposed ear lobes, cloth body/bisque lower limbs, elaborate old clothes. Ca. 1865 ....$3,000

14" "Little Girl" Parian. White bisque shoulder head, ptd blue eyes, rosy cheeks, blonde ptd hair/tiny ringlet curls on forehead/waved sides/crown curls, cloth body/bisque lower limbs/well-sculpted hands, molded-on/ptd/decorated boots with heels, original commercial costume which falls below her knees, three petticoats. Ca. 1860.....................$500

14" "Peddler" Parian Lady. Pale bisque turned shoulder head/chubby child-like face, CM, inset blue glass eyes, blonde ptd/molded curly hair/center part, cloth body/leather lower arms, original clothes, red cape, tray of wares. Ca. 1860s $4,000

14" "Scottish" Parian Lady. Bisque shoulder head, CM, inset large blue glass eyes, rosy cheek blush, blonde ptd hair/molded waves framing face/long curls cascading down back and one long sausage curl dangling down right side of front shoulder/molded-on and brightly painted cap of plaid Scottish design/elaborate molded shirt with collar and necktie, cloth body/bisque lower arms, original "Scots" costume, etc. Ca. 1869 ....$2,500

14-1/2" "Spider Web Net" Parian Lady. White bisque shoulder head, CM, ptd blue eyes, bright pink cheek blush, ptd blue eyes/red lid lines, yellow ptd/molded hair/full sides sculpted in deep ridged "crimp" waves/back hair enclosed in a "spider web net" or snood/mauve luster ruffle trim with large blue flowers/and leaves atop center section of head, cloth body/wooden lower limbs, original elaborate gown, etc. Ca. 1860s ....$3,000+

14-1/2" "Blue Hood" Parian Lady. Pale bisque face/dour expression, prim CM, well-defined ptd blue eyes, thin dark eyebrows, brown ptd/molded hairdo in a rolled puff above forehead/deep comb marks/dark blue ptd/molded hood covers most of head and all of sloping shoulders/4 sew holes (hood has separate top section hanging backward and reattached to rear shoulders), kid body/bisque lower arms, original clothing. Ca. 1850s-60s (Super-rare) ....$5,000+

14-1/2" "131,4" incised girl. Pink tinted bisque shoulder head, CM, pale orange cheek blush, huge inset blue-grey PW eyes, wide 1-stroke blonde eyebrows, orange-blonde/molded hairdo/wavy bangs/short wavy sides, cloth body/bisque lower arms/legs, old clothes. Ca. 1880 Made by C.F. Kling & Co., Germany. $750

15" "153-6" or "Black Ribbon" Parian Lady. White bisque shoulder head, CM, ptd blue eyes, blonde ptd/molded hairdo with waves covering entire head/narrow black ptd ribbon molded across top of head, kid body/brown leather arms, old pink visiting gown, etc. Neck incised: "153-6." Possibly Simon & Halbig (Halbig mold numbers). Ca. 1870s $1,200

15" "Bonnet" Parian Child. White bisque shoulder head, CM, ptd blue eyes, blonde ptd/molded hairdo/bangs, molded bonnet/pointed top/gold luster neck ribbon, sawdust-filled cloth body/bisque lower limbs, original clothes. Ca. 1865 ....$900

15" "Gesland-type" Parian Lady. Creamy bisque shoulder head, small CM, orange-pink cheek blush, small ptd blue eyes, thin 1-stroke light brown eyebrows, cafe-au-lait ptd/molded hairdo/exposed earlobes/center part with loose wavy sides and rear cadogan ornamented with unpainted beads, rare "Gesland-type" body (cloth-covered wire-armature) bisque lower limbs, old clothes. Ca. 1864 ....$2,500

15" "Glass-eyed" Parian Child. White bisque shoulder head/cup-and-saucer neck, CM, inset brown glass eyes, blonde ptd/molded hair/soft waves/bangs, cloth body/bisque lower limbs, old clothes. Ca. 1880 ....$750

15" "Glazed Net" Parian Lady. White bisque shoulder head, CM, ptd blue eyes, blonde ptd/molded blonde hairdo covered with a glazed net with a pink luster tasseled band and a glazed green feather, cloth body/bisque lower limbs/ptd flat-soled boots, original clothes. (Flat-soled slippers for ladies went out of style in the 1840s and a low heel came into vogue in the 1850s, thus flat-soled shoes on parians and chinas can be misleading and dates them earlier than their hairdos. Some slippers have a slight heel molded on the bottom. Earlier limbs were also sometimes used on later dolls.) Ca. 1850s $3,000

15" "Luster Tiara" Parian Lady. Bisque shoulder head/oval face/sloping shoulders, CM, ptd blue eyes, cafe-au-lait ptd/molded hairdo/waves on each side of center part/upswept rear hair molded in curls and coronet with luster tiara, exposed PE/earrings, kid body with wasp waist/bisque lower arms, fancy old clothes. Ca. 1860s $1,800

15" "Swivel neck" Parian Lady. Bisque shoulder head with rare swivel neck, slightly smiling CM, large vivid blue ptd eyes, rosy cheeks, PE, yellow ptd/molded hairdo smoothed away from broad high forehead in waved puffs and deep combmarks/2 large rear rolls/narrow band "secures" a mass of

curls held away from the neck, cloth body/bisque lower limbs/boots, old clothes. (This doll has a china-head twin with black painted hair and stationary neck.) Ca. 1865 ....$2,000

15-1/2" "Emma Clear" Parian. White bisque shoulder head, CM, ptd blue eyes, blonde ptd hairdo/upswept curly ringlet style/band, cloth body/bisque lower limbs/original corset, original clothes. Shoulder mark: "Humpty Dumpty//Doll Hospital." Ca. 1942 ....$750

15-1/2" Little Girl Parian. Stone bisque shoulder head, CM, ptd blue eyes, short molded blonde hair/bangs, stone bisque lower limbs/cloth body, old clothes. (This shoulder plate has molded, gold-painted bead necklace; legs have painted high-heeled boots with brown garters, and the cloth body is printed with horseshoes in colors red and blue.) Ca. 1880s $350

Glass eyed parian, PE, CM, parian lower limbs, elaborate original clothes. See parian section for prices. (Photo courtesy of Janet Johl Weissman)

16" "894x6" incised "Blue Scarf" Parian or "Queen Louise of Prussia." White bisque shoulder head, impudent rose-tinted CM, pale pink cheek blush, ptd blue eyes/black eyeliner/orange lid lines, 1-stroke eyebrows, dark orange ptd forehead and side locks/blue ptd/molded scarf draped over head and under chin, cloth body/white bisque lower limbs, old clothes. Made by Alt, Beck & Gottschalck, Germany. Ca. 1880 ....$3,500

16" "Bald" Parian Lady. White bisque shoulder head/high domed bald head, CM, inset blue glass eyes, brown plaited HHW, PE, cloth body/white bisque lower limbs, old clothes. Incised: "16." (inside rear shoulder plate). Ca. 1850s $1,300

16" "Blue Band" Parian Lady. White bisque shoulder head/long oval face, CM, light blue ptd eyes, thin blonde eyebrows, blonde ptd/molded hairdo/fat vertical curls arranged across top of head and

held by a wide glazed blue band, PE/blue earrings, cloth body/bisque lower limbs, original clothes. Incised: "14." Possibly early Kestner or Simon & Halbig. Ca. 1870s $1,700

16" "D.F./B./F.1." incised Parian Girl. Pale bisque "domed" shoulder head (bald)/narrow shoulders/throat indention/4 sew holes, deeply modeled ptd blue eyes with tiny white eye dots (to simulate glass), eyebrows ptd in 2 shades of color, blonde mohair wig, cloth body/bisque lower limbs, original clothes. Mark: "D.F.//B.//F.1." Made by De Fusseau, Bandour, Belgium, 1909-1913. (Rare) ....$1,000+

16" "Green Net" Parian Lady. Pale bisque shoulder head, tiny pastel pink CM, small ptd blue eyes/rare ptd eyelashes, blonde ptd eyebrows, pale pink cheek blush, yellow blonde ptd/molded hairdo "brushed" off forehead with delicate comb marks/gold luster band across top of head with a tassel on right side with a fringed bottom/white feather plume on left side of gold band/rear hair enclosed in a green ptd/molded net, cloth body/bisque lower limbs/gold glazed boots, elaborate old clothes. Ca. 1863 ....$3,000

16" "Simon & Halbig" incised Parian Lady. Bisque shoulder head/sloping shoulders/semi-long neck/character face, CM, inset almond-shaped blue glass eyes/upper and lower ptd eyelashes, blonde ptd/molded short hairdo/center part/exposed ears/high, deeply molded waves above forehead/rear hair sports 8 puffs and interwoven puffs at nape and sides/black molded ribbon atop head/modeled necklace with cross, cloth body/bisque lower limbs (arms), old clothes. Mark: "S&H" (in front of shoulder plate). Ca. 1870s $1,800

16-1/2" "151" incised Parian Girl. White bisque shoulder head, CM (full lips), large inset almond-shaped blue glass eyes/long ptd upper and lower eyelashes, blonde ptd/molded hairdo/center part/upswept sides/exposed ears/five forehead tendrils, PE/earrings, cloth body/white bisque lower limbs, old clothes. (This lovely face resembles mold 128, but with a different "bangs" style.) Made by Kling & Co., Germany, 1880 ....$850

17" "128" incised Parian Girl. White bisque shoulder head, CM (full lips), large inset brown PW eyes/long ptd upper and lower eyelashes, thin feathered eyebrows, PE/earrings, blonde ptd/molded hairdo/wavy bangs/exposed ears/large crown puff/black ptd comb/upswept puffs of hair, kid body/white bisque lower limbs/tiny feet with molded-on/violet tinted boots with heels, original elaborate costume, etc. (Very ornate doll; reminiscent of an old-time dance hall girl.) Ca. 1880 Made by Kling & Co., Germany, 1836+; 1870+ dolls. ... $850

17" "153,5" incised Parian Boy. Tinted bisque shoulder head/round face, CM, pale orange cheek blush, huge inset blue-grey PW eyes, molded ears, orange-blonde ptd/molded hairdo/straggly bangs, kid body/bisque lower arms, old boy clothes. Ca. 1880 Made by Kling & Co., Germany 1836+; 1870+ dolls $800

17" "5R5"/Parian Lady. White bisque shoulder head/unusual portrait face/long neck/3 strand molded bead necklace, prim CM, slender nose large inset blue glass eyes, blonde ptd/molded curly hairdo, exposed PE, cloth body/bisque lower arms, old clothes. Shoulder mark: "5R5." Probably Borgfeldt & Co., 1881-1930s. Ca. 1908 .... $950

17" "Biedermeier" Parian Lady. White bisque shoulder plate/bald pate with black spot on crown/small head/long neck, tiny CM, small ptd blue eyes, short 1-stroke eyebrows, protruding ears, brown HHW, cloth body/bisque lower limbs, original regional costume in the "Greek" peasant style with fez. Ca. 1850s incised $1,600

17" "R&C" incised Parian Lady. Mannequin-type. White bisque swivel head on white bisque shoulder head/modeled collar bone and bosom, CM, blue-grey PW eyes, white mohair wig in the high pompadour style, shapely kid body/bisque lower limbs/bare feet/well-modeled toes, original drawers, petticoat, corset. (Doll is sculpted like a mannequin for clothes display; in this instance, underwear. She has a hole in the bottom of each foot (flat soles) into which the metal rods of the round wooden base on which she stands, holds her upright (Cardonnier 1880 design patent). Pink paper label attached to the bottom of stand reads: "Poupée Statuette, systeme, Breveté, S.G.D.G., nouveau system de plied, marque deposée, busté depose..."). Shoulder plate mark reads: "R.C. DEPOSE." Made by Radiquet & Cordonnier, France, Ca. 1881 (Rare) ... $8,000+

17" "Two-Faced" Parian Lady. White bisque swivel neck on white bisque shoulder plate, oval-shaped inset blue glass eyes/sleep eyes on opposite head, CM, blonde ptd/molded hairdo/center part/deep comb marks with fullness on top and sides of head, PE, kid body/bisque lower limbs/deep shoulder plate/original beads conceal swivel neck, original silk dress, etc. Ca. 1870s .... $7,000-$10,000

17-1/2" "Straw Hat" Parian Lady. Bisque shoulder head, CM, ptd blue eyes, rosy cheeks, strawberry blonde ptd/molded hairdo with etched sides and rear curls/molded-on tan ptd "straw" hat with black ribbon band and applied flowers strewn across front brim, cloth body/bisque lower limbs, old clothes. Ca. 1868 .... $4,000

17-1/2" "Detachable Chignon" Parian Lady. Bisque shoulder head, CM, pale orange cheek blush, small inset blue glass eyes/rare ptd upper/lower eyelashes, short 1-stroke eyebrows, blonde ptd/molded hairdo/center part/deep side waves with comb marks/upswept nape hair/detachable chignon consisting of curl clusters, PE/earrings, cloth body/bisque lower limbs, elaborate original clothes. (In Victorian times ladies of style attached clusters of false hair curls to their heads. This super-rare doll symbolizes this fashion trend.) Ca. 1876 .... $8,000

18" "1288" incised Parian Child. Tinted bisque shoulder head, CM, inset blue glass eyes, heavy dark brown "French" eyebrows, blonde ptd/molded hair/scraggly bangs/side swirls/exposed earlobes only, cloth body/bisque lower limbs, old clothes. Ca. 1880 made by Alt, Beck & Gottschalck, Germany, 1854+ $950

18" "Adelina Patti" Parian Lady. White bisque shoulder head, tiny CM, inset blue cobalt glass eyes, blonde ptd hairdo/flat top/center part/winged curls on upper bangs/wavy curls on sides and rear, exposed ears, cloth body/leather arms, old clothes. (Adelina Patti 1843-1919, an operatic singer of Italian parentage, born in Madrid, Spain. The daughter of opera singers; raised in New York. Made her debut in New York as Lucia in November, 1859. Patti had black hair. Not a likeness.) Ca. 1870s $1,500

18" "Coiled Braids" Parian Lady. White bisque shoulder head/round face/med. long neck/round sloping shoulders, rosy cheeks, CM, ptd blue eyes, blonde ptd/molded hairdo with circular coiled braids directly above forehead/high molded side puffs with 5 smaller circular coiled braids in rear, cloth body/bisque lower arms, old clothes. Ca. 1870s $3,000

18" "Kaiserin Augusta Victoria" Parian Lady. Bisque shoulder head/round face/molded and ptd Iron Cross encircling semi-long neck, rosy cheeks, ptd blue eyes, blonde ptd/molded hairdo swept high off forehead and sides with many comb marks/molded curls on crown/head band of black ptd beads, white ptd/molded ruffled collar/gathered neckline, kid body, old clothes. (There is a dark hair version of this doll.) 1881 .... $1,800

18" "Necklace" Parian Lady. Bisque shoulder head, CM, rosy cheeks, ptd blue eyes, blonde ptd/molded hairdo (flat-top, puff curls at sides and back), molded necklace with cross pendant/molded earrings/molded hair ribbon with rose decoration atop head, cloth body/leather lower arms, old clothes. Ca. 1860s .... $2,000+

18" "Pink Bow" Parian Lady. White bisque shoulder head, CM, ptd blue eyes, blonde ptd/molded pompadour, PE, cloth body/leather lower arms/stitched fingers/molded bodice decorated with a pink bow at the neckline, original clothes. Ca. 1875 .... $1,500-$2,000

18" "Rosa Bonheur" Parian Lady. White bisque shoulder head/round full face/double chin, wee CM, large blue ptd eyes with white highlights, exposed ears, blonde ptd/molded hairdo/center part/severely "brushed" backwards on sides of head/molded guimpe/collar/tie highlighted with blue dots and gold trim, cloth body/bisque lower limbs, old clothes. (Rosa Bonheur always dressed in male attire.) Ca. 1860s .... $2,500-$3,000

18" "Snood" Parian Lady. Bisque shoulder head, CM, pink cheeks, ptd blue eyes, orange-blonde ptd hairdo/blue ribbon across top of head and 2 large blue molded bows in front of each ear/rear hair enclosed in a snood or net, cloth body/bisque lower limbs, old clothes. Ca. 1850s $1,200

18" "White Plume" Parian Lady. White bisque shoulder head, tiny CM, rosy cheeks, almond-shaped vivid blue ptd eyes/black eyeliner/ptd upper/lower eyelashes, exposed ears/molded-on glazed earrings ptd gold and white, rare brown ptd/molded hairdo "brushed" away from forehead with many fine brushstrokes/front waves/9 vertical rolls across head separated by 8 rows of wee gold beads and bow behind each ear/glazed white plume in front of hairdo with a molded flower at the bottom/large semi-circular gold comb holds rear curls/three-strand gold necklace with side clasps/single strand at rear of neck, cloth body/bisque lower limbs, elaborate old clothes/high-heeled glazed boots. Ca. 1865 .... $3,500+

19" "151" incised Parian Girl. White bisque shoulder head, pale pink CM, pale pink cheek blush, large inset dark blue glass eyes/ptd upper/lower lashes, dark brown feathered eyebrows, yellow ptd/molded hairdo/comb marks/bangs with pointed tips/some ear exposure, clothe body/white bisque lower limbs, old clothes. Made by C.F. Kling & Co., Germany. Ca. 1880 (Measures closer to 20") $1,000

19" "Beaded Comb" Parian Lady. White bisque shoulder head/long neck/rosy cheeks, CM, inset blue glass eyes, exposed PE/earrings, blonde ptd/molded hairdo waved high off forehead with braids behind each ear and ending in a curl/vertical rear curls/brown ptd "beaded" comb across front curls piled high atop head, cloth body/bisque lower arms, original clothes. Ca. 1877 $3,700

19" "Brown Ribbon" Parian Lady. White bisque shoulder head, tiny CM, heavily roughed rosy cheeks, vivid blue ptd eyes/fine black eyeliner/light brown lid lines/brown eyebrows, brown ptd/molded hairdo/forehead ringlets/waved full sides/wide brown ribbon band above a bustle of fat rear curls, PE/earrings, kid body, original clothes. Ca. 1875 $1,200

19" "Dolley Madison" Parian Lady. Bisque shoulder head, CM, rosy cheeks, ptd blue eyes, blonde ptd/molded hairdo/blue glazed ribbon bow in front and back of head/exposed ears ringlets bordering face, cloth body/brown leather lower arms, original clothes. Ca. 1865-73 .... $700

19" "Empress Eugenie" Parian Lady. White bisque shoulder head, tiny CM, orange-pink cheek blush, ptd blue eyes/orange lid lines, thin 1-stroke eyebrows, cafe-au-lait ptd/molded hairdo/flat-top/center part/comb marks/wide puffed sides/molded hair net/molded white blouse with collar and necktie decorated with gold and blue, kid body, old clothes. Ca. 1865 $3,000

19" "Fancy" Parian Lady. White bisque shoulder head/semi-long neck/slim face, CM, rosy cheeks, ptd blue eyes, blonde ptd/molded hairdo/circular braid and pink porcelain flowers above forehead/upswept side hair with deep comb marks/coiled and looped braids at rear of head, PE/earrings, kid body/limbs/ruffled shoulder plate decorated with red dots and gold trim, original elaborate gown, etc. (This doll with her candy box loveliness personifies the term "fancy" often given to parians in their day.) Ca. 1869 ....$3,500+

20" "182" incised Parian Girl. Tinted bisque shoulder head/round face, orange cheek blush, CM, huge inset blue glass eyes, yellow ptd/molded hairdo/straggly bangs/waved sides, kid body/bisque lower arms, old clothes. Made by Kling & Co., Germany. Ca. 1880 ....$1,000

20" "Bald" Parian Lady. White bisque shoulder head, CM, inset blue glass eyes, blonde HHW, PE/earrings, cloth body/lower limbs, original fancy silk gown, etc. Ca. 1870s (sold for ..$1,200 in 1993) $1,800

12" unmarked molded bisque boy, cloth body/bisque lower limbs, redressed. CA. 1880s $450. (Courtesy of Ruby Ellen Smith)

20" "Black hair" Parian Lady. White bisque shoulder head/oval face/pointed chin, prim CM, rosy cheeks, gold glazed molded earrings, ptd blue eyes/well-defined lid modeling, black ptd eyebrows/molded hairdo ptd black/high-ridged puffs or rolls of hair modeled around crown/2 small curls at nape, blue glazed necklace with 6 "pearls" in front of neck and blue ribbon tie at rear, cloth body/bisque lower limbs, original silk dress, etc. Ca. 1870s..$2,500

20" "Blue Scarf" Parian Lady. White bisque shoulder head/long face/high forehead/sloping shoulders, CM, ptd blue eyes, blonde ptd/molded hairdo decorated with a pink rose/blue scarf has gold luster trim/puffed sides/double bun in rear, cloth body/white bisque lower arms, elaborate clothes. Ca. 1880 ....$3,000

20" "Floral" Parian Lady. White bisque shoulder head, tiny CM, ptd blue eyes, cafe-au-lait ptd/molded hairdo/profusion of short vertical curls framing face, sides, and rear of hair/rose and leaves and other small applied flowers above the front ringlets, cloth body/bisque

lower limbs/ptd boots, original elaborate gown, etc. Ca. 1870s $1,000

20" Little Boy. Tinted bisque shoulder head, CM, ptd blue yes, blonde ptd/molded hair, rosy cheeks, cloth body/brown leather arms, original 2-pc suit, silk shirt, ribbon tie, shoes, stockings. Ca. 1880s $1,000

21" "Bald" Parian Lady. White bisque shoulder head/round full face, rosy cheeks, small CM, red nose dots, large inset almond-shaped blue glass eyes/ptd upper and lower lashes, original brown HHW styled with coronet wrapped around top of head/rear looped braids, black ptd/molded, narrow neck ribbon with inset black stone ornament/detailed molded bodice with red trim/molded shoulder bows, cloth body/leather arms, original clothes. (This rare doll has a twin with blue ptd eyes, similar hairdo ptd blonde and modeled with coronet braid and rear puff curls instead of braided loops; also identically designed breast-plate, but ptd black.) Ca. 1870s ....$3,000+

21" "Brown hair" Parian Lady. White bisque shoulder head/long oval face/long neck, pale pink cheek blush, ptd blue eyes/round eyeballs/well-defined modeling, rare brown ptd/molded hairdo/center part/flat top (width at sides in rolled puffs with 3 looped braids on nape held with a brown band decorated with 2 brown flower bows on each end), cloth body/leather arms, original clothes. Ca. 1850s $4,000

21" "Glass-eyed" Parian Lady. White bisque shoulder head, CM, rosy cheeks, inset blue glass eyes, PE/earrings, light brown ptd hair/molded ringlet curls on forehead/chignon with blue and gold bow, 6 sew holes on shoulder plate which has a molded collar with blue polka dot ruffles and gold ball trim, kid body/limbs, original gown, etc. Ca. 1870s ....$2,700-$3,000

21" "Miss Liberty" or "Tiara" Parian Lady. White bisque shoulder head, long neck/somber expression, CM, rosy cheeks, ptd blue eyes, blonde ptd/molded hairdo/small vertical curls framing wide forehead/side waves/rear bun with bands and black ribbon trailing down one shoulder/molded gold luster earrings/gold luster tiara, cloth body/bisque lower limbs/molded-on and ptd boots, original clothes. Ca. 1865 ....$2,500

21-1/2" "Removable Tiara" Parian Lady. White bisque shoulder head/sloping round shoulders/regal, haughty expression, prim CM, ptd blue eyes/black eyeliner, thin black ptd eyebrows, PE/exposed ears, light brown ptd/molded hair/deep comb marks (hair molded in waves above head and on sides above ears/deep crown comb marks/black glazed band holds 2 loops of hair in a v-shape at nape/white molded collar/brass tiara held onto head with attachments that fit into head holes, cloth body/bisque lower arms, original elaborate gown, etc. Ca. 1870s (Rare) ....$6,500-$7,500

22" "1000/11" incised "Highland Mary" Parian. White bisque shoulder head, orange ptd CM, pale orange cheek blush, inset blue glass threaded eyes, feath-

ered eyebrows/tiny upper and lower eyelashes, yellow ptd/molded hairdo with curly sides and bangs with pointed tips, cloth body/bisque lower arms/legs, old whitework dress, etc. Made by Alt, Beck & Gottschalck, Germany. Ca. 1880 ....$500-$550

22" "1304" incised "Glass-eyed" Parian Boy. White bisque shoulder head CM, inset blue glass eyes, thick dark eyebrows, blonde/molded tousled curly hair low on forehead, cloth body/bisque lower limbs, old clothes. Alt, Beck & Gottschalck, Germany. Ca. 1880 ....$1,250

22" "Dagmar" Parian Lady. White bisque shoulder head/deep sloping shoulders, rosy cheeks, CM, ptd blue eyes, blonde ptd/molded hairdo/side rolls above ears/ringlet curls across forehead/ebony and gilt diadem resembling damascene/curled chignon with matching comb, cloth body/bisque lower limbs, fancy original gown, etc. Ca. 1870s $2,700

22" "Glass-eyed" Parian Child. White bisque shoulder head/round face, CM, large inset almond-shaped brown glass eyes, 1-stroke blonde eyebrows, PE/earrings, blonde ptd/molded hairdo/curls atop and around head in the "Nellie Bly" or "Lilly Langtry" style/decorated shoulder plate/pink bow at neckline, cloth body/bisque lower limbs, original silk brocade gown, etc. Ca. 1870s $2,700

22" "Gold Beads" Parian Lady. White bisque shoulder head/long face/high forehead, CM, ptd blue eyes, brown ptd/molded hairdo decorated with many roses/side puffs/long curls on rear shoulders/gold beads in hair and around neck, cloth body/bisque lower limbs, old clothes. Ca. 1869 ....$2,500

22" "Gold Snood" Parian Lady. White bisque shoulder head/long neck/round sloping shoulders, tiny rosebud mouth, pink cheek blush, PE, ptd blue eyes/red lid lines, short orange-blonde eyebrows, orange-blonde ptd/molded hairdo/flat top/deep comb marks/waved saves/2 sausage curls on each side of neck/gold snood with gold bow atop head and gold tassels, cloth body/bisque lower limbs/gold glazed boots with tiny heels, original clothes. Ca. 1850s $3,000

22" "Removable Tiara" Parian Lady. White bisque shoulder head, CM, ptd blue eyes, PE/earrings, blonde ptd/molded hairdo/4 small ringlet curls above forehead/small ringlet or sausage curls on sides and back of head/removable brass and beaded tiara attached to head, original commercially-made cloth body/brown leather arms, original commercially-made print dress, etc. 1873 (Tiaras were called "diadems" in the Victorian era) $5,500

22-1/2" "Black Ribbon" Parian Lady. White bisque shoulder head/collar and pink ribbon bow/black ptd ribbon neck band with yellow ptd ornament, rosy cheeks, tiny CM, ptd blue eyes/black eyeliner, thin brown eyebrows, blonde ptd/molded hairdo with 2 vertical puffs above forehead in a v-shape/black ribbon band across head from ear to ear/puffs atop head and cascading downward toward nape and banded underneath by a black ptd ribbon/braided loop circles the small puffs in back/bottom hair is rolled under at nape, PE, cloth body/bisque lower arms, old clothes. Ca. 1870s (Rare) ....$5,000+

23" "Chenille Net" Parian Lady. White bisque shoulder head/oval face/molded white bodice with rounded collar/blue molded bows tiny prim CM, very pale pink cheek blush, vivid blue ptd eyes, blonde ptd/molded hairdo sculpted away from face with full sides/center part/comb marks/rear hair has a gilded diamond-shaped net bordered with gathered ribbon and gilded edges, cloth/bisque lower limbs/molded glazed boots, old clothes. Ca. 1863+ ...$2,800

23" "Fancy" Parian Lady. White bisque shoulder head, tiny cupid's bow CM, rosy cheeks, ptd blue eyes, cafe-au-lait ptd/molded hairdo/center part/waves bordering forehead/black glazed ribbon across crown of head with molded bow on right side which separates higher ridged curls on top/molded white collar covers shoulders with a V-shaped neckline which reveals black glazed neck ribbon and black button ornament with red trim, cloth body/bisque lower limbs, original black satin gown, etc. Ca. 1870 ....$3,000

23" "Glass-eyed" Parian Lady. White bisque shoulder head/sloping shoulders, CM, rosy cheeks, inset blue glass eyes, rare brown ptd/molded hairdo with clusters of curls on each side of center part/side puffs/rear curls, cloth body/bisque lower limbs, old clothes. Ca. 1860s..................................$1,500

23" "Hatted" Parian Lady. White bisque shoulder head/long neck, small CM, rosy cheeks, ptd blue eyes/red lid lines, thin light brown eyebrows, cafe-au-lait ptd/molded hairdo/center part/waves "brushed" off forehead and above exposed ears/molded-on black ptd hat with molded flowers on top and blue ribbon tied beneath chin in a large blue bow/bow ends sculpted onto upper chest and trimmed in red, cloth body/bisque lower limbs/molded-on boots, fancy original clothes. Ca. 1860s $5,000

23-1/2" "Brass Headband" Parian Lady. White bisque shoulder head, CM, rosy cheeks, inset blue glass eyes, glass earrings, blonde ptd/molded hairdo set in rows of puff curls across front of head/brass headband/hair modeled higher behind headband, cloth body/leather arms, old 2-pc outfit, etc. Ca. 1870s (Sold for $2,200 in 1992) $3,500

23-1/2" "Molded Blouse" Parian lady. Bisque shoulder head, tiny CM, rosy cheeks, ptd blue eyes, thin orange-blonde eyebrows, orange-blonde ptd/molded hairdo/ "winged" waves on each side of center part/puff curls across top of head/clusters of small sausage curls or ringlets at rear of head and nape hair brushed under/molded white blouse with glazed ruffled collar decorated with tiny blue glazed dots, original cloth body/bisque lower limbs/ptd boots with tiny heels, original elaborate gown, etc. Ca. 1870s $3,000

24" "144" incised "Kling" Parian Child. Bisque shoulder head/chubby cheeks, well-modeled CM (full lips), large almond-shaped inset blue-grey PW eyes, yellow ptd eyebrows, orange-yellow ptd hair/curly molded bangs/upswept sides/deep side comb marks/high molded crown/black ptd and molded feather plume across front of head/molded rear curls with deep swirls and comb marks/exposed ears (pierced)/molded collar outlined in red/molded yellow rose with green leaves in front of collar, cloth body/bisque lower arms/legs, elaborate original clothes. Ca. 1880 ....$1,400

24" "990" or "Pink Mob-cap" Parian Child. White bisque shoulder head/round face, CM, large ptd blue yes, protruding ears, blonde ptd/molded hair with bangs and deep side waves/molded-on light pink mobcap with pink bow, cloth body/bisque lower limbs/molded-on boots, original clothes. 1880. Made by Alt, Beck & Gottschalck, Germany. Ca. 1880 ....$750

24" "Two Comb" Parian Lady. White bisque shoulder head/semi-long neck/sloping shoulders with luster glazed white beaded neckline molded in a v-shape, red cupid's bow CM, very rosy cheeks, large almond-shaped inset blue glass eyes, yellow ptd/molded hairdo/asymmetrical arrangement of marcel waves one side of head decorated with a white gilded comb/right side "brushed" high with deep comb marks and held by a red gilded comb/exposed earlobes, cloth body/bisque lower limbs/ptd boots, old clothes. (This doll appears to be a young girl in her late teens or early twenties, and despite her gaudy cheek rouge and adornment has an aura of old-fashioned innocence.) Ca. 1870s (Sold for $5,800 in 1993) ....$6,000+

24" "W" incised "Hatted" Boy Parian. White bisque shoulder head/round face, Cm, pale pink cheek blush, modeled ears, ptd blue eyes, 1-stroke eyebrows, blonde ptd/molded hair/curly bangs

and side hair/molded white hat with blue ptd rim and 2 blue ptd medallions in front, cloth body/bisque lower limbs, old clothes. Possibly Heubach, Kampfe & Sontag, Wallendorf, Germany, 1763, porcelain factory; 1874-1894, dolls. Ca. 1874+ $2,500

25" "Glass-eyed" Parian Lady. White bisque shoulder head/semi-long neck/molded blouse with white molded collar/black glazed button, CM, inset cobalt blue glass eyes, strawberry blonde ptd/molded hairdo/high waved front hair/top curls/side braids, PE, cloth body/leather arms original clothes. Ca. 1869 ....$2,700

26" "Blue Ribbon" Parian Lady. White bisque shoulder head, tiny CM, pale pink cheek blush, ptd blue eyes/light brown lid lines, thin light brown eyebrows, blonde ptd/molded hairdo/center part/flat front waves/side fullness/exposed ears/eight fat puff curls emanate crossways from top of head to nape/blue glazed ribbon tied in a fancy rear bow (this is a "French" hairstyle), cloth body/bisque lower limbs, original clothes. Ca. 1871 ....$2,000+

27" "Diadem" Parian Lady. White bisque shoulder head, red CM, very rosy cheeks, ptd blue eyes, orange ptd/molded hairdo/"crimped" waves bordering face/thick braid across top of head adorned with a black molded hair bow/diadem across front part of hairdo set with faux sapphires and paste brilliants/long bunched sausage curls at rear of head, cloth body/leather arms, old clothes. Ca. late 1870s ....$5,000+

28" "White Ribbon" Parian Lady. Tinted bisque shoulder head, CM, rosy cheeks, ptd blue eyes, ptd/molded orange-blonde hair held high off forehead with a molded white ribbon/2 long fat curls molded onto rear of long neck, original cloth body/bisque lower limbs, original elaborate gown, etc. Ca. 1880s $2,000

29" "Corset" Parian Lady. Bisque shoulder head/semi-long neck, tiny CM, heavily roughed cheeks, ptd blue eyes/dark brown eyeliner/eyeshadow, 1 stroke eyebrows, chocolate brown/molded hairdo arranged in puff curls atop head and sides of head/swirled tendrils of hair framing face/back center part separates hair and arranges it to area behind ears in curl clusters, PE/earrings, cloth body/original corset/bisque lower limbs, elaborate original clothes. Ca. 1880s $3,500

Chapter 33

~ PLASTIC AGE DOLLS ~

History: 1954+

Horsman Dolls Inc., introduced Plastisol Dolls into the world of dolls and toys in 1946. It was indeed a new era in toymaking. At last a doll could be made that did not chip or crack. Plastic wigs could be washed and combed, and, if rooted, would not fall out. Glass and tin eyes gave sway to eyes made of plastic; real eyelashes could be replaced with molded plastic substitutes. But the doll manufacturers still weren't satisfied. They wanted a doll with a soft texture like human skin. The result was lifelike vinyl. When stuffed with cotton, vinyl was even more appealing and cuddly.

However, the soft vinyl was not as durable as they thought. It stained easily, became sticky and smelly, and discolored with age. Other plastic substances were then developed, but none were as satisfactory as the lovely hard plastic used in the 1950s, and these dolls have become very coveted by the children who grew up during those years and who have now become bona-fide collectors. Plastics were not a post World War II innovation, since natural plastics were actually developed before the wide-spread use of celluloid.

Emile Hemming, Sr., invented the first molding process in Europe ca. 1900. This formula was called cold-mold plastics. Leo Hendrick Baekeland's* Phenolic Resin was the first "synthetic" plastic. As early as the 1900s he experimented in his Yonkers, New York laboratory with a resin that would not, in time, soften and become tacky. His invention proved successful and he began production of Bakelite resins which were widely used in the industrial field. Mr. Baekeland died in 1944, shortly before its invasion into the doll and toy media (and every other media!). The celluloid doll is the plastic doll's step-child, and while the celluloid doll has always remained in the "secondary" class and not considered a "thing of great value" (with the exception of a few antique types), the plastic doll has now out-priced and out-distance the demoded old things!

*Dr. Baekeland, born in 1863 in Belgium, came to the U.S.A. in 1889.

Collecting Hints:

Plastic dolls fall into several categories: the hard plastics of the late 1940s and 1950s, the soft vinyls, the sturdier plastic/vinyls. Regardless of the medium, these dolls are more valuable and beautiful when they are found mint, in their original boxes, and wearing their original clothing. It is then we begin to realize how beautiful they really were and how fashionable and chic. However, when these same dolls are found nude, and their hair mussed, they take on a look of common cheapness. In other words, they all look alike! And, why shouldn't they? Most came from the same molds! Even Madame Alexander dressed blank dolls at the beginning of her career, as did Mollye Goldman, and so many others!

Nevertheless, the little girls who once played with these dolls have now grown older and have become bona-fide collectors, and these dolls appeal to their sense of nostalgia, just as the Depression Kiddies related to Shirley Temple, Deanna Durbin, Sonja Henie, and Jane Withers. Cissy, Barbie, Ginny, et al., have become their idols and they pay dearly to acquire them! However, to have any real value at all these dolls must be as near mint as possible and have their mint original clothes, etc. Since the Baby Boomers are still young, chances are that these dolls will retain their values for many years to come.

PLASTIC AGE DOLLS

5" "A Wee Bonnie Lassie." All Compo/jtd at neck/sh/hips, CM, blue sleep eyes, blonde ptd/molded hair, original outfit. Original box decorated with stars, reads: "Hollywood Doll." Pamphlet in box reads: "Playmate Series." Copyright 1949. H. & E.G., Lakeside, CA. Founder: Domenick Ippolite. (Dolls were made from 1942-1960. Dolls made prior to 1950 were compo; dolls made after 1950 were plastic.) 1947 MIB $100

5" "Little Bo-Peep." All hard plastic/jtd arms/cupped hands, CM, blue ptd eyes to side, brown mohair wig, original costume with "Little Bo-Peep" design on skirt. MIB. Made by Varga Doll Company. Ca. 1950 .... $25-$35

6" "Little Rascals." Spanky, Mickey, Darla, Porky, Alfalfa, Buckwheat. All hard plastic/jtd head/sh/elbows/hands, hips/knees/feet, ptd features, ptd/molded hair, original clothes. Marks: Circle and numbers on outside of circle. Made by Mego, 1972-1982. (Darla and Mickey command ..$10 more to given price. There was also a club house and accessories in this coveted set.) Ca. 1970s. Each............................ $40-$50

6" "Priscilla Doll Sewing Set". Hard plastic/pink-tinted doll with mld hair/jtd arms/stationary legs (apart). Original box contains metal scissors, thimble, needle, thread, and a variety of printed-on-clothes to be sewn together. Made by Standard Toycraft Productions, Inc., NYC. Ca. 1950s MIB.... $75

7" "Duchess" Doll. All hard plastic/jtd arms/ptd shoes, CM (some had OCM/mld teeth), blue sleep eyes (some had ptd eyes), glued-on blonde mohair wig, original long "period" gown, hat. Mark: "DUCHESS DOLL//DESIGN COPYRIGHT//1948." Ca. 1948-1950s $25

7-1/2" "Junior Miss Sewing Kit." All hard plastic/movable arms/stationary legs (apart), CM, blue ptd eyes, yellow ptd/molded hair, red ptd/molded-on shoes. Original box contains scissors, needle, cut-out fabric clothes, etc. (Box top has the same design as the 5" doll version.). Made by Hassenfeld Bros., or Hasbro, NYC. 1950s MIB $100

7-1/2" "New Ginger." Soft vinyl head, CM, blue sleep eyes/mld eyelashes, rooted blonde synthetic wig, hard plastic body jtd at neck/sh/hips, original clothes, etc. Head mark: "GINGER." Made by Cosmopolitan Doll & Toy Corp., NYC. 1956... $65

10-1/2" Crawler Baby, vinylhead/hands/feet/metal body/legs/battery operated, ca. 1940s or 1950s $75. (Courtesy of Carol Lindberg)

8" "Betsy McCall." All hard plastic/bisque-like finish/jtd at neck/sh/hips/knees, CM, blue sleep eyes, Saran wig, original clothes, etc. Mark: "McCALL (c in a circle) CORP." (This was a wardrobe doll with 18+ different costumes.) American Character Doll Co., NYC. 1957....................$200

8" "Easter Girl." All-hard plastic/jtd at neck/sh/hips/chubby legs, CM, blue sleep eyes, brown glued-on wig, original polished cotton yellow dress with lace-trimmed bodice, matching bonnet with yellow satin ribbon ties, etc. (Only 300 made; sold only in California.) 1968 Rare Mme Alexander, NYC ....$900-$1,000

8" "Ginnette." All-vinyl/jtd at neck/sh/hips/flexible fingers and toes, CM, ptd eyes (sleep eyes added in 1956), brown ptd hair, original clothes, etc. ("Tear" eyes were added in 1957. This was a washable drink-wet doll with her own bottle.) Back mark: "VOGUE DOLLS INC." 1955+ ....$175-$200

8" "Ginnette." or "Ginny Baby." (Ginnette mold with rotted wig.) Her wardrobe had separate outfits/interchangeable with Ginnette's. "Ginny Baby" came in 3 larger sizes in 1962. Mark: "VOGUE DOLLS INC." 1958..............$175-$200

8" "Ginny." All-hard plastic/jtd at neck/sh/hips, CM, blue ptd eyes, blonde wig, original clothes, etc. Mark: "VOGUE DOLLS." 1948-49.$400-$450

8" "Ginny." Far-Away Lands series. All-hard plastic, CM, blue sleep eyes/mld lashes, blonde wig, jtd at neck/sh/hips, original "Belgium" costume, head-dress, etc. Made by Vogue Dolls, Inc., Medford, Mass. 1966 ....$100+

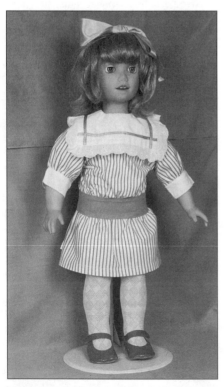

"Julie, Worlds of Wonder Doll", computerized talking doll, all original, plastic/cloth body. Ca. 1988. (Courtesy of Carol Lindberg)

8" "Ginny" Cowgirl. All-hard plastic/jtd at neck/sh/hips, CM, brown sleep eyes/ptd eyelashes, blonde wig, original black felt costume with silver trim, metal gun, black shoes with snaps. Head mark: "VOGUE DOLLS." 1950-1953...........................$400-$450

8" "Jimmy." Ginny's baby brother. All-vinyl/jtd at neck/sh/hips, CM, blue ptd eyes, brown ptd hair, original denim diaper, jeans, etc. (Other available outfits: blue cotton overalls, a cowboy set, and a clown costume. Jimmy was actually the 1955 Ginnette with ptd eyes.) Mark: "VOGUE DOLLS INC." 1958 ....$175-$200

8" "Little Genius." Hard plastic head, OM, blue-grey sleep eyes/mld eyelashes, blonde glued-on wig, vinyl body, original yellow organdy dress with blue embroidery and lace trim, white cotton eyelet slip, white flannel lace-trimmed diaper, white knitted booties. Un-

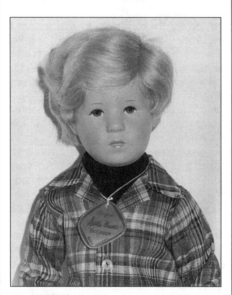

20" Kathe Kruse boy, all original, ca. 1977. (Courtesy of Herron)

marked. (Alexander's first "Baby Genius" was all-cloth, 1937.) 1957 . $300+

8" "Wendy-Ann." (Alexander-Kins.) Walker. All-hard plastic, CM, brown sleep eyes, strawberry blonde "washable" Saran wig, jtd at neck/sh/hips/walker mechanism, original "Easter Parade" outfit, hat, etc. 1954-55 Mint.........$500-$550

8" "Wendy-Ann." (Named for Mme Alexander's granddaughter.) Also called "Alexander-Kins." All-hard plastic/jtd at neck/sh/hips, CM, blue sleep eyes, strawberry blonde "washable" Saran wig, original long party gown, etc. (Non-walker.) 1953 Mint .....$500-$550

10" "Cissette." All-hard plastic/jtd at neck/sh/hips/knees, CM, blue sleep eyes, brown synthetic wig with bangs, PE/earrings, original clothes, tag, etc. Mark: none. Dress tag: "Cissette." 1957-63 Made by Madame Alexander, NYC $250

10" "Jill." (Ginny's older sister.) All-hard plastic/jtd at neck/sh/hips/knees/long limbs, CM, blue ptd eyes, auburn wig

with bangs, original pink party gown with net overlay, white plastic slippers, etc. Blue wrist tag reads: "Jill//AN ORIGINAL CREATION OF//VOGUE DOLLS, INC." 1957-60 (Discontinued 1966) Mint..................................$250

10" "Portrette Margot." All-hard plastic, blue sleep eyes, CM, blonde hair, original pink gown, tag, etc. Ca. 1970 Made by Madame Alexander, NYC. 1968-73 ....$500-$550

15" "Shrinking Violet" talking doll, all-cloth/yellow yarn hair, pull string. Mattel. 1960s $65. (Courtesy of Carol Lindberg)

10" "Sweetheart" Jill. All-vinyl/jtd body (no swivel waist), CM, blue sleep eyes, rooted brunette wig, original clothes, shoes. (This doll is more slender than the original 1957 Jill.) Head mark: "VOGUE." 1962-1963 Rare $300

(Toni's body mold is almost identical to Alexander's "Cissette's" mold, except Toni has longer legs and no knee joints.)

10-1/2" "Coty" Girl. Wardrobe Doll. All-vinyl/jtd body, CM, blue sleep eyes, platinum (white) hair that is washable and stylable, original black gown, black hat, black high heels, etc. Her box reads: "Hello I'm the new Coty Girl Doll." (Promoted Coty products/cosmetics. Additional dresses, hats, accessories, etc., could be purchased separately. A "Circle P" doll. Ca. 1950s MIB $350

10-1/2" "Ginger." Wardrobe Doll. All-vinyl/jtd body, CM, sleep eyes, blonde rooted hair, adult figure, arched feet for high-heels, original clothes, etc. Mark: "Ginger." Clothes tag reads: "Cosmopolitan Doll & Toy Corp//Jamaica, N.Y." Ginger had a complete wardrobe of dresses, hats, etc. Ca. 1950s-early 1960s. Doll only: $200

10-1/2" "Suzette." Teen-Doll. Soft vinyl head/rigid vinyl body jtd at neck/sh/hips/arched feet for high heels, CM, blue sleep eyes, blonde wig, original clothes, white plastic high-heeled slippers, etc. Mark: "Uneeda." Made by

8"-9" stuffed toy by Anna Lee, $95-$100. (Courtesy of Irene Oretga)

Dewees Cochran by Effanbee, Limited edition doll, all original, 1977 $125.

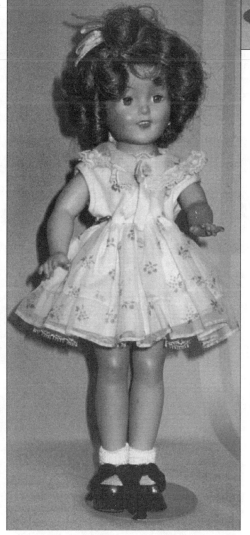

216" Unmarked composition doll, original dress, replaced wig, shoes, socks. 1940s. (Courtesy of Carol Lindberg)

12" Shirley Temple, all original, 1957. See plastic age dolls for prices. (Courtesy of Irene Ortega)

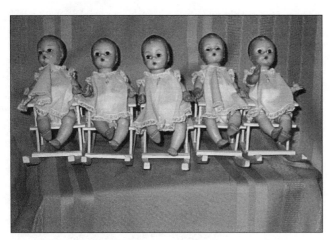

7" Fisher Quints-all original clothes, by Alexander, 1964, $475-$575. (Courtesy of Irene Ortega)

12" Buddy Lee, compo, all original, 1949. $300-$350. (Courtesy of Rosalie Purvis)

Plastic Kathe Kruse dolls, all original, 1970s. (Courtesy of Herron)

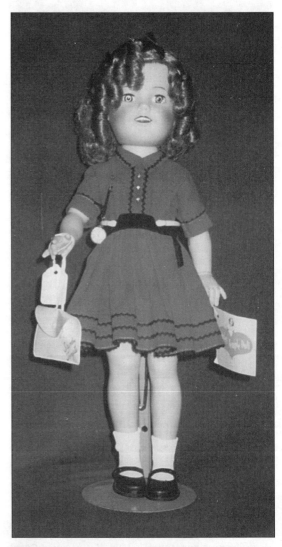

12" Shirley Temple, all original, 1957. See plastic age dolls for prices. (Courtesy of Irene Ortega)

Uneeda Doll Co., NYC, 1917-1976. Ca. late 1950s Mint.............................$135

10-1/2" "Toni." Wardrobe doll. Vinyl head/jtd plastic body, CM, blue sleep eyes, rooted wig, adult body, arched feet, original clothes, etc. Additional wardrobe sold separately in boxes, included innumerable accessories. Made by American Character Doll Co., NYC, 1919+. Mark: "American Character 1958 (in a circle)" on head/body. Doll only $250

11" "Bob." Companion to "Suzette." Teen-Doll. Soft vinyl head/rigid vinyl body jtd at neck/sh/hips, smiling CM, brown sleep eyes, brown mld hair/deep comb marks original shirt, trousers, loafers, etc. Mark: "Uneeda." Ca. late 1950s $75

Kathe Kruse girl, all original, ca. 1971. (Courtesy of Herron)

11" "Baby Precious." Negro Child. Soft black vinyl head/soft jtd vinyl body/super-flex limbs/voice box, CM, brown glassine sleep eyes, short black curly wig, original dress, bonnet, etc. Mark: "HORSMAN DOLL MFG CO., A/HORSMAN/DOLL HORSMAN, IRENE SZOR/HORSMAN" or "HORSMAN DOLLS, INC." U.S.A. made. 1950s Mint $150

11" "Little Angel." Walker. All-hard plastic/jtd at neck/sh/hips/straight legs, CM, blue sleep eyes, blonde wig, original clothes. Original box reads: "Littlest Angel V 1411//She sits-she walks-she kneels//you can wash, wave, comb and curl her hair." Made by Arranbee, NYC. Ca. 1954 MIB..............................$200

11" "Miss America." Vinyl head, CM, large round blue sleep eyes, brown synthetic rooted wig/bangs, hard plastic body jtd at neck/sh/hips/knees, original "Miss America" long gown, cape, crown, scepter, etc. Made by Schoen & Yondorf Co., NYC, early 1900s+. Ca. 1959 ....$100

11" John F. Kennedy. U.S. President. Vinyl head/hands/feet, CM, blue ptd eyes, blonde ptd/molded hair, original clothes. (Doll is seated in a rocking chair and reading a copy of *The Herald Tribune*. There is a wind-up key; when wound the chair rocks to the tune "Happy Days Are Here Again." Mark on chair bottom: "1963 Kamer Incorporated, Pat. No. 2121, 4344, 14899," and below: "709466." Made in Japan. 1963 ....$225

11-1/2" "Texaco Cheerleader Doll." Barbie-type. All plastic/jtd body, CM, blue ptd eyes, long blonde rooted wig, original clothes (2 other costumes attached to original box). Box reads: "Texas Cheerleader Doll." Doll marked: "T51 Hong Kong." (Sold at Texaco stations for $2.00. Other marks: "T20" and "T30".) 1973 MIB.................$100-$125

11-1/2" "Miss Francie." Barbie-type. All plastic/jtd body, CM, blue ptd eyes, blonde rooted hair, original gown, long gloves, "Miss Teenage Beauty Contest" banner. Ca. 1960 (Sold for $520 in 1993)..$750+

11-1/2" "Lilli" look-alike. All plastic/long neck/jtd body/shapely figure/bosom/long limbs/ptd-on black spike heeled shoes, CM, blue ptd eyes/blue eyeshadow, green ptd earrings, red hair, original swimsuit. Back mark: "MADE IN HONG KONG." (This imitation "Lilli" was made by Marx and Faber Luft, Ltd., and other Hong Kong companies.) Ca. late 1950s (Sold for $70 in 1994)..$225

11-1/2" "Barbie." First Edition. All vinyl/jtd body, CM, white irises, pointed eyebrows, blonde ponytail, gold hoop earrings, original white-striped swimsuit. Feet holes. Made by Mattel, Inc., Hawthorne, CA, 1959-1990s. 1959 Mint ....$3,000+

(Barbies have reached the "cult" stage which means that prices are speculative and will continue to rise at auctions. It is difficult to predict prices in this area of doll collecting.)

16" Mme Alexander's "Elise", all original, 1962, $350-$375.

11-1/2" "Barbie." Second Edition. All vinyl/jtd body, CM, white irises. Doll is similar to above doll except some dolls wore pearl earrings. No holes in feet. Made for 3 months. 1959-1960 Mint .... $2,800+

11-1/2" "Barbie." Third Edition. Same as above doll except for blue irises/curved eyebrows. No holes in feet. 1960 Mint .... $650+

11-1/2" "Barbie." Fourth Edition. The color of complexion changed this year from a very pale tone to a more natural flesh tone. Same doll as Third Edition Barbie. 1960 Mint.................................. $400+

15-3/4"-16-1/2" Mexican Senoritas, made in Old Mexico, early 1950s, all original. Compo shoulder heads, ptd features, black silk thread hair, straw-stuffed cloth bodies/compo lower limbs/gold ptd high-heeled shoes, original regional costumes. $65 each. (Courtesy of Herron)

11-1/2" "Barbie." Fifth Edition. Same as above Barbie except ponytail is a firmer grade of Saran. 1961 Mint .... $400+

12" "Buddy Lee." All hard plastic/jtd sh/stationary legs, smiling CM, large ptd blue eyes to side, ptd/mld hair, dressed in LEE bib overalls, shirt, cap. H.D. Lee, Inc. 1949-1962.................... $300-$350

12" "Daisy Mae." Li'l Abner comic strip character. One piece vinyl body/limbs/bosom, CM, blue sleep eyes, rooted blonde hair, original clothes. Made by Baby Berry Toy Co., NYC. Ca. 1957 .... $225

12" "Superman." All-plastic/jtd at neck/sh/waist/elbows/wrists/knees, CM, blue ptd eyes, black ptd/mld hair, original blue and red nylon costume, red nylon coat, red plastic boots. Neck mark: "D.C. Comics, Inc." 1964-77 (this doll dates to 1977) Mint $150

12" "Tammy." All-vinyl/jtd at neck/sh/hips, CM, blue ptd eyes, rooted brown hair, original clothes, shoes. Head mark: "c Ideal Toy Corp.//BS-12." (There was also a "Tammy and Her Family" paper doll book published at this time—#1997.) 1964 Mint $65

12" "Tiny Tears." Hard plastic head/rubber jtd body, OM/sleep eyes/brown ptd/mld hair, original clothes, etc. (When Tiny Tears drank water from her bottle tears came from her eyes and she wet her diaper. When IDEAL purchased this company they produced Tiny Tears in vinyl, limited edition vinyl, and bisque.) American Character Doll Co., NYC. 1950s MINT $200

168

12" Shirley Temple. All-vinyl/jtd body, OM/6 teeth, hazel sleep eyes, blonde synthetic rooted wig, original clothes, etc. Back mark: "ST-12-N." Head mark: "IDEAL DOLL//ST 12." (This size was the most common. These vinyl Shirleys were made from 1958-1961; 300,000 sold within the first 6 months.) 1958-1961 Mint............................$225

12-1/2" "Susy Goose Francie Go-Go" Bedroom set. (12-1/2"-long) white plastic bed, white telephone, white TV set, go-go cart. Ca. 1960 (Sold for $1,050 in 1993 at auction) Speculative...$1,000+

13" "Bonny Braids." Vinyl head/hard plastic body jtd at neck/sh/hips, smiling O/C mouth, large blue ptd eyes, blonde ptd/mld hair with 2 braids, original print dress, etc. Original box reads: "AMERICA'S NEW DARLING." Made by Ideal Novelty & Toy Co., Brooklyn, N.Y., 1907-1991. Ca. 1951 Doll only $225 MIB..$375

13" "Make-up Doll." Compo head, OM/teeth, large blue sleep eyes, blonde wig with looped braids over ears and ribbons, jtd compo body, original lt. blue playsuit with tie-on skirt, matching bonnet, pale blue shoes, white socks, make-up bag, etc. Body mark: "13." Probably Ideal. Ca. 1940s............$350

13" "Mammy & Pappy Yokum." One-piece vinyl body/limbs (Mammy has mld bosom), ptd features, mld hair, original clothes. Tag reads: "Al Capp//Dog Patch Family//Exclusive License//Baby Berry//Tony N.Y.C." Ca. 1957 Each $225

11-1/2" Barbie #1, original "Gay Parisienne" outfit, $1800+. (Courtesy of Connie Baca)

15-1/2"-16-3/4" Mexican Senoritas, made in Old Mexico, early 1950s. Compo shoulder heads/cloth bodies/compo limbs, original regional costumes, hat. $65 each. (Courtesy of Herron)

13" "Pete." Polly's Twin Brother. Negroid features. Brown vinyl head, OM/teeth, brown ptd eyes, black ptd/mld hair, jtd vinyl body/super-flex legs, original clothes, etc. Mark: "HORSMAN DOLL MFG. CO. A//HORSMAN//DOLL, HORSMAN, IRENE SZOR//HORSMAN" or "Horsman Dolls, Inc." U.S.A. made. 1956-58 Rare...................$200

13" "Polly." Negro Girl. Negroid features. Brown vinyl head, OM/teeth, brown ptd eyes, black ptd/mld hair/bangs/ponytail, jtd vinyl body/super-flex legs/voice box, original clothes, etc. Mark: "HORSMAN DOLL MFG. CO. A/HORSMAN//DOLL, HORSMAN, IRENE SZOR//HORSMAN..." Horsman Doll Co., NYC. U.S.A. made. Rare 1956-58.......................................$175

13" "Sunbabe." All-synthetic rubber, CM, blue ptd eyes, brown ptd/mld hair, jtd at neck/sh/hips/bent limbs, original sunsuit. Body mark: "MFD BY//THE SUN RUBBER CO.//BARBERTON, O. U.S.A.//PAT. 2118682//PAT. 2160739." Designed by Ruth E. Newton. Ca. 1950 Mint.........................$65

13" Jackie Robinson. Famous Negro Baseball Player. Black compo head, CM, brown ptd eyes, black ptd/mld hair, jtd compo body, original "Dodgers" uniform, cap, etc. Bat marked: "Louisville Sluggerbats//Hillerich S. Bradsky & Co.//Louisville, KY." Box marked: "The Jackie Robinson Doll. The most valuable player in the National League. Manufactured by Allied-Grand Doll Mfg. Do., Inc., Brooklyn, N.Y." Ca. 1950 Scarce Doll only.......$800; MIB $1,000

13" Li'l Abner. Comic strip character by Al Capp. One-piece vinyl body/limbs, large feet, OCM/mld teeth, blue ptd eyes to side, black ptd/mld hair, original clothes. Tag reads: "Al Capp//Dog Patch Family//Exclusive License//Baby Berry//Toy N.Y.C." Ca. 1957........$225

13" Martha Washington. Vinyl head, CM, blue sleep eyes/upper lashes, rooted wig, hard plastic body/limbs, original clothes, frilly bonnet, etc. Made by Ma-

dame Alexander, NYC. 1976 ....$150-$200
(This doll has the glued-on wig rare after 1950) $350

14" "Betsy McCall." All-vinyl/jtd body, CM, rooted wig, brown sleep eyes, original clothes, etc. Marked: "McCall Corp." (in a circle). (This version of Betsy is different than the below 1952 doll—a more slender body and limbs.) Made by American Character Doll Co., NYC, 1919+. 1960.......................$300-$325

14" "Betsy McCall." Soft vinyl head/hard plastic body/limbs, CM, brown sleep eyes, glued-on black Saran wig/pageboy style, original red polished cotton dress with white trim, black shoes, white socks, wrist tag. Ideal Novelty & Toy Co., Brooklyn, N.Y. Ca. 1952. $350

14" "Nancy Lee." All-hard plastic/jtd at neck/sh/hips, CM, blue sleep eyes, blonde mohair wig, original felt outfit, hat, etc. (mohair wigs ceased being made ca. 1950. Saran became the popular medium for wigs after 1950.) Made by Arranbee (R&B) Doll Co., NYC, 1922-1960. Ca. 1947-49.....$275-$300

14" Shari Lewis. All-hard plastic/jtd fashion body, CM, brown eyes, auburn wig, original clothes/tag. Made by Madame Alexander, NYC. 1959........$500-$600

23" "English Peddler Lady." Wax head, ptd features, grey mohair wig, cloth body/wax limbs, original clothes, wares, etc. Made by Lewis Sorensen, Fullerton, CA 1960s................$1,200+

23" "Miss Pepsodent." Advertising Doll. All-vinyl. (Doll has rotating teeth made like a marble. When she lies down her teeth are yellow, when she stands up her teeth turn white.) Original dress banner reads: "Miss Pepsodent." She

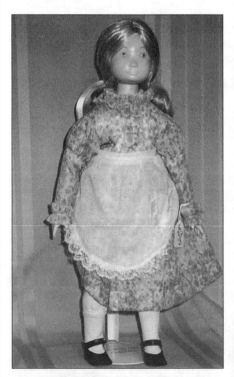

18" Suzanne Gibson's Calico Kid, vinyl, all original, early 1980s $100. (Courtesy of Irene Ortega)

has a tube of Pepsodent and a tiny brush. Made by Imperial Crown Doll Co., NYC. 1955 Mint $200

23" "Ruthie." Hard plastic head, CM, blue sleep eyes, wig, cloth body/vinylite brand plastic limbs/crier, original clothes, bonnet, box. Box number 2522. E.I. Horsman, NYC. 1954 MIB $300

24" "Paul Marie." Vinyl head, CM, blue sleep eyes, rooted blonde wig, bangs, 1-pc stuffed vinyl body/limbs, original striped skirt, blouse, stockings, high-heeled slippers. Made by Deluxe Toys (Deluxe Reading; Deluxe Toy Creations; Topper Toys, Topper Corp.) 1958 Mint (Dolls with stuffed vinyl bodies are rarely found in perfect condition, and are not as durable as hard plastic.).............. $150-$175

10" Negro Kathe Kruse children, vinyl all original, 1988-89 $240 each when new. (Courtesy of Irene Ortega)

24" "Sweet Sue." Walker. Hard plastic/vinyl scalp, CM, blue sleep eyes, rooted brown wig, jtd body/hips, original floor-length gown, etc. Head mark: "AMER. CHAR." American Character Doll co., NYC. 1953 .... $450

25" "Plassie." Hard plastic had, CM, blue sleep eyes, blond mohair wig, cloth body/hard plastic limbs/cry box, original clothes, etc. Mark: "P 400//Ideal Doll//Made in U.S.A." 1948-50 ..... $350

27" "Charming Bride." A series doll. Soft vinyl head, CM blue sleep eyes, real lashes, rooted wig, hard plastic jtd body/walker/crier, original clothes, etc. Mark: "Eegee." E. Goldberger, NYC, 1917+. Series started in 1956 to 1964. Ca. 1957 .... $400

29" "Betty, the Beautiful Bride." Stuffed vinyl/1-pc body/limbs, CM, blue sleep eyes, dark brown wig, original bridal gown, veil, etc. Head mark: "251/A-E" with "4" at the side of the head. Back mark: "A." Made by Deluxe Toys, a division of the defunct Deluxe Reading company. (A pre-Christmas sale item sold through stores from 1957-59. She was known as "Sweet Rosemary" when she wore her pink, blue, or yellow evening gown.) Ca. 1957-59 Mint ....$150-$175

30" "Bad Boy." All-hard plastic, O/C mouth, round blue sleep eyes, blonde ptd/mld hair, jtd body, original 2-pc black/white striped convict suit/cap. Square label on chest reads: "LITTLE MISTER BAD BOY" (illustration of a smiling convict). Made by Earl Pullan Limited, Canada. (Sales promotion doll for "Bad Boy" appliance store, also known as Heather Hill Appliances.) Ca 1960-61 ..... $200+

30" Marie Osmond. Television Vocalist. Vinyl head, O/C mouth/teeth, blue ptd eyes, long dark brown wig, jtd plastic body, original long pink gown, etc. Mark: "C (in a circle) OSBRO PROD. 1976 USA." Osmond Bros. Productions, Salt Lake City, Utah. 1976 (This doll is more scarce than those of her brothers.) $150

17" "Smokey the Bear", all original. $125-$175. (Courtesy of Connie Baca)

31" "Mary Ellen." Walker. All-hard plastic/jtd body, CM, blue sleep eyes, brown wig, original clothes, etc. (This doll had vinyl arms in 1955. Made for 2 years only.) Ca. 1954 Scarce $600

31" "Howdy Doody." Ventriloquist dummy. Vinyl head/hands/cloth body, original clothes, etc. Head mark: "Eegee//National Broadcasting Co., Inc. 1972." Tag reads: "Goldberger Doll Co." 1972 ....$150-$175

31" "Penny Playpal." (Pattie Playpal's little sister.) Vinyl head, CM, blue sleep eyes, rooted wig, hard vinyl body jtd at sh/hips, original clothes, etc. (Her chubby legs are slightly bowed.) Made by Ideal. N.Y. 1960 .... $300-$350

36" "Betsy McCall." All-vinyl/jtd body, smiling CM, blue sleep eyes, blonde wig, original clothes, etc. Head mark: "Mc-Call Corp." American Character Doll Co., NYC. 1960 .... $600-$650

36" "Sandy McCall." Betsy McCall's brother. All-vinyl/jtd body, CM, blue sleep eyes, lashes, ptd, mld hair, original clothes, etc. Neck mark: "McCall//Corp 1959." Made by McCall's Pattern Co. Rare.. $600

38" "Peter Playpal." All-plastic/jtd at neck/sh/hips/muscular legs/separate fingers, smiling CM, blue sleep eyes, blonde rooted hair, original brown short pants, red jacket, red knee-length stockings, black shoes cap, wrist tag. Mark: "Ideal, B35-38." (These "companion" dolls are rarely found in their original clothing. Children preferred dressing them in their own clothes, which was actually a sales gimmick. 1960.................................... $650-$700

38" "Lori Martin." Personality Doll. All plastic/jtd at sh/hips/wrists/ankles, CM, dark wig, blue sleep eyes, original clothes include blue jeans, plaid shirt, scarf, etc. Head mark: "Metro-Goldy-wn-Mayer Mfg. by Ideal Corporation." Back mark: "Ideal Toy Corp. 38." (Doll represents Lori Martin as "Velvet Brown" in the film "National Velvet" which once starred Liz Taylor in the 1940s.) $500

42" "Daddy's Girl." Companion doll. All-plastic/jtd at neck/sh/hips/long limbs/separate fingers, broad smiling mouth, sleep eyes, long brunette hair, original clothes, etc. Head mark: "Ideal Doll Corp." Early 1960s (Sold for $775 in 1987).. $800

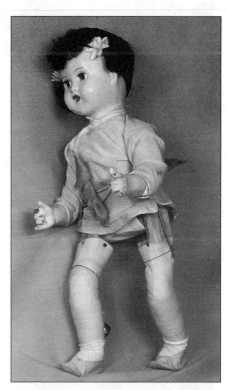

16" "Walker" (push chest area and legs walk). Compo head/hands/cloth body/legs. Unmarked. Ca. 1950s $200. (Courtesy of Carol Lindberg)

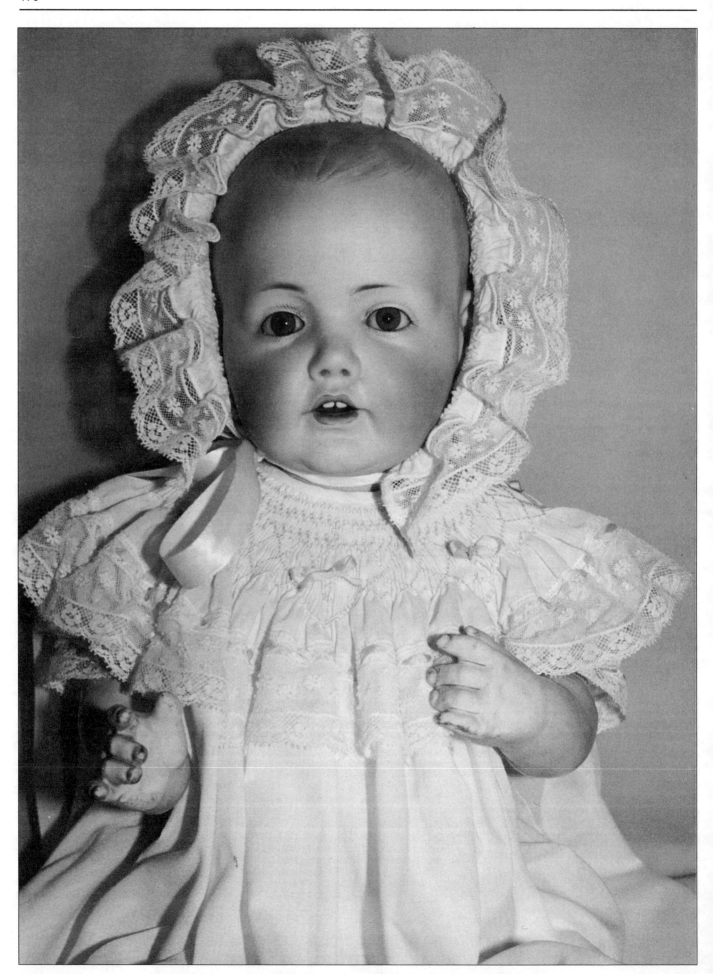

Chapter 34

~POPULAR BABY DOLLS~

History:

Why it took over a half century from 1855, when Fr. Greffier exhibited the first baby dolls at the Paris Exposition, to 1910 when the beautiful and realistic Character Babies were introduced to perfect the baby doll face and body, is beyond comprehension. The babies Fr. Greffier exhibited at the Paris Exposition in 1855 were of Japanese origin and looked Japanese, but they were soon copied in Sonneberg, not only in papier-mâché, but in bisque and china. Their odd molded hip area distinguished them from ordinary all-cloth bodied baby dolls.

The British babies modeled at this time had more natural looking faces and limbs. They were duplicated, of course, in poured wax which added to their realism. Baby dolls continued to be made in all the available mediums, but mostly with stuffed cloth bodies. These were identified by their so-called cup-and-saucer necks and not their faces which looked much too stern and mature to be called "babies." The invention of the French ball-jointed wood and composition body was a boon to the doll trade since it gave the sculptor a better advantage. He could now develop the anatomy to its fullest beauty; the result being the beautiful baby bodies seen on dolls after 1910. The baby doll craze had begun and has lasted to this day.

Collecting Hints:

Baby dolls saved the German doll companies when the character child dolls proved a dismal failure. Perhaps that is the reason why so many can be found today and in mint condition. Baby dolls flooded the American market for decades; every decade introducing a cheaper and far less interesting version. When buying a baby doll for investment purposes, seek the unusual, the mint, the all original. Baby dolls in their original clothing are difficult to find for obvious reasons, but they do exist. A baby doll in its original trunk, box, basket, or whatever with wardrobe and accessories is always a choice "find." The layette adds to its charm and allure. A mint doll in its original condition, with original clothes and trunk, is like a time-capsule it suddenly wafts us away to the past the doll's era and to childhood. And, money aside, that's what collecting is all about nostalgia!

Reproduction Alert:

Many of the old character babies and other types have been reproduced. Be wary of heads that appear too "new." Modern composition bodies differ from the old. Check arm and leg joints for wear and compare the body with an old one in your collection. Scrutinize the painting of eyelashes, eyebrows, lips, and hair. Remember, some of today's artists are even better than the artists in the old factories!

POPULAR BABY DOLLS

6-1/2" "880-17" incised "Prize Baby." All-bisque/jtd at neck/sh./hips, O/C mouth, blue glass eyes, brown ptd/molded hair, old clothes, bonnet. Incised on body: "Copr. by Mildred 'The Prize Baby' Germany, 880-17." Chest label reads: "Mildred The Prize Baby." Ca. 1910 (Sold for $1,600 in 1987 at auction.) .... $1,000+

6-1/2" Character Baby, Solid-dome bisque head, CM, blue intaglio eyes, blonde ptd hair, bent-limb compo body, old clothes. Head mark: "5/L/Heubach" (square design). 1910+ ......$375-$400

7-1/2" "150" Character Baby. All-bisque/jtd body, CM, blue glass eyes, blonde ptd/molded hair, old clothes. Made by Hertel, Schwab & Co., Germany. 1910+ $650

8" "Bonnie Babe." Bisque socket head, OM/2 lower teeth, blue glass sleep eyes, blonde mohair wig, jtd compo body, old baby dress, etc. Mark: "1393 20 Germany." Head made by Alt, Beck & Gottschalck, Germany. Distributed by George Borgfeldt, NYC. 1926 .... $1,350

8" "F.P." incised Character Baby. Bisque head, O/C mouth, small grey glass eyes, blonde HHW, BJ compo body, old clothes, bonnet. 1910+ Made by Swaine & Co., Germany. 1910+ .... $1,000-$1,350

8" "S3F1" incised Character Baby. Bisque head/2 faces (smiling and frowning), O/C mouth, ptd blue eyes/inset blue glass eyes, brown HHW, bent-limb compo body, old clothes. Mark: (Shield design with a double S in the center and a ribbon draped across the top and S 3FO.)" Made by Max Friedrich Schelhorn, Sonneberg, Germany, 1907-1925. (This mark was registered in 1908. Made dolls and parts.) Ca.1912 .... $1,000+

8" Negro "Dream Baby." Black bisque head, CM, brown glass sleep eyes, sparsely ptd black hair, cloth body/compo hands, original clothes. Mold number: "341." Made by Armand Marseille, Germany. (ARRANBEE was an importer who assembled dolls, such as in this case, with an Armand Marseille head.) 1924 .... $450

8" Negro Baby. Black bisque head/Negroid features, red CM, large ptd black eyes, molded ears, ptd black hair/3 molded tufts/red ptd and molded ribbon bows, straw-stuffed black cloth body original white cheesecloth gown with lace trim, white slip, black shoes, black stockings. Mark: "Morimura." Made by Morimura Brothers, NYC, producers and importers of dolls during World War One and afterwards. Ca. 1915-22 $250

8" Nuborn or "New Born Babe." Bisque head, CM, sleep blue glass eyes, painted dark hair, cloth body/compo hands/crier, original baby gown/metal button. Crude doll. Head designed by Jeno Juszko. (Forerunner of the Bye-Lo Baby.) 1914-25+ made by Louis Amberg & Son. $425

8-1/2" "FS & C 1295" Toddler Girl. Bisque head, OM/teeth, PN (pierced nostrils), blue glass sleep eyes, blonde HHW, BJ compo body, etc. Made by Franz Schmidt & Co., Georgenthal near Waltershausen, Thur., Germany (Simon & Halbig heads) Ca. 1910+. $500

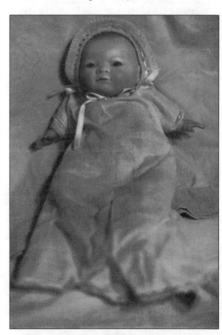

7-1/2" 8" head cir. Bye-Lo Baby. Bisque head/celluloid hands/cloth body, original clothes. Ca. 1923 $575-$625. (Courtesy of Herron)

9" "MB" incised Baby. Bisque head, OM/2 lower teeth, blue glass sleep eyes, blonde HHW, bent-limb jtd compo body, old clothes. Head mark: "MB/Japan." Made by Morimura Bros., NYC/Japan. 1915-22 .... $225

9-1/2" (head cir.) Character Baby. Bisque head, OM/teeth, blue glass sleep eyes, brown HHW, bent-limb jtd compo body, old clothes. Mark: "GB & Co.//Germany//BxF." Distributed by George Borgfeld Co., NYC 1910+ $275

17" Ernst Heubach baby, bisque head/BJ compo body, old clothes. 1910+ $525-$575. (Courtesy of Herron)

9-1/2" "P.M. 914" incised Character Toddler. Bisque head, OM/molded tongue, inset blue glass eyes, auburn mohair wig, BJ compo toddler body, old clothes. Made by Porzellanfabrik Mengersgereuth, Mengersgereuth, Germany, 1908+. (Dolls' heads made ca. 1913-1930. supplied heads to Carl Harmus and Gebruder Ohlhaver. Company sold to Robert Carl in 1925. Mark RC or R or X letters used thereafter.) 1913+ $400

10" "B.O." incised Baby. Bisque head/long neck, broad smiling mouth/molded teeth, blue-grey intaglio eyes, blonde ptd/molded hair, molded ears, BJ compo toddler body, old clothes. Made by Swaine & Co., Germany. Ca. 1910+ $2,200

10" "F.P." incised Baby Boy. Bisque head, O/C mouth, blue-grey ptd eyes, blonde ptd/molded hair, BJ compo body/straight legs/molded-on and black ptd shoes/white socks, original regional costume, cap. "S.&Co." or Swaine & Co., Huttensteinach, Sonneberg, Thur., Germany Ca. 1910+ $1,500

10" "P/M 914" incised Character Baby. Bisque head/2 dimples, OM/molded tongue/2 teeth, blue glass sleep eyes, blonde mohair wig, bent-limb jtd compo body, old clothes. Mark: "P/M 914 Germany 10 3/0." Porzellanfabrik Mengersgereuth. 1913+ $300

10" "Snookie." Vinyl head, CM, blue ptd eyes, ptd/molded hair, "Magic Skin" (soft rubber) body made in one piece, dressed. Ideal. (Same mold used for the Bucilla Thrift Kit Doll.) 1953 Good condition $75

10" Negro "Dream" Baby. Black bisque head, CM, brown glass sleep eyes, sparsely ptd black hair, bent-limb jtd compo body, original clothes. Mark: "351." Arranbee Doll Co., NYC. (Also R&B) Armand Marseille head. 1924 .... $550

10-1/4" "Gerling" Newborn Babe. Solid-dome bisque head, CM, brown glass sleep eyes, PN, blonde ptd hair, cotton-stuffed cloth body/limbs/compo hands/squeeze box, original gown. Mark: "Arthur Gerling 3//made in Germany." Made by Arthur Gerling Toy Co., NYC, London, Paris; Neustadt, Germany, 1912-1930s $700

10-1/2" "166" Baby Boy. Bisque head, OM/2 teeth, blue glass sleep eyes, light brown ptd hair, bent-limb jtd compo baby body, old clothes. Kley & Hahn, Germany. Head by Hertel, Schwab & Co. $650

10-1/2" "ABG//1361//Made in Germany//5" incised Baby. Bisque head, OM, blue glass sleep eyes, blonde mohair wig, bent-limb jtd compo body, old christening gown, bonnet. Made by alt, Beck & Gottschalck, Germany. 1910+ .... $475-$525

(Schmidt purchased Bahr & Proschild factory in 1918. Prior to that, Schmidt used heads made by Bahr & Proschild. Mein Goldherz or My Golden Heart trademark was used beginning in 1910 for Character Babies.)

11" "1418" or "Baby Aero"/ "Fly-Lo" Baby. Bisque head, CM, blue glass sleep eyes, blonde ptd/molded hair "combed" to a point on forehead, cloth body/silk over-suit with wings (some have usual cloth body), celluloid hands (some have cloth hands), Borgfeldt patent. (Represents the Spirit of Aviation.) 1928.............................. $4,000-$4,500

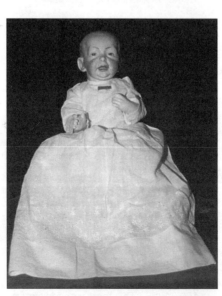

15" Kammer & Reinhardt's Baby #100, old clothes. 1909+ $900-$1,000. (Courtesy of Ruby Ellen Smith)

11" "2023/539" incised Character Baby. Solid-dome bisque head, pouty CM, blue ptd eyes, sparse blonde ptd hair, well-modeled ears, bent limb jtd compo body, old clothes. Made by Bahr & Proschild for Bruno Schmidt, Germany (head). 1910+ $2,200

11" "245" incised Negro "Hilda." Dark chocolate brown bisque head, OM/teeth, brown glass sleep eyes, black HHW, brown bent-limb jtd compo body, old clothes, bonnet. Mark: "Made in//C. Germany 7.//245//J.D.K.//1914 C (in a circle)//Hilda//Ges. gesch." 1914+ .... $4,000-$4,600

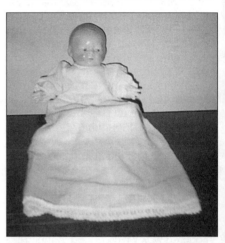

12" Tynie Baby. E.I. Horsman. Compo head/hands/cloth body/legs. Original clothing. Mark: "(2) 1924. E.T.H." 1924 $275-$300. (Courtesy of Ruby Ellen Smith)

11" "580" Character Baby. Bisque head/voice box inside head, O/C, mouth, blue glass sleep eyes, BJ compo body, old clothes. Made by Armand Marseille, Germany. 1910+ $1,200

11" "99" incised Character Baby. Bisque head, OM/teeth, brown glass sleep eyes, brown HHW, BJ compo body (toddler), old clothes, etc. Made by Konig & Wernicke, Waltershausen, Thuringia, Germany. 1912+ $950-$975

11" (long) "Bonnie Babe." Bisque head/beautiful coloring, broad smiling OM/teeth, blue glass sleep eyes, blonde ptd/molded hair, cloth body/compo arms, original factory-made gown, bonnet, etc. Mark: "Copr by Georgene Averill Germany 1005/3652 1386." (head by Alt, Beck, & Gottschalck; body by K&K Toy Co.; Borgfeldt distributor, NYC) 1926 .... $1,250

11-1/2" "386-8/O" incised Baby. Bisque dome-shaped head/pretty face, OM/2 molded-in teeth, blue glass sleep eyes, blonde ptd/molded hair, cloth body/celluloid hands, original clothes, bonnet, etc. Made in Germany. Maker unknown. 1925+ $350

11-1/2" (long) Two-faced Bye-Lo. Bisque head (10-1/2" cir.)/one face has CM and the other face has an OM/2 teeth, brown glass sleep eyes (both faces), orange ptd hair, flange neck/cloth body/celluloid hands, old baby gown. (Some of these dolls measure 11" long.) 1923+ .... $5,000+

12" "152" Character Baby. Bisque head, OM/2 molded upper teeth/felt tongue, inset blue glass eyes, blonde mohair wig, bent-limb jtd compo body, old clothes, bonnet. Mark: "Made in Germany//152//4." Made by Hertel, Schwab & Co., Germany. 1910+ $550

12" "Bucilla Thrift Kit Doll." Baby-type. All hard plastic, CM, blue sleep eyes, ptd/molded hair, original outfit. Back mark: "Ideal doll." (These dolls originally came with kits that contained fabric for making various outfits, such as a christening gown, etc. The dolls and kits could usually be purchased wherever Bucilla products were sold or one could order them from the Bucilla firm.) 1951 Doll only $100

12" "Century" Baby. Pink bisque head, CM, small squinty blue glass eyes, ptd blonde hair, cloth body/compo limbs, old baby clothes. (This doll has a combination Bye-Lo/Dream Baby persona.) Mark: "K (in a diamond shape) Germany//CENTURY DOLL CO. O." 1925 ....$750

12" "Tynie Baby." Solid-dome bisque head, tiny CM, tiny blue glass sleep eyes, ptd blonde hair, cloth body/compo arms, original clothes, bonnet, etc. Mark: "C (in a circle) 1924 E.I. Horsman Inc. Made in Germany." Designed by Bernard Lipfert. 1924 (Resembles Bye-Lo) ....$900-$950

12" Bye-Lo Baby. Compo head, CM, blue sleep eyes, blonde ptd/molded hair cloth body (stamped)/curved cloth legs/crier/celluloid hands, original clothes, bonnet. Mark: "Grace Storey Putnam." 1924 ....$450

12" (head cir.) Bye-Lo. Bisque head, CM, rosy cheeks, rare ptd blue eyes, orange ptd hair, bent-limb compo baby body, original white gown, blue Bye-Lo pin. Mark: "Copyright G.S. Putnam, 1922, made in Germany, 1369/30." 1922-23 ....$5,000+

12" (long) Bye-Lo. Bisque head, OM/2 upper teeth, blue glass flirty eyes, blonde ptd/molded hair, cloth body/celluloid hands, original clothes. Mark: "Copr. by Grace S. Putnam//Made in Germany, 1373/30." Ca. 1923 ....$5,000

12" "173" Googly. Bisque head, watermelon mouth, blue glass flirty eyes, blonde ptd/molded hair, BJ compo toddler body, old clothes. Hertel, Schwab & Co., Germany. (Head for Strobel & Wilkin's "Jubilee" line. Other mold numbers in this googly line: 163, 165, 172.) 1910+ $5,500

12-1/2" (head cir.) 16" (long). Mulatto Bye-Lo. Brown bisque head, CM, dark brown glass sleep eyes, black ptd hair, flange neck, brown cloth body/brown celluloid hands, old baby gown. $3,000

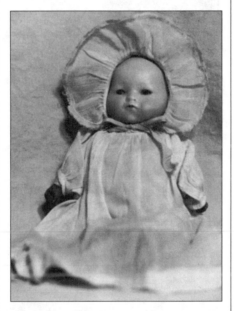

8" "My Dream Baby", bisque head, cloth body/compo hands, CM, blue sleep eyes, original clothes. Armand Marseille head. Made by Arranbee. 1924. $275 (Courtesy of Herron)

13" "160" Character Baby Girl. Bisque head/chubby cheeks, smiling O/C mouth/2 molded teeth, blonde HHW, bent-limb compo jtd body, old clothes. Made by Hertel, Schwab & Co. (100 series) for Kley & Hahn, Ohrdruf, Thur., Germany. 1910+ ....$600-$625

13" "247" Character Baby. Bisque head/chubby face/double chin, OM/2 upper teeth, blue glass sleep eyes, brown HHW, bent-limb jtd compo body, old clothes. Mark: "Germany//247//J.D.K." 1910+ . $2,000-$2,100

13" Pouty Baby. Solid-dome bisque head (pale coloring), CM, small blue glass sleep eyes, blonde ptd hair, cloth body/compo limbs, old christening gown, etc. Made by Schoenau & Hoffmeister, Porzellanfabrik Burggrub, Burggrub, Bavaria, Germany, 1901+. 1925 ....$900

13-1/2" "2096-0" incised Baby. Solid-dome bisque head, OM, blue glass eyes, well-modeled ears, blonde ptd hair, BJ compo jtd body, original clothes. (Often called "Tommy Tucker" by collectors. This head bears a faint resemblance to the Francois Duquenois baby head sculpture.) Bruno Schmidt owned this mold, but Bahr & Proschild made the heads for them.) Ca. 1898+ ....$1,350-$1,400

14" "142" Character Baby Boy. Solid-dome bisque head, O/C mouth, brown ptd intaglio eyes, blonde ptd hair, large protruding ears, rosy cheeks, jtd kid body/upper arms/legs/compo lower arms, old clothes. Mark: "DRGM 4428107." Hertel, Schwab & Co., Germany. 1910+ (Mold numbers 150, 163, 165 and 173 are Character Babies made by Hertel, Schwab & Co., and often attributed to Kestner.) ..$650-$700

14" "154" Character Baby Boy. Pale bisque head, CM, blue glass sleep eyes, blonde ptd/molded hair, bent-limb jtd compo body, old clothes. (This head resembles the Fiammingo bust.) Made by Hertel, Schwab & Co., Germany. 1910+ $2,600

16" J.D.K. Baby, bisque head/BJ compo body, O/M/2 teeth, blue sleep eyes, blonde mohair wig, old christening gown. Mark: "Made in Germany J.D.K. 211." 1910+ $900-$950. (Courtesy of Ruby Ellen Smith)

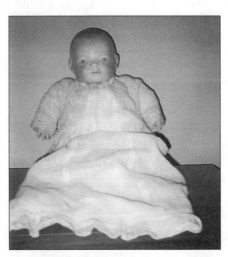

11" (head cir.) Bye-Lo, bisque head, cloth body/celluloid hands, brown sleep eyes, brown ptd hair, original tagged gown. Ca. 1923 $550-$650. (Courtesy of Ruby Ellen Smith)

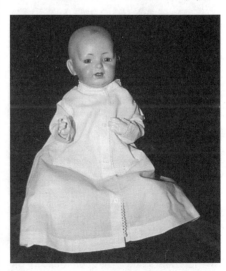

16" J.D.K. or "Kestner" Baby, bisque head, OM/2 teeth, blue glass eyes, blonde ptd hair, 5-pc bent-limb compo body, old clothes. Mark: "JDK-12 Made in Germany." 1910+ $800. (Courtesy of Ruby Ellen Smith)

19" K (star R/Simon & Halbig Character baby 126, bisque head, bent-limb compo body, flirty glass eyes, old clothes. 1909+ $900-$950. (Courtesy of Connie Baca)

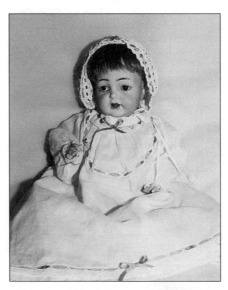

11" Simon & Halbig 122 K (star) R baby, bisque head, O/C mouth, brown sleep eyes, original brown HHW, bent-limb compo body, original clothes. 1909+ $800-$850. (Courtesy of D. Kay Crow)

13" Heubach-Kopplesdorg 317-3/O marked baby, bisque head, OM/tongue teeth, brown sleep eyes, brown HHW, bent-limb compo body, original dress, antique bonnet. 1910+ $500-$525. (Courtesy of D. Kay Crow)

12" head cir. "My Dream Baby" with Armand Marseille bisque head, old clothes. 1924 $475-$500. (Courtesy of Connie Baca)

12" "A2M 341" marked baby (Armand Marseille), bisque head, CM, blue sleep eyes, cloth body/compo hands, original clothes, etc. This is still another "My Dream Baby." $475-$500. (Courtesy of D. Kay Crow)

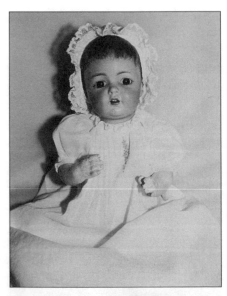

12" K (star) R/Simon & Halbig 121 baby, bisque head, OM/teeth, brown sleep eyes, brown HHW, bent-limb compo body, old or original clothes. 1909+ $800-$850. (Courtesy of D. Kay Crow)

14" "A.4M." incised Character Baby. Bisque head, OM/4 lower teeth, blue glass sleep eyes, brown mohair wig, bent-limb jtd compo body, old clothes, etc. Made by Armand Marseille, Germany. 1910+ $500

14" (long) Schoenhut Bye-Lo. Wood head (13" cir.) 1925 .... $2,000

14" "Century" Baby. Pale bisque solid-dome head/round face, smiling O/C mouth/2 molded upper teeth/molded red tongue, rosy cheeks, small squinty blue glass sleep eyes, blonde ptd/molded hair, cloth body/compo limbs, original clothes. Mark: "Century doll Co.//Kestner Germany." 1925 (Another Bye-Lo inspiration.) $950

15" "165-5" incised Character Baby. Bisque head, small smiling watermelon mouth, round grey glass sleep/googly eyes, blonde mohair wig, bent-limb jtd compo body, old clothes, bonnet. Made by Hertel, Schwab & Co., Germany, for Strobel & Wilkin, Germany. 1911+ $5,500

15" "211" Character Baby. Bisque head/chubby expressive face/double chin, OM/molded gums/2 tiny lower teeth, brown glass sleep eyes, brown HHW, large ears, BJ bent-limb body, old clothes. 1910+ by J.D. Kestner .... $900-$1,000

15" "619" incised Character Baby. Pale bisque head/double chin/pretty face, OM/teeth, blue glass sleep eyes, blonde ptd/molded hair, bent-limb jtd compo body, old christening gown, bonnet, etc. Mark: "Germany (BXP) 619-5." Made by Bahr & Proschild, Germany. 1910 .... $750

15" "AMUSO" Toddler. Bisque head, OM/2 teeth/tongue, blue glass flirty eyes (move from side to side; activated by pulling a string under each ear), BJ compo toddler body, blonde HHW/squeak box inside head, old clothes. Head mark: "AMUSO Co. 32 Made in Germany." August Moller & Sohn, Goergenthal, Germany 1915+. Trademark AMUSO registered in 1925.

9"-151 Girl (Hertel, Schwab & Co.), $475-$525; 10"-151 boy (Hertel & Schwab & Co.), $475-$525. 1910+. (Courtesy of Irene Ortega)

(This firm used mold numbers 100 and 1920. Their moving eye patent dates to 1911.) 1925+ .... $600-$700

15" "Bye-Lo." Bisque head, CM, blue glass sleep eyes, orange-blonde ptd hair, rare bent-limb jtd compo body, original clothes. Incised: "1369." Made by Alt, Beck & Gottschalck, Nauendorf, Thur., Germany, 1854+. (This company made dolls until 1941. At its peak, it employed 300 factory workers and 100 cottage workers.) 1923+ $1,500

15" "Bye-Lo." Compo head, ptd features/hair, cloth body/compo hands, original white cotton gown trimmed with lace, etc. Original pin reads: "Bye-Lo Baby Grace Storey Putnam." Made by Cameo Doll Co., NYC 1924 $650-$750

15" "Gerling" Baby. Round solid-dome bisque head, tiny OM, PN, blue ptd eyes, blonde hair, bent-limb jtd compo body, old christening gown. (Resembles the Bye-Lo.) Made by Gerling Toy Co., NYC, London, Paris, Neustadt near Coburg, Thur., Germany, 1912-1930s. 1925 .... $1,000+

15" "Jutta" Baby. Bisque head, OM/teeth, blue glass sleep eyes, ptd blonde hair, bent-limb jtd compo body/plaster limbs, old clothes. Mark: "1920/9 1/2//Jutta Baby//Dressel//5." Cuno & Otto Dressel, Germany. (Heads by Ernst Heubach, Armand Marseille, Simon & Halbig.) 1910-1922 (This head by Simon & Halbig) .... $750-$800

15" (head cir.) "Nursing Baby." Solid-dome bisque head, OM, blue-grey glass sleep eyes/orange ptd eyebrows, orange ptd hair, rosy cheeks, cloth body/rubber hands, old clothes, etc. Incised: "620." Imported from Germany by Arranbee Doll Co., NYC. (This doll came with a nursing bottle. Head probably by Armand Marseille.) 1924 (Sold for .... $650 in 1995.) $700-$800

15-1/2" Bye-Lo. Compo head, CM, rare brown eyes, blonde ptd/molded hair, cloth body, celluloid hands, original clothes. Made by Cameo Doll Co., NYC. 1924 .... $850

16" "1386" incised "Bonnie Babe." Bisque flange head, smiling OM/2 lower teeth, blue glass sleep eyes, blonde ptd/molded hair, cloth body (made by K&K Toy Co.)/compo lower limbs, old clothes, bonnet. Mark: "Copr. by Georgene Averill Germany 1005/3652/1386." 1926 $1,550-$1,650

16" "1386" incised "Bonnie Babe." Bisque flange head/double chin, smiling OM/2 lower teeth, blue glass sleep eyes, blonde ptd/molded hair, cloth body/bent compo arms/straight compo legs/cry box, original pink factory dress, bonnet, etc. 1926 (Newer version of above doll with original clothes.) .... $1,650-$1,850

16" "142" Character Boy Toddler. Solid-dome bisque/head, O/C mouth/teeth, brown intaglio eyes, jtd kid body/compo lower limbs, old clothes. (Hertel, Schwab & Company used this number on socket heads with bent-limb compo bodies as well.) 1910+ $700

19" J.D.K. (Kestner) Toddler (257), bisque head/BJ compo body. 1910+ $1,150-$1,300+. (Courtesy of Irene Oretga.)

16" Baby #151 (Hertel, Schwab & Co.) bisque head/BJ compo body, old clothes. 1910+ $700-$750. (Courtesy of Irene Ortega.)

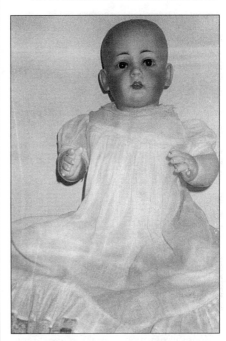

20" Kley & Hahn 169 10 Baby, bisque head, OM/teeth, bent-limb compo body, old clothes. 1902+ $1,600. (Courtesy of Connie Baca)

10" "Germany 2/O" marked baby, bisque head, OM/teeth, blue sleep eyes, bent-limb compo body, original clothes. 1910+ $400-$450. (Courtesy of D. Kay Crow)

16" "172.3" incised Googley Baby. Bisque head, watermelon mouth, round shaped brown sleep/googly eyes, rosy cheeks, blonde ptd/brush-stroked hair, bent-limb jtd compo body, old clothes. Head mark: "172.3" made by Hertel, Schwab & Co., Germany. Ca. 1915 ....$5,500

16" "Bebe Tout-en-Bois." All-wood, CM, blue ptd eyes, black ptd hair/brush-strokes, modeled ears, 5-pc jtd wood body, original night dress. (This is the baby type.) Probably Rudolf Schneider, Germany. 1901-14 ....$600

16" Bye-Lo. Vinyl head, CM, blue ptd eyes, blonde ptd hair, well-sculpted ears, cloth body/limbs, original white nylon gown, bonnet. Mark: "3/Horsman Dolls, Inc./C (in a circle) 1972." Designed by

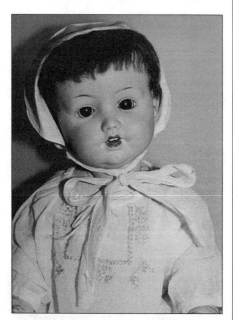

19" Herm Steiner baby, bisque head, OM/teeth, dimples, brown glass sleep eyes, brown HHW, bent-limb compo body, original clothes, bonnet. 1910+ $700-$800. (Courtesy of D. Kay Crow)

Irene Szor who designed dolls for Horsman since the 1950s. This doll bears no resemblance to the Putnam Bye-Lo. Original box reads: "A Genuine Reproduction Bye-Lo Baby 1925." Horsman made imitation Bye-Los in 1924, both in bisque and compo that did resemble the real Bye-Lo Baby.) 1972 MIB $150

16" (long) Bye-Lo. Vinyl head (12" cir.) CM, ptd blue eyes, cloth body/vinyl limbs, original pink flannel nightgown. Head mark: "C" (in a circle) Grace Storey Putnam. Cameo Doll Co., NYC (Mrs. Putnam felt that plastic or vinyl was the ideal medium for doll-making, due to its soft realism.) 1948 (Mint) $250

16-1/2" "H.V.B." incised Two-face Baby. Sleep/Wake Faces. Pale bisque solid-dome head/pretty "wake" face/sleep face, slightly smiling CM/puckered CM, tiny inset blue glass eyes/closed molded lids, ears for both faces sculpted together at lobes, dark ptd hair, crude cloth body/compo hands, old factory-made clothes. ("H.V.B." stands for Hermann von Berg, Huttensteinach, Germany; originally set eyes in dolls' heads and sold wigs, later supplied doll parts to Sonneberg factories. He moved to a larger factory in 1913. In 1918 he advertised babies and jointed dolls. His association with Schoenau & Hoffmeister is ca. 1923. His babies have the incised "H.V.B. 500" mark. This doll resembles My Dream Baby. Similar versions have painted blonde hair.) Ca. 1925 ....$1,000+

17" "151" Character Baby. Solid-dome pale bisque head, O/C mouth/molded tongue, blue glass sleep eyes/finely ptd upper and lower lashes, blonde ptd hair, bent-limb jtd combo body, old clothes, bonnet. Hertel, Schwab & Co., Germany. 1910+ $750

17" "152" Character Baby. Bisque head. OM/teeth, blue glass sleep eyes, blonde ptd/molded hair, bent-limb jtd compo body, old clothes, etc. 1910 Hertel, Schwab & Co. 1910+ $750

17" "154" Character Toddler Boy. Bisque head, CM, blue glass sleep eyes, blonde ptd/molded hair, BJ compo toddler body, old "boy" clothes, etc. Made by Hertel, Schwab & Co., Germany, for Kley & Hahn. 1910+ $2,800

17" "166" Character Toddler Boy. Bisque head, CM, small blue glass sleep eyes, blonde ptd/molded hair, BJ compo toddler body, old "boy" clothes, etc. Head made by Hertel, Schwab & Co. for Kley & Hahn. 1910+ $2,800

17" "800" incised Baby. Bye-Lo look-alike. Solid-dome pale bisque head, CM, small blue glass sleep eyes, blonde ptd sparse hair, bent-limb compo body, old christening dress, etc. Probably Kammer & Reinhardt. 1925 ....$1,000+

18" "12" incised Baby. Bisque head, O/C mouth, skin wig, brown glass sleep eyes, bent-limb jtd compo body, old batiste dress, etc. Mark: "Simon-Halbig//12." 1909-1930s $950

18" "126" Character Baby. Pale bisque head/round face/double chin, OM, blue glass sleep eyes, brown HHW, bent-limb jtd compo body, original long white cotton baby gown, etc. Kammer & Reinhardt (head by Simon & Halbig).

This was K (star) R's most popular mold number. 1909+ $875

18" "2072" Character Baby. Pale bisque head/open crown, OM, blue glass sleep eyes, brown HHW, bent-limb jtd compo body, original clothes, etc. Made by Bahr & Proschild for Bruno Schmidt, Waltershausen, Thur., Germany. 1910+ ....$3,400-$3,800

18" "231" or "Fany." Bisque head/chubby face/double chin, small CM, blue glass eyes, well-modelled ears, ptd/molded "flocked" hair, bent limb jtd compo body, old clothes, etc. (Inspired by the Duquesnois sculpture.) 1910+ ....$8,500-$9,000

18" "Baby Coos." Hard plastic head, CM, blue sleep eyes, blonde ptd hair, "Magic Skin" vinyl body/limbs (has not turned brown), original clothes, etc. Ideal Toy Co., New York. 1951 ....$65-$85

18" (head cir.) Life-Size Bye-Lo. Bisque head/flange neck, CM, blue glass sleep eyes, orange ptd hair, cloth body/celluloid hands, original baby gown, etc. Ca. 1923 ....$1,700-$1,800

18-1/2" "Gerling" Baby. Bisque head (resembles the Bye-Lo), flange neck, CM/PN, ptd blonde hair, cloth body/compo limbs, original clothes. Mark: "ARTHUR A GERLING." Ca. 1924+ $1,200

19" "169" Character Boy Toddler. Bisque head, CM, small brown glass sleep eyes, brown HHW, Bj compo toddler body, old clothes. Made by Hertel, Schwab & Company for Kley & Hahn, Germany. 1910+ ....$3,700-$4,200

19" "2048" Character Baby. Bisque head, CM, blue glass sleep eyes, blonde ptd/molded hair, bent-limb jtd compo body, old clothes. Made by Bruno Schmidt, Waltershausen, Thur., Ger-

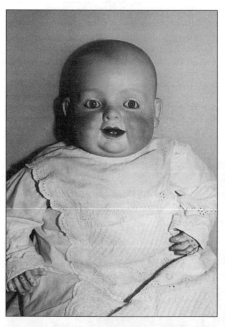

16" "Copyright by Georgene Averill" marked baby (1005/3652), bisque head, OM/teeth/tongue, ptd/mld hair, blue sleep eyes, cloth body/compo limbs, antique christening gown and petticoat. 1926+ $1,500-$1,700. (Courtesy of D. Kay Crow)

many. Heads by Bahr & Proschild, Ohrdruf, Thur., Germany. $2,700

19" "Baby Jean." Bisque head, OM/2 upper teeth, inset blue glass eyes, blonde/ptd/molded hair, bent-limb jtd compo body, old clothes. Mark: "JDK Made in Germany." (Resembles Hilda.) 1910-12 ....$1,750-$1,850

19" "Kiddie Pal Dolly." Compo shoulder head, O/C mouth/2 upper teeth, ptd blue eyes, blonde ptd/molded hair, cloth body/bent rubber arms/bent compo legs, original clothes. Mark: "Kiddie Pal Dolly." Made by Regal Doll Mfg., Co., Inc. NYC, Jersey City, N.J., 1918-1930s (German American Doll Co., successors before 1918.) Ca. 1925+ $600

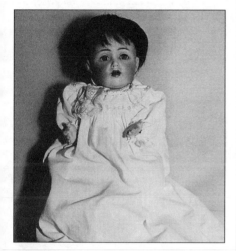

9" "Made in Germany J.D.K. 257" marked baby (Kestner), bisque head, OM/teeth/tongue, blue glass sleep eyes, bent-limb compo body, original clothes. 1910+ $700-$800. (D. Kay Crow)

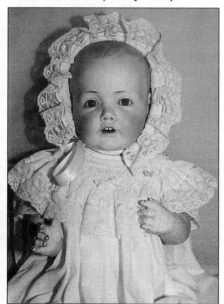

20" "Hilda" by J.D. Kestner, Germany, pale bisque head, OM/teeth, blue sleep eyes, blonde ptd hair, bent-limb compo body, old baby clothes. Mark: "Hilda/c/JDK Jr. 1914/Gesgesch 1914/Made in Germany." 1914+ $5,500. (Courtesy of D. Kay Crow)

19" "Lori" and "D" incised Character Baby. Pale bisque head, O/C mouth, blue glass sleep eyes, blonde ptd/molded hair, bent-limb jtd compo body, old clothes. "S.&Co." or Swaine & Co., Huttensteinach, Sonneberg, Thur., Germany 1910+ ....$2,000-$2,400

19" "Nippon" Baby. Hilda look-alike. Bisque head, OM/teeth/tongue, blue glass eyes, blonde ptd/molded hair, bent-limb jtd compo body, old clothes. Head mark: "B8 RE (in a triangle) NIPPON." 1918-22 (This is a repro "Hilda," made in Japan.) $1,000

20" "100" Character Girl. Bisque head/expressive face, OM/lower teeth, large brown glass flirty eyes, brown HHW, BJ compo toddler body, old clothes, etc. Made by Konig & Wernicke with head by Hertel, Schwab & Co., Germany. 1912+ ....$1,750-$1,800

20" "10735" or "Adlon" Character Boy. Pale bisque head/very realistic face/somber expression/double chin/full cheeks, brown glass sleep eyes/CM/auburn HHW, BJ compo toddler body, old clothes, hat, etc. (The name "Adlon" was advertised by Otto Schamberger, Sonneberg, Thur., Germany, in 1922. Head was inspired by the Duquesnois sculpture.) Incised: "Adlon 5 (in a square)." 1922-1925 ....$1,500-$1,800

20" "151" Character Baby. Solid-dome pale bisque head, O/C mouth/molded tongue, blue glass sleep eyes, blonde ptd/molded hair, bent-limb jtd compo body, old clothes. Hertel, Schwab & Co., Germany. 1910+ $850

20" "166" Character Baby Boy. Bisque head, OM/teeth, small blue glass sleep eyes, blonde ptd/molded hair, bent-limb jtd compo body, old clothes. Head mark by Hertel, Schwab & Co., for Kley & Hahn. 1910 $1,650 ($1,650)

20" "769" Character Baby. Bisque head, OM, blue glass sleep eyes, brown mohair wig, bent-limb jtd compo body, old clothes, etc. Mark: "Porzellan Fabrik-Burggrub//769//4//Germany." Made by Schoenau & Hoffmeister, 1901+. 1910+ ....$750-$800

20" "924" Character Baby. Bisque head, OM/teeth, blue glass sleep eyes, blonde HHW, bent-limb jtd compo body, old clothes, etc. Made by Porzellanfabrik Mengersgersgereuth, Mengersgereuth, Germany, 1908+. (Supplied heads to G. Ohlhaver and C. Harmus.) 1913-1930 ....$950

20" "Melitta" incised Baby. Bisque head, OM/teeth, pale blue glass sleep eyes, blonde mohair wig, PN, bent-limb jtd compo body, old clothes. Mark: "Melitta//A. Germany M.//12." Edmund Edelmann, Sonneberg, Thur., Germany, 1903+. (Made bisque and celluloid dolls. "Melitta" head was made by Armand Marseille.) 1910+ ....$900-$1,000

21" "201" incised Character Baby. Bisque head, OM/2 upper teeth, blue glass sleep eyes/real eyelashes, blonde HHW, bent-limb jtd compo body, old clothes. Head Mark: "201//SQ/Germany//9." Made by Schutzmeister & Quendt, Boilstadt, Thur., Germany, 1889-1930s. (Made heads for Kammer & Reinhardt, Welsch & Co., and Wolf & Co; became part of the Bing conglom-

erate in 1918. Other mold numbers: 101, 102, 201, 204, 252, 300, 301, 1376.) 1920s ....$750-$800

21" "352" incised "Rockaby Baby." Solid-dome bisque head, smiling OM/flutter tongue, blue glass sleep eyes, blonde ptd hair, bent-limb jtd compo body, old clothes. 1924+ made by Armand Marseille. $700

22" "1361" incised Character Baby. Bisque head, OM/teeth, blue glass sleep eyes/real eyelashes, brown HHW, bent-limb jtd compo body, old clothes. Made by Alt, Beck & Gottschalck, Nauendorf near Ohrdruf, Thur., Germany, 1854+. 1910+ $1,100

22" "208" Character Toddler. Bisque head, OM/2 upper teeth, dimples, blue glass sleep eyes, blonde HHW, jtd compo body/limbs, old clothes. Mark: "C.P. 208/50." Catterfelder Puppenfabrik, Germany, 1902+. 1910+ $1,000

22" "232" or "Lori" Baby. Solid-dome bisque head, OM, blue glass sleep eyes, blonde ptd hair, bent-limb jtd compo body, original white gown; original wicker hamper and extra clothes, i.e., embroidered dresses, knitted dresses, bonnets, booties, coats, etc. Mint. Never played with. Swaine & Co., Germany, 1910-1930. Ca. 1920s $4,000

22" "263" Character Baby. Bisque head, OM/2 teeth/tongue, brown glass sleep eyes, blonde HHW, bent-limb jtd compo body, old baby gown, etc. Mark: "263//CP//55//Made in Germany." Catterfelder Puppenfabrik, Catterfield, Thur., Germany 1902+. (Heads by J.D. Kestner) 1910+ ....$1,000-$1,100

22" "X" incised "Revalo" Baby. Lovely compo head, OM/teeth, blue glass sleep eyes, real eyelashes, ptd/molded brown hair, cloth body with zipper (rub-

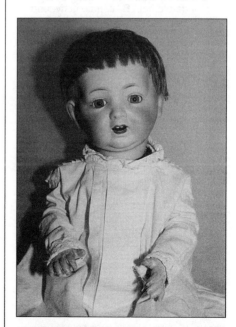

16" Morimura Bros. Baby, bisque head, OM/teeth, blue sleep eyes, OM/teeth, blonde HHW, bent-limb compo body, old clothes. Morimura Bros., NYC, was a Japanese import firm. 1915-1922. $375-$425. (Courtesy of D. Kay Crow)

ber balloon inside), compo lower limbs, original pink organdy dress, flaring bonnet, etc. Mint. Head mark: "X" (inside a circle). Gebruder Ohlhaver, Germany. Ca. 1925-35 (Rare) $800

23" "2072" incised Character Girl. Pale bisque head/open crown, wee CM, brown glass sleep eyes, brown HHW, BJ compo toddler body, old clothes. Made by Bahr & Proschild for Bruno Schmidt. (Duquenois likeness) 1910+ .... $5,500+

23" "98" incised Character Baby. Pale bisque head/chubby cheeks, OM, large blue glass sleep eyes, PN, short curved eyebrows, blonde HHW, bent-limb jtd compo body, old clothes. Head by Hertel, Schwab & Co., for Koenig & Wernicke. (This pretty baby has the desirable "follow" eyes.) 1912+ .... $1,250-$1,300

24" "158" Character Baby Boy. Bisque head, OM/teeth/tongue, blue glass sleep eyes, blonde ptd/molded hair, BJ compo toddler body, old clothes. Made by Hertel, Schwab & Co. for Kley & Hahn. 1910+ $2,250

24" "167" Character Boy Toddler. Bisque head, O/C mouth, blue glass sleep eyes, blonde HHW, Bj compo toddler body, old clothes. Made by Hertel, Schwab & Co., for Kley & Hahn. 1910+ $2,300

24" "624" incised Character Baby. Bisque head/chubby face, O/C mouth, blue glass sleep eyes, brown HHW, bent-limb jtd compo body, old clothes. Made by Bahr & Proschild, Germany. 1910+ $1,350

24" "AM/Germany" incised Character Baby. Rare ptd pottery head, solid-dome, OM/teeth, brown glass sleep eyes, blonde ptd hair, BJ compo body, original clothes. (Very pretty face.) Armand Marseille, Germany. Ca. 1910+ (sold for $250 in 1986)......................... $650

24" "My Dream Baby." Bisque head, OM/teeth, blue glass sleep eyes, blonde ptd hair, bent-limb jtd compo body, old white cotton open-work batiste baby dress. Head Mark: "A./M./Germany/351/8K." Imported by Arranbee Doll Co., NYC. Armand Marseille head. 1924 .... $900

26" "1361" incised Character Baby. Large bisque head/chubby face, OM/2 teeth/tongue, flirty brown glass eyes, brown HHW, bent-limb jtd compo body,

17" Negro "My Dream Baby" #351, black bisque head, OM/teeth, brown glass sleep eyes, black ptd hair, black bent-limb compo body, original clothes. $800-$850. (Courtesy of Victoria Rose, England)

old clothes, bonnet. Made by Alt, Beck & Gottschalck, Germany.......... $1,400

26" "152" Character Baby. Bisque head, OM/4 upper teeth/molded tongue, brown glass sleep eyes, blonde HHW, bent-limb jtd compo body, old clothes. Mark: "Made in Germany 152-13." Hertel, Schwab & Co., Germany 1910+ $1,200

26" Life-Size Baby. Fine quality bisque head (17" cir.), OM/2 teeth, blue glass sleep eyes, brown HHW, bent-limb jtd compo body, original lawn christening gown, etc. Crown mark: "G.B." George Borgfeldt & Co., NYC, 1881+. Distributor of German heads/Japanese heads (dolls); opened the American market. (This appears to be a Kestner head.) 1910+ $850

30" "1295" incised Character Boy Toddler. Large bisque head, OM/teeth, brown glass sleep eyes, brown skin wig, BJ compo toddler body/bent arms, original clothes. Made by Franz Schmidt & Co., Germany. 1910 .... $2,700

14" Kammer & Reinhardt's "Baby 100" twins, original clothes, bisque heads, O/C mouths, blonde ptd hair, blue ptd eyes. Purchased from their original owners who were twins. $900-$1,000 each. (Courtesy of Victoria Rose, England)

Chapter 35

~ROHMER (MAISON)~

History: 1856-1880

Marie Leontine Rohmer, 24, Boulevard Poissonniere, Paris, 1856+; 23, rue de Choiseul, Paris, 1870; 33, rue du Terrage, Paris, 1875 (with Reidmeister). Mlle. Rohmer, born 13 January, 1829, in Strasbourg, France, the daughter of a medical doctor. She opened her first doll factory in 1856, and was issued as many as six patents and additions from March 1857 to May 1858. Early dolls were stamped (in an oval) on the body with the words: "Mme Rohmer//Boulevard Poissonniere 24 PARIS." She married a civil engineer, M. Vuillaume, in 1859. Her dolls were so similar to those produced by Mlle. Huret of Paris, that it is sometimes difficult to differentiate the two when found unmarked. Both ladies specialized in Parisiennes with luxury trousseaux and trunks. Obviously both ladies used German heads on their early dolls made by the same supplier. When Madame Vuillaume's sister married, Reidmeister, a doll-maker, it was a most fortunate union until the madame (Rohmer) and Reidmeister designed and produced dolls conceived of punched-out metal which were articulated similarly to those made by Huret in gutta-percha. Mlle. Huret sued in the courts and won the case. Reidmeister and Rohmer were modestly fined and were told to destroy the dolls. Rohmer continued to manufacture custom-made dolls at the Poissonniere address until 1870. (She exhibited her dolls at the Paris Exposition in 1867.)

Since the Rohmer poupees were outfitted on the rue de Choiseul, she moved her factory to the famous street in 1870. Five years later, she made her final move to 33, rue du Terrage, where her brother-in-law, Reidmeister, had a toy store. She ceased business altogether in 1880. The popularity of the grand Pandore, the Parisienne, was beginning to diminish at this time.

Collecting Hints:

The Rohmer Parisienne is in the same league as those of Huret, Jumeau, and Bru, but even more rare because they were made for a shorter period of time. Sizes vary from 12" to 29." There are shoulder heads, swivel heads on shoulder plates, kid bodies, china or bisque heads and lower limbs, or heads on kid bodies with leather legs and arms. Some Rohmers have gutta-percha arms. Eyes were either inset blue glass eyes or blue painted eyes. Original clothes always add to the value of any doll, but especially the French doll, since the clothes are usually well-made and elaborate. Whereas some early Hurets are found unmarked, the Rohmer is usually marked on the chest or stomach with the Rohmer oval stamp.

Reproduction Alert:

To my knowledge the Rohmer Parisiennes have not been reproduced, possibly due to their lack of universal popularity and complicated body structure. However, most of the rare French dolls have been reproduced. Remember, old kid bodies are worn and smell old.

ROHMER (MAISON)

13-1/4" Parisienne. Lady-type. China swivel head on china shoulder-plate, CM, ptd blue eyes, blonde mohair wig, kid body/china lower arms, old clothes, etc. Mark: "Mme ROHMER//BREVETE SGDG PARIS (in an oval)." (Sold for $6,400 in 1991 at auction) Ca. 1860
.... $7,000+

13-1/2" Parisienne. Child-type. Pale bisque swivel head on pale bisque shoulder plate, CM, ptd blue eyes/large black pupils, pale pink cheeks, blonde mohair wig, kid body/bent bisque lower limbs/kid-over-wood upper limbs, original brown printed cloth gown trimmed with lace, etc. Mark: oval ROHMER stamp on chest. Ca. 1860 .... $7,500

15" Parisienne. Lady-type. White china swivel head on white china shoulder plate, red CM, bright red rouge spots on chubby cheeks, ptd blue eyes/thin brown eyebrows, blonde curly mohair wig, kid body/white china lower arms/ball and socket lower legs/kid-over-wood upper arms, original clothes, hat, etc. Ca. 1860s (Marked) $8,000

15" Parisienne. Lady-type. Pink luster or pink tinted china shoulder head, CM, inset blue glass eyes, rosy cheeks, blonde skin wig, PE, kid body/pink luster lower arms/rare bare feet with toe detail, original elaborate clothes, hat, stockings, leather shoes. 1857 (Sold for $6,750 in 1990) (Marked) . $10,000

16" Parisienne Parian Lady. White bisque swivel head on white bisque shoulder plate, CM, large inset cobalt blue eyes, blonde mohair wig, orange-pink cheek blush, kid body/white bisque lower arms, original clothes, hat, etc. Ca. 1860s (Marked) $10,000

17" Parisienne. Lady-type. China shoulder head/cup-and-saucer neck, CM, ptd blue eyes, blonde skin wig/cork pate, kid body/kid-over-wood upper arms/bent china lower arms/ball and socket lower legs/2 eyelets in front of lower body and upper leg with ribbon ties, original clothes, boots, etc. original clothes, hat etc. (The ribbon ties or laces connect with hooks in the knees which help the doll sit without falling backwards. Patent 31,342 registered July 7, 1857.). Ca. 1857+ $12,000

18" Parisienne. Little girl-type. China swivel head on china shoulder plate, CM, ptd blue eyes, blonde skin wig, rare kid-over-wood body/chubby legs/china lower arms, original clothes, shoes, etc. Ca. 1860s (Marked) (Sold for $4,800 in 1981) $12,000

20" Parisienne. Little girl-type. Bisque swivel head on bisque shoulder plate, CM, inset blue PW eyes, pale pink cheek blush, thin light brown eyebrows, brown HHW, kid body/bent china lower arms with lovely hands/ball-and-socket jtd knees, old clothes, etc. Ca. 1870s $12,000

20" Parisienne. Male. Bisque swivel head on bisque shoulder plate, CM, inset blue glass eyes, short brown HHW, shapely kid body/2 eyelets in lower torso and upper legs with ribbon ties to adjust jtd knees to sitting position/bisque lower arms, original male costume, hat. Ca. 1866 (Marked) $15,000

29" Parisienne. Lady-type. Pink luster china shoulder head, CM, inset cobalt blue glass eyes, auburn HHW, kid body/pink luster lower arms, gorgeous original clothes, hat, shoes, stockings. Rare size. (Marked) Ca. 1860s $20,000

Chapter 36

~SCHOENAU & HOFFMEISTER~

History: 1901-1953

Schoenau & Hoffmeister, Burggrub, Bavaria, Germany (Porzellanfabrik Burggrub), 1901-1953. The firm of Schoenau & Hoffmeister was founded in 1901. They made both dolls' heads and complete dolls. They also made bisque heads for other companies, including Canzler & Hoffman, Cuno & Otto Dressel, and Ernst Maar. Trademarks used by SH: "Das lachende Baby," "Hanna," "Kunstlerkopf," "My Cherub," "Princess Elizabeth," and "Viola." Some heads only bear initials: "DALABA" for "Das lachende Baby" and "MB" for "MY CHERUB." The initials "NKB" and "WSB" with "SHPB" are found on a Character Baby. Dolls manufactured after 1930 are incised "Porzellan-fabrik Burggrub" with numbers 169 or 170 and sometimes "Spezial." The dates 1904, 1906, 1909, 1914, 1916, 1923, 1930, which appear on their dolls, may well be the date of first issue.

Collecting Hints:

SH dolls run the price gamut, from the medium price range of under $1,000 to around $3,000 (mold numbers 1906, 1909, 4000, 4600, 5000, 5500, 5700, 169, 769, Kunstlerkopf, Hanna, etc.), to the more advanced collector range, which includes such types as "Princess Elizabeth" and "Das Lachende Baby." These have more character than the ordinary "dolly faces," which are more for the beginning collector. One of my favorite German dolls was made by this factory, and although I sold her long ago, I still miss her.

Reproduction Alert:

It is doubtful these dolls would be reproduced, with the possible exception of "Princess Elizabeth."

SCHOENAU & HOFFMEISTER

11"   Chinese Boy. Bisque head, OM/6 teeth, inset brown glass eyes/slanted shape, black mohair wig, BJ compo body, original costume, hat, shoes, stockings. Ca. 1901+ $950

12-1/2" "Marotte" Girl. Bisque head, OM/teeth, inset blue glass eyes, blonde lamb's wool wig, pleated/lace-trimmed tarleton skirt/ivory brocade over-dress with red trim, straw hat with red plume. Twirl the stick handle and hear the tune! Mark: "S (star design PB) H." Ca. 1901+ $750

12-1/2" Pouty Baby. Solid-dome bisque head, pouty CM, wee blue glass sleep eyes, blonde ptd hair, cloth body/compo limbs, original clothes. (This baby measures closer to 12". Ca. 1925 $950

14"   "5800" incised Girl. Bisque head, OM, brown glass sleep eyes, brown HHW, BJ compo body, original clothes, etc. 1901+ $450

14"   "Hanna." Polynesian. Dark bisque head, OM/2 teeth, brown glass sleep eyes, black HHW, bent-limb jtd compo body, original clothes. .... $800-$850

14"   "Hanna" toddler: .... $1,000-$1,100

14"   "170" incised girl. Painted bisque head, OM/2 teeth, blue glass sleep eyes, brown mohair wig, BJ compo body, original Zeeland/Holland costume, head-dress, etc. Mark: ,"SPBH (star encircling the PB initials) 170 3/0." Ca. 1930s $250

15"   "169" incised Character Baby. Bisque head, OM, blue glass sleep eyes, blonde mohair wig, bent-limb jtd compo body, original clothes. ("Burrgrub Baby" or "Porzellanfabrik Burggrub.") Ca. 1930+ $650

15"   "769" incised Character Baby. Bisque head, OM, brown glass sleep eyes, brown mohair wig, bent-limb jtd compo body, original clothes. (Another "Burggrub Baby.") Ca. 1910+ $650

17"   "Princess Elizabeth." Bisque head, OM/teeth, blue glass sleep eyes, blonde mohair wig, 5-pc. jtd compo body, original clothes. Mark: "Porzellanfabrik Burggrub/Princess Elizabeth." Ca. 1932 .... $2,000-$2,200

17"   "H.v.B. 500" incised Two-Faced Baby. Solid-dome bisque head/sleep-wake faces, smiling CM/somber CM, tiny inset blue glass eyes/closed/molded eyes, ears for both faces molded together, dark ptd hair, flange neck, crude cloth body/legs/compo arms, old baby dress. ("H.V.B." are the initials of Hermann von Berg, Huttensteinach, 1904. He supplied doll parts to Sonneberg factories; originally sold wigs and set eyes in German doll heads. He moved into a larger building at Koppelsdorf in 1912. His association with Schoenau & Hoffmeister dates to ca. 1923. This doll resembles the popular "My Dream Baby.") 1924+ $850

12" "SH-PB (in a star) 100-10" incised girl. Bisque shoulder head, OM/teeth, brown glass eyes, blonde mohair wig, kid body/bisque lower arms, redressed. 1901+ $350. (Courtesy of Ruby Ellen Smith)

23" "1909 SH" incised girl. Bisque head, OM/teeth, blue glass sleep eyes, brown mohair wig, BJ compo body, dressed by Virginia Yates. 1901+ $650-$700. (Courtesy of Virginia Yates)

Chapter 37

~ALBERT SHOENHUT~

History: 1872-1936

Albert Shoenhut (1849-1912) was a pioneer in the founding of the toy industry in America. When he died suddenly in his Philadelphia home in 1912, his subsequent funeral attracted several thousand people, including hundreds of children. It was one of the largest private funerals ever held in the city. The German born toymaker was only sixty-three, but had already become a legend in the world of playthings.

Albert Schoenhut came to America at age seventeen. His traveling companion was John Doll, the father of John E. Doll, who was the toy buyer for the Wanamker establishment. Being interested in the toy trade, young Albert settled in Philadelphia where he found employment with John Deiser & Company who was then making rocking horses and similar items. He remained with the firm for six years, learning the business thoroughly. Toy pianos were popular at the time, the notes of which were made of glass plates glued on strings. This disturbed Schoenhut to such an extent that his inventive mind sought a more durable devise; the result being the steel plate piano which became standard thenceforward. The success and acceptance of the innovation inspired the young man and gave him the encouragement to open his own factory and manufacture the new-type piano. He married in 1870, and his wife became his business partner. As fate would have it, his first customer was none other than Strasburger Pfeiffer & Company, who would remain loyal to the Schoenhuts for many years to come.

The Schoenhuts were astounded by the rapid growth of their little business, and as the years passed they continued to add new products. Their first doll-like figures were introduced with the Humpty Dumpty Circus in 1903. In 1908, Rolly Dolly was born. Rolly Dolly was similar to the popular Roly Poly types, but with improvements. In 1911, the "All-Wood Perfection Art Doll" was unveiled. These dolls were highly acclaimed, and when Schoenhut died the following year, it could well have been the end of an era, but instead it was just the beginning.

The patent for the wooden doll with the spring joints was applied for in 1908 and granted in 1911. Every doll was marked with the patent data as a means of identification. Some dolls had paper labels glued on their back or were incised. Mail order catalogs date to 1911. The dolls had somber faces similar to the Kammer & Reinhardt line. The dolls with the carved hair were the "economy" types. The boys wore a plain union suit, stockings and shoes. The girls sported stockinette union suits, stockings and shoes. The girl's union suits were trimmed with lace and adorned with a small bow; their shoes ornamented with a buckle. The boy's union suits had a round neck and the girl's union suits had a V-shaped neck. A stand came with the doll. Expensive dolls wore wigs which were nailed to the head or stapled. Heads were solid wood and hand-painted. Later dolls had hollow heads with an open mouth and sleep eyes. Bodies and parts were turned on a lathe, and when completed, were sealed with varnish or shellac. Heads and hands were left "natural" for a more realistic appearance.

Collecting Hints:

Early Schoenhut dolls are the most desirable since the supply was more limited due to the unpopularity of character dolls at the time. An early type in good or mint condition and wearing original or old clothes, shoes, stockings, etc. is worth an added $2,000 or more to the prices given in this section. So study your doll carefully before you sell it. On the other hand, regardless of the age of the doll, if it is badly chipped or has been completely repainted, especially the face, it is worth only what you are able to sell it for. A face that has been lightly retouched is not in danger, however. When dressing these priceless old relics, adhere to original styles and modes of the day. Better still, dress them in old fabrics and trim for a more "authentic" look and you will enhance their value when you sell them. Adolph Graziano sculpted the models for the original line of Schoenhut dolls (characters). But

when sales dropped, he was replaced in 1912 by "Mr. Leslie." Mr. Leslie left the firm in 1916. Harry E. Schoenhut sculpted some of the later dolls.

ALBERT SCHOENHUT & CO.

8-1/2" Happy Hooligan. Round 1-pc head/protruding eyes, broad smile, blue ptd eyes, dowel thumbs, original yellow coat/black trousers. Ca. 1915-20 (Sold for $850 in 1993)
.... $1,000+

8"-9" Circus Performers/Figures. Humpty Dumpty Circus. Turned hardwood/brightly painted/articulated (elastic joints/slots in hands for posing and holding objects. Copyright 1903 in United States, Germany, England. Clowns $165+; ringmaster-$295+; Max-$650+. (The circus came in a redwood box with a labeled front (label in front) No.
.... 20/27.)

8"-9" Humpty Dumpty Circus Animals. Turned hardwood/brightly painted,/articulated (elastic jts). Copyright in 1903 in Germany, England. Prices vary from $165+ for a donkey to $950+ for a rhinoceros; horse $195+; hippopotamus $775. (Furniture $35-$50 each; props $35-50 each).

9" Theodore (Teddy) Roosevelt. American President. All wood/jtd limbs, ptd features/mustache, black ptd hair, original khaki hunting outfit, hat, gun. Ca. 1915-20 (sold for $1,500 in 1993 and $2,970 in 1995) .... $2,500+

9-1/4" "Maggie." Maggie & Jiggs cartoon characters. All wood/jtd, ptd features, ptd/molded hair/topknot, original 2-pc cotton dress, rolling pin. 1918
.... $600

11" "Walker" Girl. Wood head, O/C mouth, brown ptd eyes, blonde mohair wig, wood body jtd at neck sh. by spring units/legs jtd at hips in a slot/no holes the feet/shoes designed at an angle for easier walking, original clothes, etc. Ca. 1919-1930 .... $700-$800

12" "107" Baby. Wood head, CM, large blue ptd eyes, brown mohair wig, spring jtd wooden (toddler) body, old clothes, etc. (These faces were designed by H.E. Schoenhut in 1913 and were taken from a clay mold of Bill Schoenhut at 9 months by his Uncle Harry Edison Schoenhut.) Ca. 1913-1930
.... $1,000-$1,200

12" Baby. Wood head, CM, blue ptd eyes, blonde mohair wig, bent-limb body, old clothes. Ca. 1913-1930 ..... $650-$700

12" Clothespin Boy. Round wood head, smiling mouth (a curved line), black "dot" eyes, red yarn hair/Dutch-cut style, wood body/legs/flat feet/clothespin-type arms, 2-pc pantsuit/belt. Ca.

1935 (Sold for $85 at auction in 1993) $165

12" Clothespin Girl. Round wooden head, red heart-shaped mouth, round blue ptd eyes, yellow yarn shoulder-length hair/curled bangs/page boy style, wood body/legs/flat feet, clothespin-type arms, original 2-pc pantsuit/belt. Ca. 1935 (Sold for $85 in 1993) $165

14" "102" Character Girl. (Dead). Wood head, CM, brown ptd/eyes, intaglio light brown ptd hair/center part/loose braid at the back decorated with a pink bow in the middle (some had blue bows), spring jtd wooden body, original clothes, etc. (This doll came in 4 sizes: 14" (Dead); 16" (Deafen); 19" (Dealer); 21" (Dear). These are code names used by telegraph operators who used a key punching system. Words or names could be telegraphed with more accuracy than numbers when filling orders Ca. 1916 (good condition) ....$2,000-$2,400+

14" "14/101" Character Girl. (Deacon). Wood head, smiling O/C mouth/teeth, brown ptd intaglio eyes, brown ptd/short carved hair, spring jtd wooden body, original clothes, etc. (In 1916 catalog size 16" named "Deaf" by code.) Ca. 1916+ (Good condition) ....$2,000-$2,400

14" "205" Character Boy. Wood head, CM, brown ptd intaglio eyes, brown ptd/carved hair swirled to side, spring jtd wooden body, original clothes, etc. (Face somewhat similar to 207 except eyes are larger. Came in 4 sizes.) Ca. 1912-1930 (Good condition) ....$2,000-$2,400

14" "207" Character Boy. Wood head, defiant CM, small blue ptd intaglio eyes, short brown ptd/carved hair with forelocks/deep comb marks, spring jtd wooden body, original clothes, etc. Ca. 1912-1915 (Good condition) ....$2,000-$2,400+

14" "310" Character Girl. Wood head/full face, CM, small blue ptd intaglio eyes, blonde HHW, spring jtd wooden body, original clothes, etc. (This doll has full or "thick" lips. Came in 4 sizes.) Ca. 1914-1920 (Good condition) ....$1,100-$1,500+

14" "316" doll-face girl. Wood head, O/C mouth/carved teeth, brown decal eyes, brown mohair wig, spring jtd wooden body, original clothes, etc. (Came in sized: 14", 16", 19", 21". These dolls were made to compete with the German open-mouth doll-face dolls and had decal eyes made to simulate glass.) Ca. 1915-1930 (Good condition) ....$800-$900

14" Character Boy. Wood head, somber CM, brown ptd intaglio eyes, brown ptd/carved earlobe-length hair, spring jtd wooden body, original clothes, etc. Ca. 1911-1930 (Good condition).........$2,000-$2,400

14" Character Girl. Toddler. Wood head, smiling O/C mouth/5 ptd teeth, chubby cheeks, blue ptd intaglio eyes, blonde ptd/carved short windblown bob/carved side ribbon, spring jtd wooden body, old clothes, etc. Ca. 1911-1930 (Good condition) ....$2,000-$2,400

14" Character Girl. Wood head, CM, brown ptd intaglio eyes, dark blonde ptd/carved side hair and fore-

locks/ptd/carved bathing cap with chin strap and decorated with stars and stripes, spring jtd wooden body, original clothes, etc. Ca. 1911 (Good condition) $3,000

14" Character Girl. Wood head, smiling CM, blue ptd intaglio eyes, blonde ptd/deeply carved hair/center part/rear intertwined braid/large bow, spring jtd wooden body, original clothes, etc. Ca. 1911-1930 (Good condition) ....$2,000-$2,400

14" Character Girl. Wood head, somber CM, brown ptd intaglio eyes, brown ptd/simply carved short hair/carved ribbon above front hairline, spring jtd wooden body, old clothes, etc. Ca. 1911-1930 (Good condition) ....$2,000-$2,400

15"-17" "Ma-Ma" Doll. Wood head/papier-mâché yoke, CM, blue ptd eyes, brown mohair wig, cloth body/wood hands/voice box, original clothes, etc. Designed by Harry F. Schoenhut. Mark: "H.E. SCHOENHUT 1913 (in a circle) C (in a circle) 1925." $700-$800

15" "103" Character Girl. Wood head, CM, blue ptd intaglio eyes, brown ptd/carved hair with blue ribbon band, spring jtd wooden body, original clothes, etc. Ca. 1916 (Good condition) ....$2,000-$2,400

15" "312" Character Girl. MIB. Doll tied inside box with cloth tapes; her stand is also tied into the box. Original chemise and shoes (on the doll); Wears a short, blonde mohair wig. Ca. 1911-1930 Mint (sold for $2,500 in 1995) $3,500

15" "Nature Baby." Wood head, O/C mouth, blue ptd eyes, blonde ptd hair, bent-limb wood body jtd at neck/sh./hips (5 spring units), old clothes. Schoenhut decal on her back. Ca. 1913 ....$850-$900+

15" "Snickelfritz." Character Infant Boy. Wood head/very expressive crying face, O/C mouth/upper/lower carved teeth, well-modeled large ears, blue ptd "squinty" intaglio eyes, brown ptd/molded short hair/deep comb marks, spring jtd wooden body, original baby clothes. Trademark registered in U.S.A. in 1911. Ca. 1911-1914 ...$2,700-$3,000

15" "Tootsie Wootsie." Character Boy. Wood head, CM, blue ptd intaglio eyes, brown ptd/molded hair, spring jtd wooden body, original clothes, etc. Ca. 1911-1930 $3,500

15" Character Girl. Wood head, CM, brown ptd intaglio eyes, light brown ptd/carved hair, spring jtd wooden body, original coral and white 3-pc outfit, etc. Blue and orange pin reads: "Schoenhut Art Wood Doll USA." Ca. 1915-20 (good condition) ....$2,000-$2,400

15-1/2" "Sleep-eyed" Girl. Dolly face. Wood head, O/C mouth/carved teeth, long brown HHW, spring jtd wooden body, old clothes. Ca. 1920-1930 (Good condition) $1,000

16" "100" Character Girl. (Daddy). Wood head, CM, blue intaglio eyes, black ptd/carved hair/bangs/short sides cover ears in a "Dutch" cut, spring jtd wooden body, old clothes, etc. Ca. 1911-1930 (Good condition) ....$2,000-$2,400

16" "16/203" Character Boy. Wood head, smiling O/C mouth/carved teeth, cheek dimples, blue ptd intaglio eyes, blonde ptd short carved hair/deep comb marks/straggly forehead locks, spring jtd wooden body, original clothes, etc. (Face similar to 203 except for dimples.) Ca. 1915-1919 (Good condition) ....$2,000-$2,400+

16" "16/705" Character Girl. (Resembles Kammer & Reinhardt's 114 mold.) Wood head, pouty CM, small blue ptd intaglio eyes, original blonde mohair wig, spring jtd wooden body, original clothes, etc. (No. "16/705" is for the dressed catalog version, and not the head number.) Ca. 1911-1912 (Good condition) ....$1,200-$1,600+

16" "201" Character Boy. (Daggle) wood head, somber CM, blue ptd/intaglio eyes, orange blonde ptd/carved hair "brushed" casually forward on face, large ears, spring jtd wooden body, original clothes, etc. Ca. 1911-1914 (1930) (Good condition) ....$2,000-$2,400+

16" "202" Character Boy. (Dagoba). Wood head, CM, blonde ptd/carved hair spring jtd wooden body, original clothes, etc. ("Dagoba" was a code name for filling telegraph orders.) Ca. 1911+ ....$2,000-$2,400+

16" "204" Character Boy. Wood head, sad CM, blue ptd intaglio eyes, brown ptd/carved short hair/forelock lock/deep comb marks, spring jtd wooden body, original clothes, etc. Ca. 1915-1930 (Good condition) .... $2,000-$2,400

16" "300" Character Girl. Wood head/chubby cheeks, sad CM, blue ptd intaglio eyes, blonde HHW, spring jtd wooden body, original clothes, etc. Ca. 1911-1923 (Good condition) ....$1,100-$1,500+

16" "301" Character Girl. (Daily). Wood head, faintly smiling CM, blue ptd intaglio eyes, brown mohair wig, spring jtd wooden body, original clothes, etc. 1911+ (Mint) ....$1,900-$2,400+

16" "403" Character "Soldier" Boy. Wood head, sullen CM, blue ptd eyes (intaglio), blonde HHW, spring jtd wooden body, original uniform, etc. Ca. 1915-1917 (Mint) ....$1,900-$2,400

16" "Chinese" Man. Wood head, orange ptd CM, black ptd intaglio eyes/thick black eyebrows, large ears, black ptd/carved hair, spring jtd wooden body, original black silk Chinese outfit, etc. (This is the stock head used on the familiar 19" mannequin doll and placed on a child's body to simulate the shorter Oriental body structure). Ca. 1915+ .....$2,500+

16" "Dolly face" girl. Wood head, O/C mouth/carved teeth, blue-green decal eyes, blonde mohair wig, spring jtd wooden body, original pinkcheek dress, shoes, socks, badge pin, etc. Ca. 1915 (Mint) ....$1000-$1,100

16" Oriental Boy. Wood head, CM, dark brown ptd eyes, black mohair wig, bent-limb baby body, original elaborate costume, head-dress, shoes, socks. Ca. 1913-30 ....$3,000+

16" Oriental Girl. Wood head, CM, dark brown ptd/eyes, black mohair wig, bent-limb baby body, original elaborate costume, head-dress, shoes, socks, etc. Ca. 1913-30 ....$3,000

Chapter 38

~ SIMON & HALBIG ~

History: 1870-1920+

Simon & Halbig, Grafenhain near Ohrdruf, Thuringia, Germany, 1870-1920. Simon of Hildburghausen and Halbig companies merged and called their factory Simon & Halbig. Although they made complete dolls in small quantities, they specialized in dolls' heads and parts. These were made in bisque, composition and celluloid. They also made all bisque dolls. Like most of the early doll manufacturers, they made doll types that were popular during their times, i.e., parians, molded hairdo bisques and limbs, lady dolls, Parisiennes, and, later child and baby dolls, including "bathing" dolls. The United States was their biggest buyer of dolls, with Germany and France running a close second.

Heads marked "DEP" (Deponiertes Geschmacksmuster) were made for the French trade and assembled in France with French paperweight eyes, French wigs, French bodies, and French-made clothing. There were two versions of some heads one for the mass-market and one for the French. The mass-market head(s) had German glass eyes, German wigs, German bodies, and costumed in Germany in cheap commercial finery—if at all. (Usually a chemise.) German-made heads designed for the French market were painted similarly to the finest French dolls of the moment Jumeau, Bru, A.T., etc. Even the bisque was of the finest, palest, and smoothest "French" quality. Of course, these dolls were sold in France as "French dolls."

After 1900 Simon & Halbig made most of the French heads (until World War One), but they were not always up to previous standards. Not until 1910, did Simon & Halbig glean their just rewards, and this came in the guise of "character" heads (100 series) for Kammer & Reinhardt, who subsequently purchased the Simon & Halbig company in 1920.

An interesting footnote in the Simon & Halbig doll history is their participation in the creation of a doll head sculpted in the likeness of the silent screen's greatest star, America's Sweetheart, Mary Pickford. The clay model was sculpted from photographs by Berlin artist Lilly Baitz. Miss Baitz was well-known for her dolls of theatrical folk. She exhibited at the Leipzig Fair in 1919. The S&H factory poured the head in the finest bisque and painted the features. The doll had inset glass eyes, real eyelashes, dark brown eyeshadow, feathered eyebrows, an open-closed mouth with painted teeth, a luxurious long-curl dark blonde mohair wig, and a ball-jointed composition and wood body. It was dressed in a whitework dress. The doll was made circa 1922.

Collecting Hints:

A Simon & Halbig doll is not a "poor man's" French doll, but a doll as fine as any good-quality French doll. In fact, it is just as much a "French doll" as is a Jules Steiner, which is actually more a German doll than a true French doll. Confusing? It need not be. Simon & Halbig made not only a wide range of dolly-face dolls but the more serious character heads that today's collectors spend their all on. They catered tot he French market, and S&H heads are frequently found on marked Jumeau bodies. A few tips: 1000 number series began in 1889 with 1008. 1079 (GM registration in 1892). The earliest S&H marks depicts a seated Chinese. It was registered in 1875. DEP incised with the mark dates the doll after 1887. The mark SH (minus the ampersand) supposedly dates a doll prior to 1905.

Simon & Halbig made heads for the following companies: C.M. Bergmann, Carl Bergner, Cuno & Otto Dressel, R. Eekhoff, Fleischmann & Bloedel, Hamburger & Co., Heinrich Handwerck, Adolf Hulss, Jumeau, Louis Lindner, Roullet & Decamps, Franz Schmidt, S.F.B.J., Carl Trautmann, Welsch & Co., Hugo Wiegand, Wiesenthal Schindel & Kallenberg, Adolph Wislizenus.

SIMON & HALBIG

7" Chinese Baby Girl. Bisque socket head, OM/teeth, inset brown glass eyes, black HHW, jtd.. bisque body/limbs, original 2-pc outfit, elaborate head-dress, shoes. Ca. 1900+ $1,200

7" 1079 Girl. Bisque head, OM/teeth, blue glass sleep eyes, unpierced ears, brown mohair wig, cheap 5-pc compo. body/black ptd.. double-strap shoes/white stockings, old clothes. Mark: "1079 Halbig S&H Germany 4/0." Ca. 1889-1930s $350

9" 939 Girl. Bisque head, CM, spiral-threaded blue glass eyes, blonde mohair wig, jtd.. bisque body, original clothes, hat, ptd./molded shoes with ankle straps/stockings. 1880s or early 1900s $2,600

9-1/2" "S7H" Girl. Bisque shoulder head, CM, inset brown glass eyes, long HHW, PE, cloth body/bisque lower arms, old clothes, etc. Incised on front shoulder plate: "S7H." Ca. 1870s $800

10" "SH 950" Character Boy. Pale bisque head, CM, inset brown glass eyes, PE, light blonde mohair wig, original cloth body/bisque lower arms, original clothes, hat, etc. Ca. 1880+ $800-$850

11" "1079" Girl. Pale bisque head/smooth texture, OM/molded teeth, huge inset brown glass eyes, PE, blonde mohair wig, BJ "French-made" body, old clothes, etc. Mark: "S&H 1079 DEP 2 1/2 Germany." Ca. 1889-1930s .... $725-$825

11" "1160" Young Lady. "Little Women" type. Pale bisque shoulder head, CM, inset brown glass eyes, brown HHW, PE, cloth body/bisque limbs/black ptd.. boots/blue ptd.. garters, original clothes, hat. Ca. 1900 .... $525-$550

26-3/4" "S//H 1010 DEP" incised girl. Bisque shoulder head, OM/teeth, blonde HHW, PE, blue glass sleep eyes, kid body/bisque lower arms, old clothes, hat, etc. 1889+ $1,100-$1,200. (Courtesy of Herron)

11" "1269" Girl. Bisque head, OM/teeth, brown glass sleep eyes, PE, blonde mohair wig, BJ compo. body, old clothes, etc. Ca. 1889-1930s $700

11" Negro Character Girl. Light brown bisque head, OM/4 upper teeth, brown glass sleep eyes, original kinky black mohair wig/cork pate, dark brown ptd../jtd.. compo. body, old clothes, etc. Incised: "1358//1/2." Ca. 1890s $6,000

11-1/2" "1160-1" Young Lady. "Little Women" type. Bisque shoulder head, CM, inset blue glass eyes, blonde mohair wig, PE, kid body/bisque lower arms, original gown, etc. Head mark: "S&H 1160-1." Ca. 1900 ....$550

13" "10SH2" Girl. Bisque shoulder head, OM/teeth, brown glass sleep eyes, blonde HHW, kid body/bisque lower arms, old clothes, etc. Ca. 1889-1930s $625

13" "939" Girl. Pale bisque socket head, OM/teeth, blue glass sleep eyes, brown mohair wig, PE, BJ compo. body, old clothes, etc. Ca. 1889-1930s ...$1,650

14" "1368" Negro Boy. Black bisque socket head, OM/teeth (thick lips), black curly mohair wig, black BJ compo. body, old clothes, etc. Ca. 1890s (Sold for $3,100 in 1992) $4,000

14-1/2" "1249" or "Santa." Bisque swivel head on bisque shoulder plate. OM/teeth, inset brown glass eyes, PE, blonde HHW, kid body/compo. jtd.. arms, old clothes, etc. Ca. 1889-1930s $1,200

15" "1469" Can-Can Dancer. Bisque head, CM, brown glass sleep eyes, brown mohair wig, PE, BJ compo. lady body/bosom/slim limbs, original French "Can-Can" costume: long black moiré print dress with full skirt, skirt lined with pink and blue ruffles, strapless top, short cotton drawers, black lace stockings/black satin garter belt, bronze-colored high-heeled pumps, black velvet

hat with red plume, etc. Ca. 1910+ ....$3,700-$4,700

15" "Dep. 6" Oriental Girl. Bisque head, OM, brown glass sleep eyes, PE, black mohair wig, BJ compo. body, original clothes. Mark: "Germany Dep. 6." Ca. 1900+ $2,800

15" "S 5 H" Character Girl. Pale bisque head, CM, blue glass sleep eyes, waxed eyelids, PI ears, blonde mohair wig, sawdust-stuffed cloth body/stiff cloth legs/bisque lower arms, original French "regional" costume, headdress, etc. Ca. 1879 ....$2,000+

15" "S&H/Heinrich Handwerck" Girl. Bisque head, OM/teeth, blue glass sleep eyes, PE, blonde mohair wig, BJ compo. body, old clothes, Ca. 1885+ ....$800-$850

15" Parisienne. Pale bisque swivel head on pale bisque shoulder plate, CM, inset blue PW eyes, blonde mohair wig, PE, gusseted kid body/small waist/wide hips, original "French-made" clothes, hat, boots, etc. (This doll resembles a Jumeau and was obviously dressed in France for the French trade.) 1870s (Price includes original clothes, etc.) $3,500

16" "116/A" Character Boy. Bisque head/chubby cheeks, smiling O/C mouth/upper teeth, inset blue glass eyes, blonde mohair wig, bent-limb compo. body, old clothes, etc. Ca. 1909+ (Bisque head by S&H for Kammer & Reinhardt who purchased the company in 1920.) $2,800

16-1/2" "1010" Girl. Bisque shoulder head, OM/teeth, blue glass sleep eyes, blonde mohair wig, PE, kid body/bisque lower arms, old clothes, etc. Ca. 1889-1930s $750

17" "1009" Girl. Bisque socket head, OM/6 teeth, blue glass sleep eyes, blonde mohair wig, BJ compo./wood body, old clothes, etc. Head mark: "S&H 1009//DEP Germany 5 1/2." (The 1009 mold numbers were registered in 1889.) Ca. 1889+ $1,300

17" "1039" Dolly-face Girl. Walker. Lovely bisque socket head, OM/teeth, blue glass sleep eyes, sausage curl HHW, jtd.. compo. (working) mechanical body/key, original whitework dress, etc. Ca. 1889-1930s $2,200

17" "1248" Negro Girl. Very dark bisque head (dolly face), OM/teeth, red ptd.. OM, dark brown glass sleep eyes, black mohair wig, dark brown BJ compo. body, old clothes, etc. Mark: "1248." Ca. 1889-1930s $2,000

17-1/2" "Le Petite Parisien" Girl. Bisque head, OM/teeth, blue glass sleep eyes, blonde mohair wig, PE, BJ compo. body, original silk dress, bonnet, etc. Incised: "Simon Halbig//K (star) R//13." Paper label on body reads: "Le Petite Parisien 1889." 1889 ....$1,500

17-1/2" "S&H" incised lady. Pale bisque shoulder head, CM, inset almond-shaped blue glass eyes, PI ears (pierced in), blonde mohair wig, original cloth body/bisque arms with molded elbow ball that fits into socket on upper arm, original clothes, etc. Mark: "S&H" on front shoulder plate. 1870s $2,000+

18" "1078" Character Girl. Bisque head, OM/teeth, blue glass sleep eyes, brown mohair wig, PE, BJ compo. body, elaborate French "regional" costume, head-dress, etc. Incised: "1078 S&H 5." Box label reads: "Grand Bazar nouvelles Galeries/Colmar." Ca. 1900 MIB ....$2,000+

22" "SH 1079-10. DEP" incised girl. 1889-1930s. $950-$1,100. (Courtesy of D. Kay Crow)

22" Simon & Halbig lady doll. Bisque head, OM/teeth, blue glass sleep eyes, brown HHW, PE, BJ compo body/mld bosom, costumed in replica of real bride's gown. Ca. 1910 $2,500. (Courtesy of D. Kay Crow)

16" "Simon & Halbig/K (star) R/39" incised girl. Bisque head, OM/teeth, blue glass sleep eyes, brown wig, PE, BJ compo body, old clothes. 1895+ $850-$900. (Courtesy of D. Kay Crow)

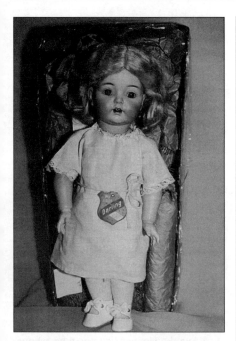

15" "Simon & Halbig 121/36" incised girl. Bisque head, OM/teeth, blue glass sleep eyes, blonde mohair wig, BJ compo toddler body, original chemise, etc. Tag reads: "My Little Darling." Box label reads: "My Little Darling//K (star) R." $2,000. (Courtesy of D. Kay Crow)

18" "1329" Burmese Girl. Yellow bisque head, OM/4 teeth, brown glass sleep eyes, black mohair wig/original set/flowers/beads/tassels, PE/earrings, yellow tinted BJ compo. body, original red silk embroidered kimono, long trousers, tiny feet with original platform soles, etc. Mark: "1329 Germany Simon & Halbig S&H 5." Ca. 1915 $3,500

18" "1428" Character Toddler. Bisque head, O/C mouth, blue glass sleep eyes, brown HHW, BJ compo. body (toddler type), old clothes, bonnet, etc. (This is a rather ugly baby, but a rare one.) Ca. 1909+ ....$3,000-$3,200

18" "Germany//Simon & Halbig//S&H//6" Negro Girl. Black baked-in bisque head/Negroid features, OM/small teeth/very thick lips, dark brown glass sleep eyes/black eye wax, PE long earrings, black curly mohair wig, black BJ compo. body/no wooden parts, old clothes, etc. Ca. 1900 ....$3,500

18" "S 10 H//949" Girl. Bisque head/"oily" finish, CM, inset brown glass eyes, brown HHW, PI ears, BJ compo. body/voice box/pull strings, old clothes, etc. Ca. 1879 ....$3,000

18" "S7H" Molded Bisque or Parian. Pale bisque shoulder head, CM, large blue ptd.. eyes, blonde ptd../molded hair with a black molded band or ribbon across top of head, original cloth body/bisque lower arms, old clothes. Mark: "S 7 H." 1870s $1,800

19" "1049" Girl. Bisque head, OM/teeth, blue glass eyes, brown mohair wig, BJ compo. body, old clothes, etc. Mark: "Heinrich Handwerck/Simon & Halbig." (Forehead has a "W" incised which means "Wimpern" or in German "Wimper" meaning "eyelash"; found on

dolls with fur and painted eyelashes.) Ca. 1885+ $850

19" "1080" or "Dainty Dorothy." Bisque shoulder head, OM/4 teeth, blue glass sleep eyes, blonde mohair wig, PE, kid body/rivets, bisque lower arms, original clothes, etc. Head mark: "Germany/Simon & Halbig/1080. S & H 7." Body sticker reads: "Dainty Dorothy copyright 1910 Germany." (Sears & Roebuck catalogs advertised "Dainty Dorothy" dolls from 1910-1930. They were not only made by Simon & Halbig, but J.D. Kestner, Gerbruder Heubach, and Armand Marseille.) Ca. 1910+ $750

19" "1358" Negro Girl. Light brown bisque head, red-orange OM/teeth (6), large brown glass sleep eyes, black molded/feathered eyebrows, long black mohair wig, PE, BJ compo. brown body, original clothes, hat, etc. Ca. 1889+ ....$8,5000-$9,000

19" "739" Negro Girl. Black bisque head, OM/teeth, inset brown glass eyes, thick black eyebrows, black fur wig, PE, brown BJ body, old clothes, etc. Mark: "Simon Halbig (in red ink on buttocks); "Handwerck" (on head) "S 11 H 739 Dep." Ca. 1880+ ....$3,000-$3,500

19" "939" Character Girl. Pale bisque head, CM, inset huge blue threaded bulging glass eyes, heavy dark "French" eyebrows, BJ "French" body/straight wrists/closed finger, original "French-made" clothes, etc. (The body is painted yellow, typical of the bodies the Germans used for the French market. It also has the large French hands.) Ca. 1897 ....$3,500

20" "1079" Girl. Bisque head/poor quality/high coloring, OM/teeth, inset blue glass threaded eyes, blonde mohair wig, ordinary eyebrow painting, BJ compo. body, old clothes, etc. (This version of the below doll was made for the mass-market, and is a cheaper doll in every aspect.) Mark: "1079//S&H" (script)//DEP.//8//Germany............$850

20" "1079" Girl. Pale bisque head/double chin, OM/teeth, large blue PW eyes, thick dark brown eyebrows/straight bottoms/molded-in eyebrow ridge (earlier dolls did not have this feature), 2 rear holes for stringing, auburn mohair wig, BJ compo. body, old clothes, etc. (This lovely doll has the fine early bisque, delicate French coloring and painting. Made for the French trade.) 1889-1930s Mark: "1079//S&H" (script)//DEP.//8" ....$950-$1,000

20" "1099" Japanese Girl. Olive bisque head, OM/teeth, slanted brown glass sleep eyes/arched brows, double chin, black mohair wig, BJ compo. body/lovely hands, original silk kimono, head-dress, etc. Early 20th c. ....$3,400-$3,700

20" "119" Girl. Pale bisque head/double chin/dimple, OM/teeth, brown HHW, PI ears, BJ compo. body, old clothes, etc. Ca. 1885+ Mark: "S&H 110//DEP." (S&H head on Handwerck body.) $1,000

20" "719" Character Girl. Pale bisque head/pointed chin with dimple, CM, large blue threaded glass eyes, heavy dark French eyebrows, dark brown

HHW, BJ compo. body, old clothes, etc. Mark: "S&H (in script) 719 DEP." Ca. 1879 ....$3,700-$4,000

20" "750" Character Girl. Solid-dome bisque turned shoulder head, CM, large inset blue PW eyes, blonde mohair wig, kid body/bisque lower arms, old clothes, etc. Mark: "S 7 H 750 DEP." ca. 1880s+ $2,200

20" "939" Girl. Bisque head, OM/2 square teeth (uppers)/1 square lower tooth, brown PW eyes, PE, blonde mohair wig, BJ compo. body, old clothes, etc. Mark: "S 12 H 939." Ca. 1889-1930s $2,500

20" "949" Girl. Pale bisque head, OM/teeth, inset blue PW eyes, PE, brown mohair wig, BJ compo. body, old clothes, etc. Ca. 1889-1930s ... $2,400

21" "Simon & Halbig//K (star) R//65" incised girl. Oily bisque head, OM/teeth, blue glass sleep eyes, brown HHW, BJ compo body, old clothes, etc. $1,000-$1,200. (Courtesy of D. Kay Crow)

21" "1079" World War One Nurse. Bisque head, OM/teeth, blue glass sleep eyes, blond mohair wig, BJ compo. body, original WW 1 nurse uniform, head-dress, hot water bottle, thermometer, etc. Ca. 1915 ....$3,000

21" "1159" Lady. Bisque head, OM/teeth, inset blue glass eyes, blonde mohair wig, PE, BJ lady body/bosom/slim limbs, original clothes. Ca. 1910 ....$2,500

21" "739" Negro Girl. Black bisque head (non-ethnic features), CM, large inset dark brown glass eyes, black curly mohair wig, BJ compo. body, old clothes, etc. Ca. 1880+ $3,700

21-1/4" "920" Girl. Bisque shoulder head, O/C mouth, inset blue glass eyes, blonde mohair wig, PE, gusseted kid body/bisque lower arms, old clothes, etc. Ca. 1880+ $2,200

22" "1159" Gibson Girl. Bisque head, OM/teeth, brown glass sleep eyes, brown mohair wig set in the "Gibson Girl" style, PE, BJ "French-type" compo. body/small waist/hips/bosom, original cotton print long dress, chemise, drawers, high-button shoes, stockings. Mark: "S&H 1159." Ca. 1910 ..$2,500+

22" "1299" Character Girl. Bisque head/chubby cheeks, OM/teeth, blue glass sleep eyes, blonde mohair wig, BJ compo. body, old clothes, etc. Ca. 1909 ....$2,200

22" "151" Character Boy. Bisque head, O/C mouth/molded teeth, brown glass eyes, brown HHW, BJ compo. body, old clothes. Ca. 1910+ (Sold for $3,200 in 1989.) ....$10,000-$11,000

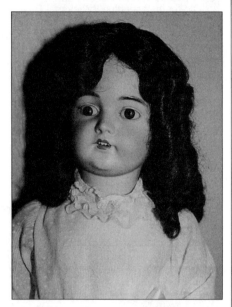

31" "S&H/1079/DEP//Germany//14" incised girl. 1889-1930s $1,500-$1,600. (Courtesy of D. Kay Crow)

22" Edison Phonograph Doll. Bisque head #719, OM/teeth, blue glass sleep eyes, blonde mohair wig, metal body holds talking mechanism (13 patent dates on body, 1878-89)/wood jtd.. limbs/compo. hands/feet, original clothes, etc. (According to Mr. Melvin Weig, Supt. Edison Laboratory National Monument, Orange, N.J., 1962, the Edison Talking Dolls were made in West Orange for only 18 months, 1889-90, in sizes 22" only, with a metal body and compo. limbs. The wax records of 1889-90 were rather fragile for toy use, thus were short-lived; reason so few are found nowadays. Mr. Edison's first talking dolls bore non resemblance to this doll.) Workable. Rare. 1899-90 ....$5,000+

22" Negro Girl. Chocolate brown bisque head, OM/teeth, brown PW eyes, original black curly mohair wig, PE, back BJ compo. body, original red silk dress with long sleeves and lace trim, matching hat, stockings, shoes (marked "France"). Head mark: "S 12 H 739 DEP." Ca. 1910 (This is an elaborate version of number 739 made for the French trade.) ....$4,000-$4,500

22-1/2" "570" or "Baby Blanche." Pale bisque head, OM/teeth, brown glass sleep eyes, blonde mohair wig, PE, BJ

compo. body, old clothes, bonnet, etc. Ca. 1889-1930s ....$900-$950

23" "550" Girl. Bisque head, OM/teeth, blue glass sleep eyes, blonde mohair wig, PE, BJ compo. body, old clothes, etc. Mark: "550//Germany, C//Simon & Halbig/S&H." Ca. 1889-1930s $975

23" "S 12 H" Parian. Pale bisque shoulder head/double chine/chin dimples/mumps cheeks, CM, pale pink cheek blush, dark "French" eyebrows, blonde ptd../molded hairdo/curly bangs/short rear hair, exposed PE/earrings, inset dark brown glass eyes, kid body/limbs, old clothes. Mark: "S 12 H Simon & Halbig." Ca. 1870s $2,700

24" "1080" Dolly-face Girl. Bisque shoulder head, OM/teeth, brown glass sleep eyes, blonde mohair wig, PE, kid body/bisque lower arms, old clothes, etc. Ca. 1889-1930s $950

24" "1159" Lady. Bisque head/long neck, OM/teeth, brown glass sleep eyes, blonde mohair wig, PE, BJ wood "lady" body/bosom/slim limbs, original corset, petticoat, lingerie cap, shoes, stockings. (Another variation in original costume and size of this mold numbered lady. This particular doll used to display underwear in a corsetier's shop.) Ca. 1910 (Sold for $3,200 in 1992) $4,000

24" "1250" Girl. Bisque head, OM/teeth, brown glass sleep eyes, brown HHW, PE, BJ compo. body, old whitework dress, etc. 1889-1930s $1,200

24" "540" or "Baby Blanche." Bisque head, OM/teeth, blue glass sleep eyes, blonde mohair wig, PE, BJ compo. body, old clothes, etc. Ca. 1889-1930s $975

24" "719" Character Girl. Bisque shoulder head, CM, inset brown glass eyes, auburn HHW, PE, pink kid body/compo. upper arms/bisque lower arms, old whitework and lace dress, etc. Head mark: "Simon & Halbig//719-S 13 H." 1879 ....$4,000

24" "719" Character Girl. Early pale bisque head, CM, delicate cheek coloring, thick brown eyebrows, inset brown glass eyes, PE, brown HHW, BJ compo. wood body, old clothes, etc. Ca. 1879 ....$4,500

24" "1489" or "Erika" Toddler. Bisque head/chubby cheeks, OM/2 teeth, blue glass sleep eyes, blonde mohair wig, PE, B compo. toddler body, old clothes, etc. Ca. 1889-1930s $5,000

24" "1079" Girl. Bisque head, OM/teeth, brown glass sleep eyes, brown mohair wig, PE, chin dimple, BJ compo. body, old clothes, hat, etc. Mark: "S&H. 1079//DEP Germany 13/" Ca. 1889-1930s $1,150

25" "908" Parisienne. Bisque swivel head on bisque shoulder plate/"oily" texture, OM/teeth, blue-grey glass threaded sleep eyes/shiny eyebrows, blonde mohair wig/glued-on cork pate, PT ears, kid body/cloth and kid over-jackets/kid limbs, hand-sewn lower legs/toe stitching/stitched fingers, old clothes, etc. Ca. 1880 ....$2,500

25" "939" Girl. Pale bisque head, CM, inset blue PW eyes, brown HHW, PE, heavy dark eyebrows, chunky German

BJ compo. body/straight wrists, old clothes, etc. Ca. 1879... $4,000-$4,500

25-1/2" "S 14 H//949" Character Girl. Solid-dome "Belton-type" bisque head has small holes), CM, blue glass sleep eyes, blonde mohair wig, PE, BJ compo. body, old clothes, etc. Ca. 1879 ....$3,400

26" "939" Girl. "Belton-type" bisque head, CM, inset blue PW eyes, blonde mohair wig, PE, BJ "French" compo./wood body/straight wrists, old whitework cotton dress, bonnet, etc. Mark: S 15 H 939" (This doll has a "Jumeau" look and was made for the French market). Ca. 1879 ....$5,500

26" "CM Bergmann" Girl. Bisque head, OM/teeth, blue glass sleep eyes, brown mohair wig, PE, BJ compo. body, old clothes, etc. Mark: "CM BERGMANN/SIMON & HALBIG/12." (Choice Bermann as it is also inscribed with the name "Simon & Halbig." Charles M. Bergmann had a doll factory in Waltershausen, Thur., Germany. He was an American cowboy before he turned dollmaker. Upon his return to Germany he worked for two German firms where he learned the business thoroughly. He registered patents for designs for ball-jointed bodies.) Ca. 1888+ ... $800

26" "S & C" Girl. Bisque socket head, OM/teeth, brown glass sleep eyes, brown mohair wig, PE, BJ "Jumeau" marked compo. body, old white-work dress, etc. Made by Franz Schmidt & Co., Georgenthal near Waltershausen, Thur., Germany (used S&H heads). Ca. 1890+ $1,000

26-1/2" "66" Dolly-face Girl. Bisque head, OM/4 teeth, brown glass sleep eyes, brown HHW, PE, BJ compo. body, old clothes, etc. Mark: "K (star) R Simon & Halbig//66." Ca. 1908................$1,300

27" "939" Girl. Bisque head, CM, large brown glass eyes, brown mohair wig, PE, BJ body/compo./wood, old clothes, etc. Ca. 1879 ....$5,500

16" "K (star) R//Simon Halbig//117/A" incised girl or "Mein Liebling." $4,000-$4,500. (Courtesy of D. Kay Crow)

28" "1079" Girl. Pale bisque swivel head on pale bisque shoulder plate, OM/teeth, large brown glass sleep eyes, blonde mohair wig, PE, kid body/bisque lower arms, old clothes, hat, etc. (Front shoulder plate incised: "SH 1041 13." Head and shoulder plate original to doll. Shoulder plate lined with kid leather.) Ca. 1889-1930s $1,350

28" "1339" Character Girl. Bisque head/pug nose/dimpled chine, OM/4 upper teeth, brown glass sleep eyes, protruding PE, blonde HHW, BJ compo./wood body/attached compo. shoulder plate, old clothes, etc. Head mark: "1339//S&H//LL & S//13." Body mark: "D.R.G.M.//357529." (L.L. & S. mark attributed to Louis Lindner & Son of the famous Lindner family, Sonneberg, Thur., Germany, 1863-1914.) Ca. 1909 ....$2,700

28" "DEP" Negro Girl. Brown bisque head, OM/teeth, large brown glass flirty eyes, real lashes, black mohair wig, PE, brown BJ compo. body, old clothes, etc. Mark: "S&H DEP, 14, Germany." Ca. 1905 ....$5,000+

29" "1348" Girl. Bisque head, OM/teeth, blue glass sleep eyes, blonde HHW, PE, BJ compo. body, old clothes, etc. Head mark: "1348//Jutta//Simon & Halbig." Ca. 1910 (Cuno, & Otto Dressel, Germany, commissioned other doll companies to make heads under their trademark. The name JUTTA was registered in 1907, and is found on various dolls, including character babies. The number 1348 in considered rare.) Ca. 1910 ....$2,000

30" "C.M. Bergmann" Girl. Bisque head, OM/teeth, blue glass sleep eyes, brown HHW, PE, BJ compo. body/long slender legs, old clothes, etc. Mark: "C.M. Bergmann/Simon & Halbig 14." (Christopher Bergmann worked for Handwerck before establishing his own factory in Waltershausen, Thuringia, Germany, in 1888. He had been a cowboy and miner in America, and a lawyer's clerk in Waltershausen. The Bergmann factory only made bodies. They purchased heads from Simon & Halbig, Armand Marseille, and Alt, Beck & Gottschalck. They used S&H heads exclusively in the 1920s on their expensive dolls. They went bankrupt in 1931. Ca. late 1920s (1920s) $1,250

30" "1079" Dolly-face Girl. Bisque head, OM/teeth, brown glass sleep eyes, auburn HHW, PE, BJ compo. body, original whitework dress with tucking, etc. Ca. 1889-1930s $1,600

31" "C.M. Bergmann" Girl. Bisque head by S&H, OM/teeth, inset brown glass eyes/lashes, inset fur eyebrows, BJ compo. body, old whitework dress with eyelet and lace yoke, etc. Ca. 1910+ $1,300

33" "1249" Dolly-face Girl. Bisque head, OM/teeth, blue glass sleep eyes, brown HHW, PE, BJ compo. body, old whitework dress with a high waist, etc. Ca. 1889-1930s $2,500

34" "939" Girl. Bisque head, OM/teeth, blue glass sleep eyes, brown mohair wig, PE, BJ compo. body, old clothes, etc. Ca. 1889-1930s $3,500

34" "979" Girl. Bisque head, OM/teeth, almond-shaped inset blue PW eyes, dimpled chin, old blonde HHW, PE, BJ compo. wood body, old or original "French" clothes, etc. (This doll has a "French" persona.) Ca. 1889-1930s $3,600

36" "1079" Girl. Bisque head, OM/teeth, brown glass sleep eyes, brown HHW, PE, BJ compo. body, old clothes, etc. Ca. 1889-1930s $2,500

42" "949" Girl. Lovely bisque socket head, OM/teeth, brown glass sleep eyes, brown HHW, PE, BJ compo. body, old clothes, etc. Ca. 1910 ....$4,300

Chapter 39

∼ STEIFF ∼

History: 1892-1990s

Margarete Steiff (1847-1909); Giengen, Wurtemberg, Germany. Fraulein Steiff's soft toy making career began by accident. A polio victim and a cripple, she had been confined to a wheelchair since childhood, having contacted the fatal illness at the age of eighteen months. Being skilled with the needle, she began making stuffed elephants which she gave away to the neighborhood children. Her elephants were so well-made and unique that friends and relatives encouraged her to open a small business. She hired a few women to help her sew and assemble the animals she designed. These were made from felt pieces given to her by a local felt factory. Her felt dolls date to around 1892 and were made until 1914. These comic characters varied in size; the largest "display" figures measuring from four-to-six feet. Jean Doin, who wrote "Renaissance de la Poupee Francaise" (Gazette des Beaux Arts, 1916), would describe them as "little horrors."

Although homely and simplistic, they did possess a peculiar Germanic sense of humor. Steiff catalogs advertised dolls with "un-breakable" mask faces as early as 1892. There were 21 different character types, 10-inches tall, and were similar to dolls made by Cuno & Otto Dressel during this period. The Steiffs must have been dissatisfied with the heads of these dolls, because an 1897 catalog illustrated dolls with bisque heads. In 1902, Richard Steiff expressed his dislike of the dolls, and in 1903 new designs were introduced. These dolls were more original than the old-fashioned type the company had been making. They had velvet or felt bodies, velvet faces, hand-painted features, button eyes, and well-made costumes. Their amusing countenance, large feet, and durability, set them apart from ordinary dolls; especially since they caricaturized the eccentricities of the common folk. Their comic-strip and storybook characters date from 1904.

Albert Schlopsnies, a Munich artist and advertising expert, designed many of Steiff's dolls (1910-1924). He broadened the line with cowboys, Indians, Eskimos, etc. Margarete Steiff died in 1909 and business dwindled during World War One. The Schlopsnies Doll sported the popular "celluloid" head in 1921. It was manufactured until 1925. The pressed mask faces were made from 1925 to 1938; the seam was at the back of the neck. The Steiff company was still active. Their new designs, Alice with Rabbit, Peter with Goat, and Siegfried with Dragon were issued in editions of 600 each.

Collecting Hints:

Now that doll collecting has become and international hobby, or, better still, and "investment program," Steiff dolls, like all of the most coveted types, has moved out of the realm and reach of the average pocketbook and has moved into the big money circles. Fewer women dolls were made than men dolls, so these are considered rare and in demand. Other desirable types include children's book characters, comic-strip characters, and tradespeople. All original costumes and accessories add to a doll's value. Dolls made during the period 1900-1920 are highly sought and prices vary from $1,000 - $5,000+. Auction prices continue to surprise even the most jaded collector.

Reproduction Alert:

Steiff has reproduced some of its more popular designed from the past, including: Tennis Lady Bette(1986), Mr. Councellor (1986), Gentleman in Morning Coat (1986), Coloro the Clown (1988), Onkel Sam (1994). Reproductions of old dolls are always expensive, but when the original company reproduces a doll, a collector is assured that it is not a fraud made in a third world country without authorization, hence future value is more intact.

STEIFF

10-1/2" Tyrolean Boy and Girl. All-felt/jdt body, CM, inset blue glass eyes, blonde mohair wigs, original short trousers, jacket, hat, etc. (ear clip incised "Steiff"); girl wears original outfit, hat, etc. (ear clip incised "Steiff."). ... $1,600

10-1/2" Policeman. Molded felt face/jtd felt body, CM, button eyes, original blue uniform, cap, etc. This clockwork doll walks forward and backwards when wound. Ca. 1913.................... $2,000+

10-1/2" Hedgehogs. Male and Female. Film characters created by Ferdinand Diehl in 1937. Molded rubber heads, CM, black ptd eyes/nose, "fur" hair, felt bodies/semi-articulated, felt and cotton (removable) clothes. 1952+ $500

12""Dach." Molded felt face/face seam/felt body jtd at neck/sh/hips, black button eyes, CM, ptd gray hair, large ears/Steiff button in each, original outfit has marked "Steiff" buttons, hat, shoes, holds horn. (Musician in "The Village Band." Early 1900s $3,000

13"........ Dutch Girl. Molded felt face/center seam/jtd felt body, CM, inset dark blue glass eyes, blonde mohair wig, original "Dutch" costume, large wooden shoes, etc. Ca. 1913 $1,400

14""Bill Stickers." Argentine Cowboy. Molded felt face/jtd felt body, face seam, CM, black moustache, inset blue bead eyes, button in ear, black mohair wig, original 2-pc cowboy outfit, neckerchief, etc. 1920 .... $3,000

14"English Postman. Series 1. Molded velvet face/fat felt jtd body, CM, button eyes, long nose, applied ears, skinny concave legs/long pointed shoes, original black felt uniform, hat shoes, white mail sack, etc. Ca. 1903 .... $3,000

15" Character Man. Molded felt face/center seam, red "line" CM, button eyes, straggly black wool hair, "Steiff" button in each protruding ear, jtd felt body/limbs/separated fingers, original black trousers, blue jacket, red shirt with 16 "Steiff" buttons, black hat, black boots. Early 1900s $3,000

15" Little Girl. Molded felt face/seam/jtd felt body/stitched fingers/separate thumb/long feet with brown felt shoes, O/C mouth, button eyes, brown wool hair (pigtails), original pink dress decorated with lace, etc. Ca. 1910 ... $1,700

15" Scotsman. Molded felt face/center seam, CM, button eyes, black ptd hair, jtd felt body, original yellow felt jacket, brown cotton-plaid kilts, hat, shoes, etc. Ca. 1920s $2,000

17" "Old Mother Hubbard." Molded velvet face/long nose/pointed chin, face seam, CM, button eyes, gray mohair wig, jtd felt body, original dress, apron, cape, pointed black felt hat, etc. Ca. 1909-1914 Rare........................ $4,000

17" Clown. Male. Molded felt face/center seam, CM, button eyes, mohair wig, protruding ears, excelsior stuffed jtd body/swivel neck, original felt outfit, long over-sized shoes wit spats, hat, etc. Ca. 1913 .... $2,500

17" Teddy Bear. Golden mohair fur/hump/growler/ear button/swivel head, black stitched mouth/nose/claws, dark brown eyes. $9,000

Chapter 40

~ JULES NICOLAS STEINER ~

History:

Jules Nicolas Steiner or "Societé Steiner", 1855-1908+. Although J.N. Steiner had a doll factory in Paris where they assembled parts, it was not entirely a "French" firm, having German affiliations, and a doll factory in Germany where they made bisque heads and bodies. Their dolls were also dressed in Paris in fancy French finery and sold in Paris stores. Steiner made many early dolls that were later called "bébés", and claimed to have been the originator of same. Was his the German factory that made the first Jumeau heads? Certainly the Steiner doll had a definite Jumeau persona. His earliest poupées (marked) had the wax-over-mache or compo heads and were of the mechanical types, being walkers, kickers, and criers. The company changed hands many times in later years: A. Lafosse, 1892: Jules Mettais, 1902; E. Daspres, 1906. Steiner marks varied with the change of owners: Baby, 1899; Bébé Liege, 1899; Bébé Marcheur, 1890; Bébé Model, 1901; Bébé Phénix, 1895; Bébé Premier Pas, 1890; La Patricienne, 1908; Le Parisien, 1892; Le Phénix, 1899; Mascotte, 1901; Phénix Bébé or Phénix-Baby, 1899; Poupée Merveilleuse, 1899. In 1908 E. Daspres advertised "La Particienne" as a "worldly doll."

Collecting Hints:

The Steiner, like the Jumeau, Bru, etc., is and old fashioned custom-made doll and all Steiners are a good investment. Here are a few characteristics to look for: the eyelashes are much heavier painted that most French dolls, with a deep indentation around the upper lids. The painting at the edge of the eye is also heavy (the early mechanicals are the exception). Not all Steiners have cork pates. Many pates are made of pressed cardboard or of a matrix substance (some are purple in color). There is also a purple paint beneath the flesh paint on the bodies. Early Steiners have hands that are short and stubby with wide-apart fingers. Later hands were modeled for the jointed wrists and are much more attractive and natural looking. Another oddity: fin-

gers are almost all the same length (small Steiners have their fingers jointed together). Sometimes the big toe on feet is separate from the others. Steiner bodies are slender and lightweight, yet sturdy and durable. Some collectors believe that the purple paint used (or dipped) on the bodies was a preservative since the rolled paper inside the fingers is also purple. Negro Steiners are very rare.

Reproduction Alert:

Some of the early, choice Steiners have been reproduced.

JULES NICOLAS STEINER

8" Bébé. Bisque head, CM, grey glass sleep eyes, blonde mohair wig, BJ compo body/straight wrists, original clothes, straw hat with flower trim, etc. Ca. 1900 (Sold for....... $3,090 in 1989) $4,500

8-1/2" "C" series Bébé. Bisque head, CM, brown glass sleep eyes/Bourgoin-type lever, brown mohair wig, PE, BJ compo body/straight wrists, original clothes/trunk with Nain Bleu label. Ca. 1880s $7,500

9" "3/0" incised Bébé. Early pale bisque head/round face/head opening, CM, inset blue PW eyes (early type threading), PI ears, BJ compo body/straight wrists, original clothes, etc. Ca. 1880s .... $5,000-$5,500

10" "Ste C 3/0" incised Bébé (Boy). Bisque head/ "mumps cheeks," CM, large inset bulbous blue PW eyes, brown skin wig, PE, BJ compo body/straight wrists/early stubby fingers, original navy sailor suit, straw boater, ivory whistle, chemise, shoes, socks. Head stamp: "Steiner Bte S.G.D.G. Bourgoin." Buttocks stamp: "J.St. Caduceus." Ca. 1880s $4,500

10-1/2" "Le Parisien" Bébé. Bisque head, CM, inset blue PW eyes, thick eyebrows (almost join in the middle), blonde mohair wig, PE, old clothes, bonnet, etc. Incised: "Medaille d'Or Paris." Ca. 1900+ $3,200

10-1/2" "C" series Bébé. Bisque head, CM, blue glass sleep eyes/lever, blonde skin wig, PE, BJ compo body/straight wrists, original blue satin dress, etc. Mark: "Ste C 3/0." 1880s $4,500

10-1/2" Negro Bébé. Black bisque head, OM/teeth, brown PW eyes, black curly mohair wig, PE, BJ compo body, original pink cotton dress, bonnet, etc. Mark: "J.Steiner Bte. SGDG. Paris." Ca. early 1900s $2,200

10-1/2" "Steiner Paris 3" incised Bébé. Bisque head/round face, OM, blue PW eyes, dark brown HHW, PE, BJ compo body, old clothes, etc. Ca. 1890s (late) $1,500

11" "Ste A 2/0" incised "Bourgoin" Bébé. Pale bisque head, brown glass eyes/lever, blonde mohair wig, PE, BJ compo body/straight wrists, original clothes, etc. Mark: "Ste A 2/0"; "Bourgoin" (on one side of head) and "J.Steiner, S.G.D.G." (in red script on the opposite side of head) 1880s (Coarse bisque) $4,500

13" Bébé. Bisque head, CM, inset blue PW eyes, blonde mohair wig, PE, BJ compo body, original fancy blue silk 2-pc dress/matching hat, etc. Mark: "J. Steiner. Bte SGDG Paris..." Ca. 1890 .... $4,200

13" "O" incised Bébé. Early pale bisque head/round face/head opening with cork plug, CM, inset blue PW eyes (early type threading), PI ears, blonde skin wig, BJ compo body/straight wrists, original clothes, bonnet, etc. (The "O" and "3/0" markings were used before the Steiner name was incised on heads. Early mechanical heads were not usually marked. The "Steiner" name was impressed on the mechanism.) Ca. 1880s $5,000

14" "Fre, A.7" incised Boy. Pale bisque head, CM, inset blue PW eyes, blonde skin wig, BJ compo body/straight wrists, original uniform: red wool trousers, black wool jacket (both trimmed with gold braid), etc. Mark: "Steiner, Paris, Fre, A.7." Body Mark: "Bébé Steiner." 1887 .... $5,000-$5,300

14" "Taufling" Bébé. Pale bisque shoulder head, CM, inset blue PW eyes, blonde skin wig, bisque hips/upper thighs/lower limbs/cloth mid-section/upper limbs, original dress. Ca. 1870s $5,500

15" "Ste" Bébé. Bisque head, CM, large blue glass sleep eyes/lever (marked "Steiner"), rosy cheeks, blonde mohair wig, PE, BJ compo body/straight wrists, original white cotton christening dress, underclothes, bonnet. Incised: "Ste CO J. Steiner//J. Bourgoin." (Suppose to be a baby, but the face is that of a much older child; has a "Jumeau" look.) 1880s .... $6,000-$6,500

15" "Taufling" Bébé. Pale bisque shoulder head, CM, inset blue PW eyes/blue liner, blonde mohair wig, bisque hips/upper thighs/lower limbs/twill joined, original white christening gown, bonnet. Ca. 1870s $5,700

15" Parisienne. Bisque shoulder head, OM/2 rows of teeth, large inset almond-shaped PW eyes, blonde mohair wig, cardboard/cone-shaped body/walking mechanism/key wind/bisque lower arms, original clothes. Label reads: "J.Steiner." Ca. 1890a $6,000

15" Parisienne. Walzer. Pale pressed bisque shoulder head, CM, inset almond-shaped blue PW eyes, blonde mohair wig, PE carton body/bisque lower arms/walking mechanism is located in her cardboard base/when activates (wound) she waltzes in a circle and her arms move up and down, original silk dress. Ca. 1890s $6,000

16" "C" series Bébé. Bisque head, CM, large blue PW eyes, brown mohair wig, PE, BJ compo body/straight wrists, original clothes, etc. 1887+ $6,500

16" "Fre A.9." incised Bébé. Pale bisque head, CM, large inset blue PW eyes, blonde mohair wig, PE, BJ wood/compo body/straight wrists, original beige silk dress, bonnet, etc. Mark: "Steiner/Paris/Fre A. 9." 1887+ $5,200

17" "Fre A-9" incised Bébé. Bisque head, CM, inset PW eyes, blonde mohair wig, PE, BJ compo body, old clothes, etc. Mark: "J.N. Steiner//Br te SGDG//Paris//Fre A-9." Body stamped: "Medaile d'Or//1889//La Petite Parisien//Bébé Steiner." 1889+ $5,200

19" "G" series Bébé. Bisque head, CM, rosy cheeks, large inset blue PW eyes, blonde mohair wig, BJ compo body/straight wrists, original ecru wool challis dress with lace trim, matching bonnet, etc. Incised: "Steiner Bte. S.G.D.G. J. Bourgoin." Ca. 1880s (Rarest of the Steiners) .... $20,000+

19" Ste C. 5" incised Bébé. Pale bisque head, CM, almond-shaped blue PW eyes, blonde mohair wig, PE, BJ papier-mâché body, old clothes, etc. Blue body stamp reads: "Le Petite Parisien J. St. Bte. S.G.D.G. J.B. Succe, Paris." 1892+ .... $5,500-$6,000

20" "Bébé Parlant Automatique" or "Kicking/Speaking" Bébé. Wax-over-mâché head, small puckered OM/2 square upper/lower teeth, blue glass sleep eyes (open and close when arms are raised and lowered), blonde skin wig, carton body/white kid upper legs glued to body/compo lower limbs/well-modeled feet and hands/voice box/key wind, original christening dress, underwear, bonnet. Ca. 1862+ $3,000

20" "Clockwork" Bébé. Early pale bisque head, tiny CM, inset blue glass eyes, skimpy skin wig, cloth covered carton upper body/kid lower body/compo limbs/arms pegged to body/upper legs attached with kid, original clothes. Ca. 1870s $2,500

21" "Kicker" Bébé. Bisque head, CM, blue threaded glass eyes, blonde mohair wig, compo body/compo arms/lower legs/cloth upper legs, mechanical key-wind, original fancy silk dress, long black stockings, black leather shoes, etc. (She kicks and cries when wound.) Ca. 1890 .... $2,500

21" "Le Parisien" stamped Bébé. Bisque head, CM, green glass sleep eyes/lever operated, thick brown eyebrows, blonde mohair wig, PE, BJ compo body, original velvet cafe-aut-lait colored outfit, bonnet, etc. Mark: "A-13." Ca. 1900 .... $6,000

21" Bébé. Bisque head, blue glass sleep eyes operated by wire mechanism, OM/teeth, blonde mohair wig, compo jtd body/crier, old long dress, cap, etc. Head incised: "Figure B Steiner Bte." Ca. 1900 (Sold for $5,500) .. $6,000+

22" "Figure A" Bébé. Bisque head, CM, dark brown glass sleep eyes/lever mechanism at rear of head, brown mohair wig, BJ compo body, original maroon silk dress, hat, etc. Mark: "J. Steiner Bte SGDG Paris Fre A 15." Ca. 1887+ $6,500

22" "Le Parisien" Bébé. Bisque head, CM, inset blue PW eyes, brown HHW, BJ compo body, original clothes, etc. Head mark: "A-13." Ca. early 1900s . $6,000

22-1/2" "A" series "Bourgoin" Bébé. Size 4. Pale bisque head, tiny CM, large blue PW eyes, PE, BJ compo body/straight wrists, original clothes, hat, etc. Ca. 1880s $8,100

24" "A No. 5" Bébé. Bisque head, CM, brown PW eyes, applied PE, brown mohair wig, BJ (signed "Steiner") compo body, old clothes, bonnet, etc. Mark: "A No. 5 J. Steiner Bte. S.G.D.G. Paris." Ca. 1887+ $7,000

24" "Figure A" Bébé. Bisque head (sad expression), CM, inset blue PW eyes, blonde mohair wig, BJ compo body, original clothes, etc. Mark: "J. Steiner Bte, SGDG Paris Fre A-17." Ca. 1887+ $7,000

24" "Taufling" Bébé. Bisque shoulder head, CM, flat ears, thin "blonde" eyebrows, blonde skin wig, cobalt blue PW eyes, bisque hips/upper thighs/lower limbs/fabric joined, original white christening gown, bonnet, etc. (Typical mature-looking Steiner face on a "baby" doll.) Ca. 1870s $7,000

25" "BN 5" Bébé. Pale bisque head, OM/2 rows of teeth, brown mohair wig/cardboard pate, PE, BJ compo body/straight wrists/cry box, old clothes, bonnet, etc. Mark: "BN 5 J. Steiner SDGD Paris." Ca. 1890 $6,500

25" "Figure B" Bébé. Bisque head, OM/lower teeth, large inset blue PW eyes, thick light brown eyebrows, blonde mohair wig, PE, old clothes, etc. Mark: "J. Steiner Bte S.G.D.G. Paris." Ca. 1900+ $6,500

28" "A" series Bébé. Bisque head, CM, inset blue PW eyes/open and closed by a wire lever mechanism, brown mohair wig, PE, BJ compo/wood body/straight wrists, original green silk taffeta dress with lace trim, original shoes, stockings, etc. Ca. 1880s $10,500

28" "A-19" or "Le Parisien." Bisque head/full lower cheeks/cardboard pate, CM, large inset blue PW eyes, brown mohair wig, PE, BJ compo body, original clothes, etc. Incised: "A19 PARIS." Ca. 1892+ $7,500

28" "C" series Bébé. Bisque head, tiny CM, large inset almond-shaped PW eyes, blonde mohair wig, PE, BJ compo body/straight wrists, original dress, bonnet, etc. Ca. 1880s $10,100

28" "F1 RE A 19" incised Bébé. Pale bisque head, CM, inset large brown PW eyes, dark brown HHW, PE, BJ compo body, old clothes, etc. Mark: "J. Steiner//Bte S.G.D.G.//F 1 Re A 19." Ca. 1887+ $8,000

28" Bébé. Bisque head, CM, large inset brown PW eyes, light blonde sausage curl HHW, PE, BJ compo body, original elaborate lace dress decorated with pink ribbons, etc. Head Mark: "J. Steiner Bte S.G.D.G. Paris." Ca. 1900 .... $8,000-$8,500

29" "C" series "Bourgoin" Bébé. Bisque head, CM, wire-operated sleep eyes (made of porcelain with glass pupils), blonde HHW, PE, BJ compo body/straight wrists, old clothes, coat, hat, etc. Ca. 1880s . $10,000-$10,300

34" "J. Steiner" incised Bébé. Bisque head, CM, inset blue PW eyes, brown HHW, PE, BJ compo body/straight wrists, old clothes, hat, etc. Ca. 1880s .. $13,000

34" "No. 7" incised Bébé. Bisque head/long neck, CM, blue glass sleep eyes/wire motivated/lever, blonde HHW, PE, BJ "Steiner" marked compo body/beautiful bisque hands with separate fingers/fingernail detail, original elaborate clothes, hat, etc. Mark: "Figure Co, No.7, Steiner by S.G.D.G., Paris." (Purple matrix-type pate incised "7".) Ca. 1880s .... $13,000-$13,500

38" Mannequin. Bisque head, CM, inset blue PW eyes, blonde mohair wig, PE, BJ compo body, original clothes, etc. Ca. 1880s $16,000

Chapter 41

~ TINIES ~

History:

Tiny dolls have always been made, not only for play, but as decorative items and effigies. The commercialization of these pocket-sized companions began circa 1880 (earlier for doll's house size china-head dolls). This date is given for convenience, but one thing is certain: the earliest dolls ever made were the best made, and more care was given to merchandising and packaging. The loveliest and best quality were made by Kestner, and he probably made those we now refer to as "French." Armand Marseille, Simon & Halbig, Kammer & Reinhardt, and other German companies made their share of tinies once the demand for them increased. Jumeau probably made some of the early unmarked types, as well.

These wee dolls were always favorites with the child; being so small they fit snugly in tiny apron pockets. They also suited the small scale furniture designed for the doll's house. The best of the lot spanned the decades between 1880 and 1900. After the war, Japan cornered the small doll market. They purchased German molds, duplicated dolls made in Germany, and even created their own types. These dolls were sold to the dime-store chains until World War Two. After the war, the dolls were incised "Made in Occupied Japan" (Shackman labels appeared on many Japan-made dolls). Despite the Plastic Age, bisque dolls in the smaller sizes have never ceased being made—and will always be collectible—old or new.

Collecting Hints:

The most desirable of the "tinies" are now the most expensive: French and French-types, Kestners, Simon & Halbig, Heubach, etc. "Name" dolls also come in this category: "Bye-Los," "Orsini," "Kewpies"; Kestner "Orientals," some of the "googlies," etc. Smooth bisque quality, bare feet, jointed limbs (elbows, knees), original wigs and clothes, etc., make for a valuable doll, as do marks and labels (Kestner's crown seal). These dolls are not rare, there are just more people collecting them for their "value."

Reproduction Alert:

The "tiny" has been the most reproduced of all dolls, and there are so many "experts" in the porcelain doll-making arena that their output could fool an expert; especially since some of the famous dolls of the past, like the wee Bye-Lo babies, have been reproduced with the original incised marks left intact. When in doubt look inside the neck and limb holes and study the stringing loops and elastic. Also scrutinize the painting of eyes and eyebrows. Compare your old doll with the new one you intend to buy. As I've said before, when in doubt—don't buy. Kewpies, Scootles, Snow Babies, Happifats, Shirley Temples (Made in Japan originally), Heubachs, are some of the dolls reproduced in modern times by amateur doll-makers.

TINIES

(DOLLS UNDER 10-INCHES)

2"-4" Doll's House Dolls. Set of 10 includes Father, Mother, Grandparents, Children, Servants. Painted stockinet faces, wire-armature bodies wrapped with cloth/metal feet, wigs, oriental clothes. Tag on each doll reads: "Made in England/Grecon/London." Made by Margarete Cohn, a German, in England. (Cohn's dolls date to the 1920s.) Ca. 1940s (She was still making dolls in the 1950s) $225 set/10

2-1/2" "Chi-Chi-Chi." All bisque nodder/head to side, CM, blue ptd. eyes to side, hands holding outstretched skirt/ptd. shoes/body modeled in one piece. (Only head nods.) Made by Jeanne I. Orsini, NYC, 1916-1930s .... $1,000+

2-3/4" "Perry Winkle." Boy with Buster Brown hair style. Character in the comic strip "Winnie Winkle" by Martin A. Branner. all bisque/nodder of "Knotter"/head knotted to body with a string which goes through body and knotted at buttocks/painted-on clothes/ptd. features. Incised: "Perry Winkle by Banner." 1929 .... $85

3-1/4" "Kicking" Bye-Lo. All bisque, ptd. features, ptd. hair, reclines on a pink papier-mâché Easter egg on a stuffed cushion/baby bottle/original chest sticker. (These are called "Action Bye-Los" and were quite common in there day.) Ca. 1925+ $375-475

3-1/2" "125-8" Belton-type "Oriental" Girl. All bisque/jtd at neck/sh./hips, CM, slanted inset brown glass eyes,

well-defined ears, black mohair wig, oriental silk costume. Mark: "125-8." (French face). Ca. 1875+ $750

3-1/2" Happifat Girl. All bisque/movable arms only, ptd./molded-on dress with ribbon near bottom and low in back. Back sticker reads: "Happifat Nippon." (Borgfeldt registered Happifat trademark in 1913-1921. Dolls were all bisque or compo with cloth bodies. The dolls were based on Kate Jordan's illustrations in John Martin's books. Germany made the all-bisque Happifats. Amberg acquired the Happifat patent in 1921.) Ca. WW 1 (boy or Girl) .... $300 - $400

3-7/8" "Dionne Quintuplets." Al bisque/movable arms only/apart legs, red CM, gold and silver/molded "Dutch-cut" bob, ptd. blue eyes, original silk glued-on skirt/silk floss tops. Dolls and skirts marked: "Made in Japan".

6-1/2" "Mon Tresor" marked lady. Bisque head, OM/4 teeth, inset blue glass eyes, brown HHW wig, stub at waist/no lower body or legs, original clothes, hat. Novelty type doll. French $300. (Courtesy of Carol Lindberg)

(This was Japan's version of the Quints with just enough "difference" to skirt the issue of copyright infringement.) Ca. 1939 MIB $125

4" "Dionne Quintuplets." All bisque/movable arms only/apart legs, CM, ptd. features, orange-blonde ptd./molded hair with bangs, original white silk dress with hem seams of different colors. Neck marks: "Foreign." Box mark: "No. 35 N 35." "Quintuplets" imprinted on box top. MIB Ca. 1939-40 .... $125

6-1/2" "A 13/O M" marked girl. Bisque swivel head, OM/teeth, inset blue glass eyes, brown HHW, compo body/lt. brown ptd/mld shoes/socks, old clothes. Full mark: "Germany//390//A 13/OM." 1890s $225. (Courtesy of D. Kay Crow)

4" Bye-Lo Baby. All bisque/jtd at sh./hips, CM, inset blue glass eyes, blonde ptd. hair, chest sticker, complete/original layette: dress, bonnet, slip, hood, hooded sacque-like enclosure, booties. Ca. 1925+ $1,000

4-1/2" "GK44-12" incised Girl. Bisque head, OM/molded teeth, inset blue glass eyes, blonde mohair wig, 11-pc compo body, original clothes. Ca. 1890+ Made by Gebruder Kuhnlenz, Germany, 1884+ .... $400 - $500

4-1/2" "Googly" Girl. Bisque head/open crown, watermelon mouth, blue sleep glass eyes, blonde mohair wig, bisque body jtd at sh./hips/ptd. shoe and socks, original clothes, bonnet. Mark: "217/11; 11 on inside of each arm; 217 and 11 on inside of each leg. Made by Wm. Goebel, Germany. Ca. 1908+ .... $600 - $625

4-1/2" Bye-Lo Baby. All bisque/jtd at sh./hips, CM, rare brown glass eyes, brown mohair wig/bangs, old hand-made nightgown. Round dark green paper label on chest reads: "BYE-LO BABY G.S. PUTNAM.."; Back mark: "Copr. by Grace S. Putnam." 1925+ .... $1,000+

4-1/2" Bye-Lo. All bisque/jtd at sh./hips, CM, blue glass eyes, blonde mohair wig, bangs, old handmade nightgown. Round dark green paper label on chest reads: "BYE-LO BABY G.S. PUTNAM..."; Back mark: "Copr. by G.S. Putnam." Ca. 1925+ .... $800-$850

4-1/2" MIBS. All bisque/jtd at sh./hips/ptd./molded shoes/socks, CM, blue ptd. eyes, blonde ptd./molded short curly hair/forelock, original dress, underwear. Mark: "LA&S 1921 GERMANY." Paper label on chest reads: "PLEASE LOVE ME I' M MIBS." 1921 (MIBS-3" $275 - $300) ...... $400-$425

4-1/2" Frozen Charlotte. All china/no movable parts/bent arms/apart legs, CM, blue ptd. eyes, black ptd./molded hair. Nude. Made in Germany Ca. 1850s $150

4-1/2" "Our Fairy." All bisque/movable arms/together legs, smiling mouth, inset brown glass eyes, brown HHW/bangs, original clothes. Body sticker reads: "Our Fairy/Germany" (in a circle design with sprigs of leaves on each side of "Our Fairy" and tiny wings at bottom of sprigs.) Nude. Made by Louis Wolf & Co., Germany. Ca. 1914 .... $800

4-1/2" "10" incised Girl. Bisque head, CM, blue glass sleep eyes, blonde mohair wig, bisque body jtd at sh./hips/black ptd./molded shoes with ankle-straps and knee-length white ribbed stockings, old clothes, bonnet Body mark: "Made in//Germany." Limbs mark: "10." Ca. 1890s $375

4-1/2" "390" incised Girl. Crude bisque head, CM, blue glass sleep eyes, brown mohair wig, jtd compo body, original cheap commercial dress/undies/ptd.-on black shoes with ankle straps/white socks. Ca. Early 1900s (Rare size) Made by Armand Marseille, Germany $175

4-1/2" "Priscilla's Sewing Set" #1215. Dionne Quints. All bisque/movable bent arms, blonde ptd./molded curly hair,

6" early dolls house dolls (Male Chef-5"). Left to right: Maid-$300; housekeeper-$500-$550; young girl (center) $250; lady, $450; male "chef" $350. Ca. 1890s. (Courtesy of D. Kay Crow)

CM, blue ptd. eyes, pink and aqua swimsuits. Dresses are printed on cloth, uncut, unseamed. (This boxed set has the Dionne Quintuplets on the top.) Made by J. Pressman Co., Inc., NYC. 1930s (MIB) $175

4-1/2" "Playtime Dresses for Dolly" #2526. All bisque/jtd at sh./hips, ptd. features, blonde ptd. hair, baby-type. Original box contains metal scissors, embroidery, hoops thread, dresses/rompers, etc.; printed on cloth to be cut-out, sewn together, and embroidered. Instruction booklet entitled: "My First Lesson in the Art of Embroidery." Made by Transogram Co., Inc. NYC. Ca. 1920s (MIB) $125

6" Heubach boy, marked "Heubach" in the square, ptd features, all original. Gebruder Heubach, Germany. 1910+. (Courtesy of D. Kay Crow)

5" "310" incised Girl. All bisque/swivel neck/jtd at sh./hips, CM, large inset blue glass eyes, blonde mohair wig, original clothes/black ptd./molded on shoes and socks. Possibly Armand Marseille, Germany Ca. 1925 (Good quality) $650

5" "French" Crawler. (Doll in crawling position). All bisque, jtd at neck/sh./hips, CM, inset blue glass eyes, brown HHW, nude. (Legs bent at knees.) Unmarked French. Ca. 1880s $1,500

5" "French-type" Girl. Solid-dome bisque head, red CM, rosy cheeks, inset blue glass eyes, blonde mohair wig, bisque body jtd at kid-lined swivel neck/sh./hips/pink ptd./molded shoes

6-1/2" Bisque child marked "14" (French persona), card-type body, CM, inset blue glass eyes, blonde wig, ptd brown shoes/black ptd socks; $125; antique buggy, tiny bisque doll. (Courtesy of D. Kay Crow)

French bisque head dolls marked: "SFBJ//60." Dolls have inset glass eyes, cloth bodies, original costumes. 10" doll dressed in Lorraine provincial costume; 11" doll dressed in Alsace costume; 10" doll dressed in Martinique costume. 1917+ $700-$800 each. (Courtesy of D. Kay Crow)

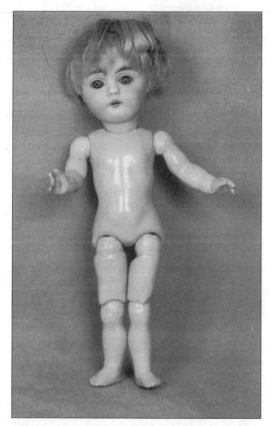

6-1/2" Kestner. Mark: "Made in Germany 143." Sleep glass eyes, blonde mohair wig, OM/teeth. 1909+ $800-$825. (Courtesy of Carol Lindberg)

Left to right: 5"-pink tint frozen Charlotte, $400. 4" "Covered Wagon" hairdo frozen Charlotte, $175; 4-3/4" Bonnet Charlotte, $375 all 19th century. 1850s+. (Courtesy of D. Kay Crow)

and white socks, original dress, undies. Made in Germany. Ca. 1880s ....$750 - $800

5" "Gold Medal Dresses for dolly." 5 all bisque Japanese-made dolls/movable arms only/together legs/red ptd.-on bathing suits, CM, blue ptd. eyes to side, blonde ptd./molded curly hair, original box contains fabric, needle, threads, etc. (These are the dolls we call "Betty Boop" types today, but they are not!) Made by Transogram C., Inc., NYC. Ca. 1920s $225

5" "Nancy Ann" Cowgirl. Painted bisque head, CM, blue ptd. eyes, blonde mohair wig, bisque body jtd at sh./hips/black ptd. boots (ribbed socks ptd. clack to simulate boot tops), original black trousers, brown leather chaps, plaid skirt, red ribbon tied around neck, black felt cowboy hat. Back mark: "STORY//BOOK/DOLL//USA." Original red box with large white polka dots. Box label reads: "Masquerade Series//Cowboy//62." Ca. 1940 (MIB) Gold Sticker ....$225 - $250

6" "S&H/K (star) R" marked boy. Bisque head, OM/teeth, inset blue glass eyes, brown HHW, compo body/mld double-strap shoes/white socks, old clothes. 1895+ $525-$550. (Courtesy of D. Kay Crow)

5" "O" incised Kestner Girl. All bisque/swivel neck/jtd at sh./hips, CM, inset blue glass eyes, blonde mohair wig, original dress, undies/ptd. on/molded shoes and socks. Ca. 1880s (Sold for $1,200 in 1989 at auction) $1,500

5" French Boy. All cloth, well-modeled features, CM, blue ptd. eyes, modeled ears, blonde ptd. hair, cloth body jtd at neck/sh./hips/bent legs, lovely original clothes. Upside down mark on back: "MADE IN FRANCE." Rare and unusual. Ca. 1920s $150

5" French Fruit-Pedlar Lady. Papier-mâché shoulder head, crudely ptd. features, black ptd. short hair covered with original paper turban, original handmade cloth body/mâché legs/well-made leather hands, original paper dress, apron, paper lace fichu, original mâché, tray with remnants of original mâché fruit (attached to original stand). This doll's face is not well-sculpted. Made in France. Ca. early 19th c. Price speculative $500

5" French Girl. All bisque/jtd at neck/sh./hips, CM, inset blue glass eyes, old clothes. Mark: "(Anchor)France/5/0." Lanternier, Limoges, France, 1915-24. (Not the finest quality) $350

5-1/2" "6-13" incised Negro Girl. All black bisque/swivel neck/French molded stringing loops/jtd at sh./hips, CM, inset black glass eyes, black HHW, old clothes. Mark: "6-13." 1880-1910 $700

5-1/2" "Bonnie Babe." All bisque/swivel neck/jtd limbs, smiling OM/2 lower teeth/tongue, blue glass sleep eyes, blonde ptd./molded hair, modeled ears, molded blue shoes, old clothes. Unmarked. Round paper label on chest: "BONNIE BABE COP R. BY GEORGENE AVERILL..." Made by Georgene Averill, NYC. 1926 ....$900

5-1/2" French Girl. Pale bisque swivel head, CM, inset blue glass eyes, blonde mohair wig, long bisque body/straight bisque legs (no joints)/bare feet/bisque arms with ball-joints at elbows, original clothes. Ca. 1880+ $3,000

5-1/2" "Hatted" Parian Lady. White bisque shoulder head, CM, rosy cheeks, blue ptd. eyes/black pupil dots/red lid lines, small yellow ptd. "Empress" hat with molded pink luster plume/black ptd. curls/exposed ears, cloth body/bisque lower limbs/black ptd. boots, elaborate original clothes. Ca. 1860 ....$350

5-3/4" "Elizabeth/6//0/Heubach//Germany" incised Googly. Bisque head, smiling CM, brown glass sleep eyes, blonde HHW, cardboard body/ptd. limbs/black ptd. ankle-strap shoes, original clothes: felt dress/hat, gauze undies. Gebruder Heubach, Germany. Ca. 1911+ ....$1,750 - $1,950

6" "S&H" Girl. Solid-dome bisque swivel head on bisque shoulder plate, CM, inset blue glass eyes, blonde mohair wig, cloth body/bisque lower limbs/bare feet, old clothes. (Unmarked version of a similar marked S&H type.) Ca. 1870s $400

6" Topsy-Turvey Baby. Bisque heads, O/C mouth (crying)/smiling CM, blue ptd.

eyes, blonde ptd./molded hair, origin dark blue satin jester's costume with hood/gold trim. Made in Germany. Ca. 1880s (Sold for $2,820 in 1989 at auction; estimate $1,200) $2,000

6" "189" incised Kestner Girl. Googly. Bisque head, watermelon mouth, large blue glass eyes to side, blonde mohair wig, 5-pc compo body, (Sold for $1,200 in 1989 at auction) ....$2,000+

6" French Girl. Bisque head/long neck/open crown/pate, pink CM, inset brown glass eyes, brown HHW, bisque body/long torso/long unjtd legs/bare

7" "250" incised Heubach/Koppelsdorf child. Bisque head, OM/teeth, blue glass sleep eyes, compo body, blonde HHW, modern clothes. 1888+ $235. (Courtesy of Carol Lindberg)

feet/long bisque arms with wooden joints/peg strung, original ecru lace dress trimmed with lace, petticoat, drawers. Unmarked. Ca. 1880s ..$3,000-$3,200

6" "1907" incised Boy. Bisque swivel head, OM/teeth, inset blue glass eyes, brown mohair wig, compo body jtd at sh./hips/ptd. shoes/straight legs, original trousers, jacket, hat, etc. Mark: "D.E.P. R/A Recknagel 1907." Made by Th. Recknagel, Germany. Ca. 1890s - WW 1 (DEP means Depoiniert or registered design) ....$175-$185

6-1/2" "S//W//S" incised Girl. Googly. Bisque head, watermelon mouth, large blue glass eyes, blonde mohair wig, compo Body jtd at neck/sh./hips/ptd. limbs/tan ptd. ankle-strap shoes, old dress. Made by Strobel and Wilkin, Cincinnati, Ohio, NYC, 1864-1930s. Ca. 1911+..$600

6-1/2" "R 45//A/13/0" incised Girl. Googly. Bisque head/wire-strung, watermelon mouth, blue ptd. intaglio eyes to side, blonde ptd./molded bob/no bangs, cardboard body jtd at neck/ /hips/tan ptd. shoes/black ptd. socks, old dress. Made by Th. Recknagel, Germany. 1911+...$650

6-1/2" "306/0 11//95 HEUBACH 94//Germany" incised Child. Googly. Bisque head, watermelon mouth, blue ptd. eyes to side, blonde ptd. hair/molded forelock, sturdy compo body jtd at neck/sh./hips/black ptd. ankle-strap shoes, felt dress with white collar and black sateen belt. Made by Ernst Heubach, Germany, 1887+. Ca. 1911+..$650

6-1/2" "PM 950" incised Boy. Googly. Bisque head, watermelon mouth, blue glass eyes, modeled ears, brown HHW, chubby toddler body/jtd compo factory-made clothes. Made by Porzellanfabrik Mengersgereuth, Germany, 1908+. Ca. 1913+.................$850-900

6-1/2" "Sonny." All-bisque/jtd body, CM, brown glass sleep eyes, blonde ptd./molded hair, old romper suit (original). Made by Georgene Averill, NYC/Germany. Ca. 1920 ....$3,000-$4,000

6-1/2" Dionne Quintuplets. All-compo/jtd at neck/sh./hips, CM, blue ptd. eyes, brown ptd. hair, original diapers. Head mark: "EFFanBEE." Back mark: "EF-FanBEE/Baby Tinyette." Ca. 1938-39 (5 dolls) Each.......................$350-$450

7" "133/S//H//Germany//2" incised Girl. Googly Bisque head, watermelon mouth, brown glass sleep eyes, blonde mohair wig/card dome, cardboard body/ptd. limbs, old clothes. (Resembles A.M.'s 323 mold) Made by Hermann Steiner, Sonneberg, Thur., Germany. 1924 (Well known for their googlies.) ....$1,000-$1,100

7" "155" incised Kestner. Bisque head, CM, inset blue glass eyes, blonde mohair wig, 5-pc jtd compo body, original silk dress, undies. Ca. 1892......$900-$950

7" "83//125" incised Girl. All-bisque/jtd at sh./hips/straight legs/black ptd. ankle-strap shoes/knee-length white ptd. ribbed stockings, CM, blue glass sleep eyes, blonde HHW, old clothes. Head mark: "83//125" and "16 0/2." Back stamp: "Germany." Made by an elderly German woman in East Germany, near Bonn. (Some dolls have set glass eyes) 1951 ....$200

7" "9573/5//0/HEUBACH//Germany" incised Girl. Bisque head/2 holes over each ear, smiling CM, brown glass sleep eyes, cardboard body/ptd. limbs/black ptd. ankle-strap shoes, original dress. Made by G. Heubach, Germany. Ca. 1911+ ....$1,100-$1,200

7" "Baby Bud." All-bisque, smiling O/C mouth, blue ptd. eyes to side, brown ptd. hair/high forehead/single forelock, molded-on clothes/stationary legs/movable arms. Mark: "Germany." (Smooth Kestner bisque) "Baby Bud" trademark registered in Germany by Butler Bros., NYC. 1915+ $750

7" "Barefoot" Kestner. All-bisque/jtd at neck/sh./hips/chubby body/wide hips/chubby thighs/bare feet, CM, inset blue glass eyes, blonde mohair wig. Nude. Ca. 1880-1910....$2,800-$3,000

7" "Boy on Rabbit." Bisque head/soft-stuffed body/wired "stick" arms, original clothes, hat. Basket strapped to boy's back once held Easter candy eggs. Mark: "4600 20 PB (in a 5-point star) SH. Made by Schoenau & Hoffmeister, Germany. Ca. 1901+ $300

7" "Little Imp." All-bisque, smiling CM, blue ptd. eyes, bald head/movable arms/together legs/nude. Made by Max Illfelder for B. Illfelder & Co., NYC. Ca. 1910+ ....$250-$300

7" "Quintuplets Playset and Sewing Outfit." (This boxed set has the Dionne Quints on the top, although the five mint Japan-made dolls in the box have curly blonde molded/ptd. hair and do not resemble them.) All-bisque/movable bent arms, ptd. features, blonde ptd./molded hairdos, pink and aqua swimsuits. Dresses are printed on fabric, uncut, unseamed sides. Made by J. Pressman Co., Inc., NYC. Ca. 1939 ....$225

7" Bathing Beauty. Figurine. All-bisque/reclining in a swimming position/ptd. yellow cap/yellow sand shoes/white, green, blue swim suit. (These dolls were inspired by champion swimmer, Annette Kellerman.) (Quality) Ca. 1909+..................................$700-$750

7" Bonn Girl. All-bisque, O/c mouth/ptd. teeth, blue glass sleep eyes, blonde mohair wig, movable limbs/loop strung/black ptd. shoes with ankle-straps and white ribbed knee-length

8-1/2" "Armand Marseille//Germany//390//A 10/O M." marked girl. Bisque swivel head, OM/teeth, blue glass sleep eyes, brown HHW, compo body/mld-on it brown shoes/white socks, original clothes. $250-$300. (Courtesy of D. Kay Crow)

stockings with red striped tops/coarse bisque. Head mark: "83/150/18."Marks inside limbs: "83/150." Made by an elderly German woman in East Germany, near Bonn. 1951 ....$200

7" Little Boy. All-bisque/stationary head/jtd at sh./hips, CM, blue ptd. eyes, blonde ptd./molded short wavy hairdo/wavy bangs, modeled ears, old clothes/ptd. brown shoes with ankle-straps/short white ribbed socks. Ca. 1880-1910 ....$325

7" Little Girl. Bisque head/open crown, CM, rosy cheeks, inset blue glass threaded eyes/black pupils, brown HHW, original turned-wood body/long torso/sparse hip area/bent bisque arms/bulbous bisque legs/ ptd.-on high-top boots and stockings/ribbon tied head and limbs, original cotton dress, undies, straw hat. Unmarked. Germany. (Probably an experimental doll made for the cheaper mass-market, although the bisque head is smooth quality, the bisque of the limbs is coarse, the painting amateurish.) Ca. 1880-90s. (Rare).. $1,000

7-1/2" "10542/4//0/HEUBACH//Germany" incised Girl. Googly. Bisque head/ two holes above ears, CM, blue glass sleep eyes, blonde mohair wig, compo jtd body/jtd at sh./hips/tan ptd. ankle-strap shoes/orange socks, old clothes. Gebruder Heubach, Germany. CA. 1911+ $950

7-1/2" "R46//A/12/0" incised Girl. Googly. Bisque head/wire strung, watermelon mouth, blue ptd. intaglio eyes, blonde ptd./molded bob/no bangs/blue ptd. band, compo body jtd at neck/sh./hips/blue ptd. shoes with gold flecked buckles, old dress. Made by Th. Recknagel, Germany. Ca. 1911+ $750

7-1/2" "Germany//EH 27X15//0//D.R.G.M." incised Boy. Googly. Bisque head, watermelon mouth, blue ptd. eyes to side (half-pupils), blonde ptd./molded hair/ears, compo body jtd at neck/sh./hips/bare feet, old romper suit. Made by Ernst Heubach, Germany. Ca. 1911+ $750

7-1/2" Fashionable Lady. Turned bisque shoulder/head bald dome, CM, blue ptd. eyes, strawberry blonde mohair wig (Gibson style), shapely cloth body/bent bisque arms (jtd at shoulders)?bisque lower legs/ molded high-heeled slippers with bows, original period clothes, black velvet hat, etc. Shoulder mark: "1550-11/0." Box label reads: "Dame in Strassenkieid 1417/8." Dress sticker reads: "Manufactured for FAO Schwarz Toys, Fifth Avenue and Thirty First Street, New York." Made in Germany. Ca. 1910 (MIB) $1,500

7-1/2" Toddles. "Air Corps Officer." All-compo/jtd neck/sh./hips, CM, blue ptd. eyes to side, blonde mohair wig, original 2-toned uniform, pilot wings pin, cap. Made by Vogue Dolls Inc., Medford, Mass., 1937-48. (These dolls were originally called "Toodles.") Ca. WWII ....$400-$450

7-1/2" Toddles. "Naval Captain." All-compo/jtd at neck/sh./hips, CM, brown ptd. eyes to side, blonde mohair wig, original white pants, blue coat with gold braid, white cap. Made by Vogue Dolls.

7" All-bisque Bye-Lo baby, brown sleep eyes, original clothes/pacifier. Mark: "6-16 copyr. Grace Storey Putnam Germany." 1925+ $900-$1,000+. (Courtesy of Ruby Ellen Smith)

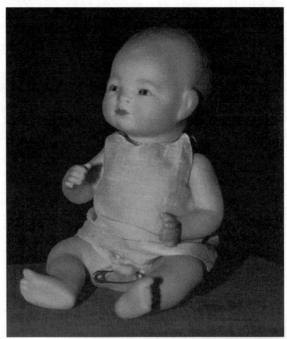

7" "Simon & Halbig/1079" marked girl. Bisque swivel head, CM, inset blue glass eyes, brown HHW, compo body/lt. brown ptd shoes/socks redressed. 1889+ $525-$550. (D. Kay Crow)

9" "U" marked child. Bisque head, inset glass eyes, CM, brown HHW, compo body/mld/ptd boots, original clothes. Ca. 1890s $475 (Courtesy of Carol Lindberg)

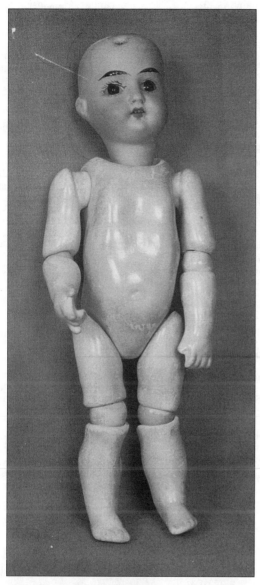

8" "1075/S&H/Germany" marked girl. Pale bisque head, OM/teeth, inset blue glass eyes, blonde mohair wig, compo body/lt. brown ptd shoes/socks, redressed in old fabrics. 1889+ $525-$550. (D. R. Crow)

8" "1903//16/O" marked German child. Bisque head, OM, blue glass eyes, BJ compo body. Possibly Armand Marseille. 1903 $265. (Courtesy of Carol Lindberg)

8-1/2" German bisque head googly girl marked "A 11/OM 1911." Bisque socket head, CM, blue glass eyes, blonde wig, cloth body/bisque arms/legs, dressed. 1911+ Armand Marseille. $1,000. (Courtesy of D. Kay Crow)

Inc., Medford, Mass, 1937-48. Ca. WWII ....$400-$450

7-1/2" Toddles. "Civilian Air Raid Warden." All compo/jtd at neck/sh./hips, CM, blue ptd. eyes to side, blonde mohair wig, original blue denim trousers and coat, white arm band with letter "CD" (Civilian Defense). Right shoe reads: "Air Raid Warden." Made by Vogue. Ca. WWII ....$400-$450

7-1/2" Toddles. "Draf-Tee." All compo/jtd at neck/sh./hips, CM, blue ptd. eyes to side, brown mohair wig, original ""sol-dier" uniform, belt, pistol, Pershing cap. "Draf-Tee" printed on one shoe. Vogue. Ca. WWII..............................$400-$450

7-3/4" "Bonnet" Parian Lady. Bisque shoul-der head/long oval face/long neck/slop-ing shoulders, CM, blue ptd. eyes/red lid lines. Light blonde/molded wavy hair/center part/molded light tan bonnet with a high brim/ribbon bow below chin/pink luster plume at rear of bonnet, original cloth body/bisque lower limbs/brown ptd./molded boots with heels. Ca. 1867 ....$700

8" "101" incised Girl. Bisque head, OM/3 teeth, blue glass sleep eyes, blonde mohair wig, slim compo jtd body, old clothes. Mark: "K (star)R//101 810." (Flapper type). 1920s..........$450-$550

8" "1393" incised "Bonnie Babe." Bisque head, OM, rosy cheeks, small blue glass eyes, blonde mohair wig, jtd com-po body, original clothes, bonnet, etc. Made by Alt, Beck & Gottschalck (ABG), Germany, 1854+ (porcelain makers); exported heads to U.S.A. ca. 1882; made dolls' heads ca. 1910-1941. Probably made the all-bisque Bonnie Babes a s well. 1926 ....$1,350-$1,450

8" "154" incised Girl. Bisque shoulder head/solid dome/ small rear crown holes, OM/4 molded teeth, inset blue glass eyes, blonde mohair wig, kid body/hip and knee gussets/stumpy feet, old clothes. Head mark: "154 dep 3/0" and "Made in Germany." Made by J.D. Kestner, Germany. Ca. 1900 ....$350-$400

8" "Heubach" Boy. Bisque head/open dome, OM/teeth, inset blue glass eyes, compo body jtd at neck/sh./hips, old clothes. Mark: "5/OD" (over a square). Gebruder Heubach, Germany. Ca. 1910+..$1,400

8" "Pet Name" China. China shoulder head, CM, blue ptd. eyes, black ptd/molded hairdo, cloth body/china lower limbs, original clothes. Name: "Ethel." (About twelve names in this series; imprinted on shirtwaist.) Ca. 1905-1930s $150

8" Bye-Lo. All-bisque/rare swivel neck/jtd at sh./hips, CM, blue glass eyes, blonde mohair wig/bangs, old clothes. Dark green paper label on chest reads: "BYE-LO BABY G.S. PUTNAM (C in a circle) GERMANY." Back Mark: "Copr. By Grace S. Putnam, Germany." Ca. 1925 ....$1,300-$1,400

8" Bye-Lo. Look-alike. Bisque flange head, CM, blue glass sleep eyes, blonde ptd/molded hair, cloth body/straight legs/compo hands, original gown, bon-net. Mark: "Germany//H//." Made by

Hermann Steiner, Germany, 1920+. Ca. 1921+ $350

8" HEbee-SHEbee. All-bisque/jtd arms/molded clothes/molded pink boo-ties (boy's shoes were blue) with two holes for insertion of ribbon, ptd. fea-tures. Mark: "Germany" (at base of baby shirt). Charles Twelvetrees de-signer (illustrations appeared in *Pictori-al Review* magazine). These dolls were made in compo in the U.S.A. and repro-duced in bisque in Japan. Ca. 1920s (rare size).........................$900-$1,100

8" Lady Clown. Bisque head, CM, blue ptd. eyes, wood/cloth body. Original clothes. (She holds an articulated pa-pier-mâché/cloth squeak toy doll and sits on a wooden chair attached to a wooden base.) Ca. 1870s, Made in Germany. $800

8" Mme. Alexander. Doll furniture scaled to 8" size dolls. (Alexander-kins). 4-pc to one set, white vanity with matching chair. This furniture was sold through FAO Schwarz Co., NYC, and adver-tised in their yearly catalogs. Ca. 1950s-1960s 4-pc set $500; vanity w/chair ....$50-$75

8-1/2" Gibson Girl. Bisque shoulder head, CM, blue ptd. eyes, blonde mohair wig/Gibson style, cloth body/bisque lower limbs, original white challis floor-length gown with scalloped edg-es, etc. Mark: "Kling." Early 20th century. $350

8-1/2" "My Dream Baby." Bisque head, CM, blue glass eyes, blonde ptd. hair, cloth body/celluloid hands, original gown, etc. Made by Armand Marseille, Ger-many, for Arranbee Doll Co., NYC. 1924..................................$300-$325+

8-1/2" "Hatted" Parian Man. Pale bisque shoulder head/sloping shoulders/mold-ed-on military-type hat (brown) with high top and chin strap/molded red em-blem frontal design/black strands of hair brush-stroked forward on each side of forehead, CM, blue ptd. eyes, original cloth body/bisque lower limbs/brown ptd. boots/original "mili-tary" costume. (The hat has a "textured" finish to simulate felt). Ca. 1850s ....$800+

8-1/2" Boy Clown. White bisque head, O/C mouth/molded teeth, blue ptd. eyes, brown HHW, 5-pc compo body/ptd shoes and socks, original 2-pc yellow outfit with two blue pompons and red neck ruff, military hat with blue pompon. Mark: "Germany//Herm Steiner//16/0." Ca. 1920+ ....$350-$400

8-1/2" "Bonnet" Girl. Stone bisque shoulder head, CM, Blue ptd. eyes, blonde ptd./molded hair/molded-on blue ptd. bonnet with gold trim, cloth body/bisque lower arms/legs, old clothes. Ca. 1890s $300

8-1/2" "2/2" incised "Two-faced" Girl. All bisque, O/C mouth/molded upper teeth and tongue (cry and calm faces), blue ptd. eyes, swivel neck/movable limbs/black ptd. shoes with two straps/white ptd. socks with blue dots/elastic-strung wooden pegs/kid-lined neck and leg joints, orig-

inal clothes. Mark inside right arm: "2/2." ....$1,000-$2,000

9" "208" incised Kestner Girl. All-bisque/jtd at sh./hips, OM/teeth, blue glass sleep eyes, brown HHW, original clothes/black ptd. shoes with an-kle-straps/long white ptd. stockings. Rare size. ....$900-$1,000

9" "4418" incised Girl. Bisque head/long neck, OM, blue glass sleep eyes, brown HHW, mâché jtd body/limbs, old clothes. Mark: "Germany 4418." Made by Schoenau & Hoffmeister, Germany, 1884+. Ca. 1910 ....$475-$525

9-1/2" "102" incised Girl. So-called "Wres-tler." All-bisque/jtd at neck/sh./hips/loop strung, blue glass eyes, OM/teeth, blonde HHW, ptd/molded boots with heels/white ptd. stockings, original clothes. (These shapely and plumpish little dolls are called "Wrestlers" by col-lectors due to the seeming muscularity of their little bodies and legs, but they look more like the ladies in musical comedies so popular in that day. The numbers "102" were used by both Kam-mer & Reinhardt and Schutzmeister & Quendt, Boilstadt, Germany.) 1889+ ....$2,300-$2,700

9-1/2" "Snow Baby." Bisque head/hands/feet/compo body covered by a peaked fur hood and fur suit, OM/teeth, inset blue glass eyes, no vis-ible wig. Possibly made by Armand Marseille, Germany. Ca. 1890s ... $325

10" Edwardian Lady. Bisque shoulder head, OM/teeth, inset blue glass eyes, cheap cloth body/compo lower limbs (poorly sculpted hands)/long bisque neck with throat indentation/well-mod-eled breastplate, original ecru-colored silk and lace gown. Mark: "792.7." Ger-many. Ca. 1906 ....$1,200

6" Reproduction bisque Peddler lady with tiny all-bisque dolls in her sales basket. Modern. (Courtesy of Carol Lindberg)

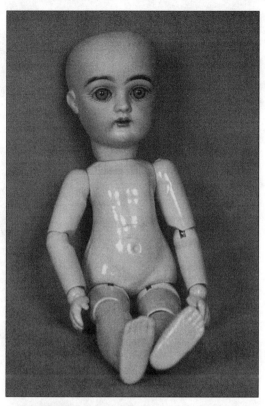

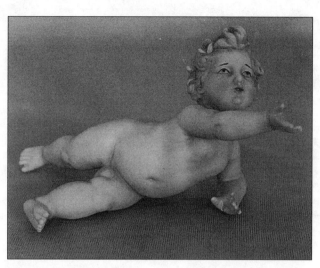

6" long. Piano baby, all bisque/fine quality. German. 19th c. $350. (Courtesy of Herron)

9-1/2" Bisque head, OM/teeth, blue glass sleep eyes, BJ compo body, mark; "Made in Germany" (on rim of back of head). Ca. 1890s $300-$350. (Courtesy of Carol Lindberg)

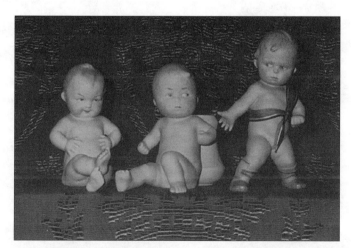

7-1/2" standing Piano Baby, $400; seated Piano babies, $350 each Made by G. Heubach, Germany. (Courtesy Linda Martinez Bassi)

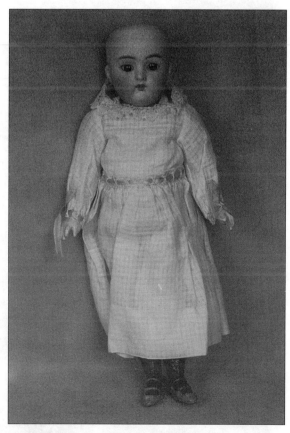

9" "L//S&H//K (star) R//23" marked girl. Bisque head, OM/teeth, blue glass sleep eyes, 5-pc compo body/ptd-on shoes/socks, original clothes. $525-$575. (Courtesy of Carol Lindberg)

Chapter 42

WAX AND WAX-OVER DOLLS

History:

Wax has always been a readily accessible modeling medium for the sculptor. It is also translucent like human skin which makes it ideal for portraiture. Cellini, the 16th-century artist, made wax effigies of the deceased nobility for display in chapels and churches. As early as 1550 Giorgio Vasari wrote in *The Lives of the Most Excellent Italian Architects, Painters, and Sculptors* that the art of wax modeling was "on the decline."

The Benintendi family of Florence had been well-known for their wax works for several generations. Orsini Benintendi had been assisted by the painter Andrea del Versocchio (1435-1488). Benintendi's figures had thickly poured heads, hands, and feet, though hollow within, and were painted with oil paints for realism. Hair wigs were used. Clothes were dipped in wax in layers. This kept them from rotting.

Angel Pio (1690-1769) of Bologna, a pupil of Ferrari, was renown for his ability to depict perfect portrait likenesses of famous people. He also made dolls, being the first to insert glass eyes and to implant human hair into the scalps. He also dressed his dolls.

Anna Morandi (1716-1774), Bologna, was a famous sculptor who, with her husband, Giovanni, Manzolini, worked for Ercole Lelli. Lelli made wax anatomical models. This trio later established an entire museum collection of their works which was financed by Pope Benedetto XIV, the former Archbishop of Bologna. Manzolini used life-like colors in tinting the wax and had a secret formula for hardening and preserving it.

Johann Schalch (1623-1704) billed himself as the "Eighth Wonder of the World." His first waxworks exhibition was in London in 1685. He is best known for making glass eyes and for his optical apparatus. He was a pet of royalty, and his death mask of Queen Mary (1694) caused quite a stir.

Mrs. Salmon (1650-1740), England, was famous for her permanent waxworks near St. Martin's and later on Fleet Street. She was not only a wax modeler, but a toymaker as well. In her old age she taught the art to others.

The famous Irish couple Mr. and Mrs. Sylvester who worked in Dublin and Edinburgh (1780-1794), were so skilled at their trade they could model an exact likeness on the spot. If the sitter wasn't satisfied, no money was expected for the chore. Other noted early wax modelers were Samuel Percy (1750-1820) who specialized in colored wax profiles and tableaux, John Flaxman (1755-1826) who designed classical cameos and portrait medallions.

Wax dolls were made in Italy, France, Spain, England, Germany and in other countries in the 16th and 17th and 18th centuries, but little mention is found of them; only their dolls live on in museums as testimony of their skill and the beauty of their dolls. Domencio Pierotti, of the famous wax doll-making family, was selling dolls at the Pantheon in London as early as 1793. Only two of his eleven children would follow in his footsteps: Henry and later, Giovanni (1847). Henry would be the most famous. It was the beginning of wax doll-making in England.

Collecting Hints:

When paying extremely high prices for wax dolls look for good coloring, realistic faces, original body and parts. Undress the doll and see if the shoulder plate is still glued intact to the body. Embedded hair and original clothing adds to the doll's value, as do body marks, which are rare. Ordinary wax dolls should sell for less. Poured wax dolls are more expensive than a wax-over type. Babies are more common than little girls and little boys. Lady dolls and gentlemen are also considered good buys. Babies with realistic

Young Marie Antoinette, age 13, wax shoulder head/lower limbs, cloth body, ptd features, white mohair wig, original clothes. One-of-a-kind by Sheila Wallace McKay $1,000+.

Louis XV. Wax shoulder head/lower limbs/cloth body, original clothes, ptd features, white mohair wig. One-of-a-kind by Shelia Wallace McKay $1,000+.

faces and good modeling sell for more money than a bland type.

Wax dolls can be gently cleaned with cold cream. When rubbing the face keep the cloth away from the painted parts of the face. Rewaxing a head should be left to an expert and ask to see examples of his work before leaving a doll for restoration. Old cracks in the face of an ancient doll should be left alone. Purists do not mind cracks and signs of wear.

Reproduction Alert:

Antique wax dolls were reproduced in England in modern times, but they were signed and sold as such. Modern wax doll-makers like Lewis Sorensen also tried to duplicate them. Mr. Sorensen signed his on the inside of the shoulder plate. It should never be difficult to mistake the old for the new. Old dolls reveal wear and tear, and the wax is usually dented and marred by scratching, etc.

WAX AND WAX-OVER DOLLS

4-1/2" Half-doll Lady. Turned wax shoulder head/long neck/molded bosom, CM, inset blue glass eyes, HHW attached with pins and nails, wax lower arms/lovely hands/rolled 18th c. newspaper serves as upper arms, original costume pinned to body. (Doll mounted to a wooden base.) Probably German. 18th c. ....$2,000+

6" "Egg" Baby. Baby Girl emerging from Egg Shell. Solid wax/no movable parts, inset blue glass eyes, CM, inserted soft blonde mohair ringlets, original dress, frilly bonnet, papier-mâché egg with flower design. Unmarked. German. 19th c. ....$1,000+

8" Dolls' House Lady. Poured wax shoulder head/sloping shoulders, CM, inset blue glass eyes, white mohair wig, solid wax hands, cloth body/limbs, original pale blue silk brocade dress, underclothes. Ca. 1750s................................$1,500

8" French Half-doll Lady. Poured wax to waist/molded bosom/lovely face, O/C mouth/ptd teeth, large ptd brown eyes/ptd upper and lower lashes, poured wax bent arms/peg jtd, brown mohair wig/elaborately curled (one long curl dangling in front of shoulder and the other tight curls piled atop head in a late 1870s pompadour). Head slightly turned and raised upward. Another version of this doll wears a yellow-blonde mohair wig and has her head turned to right side and ptd blue eyes. Made in Paris, France. 1920s....................$700

8-1/2" Motschmann-type Child. Wax-over-mâché shoulder head, tiny CM, inset large blue glass bulging eyes, blonde ptd/molded short hair/molded-on pork pie hat with hand-painted flower decoration around brim, compo hip and upper thigh area/compo lower limbs/cloth midsection and upper limbs, original "Scottish" out-

fit with plaid skirt, shoes, stockings, etc. Ca. 1868 ....$700

10" Flapper. Solid wax to waist/immobile, bare posed arms, cupid's bow red lips, large ptd brown eyes, brown bobbed mohair wig/headband, wire-armature lower body/cloth covered/wax lower limbs/black ptd and molded high-heeled pumps, original short "lacy" gown with shoulder straps. Doll attached to round wooden base covered with yellow velvet. Lafitte-Desirat. 1920s (France) ....$800-$1000

10" Wax-over-compo Lady. Wax-over-compo shoulder head/molded bosom, CM, black pupil-less sleep eyes/wire lever pull, brown HHW (coiled rear braids) wooden body/peg-jtd limbs, original clothes/ptd shoes and stockings. Ca. 1840s.. $750

11" "Hatted" Girl. Wax-over-mâché shoulder head, tiny red CM, large inset brown glass bulging eyes, short blonde ptd/molded curly hair/molded-on blue-ptd pork-pie hat with 3 white ptd and molded feathers on front of hat, cloth body/smooth carved wood limbs/blue ptd boots/white ptd stockings, original clothes. Ca. 1868.... $900

11" "The Wonderful Creeping Baby." Wax-over compo head, smiling O/C mouth/5 ptd teeth, ptd brown eyes, feathered brown eyebrows, blonde ptd/molded hair, cardboard body with brass clockworks mechanism/brass key/wax-over-compo limbs, original cotton dress trimmed with lace, matching lace bonnet adorned with tiny pink silk ribbons. Workable. Ives Blakeslee Co., Bridgeport, Conn. Patent date: August 29, 1871. Original wooden box reads: "The Wonderful Creeping Baby." Ca. 1871+ MIB Rare.................$2,000

Marie Antoinette Wax shoulder head/lower limbs/cloth body, ptd features, white mohair wig, original clothes, etc. One-of-a-kind originals by Sheila Wallace McKay $1,000+.

12" "Pierotti" type. Baby. Poured wax shoulder head (slightly turned), CM, large inset blue glass eyes/inserted eyelashes and eyebrows, inserted blonde HHW, cloth body/poured wax lower limbs, old clothes, etc. Body stamp: "Hamley's Regent Street Doll Emporium." Ca. 1860s....................................$1,500+

12" "Snood" Child. Wax-over-compo shoulder head, CM, inset almond-shaped dark brown glass eyes, light brown ptd/molded hairdo/molded/ptd yellow snood, Motschmann-type body/wooden lower limbs/black ptd boots, original tan lawn semi-long dress, petticoat, etc. Sonneberg, Germany. Ca. 1850 ....$900

George and Martha Washington. Wax shoulder head/lower limbs, cloth body, ptd features, white mohair wigs, original clothes, etc. One-of-a-kinds by Sheila Wallace McKay $1,000 each.

12" English Peddler. Wax-over-carved wood shoulder head, CM, wired pupil-less black sleep eyes, brown HHW set into slit atop head, kid body/carved wood lower limbs, original old blue print dress, apron, petticoat, drawers, red wood cape. (She carries a tray of original tiny objects, i.e., needles, ribbons, thimbles, thread, flowers, etc. Original glass dome. English or German. Ca. 1840s..$2,500

12" Graveyard Doll. Wax-over-mâché shoulder head, CM, blue glass sleep eyes/wire attachment for opening/closing, soft blonde HHW (probably that of the deceased child), cloth body/leather lower arms, original shroud, bonnet, etc.; original black ptd heavy concrete coffin with 2 metal hinges and lock groove. Germany. Ca. 1830s-40s rare $1,500

12" Lafitte-Desirat Bride. Wax head, CM, ptd blue eyes, light brown mohair wig, wire-armature body/kid covered lower limbs/silver ptd high-heeled slippers, original short silk satin wedding gown and tunic decorated with silver sequins, bandeau, wedding veil. Doll attached to a base covered with pink velvet, signed, dated, brief description of costume. 1915 (France) .....$1,000-$1,200

12" Peddler Lady. Wax-over-compo shoulder head, CM, inset blue glass eyes, brown mohair wig, cloth body/compo lower limbs, wears original dress, red cape, hat, etc. (Original tiny wares in original tiny basket.) Mint (Has been kept in a glass dome). Ca. 1870s ....$2,000+

13" "Mandolin" Lady. Art Nouveau type. Flesh-tinted solid wax to waist/turned head/long neck, CM, half-closed ptd blue yes, brown mohair wig, wood-block lower body with wired-on full-length solid wax shapely legs/black ptd high-heeled slippers/solid wax arms wired to shoulders/long fingers, original wispy costume, turban with feathers, wisps of curls on forehead and sides of face, wooden mandolin. Probably German. Early 20th c. ....$800-$900

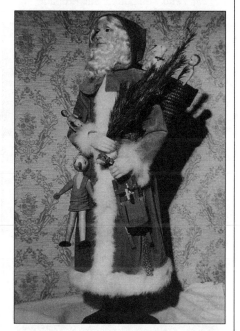

Father Christmas (24"), wax head/hands, cloth body, original clothes, etc. Made by Lewis Sorensen, 1960s $1,500.

13" English Peddler. Poured wax shoulder head, simple round face, tiny CM, inset brown pupil-less glass eyes, wispy brown mohair wig, cloth body/leather lower arms, original dress, apron, cape, etc. (She carries 3 baskets of original tiny wares.) Unmarked. English or German. Ca. 1830s.........................$2,500

13" Lafitte-Desirat Parisienne. Turned solid wax shoulder head, CM, blonde mohair wig, wire-armature body covered with layers of paper padded to form a shape/kid leather arms, original clothes, hat, etc. Doll attached to a round wooden base covered with yellow velvet and signed: "A la Pensee, 5 Faubourg Saint Honore, Paris." (Henri La Pensee was a well-known Parisian couturier.) Also signed on the base is the tradename "Lafitte-Desirat" which is the combined married surnames of sisters Louise Daussat Lafitte and Augusta Daussat Desirat, who created and costumed style dolls by hand and used wax heads made by Monsieur Grevin of the Musee de Grevin Wax Works Mu-

seum. (The dolls varied in size from 10-13-inches tall.) Ca. 1910....$1,000+

13-1/2"Art Deco Boudoir Lady. Poured wax to waist/turned head, O/C mouth/white space, ptd blue eyes, inserted brown HHW, wired lower cloth body in a seated position/wired poured wax lower limbs, original chiffon gown. 1920s (German) ....$1,000+

13-1/2"Wax-over-wood lady. Thick wax-over-wood head, wee CM, inset small black pupil-less glass eyes, light brown HHW, wooden body/peg-jtd limbs, original silk dress, etc. Ca. 1840s (German) ....$2,000+

13-1/2"Lady Doll. Wax-over-compo shoulder head/long oval face/pointed chin, modeled neck glands, CM, large inset blue glass eyes, blonde mohair wig, cloth body/wooden lower limbs/spoon hands/blue ptd boots, original red woolen dress/lace trim, cheap muslin over-skirt, etc. Probably German. Ca. 1850s ....$1,000+

13-1/2"Lady Doll. Wax-over-compo shoulder head, wee prim CM, round face shape, inset black pupil-less glass eyes, brown HHW pinned to crown, cloth body/pink leather limbs, original pink net dress, straw hat, etc. German Ca. 1830s or earlier..................$1,200

14" "Swaddling" Baby. Christ Child Church Figure. All solid carved ptd wax/no limbs, ptd blue eyes, CM, brown ptd hair bordering edges of carved wooden bonnet, elaborately carved lower area. Italy. 18th c. ....$2,000+

14" Motschmann or "Taufling" Baby. Wax-over-mâché shoulder head and upper torso/lower limbs/hips and upper leg area/cloth upper limbs and stomach area, CM, inset blue glass eyes, blonde skin wig, original christening clothes, bonnet. 1850s (Good condition) $1,500

14-1/2"head cir. Bye-Lo Baby. Poured wax head/oil ptd, CM, squinty blue ptd eyes, Cloth body/flange neck/sateen mitt hands, old clothes. Mark: "Grace Storey/22." Ca. 1922 ....$900-$1,000

14-1/2"head cir. Bye-Lo Baby. Wax head, CM, squinty blue ptd eyes, dark oil ptd hair, orange-pink muslin body/legs/pink sateen arms with mitten hands/no voice box, old clothes. (Earliest wax head Bye-Los had mitten hands, later ones had celluloid hands, voice boxes. One rare wax Bye-Lo was 8-inches long.) Mark: "Grace Storey 22." 1922 ....$900-$1,000

14-1/2"head cir. Bye-Lo "Sleeping" Baby. Wax head, CM, closed eyes, cloth body, old clothes, bonnet. (Only 250 of these were made.) Rare Ca. 1922 ....$5,000

14-1/2"Montanari-type Girl. Poured wax shoulder head, CM, inset blue glass eyes, inserted blonde mohair wig, cloth body/poured wax lower limbs, original cloth body, original silk dress with lace trim. Ca. 1870 ....$1,300

14-3/4" "Montanari" Girl. Baby. Poured wax shoulder head, CM, onset blue glass eyes, embedded blonde HHW, cloth body/poured wax lower limbs, original long white cotton christening gown, bonnet, etc. Lower torso ink marked: "Montanari." Original wooden box; label

has name Madame Montanari. Ca. 1851 MIB $2,500

15" "E" marked Lady. Poured wax shoulder head, CM, inset blue glass eyes, blonde HHW (individual hairs inserted into scalp around hairline; wig covers remainder of head; attached with glue and nails), well-constructed kid gusseted body/limbs, original clothes, etc. Oval paper sticker on rear shoulder plate reads: "E." Ca. 1860s (English) Made by John Edwards, London. 1868+ Super-rare ....$2,000+

15" Queen Victoria. Poured wax shoulder head/deep chest modeling, CM, small ptd blue eyes, inserted HHW with looped side braids and coiled rear braided bun, cloth body/legs/poured wax lower arms/separated fingers, original elaborate costume, etc. Made by Madame Montanari. (An obvious Queen Victoria doll; slight resemblance.) 1850s $3,000

15" Slit-head Lady. Poured wax shoulder head, CM, inset brown pupil-less glass eyes, long curl HHW inserted through slit head atop head, cloth body/legs/leather arms, old clothes. English. Ca. 1830s+ $1,000

15-1/2" "Bonnet" Wax Lady. Wax-over-mâché shoulder head, CM, inset brown pupil-less brown glass eyes, blonde mohair wig glued under brim of hat/molded-on "Empress" style hat with a pink band and yellow ptd plume, cloth body/compo lower limbs/ptd and molded-on boots, old clothes. (Although this "lady" is dressed like an adult and wears a "lady" hat, her round baby face is probably that of a child. Little girls wore similar style hats and dressed like adults.) Ca. 1859-1865 ....$2,700

16" "Pumpkin" Head Lady. Wax-over-compo shoulder head, CM, inset brown pupil-less glass eyes, ptd light

14" Poured wax to waist lady (wax lower arms), attached to wooden stand, embedded auburn HHW, ptd features, old clothes. Marked on bottom: "Made in Germany 1". Early 20th century $600. (Courtesy of Herron)

206

blonde/molded hairdo, original cloth body/squeak-box in chest/wooden lower limbs/ptd flat-soled shoes, old cotton print dress, etc. Ca. 1860s $450

16" Lady. Poured wax turned shoulder head, CM, light blue PW eyes, inserted blonde mohair wig styled in a high pompadour, PE/earrings, cloth body/poured wax lower arms/compo lower legs with molded boots and stockings, original

21" "Isobelle", wax-over-compo shoulder head/lower limbs/cloth body, CM, inset blue glass eyes, blonde mohair wig, original clothes, etc. Ca. 1870s $650. (Courtesy of Victoria Rose, England)

13" "Ginette", wax-over-compo, OM/4 teeth, inset blonde mohair wig, cloth body/compo lower limbs, old clothes. Ca. 1870s $350-$400. (Courtesy of Victoria Rose, England)

21" "Isobelle" and 13" "Ginette" (close-up of above dolls). (Courtesy of Victoria Rose, England)

clothes. Unmarked. English. Ca. 1870s $1,700

16-1/2" "Hatted" Girl. Wax-over-mâché shoulder head, tiny pink CM, inset blue glass bulging eyes, yellow ptd/molded-on "Empress" style hat trimmed in green with applied fabric flowers and gilt trim/blonde mohair curls inserted beneath edges of hat, cloth body/compo lower arms/carved wood lower legs/green molded and ptd boots, original clothes. Ca. 1860 .... $2,700

18" "Alice". Wax-over-mâché shoulder head, CM, inset blue glass eyes, blonde ptd/molded short hair with blue ptd ribbon across top of head, cloth body/compo lower limbs, original clothes. Ca. 1850s $850

18" "Hatted" Boy. Wax-over-mâché shoulder head, red CM, inset blue glass bulging eyes, short black ptd/molded curly hair/molded-on orange ptd toque with blue trim and molded and ptd blue feather, cloth body/smooth carved wood limbs/brown ptd boots, original outfit. Ca. 1868 .... $850

18" "Jointed" French Lady Style Doll. Poured wax shoulder head deep shoulder modeling with a hint of bosom/round face, CM, rosy cheeks, inset blue glass bulging eyes, glued-on braided brown HHW, shapely kid-over-carton-moule body/carton-moule upper limbs/wood jts at elbows and knees/poured wax lower arms/carton-moule lower legs/jts at elbows, hips, knees, ankles, original elaborate French-made costume, stockings, boots. Early 1870s ... $4,500

18" "Laughing" Child. Poured wax shoulder head, OM with curved slit/4 molded upper teeth/pink molded tongue, inset blue glass eyes, inserted lashes/brows, blonde mohair wig inserted into scalp in small bunches in concentric circles around the head, cloth body with metal grommets/poured wax 3/4 arms and legs above knees, original clothes, etc. Mark: oval purple ink stamp and "Mrs. Peck. The Doll's home-131 Regent Street-London, W-dolls and Toys of all Descriptions repaired." Made by Lucy Peck, London, England. 1893+ $4,000

18" "Peacock's" Girl. Poured wax shoulder head/short neck/deep chest modeling, sullen CM, inset blue glass eyes, embedded mohair blonde wig, cloth body/wax lower limbs, original fancy full-length gown, etc. Mark: "From//PEACOCK'S//the Rocking Horse//525 New Oxford St.//Corner of Bloomsbury St.//London, W.C." Super-rare Ca. 1860s $3,000

18" "Pumpkin" Head Girl. Wax-over-compo shoulder head, CM, almond-shaped inset dark pupil-less glass eyes, blonde ptd/molded hairdo/hair band, cloth body/carved wood lower limbs/black ptd high-top boots, original flannel dress, etc. Ca. 1860s-70s $500

18" Christmas Tree Fairy. Poured wax shoulder head, CM, inset large blue glass eyes, embedded ankle-length straight blonde HHW, cloth body/poured wax lower limbs/bare feet, original gauze dress trimmed with tinsel-like glitter at neck and hemline,

crown with stars made of the tinsel glitter. Mark: "Pierotti." Ca. 1900 . $3,000+

18" Lady Bride. Poured wax shoulder head/round chubby face, CM, light blue glass eyes, dark blonde HHW (inserted)/laid-on eyelashes, cloth body/chubby poured wax lower limbs, original white silk organdy bridal gown, etc. Unmarked Montanari. Ca. 1860s .. $3,500

18" Little Girl. Poured wax shoulder head, OM/teeth, inset blue glass eyes, embedded blonde HHW, cloth body/poured wax lower limbs, original clothes, etc. Unmarked. Probably English Ca. 1880s .... $2,000+

18-1/2" Edwardian Lady. Slightly turned poured wax shoulder head, CM, inset blue glass eyes, embedded auburn HHW, cloth body/poured wax lower limbs, original silk gown trimmed with lace and wee pearls, etc. Probably unmarked Pierotti, England. Ca. 1900+ $2,000

18-1/2" Queen Victoria. Poured wax shoulder head, CM, inset blue glass eyes, embedded dark HHW, cloth body/poured wax lower limbs, original floor-length silk gown, fur-trimmed cape, crown, etc. Unmarked Montanari. Ca. 1860s .... $4,000-$5,000

19" "Wire-eyed" Child. Wax-over-mâché shoulder head, red CM, delicate facial coloring, blue glass sleep eyes activated by a wire concealed in one of her wrists, glued-on blonde HHW (sausage curls), cloth body/wax-over-mâché limbs/fingernail and toe detail, original dress, etc. Ca. 1840s Excellent condition $1,200

19" Infant. Poured wax shoulder head, CM, rare blue ptd eyes, inserted soft blonde mohair, cloth body/poured wax lower limbs, original tucked white baby gown, lace-trimmed cape, etc. Signed: "Pierotti." Ca. 1849+ ..... $1,500-$1,800

20" "Lucy", poured wax shoulder head, CM, inset blue glass eyes, embedded blonde HHW, cloth body/poured wax lower limbs, original clothes, etc. Stamped on cloth body with "Lucy Peck" stamp. Lucy Peck, London, 1891-1921. $2,000. (Courtesy of Victoria Rose, England)

23" Wax-over-compo shoulder head, CM, inset brown glass eyes, blonde HHW embedded into scalp through slit in center of head, straw-stuffed cloth body/leather arms/wire inside body opens and closes eyes, original clothes. 1830s-1840s $1,600. (Courtesy of D. Kay Crow)

19" Lady Bride. Poured wax head/hands, inset blue glass eyes, inserted blonde hair/eyebrows, stout cloth body with large bosom/cloth limbs, original fancy bridal outfit, veil, etc. Mark: Charles Marsh stamp and the Royal Warrant. Ca. 1880s..............................$2,700+

19-1/4" Queen Victoria. Portrait doll. Poured wax shoulder head, CM, inset blue glass eyes, inserted grey HHW, cloth body/long wax arms, original dress, etc. Late 19th c. Rare (Possibly Lucy Peck) ....$2,000+

19-1/2" Early "Kicking" Baby. Wax-over-mâché shoulder head, OM/4 inset teeth, cobalt blue glass eye/outlined with black paint, round bald head with ptd ringlets above and behind ears, carton body covered with fabric/wood box situated in lower front section of body (when a wooden knob is pushed the legs kick, the arms move, and baby squeaks), cloth upper limbs/poured wax lower limbs (arms are bent), original christening gown, bonnet, etc. Possibly German. Ca. 1850s $2,000

19-1/2" Crying Baby. Pink tinted poured wax shoulder head/deep chest modeling, wide open O/C mouth/tongue, closed eyes/inserted blonde eyelashes, blonde inserted HHW, cloth body/poured wax lower limbs, original christening gown, bonnet, etc. Mark: "John Edwards". John Edwards, London. Ca. 1868+ Rare ....$3,000+

20" "Hatted" Girl. Wax-over-compo shoulder head, tiny CM, ptd blue eyes, brown ptd/molded hairdo enclosed in a gold ptd snood with large orchid ptd bow molded above right ear/molded-on "Empress" style flocked hat with a rolled brim/large pink molded bow in front of hat and molded white ostrich

plume on right side/exposed ears with gold touched and molded earrings, cloth body/carved wood lower limbs, original clothes. Ca. 1860 Rare type (German) $3,500

20" "Reinforced" Wax Girl. Slightly turned poured wax shoulder head (reinforced from within with plaster), CM, inset blue glass eyes, inserted human hair around front hairline/nailed-on wig cap covers bald area, cloth body/wax-over-mâché lower limbs, old clothes, etc. (When poured wax dolls became popular in England, Heinrich Stier, Sonneberg, Germany, studied wax-doll-making in London, and returned to Sonnenberg to experiment with his new formulas and methods for creating durable dolls. He advertised his dolls in 1868. Despite their beauty, the German-made wax dolls never compared to those made in England.) Made in Germany. 1870s $2,700

20" Elizabeth I. Portrait Doll. Poured wax shoulder head, CM, almond-shaped inset blue glass eyes, embedded red HHW, cloth body/poured wax lower limbs, original court costume including crown, etc. (Supposedly Elizabeth I as a child, although it does not resemble the early paintings of her in childhood.) Unmarked Pierotti. Ca. 1850s super-rare ....$4,000+

20" Infant. Poured wax shoulder head, CM, inset brown glass eyes, embedded soft blonde HHW, cloth body/poured wax lower limbs, original clothes, bonnet, etc. Mark: Hamley store label. Pierotti. Ca. late 1890s........................$2,000+

20" Infant. Turned poured wax shoulder head, sullen CM, small inset blue glass eyes/inserted eyelashes and eyebrows, soft light brown baby hair, cloth body/poured wax lower limbs, old clothes, etc. (pelisse, ruched bonnet, etc.) Mark: "Pierotti." Ca. 1880s ....$2,000+

20" Lady. Poured wax shoulder head, CM, large ptd brown eyes, slightly modeled ears, black ptd hair (hair painted on round dome-shaped head; has center part/flat top/2 corkscrew curls in front of ears and back of head), cloth body/poured wax lower limbs, original gauze dress, chemise, petticoat, drawers, etc. Ca. 1812 ....$4,000+

20" Little Girl. Poured wax shoulder head, CM, inset light blue PW eyes, embedded eyelashes/eyebrows, embedded waist-length blonde human hair inset into scalp 6 hairs to slit, cloth body with narrow waist/horsehair stuffed/poured wax lower limbs/wax parts sewn to body with tape pulled through metal eyelets, original clothes, no shoes. Made in England. Unmarked. Ca. 1890..............................$1,900-$2,200

20" Little Girl. Wax-over-compo swivel head on wax-over-compo shoulder plate, CM, inset blue glass eyes, blonde skin wig, cloth body/wax-over-compo limbs/ptd/molded boots, original clothes, hat, etc. Unmarked. Possibly German. Ca. 1870s Rare type $1,500

20-1/2" Little Girl. Poured wax shoulder head/deep chest modeling, CM, inset blue glass eyes/embedded eyelashes,

embedded waist-length center-parted HHW, cloth body/poured wax lower limbs, original silk and lace dress, purple boots, etc. Gorgeous doll (very human appearing). Mark: "Chas Marsh Model Wax Baby Doll Manufacturer, 114 Fulham Road S.W. Dolls cleaned and repaired." Ca. 1880............$3,000

20-1/2" "Hatted" Lady. Wax-over-mâché shoulder head/slim oval face shape, CM, large inset brown glass eyes, dark blue flocked/molded-on riding hat/inserted "real" feather/inserted human hair curls above ear/rear human hair braided and coiled into a chignon and covered by a real "snood", cloth body/carved wood lower limbs, original clothes. Ca. 1868 Rare type (German) $4,000

15" Poured wax Oriental man. Wax shoulder head, CM, inset glass eyes, glued-on mohair wig, PE, straw-stuffed cloth body/wax hands, original clothes, etc. Ca. 1850s $1,500. (Courtesy of D. Kay Crow)

20-1/2" "Bonnet" Girl. Wax-over-mâché shoulder head, CM, pale pink cheek blush, large inset dark brown glass bulging eyes, curly blonde HHW inserted at rear of bonnet and around forehead area/yellow ptd flat-shaped bonnet with molded and ptd roses and leaves on right side and black ptd ribbon with a bow tied under the chin and long flowing ribbon ends ptd on the upper chest, cloth body/wax-over-compo lower limbs, original clothes, etc. Ca. 1850s Rare type (German) $4,000

20-1/2" "Hatted" Girl. Wax-over-mâché shoulder head, CM, inset brown pupil-less glass eyes, blonde ptd/molded short hair/molded-on toque, cloth body/compo lower limbs/molded-on/ptd boots, original dress, coat, etc. 1860s (German)................$3,000

21" Infant. Poured wax shoulder head, CM, inset blue glass eyes, inset soft blonde HHW, cloth body/poured wax lower limbs/well-defined hands and feet, original clothes, bonnet. Mark on lower left side of torso: "Montanari//13 Charles St.,//Soho Sq.//London." Ca. 1850s ....$2,500+

21" Lady. Portrait-type. Poured wax shoulder head (turned), CM, inset blue glass eyes, embedded soft blonde hair, earrings, old muslin body/poured wax lower limbs/sloping wax shoulders, original net and gauze dress, etc. unmarked. England. Ca. 1870 ....$4,500

22" "Snood" Lady. Wax-over-mâché shoulder head, slightly smiling CM, dark brown glass eyes with black pupils/wire lever in the lower back area opens and closes the eyes, rosy cheeks, black ptd/molded hairdo "brushed" back over forehead and concealed by a rear black snood, exposed ears, cloth body/carved wood lower limbs/orange ptd flat-soled boots trimmed at tops with blue paint, original clothes. 1850s Rare type (German) $1,600

22" Lady. Poured wax turned shoulder head/rounded shoulders/molded bosom/lovely face (resembles a Gibson Girl), CM, inset blue glass eyes, inserted blonde HHW styled in high pompadour, cloth body/poured wax lower limbs, original elaborate costume, etc. English. Probably Pierotti. 1870s ....$4,000+

22" Little Girl. Poured wax shoulder head, CM, inset blue glass eyes, soft blonde mohair wig (inserted into scalp), cloth body/poured wax lower limbs, original clothes, etc. Body stamp reads: "MRS PECK//THE DOLL'S HOME//131 REGENT STREET/LONDON, W//DOLLS AND TOYS OF ALL DESCRIPTIONS REPAIRED." Mrs. Lucy Peck, London, 1891-1930. Ca. 1890s ..$2,700-$3,000

22" Little Girl. Poured wax shoulder head, CM, inset brown glass eyes, bald head with glued-on HHW, cloth body/poured wax lower limbs, old clothes, etc. English or German. Unmarked. Ca. 1865 ....$2,500

22" Realistic Infant. Poured wax shoulder head, CM, inset blue glass eyes, embedded brown HHW, cloth body/poured wax lower limbs, original floor-length gown, lace cap, etc. (Well-modeled, realistic face and shoulders.) English. Unmarked ....$2,000+

23" "Pumpkin" head girl. Wax-over-compo shoulder head/cup-and-saucer neck, OM/lower teeth, inset blue glass eyes, orange ptd hair molded in a pompadour fat curls behind ears, cloth body/compo lower limbs, old clothes. Ca. 1870s Rare type $700

23-1/2" "Wire-eyed" Girl. Young lady type. Poured wax shoulder head, CM, rosy cheeks, blue glass sleep eyes, brown HHW, cloth body/wasp waist/poured wax lower limbs/wire for opening and closing eyes, original clothes, etc. Unmarked. English. Ca. 1850s......$2,500

23-1/2"Little Girl. Poured wax shoulder head, CM, inset large blue glass eyes/eyelid modeling/inserted eyelash-

es and thick eyebrows, cloth body/poured wax lower limbs/closed fingers/dimpled knuckles, original clothes, hat, etc. (Meech dolls are easy to identify by their large owlish eyes.) Rubber stamp mark: "H.J. Meech//Dolls Cleaned & Repaired//So Kensington Road//London. S.E.I." (in an oval). Ca. 1850s Rare........$4,000+

14-1/2" turned head poured wax lady (wax to waist), poured wax lower arms, cloth lower body, O/C mouth/mld teeth, ptd blue eyes, inset blonde HHW, redressed. Ca. 1910 $600. (Courtesy of Herron)

14-1/2" Close-up of above doll. Turned wax head (wax to waist), O/C mouth/mld teeth, blue ptd eyes, blonde HHW inserted hair by hair into scalp, wax lower arms, cloth lower body/legs, redressed. Blue ribbon winner. Early 20th c. $600 (Courtesy of Herron, photo by Mike Trompak, Timeless Images, Albuquerque, N.M.)

24" Lady. Wax-over-compo shoulder head/round face (looks German), smirking CM, inset pale blue glass eyes, brown mohair inserted into slits in center of head, cloth body/leather arms, original late 18th c. style outfit: elaborate lace-trimmed velvet jacket over a white muslin gown, etc. Ca. 1825 ....$1,200

24" Lady. Wax-over-mâché shoulder head, OM/upper and lower teeth, black pupil-less glass eyes, PN, black HHW, pink kid body/jtd at shoulders only, original hand-made silk dress, etc. (This lady has a high forehead and sparse ptd black hair with fine brush marks under the original nailed-on wig.) 1850s $2,600

24" Little Girl. Child Model Wax Doll. Poured wax shoulder head/slightly turned, OM/teeth, inset blue glass eyes, inserted blonde mohair wig, hair-stuffed cloth body/compo lower limbs, original whitework and lace dress, etc. Thigh mark: "Holz-Masse." Original box marked: "Marshall and Snelgrove" (famous old London department store) and "Child Model Wax Doll." Cuno & Otto Dressel, Sonneberg, Gernay. Ca. 1875+ Rare type... $3,000

24-1/2"Little Girl. Wax-over-compo shoulder head, tiny CM, inset blue glass eyes, HHW inserted into center head slit, cloth body/leather lower arms, old clothes, etc. Paper label reads: "Imported & Sold by Charles Dummig, NO. 812 Chestnut St., Philadelphia." Ca. 1848-65 ....$1,400

24-1/2"Queen Victoria. Poured wax shoulder head, CM, inset blue glass eyes, embedded light brown hair braided in coils over each ear and rear coiled bun, cloth body/legs/poured wax 3/4 arms, original lace trimmed gown, etc. Mark: "Madame Montanari" and "Soho Bazaar." Ca. 1851 ....$6,000

25" Little Girl. Poured wax shoulder head, OM/upper teeth, inset blue striated glass eyes, embedded blonde HHW, cloth body/wax lower limbs, original organdy dress, hat etc. Stamped on lower front part of body: "A. Bazzoni-Maker." (Anthony Bazzoni, Italian born, made wax dolls in England, ca. 1832-1855; known for his famous "Speaking Doll" which said "mamma" and "pappa". He had a showroom where he displayed his dolls. He also made wax-over-compo dolls with glued-on hair wigs.) Super-rare. Ca. 1850s $6,500

25" "Wire-eyed" Baby Girl. Poured wax shoulder head, CM, large blue glass sleep eyes/wire lever, inserted brown HHW, original cloth body/poured wax lower limbs, original clothes, bonnet, etc. Body mark: "FROM MRS. PECK THE DOLL'S HOME 131 REGENT STREET W." Ca. 1890s Rare type. $4,000

26-1/2"Victorian Lady. Wax-over-mâché shoulder head/top of arm modeling and modeled below bosom, tilted head, slightly smiling CM, large inset blue glass eyes, brown HW (sausage curls), cloth body/wax-over-compo lower arms/cloth legs, original white cotton gown, petticoat, pantalets, etc. Ca. 1849 Rare type $3,000

Chapter 43

～ WOODEN DOLLS ～

History:

Wooden dolls made prior to the 17th century are difficult to find if they exist at all! The crude "toy" types were discarded and rotted away, and the more artistically carved pieces made by craftsmen for the church and window display (lay figures) wound up in exclusive collections to be seen by very few. It was during this period that gesso and varnish was introduced, and the ball-and-socket was invented for posing the dress mannequins.

The evolution of the wooden doll began slowly, reaching a zenith of perfection and beauty during the William and Mary Period (1689-94), and the Queen Anne Period (1702-14). Mass-production during the Georgian Period (mid-to-late 1700s), cheapened the playdoll, and we find two types being made: those for the wealthy or elite and those for the working class or poor. The mortise-and-tenon peg jointed wooden doll became popular in the 19th century, but as the century wore on and other doll types came to the fore, it, too, became nothing more than a hastily conceived product, and by the end of the century, was one of the crudest and cheapest dolls on the market. It was truly the "poor child's" toy, but it was dearly loved. The turned woodens continued to be made in this century despite declining sales. Today their only claim to fame is the simple fact that fanciers of primitive wooden dolls seek them for their collections as an "example" of a late wooden doll.

Collecting Hints:

In the 1950s and 1960s, one could still find wooden dolls made during the periods, William and Mary, Queen Anne, and Georgian, etc., in junk shops, secondhand stores, and in ordinary antiques shops and auctions. Collectors like Ruth Campbell Williams and Helen Hinckley put wooden dolls on the "collecting map," so to speak.

The more publicity a doll gets, the more scarce and expensive it becomes. Everyone wants it! Nowadays, one is fortunate to even glimpse one of these old relics in a museum, and when it does make its esteemed debut it is usually at an auction like Sothe-

by's; the price prohibitive, except to those of super wealth. But prices vary; the dolls sell both below and above estimate. The peg woodens with the tuck combs are very charming and still priced within reach of the average collector. Unusual faces, pretty faces, well-made dolls, and dolls with their original or near original finery are the most desirable.

WOODEN DOLLS

1-1/2" Peg Wooden. All-wood/jtd at sh/hips/knees/carved hands with separate thumbs/carved feet with flat-heeled/black ptd shoes/well-ptd features, black old hair with curled sides and carved rear bun, original blue silk dress, white silk pantalets. Ca. 1846 .... $200

4" Normandy Seashell Lady. Early papier-mâché head, ptd features, black ptd/molded hairdo, jtd wood body, original outfit decorated entirely with wee seashells of various colors, seashell head-dress. Ca. 1850s ......$600-$700

4" Tuck Comb Lady. All-wood/jtd limbs, black ptd hair/2 spit curls on each side of face, CM, blue ptd eyes, original ecru gown with puff sleeves. Early 19th c. $350

7-1/2" Schoenhut Strongman, bisque head, wooden body/movable limbs, black ptd/mld hair, long black flat wooden shoes, purple and gold felt costume trimmed in gold. See Schoenhut section for prices. (Courtesy of D. Kay Crow)

5" Georgian Period Lady. All-wood/jtd at sh/hips/gesso ptd head, HHW, straight red CM, black pupil-less glass eyes, "dotted" eyebrows/lashes, large carved hands, original costume has long-sleeved bodice and wide-pan-niered skirt. Ca. 1775 .... $1,000+

6" Grodner Tal Lady. All carved wood/jtd stick-like limbs/round head, wee CM, ptd blue eyes, two-toned brown ptd hair, original "Welsh" clothes: red wool cape, brown cotton dress, white apron, green with brown trim hat. Ca. 1820s-30s $800

6-1/2" Late Peg Wooden Child. all-wood/jtd at sh/hips/knees/unjtd arms, red dash CM, red rouge spots, black ptd eyes/eyebrows, black ptd hair (no particular style), white ptd head/shoulders/lower limbs/black ptd shoes, original cheap cotton print dress, underwear. Germany or Austria. Ca. late 1890s $225

8-1/2" Georgian Period Lady. Molded plaster face, red ptd CM, dark brown HHW, blue glass eyes, red rouge spots, wood body/cloth limbs, original high-waisted white embroidery net dress (lined with red ribbons), white linen hat. Ca. 1790s $1,400

8-1/2" Jiminy Cricket. All-wood/jtd body, ptd features, ptd/molded clothes/shoes, molded hat with felt brim, felt collar, umbrella. Ideal Toy Co., Hollis, NY 1940 .... $550

9-1/4" Queen Anne Period lady. Carved wood head/jtd wooden body/leather arms, tiny straight red ptd mouth, inset brown pupil-less glass eyes, dotted eyebrows/eyelashes, vivid round rouge spots, brown HHW sewn to a line cap, very old clothes. Ca. 1700 ..... $12,000

9-1/4" Tuck Comb or French Restoration Lady. Oval-shaped face, ptd features, black ptd hair/spit curls at each temple/yellow tuck comb, round shoulder jts/peg jts at elbows/knees/hips, original ornate sheer dress, pantalets. Made in Grodner Tal, Germany. Ca. 1820 .... $1,150

9-1/2" Swaddling Baby. All-wood, carved in 1-pc/no jtd or limbs, torso carved with flower designs and painted. Made in Bohemia. Late 18th c. $2,000

9-1/2" "Red Body" Lady. Wood head/red ptd turned body in 1-pc, ptd features, "stub" nose, black ptd hair, straight wooden limbs/leather jts, old clothes. Made in Bohemia. Late 19th c. . $350+

9-1/2" Late Peg Wooden Lady. All-wood/jtd at sh/hips/knees/unjointed arms, red dash mouth. black ptd eyes/eyebrows, black ptd hair (no style), white ptd head/sh/black ptd shoes, undressed. Germany or Austria. Ca. late 1890s $375

10" Autoperipatetikos. Walking Doll. Lady type. Beautiful wood-carved head/gesso finished/ptd, wired and very detailed wood hands, brass walking mechanism/clock key windup, wood legs attached to wood base. Green paper label on base reads: "Patented July 15, 1862; also in Europe 20 Dec. 1862." Enoch Rice Morrison, NYC; also made by Martin & Runyan of London. (These dolls came with heads of bisque, china, , cloth, and carved wood.) 1862+ $3,000

10" Hopi Indian Katchina Doll. All carved wood (hand-made), black mask, blue jeans/vest, holds a dance rattle and staff. Inscribed on back: "Power Man." Ca. 1960 ....$350

10-1/2"Queen Anne Period Lady. Oval face/carved wood head/jtd body/cloth upper arms, smiling red CM, ptd brown eyes, brown HHW, dotted eyebrows/eyelashes, original long dress of wool with gallon trim, fontage, 2 petticoats (outer petticoat has embroidered flower design), stockings simulated with bands of cotton wound around legs. Ca. 1710......................$12,500

11" Peg Wooden Peddler Lady. Hand-carved wooden type, painted features, brown HHW, original dress, cape, hat, etc. (Tray of original miniature wares held by a neck cord.) Doll sealed in her original glass dome. Mint. 1830s $2,500

11" Pinocchio. All wood/multi-jtd body/long neck, compo head smiling mouth, round ptd eyes, black ptd hair, molded/ptd clothes, yellow felt hat, silk bow tie, ptd shoes, metal pin. Ideal Toy Co., Hollis, N.Y. Ca. 1940 ....$550-$575

11"& 5" "Nursemaid and Child." Door of Hope Mission. Hand-carved pear wood heads/hands, CM, ptd brown eyes, black ptd hair. The nursemaid or "amah" wears original white cotton tunic with long sleeves and embroidered collar, blue trousers, embroidered silk head covering, red silk print leggings. (Child strapped to Nursemaid's back with red binding cord; wears cotton and silk clothing.) Made by Door of Hope Mission carvers from Ning-Po, China. Label reads: "Made in China." 1914+ $950

11-1/2"Chinese Farmer. Door of Hope Mission. Carved pear wood head/arms/bald head/cap, ptd features, cloth body, hand-made clothes, original pitchfork. Tag reads: "Made in China." Made by Door of Hope Mission carvers from Ning-Po, China. (The Door of Hope was a Christian mission, Shanghai, China. The girls associated with the charity dressed the wooden dolls that were made by the Ning-Po carvers. Wooden hands date dolls made from 1914, although the dolls were made as early as 1901.) 1901+ $700

11-1/2"Black Dancing Dan. All-wood/paper lithographed face/springwire attached to head enables a nodding movement/metal pin jtds/wire handle in rear. (This Dancing Dan is dressed as a hotel bell captain. He holds a message tray. Other Dancing Dans are dressed as railroad porters and hold a tray of dishes. A Dancing Dan with jointed elbows holds a cane.) Atlas Doll & Toy Co., distributed by Hoest & Henderson, NYC. 1926-27 ....$200

11-1/2"Dolomite Peg Wooden. All wood/jtd at sh/elbows/hips/knees, white ptd head/sh/arms/legs/red ptd shoes, tiny red CM, red rouge spots, tiny carved nose, black ptd eyes, black ptd hair (no style). Undressed. Made in the Dolomite Mountains. Ca. 1900-14.......$100

12" Empire Period Grodner Tal Lady. All-wood/jtd body, tiny red CM, tiny ptd brown eyes, carved PE/earrings, black ptd hair/center part/large spit curls over each temple, rosy cheeks/long neck, old high-waisted Empire gown with short puff sleeves, red ptd shoes, etc. Germany. Ca. 1815 ....$1,600

12" Georgian Period Lady. Round wooden head/tapered jawline, red ptd mouth with straight lines at the corners, red rough spots, large almond-shaped inset brown glass eyes, dotted eyebrows/eyelashes, nailed-on brown HHW, wood body jtd at hips/leather arms, early clothes which may be original. English. Ca. 1750s $2,700

11" All-wood "Selina", hand-carved by Fred Thompson, NIADA, all original, 1975 $500. (Courtesy of D. Kay Crow)

12" Greenland Eskimo. All hand-carved wood, ptd features, black HHW, static body/moveable wrists, fancy original clothes, boots, leggings, hooded parka. (Hair is wound in a topknot.) $500

12" Grodner Tal Lady. All-wood/white leather jts nailed to moveable parts, red ptd CM, ptd blue eyes, carved nose/red nose dots, black ptd/carved simple hairdo, white ptd head/sh/arms/brown ptd flat-soled shoes/orange ptd body, original calico dress, underwear, nailed-on hat. Ca. 1838-40. Germany $1,650

12" Joel Ellis Lady. Wood head, ptd features, black ptd/short molded hairdo wood body jtd at neck/sh/elbows/hips/knees (mortise and tenon jtd), metal hands/feet/black ptd high-top shoes/white ptd stockings. Made by Cooperative Mfg. Co., Springfield, Vermont. Ca. 1873 ....$1,200

12-1/4"Zuni Kachina Doll. Carved pine/horns/blue face mask/hand-ptd skirt. Ca. 1950 ....$400

12-1/2"Joel Ellis Lady. Rock maple wood head, CM, ptd blue eye, rare red ptd/molded hair, rock maple wood jtd body/metal hands and feet/black ptd shoes/white ptd stockings, undressed. The Cooperative Mfg. Co., Springfield, Vt. 1873 ....$1,500

12-1/2"Wm. and Mary Wooden Lady Doll. Round wooden head, red CM, black ptd eyes, brightly roughed cheeks, red nostril dots, brown HHW, wooden body/swivel neck/cloth upper arms/wooden lower arms/legs jtd at hip and knees/lower legs ptd black, original silk gown/braid appliqué train/bodice, linen underskirt, silk gauze cap nailed to wig and head. Ca. 1690 ... $50,000+

13" Bébé Tout-en-Bois. All-wood/jtd at neck/sh/elbows/hips/long narrow body/long straight legs/spoon-shaped hands with separate thumb, red CM, round red rouge spots on cheeks, large inset blue glass eyes, brown mohair wig, old clothes. (Body is turned-wood type). Probably Rudolf Schneider, Germany. 1901-14 ....$550-$600

13" Charles II Lady. All-wood/jtd at neck/hips/knees/wood lower arms/fork-like fingers/cloth upper arms, smiling CM, brown ptd eyes/white dots, rouge spots, blonde mohair wig (nailed on), original silk bodice trimmed with silver gilt braid, silk over-and-under skirts trimmed with silver gilt braid, linen shifts, printed shift, silk cap, white stockings, leather shoes. Ca. 1680 ....$50,000+

13" George III Lady. Wood head/body/straight wooden legs with block feet/short blue skin wig, pink floral print cotton dress. English. Ca. 1810 ....$1,800

13" Jumeau-type Bébé. Wood head/hollow interior, CM, inset blue glass eyes, brown mohair wig, BJ wood body, original clothes, etc. (This doll resembles an early Jumeau.) Ca. 1860s $2,000+

13-1/2" Napoleon. Portrait type. Plaster-on-wood head, CM, ptd blue eyes, wooden body jtd at sh/elbows/solid wood from waist down/wire hoop through top of head for neck articulation, original machine-stitched clothes, brass-capped buttons, etc. (Wears accurately scaled clothes: Cross and Star of the Great Eagle, the Knight Cross of the Order of the Iron Crown, decoration, saber; uniform Napoleon wore in several famous portraits.) French label. Ca. 1900 or earlier $5,000

14" (18" with pointed hat) German Court Clown. Male. Carved wood head, red smiling CM, long nose, red marks on each cheek, black eyebrows, ptd blue eyes, wooden body with metal cone extending from the back into which a red wooden handle is inserted for animation (jester or clown walks, head turns from side to side), crude wooden legs/well-sculpted hands, original commercially-made costume, green stuffed hat with pompon, lamb's wool wig. Ca. 1870s ....$2,000+

14" Baby #100 look-alike. Wood swivel head, O/C mouth, ptd blue intaglio eyes, dark brown ptd hair/brush-strokes, bent-limb compo body, old clothes. (Baby #100 started the character series for Kammer & Reinhardt bisque-head character dolls ca. 1911. It was supposedly a likeness of Kaiser Wilhelm as a baby, when, in actuality, it was a likeness of the sculptor's own child. Ugly doll.) 1911+ $1,500

14" Court Gentleman. All hand-carved wood/wire jtd hips/wire-loop jts at sh/elbows, CM, blue ptd/carved eyes with lids, pale blonde ptd/carved hairdo with 2 side curls and a real curl, carved and ptd genitals (over-sized), original silk trousers, brocade vest, lace-trimmed silk brocade jacket, etc./black ptd/carved shoes/white ptd stockings. (This male doll is a companion to the below lady doll. The facial expressions of both dolls is serious rather than amorous.) Ca. 1776+ (or 1890s+) $5,000+

14" Court Lady or Marie Antoinette. All hand-carved wood/mortise and tenon jts at the hips/wire-loop jts as sh/elbows/knees, CM, blue ptd/carved eyes with lids, light yellow ptd high pompadour-style hairdo with rolled curls on each side of long neck, carved and ptd genitals, original elaborate and detailed costume, hat, etc. (These strange caricature dolls were made similarly to puppets, and were supposedly used in the decadent French court during Marie Antoinette's reign for lewd entertainment. There were both men and women depicting well-known people in the court. There were either other sets carved similarly or later made in the 1890s, as various examples surface from time to time.) Ca. 1776+ (or 1890s+) ....$5,000+

24" Carved wood lady, ptd features, carved hair, leather body, wood stick hands, crude carved fingers, original clothes (layers of petticoats, elaborate bonnet with handmade roses. 18th century $7,000-$8,000+. (Courtesy of D. Kay Crow)

15" (17" with pointed hat) German Boy clown. Flesh-colored bisque head/dimple/fired-on facial marks, O/C mouth/teeth, dark brown glass eyes open/close when stomach squeeze-box is pressed/arms open and close simultaneously, mohair wig, wood and wire body/limbs, original red, blue, yellow cotton print close suit with gold and white lace trim, red painted stockings, black ptd shoes. Mark: "H3." Ca. 1870s $1,200

15" Bébé Tout en bois. Carved wood head, OM/teeth, brown sleep glass eyes, brown mohair wig, BJ compo body, original cheap chemise. Tag reads: "Incassable Tout en bois." Made in Germany for the French market. Ca. 1901-14 ....$750-$800

11-1/2" 11-3/4" Dolomite Peg-woodens, late 19th c. or early 20th c. $100-$125 each. (Courtesy of Herron)

15" Joel Ellis Lady. Rock maple wood head, CM, ptd blue eyes, blonde ptd/molded hairdo, jtd rock maple wood body/pewter hands/feet, original clothes. The Co-operative Mfg., Co., Springsfield, VT. (Joel Ellis was granted a patent for the mortise-and-tenon joint, May 20, 1873. Dolls were manufactured for only 1 year. Early Ellis dolls have black ptd feet simulating shoes. Later dolls have blue ptd feet. The eyes were painted by two young artists, Misses Abbie and Emma Woodbury, daughters of Deacon Joel Woodbury of North Springfield. The dolls were made in 3 sizes: 12", 15", 18". When a Negro doll was ordered, a white doll was simply painted black. the latter types are extremely rare.) 1873 ....$1,700

15-1/2"Wooden head and narrow sloping shoulders in one piece, thin CM, inset almond-shaped blue glass eyes, carved nose, red rouge spots, brown HHW, woody body jtd at hips and knees/wood lower arms/cloth upper arms/wood legs, original cotton high-waisted gown with half sleeves, etc. Ca. 1800-1805 ....$2,000+

16" Bébé Bijou. Little Girl type. wood head/gesso covered/oil ptd/varnished (appears to be machine-carved), CM,

PW eyes (set in with beeswax and sealing wax), brown mohair wig nailed onto head, lathe-turned body/limbs/straight wrists (some have jointed wrists), original dress of white scrim with wide diagonal waist ribbon (reads: "Tete & Corp bois"; translated: "head and body of wood"); printed on the stiff white shift in lavender ink: "Bébé Bijou Exclusivement Francaise Brevete S.G.D.G. Paris." Pierre Levy Co., 67 rue de Turenne, Paris, July 18, 1919. 1919+ $1,500

16" First Empire or French Consulate Period Lady. Grodner Tal type. All wood/Heinrich Stier-type ball-and-socket jts, oval face/long neck/narrow shoulders/long limbs (head, shoulders and lower limbs painted a cream color, the rest of the body and limbs painted brown and varnished), CM, ptd blue eyes, black-brown ptd hair with a profusion of spit curls bordering forehead/carved tuck comb, old or original clothes, fancy hat. Germany. Ca. 1810 ....$1,900

16" French Revolution Lady. Carved wood head/gesso covered/ptd, round head shape, thin red lips, inset black pupil-less glass eyes, dotted eyebrows/lashes, red rouge spots, brown HHW tacked to head, skittle-shaped wooden body/flat wood arms/paddle hands/outlined fingers/articulated wooden lower legs, old or original clothes. Near mint condition. English. ca. 1790 ....$5,500

16" Lady or "Pauline" type. Exquisitely carved wooden shoulder head/gesso covered/ptd, CM, ptd blue eyes, thin eyebrows, modeled ears, long neck, brown HHW/kid body/leather arms, original or old muslin dress, pantalets, shoes, stockings. Probably French. Ca. 1840s $1,500

16-1/4"Gentleman. Carved wood head, smiling CM, ptd brown eyes, brown HHW, cloth body and upper limbs/carved wood lower limbs, dressed lavishly in all original clothing, hat (tricorn hat, shirt, jacket, trousers, stockings, leather shoes.) Ca. 1690s/early 18th c. ....$50,000+

17" "Pregnant" Lady. Head and body carved in one piece/long neck/oval face, CM, ptd blue eyes, black ptd hair, long slender limbs jtd at sh/hips/fingers carved together with a separate thumb/black ptd low-heeled slippers/bulging stomacher, original clothes. Ca. early 19th century $2,500+

17" Georgian Period Lady. Elegantly carved head/long neck/sloping shoulders, CM, ptd blue eyes, dark brown HHW styles in elaborate pompadour, fully articulated wooden body/forked fingers/painted shoes, old silk floral print silk brocade open robe, matching petticoat, stomacher, etc. Ca. 1760s. ....$20,000+

17" Georgian Period Lady. Round wooden head/gesso ptd, inset black pupil-less black glass eyes, dotted eyelashes/eyebrows, black ptd hair, red rouge spots, cloth body/upper arms/wood lower limbs/forked hands/hooved feet, original fancy mobcap, long dress, short cape, etc. Ca. late 1700s $5,000

17" Queen Anne Mechanical. Ptd wood head, CM, black pupil-less glass eyes, wood torso/limbs/fixed arms to elbows with movement downward/ivory hands, mechanism housed in wooden bell arrangement (brass works). When wound, doll rolls around the floor and turns from side to side with arms raised and lowered, original brocade gown, lace cap. English. Ca. early 1700s ....$30,000+

17" Wm. and Mary Period Lady. Wood head, CM, ptd blue eyes, brown HHW, papier-mâché body/legs/feet/wired arms/forked wooden hands, original embroidered silk shift, under-shift, silver thread stomacher, silk petticoat, robe, fontage. Ca. 1690 ....$50,000

18-1/2"First Empire Lady. Round head/gesso covered/ptd, inset glass eyes, red rouge spots, tiny CM, brown mohair wig, pointed body, original gown, kid slippers, etc. Ca. 1800 ($3,168 gleaned at Sotheby's London in 1990) $4,000

19" First Empire Lady. oval wooden face, CM, ptd blue eyes, black ptd hair/spit-curls bordering face/topknot encircled by a band, earrings, peg-jtd wooden body/black ptd shoes, original clothes (drawers show beneath dress). Grodner Tal, Germany. Early 19th c. ($10,164.00 at auction in 1991.) ....$4,500+

19" George 111 Lady. Round wood head/gesso covered face, long neck, almond-shaped inset brown glass eyes, thin ptd eyebrows, wee smiling mouth, nailed-on auburn HHW, wood body/limbs/disc-jtd arms/legs jtd at the knees, original white muslin gown, linen shift, mob cap. Ca. 1765 ...$5,000+

20" Georgian Period Lady. All wood/wood legs peg-jtd at hips and knees/upper arms are wire attachment to carved wooden lower arms/fork fingers/long neck/long face with a high round forehead and full cheeks, pink ptd CM, pale rose rouge spots, inset brown pupil-less glass eyes/dotted eyebrows and lashes, nailed-on dark brown HHW, very early or original clothes: silk dress with rear lacings, full skirt, quilted silk petticoat, quilted cap. (These dolls are distinguished by their broad shoulder and hips and small waists.) English. Ca. 1750s ....$5,000+

20" Queen Anne Period Lady. head/body carved in one piece/jtd legs/wood lower arms/cloth upper arms/all gesso ptd/varnished, wee red CM, huge inset brown pupil-less glass eyes, brown HHW, long dotted eyebrows/lashes/dots under eye, no rouge spots, original low-cut plain bodice 9bosom concealed by a neckerchief), plain matching skirt, apron, plain underclothes, bonnet. Ca. 1725 ....$25,000+

22" "Top" Wooden. Lady-type. All wood/jtd body/skittle shaped head, tiny red CM, rosy cheeks, ptd blue eyes, sharp-carved nose, black ptd "cap" hair/no spit curls, long jtd limbs/knob hands and feet, old elaborate costume, head-dress. (This lady has a very severe, crudely painted face with bright rough spots. This was the era when the jointed wooden doll has passed her

prime and popularity and was hastily conceived.) Ca. 1870s ....$1,000+

22" First Empire Lady. Oval-shaped wooden head, tiny red CM, ptd blue eyes, modeled ears/earrings, black ptd/molded hair/center part/spit curls/yellow tuck comb, mortise-and-tenon peg-jtd wooden body/limbs, original clothes. Early 19th c. $3,000

13-1/2" "Quail Kachina" by V. Kasuse, New Mexico, ca. 1950s $395. (Courtesy of Herron)

25-1/4"George 11 English Lady. Round wood head/gesso/ptd a whitish hue, tiny red prim CM, round red rouge spots, thin carved nose, thin arched eyebrows/dotted eyelashes, inset dark brown pupil-less glass eyes, auburn HHW nailed to head, carved wood body/narrow waist/square pegged hips and knees/simple wood feet, cloth upper arms/wood lower arms/long flat fingers, original or very old 2-pc ivory satin gown with floral print, cotton petticoat, corset, crocheted stockings, leather shoes, original mitts, mobcap. Ca. 1740-60.....................$9,000-$10,000+

27" First Empire Lady. All-wood jtd, carved features, smiling CM, very short ptd black hair with spit curls bordering oval face, ptd blue eyes, exposed/carved ears, German joint at elbows/mortise-and-tenon jts, original sheer white, embroidered long dress with V-neck and short puffed sleeves, pointed-toe shoes. Ca. 1810-15 ....$5,000+

27-1/4"French Revolution Lady. Carved/ptd wooden head/body/narrow waist/jtd legs/white kid arms, tiny CM, inset dark brown enamel eyes, brown HHW, original or old floral print dress, matching bonnet, shoes, stockings. Ca. 1790 (1996 auction price: $6,000) ..$8,000+

28" "French" Lady. Carved wooden head/torso/large head/black ptd/molded necklace, small CM, ptd blue eyes, large exposed ears, black ptd hair/downward brushstrokes bordering

face (this effect gives the appearance of uneven bangs), body jtd at sh/elbows/hips/knees/long skinny limbs/ptd shoes/torso covered with kid leather, old clothes. Ca. 1800 (1985 auction price: $16,000; estimate ....$4,000) $20,000+

28" Hugo Hugo Lady. 1930's replica of 18th c. woodens. Turned wood head/body/cloth jts at sh/elbows/mortise-and-tenon jts at hips/knees/black ptd shoes, tiny ptd straight red mouth, compo molded nose, inset threaded blue glass eyes fixed with composition, brown long curl HHW, original clothes in 18th c. style. Hugo Hugo, London, England. 1930s.......................$1,000+

28" Lady with Cone-shaped Hat. all carved wood/jtd arms/embossed and painted, CM. ptd blue eyes, sparse brown HHW, molded cloth and plaster ankle-length, ornate dress, cone-shaped, pointed felt hat. English. Ca. 1800. ....$2,500

30" First Empire Lady. Lovely carved face (not the typical face), CM, ptd blue eyes, black ptd hair/center part/spit curls in front and below ears, articulated wood body (ball/socket joints with hooks attached to knees)/wood limbs, original costume, hat. (The knee hooks allow for free standing.) Ca. 1810 ....$10,000+

31" Dressmaker's Mannequin. All-carved wood/ptd/jtd at sh/elbows/well-shaped hands, lovely carved wood face/long neck, delicate feminine features, CM, ptd blue eyes, jute wig, hourglass figure carved to base of torso/cage bottom consisting of 6 slates nailed to round wooden bottom, original clothes, hat. Ca. 18th c. ....$10,000+

31" First Empire Lady. All-wood/ball-and-socket jts/knee hooks for standing/finely ptd face on gesso and varnished, tiny pink CM, almond-shaped brown ptd eyes/black pupils/dotted eyebrows, black ptd hair with brown brushstrokes bordering forehead simulating waves and swirled into 2 huge spit curls before each ear, original "Empire" gown, hat, etc. (Dotted eyebrows were rarely used at this time.) Possibly French. $15,000

33" Madonna. Religious figure. Carved wood head and body to waist/realistic facial detail, long neck, CM, ptd blue eyes, carved ears, jtd at sh/elbows/small waist/wide round hip area/cage bottom or 6 slates nailed to a round wooden base/hook fasteners, brown HHW nailed-on, original brocade dress, etc. Spanish. 18th c. . $10,000+

33" French "Pandora" Lady. Fashion type. Portrait face/long neck, red CM, ptd brown eyes/carved eyelids, well-carved nose/ears, blonde skin wig, head/upper body carved in one piece/arms peg-jtd at sh/realistic carved wood hands with separated fingers/cone-shaped lower body, original silk "Watteau sacque" style gown with printed flowers, box pleats, lace-trimmed sleeves and skirt, etc. (This is the type Pandora sent to Marie Antoinette to select the fashions of the day. It is life-like and carved by an expert artist, with a realistic face and graceful lady hands.) Ca. late 18th c. ....$12,000+

ARTIST DOLLS

30-1/2" Mile Gabrielle Dorziat of the Comedia Francaise, Paris, 1915. Sculpted and costumed by R. Lane Herron, one-of-a-kind. $1,500.

24" Spanish Opera diva, Maria Felicia Malibran, ca. 1830s, Spain. All original, one-of-a-kind by R. Lane Herron. $1,500.

26" The original Gibson Girl, Evelyn Nesbit Thaw, ca. 1906. All original, one-of-a-kind by R. Lane Herron. $1,500.

112-1/2" Gibson Girl, all original, by Corliss Ann Sinclair, California. One-of-a-kind doll. $350 (Super Sculpey) (Courtesy of Herron)

24" Profile view of Opera diva, Maria Felicia Malibran, ca. 1830s. All original, one-of-a-kind by R. Lane Herron. $1,500.

25" Ninon de L'Enclos, historic personality, ca. 1630, all original, one-of-a-kind doll by R. Lane Herron. $1,500.

8" Negro babies, all-porcelain/jtd bodies, by June Rose Gale, England, BDA. $150 each.

20" "Missy." Porcelain. Limited Edition. By Irene Ortega. $485.

18" All porcelain Jester, multi-jointed, by Judy Condon, NIADA, 1975..

28" Close-up of Rebecca or "Rosy", porcelain head/BJ compo body LTD 25, Original by John and Angela Barker, England. $1,800.

20" "Morning Star." Porcelain. Limited Edition. By Irene Ortega. $475.

21" "Memories" by Irene Ortega. Cernit lady. One-of-a-kind $650.

26" "Dawn", LTD 25, porcelain/BJ compo body, Victorian silk tartan dress. Original by John and Angela Barker, England. $1,800.

33" Gemma, LTD 50, porcelain/BJ compo body, Cinderella type ball gown. Original by John and Angela Barker, England. $2,750.

2The Infanta or Princess Margarita, the Spanish Royal Princess painted by Valeazquez in "Las Meninas" (the Serving Woman). Porcelain original by June Rose Gale, England. $600.

Alice in Wonderland, porcelain, original by June Rose Gale, BDA, England $600.

MISC. DOLLS

28-1/2" Ideal doll, all original, ca. 1952, $200 (Herron collection)

Jumeau Parian bébé circa 1845. Wooden body with music box, basket with kitten, brown eyes, blonde wig, original wine-colored satin dress. $25,000+.

17" Reproduction "Tete Jumeau" by Peggy Leighninger, Colo., all bisque. (Herron collection)

Bébés Marcheurs-parlant, all original, Paris, 1950s. (Courtesy of Herron)

122" "301" incised Bébé. Bisque head, OM/teeth, inset brown glass eyes, blonde mohair wig, BJ compo body, redressed. $1,350-$1,450 1899+. (Courtesy of D. Kay Crow)

SFBJ Bébés, 1950s, all original. (Courtesy of Herron)

14-1/2" "60" incised Bébé. Bisque head, OM/teeth, inset blue glass eyes, BJ compo body, original clothes, etc. 1899 ca. 1917+ $750-$800. (Courtesy of D. Kay Crow)

BIBLIOGRAPHY

Antiques & Collecting magazine, Chicago, IL

Antique Trader Weekly, Dubuque, Iowa

Anuaire Official Des Jouets & Jeux Francaise, 1892-1893, Chambre Syndicale

Annuaire du Commerce, Paris, France, 19th century

Art & Decoration magazine, Rare Modern Porcelain by Lenci of Italy Famous for Subtle
   AnimalPortraiture, September, 1931

Art & Decoration magazine, Little Mary, Queen of Heaven (Lenci Madonnas),
   December, 1936

Borger, Mona, Chinas, *Dolls for Study and Admiration*, Borger Publications,
   San Francisco,CA,1983

Cieslik, Jurgen and Marianne, *German Doll Encyclopedia 1800-1939*,
   Hobby House Press,Cumberland, Maryland, 1985

Coleman, Dorothy S., Elizabeth Ann, Evelyn Jane, *The Collector's Book of
   Dolls' Clothes*,Crown Publishers, Inc., NYC, 1975

Contemporary Doll Collector, Livonia, MI

Crafts & Hobbies magazine, Making Life-Size Dolls from wax, (Lewis Sorensen
   story), by Wally Schulz, January, 1953 (Publisher unknown)

Das Spielzeug (toy magazine), Germany

Davis, Nina S., *Classics of the Doll World*, Pelican Publishing Co., New Orleans,
   LA, 1959

Doll, West Sussex, England

Dolls, New York, New York

Doll Artisan Guild, Oneonta, New York

Doll Castle News, Washington, NJ

Doll Reader, Cumberland, Maryland

Du Bois, J. Harry, *Plastics History*, U.S.A., Cahners Publishing Co., Inc.,
   Boston, Mass., 1972

Ella Smith Doll Company catalog, Roanoke, Ala., 1920

Gimbel Brothers catalogs, 1900+

Greg Catalog of Collections of Dolls & Dolls' Houses, R. Bates, Ltd., Manchester,
   England,1900s

Guptill, Elizabeth F., *The Dolls' Symposium*, March Bros., 1911

Hart, Luella Tilton, *The Japanese Doll*, E.A. Fisher, Middleton, Ct., *1952*

Heubach Character Dolls and Figurines, Hobby House Press, Cumberland,
   Maryland, 1992

Kammer & Reinhardt, *Fabrik des Gelenpuppen 'Mein Liebling'*, Waltershausen I.
   TN. Germany, 1911

Kester, Philipp, *DOLLS-ART OF ALL RAGES*, International Studio, July, 192

La Poupee Modele monthly magazine, Paris, France, 1863-1924

La Poupee Modele, *Journal des Petites Filles (V.1-61)*, 1863-Sept. 15, 1924.
(Merged with Mon Journal Bureau die Journal des Demoiselles, Paris.)

Low, Frances, *Queen Victoria's Dolls*, George Newnes, (Strand magazine
reprint, 1892-1894), Stephen McIntyre, Canada

Lowe, Mary A., *The Use of Dolls in Child Training*, Abingdon Press, N.Y., Cincinnati, 1921

Macy department store catalogs, 1880's+

Madame Hendren Dolls Catalog, Averill Mfg. Co., NYC, 1920

Maitland, Julia Charlotte (Barrett), *The Doll and Her Friends: Or Memories of the Lady
Seraphina*, Ticknor, Read and Fields, Boston, Mass., 1852

Marshall Fields catalogs, 1880's+

Mills, Mrs. W.H., *The Story of Old Dolls and How to Make New Ones*, Doubleday
& Co., N.Y. 1940

Montgomery Ward & Co., catalogs, 1890s+

Morrison, Lucille (Phillips), *Doll Dreams*, Holly Crafters, inc., Hollywood, CA, 1932

National Doll World, Berne, Indiana

Pardella, Edward R., *Shirley Temple Dolls and Fashions*, Schiffer Publishing Ltd.,
West Chester, PA

Playthings (trade magazine), McCready Publishing Co, NYC, 1903-1968;
Geyer-McAllister Publications, Inc., NYC, 1968+

Playthings Directory, 1952-1953

Robinson, Julia A., *Dolls: An Anthology*, Albert Whitman Co., 1938

Starr, Laura B., *The Doll Book*, The Outing Publishing Co., 1908

Tarnowska, Maree, *Fashion Dolls*, Hobby House Press, Inc., Cumberland,
Maryland 1986

Theimer, Francois, *The Jumeau Book* (English edition by Florence Theriault,
Gold Horse Publishing Co.) 1993

Tucker, Elizabeth S., *My Dolls*, L. Prang and Co., Boston, 1889

Yamada, Tokukei, *Japanese Dolls*, Japan Travel Bureau, Kyodo Printing Co.,
Tokyo, 1955

ABOUT THE AUTHOR

R. LANE HERRON is not only a well-known doll authority and historian, but one of the pioneers of the hobby. He was the first writer to introduce the modern doll artist (and the foreign doll artist) in the columns he wrote for such magazines as Spinning Wheel, Antiques Journal, Antiques Trader, Collectors News, etc. He was also the first person to originate a paper doll series in the collectors' magazines. His portrait dolls of famous personages of the past (old-time stage and screen stars, authors, royalty, etc.) are unequalled for their beauty and authenticity. Yet, it didn't all happen by chance. It was the end result of much hard work and dedication. At age four years, he was attending auctions and visiting antiques shops with his father who knew many people in the business. Instead of getting only new toys for Christmas, he was given antique dolls and toys as well (none of which were ever retained). But his real interest in old dolls as a collectible or as a "hobby", began during his high school years when he wrote a letter to Janet Johl, who had written books on the subject. His friendship with Clara H. Fawcett and Luella Hart, well-known doll historians, also proved invaluable. (Mrs. Fawcett encouraged him to write about dolls.) In the ensuing years, he not only collected dolls, but inspected hundreds of thousands in museums and collections. He collected vintage books and articles, studied patents and trademarks, travelled abroad, and kept records of the rare, unusual, and even the more common types. He has written for all the leading antiques/collectible and doll magazines. He has regular doll columns in Collectors News and Doll Castle News, and freelances for other magazines, including Antiques & Collecting magazine in Chicago, Illinois.

Other books by Herron: *Much Ado About Dolls* (1979), *Herron's Price Guide To Dolls & Paper Dolls* (1982), and *Herron's Price Guide To Dolls* (1990). These were published by Wallace-Homestead Book Company.

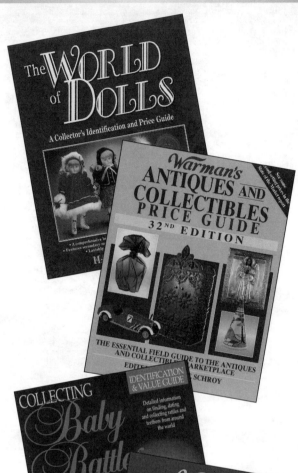

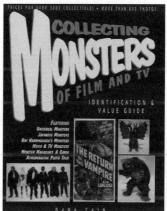